Automated Secure Computing for Next-Generation Systems

Scrivener Publishing
100 Cummings Center, Suite 541J
Beverly, MA 01915-6106

Publishers at Scrivener
Martin Scrivener (martin@scrivenerpublishing.com)
Phillip Carmical (pcarmical@scrivenerpublishing.com)

Automated Secure Computing for Next-Generation Systems

Edited by

Amit Kumar Tyagi

National Institute of Fashion Technology, New Delhi, India

Scrivener
Publishing

WILEY

Wiley Global Headquarters
111 River Street, Hoboken, NJ 07030, USA

For details of our global editorial offices, customer services, and more information about Wiley products visit us at www.wiley.com.

Limit of Liability/Disclaimer of Warranty
While the publisher and authors have used their best efforts in preparing this work, they make no representations or warranties with respect to the accuracy or completeness of the contents of this work and specifically disclaim all warranties, including without limitation any implied warranties of merchant-ability or fitness for a particular purpose. No warranty may be created or extended by sales representatives, written sales materials, or promotional statements for this work. The fact that an organization, website, or product is referred to in this work as a citation and/or potential source of further information does not mean that the publisher and authors endorse the information or services the organization, website, or product may provide or recommendations it may make. This work is sold with the understanding that the publisher is not engaged in rendering professional services. The advice and strategies contained herein may not be suitable for your situation. You should consult with a specialist where appropriate. Neither the publisher nor authors shall be liable for any loss of profit or any other commercial damages, including but not limited to special, incidental, consequential, or other damages. Further, readers should be aware that websites listed in this work may have changed or disappeared between when this work was written and when it is read.

Library of Congress Cataloging-in-Publication Data

ISBN 978-1-394-213597

Cover images: Russell Richardson
Cover design by Pixabay.Com

Set in size of 11pt and Minion Pro by Manila Typesetting Company, Makati, Philippines

Printed in the USA

10 9 8 7 6 5 4 3 2 1

Contents

4 Artificial Intelligence–Blockchain-Enabled–Internet of Things-Based Cloud Applications for Next-Generation Society   **65**

V. Hemamalini, Anand Kumar Mishra, Amit Kumar Tyagi and Vijayalakshmi Kakulapati

5 Artificial Intelligence for Cyber Security: Current Trends and Future Challenges   **83**

Meghna Manoj Nair, Atharva Deshmukh and Amit Kumar Tyagi

Preface

Security is always a primary concern to each application and sector. In the last decade, many techniques and frameworks have been suggested by several researchers to improve security (data, information, and network). Due to rapid improvement in industry automation, however, systems need to be secured more quickly and efficiently. Artificial Intelligence (AI) and Machine Learning (ML) have been put thoroughly into practice to enhance continuity, cybersecurity, and security in cloud computing, internet services, and the Internet of Things and its related applications. Computer vision based algorithms, such as ML and AI, are used to track complex cyber threats that cannot be readily identified by conventional detection methods. It is important to explore the best ways to incorporate the suggested solutions to improve their accuracy while reducing their learning cost.

During implementation, the most difficult challenge is determining how to exploit AI and ML algorithms for improved safe service computation while maintaining the user's privacy. The robustness of AI and deep learning, as well as the reliability and privacy of data, is an important part of modern computing. It is essential to determine the security issues of using AI to protect systems or ML-based automated intelligent systems. To enforce them in reality, privacy would have to be maintained throughout the implementation process.

This book presents groundbreaking applications and undisclosed work related to artificial intelligence and machine learning for more stable and privacy focused computing. By reflecting on the role of machine learning in information, cyber, and data security, the book outlines recent developments in the security domain with artificial intelligence, machine learning, and privacy-preserving methods and strategies. To make computation more secure and confidential, the book provides ways to experiment, conceptualize, and theorize about issues that include AI and machine learning for improved security and preserve privacy in next-generation-based automated and intelligent systems. Hence, this book provides a detailed description about the role of AI, ML, etc., in automated and intelligent systems used for solving critical issues in various sectors of modern society. In summary, this book includes all possible topics based on machine empowered solutions for next generation secure systems.

Amit Kumar Tyagi
October 2023

Acknowledgements

First, we extend our gratitude to our family members, friends, and supervisors who stood by us as advisors during the completion of this book. Also, we thank our almighty God who inspired us to write this book. Furthermore, we thank Wiley and Scrivener Publishing, who have provided continuous support; and our colleagues with whom we have worked inside the college and university system, as well as those outside of academia who have provided their endless support toward completing this book.

Finally, we wish to thank our Respected Madam, Prof. G Aghila, Prof. Siva Sathya, our Respected Sir Prof. N Sreenath, and Prof. Aswani Kumar Cherukuri, for their valuable input and help in completing this book.

Amit Kumar Tyagi
October 2023

Part 1
FUNDAMENTALS

Digital Twin Technology: Necessity of the Future in Education and Beyond

Robertas Damaševičius[1]* and Ligita Zailskaitė-Jakštė[2]

¹Department of Applied Informatics, Vytautas Magnus University, Kaunas, Lithuania
²Department of Multimedia Engineering, Kaunas University of Technology, Kaunas, Lithuania

Abstract

This chapter provides an overview of digital twin technology (DTT) and its applications in various industries including education. DTT involves the creation of exact digital replicas of physical entities that can reflect real-time changes in the underlying entity. The chapter explores the potential of DTT for enhancing the learning experience and improving the educational outcomes through immersive hands-on learning, replication of real-world scenarios for scientific inquiry and problem-solving, and personalization of the learning process. The chapter also examines the challenges of implementing DTT in education, including technical, pedagogical, ethical, and privacy concerns. It also discusses the potential of DTT for shaping the future of education and beyond as well as future research directions.

Keywords: Digital twin technology, education, virtual reality, avatar, immersive learning, personalized learning, real-world scenarios

1.1 Introduction

Digital twin technology (DTT) allows the creation of an exact digital replica of a physical entity and continuously feeds it with real-time data from integrated sensors and other devices [6]. The foundation of DTT is the ability to simulate the behavior of a physical entity in a virtual environment [62]. By gathering data from sensors and other devices, the digital twin is able to mirror the actions, interactions, and changes of the underlying physical entity in cyberspace [61]. This real-time data flow creates a bridge between the physical and digital worlds, allowing us to understand and predict the behavior of the physical entity in ways that were never before possible [72]. However, the true power of DTT lies in its ability to go beyond mere observation and prediction. With the use of advanced algorithms and simulations, the digital twin can be used to improve the performance of the physical entity and even to control it in real time. This opens up new possibilities for innovation and optimization in fields such as manufacturing, transportation, healthcare, etc. [10]. It can change

---

Corresponding author: robertas.damasevicius@vdu.lt

Amit Kumar Tyagi (ed.) Automated Secure Computing for Next-Generation Systems, (3–22) © 2024 Scrivener Publishing LLC

the way we design, build, and operate the systems that shape our world, and it is a necessary component for the Industry 4.0 Revolution [35], the future of education, and beyond. DTT has a wide range of applications across various industries. Some of the most notable applications include the following:

- Manufacturing: DTT can be used to optimize the performance of production lines and machines by simulating and predicting their behavior under different conditions. This can help to identify and resolve bottlenecks, reduce downtime, and improve overall efficiency [18].
- Transportation: DTT can optimize the performance of transportation systems, such as trains, buses, and logistics networks [52]. By simulating and predicting the behavior of these systems, it is possible to identify and resolve issues, improve efficiency, and reduce costs.
- Healthcare: DTT can be used to optimize the performance of medical equipment, such as MRI scanners and X-ray machines, and to simulate and predict the behavior of patients [31], which can reduce costs and improve patient outcomes.
- Aerospace: DTT can be used in the aerospace industry to optimize the performance of aircraft and spacecraft by simulating and predicting their behavior under different conditions [41]. This can help to improve safety and increase efficiency.
- Infrastructure design: DTT can be used to optimize the performance of buildings, bridges, and other structures by simulating and predicting their behavior under different conditions [5]. This can help to reduce costs and improve safety.
- Smart cities: DTT can be used to optimize the performance of smart cities by simulating and predicting the behavior of infrastructure, transportation systems, and other key components of the city [64]. This can help to reduce costs, improve safety, and increase efficiency.
- Agriculture: DTT can be used to improve the efficiency and productivity of agricultural operations by optimizing planting, irrigation, and fertilization schedules, monitoring the health and well-being of livestock, monitoring and optimizing the performance of agricultural equipment, creating accurate weather forecasts, creating predictive models of crop yields, and monitoring the farm remotely. This can help farmers in making more informed decisions and can improve the overall efficiency and productivity of their work [46].
- Energy and utilities: DTT can be used to optimize the performance of energy and utility systems, such as power plants, water treatment facilities, and pipelines (see "Teaching Factory" [44]). By simulating and predicting their behavior under different conditions, one can identify and resolve issues, improve efficiency, and reduce costs.
- Retail: DTT can be used to optimize the performance of retail operations, such as stores, warehouses, and logistics networks [19]. By simulating and predicting their behavior under different conditions, it is possible to identify and resolve issues, improve efficiency, and reduce costs.

These are just a few examples of the many different applications of DTT across various industries. As technology continues to advance and the data generated by digital twin systems becomes more accurate, the potential for DTT to improve business processes, reduce costs, and increase efficiency is expected to continue to grow [55].

The aim of this chapter is to examine the role and impact of DTT in shaping the future of education and beyond. It aims to provide an overview of DTT and its applications in various industries and delve into the specific ways in which DTT can be utilized in education. The chapter explores the potential of DTT to support the evolution of intelligence and personalization in education and discusses the challenges and limitations that must be considered in the implementation of DTT in education.

The novelty of this chapter is that it provides a comprehensive examination of DTT and its potential impact on education, which has not been fully explored before. This chapter brings together the latest research and developments in DTT and education to present a holistic view of the current state of the field. The chapter also discusses the challenges and limitations that must be considered in the implementation of DTT in education, which is an important aspect that is rarely highlighted in other studies.

The contribution of this chapter is that it highlights the potential of DTT to shape the future of education and beyond. It argues that DTT is a necessary component for enhancing the learning experience and improving outcomes and that its potential must be fully realized in order to achieve this. The chapter contributes to the understanding of the challenges and limitations that must be considered in the implementation of DTT in education. By highlighting these challenges, the chapter aims to help researchers and practitioners navigate them and ensures that DTT is implemented in the most effective way possible.

1.2 Digital Twins in Education

1.2.1 Virtual Reality for Immersive Learning

Virtual reality (VR) and computer vision (CV) are two technologies that can be used to enhance the learning experience through immersive hands-on learning when combined with DTT. VR is an artificial simulation of a 3D environment which a person can explore and interact with [51]. VR can be used to create immersive and interactive learning environments that allow students to experience and interact with virtual objects and scenarios as if they were real [36]. This allows students to have hands-on experience in simulations and helps them to better understand and retain the teaching material [66]. CV is a field of artificial intelligence (AI) that deals with the development of systems that can interpret and understand visual information [23]. CV can be used to enhance the realism of virtual environments and to track the movement of students in VR. This allows students to interact with virtual environments in a more natural and intuitive way and enhances the sense of immersion in the learning experience [65].

When combined with DTT, VR and CV can be used to create immersive learning environments that replicate real-world scenarios [58]. This allows students to practice and experience the material in a realistic way and helps them to better assimilate and retain the material—for example, in a medical education context, students can practice performing surgeries in a VR environment that replicates a real-world scenario, which can help them to better understand and retain the material and also to be better prepared for real-world scenarios. The use of VR and CV in combination with DTT also allows for the creation of personalized learning experiences—for example, using CV methods, the system can track and analyze the student's movements and interactions in the virtual environment and provide feedback and guidance accordingly. This allows for more individualized instruction and support and can help students to learn at their own pace.

Another advantage of using VR and CV in combination with DTT is the ability to conduct experimentation and scientific inquiry in a safe and controlled environment—for example, in a physics class, students can conduct experiments in a virtual environment that replicates the real-world scenario and test different variables and conditions. This allows the students to explore and understand scientific concepts in a more interactive and engaging way and can help them to better understand and retain the material. In DTT, avatars [47] can be used to represent real-world objects and entities, such as vehicles, buildings, or even entire cities. An avatar refers to a digital representation of a person typically used in VR environments and simulations. They can also be used to represent virtual entities, such as robots, drones, or even abstract concepts. Avatars can be used to simulate human behavior and interactions in digital twin scenarios. They can also be used as a way for users to interact and communicate with the virtual environment and with other avatars. Avatars can be created in a variety of forms, such as 3D models, digital characters, or even simple icons. They can be customized to represent the user's physical characteristics, such as height, weight, and facial features. They can also be programmed to exhibit different behaviors, movements, and expressions to simulate human-like interactions. Avatars can be controlled by the user, or they can be programmed to operate autonomously and exhibit behaviors based on rules and algorithms. In this way, the avatars can be used to simulate real-world scenarios and help users to understand complex systems or processes and to make predictions about the behavior of these systems.

DTT also provides a key component for the metaverse. The metaverse is a term used to describe a virtual universe that combines elements of the real world and the digital world [3]. It is a concept that represents an extension of the Internet where users can perform actions in virtual environments with digital objects and other users in a seamless and immersive way. DTT is a key enabler for the metaverse, as it allows for the creation of exact digital replicas of real-world objects, environments, and systems that can be used to connect the physical and virtual worlds and provide a more immersive and realistic experience for users in the metaverse.

1.2.2 Delivery of Remote Education

The importance of remote education has grown in recent years especially due to the COVID-19 pandemic [56]. DTT can be used to enable and support the delivery of remote education (distance/online teaching) in a number of ways, namely:

- Virtual classrooms: DTT can be used to create virtual classrooms that mimic the physical classroom environment. It can provide students with a sense of presence and engagement and enable real-time interactions with the teacher and other students [8].

- Real-time monitoring and feedback: DTT can be used to monitor student engagement, progress, and understanding and provide real-time feedback to the teacher and student [54]. This can help to ensure that the student is keeping pace with the class and addressing any gaps in understanding.
- Collaborative learning: DTT can be used to create collaborative learning environments that allow students to work together on projects, assignments, and simulations [60]. This can help to promote teamwork and collaboration and can make the remote learning experience more enjoyable and interactive.
- Remote access: DTT can provide remote access to educational resources, which can enable students to learn from anywhere at any time [50, 68].

DTT can be used to support the delivery of remote education by providing students with a sense of presence and engagement, real-time monitoring and feedback, personalized learning, simulation-based learning, collaborative learning, and remote access to educational resources. This can help to improve the effectiveness and efficiency of distance/online teaching and can make the learning experience more interactive and engaging for students.

1.2.3   Replication of Real-World Scenarios

DTT is increasingly being used to replicate real-world scenarios for scientific inquiry and problem-solving. The ability to create an exact digital replica of a physical entity or process and feeding it with real-time data from sensors and other devices allow for a wide range of experimentation and exploration in a safe and controlled environment. One of the advantages of using DTT for scientific inquiry and problem-solving is the ability to replicate real-world scenarios in a virtual environment. This allows for the testing and exploration of different variables and conditions without the need for expensive and time-consuming physical experiments, e.g., in engineering, scientists can use DTT to simulate the behavior of a bridge under different loads and conditions, which would be expensive and dangerous to replicate in the real world. DTT can also be used to replicate real-world scenarios in healthcare—for example, DTT can be used to simulate the state of a patient's body under different medical treatments, which would be impossible to replicate in the real world. This allows for the exploration of different treatment options and can help to identify an effective treatment for a particular patient. In education, DTT can be used to replicate real-world scenarios for scientific inquiry and problem-solving—for example, students can use DTT to explore and experiment with different ecological environments and the impact of biodiversity on the ecosystem without the need for expensive and time-consuming field trips. This allows for the development of scientific inquiry and problem-solving skills and can help students to better understand and retain the material.

1.2.4   Promote Intelligences and Personalization

The use of DTT in the education system can provide a comprehensive approach to the digitalization of education, setting new goals and changing the educational process [37]. By creating a digital twin of the learner, the system can be used to improve the digitalization of the learning process and the entire educational organization by automatically searching for suitable disciplines, learning technologies, and forming individual educational trajectories.

The data collected can also be used for recruitment, career guidance, and management activities of the educational organization [1].

Specifically, DTT has the potential to promote multiple intelligences [32] and personalization in education through the use of immersive and interactive learning environments. By providing students with a virtual environment that replicates real-world scenarios, DTT can help to develop students' spatial intelligence as they navigate and interact with the virtual environment. DTT can help to develop students' logical–mathematical intelligence as they conduct experimentation and problem-solving in the virtual environment. DTT can also be used to promote the development of interpersonal and intrapersonal intelligences through the use of personal virtual tutors. Personal virtual tutors [34] can be used to provide individualized instruction and support and can help students develop their social and emotional intelligence, as they interact with the virtual tutor, and to provide feedback and guidance, which can help students develop their self-awareness and self-regulation. DTT also allows for personalization in education by allowing students to interact with learning resources that are tailored to their individual needs. Through the use of intelligent recommendations and learning analytics, DTT can help to identify and provide students with learning resources that are best suited to their individual needs. This can help to promote personalization in education and can lead to better learning outcomes.

Therefore, DTT has the potential to support personalization by providing students with immersive and interactive learning environments, personal virtual tutors, and personalized learning resources. DTT can help to enhance the learning experience and improve outcomes. DTT can also help to foster a more engaging and interactive learning experience, as it allows students to conduct experimentation, scientific inquiry, and problem-solving in a safe and controlled environment. This can help to develop critical thinking and problem-solving skills and can help students better understand and retain the material. Furthermore, it can provide an effective way for students to practice and experience the material in a realistic way, which can lead to better understanding, retention, and preparation for real-world scenarios.

1.3   Examples and Case Studies

1.3.1   Examples of DTT in Education

DTT is increasingly being used in education to enhance the learning experience and improve outcomes. Some examples of DTT in education include the following:

- Virtual labs: DTT can be used to create virtual labs that replicate real-world scenarios, allowing students to conduct experiments and explore scientific concepts in a safe and controlled environment without the need for expensive and time-consuming field trips [29, 57].
- Language learning: DTT can be used to create immersive and interactive language learning environments that replicate real-world scenarios—for example, students can use DTT to explore and interact with virtual environments that simulate different cultures and languages, which can help to improve their understanding and retention of the material [15].

- Science, Technology, and Mathematics (STEM) education: DTT can be used to create immersive and interactive STEM learning environments that replicate real-world scenarios—for example, students can use DTT to explore and interact with virtual environments that simulate different engineering or physics concepts [16] or control robots [11], which can improve their understanding and retention of the material.

- Serious educational games: DTT can be used to create immersive and inter-active learning experiences that closely mimic real-world scenarios [38]—for example, a digital twin of a factory or power plant can be used in a game that teaches students about industrial processes and systems. The game can include challenges and puzzles that require players to apply their knowledge of the systems to solve problems [40], and the digital twin can be used to provide feedback and guidance on their performance. Additionally, digital twins can be used in games that teach subjects like physics, engineering [13], and architecture by allowing players to create and experiment with virtual models of processes, structures, and systems [12, 16].

- Architecture and design education: DTT can be used to create virtual models of buildings and other structures for architectural design, engineering, and construction education [63]. This allows students to explore and experiment with different design options in a safe and controlled environment, thus improving their understanding and retention of the material.

- Virtual field trips: DTT can be used to create virtual field trips that replicate real-world scenarios, allowing students to explore different locations and historical sites without the need for expensive and time-consuming physical trips. This can help to expand students' knowledge and understanding of different cultures and historical events.

- Professional training: DTT can be used to create virtual training environments that replicate real-world scenarios, allowing students to practice in a realistic way [42]—for example, in fields such as aviation, engineering, and manufacturing, students can use DTT to practice operating equipment and machinery, which can help to prepare them for real-world scenarios and improve their understanding and retention of the material.

- Space education: DTT can be used to create virtual environments that replicate space and planetary environments, allowing students to explore and understand scientific concepts related to space and astronomy. This can help to develop students' spatial intelligence [69] as well as their understanding of scientific concepts related to space.

- Art and design education: DTT can be used to replicate real-world art and design scenarios, allowing students to explore and experiment with different design options in a safe and controlled virtual environment [59]. This can help to improve their understanding and retention of the material and develop their creative talents.

These are some examples of how DTT is being used in education to enhance the learning experience and improve outcomes. As technology continues to advance, DTT is expected to play an increasingly important role in shaping the future of education.

1.3.2   Digital Twin-Based Educational Systems

There are several specific examples of digital twin-based educational systems that are currently being used or developed in various fields of education, namely:

- Virtual anatomy lab [4] allows medical students to explore and study the human body in a virtual environment. The system uses 3D imaging and VR technology to create a digital replica of the human body which students can interact with and explore in a safe and controlled environment.
- Virtual ship design platform [48] allows engineering students to design and test virtual ships in a virtual environment. The system uses DTT to create a replica of the ship which students can use to explore different design options and test the ship's performance in a variety of conditions.
- Virtual chemistry lab [21] allows students to conduct experiments and explore scientific concepts in a virtual environment. The system creates a replica of a chemistry lab which students can use to explore different chemical reactions and test different variables in a safe and controlled environment.
- Virtual field trips can be used to take students to different historical sites or geographical locations without the need for physical field trips [3]. This can be done by creating virtual environments that replicate real-world scenarios which students can explore and interact with using VR technology.
- Virtual nature is an example of a digital twin-based educational system that simulates natural environments and ecosystems [26]. It allows students to explore and interact with virtual representations of real-world natural environments, such as forests, oceans, and wetlands. The system can be used to teach subjects such as biology, ecology, and environmental science. The virtual nature system can be accessed through VR technology which provides an immersive and interactive experience for students. They can explore virtual environments and observe the behavior of virtual plants and animals in real time, thus simulating the natural world. This allows students to observe and study natural phenomena that may be difficult or impossible to observe in the real world, such as the behavior of rare or endangered species or the effects of climate change on ecosystems. The digital twin-based nature system also allows for experimentation and data collection—for example, students can conduct virtual experiments to study the impact of different variables on the ecosystem, such as the introduction of new species, changes in temperature, or pollution. This enables them to explore cause-and-effect relationships and develop scientific inquiry skills [43]. Moreover, virtual nature can also be used as an interactive and engaging way to teach conservation and sustainability, as learners can explore the impacts of human activities on the environment and the effects of different conservation strategies.
- Virtual manufacturing system [7] allows students to practice and experience the material in a realistic way. This can be done by creating virtual environments that replicate real-world manufacturing scenarios which students can explore and interact with using VR technology.

- Virtual power plant allows students to explore and understand the complexities of power generation and distribution. The students use a replica of a power plant to explore different power generation options, test different configurations, and understand the impact of various parameters on the power plant's performance in a simulated environment [22].
- Virtual construction site [70] allows students to learn about construction management and engineering by exploring and interacting with a virtual replica of a construction site. The system uses DTT to create a replica of a construction site which students can use to explore different construction options, test different configurations, and understand the impact of various parameters on the construction project's performance.
- Virtual aerospace [45] allows students to learn about aerospace engineering by exploring and interacting with virtual replicas of aircrafts and spaceships. The system uses DTT to create a replica of an aircraft which students can use to explore different design options, test different configurations, and understand the impact of various parameters on the aircraft's performance.
- Virtual automotive [30] allows students to learn about automotive engineering by exploring and interacting with virtual replicas of cars and trucks. The system uses DTT to create a replica of a car or truck which students can use to explore different design options, test different configurations, and understand the impact of various parameters on the car's or truck's performance.
- Virtual disaster response allows students to learn about emergency management and response by exploring and interacting with virtual replicas of disaster scenarios. The system uses DTT to create a replica of a disaster scenario which students can use to explore different response options, test different configurations, and understand the impact of various parameters on the disaster response's performance.
- Virtual library is a virtual representation of the physical library space and its collections. This can include a 3D model of the library building as well as digital representations of the books, journals, and other materials in the library's collection. This digital twin can be used in a variety of ways to enhance the user experience in a virtual library—for example, it can be used to provide virtual tours of the library space, allowing users to explore the library and its collections from the comfort of their own homes. It can also be used to create interactive exhibits, games, and educational resources that allow users to learn more about the library's collections in an engaging and interactive way. Additionally, digital twin can be used to track and analyze the usage of the library, such as the number of visitors, the most popular books and resources, and the busiest hours of the day, which can be used for library planning and decision making [28].
- Virtual museum is a virtual representation of the physical museum space and its collections. This can include a 3D model of the museum building and digital representations of the artifacts, artworks, and other objects in the museum's collection. This digital twin can be used in a variety of ways to enhance the user experience in a virtual museum—for example, it can be used to provide virtual tours of the museum space, allowing users to explore

the museum and its collections from the comfort of their own homes. It can also be used to create interactive exhibits, games, and educational resources that allow users to learn more about the museum's collections in an engaging and interactive way [33].

These are some examples of digital twin-based educational systems that are currently being used or developed in different fields of education. They are helping to enhance the learning experience and improve outcomes by providing students with immersive and interactive learning environments and allowing them to conduct experimentation and problem-solving in a safe and controlled environment [17].

1.4   Discussion

We evaluate the effectiveness of DTT for education in terms of five main outcomes of learning (intellectual skills, cognitive strategy, verbal information, motor skills, and attitude) [24] as follows:

- Intellectual skills: DTT can be used to create virtual simulations of real-world scenarios that can be used to teach a wide range of concepts, rules, and procedures—for example, a digital twin of a manufacturing facility can be used to teach students about industrial processes, or a digital twin of a city can be used to teach students about urban planning. These simulations can provide a more interactive and engaging learning experience, allowing students to apply their knowledge in a realistic setting.
- Cognitive strategy: DTT can be used to create personalized learning experiences that adapt to the individual needs and learning style of each student—for example, DTT can be used to create virtual tutors that can interact with students and provide feedback and guidance based on their performance. This can help students to develop their own cognitive strategies for learning and problem-solving.
- Verbal information: DTT can be used to create virtual environments that allow students to interact with and explore a wide range of information—for example, a digital twin of a historical site can be used to provide students with information about the history and culture of the site. This can help students to better understand and retain verbal information by providing a more interactive and engaging learning experience.
- Motor skills: DTT can be used to create virtual simulations of real-world tasks that can be used to teach students a wide range of motor skills—for example, a digital twin of a surgical procedure can be used to teach students about surgical techniques, or a digital twin of a sports training facility can be used to teach students about physical conditioning. These simulations can provide students with a safe and controlled environment in which to practice and develop their motor skills.
- Attitude: DTT can be used to create virtual environments for teaching students about different attitudes and perspectives—for example, a digital twin

of a city can be used to teach students about different cultures and customs, or a digital twin of an ecosystem can be used to teach students about conservation and sustainability. These simulations can provide students with a deeper comprehension of the subject matter and can help to develop positive attitudes and behaviors.

As a result, DTT can be used to support all five types of learning outcomes by providing students with interactive and engaging learning experiences that allow them to explore, practice, and apply their knowledge in realistic settings. By using DTT, educators can create personalized and adaptive learning experiences that support the development of intellectual skills, cognitive strategies, verbal information, motor skills, and attitudes. Additionally, the use of DTT can also support the development of other important skills such as collaboration, critical thinking, and problem-solving, which are essential for success in today's digital economy.

Other criteria are based on the levels of Revised Blooms' Taxonomy (RBT) [9]. DTT can support learning objectives across all levels of RBT, namely:

- Remembering: DTT can create interactive and engaging learning experiences that help learners remember and recall information—for example, learners can use DTT to explore virtual environments which can help them to remember and recall information about a specific topic or subject.
- Understanding: DTT can help learners understand complex concepts and ideas—for example, learners can use DTT to interact with virtual models of physical systems which can help them understand how the systems work and how different variables affect the system's performance.
- Applying: DTT can help learners adopt their skills and knowledge to real-life problems—for example, learners can use DTT to practice and apply their knowledge in virtual simulations of real-world scenarios.
- Analyzing: DTT can support the analysis of information and data—for example, learners can use DTT to analyze data from virtual experiments or simulations and make predictions based on the data.
- Evaluating: DTT can support the evaluation of information and data—for example, learners can use DTT to evaluate the results of virtual experiments or simulations and make judgments about the quality of the data.

1.5   Challenges and Limitations

1.5.1   Technical Challenges

There are several technical challenges that need to be considered when implementing DTT in education. Some of these challenges include the following:

- Data management: One of the main challenges of implementing DTT in education is the management of large amounts of data. Digital twins require real-time data updates to be accurate, and this data needs to be stored and managed in an efficient way. This can be a complex and time-consuming task, particularly in educational environments where large amounts of data are generated [2].

- Integration with existing systems: Another challenge is integrating DTT with existing systems and infrastructure. Educational institutions often have existing systems and technologies in place that need to be integrated with DTT to provide a seamless and effective learning experience.
- Hardware and software requirements: DTT requires a significant investment in hardware and software, including high-performance computers, sensors, and VR equipment. This can be a significant challenge for educational institutions, particularly those with limited budgets.
- Scalability: DTT can be complex and resource-intensive, making it difficult to scale up to meet the needs of large numbers of students or multiple educational institutions. This can be a significant challenge when implementing DTT in education.
- Cybersecurity: DTT is vulnerable to cyber threats, and educational institutions need to take measures to protect their digital twins from cyberattacks and data breaches.
- Limited expertise: Many institutions may lack the necessary expertise and experience to implement DTT in education. This can pose a significant challenge, particularly for smaller institutions that may not have the resources to train staff or hire specialized personnel.
- Limited access to technology: DTT is still a relatively new technology which can be difficult for students with limited access to technology to use and understand.

These are the technical challenges that need to be considered when implementing DTT in education. However, these challenges can be overcome with careful planning, investment in technology, and collaboration with experts in the field.

1.5.2 Pedagogical Challenges

In addition to the technical challenges of using DTT in education, several pedagogical challenges that also need to be considered are as follows:

- Adapting teaching methods: One of the main challenges of implementing DTT in education is adapting teaching methods to make use of the technology. DTT can provide new and interactive ways of learning, but educators need to be trained on how to effectively use and integrate the technology in the classroom.
- Personalization of learning: DTT can provide an opportunity for the personalization of learning, but educators need to be trained on how to use the technology to provide personalized learning experiences for each student.
- Curriculum development: Another challenge is developing a curriculum that effectively makes use of DTT. Educators need to be able to create learning

activities and assessments that are appropriate for the technology and that are aligned with educational goals and objectives.

- Assessment and evaluation: DTT can provide new opportunities for assessment and evaluation, but educators need to be trained on how to use the technology to assess student learning and progress in a meaningful way.
- Collaboration and teamwork: DTT can be used to facilitate collaborative learning [53] and teamwork [25], but educators need to be trained on how to use the technology to support these activities in the classroom.
- Limited access to technology: DTT is still a relatively new and complex technology which can be difficult for students with limited access to technology to use and understand.
- Limited resources and funding: Many institutions may lack the necessary resources and funding to implement DTT in education. This can pose a significant challenge particularly for smaller institutions that may not have the resources to invest in technology and training.
- Limited support and professional development: many institutions may lack the necessary support and professional development to effectively implement DTT in education.
- Limited understanding of the technology: Many educators may lack the understanding and knowledge of DTT, which can make it difficult for them to effectively implement it in the classroom.
- Limited curriculum alignment: DTT may not align with the current curriculum, which can make it difficult for educators to integrate it into their teaching methods and assessments.
- Limited access to real-world scenarios: DTT can be used to replicate real-world scenarios for scientific inquiry and problem-solving, but limited access can make it difficult for educators to utilize the technology in their teaching.

These are some of the pedagogical challenges that need to be considered when implementing DTT in education. However, with proper planning, investment in technology, and professional development, these challenges can be overcome through collaboration and partnerships between educators and technology experts, and DTT can provide new and exciting opportunities for learning, assessment and collaboration, and the design of effective digital twin-based educational systems that align with the curriculum and meet the needs of educators, students, and institutions.

1.5.3 Ethical and Privacy Concerns

DTT has the potential to revolutionize education, but it also raises a number of ethical and privacy concerns that need to be considered, which include the following:

- Data privacy: DTT requires the collection and use of large amounts of personal data, including student information, learning activities, and performance data. This data must be protected to ensure that student privacy is not compromised.

- Data security: DTT requires the storage and management of large amounts of data which must be kept secure to prevent data breaches and cyberattacks.
- Data ownership: DTT can produce a lot of data, and it is important to determine who owns this data and how it can be used.
- Informed consent: DTT can collect a lot of personal data, so one needs to get informed consent from students and their parents before collecting this data.
- Bias: DTT can perpetuate and amplify bias, particularly if it is not properly designed and implemented.
- Access and equity: DTT requires access to technology and Internet, and students who do not have access to these resources may be disadvantaged.
- Transparency: DTT can be complex and opaque, and it is important to ensure that students and their parents understand how the technology works and how their data is being used.
- Technical challenges: DTT is still a relatively new and complex technology which can be difficult for students with limited access to technology to use and understand.

By considering these ethical and privacy concerns, educators and institutions can design and implement DTT in a way that respects student privacy and promotes equity and transparency in the use of technology.

1.5.4   Future Research Directions

DTT is a rapidly evolving field with many potential future research directions and possibilities. Some of these include the following:

- Advanced data analytics: DTT generates a lot of data, and research can focus on developing advanced analytics techniques to extract valuable insights from this data.
- Predictive modeling: DTT can be used to forecast the future state of systems and processes. Future research can focus on developing predictive models for optimizing system performance and predicting potential failures.
- AI and machine learning: DTT can be used to train AI and machine learning models [39]. Future research can focus on developing AI-based digital twin systems that can learn from data and adapt to changing conditions [71] or perform data mining for further analysis [49].
- Human–computer interaction: DTT can be used to create immersive and interactive virtual environments. Future research can focus on developing new human–computer interaction techniques that can be used to develop more engaging and realistic virtual environments.
- Real-time data integration: DTT requires real-time data integration to keep the digital twin in sync with the physical twin. Future research can focus on developing new sensor technologies and data integration techniques that can be used to improve the accuracy and timeliness of digital twin data.
- Cybersecurity: DTT requires the storage and management of large amounts of data which must be kept secure to prevent data breaches and cyberattacks.

Future research can focus on developing new cybersecurity techniques that can be used to protect digital twin systems and data.

- Interoperability: DTT is often used in conjunction with other systems and technologies. Future research can focus on developing new interoperability standards and protocols that can be used to connect digital twin systems with other systems and technologies.
- Ethics and privacy: DTT raises a number of ethical and privacy concerns, such as informed consent, data privacy and security, data ownership, bias, access, and transparency. Future research can focus on addressing these concerns and developing new guidelines for the ethical use of DTT.

In summary, DTT is a promising field with many potential future research directions which can lead to the development of more advanced and sophisticated digital twin systems that can be used in various fields and industries. Additionally, digital twins can be used to simulate human cognitive and emotional processes, helping researchers and developers to understand and enhance human mental capabilities. In this way, digital twins can be used to support research on brain–computer interfaces, artificial intelligence, and other technologies that aim to augment human intelligence and capabilities. Moreover, DTT can be seen as a tool to support the goals of transhumanism [27] by providing new ways to enhance human capabilities and understanding.

1.6   Conclusion

DTT has the potential to revolutionize education by providing new and interactive ways of learning, personalization of learning, and the ability to replicate real-world scenarios for scientific inquiry and problem-solving. The technology can also be used to facilitate collaboration and teamwork and to provide new opportunities for assessment and evaluation. DTT can also be used in various industries, such as infrastructure design, manufacturing, and patient treatments. However, there are several technical, pedagogical, and ethical challenges that need to be considered when implementing DTT in education. These include data management, integration with existing systems, hardware and software requirements, scalability, cybersecurity, limited expertise, limited access to technology, and limited resources and funding. By addressing these challenges, DTT can provide new and exciting opportunities for learning, assessment, and collaboration while also aligning with the curriculum and meeting the needs of educators, students, and institutions. DTT is a necessary step for shaping the future of education and beyond, but it must be implemented with careful consideration of technical, pedagogical, ethical, and privacy concerns. With proper planning, investment in technology, and professional development, DTT can provide new and exciting opportunities for learning and beyond.

DTT has the potential to enhance the learning experience and improve educational outcomes by providing new and interactive ways of learning. It can provide immersive hands-on learning through VR and CV, which can lead to more comprehensive perception, dynamic intelligence, and virtual–real integration. This can provide new possibilities for innovation in learning environments and resources and educational content and will definitely promote profound changes in education and empower the future of education.

DTT can also be used to replicate real-world scenarios for scientific inquiry and problem-solving, which can help students develop critical thinking and problem-solving skills. This can be particularly effective in STEM fields where students can conduct experiments and simulations that would be difficult or impossible to replicate in the real world [20]. DTT can provide opportunities for personalization of learning [73], as students can interact with virtual tutors, access learning resources that suit their needs with the help of intelligent recommendations and learning analytics, and develop their creative talents. This can help students develop their multiple intelligences and tailor their learning experience to their unique needs and interests [14]. DTT can improve educational outcomes by providing new opportunities for assessment and evaluation. Educators can use the technology to monitor student progress and provide immediate feedback, which can help students improve their performance. As a result, DTT has a great potential to enhance the learning experience and improve educational outcomes by providing new and interactive ways of learning, replicating real-world scenarios for scientific inquiry and problem-solving [67], providing opportunities for personalization of learning, and providing new opportunities for assessment and evaluation.

References

1. Adewumi, A., Laleye, O., Misra, S., Maskeliunas, R. *et al.*, Automating the process of faculty evaluation in a private higher institution, in: *AISC of Advances in Intelligent Systems and Computing*, vol. 1181, 2021.
2. Ahmad, S.F., Alam, M.M., Rahmat, M.K., Mubarik, M.S., Hyder, S., II, Academic and administrative role of artificial intelligence in education. *Sustainability*, 14, 3, 2022.
3. Al-Ghaili, A.M., Kasim, H., Al-Hada, N.M., Hassan, Z.B., Othman, M., Tharik, J.H., Kasmani, R.M., Shayea, I., A review of metaverse's definitions, architecture, applications, challenges, issues, solutions, and future trends. *IEEE Access*, 10, 125835–125866, 2022.
4. Alkhammash, L., Pennfather, P., Dixit, I., Jeon, S., Shao, A., Liu, E., Swic, S., Zhang, S., Li, J., Kvaale, A. *et al.*, Design principles for vanvr app: A virtual anatomy lab. *FASEB J.*, 36, 2022.
5. Bado, M.F., Tonelli, D., Poli, F., Zonta, D., Casas, J.R., Digital twin for civil engineering systems: An exploratory review for distributed sensing updating. *Sensors*, 22, 9, 2022.
6. Barricelli, B.R., Casiraghi, E., Fogli, D., A survey on digital twin: Definitions, characteristics, applications, and design implications. *IEEE Access*, 7, 2019.
7. Bharath, V.G. and Rajashekar, P., Virtual manufacturing: A review, in: *National Conference Emerging Research Areas Mechanical Engineering Conference Proceedings*, pp. 355–364, 2015.
8. Bhute, V.J., Inguva, P., Shah, U., Brechtelsbauer, C., Transforming traditional teaching laboratories for effective remote delivery—A review. *Educ. Chem. Eng.*, 35, 96–104, 2021.
9. Bloom, B.S. and Krathwohl, D.R., *Taxonomy of educational objectives: The classification of educational goals*. Book 1, Cognitive Domain, Longman, New York, NY, USA, 2020.
10. Botın-Sanabria, D.M., Mihaita, S., Peimbert-Garcıa, R.E., Ramırez-Moreno, M.A., Ramırez-Mendoza, R.A., Lozoya-Santos, J.J., Digital twin technology challenges and applications: A comprehensive review. *Remote Sens.*, 14, 6, 2022.
11. Burbaite, R., Stuikys, V., Damasevicius, R., Educational robots as collaborative learning objects for teaching computer science, in: *ICSSE 2013 - IEEE International Conference on System Science and Engineering, Proceedings*, pp. 211–216, 2013.
12. Buzys, R., Maskeliunas, R. *et al.*, Cloudification of virtual reality gliding simulation game. *Information*, 9, 12, 2018.

13. Chacon, R., Sanchez-Juny, M., Real, E., Gironella, F.X., Puigagut, J., Ledesma, A., Digital twins in civil and environmental engineering classrooms, in: *4th International Conference on Civil Engineering Education: Challenges for the Third Millennium*, pp. 290–299, 2018.

14. Chen, Y., Gong, Z., Xing, Q., Research on the construction of graphical data intelligence education driven by digital intelligence integration, in: *LNCS of Lecture Notes in Computer Science*, vol. 13517, 2022.

15. Cho, Y., Hsu, H.N., Zheng, Z., Trinh, E.E., Jang, H., Cheng, Y., Research based on affective filter theory: Is social vr an effective tool for learning a second language?, in: *8th International Conference of the Immersive Learning Research Network, iLRN 2022*, 2022.

16. Danevicius, E., Maskeliunas, R. *et al.*, A soft body physics simulator with computational offloading to the cloud, *Information*, 9, 12, 2018.

17. David, J., Lobov, A., Lanz, M., Learning experiences involving digital twins, in: *Proceedings: IECON 2018 - 44th Annual Conference of the IEEE Industrial Electronics Society*, pp. 3681–3686, 2018.

18. David, J., Lobov, A., Lanz, M., Leveraging digital twins for assisted learning of flexible manufacturing systems, in: *IEEE 16th International Conference on Industrial Informatics, INDIN 2018*, pp. 529–535, 2018.

19. Defraeye, T., Shrivastava, C., Berry, T., Verboven, P., Onwude, D., Schudel, S., Buhlmann, A., Cronje, P., Rossi, R.M., Digital twins are coming: Will we need them in supply chains of fresh horticultural produce? *Trends Food Sci. Technol.*, 109, 245–258, 2021.

20. Deniz, S., Muller, U.C., Steiner, I., Sergi, T., Online (remote) teaching for laboratory based courses using "digital twins" of the experiments. *J. Eng. Gas Turbines Power*, 144, 5, 2022.

21. Duan, X., Kang, S.-J., Choi, J., II, Kim, S.K., Mixed reality system for virtual chemistry lab. *KSII Trans. Internet Inf. Syst. (TIIS)*, 14, 4, 1673–1688, 2020.

22. Eriksson, K., Alsaleh, A., Behzad Far, S., Stjern, D., Applying digital twin technology in higher education: An automation line case study, in: *Advances in Transdisciplinary Engineering*, vol. 21, pp. 461–472, 2022.

23. Feng, X., Jiang, Y., Yang, X., Du, M., Li, X., Computer vision algorithms and hardware implementations: A survey. *Integration*, 69, 309–320, 2019.

24. Gagne, R.M., Learning outcomes and their effects: Useful categories of human performance. *Am. Psychol.*, 39, 4, 377, 1984.

25. Gutierrez, K.S., Kidd, J.J., Lee, M.J., Pazos, P., Kaipa, K., Ringleb, S., II, Ayala, O., Undergraduate engineering and education students reflect on their interdisciplinary teamwork experiences following transition to virtual instruction caused by covid-19. *Educ. Sci.*, 12, 9, 2022.

26. Harrington, M.C.R., Jones, C., Peters, C., Virtual nature as a digital twin botanically correct 3D ar and vr optimized low-polygon and photogrammetry high-polygon plant models: A short overview of construction methods, in: *ACM SIGGRAPH 2022 Educator's Forum*, pp. 1–2, 2022.

27. Huberman, J., *Transhumanism: From ancestors to avatars*, Cambridge University Press, Cambridge, UK, 2020.

28. Iakovides, N., Lazarou, A., Kyriakou, P., Aristidou, A., Virtual library in the concept of digital twin, in: *2022 International Conference on Interactive Media, Smart Systems and Emerging Technologies, IMET 2022*, 2022.

29. Jacko, P., Beres, M., Kovacova, I., Molnar, J., Vince, T., Dziak, J., Fecko, B., Gans, S., Kovac, D., Remote iot education laboratory for microcontrollers based on the stm32 chips. *Sensors*, 22, 4, 2022.

30. Jahn, S., Weiss, N., Akcakoca, U., Mottok, J., Under the hood-a concept for virtualized automotive security education, in: *EDULEARN21 Proceedings*, pp. 6109–6118, IATED, 2021.

31. Kamel Boulos, M.N. and Zhang, P., Digital twins: From personalised medicine to precision public health. *J. Personalized Med.*, 11, 8, 2021.

32. Kezar, A., Theory of multiple intelligences: Implications for higher education. *Innovative Higher Educ.*, 26, 2, 141–154, 2001.

33. Khundam, C. and Noel, F., Storytelling framework with adaptive interaction system for interactive content in virtual museum. *ECTI Trans. Comput. Inf. Technol.*, 15, 1, 34–49, 2021.

34. Kokane, A., Singhal, H., Mukherjee, S., Ram Mohana Reddy, G., Effective e-learning using 3D virtual tutors and webrtc based multimedia chat, in: *2014 International Conference on Recent Trends in Information Technology*, IEEE, pp. 1–6, 2014.

35. Makarova, I., Mustafina, J., Buyvol, P., Mukhametdinov, E., Mavrin, V., Digitalization of Engineering Education in Training for Industry 4.0, in: *LNNS of Lecture Notes in Networks and Systems*, vol. 389, 2022.

36. Makarova, I., Parsin, G., Boyko, A., Buyvol, P., Virtual reality laboratory as a factor in increasing engineering students' motivation, in: *LNNS of Lecture Notes in Networks and Systems*, vol. 524, 2023.

37. Martynov, V., Filosova, E., Egorova, Y., Information architecture to support engineering education in the era of industry 4.0, in: *2022 6th International Conference on Information Technologies in Engineering Education, Inforino 2022*, 2022.

38. Maskeliunas, R., Damasevicius, R., Lethin, C., Paulauskas, A., Esposito, A., Catena, M., Aschettino, V., Serious game ido: Towards better education in dementia care. *Information*, 10, 11, 2019.

39. Maskeliunas, R., Damasevicius, R., Paulauskas, A., Ceravolo, M.G., Charalambous, M., Kambanaros, M., Pampoulou, E., Barbabella, F., Poli, A., Carvalho, C.V., Deep reinforcement learning-based itrain serious game for caregivers dealing with post-stroke patients. *Information*, 13, 12, 2022.

40. Maskeliunas, R., Kulikajevas, A., Blazauskas, T. *et al.*, An interactive serious mobile game for supporting the learning of programming in javascript in the context of eco-friendly city management. *Computers*, 9, 4, 1–18, 2020.

41. Meng, S., Ye, Y., Yang, Q., Huang, Z., Xie, W., Digital twin and its aerospace applications. *Hangkong Xuebao/Acta Aeronautica Astronautica Sin.*, 41, 9, 2020.

42. Moskaliuk, J., Bertram, J., Cress, U., Training in virtual environments: Putting theory into practice. *Ergonomics*, 56, 2, 195–204, February 2013.

43. Mostajeran, F., Fischer, M., Steinicke, F., Kuhn, S., Effects of exposure to immersive computer-generated virtual nature and control environments on affect and cognition. *Sci. Rep.*, 13, 1, 2023.

44. Mourtzis, D., Panopoulos, N., Angelopoulos, J., A hybrid teaching factory model towards personalized education 4.0. *Int. J. Comput. Integr. Manuf.*, 2022.

45. Mu, Z., Liu, M., Tan, Z., On the interactive display of virtual aerospace museum based on virtual reality, in: *2018 International Conference on Robots & Intelligent System (ICRIS)*, IEEE, pp. 144–146, 2018.

46. Nasirahmadi, A. and Hensel, O., Toward the next generation of digitalization in agriculture based on digital twin paradigm. *Sensors*, 22, 2, 2022.

47. Nowak, K.L. and Fox, J., Avatars and computer-mediated communication: A review of the definitions, uses, and effects of digital representations. *Rev. Commun. Res.*, 6, 30–53, 2018.

48. Oh, Y.-J. and Kim, E.-K., Efficient 3D model visualization system of design drawing based on mobile augmented reality, in: *Advances in Computer Science and its Applications*, pp. 805–810, Springer, Berlin, Heidelberg, 2014.

49. Okewu, E., Adewole, P., Misra, S. *et al.*, Artificial neural networks for educational data mining in higher education: A systematic literature review. *Appl. Artif. Intell.*, 35, 13, 983–1021, 2021.

50. Pang, D., Cui, S., Yang, G., Remote laboratory as an educational tool in robotics experimental course. *Int. J. Emerging Technol. Learn.*, 17, 21, 230–245, 2022.

51. Pellas, N., Dengel, A., Christopoulos, A., A scoping review of immersive virtual reality in stem education. *IEEE Trans. Learn. Technol.*, 13, 4, 748–761, 2020.

52. Piromalis, D. and Kantaros, A., Digital twins in the automotive industry: The road toward physical-digital convergence. *Appl. Syst. Innovation*, 5, 4, 2022.

53. Plauska, I. and Damasevicius, R., Educational robots for Internet-of-Things supported collaborative learning, in: *of Communications in Computer and Information Science*, vol. 465, 2014.

54. Qamsane, Y., Chen, C.-Y., Balta, E.C., Kao, B.-C., Mohan, S., Moyne, J., Tilbury, D., Barton, K., A unified digital twin framework for real-time monitoring and evaluation of smart manufacturing systems, in: *2019 IEEE 15th International Conference on Automation Science and Engineering (CASE)*, IEEE, August 2019.

55. Qian, C., Liu, X., Ripley, C., Qian, M., Liang, F., Yu, W., Digital twin—Cyber replica of physical things: Architecture, applications and future research directions. *Future Internet*, 14, 2, 2022.

56. Rassudov, L. and Korunets, A., Covid-19 pandemic challenges for engineering education, in: *2020 11th International Conference on Electrical Power Drive Systems (ICEPDS 2020)*, 2020.

57. Rassudov, L. and Korunets, A., Virtual labs: An effective engineering education tool for remote learning and not only, in: *International Workshop on Electric Drives (IWED)*, vol. 2022-January, 2022.

58. Ruutmann, T., Witt, E., Olowa, T., Puolitaival, T., Bragadin, M., Evaluation of immersive project-based learning experiences, in: *International CDIO Conference*, pp. 313–323, 2022.

59. Sagun, A., Potential use of virtual environments in design education. *Turkish Online J. Design Art Commun.*, 1, 2, 25–33, 2011.

60. Salimi, F.-F., Salimi, F., Taghipoor, H., Mokhtarname, R., Safavi, A.A., Urbas, L., Active learning on the collaborative digital twin of the process plants, in: *2022 IEEE Global Engineering Education Conference (EDUCON)*, IEEE, March 2022.

61. Saracco, R., Digital twins: Bridging physical space and cyberspace. *Computer*, 52, 12, 58–64, 2019.

62. Segovia, M. and Garcia-Alfaro, J., Design, modeling and implementation of digital twins. *Sensors*, 22, 14, 5396, Jul 2022.

63. Sepasgozar, S.M.E., Digital twin and web-based virtual gaming technologies for online education: A case of construction management and engineering. *Appl. Sci.*, 10, 13, 2020.

64. Shahat, E., Hyun, C.T., Yeom, C., City digital twin potentials: A review and research agenda. *Sustainability*, 13, 6, 2021.

65. Soliman, M., Pedagogical intelligence in virtual reality environments, in: *Lecture Notes in Networks and Systems*, vol. 456, 2022.

66. Spitzer, B.O., Ma, J.H., Erdogmus, E., Kreimer, B., Ryherd, E., Diefes-Dux, H., Framework for the use of extended reality modalities in aec education. *Buildings*, 12, 12, 2022.

67. Swacha, J., Maskeliunas, R. *et al.*, Introducing sustainable development topics into computer science education: Design and evaluation of the eco jsity game. *Sustainability*, 13, 8, 2021.

68. Tang, H., Implementing open educational resources in digital education. *Educ. Technol. Res. Dev.*, 69, 1, 389–392, November 2020.

69. Velazquez, F.C. and Mendez, G.M., Systematic review of the development of spatial intelligence through augmented reality in stem knowledge areas. *Mathematics*, 9, 23, 2021.

70. Wilkins, B. and Barrett, J., The virtual construction site: A web-based teaching/learning environment in construction technology. *Autom. Constr.*, 10, 1, 169–179, 2000.

71. Wogu, I.A.P., Misra, S., Assibong, P.A. *et al.*, Artificial intelligence, smart classrooms and online education in the 21st century: Implications for human development. *J. Cases Inf. Technol.*, 21, 3, 66–79, 2019.
72. Yang, B., Yang, S., Lv, Z., Wang, F., Olofsson, T., Application of digital twins and metaverse in the field of fluid machinery pumps and fans: A review. *Sensors*, 22, 23, 9294, Nov 2022.
73. Zhang, Y., Pang, L., Wang, D., Liu, S., Influences of digital twin technology on learning effect. *J. Eng. Sci. Technol. Rev.*, 15, 4, 140–145, 2022.

An Intersection Between Machine Learning, Security, and Privacy

Hareharan P.K.[1]*, Kanishka J.[2] and Subaasri D.[2]

*[1]Department of Information Technology Bannari Amman Institute of Technology,
Erode, Tamil Nadu, India*
*[2]Department of Information Science and Engineering Bannari Amman Institute of Technology,
Erode, Tamil Nadu, India*

Abstract

For people across the globe, online media is a programmer's toy as a result of the rapid development of digital threats and the consequent lack of current security and protection solutions. Concerns about security and protection are being addressed using blockchain technologies and machine language calculations. A few studies have looked at both blockchain strategies and calculations in machine language. Last but not least, we cover security and protection difficulties in the field using machine language calculations and blockchain methods, and we highlight and educate many snags and future test subjects. Due to the inclusion of devices in numerous apps, concerns over the safety and security of the customers have intensified. Blockchain techniques are becoming increasingly used in current IoT applications to handle security and protection problems. However, these investigations use machine learning or blockchain techniques to deal with security or protection issues, necessitating a comprehensive assessment of current initiatives to deal with security and protection issues using machine learning and blockchain techniques.

Keywords: Security, machine learning, deep learning, artificial intelligence

2.1 Introduction

The era was changed by the automation of machine learning on business cloud platforms, which embodied the future of technological device learning and increased computational power—for instance, statistical analysis powered by machine learning has fundamentally altered how healthcare and finance are implemented. Massive amounts of data are consumed by detection and tracking structures in the safety domain, which then extract previously unavailable information that can be used. Despite these remarkable developments, the technical community still lacks a thorough understanding of the flaws in the

*Corresponding author: hareharan.it21@bitsathy.ac.in

Amit Kumar Tyagi (ed.) Automated Secure Computing for Next-Generation Systems, (23–42) © 2024 Scrivener Publishing LLC

way machine-learning-based systems are built and how to guard against them. We must therefore create technology for safety and security [1].

Such behaviors, however, are not ignored for very long. Many studies have attempted to better understand the harms, issues, attacks, and defenses of machine learning-based systems. However, this study is divided into many research communities, such as machine learning, security, statistics, and computational concepts. There might not, however, be a single lexicon or level of technical proficiency that covers these topics. Our endeavor to systematize the myriad safety and privacy challenges included in machine learning is motivated and guided by fragmentation.

The safety and privacy of structures that integrate machine learning are therefore approximated by providing a unified chance version to allow structured interpretation (Section 2.3). This version differs from earlier attempts by considering all of the major facts at once, so machine learning is now a component rather than a standalone algorithm. The task is to classify offenses and defenses that are accepted by the technological community. In Section 2.4, we learn about the challenging circumstances of doing research in a complex setting. In addition to earlier research in these fields, we provide instances and arguments that make recent advancements in a meaningful and substantial way.

2.2   Machine Learning

We can start this section by explaining the definition of machine learning and by quickly measuring the system's performance of the used exercise equipment (for solving real-world problems). Think about the specifics of the task's analysis as well as the certain aspects of its realistic implementation. This article establishes a common understanding in this field, principally based on a random model that captures attack surface trends, adversary targets, and workable security and attack capabilities based on tool analysis-based systems [2]. Device inspection systems can be used to gather attack and defense intelligence using this security approach. This work highlights major ideas and emphasizes their importance as takeaways for this new area of study. It is a good idea to view the device's investigation-based system via the standard CIA prisms (data protection, integrity, and availability) while examining safety and privacy in this field. In this task, privacy is determined by the information's model or reputation. Attacks on model confidentiality expose its shape and parameters (a crucial conceptual characteristic) as well as the data required to train and assess it (such as details about the character in question). The key is that the latter strategy's beauty can jeopardize the source's privacy, especially if the model's users are not trusted. When a medical diagnosis model is trained using the impacted character's clinical data, this might be quite delicate. Attacks that consistently cause their opponent's preferred expenditure or behavior are known as consistency attacks. It is frequently finished by the gadget learning, honing, or modifying the data it is projecting. Such attacks fall under availability if they aim to restrict legitimate customers' access to a broad range of model output or the tool's capabilities.

When comparing security and privacy, the 2D perspective acknowledges pipeline gadget research and focuses on attacks and defences. Here we should recall the machine learning loop. An attack on education is often researched in an effort to persuade the alteration of educational patterns and closely related learning research systems. The inference period's (runtime) attack is more varied. Oracle attacks extract the version itself, while the adversary utilizes explosive attacks to produce an intense output. Defense army technological advancements in the area of gadget research are anticipated to be made. I can recall numerous requests for shields. The first is distribution drift wellness, which attempts to maintain overall performance even as distribution formation and execution times change. The second one helps to formally preserve privacy and reduces the number of documents that can be discovered [3].

2.2.1   Overview of Machine Learning

This section will discuss a few essential components of machine learning in detail [4], namely:

Supervised Learning: By giving styles or selection methods that represent the prevalent correlations in the data, machine learning makes it easier to evaluate (often big) datasets. Based on the kinds of statistics that can be used to evaluate them, machine learning approaches are typically divided into three groups. Schooling examples can be provided to supervise learning operations in the form of inputs that are categorized with corresponding outputs. The objective is to create a version that associates inputs—even hidden inputs—with outputs. If the assignment's end area was categorical, it is known as classification; if it was cardinal, it is known as regression. The following are some examples of supervised study duties: device translation, item popularity in photos, and filtering of unsolicited mail.

Unsupervised Training: The technique's project is unsupervised when it is given unnamed inputs. This includes issues like clustering factors based on similarity measures, applying dimension discounts on task information in decreasing directional subspaces, and version pre-schooling. Combining, for example, can be used to find anomalies.

Reinforcement training: Information inside the series of acts, inspections, and incentives are included in the scope of reinforcement learning (RL) (e.g., video game works). The purpose of RL is to provide a framework for operating in a given environment, and it is a branch of machine learning focused with planning and management. In the real world, dealers pick up knowledge through doing and observing what is going on around them. Go champion man was recently defeated by a machine thanks to learning combining unsupervised and supervised methods. There are numerous publications that cover this vast topic, which readers interested in machine learning surveys may find informative. The majority of machine learning security and privacy research has thus far been done in controlled contexts, as will be explained in Sections 4 and 5. We offer beneficial results in more widely used scenarios since safety concerns are still important for both uncontrolled and reinforced learning.

2.2.2   Machine Learning Stages: Training and Inference

It is helpful to distinguish between the learning level at which a version is discovered by entering information and the inference level at which the skilled version is applied to a task [5].

Training: Majority of the machine learning models can be thought of as capacities, or h(x) functions, that take an input, or x, and specify them using a vector. The output h(x) is a prediction provided by the version for x of a few valuable items. Commonly, x is represented as a feature vector, which is a set of values. The area of capabilities H is the collection of candidate hypotheses. To choose a set of rules for studying, a set of educational data is used. When a research is supervised, the settings are changed to match version predictions h(x) with the anticipated output y as indicated by the dataset means. To do this, a loss characteristic that captures the difference between h(x) and the associated y is reduced. In order to assess the level of adaptation of the version (overall performance on unknown information), the version's performance is then assessed using a check dataset that is distinct from the education dataset. A firm list of categorized information stored excellently from educational material can be used to examine version correctness with recognition to validate information for a controlled problem—for example, in the infection category (see above), precision may be referred to as the percentage of predictions h(x) that matched the label y (malware or benign) connected to the executable x in the check dataset. The purpose of education is to prescribe motions that yield the best predicted praise for entry records x, and h(x) encrypts an approach in reinforcement learning. When learning is done via the Internet (controlled, uncontrolled, or reinforcement), settings are updated as new educational factors become accessible [6].

Inference: Once the instructional process is complete, the version is used to make predictions based on inputs that were not seen earlier. In other words, the version calculates h(x) with entirely new inputs x, while the parameter costs remain constant. The version in our malicious category example guesses the label for each program x. The most typical placement for category in the model prediction is a vector that provides a probability for each problem magnificence, describing how likely it is that the center belongs to that magnificence. For the unrestricted network intrusion detection procedure, the version may choose to return to the sample illustration h(x), which concerns a brand-new entrance community visitor [7]. Figure 2.1, given below, elucidates the difference between the training and inference phases involved in the development of any model.

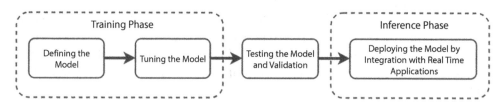

Figure 2.1 Training and inference phase of a model.

2.3   Threat Model

The protection of any machine from hostile situations to guard against the machine's possibilities of dwindling are counted with admiration. This section discusses the scope and significance of chance models in machine learning structures along with how to map the range of security models. It begins by determining the attack surface of machine learning structures to predict where and how an opponent will arrive. Make an effort to damage the device. The next component builds on the prior ones as they improve the chance version. Additionally, they draw on recent trends such as hostile incidents and club attacks based on inference.

2.3.1   Attack Model of Machine Learning

The machine's purpose is a consideration in the machine and system study. As a result, such structures can be seen on a fact pathway with a broad definition for analysis. By using version, the virtual domain manages the sensor's or the factory's position functions, and the output is sent to an external machine or consumer act. In general, this pipeline consists of the self-contained vehicle, the (center) regional invasion recognition structure, and the (below) structure. The machine learning framework extracts model inputs through sensors (images from videos, community postings) as well as functions (pixels, flows). A version's meaning was relocated and interpreted (by the character and community-sort vehicle prevention, IP fate site vision). The machine's base can recognize and describe the information on the processing pipeline in this case. The adversary has the ability to damage the version, control the fact assembly, or manipulate the output, keeping in mind that the version teaches both offline and online procedures. The education facts employed to investigate the version include vectors of functions that are used as inputs at various points in inference alongside the projected estimates for autonomous learning outcomes. As was previously discussed, the process of series and confirmation approaches offer every other attack surface; adversaries who can influence the series procedure can do so to produce targeted version acts because it may progressively change the version using carefully constructed real-time input. A challenge that is tied to an online situation could be highly destructive. Domain names, spam email, and community penetration have all been cited as examples of such cyber-attacks on anomaly detectors [8].

2.3.2   Trust Model

The extent of any ML-based device's dissemination, which has to do with agreement, greatly influences how the device's accepted version is determined. To briefly summarize, we may use the many lessons learned by artists to a machine learning system that has been deployed and is based on an entire device. First, there are information proprietors who own the data or are custodians. An example would be an IT firm implementing a facial recognition system as a supplier of authenticity. Second, there are companies that combine devices and algorithms; for example, the companies that guarantee the legitimacy of software programmes. Third, taking into account the patrons of the business, there may be customers of the service provider for the device and outsiders may also be involved. It is important to keep in mind that there may be multiple consumers, carriers, data owners, or outside parties concerned with a specific deployment. An acceptance version for the specified device assigns a level of acceptance to each and every actor in the application. Any character may be trusted, deemed hazardous, or partially relied upon (to perform or cease to perform acts of goodness). These assumptions are added together to create the accepted version of the bureaucracy, and this highlights the potential ways that evil actors could attack the device [9].

This is not an attempt to understand a particular acceptance model or a collection of "good" acceptance models in this study (perhaps an impossible task), but rather to concentrate on the hazards posed by evil actors. As a result, insight into every assumption is made possible with a version that is suitable for a certain distribution.

2.3.3   Machine Learning Capabilities in a Differential Environment

The motions and information that the adversary has access to are also used to describe a risk version. The notion of security is formulated in consideration of stronger or weaker enemies who have more or much less access to the system and its data. The word "skills" relates to the what and the how of available attacks and, on a risk scale, specifies the potential attack routes. An inner opponent might have access to the versions, for instance, in the identification of community incursions. You might be able to get away with it if your eavesdropping opponent is weaker because they are trained to distinguish attacks by consistent behavior and additionally have better access to transmission control protocol (TCP) dumps of the traffic in the neighborhood. This place always has the same attack floor, but an intruder with extra knowledge is a carefully controlled resource and acts as a stronger opponent. We identify various attacker skills in machine learning systems with regard to implication and training processes [10].

Phase of Inference: Exploratory attacks at inference time no longer modify the targeted version but, rather, both because it provides outputs that the adversary has predetermined (for example, integrity is a quality). White box and black box attacks are two subcategories of inference section attacks. In white box attacks, the enemy has limited knowledge of the version or its unique educational data, likely due to unreliable actors inside the data processing pipeline. Utilizing the following data can make white box attacks more prevalent: information about the model architecture (set of rules and shape of the hypothesis h), properties of the models (weights), educational data, and different combinations of these. In order to learn more about the target, the adversary uses the data that is readily available. An adversary who has access to the version and its parameters, for example, can also find a functional area where the model has a high error rate and take advantage of that by changing an input into that area, as in hostile instance crafting.

Contrarily, no information about the version is expected from black box attacks. In these attacks, the adversary uses information about the environment or other sources to determine the version susceptibility. In the fountain technique, for instance, a version is investigated via a series of carefully prepared inputs and outputs because there is a lot of information on Oracle which are effective. Due to the generalizability of possessions made possible by the use of numerous version architectures, a version can be built using input/output pairings, and relatively less information is required [11].

Phase of Training: On the other hand, black box attacks are not likely to reveal anything about the version. In those attacks, the attacker leverages environmental data or information from other sources to ascertain the version susceptibility—for instance, in the fountain technique, a version is examined using a number of meticulously crafted inputs and outputs. Oracle attacks are successful because Oracle has a lot of information. A version can be created utilizing input/output pairs, and only a comparatively little bit information is needed due to the generalizability of possessions made possible by the usage of various version architectures.

There are numerous attack methods for altering the version. The first modifies the education statistics either by injecting hostile data into the existing data (a process known as injection), using a malicious user, or by directly changing the education statistics on the spot (a process known as modification), either through direct attacks or through a section of a trusted data stream. Finally, adversaries may occasionally be able to influence algorithmic learning without causing a problem by cooperating with a trusted machine learning education component. It goes without saying that opponents who modify their understanding of sound judgement (and thereby create their own version) are incredibly successful and challenging to encounter [12].

2.3.4   Opposite Views of Machine Learning in Security

In addition to a fourth quality, privacy, seems to be having an impact on confidentiality, integrity, and availability. An intriguing dichotomy appears when considering this course of action: Attacks on tool intersections are carefully related in terms of goal and strategy, as well as security and safety. Both security and authenticity may be safeguarded. Everyone is aware of the machine learning notion of volume, as well as the entire tool used to implement it. However, accessibility is a problem that isn't unique to a certain product but affects how well a tool functions in a particular environment. Creating and enforcing regulations is another option depending on the ambient noise level. Although important, the security of the machine learning system is insufficient to warrant the creation of environmental legislation. For instance, a self-driving cars' visual system needs to be dependable and accessible. To ensure that unique cars may access the road, nevertheless, this is no longer sufficient. This problem is outside the scope of the inquiry and necessitates extra treatment along the lines of what Tyagi *et al.*, suggested several works [26] for concerns about privacy protection. The paper then goes on to explain the many forms of bad goals connected to each vulnerability.

Privacy and Confidentiality: Threats on anonymity and security are focused on the edition and documents. Indeed, the opponent is a version includes unreliable individual, that could try and retrieve facts approximately from the version. Those attacks typically disappear beneath the cover of secrecy. If the clients and intellectual assets that the machine learning model claims to represent aren't reliable on by the model owner, it is necessary that the model and its specifications stay private, for instance in financial market networks.

Contrarily, since version owners can no longer be relied upon by way of version users, those users may need to protect the confidentiality of their records from the version owner or the privacy of their records from attacks mounted by other version users. Regardless of the outcome, there are attacks and safeguards for privacy that have to do with revealing and preventing an exposure. Differentiating between two thoughts that are the outcome of the agreed version is difficult. Machine learning models have the ability to memorise and retain information from these educational records. As a result, it is difficult to guarantee that a person's participation in a dataset won't compromise their privacy. The use of the model's predictions, getting better of partially recognised sources, ending with the variant along with image maximum retrieval of educational records (possibly missing pieces), and adversaries acting club test are potential threats.

Accessibility and Reliability: There were also attacks on the availability and integrity of version outputs. Here, the adversary's chosen behavior is the goal to be set off. Attacks attempting authenticity attacks focus on changing the output of versions. The validity of the reasoning approach is undermined. The integrity of the authentication process is affected, for instance, by attacks that attempt to trigger bogus advantages in a negative circumstance popularity machine. Attacks based on availability aim to lower the bar of excellence (for instance, self-belief or coherence), overall effectiveness (for instance, speed), or access (for instance, service interruption). These three elements are intricately linked to one another. Although the goals of these attacks' instructions may differ from one another, the manner in which the adversary achieves his or her goals is typically the same. In the middle of an interest, for example, machine learning requires a high level of honesty, and repeatability is one of the most crucial plainly successful characteristics.

However, investigations have shown that attackers who are able to change educational or citation sources can endanger the reliability of machine learning systems. First, a competitor can serve as the machine learning version's self-confidence's focal point. Reducing this fee may also alter the behavior of the whole machine. For instance, an intrusion detection device may only increase an alarm if its confidence exceeds a particular level. Input misprocessing aims to trick the version into producing wrong outputs for a select few inputs, either altered at the pipeline's entrance or on the version's core directly. The wrong outputs vary depending on the type of enterprise. A ML classifier may identify noise confidently or assign the erroneous elegance to a good image. It can result in a pointless center illustration for an unmanaged characteristic extractor. Given the state of the environment, a reinforcement learning agent may behave in an unwise manner. Although the adversary can entirely corrupt the enter-output mapping, it can still control the version and the behavior of the machine—for instance, it can force a car's computer vision system to interpret a traffic sign incorrectly, which will cause the car to accelerate from the side [13].

2.4 Training in a Differential Environment

The learning process is completely fine because the features of the hypothesis are also perfectly fine. The analyzed dataset is probably open to modification by antagonists. This situation resembles a poisonous attack and is an example of learning that is occasionally negative. Among those scenarios, intrusion detection structures are a well-known example. Poisoning attacks modify the learning dataset by adding, deleting, or altering variables with the intention of changing the decision-making barriers of the focused version, thereby focusing on the integrity of the learning system in accordance with the risk variant. It goes without saying that such a powerful adversary might convince students to look into any imaginable aspect, rendering the service entirely unavailable. Therefore, there will always be a foe in every one of their attacks. Adjustments to the educational files and the emergence of an incompatibility among the sources that were used for deduction and schooling could be signs that the distribution that produced the data on schooling has changed. They provide a line of work that expands on that assertion and advise learning distribution drift-resistant strategies. Surveying the literature, we find that studies almost exclusively discuss poisoning attacks against classifiers (supervised models trained on categorized data). However, if an effort is made to generalize the findings to various machine learning tasks (see Section 2.2), it is found that some of the properties that are overlooked by reinforcement learning algorithms may also be applicable to the methodologies discussed below. It is an illustration of the case made for Alpha Go [14].

2.4.1   Achieving Integrity

As far as big analytics goes, that undesirable capability may be interpreted as the ability to change a small piece of both the schooling and the demographic data. Perhaps one of its most important consequences asserts that achieving a blunders price of inference necessitates $\beta \leq 1+$ for any learning method—for example, the opponent manipulation price should be less than 10% to achieve 90% accuracy (=0.1). The following attempts investigate this outcome from a practical standpoint and present poisoning attacks against machine learning systems. This section is organized around the negative qualities mentioned in the previous section. Unlike a few attacks at inference education, time attacks nearly usually require a few diplomas of expertise, approximately the gaining knowledge of procedure, which is a good way to disrupt it through manipulations of the data [15].

Label Manipulation: Attackers' attack surfaces are constrained when they can only alter the labelling records in the education dataset. Given a partial or full understanding of the learning set of rules employed by the defence, they must identify the labels in the facts that are the most destructive to alter. The fundamental approach for one set of education statistics is to disrupt the labels (i.e., generate inventive labels at random). In fact, Biggio found that manipulating 40% of specific education labels at random was sufficient to lower the overall inference performance of SVM (Support Vector Machine) classifiers. It is unknown whether this attack may be used against inter-analyzers that have more than two transmission subtypes (they only considered binary jobs, where exchanging labels is certain to be extremely hazardous to the version). Heuristics increase the likelihood that the enemy will succeed. Biggio *et al.* found that the model performs worse during inference when self-belief-related components are poisoned. In essence, they reduce the fraction of harmful elements by around 10%, decreasing accuracy, when compared with random label flipping. These attacks entail the construction of a new machine learning model for each probable candidate hazardous factor in order to assess the candidate's effect on the overall performance of the existing version during inference. This costly computation expense can be established using the typically unrecognized relation between overall performance metrics gathered at the educational and examination statistics. SVMs were used by Xiao *et al.* to locate the near-best units of labels that needed to be flipped for patterns when such relation is well understood.

Input Manipulation: The attacker can alter the entry functions of schooling factors processed with the aid of the version, in addition to its labels, in this risk version. These works presume knowledge of the learning set of rules and the schooling set of rules, poisoning the research inputs directly. The attack surface of a machine learning model is commonly aggravated while studying online, that is, with fresh schooling components introduced by staring at the environment in which the gadget matures. The majority of efforts on this proximity awareness is on clustering models, where adversaries' intuitive technique is to gently relocate the center of the cluster to have variables categorized mistakenly as inference. Loft *et al.* introduce poisoned factors into a dataset used for anomaly identification and show how this gradually moves the choice boundary of a centroid version, i.e., a version that identifies a check entry as malicious when it is miles away from the empirical mean of the data. This version is found in a web-based manner, with fresh schooling records being collected at regular intervals and attribute values θ being calculated on a sliding window of those records. Poisoning factors are discovered by solving a linear programming problem that optimizes the centroid's displacement. This approach takes advantage of the simplicity of centroid models, which essentially compute the empirical estimate of education data by evaluating Euclidean distances. This attack will not be used while courting among educational documents, and the version will not be as explicit. Later, the concept was explored in the context of malware clustering: malware is modified to contain additional behavioral capabilities that identify it among existing clusters inside the version's entrance domain, reducing the distance between clusters in the process.

For this, we can introduce a new attack that uses gradient ascent to identify poisoning variables in the model's check mistakes. When such inputs were added to the schooling, it resulted in a decrease in subclass accurate at inference. Their technique is (at least theoretically) unique to support vector machines (SVMs) because it is predicated on the presence of a closed-shape formula for the model's check errors, which, in their case, originates from the idea that assistance vector2 does not alternate owing to poisoning factor insertion. Mei *et al.* belong to this category of approaches, but they derive the gradient ascent formula using a bilevel optimization problem (in addition to label flipping attacks). Later, this equal gradient ascent method was adapted for use with characteristic choosing methods such as LASSO. Manipulation of learning inputs in this way is also an effective way to create goal reinforcement learning agents. Behzadan *et al.* demonstrated that gradient ascent tactics developed in the context of negative instances (see Section 2.5 for a more detailed description of those strategies) could lead to the agent learning the erroneous policy.

Poisoning of the Learning Inputs in an Indirect Manner: Adversaries who do not have access to the pre-processed statistics must poison the model's training statistics before it is pre-processed. Perdisci *et al.*, for example, prevented polygraph, a computer virus signature technology tool, from learning major signatures by disrupting computer virus site visits flows. Polygraph combines a go with the drift tokenizes with a classifier that determines if a go with the drift must be contained within the signature. Mutant worms have noisy visitor flows to ensure as its blockchain-enabled representations are no longer indicative of the computer virus's visitor flow, and they control the classifier's criterion for using signatures to flag worms. As a result of the attack, polygraph is driven to construct signatures with tokens that do not conform to boundary conditions of the computer virus's behavior.

2.5   Inferring in Adversarial Attack

For example, consider the adversary which can be focused on a device that detects intrusion regulations had been discovered and corrected. This attacker can be inquisitive about constructing a variant of its attack with a purpose to right away steer clear of detection at runtime. Strong white field attackers have gotten the right of entry to the version elements (as examples, that of structure and dimensions), although dark-skinned opponents are limited to communicating with the divination variant (as example through filing entries and looking at the version's expectations). In real life, talents vary on a continuum among those extremes. That attitude is wanted to shape that existing period [16].

2.5.1   Combatants in the White Box Model

The white box model has different levels of version access which can be affected by many attacks. This high probability version enables the enemy to conduct particularly deadly attacks. White box access is not always implausible, but it is typically difficult to achieve—for example, opposite opponents might be able to improve the feature's insides (or example, attribute choices) through technology in order to gain white box access. For example, machine learning techniques based on data sources have been condensed and implemented on mobile phones [17].

Integrity: To aim for the integrity of an inference system's prediction, opponents modify the deeds of the machine learning version. That might be seen as improving the dispersion which creates judgment data. The strategies, which inherently involve modifying current sources, are described first. Then, they explore the concept of remembering oblique perturbations that can withstand the various preprocessing levels in the system's records pipeline, even in the presence of variant data inputs. In this case, attackers control the important parameters collected by the variation right away. The opponent's goal, for example, could be to have a classification attribute the wrong score to variables. The timeframe opposite scenario was developed by companies that can also hire employees to examine comparable information. Those who formalize the search for opposite cases as a minimizing issue, comparable to the contemporaneous job:

$$\arg\min{}_r h(x + r) = l \text{ s.t. } x^* = x + r \in D \rightarrow \tag{2.1}$$

A correctly labeled center X is distributed using R to generate an opposing occurrence X that remains within the centers of region D but is granted the aim tag L. Whenever it comes to the goal L, this attack is a misunderstanding of the origin (additionally called centered within the side literature). When 1 can be any label one-of-a-kind according to h (x), the attack is stated with an easy misunderstanding (every now and then to be untargeted). The first magnificence of attack strategies aims to enhance the efficacy. They have been the primary way to discover that an extensive variety of ML models, along with deep neural networks with modern-day accuracy on imaginative and perceptive duties, have been mis-led and are oblivious of disturbances. These were discussed by the method of Carlini *et al.* within a one-of-a-kind optimizer by encrypting area requirements like a constant substi-tute. This is significantly the circumstance of the quick slope symbol methodology provided through the use of direction of the methods of Goodfellow *et al.*

Modification of Variant Information in an Ambiguous Way: Whenever the opponent is unable to control the important parameters that are being used as the iteration parame-ters simultaneously, it needs to find conserved aberrations with the help of the information processing that comes before the classifiers in a typical standard focused approach. Kurakin *et al.* demonstrated how printouts of hostile cases generated using the short gradient signal set of rules were still misidentified when an item reputation version was used. They supplied the model images of the printers, re-creating the customary or before the stage of a laptop's inventive and visionary console's information pipelines. They also discovered that certain physiologically adversarial cases were impervious to well before curvatures such as fogging or assessment changes. Sharif *et al.* used the tool to determine adversarial cases that can be exposed on photo chromic lenses that, when worn with the aid of a protagonist, cause its appearance to be misidentified also with the assistance of a face repute copy. Incorporating ramifications to assure that the disturbances are physically realizable (i.e., printed) in Eq. 2.1 is sufficient to prevent behavior categorization efforts (the countenance is mislabeled in any erroneous category) as well as larger restricted volumetric reference discrimination threats (in an assigned aim category, the aspect is incorrectly categorized).

Beyond Classification: It examines autoregressive models, where the test x_t collection's test $x_t = k_i = 1\ c_i x t_i$ depends on earlier good realizations of x. Such tendencies are common in economic forecasting. An adversary manipulates the entry information within the con-fines of the existing market to obtain their favored forecast. The specialists suggest sus-tainable technology and transform the adversary's manipulating problem into a nonlinear optimizer. Using antagonistic instances, recurrent neural networks are expanded. Huang *et al.* showed that an RL agent is unresponsive to adversarial changes in behavior once it has been trained. The adversary successfully induces the agency to act inappropriately either immediately or later by creating "undercover agents" that operate effectively after the envi-ronment has been disturbed for several time cycles before engaging in a wrongdoing [18].

Confidentiality and Privacy: Since the opponent now has access to the form charac-teristics, operations in their dangerous white area edition are inconsequential. As men-tioned previously, the antagonists concentrated on the privateness of facts manipulated with the aid of using a ML gadget are inquisitive about recuperating records, approximately the schooling facts. The only attack towards facts is composed in acting a membership test, i.e., understand whether or not a selected item has changed while in use in a released school dataset. Stronger parties, additionally, are searching to extract absolutely or, in part, unknown schooling points. Few attacks are performed within the side of the white field risk version, as the black field version is more practical for privateness. Economic information as inferred by Ateniese *et al.* is approximately the schooling facts on an educated version $h\theta$, that is, whether or not its schooling facts confirmed a positive statistical assets. Their attack generates numerous datasets, in which a few show off the statistical assets and most do not agree. A version is self-taught on all knowledge. The adversary then trains a contextual model using these patterns as parameters to make forecasts based on real-world data. The contextual is used to the variation in order to accomplish the previous unfavorable purpose.

The requirement is that all categories conduct research using the same approach as the versions that have been implemented.

2.5.2 Insurgencies in the Black Box Model

No matter how long the internal parts of the black box model or its components have been used to attack them, that does not include the strategies mentioned in Section 5.1, such as authenticity attacks, which required the offender to compute grades by describing the usage of versions H and its justifications. On the other hand, black-field access may be riskier because it just requires access to outputs and responses. An adversary trying to breach into a computer network, for instance, virtually never has access to the anti-malware program's specifications, but they can occasionally see how it responds to outreach initiatives. Similarly, attacks are a behavior. Nets must carry out research in order to decide on specific contextual monitoring and response requirements and employ suitable techniques. The structure of computer software is the same regardless of the industry it is utilized in. Even if there were heuristics specific to some programs, as those for sorting spam mail, a common expression of danger to opponents is a black pitch. It is the sole technique to circumvent an oracle, according to the cryptography community: the adversary can pose questions to the machine learning version and examine the results for any chosen input. This mostly applies to the increasingly well-known business environment of machine learning computing infrastructures, wherein the version is a possibility made available by a question. If the opponent is knowledgeable of the objective models, they can construct the model using comparable amounts of inquiry data as utilized in education rather than having access to the education facts and machine learning algorithm. As a result, when assessing different attacks, one of the most important factors to take into account is the variety of archon requests as well as the datasets supplied by the database.

Integrity: Through Java, the adversary can access the model. The fee attribute is connected to the modification of an input X to an aim illustration X. A feature that the commissioner possesses is a calculated difference between x and x. In order to have such a damaging input deemed innocuous, the machine learning computer must be given a quadratic set of questions to answer. This method is known as ACRE learning. Continuous capacities have been shown to allow for ACRE user-friendliness, but they also make the problem NP-hard. Although the pricing element similarly affects ACRE understandability, it presents a special challenge when trying to reverse-engineer the idea. Nelson *et al.*, who are experts on this topic, point out a weakness in convex-inducing classifiers: those that treat a subset as one.

Manipulated: Versions extractor operations have shown that opponents with access to sufficient credentials can gain access to a lot of data about the underneath black model. Xu *et al.* use an algorithm in these situations. The oracle's grandeur chances forecasts are used to explain the safety of the gene versions obtained by mutation. The process prevents a randomized woodland area and malware using SVM. Determining genomic editions, on the other hand, is a challenge for problems with a broader range of enter functions. It is far more difficult for the opponent to extract information about the decision function when they do not have access to a pre-determined requirement for detecting input disturbances that result in erroneous forecasts. In the following works, the opponent just looks at the first and last stages of the pipelines, such as the input (that you create) and the conclusion label in type jobs. Szegedy *et al.* first established an opposing example generalization: that is, commodities that are created to be incorrectly classified *via* the use of a version are very likely to be miscategorized through the use of a limited version. Even if patterns are established primarily on individual information, this capability asset remains. Presuming that the opponent has access to substitute data, Laskov *et al.* investigated the process of training a substitute rendition for the targeted ones. To get around a malicious PDF scanner, they use a semantic flaw: they inject multiple features which are not read by PDF fragment shaders. As a result, their attack does not translate well to diverse technology web addresses or styles.

Data Pipeline Manipulated: It is confirmed experimentally that transferability holds notwithstanding the preprocessing tiers of the model's facts pipelines. In fact, it was assessed that physiological hostile instances (i.e., prints of an adversarial photo), per day in the edition in which they were created, focused on an extraordinary version utilized by a cell phone app to apprehend entities. These effects display more than bodily published dependable fluctuations. Each version was initially focused on, with the first version being concentrated on first, followed by the second version known as the black-field version.

Model Recovery: Obtaining machine learning models has security practices comparable to immediate privacy issues such as trade secrets, as trends have shown that people memorize educational content to some level. Tramer *et al.* show how to obtain version attributes from its predicted annotations. Their technique is applying formula patching to improve the attributes of units from a specific team (x, h(x)). While it is simple, the technique is easy to adapt in scenarios in which the opponent loses access to the back and shoulders possibilities for each class, i.e., just before it can only gain access here to labeling. These bring up the possibility of future research into how to construct more realistic extracting procedures.

2.6   Machine Learning Methods That Are Sustainable, Private, and Accountable

Users highlight attempts at the intersection of privacy and security with machine learning which may be utilized for mitigating them (Section 2.5) after describing attacks on schools in Section 2.4 and considering the assumption in Section 2.5. The seemingly different dreams of (a) distribution drift resistance, (b) acquiring confidentiality variations as well as (c) liabilities and accountability have commonalities. Most of these challenges are largely unsolved, and as a result, we get useful information for future research.

2.6.1   Robustness of Models to Distribution Drifts

Following Sections 2.4 and 2.5 on school attacks and assumptions, Section 2.5 highlights projects at the intersection with privacy, security, and machine learning that can be utilized to mitigate them. The seemingly unrelated dreams of (a) distribution drift resistance, (b) studying confidentiality models, and (c) equality with accountability are discovered to be linked. Several of these difficulties are largely unanswered; as result, users obtain insights that will aid future research [19].

Safeguarding From Assaults on Practice Time

Most mentorship defense mechanisms work under the presumption that harmful information is actually outside the realm of input sharing predictions. Some people build PCA poison detection algorithms that are resistant to toxifying using powerful analytics. To reduce the impact of outliers on the training distribution rather than just the quality deviation, they restrict a PCA strategy to search for a path whose projections maximize a univariate dispersion, live, largely continuous testing vision pursuit estimation method. Similar methods are used by Biggio *et al.*, who reduce the accuracy of the linear model by adding a control parameter. This lessens the vulnerability of the SVM to name preparation changes. In contrast to earlier AN attempts, their methodology has little impact. To train cubic-centimeter designs, these include the usage of fully connected layers in the optimization problems that are addressed. By doing this, the criticality that an attacker might use is eliminated. As an alternative, they advise victimization and obfuscation, in which the secured hides some specifics or a piece of the model's knowledge. However, this goes against Kerckhoffs' list of fundamental security principles. By combining this line of research's findings with a categorization model that seeks to dramatically minimize data points that are not part of a workable collection, Steindhardt *et al.* also expanded the field of study [20].

Defending Yourself Against Presumption Time Attacks

The inherent complexity of machine learning hypotheses output surfaces contributes to the difficulty of achieving ruggedness to compared trickery at supposition; however, a dilemma appears out from assertion that somehow this sophistication is required to associate modeling ability ample to teach strong fashions, which would also suggest an essential drawback for the defender defending against logical deduction attacks. We explain why mechanisms that clean version outputs in infinitesimal neighborhoods of the education information fail to ensure integrity, and then we present defenses that are effective in the face of large perturbations, defending with the aid of gradient protecting most integrity attacks. Since the assailant can recognize slight disturbances, it can result in huge changes inside the model's output, a natural resistance strategy is to reduce the sensitivity of models to slight tweaks done to their input and output. Such vulnerability is predicted by employing calculating first the order effect. A secure variation of security replacement version application of interchangeability on a small scale is deployed. The tried defense edition is clean in communities of academic focuses, i.e., the differences of such edition emits of regarding itself to components are 0; the unauthorized user has no idea as well where to begin for opposing case studies. However, this same entity can just use polymeric editions shading to find opposing instances that switch back towards the preserved version [21].

Defending in Opposition to Large Perturbations

Szegedy *et al.* first cautioned against injecting antagonistic samples, efficaciously labeled, inside the education set as a method to make the version sturdy. They confirmed that fashions geared up with this mixture of valid and antagonistic samples have been regularized and extra sturdy to adversaries in the usage of their attack. The defender minimizes the mistake among the version's predictions on antagonistic examples (computed the usage of the contemporary parameter applicants at some point of education) and the authentic labels—for example, the misclassification charge of a MNIST version is decreased from 89.4% to 17.9% on antagonistic examples. Huang *et al.* evolved the instinct at the back of antagonistic education. They formulate a minmax trouble among the adversary, making use of perturbations to every education factor to maximize the version's classification error, and gaining knowledge of manners in trying to reduce this error. The overall performance enhancements over the preceding efforts are evident but regularly statistically non-significant. Although antagonistic education defends in opposition to attacks on which the version is trained, it is far susceptible within inside the face of adaptive adversaries—for example, Moosavi *et al.* use a different heuristic to locate antagonistic examples while education and attacking. Their assessment suggests that the version is no longer sturdy in those settings.

2.6.2   Learning and Inferring With Privacy

The manner of clarifying privateness maintaining fashions is what they do now and no longer display any extra statistics, approximately the topics concerning their education facts. This is captured with the aid of using differential privateness, a rigorous framework to analyze the privateness which is furnished with the aid of using algorithms. Informally, it formulates privateness because the assets that a set of rules output does now no longer fluctuate substantially statistically for two variations of the facts differing with the aid of using the most effective one record. In case, the evidence is an education factor and some set of rules of machine learning version. A component of the ML system's pipeline must be randomized to give any form of significant privacy, like different datasets. This can be done inside the preprocessing ranges prior to the version (this is beyond the focus of this study), during the version's schooling, or during inference with the aid of randomizing the version's predictions. Random noise can be added into facts during education, and the value can be lowered by learning a set of rules or the values of taught parameters. The use of local privacy is used to formalize an example of education data randomization. Erlingsson *et al.* confirmed that an approach allows browser developers to obtain considerable and privacy-preserving usage data from customers. Chaudhuri *et al.* illustrate how learning reduces goal perturbation, i.e., the introduction of background fluctuations through the estimator (which evaluates its difference in between version assumptions and the outcomes), and can give differentiated privacy. A cacophony was created with a probability function and scaled according to version sensitivity [22].

Bassily *et al.* offer sophisticated algorithms and privacy assessments as well as references to a few publications on private learning *via* price reduction. When trained using cross-computations from stochastic parameter values, Shokri *et al.* proved whether substantial architectures, such as deep neural networks, can provide completely differential privacy guarantees. The associate technique proposed by Abadi *et al.* ensures greater differential privacy restrictions in centralized settings (a single entity trains the model). Before applying gradients determined by the learning algorithmic rule to update parameter values, it arbitrarily perturbs them. It is possible to strengthen the privacy protection on sensitive (labeled) data under multiple assumptions, particularly the availability of public and unlabeled data whose privacy does not have to be required to be preserved. To begin, (disjoint) divisions of the coaching data are used to learn an ensemble of teacher models. This newly tagged dataset will be used to train a student model. This model will be deployed openly as long as it was trained on non-public labels. To achieve differential privacy, ML's behavior may be irregular at logical thinking by introducing noise to forecasts. However, because the amount of noise contributed increases with the number of inference queries answered by the cc model, this reduces the accuracy of predictions. It is worth noting that many types of privacy are discussed throughout inference, all of which belong under the umbrella of data confidentiality.

Dowlin *et al.*, for example, uses homomorphic cryptography to encode extremely complicated information such that a neuron will obtain this without attempting to decrypt information. Even though this does not provide techniques such as data, it does protect the anonymity of each implementation method in the event that a concept user somehow does not trust the pattern owner. One of most notable disadvantages are now the efficiency burden and indeed the elliptic curve encryption's limited subset of mathematical functions, both of which place extra constraints on the cc model's proposed methodology.

2.6.3   Fairness and Accountability in Machine Learning

This transparency of machine learning raises issues about the lack of due process and accountability in model forecasts. This is critical in applications like financial and humanitarian help. Furthermore, legislative frameworks such as the European Data Protection Regulation require companies to provide justification for equation assumptions if they have a potential to create victimization data that is considered sensitive or private. We do not present a complete evaluation of the fast pace of technological progress made toward justice and accountability because of space constraints, which would need an obsessive SoK. We will concentrate on work that relates to the previously described concepts of privacy (e.g., data toxifying) and security. Fairness is crucial to process being within verifying the prediction accuracy in the physical system in the cc pipeline. It must not nurture discrimination against specific people. Coaching data is one source of bias in machine learning. It must not encourage discrimination against certain individuals—for example, an unreliable data collector can decide to use the educational system to create a model that discriminates against restricted groups. Social biases are inherently reflected in historical data. The learning algorithm, which may be adjusted through offering assurances for specific portions of the coaching data, is another source of bias. This ensures a specific meaning of honesty, such as equal or impartial diagnosis. They provide a barter between the performance and the integrity of a model. As first mentioned in Zemel *et al.* who develop an intermediate depiction, it encapsulates a customized edition of the data to talk about fair models. Fairness can be attained, according to Edwards *et al.*, by learning in competition with someone attempting to anticipate the sensitive variable from the honest model's forecast. In their technique for removing sensitive annotations from images, which they apply to both tasks, they notice parallels between fairness and privacy. Future research into the junction of fairness and the issues raised in this paper is likely to yield fruit—for example, recently recognized ties between fairness and security have led to the discovery of implicit prejudices in popular image file information sets using methodologies such as adversarial [23].

Accountability

With the internal models, responsibility justifies outcomes. Most variants can be explained by design, that is, they can be made to fit human logic. Quantitative intake impact measures were suggested to evaluate the influence of variable factors just on simulation. Principles of connection are later used to assemble deep learning toxicity attacks by injecting the figure's uncertainty coaching information. Some other way to hold people accountable is to determine the inputs the machine learning model has been to which you are more responsive. Maximizing engagement creates connections which turn on individual nerves in a system of neurons to the greatest extent possible. The difficulty is in creating artificial inputs that are human-interpretable and accurately depict the model's behavior. Model failures, such as adversarial situations, are also relevant to activation maximization. In practice, techniques identical to its use in construction input directions that result in adversarial sample misclassification by a model are used to create salient data that maximally activate specific models. On the one hand, measures for liability and transparency appear to generate better tactics of attack by increasing the opponent's expertise of how the model provides decisions. They do, however, help to get a deeper awareness of the impact of instructional material on the modeling that has been developed by the machine learning algorithm that is useful for confidential machine learning [24, 25].

2.7   Conclusion

Device data protection is a relatively new field. Exploration of machine learning-based architectures' attack floor took place. A rational foundation for thinking about their risk models is provided by this research. In general, a huge body of research from numerous clinical organizations demonstrates that many machine learning weaknesses and the defences employed to prevent them are still unknown—but that the technology for spotting them is constantly developing. The knowledge gained from this systematization of expertise helps us understand a number of delicate ideas that are all connected. Machine learning that protects privacy must first determine how sensitive its learning algorithms are to the learning data it is trained on. Controlling the sensitivity of deployed models to the data they infer from is also necessary for stable machine learning.

References

1. The White House, *Preparing for the Future of Artificial Intelligence*, Executive Office of the President, National Science and Technology Council, Committee on Technology, 2016.
2. Pfleeger, C.P. and Pfleeger, S.L., *Analyzing Computer Security: A Threat/Vulnerability/ Countermeasure Approach*, Prentice Hall, 2012.
3. Amodei, D., Olah, C., Steinhardt, J., Christiano, P., Schulman, J., Mane, D., *Concrete Problems in AI Safety*, 2016, arxiv preprint arXiv:1606.06565.
4. Ohrimenko, O., Schuster, F., Fournet, C., Mehta, A., Nowozin, S., Vaswani, K., Costa, M., Oblivious multi-party machine learning on trusted processors, in: *25th USEN Security Symposium*, 2016.
5. Murphy, K.P., *Machine Learning: A Probabilistic Perspective*, MIT Press, 2012.

6. Krizhevsky, A., Sutskever, I., Hinton, G.E., Imagenet classification with deep convolutional neural networks, in: *Advances in Neural Information Processing Systems*, pp. 1097–1105, 2012.

7. Sutskever, I., Vinyals, O., Le, Q.V., Sequence to sequence learning with neural networks, in: *Advances in Neural nformation Processing Systems*, pp. 3104–3112, 2014.

8. Drucker, H., Wu, D., Vapnik, V.N., Support vector machines for spam categorization. *IEEE Trans. Neural Netw.*, 10, 5, 1048–1054, 1999.

9. Jain, A.K., Murty, M.N., Flynn, P.J., Data clustering: Review. *ACM Comput. Surv.*, 31, 3, 264–323, 1999.

10. Krizhevsky, A. and Hinton, G., *Learning Multiple Layers of Features From Tiny Images*, 2009. Available at: https://www.cs.toronto.edu/~kriz/learning-features-2009-TR.pdf

11. Erhan, D., Bengio, Y., Courville, A., Manzagol, P.-A., Vincent, P., Bengio, S., Why does unsupervised pre-training help deep learning?. *J. Mach. Learn. Res.*, 11, 625–660, 2010.

12. Chandola, V., Banerjee, A., Kumar, V., Anomaly detection: A survey. *ACM Comput. Surv.*, 41, 3, 1–58, Jul. 30, 2009.

13. Hu, J. and Wellman, M.P., Nash Qlearning for general-sum stochastic games. *J. Mach. Learn. Res.*, 4, 1039–1069, 2003.

14. Sutton, R.S. and Barto, A.G., *Reinforcement Learning: An Introduction*, MIT Press, 1998.

15. Silver, D., Huang, A., Maddison, C.J., Guez, A., Sifre, L. *et al.*, Learning the game of go with deep neural networks and tree search. *Nature*, 529, 7587, 484–489, 2016.

16. Bishop, C.M., *Pattern Recognition and Machine Learning*, Springer, 2006. Available at: https://www.microsoft.com/en-us/research/uploads/prod/2006/01/Bishop-Pattern-Recognition-and-Machine-Learning-2006.pdf

17. Goodfellow, I., Bengio, Y., Courille, A., *Deep Learning*, Book in preparation for MIT Press, MIT Press, 2016, www.deeplearningbook.org.

18. Altman, N.S., An introduction to kernel and nearestneighbor nonparametric regression. *Am. Stat.*, 46, 3, 175–185, 1992.

19. Barreno, M., Nelson, B., Sears, R., Joseph, A.D., Tygar, J.D., Can machine learning be secure?, in: *ACM Symposium on Information, Computer and Communications Security*, pp. 16–25, 2006.

20. Huang, L., Joseph, A.D., Nelson, B., Rubinstein, B., II, Tygar, J., Adversarial machine learning, in: *4th ACM Workshop on Security and Artificial Intelligence*, pp. 43–58, 2011.

21. Papernot, N., McDaniel, P., Jha, S., Fredrikson, M., Celik, Z.B., Swami, A., The limitations of deep learning in adversarial settings, in: *1st IEEE European Symposium on Security and Privacy*, 2016.

22. Kloft, M. and Lasko, P., Online anomaly detection under adversarial impact, in: *13th International Conference on Artificial Intelligence and Statistics*, pp. 405–412, 2010.

23. Sharif, M., Bhagavatula, S., Bauer, L., Reiter, M.K., Accessorize to a crime: Real and stealthy attacks on state-of-the-art face recognition, in: *23rd ACM SIGSAC Conference on Computer and Communications Security*, pp. 1528–1540, 2016.

24. Tyagi, A., Kukreja, S., Nair, M. M., Tyagi, A.K., Machine learning: Past, present and future. *Neuroquantology.* 20, 8, 2022, DOI: 10.14704/nq.2022.20.8.NQ44468.

25. Papernot, N., McDaniel, P., Goodfellow, I., Jha, S., Celik, Z.B., Swami, A., Practical blackbox attacks against deep learning systems using adversarial examples, *ASIA CCS '17, Proceedings of the 2017 ACM on Asia Conference on Computer and Communications Security*, April 2017, Pages 506–519, https://doi.org/10.1145/3052973.3053009.

26. Tyagi, A. K., *Handbook of Research on Technical, Privacy, and Security Challenges in a Modern World.* IGI Global, 2022. DOI: 10.4018/978-1-6684-5250-9

3

Decentralized, Distributed Computing for Internet of Things-Based Cloud Applications

Roopa Devi E.M.[1*], **Shanthakumari R.**[1], **Rajadevi R.**[2], **Kayethri D.**[2] **and Aparna V.**[1]

[1]*Department of Information Technology, Kongu Engineering College (Autonomous), Perundurai, Tamil Nadu, India*
[2]*Department of Artifical Intelligence, Kongu Engineering College (Autonomous), Perundurai, Tamil Nadu, India*

Abstract

Information services frequently utilize cloud computing. However, massive Internet of Things (IoT) applications pose fresh difficulties for cloud computing infrastructures. As a solution to this issue, edge computing has been proposed as an alternative to cloud computing. Tens of billions of IoT devices can be supported, and hardware can be improved through voluntary computing, which collects underutilized network resources. This chapter offers a blockchain technology for the use of volunteer edge cloud in light of the shortcomings of conventional volunteer computing, which cannot offer real-time services, and existing volunteer clouds lack a system to pay for services. Blockchain smart contracts are used to pay for essential business processes and computing services, and container technology provides a shared operating environment. A prototype system built on top of Ethereum and KubeEdge has been introduced and provides an up-to-date overview of a voluntary blockchain-based edge cloud infrastructure. An Internet of Things has been created to manage robot formation in addition to the prototype system. Through a decrease in IoT device complexity, an increase in software development freedom, and an improvement in computing service payment, it serves as an example of the benefits of an optional edge cloud. Large-scale IoT system management has taken advantage of cloud computing. IoT multi-cloud servers typically deal with a large volume of queries. The cloud must offer the servers with outstanding flexibility, reliability, affordable cost, and essential functionality because of the fluctuating and intense workload. Traditional clouds, on the other hand, often provide cloud service abstraction of a VM, which scarcely suffices to meet these requirements. As a result of the fluctuating workload, many cloud vendors offer varying performance stability and pricing strategies. The needs of the IoT scenario cannot be adequately satisfied by a single cloud. Cooperation between several public clouds is facilitated by the JointCloud computing model. The dynamic scheduling of workloads across many clouds based on VM abstraction is still challenging though. This chapter discusses HCloud, which supports serverless computing. JointCloud application for IoT systems uses a serverless computing approach. The implementation of many serverless services on an IoT server is possible with HCloud, and these tasks are scheduled on several clouds in accordance with a schedule policy. The client defines the policy, which includes the necessary functionality, operational assets, delay, price, *etc.* Serverless services are distributed by

Corresponding author: roopadevi.it@kongu.edu

Amit Kumar Tyagi (ed.) *Automated Secure Computing for Next-Generation Systems*, (43–64) © 2024 Scrivener Publishing LLC

HCloud, on the basis of the scheduling policy, to the most suitable cloud after collecting the status of each cloud. By utilizing blockchain technology, we further assure that we cannot falsify the cloud state or inappropriately send the parts of a program out.

Keywords: Blockchain technology, volunteer edge cloud, IoT, JointCloud serverless, IoT, blockchain

3.1 Introduction to Volunteer Edge Cloud for Internet of Things Utilising Blockchain

Cloud computing has grown significantly during the last 10 years or so. Today, 83% of commercial workloads are handled by cloud computing, which is used by 90% of organisations and supported by technologies like mass storage, platform management, virtualization, and others. Installing hardware and system software in data centers allows cloud computing to distribute resources as services through the Internet, realizing the goal of computing as a utility.

The design of cloud services is confronted with additional difficulties, nevertheless, as Internet of Things applications rapidly expand. Firstly, the bulk of industrial control systems call for a millisecond or less latency between sensors and control nodes. Virtual reality applications, for example, and vehicle-to-vehicle communication, among other Internet of Things applications, demand latency of under tens of milliseconds. Such latency specifications are challenging for the current public cloud services to meet. Secondly, in terms of restrictions on network capacity: Internet of Things (IoT) devices continuously produce a lot of information—for instance, a self-driving vehicle produces 1 GB of bare facts each second. The Internet of Things has billions of connected devices, and moving data transfer to far-off data centers for processing can put a tremendous strain on network infrastructure and data center capacity. Thirdly, in terms of problems with data security—the acquisition of user privacy data is a must for IoT apps due to their nature, yet many have highlighted worries regarding data security. In order to avoid having IoT devices send all data to cloud servers, they hope that they can operate behind a managed firewall. Fourthly, in terms of lasting performance restrictions—IoT device designers frequently decide to employ software to sleep and use low-power processors. Generally speaking, we can speed up the battery life of IoT devices. In addition, taking into account the cost of the hardware, consumer devices come with less expensive processors. This indicates that IoT terminals have a limited computing capacity and need outside assistance to complete activities, although it is challenging to encrypt the information more than once before being sent to the data center.

In addition to cloud computing, cloud is overfloating to emerge as a new technology to rectify the failures in IoT. Edge computing increases connectivity (networking, computing, and capacity) to the network's edge and answers inquiries close to where information is created. Another issue that needs to be resolved is how to construct a sizable and all-encompassing edge computing infrastructure. The creation of a volunteer edge cloud, which is inspired by voluntary computing, can serve a variety of Internet of Things applications and increase community hardware utilization efficiency. On the other hand, as mentioned in the review section of this chapter, traditional volunteer computing schemes lack precise time responses, mechanisms to promote resource sharing and purchasing services, and ways to ensure that the validity of the data can be processed on various devices owned by various parties.

Basically, using a distributed ledger, attributes of decentralization, freedom, autonomy, and security are parts of blockchain technology. Blockchain is a promising technology for decentralized edge cloud computing because of these benefits. To fulfil the role of user motivation, first, construct a resource trading platform based on blockchain technology. Second, the blockchain simply keeps track of transaction records. User privacy is ensured because users are anonymous to one another. Because blockchain transaction records cannot be altered, transaction security is guaranteed. Blockchain technology, which has the potential to address many current issues, should thus be used in conjunction with voluntary cloud computing.

This study suggests a decentralized real-time edge cloud architecture for volunteer Internet of Things applications in light of the instances that the existing computing model is relevant to. Consumers, resource suppliers, a resource pool, and blockchain technology make up the suggested architecture. Consumers are the entities that make use of edge cloud services. The nodes that provide computing resources are dispersed throughout the network that are owned by various parties and supply resources to the edge cloud. A resource bank serves as the center of the volunteer edge cloud, coordinating the customer and the sellers. Blockchain technology helps to track contributions from source givers, issue instant payments, safeguard data, and other things. Additionally, based on the suggested architecture, a testbed robot formation control has been created and showed how the volunteer edge cloud built on blockchain technology may be advantageous.

The chapter is structured in different sections. Section 3.2 describes a review. Section 3.3 shows the recommended approach. Section 3.4 describes the application details. Section 3.5 describes the effective presentation.

3.2   Significance of Volunteer Edge Cloud Concept

The research has been focused on voluntary computing. The study of grid computing and volunteer computing grew significantly in the 1990s. Today, 83% of commercial workloads are handled by cloud computing, which is used by 90% of organisations and supported by technologies like mass storage, platform management, virtualization, and others as stated by W. Fellows and L. Columbus [1, 2]. The primary driving force at the time has been used for clearing the issue of inadequate single-machine processing capacity and to execute complex computing operations by using unoccupied computers on a federated network. Armburst and others stated that installing hardware and system software in data centers allows cloud computing to distribute resources as services through the Internet, realizing the goal of computing as a utility [3]. Many effective engineering projects were created during this time. The design of cloud services is confronted with additional difficulties, nevertheless, as Internet of Things applications rapidly expand as concluded by M. Chiang [4]. IoT devices continuously produce a lot of information—for instance, a self-driving vehicle produces 1 GB of bare facts each second [5]. The University of California—Berkeley developed BONIC, a highly effective distributed platform for volunteer computing. Its first purpose was to carry out the SETI. With the help of this initiative, users of home computers can contribute to the hunt for extra-terrestrial civilizations by running radio duties involving glass data analysis when it is not available in the market. Current operations of more than 30 research and technology initiatives are carried out using the open computing platform BONIC. The University of California—Berkeley developed BONIC [6], a highly effective distributed platform for volunteer computing. Its first purpose was to carry out the SETI.

Another open-source computing platform is XtremWeb-HEP from the University of Paris Sud [7]. It was made to help scientists at Pierre Auger Observatory with their high-performance computing requirements. Worker and server are the two components of XtremWeb, which was created in Java. Its features include great scalability, error tolerance, and support for multiple applications. According to actual requirements, it has created a special protocol for communication and a system for operating local codes for security. Volunteer computing at the time was designed for cases of offline computing; it was not applicable for precise time services like IoT applications.

A.M. Khan, along with his teammates, developed a cloud [8]. The creation of a volunteer edge cloud, which is inspired by voluntary computing, can serve a variety of Internet of Things applications and increase community hardware utilization efficiency. Due to distributed data heavy applications' poor efficiency, an architecture for deploying servers has been suggested. It employs voluntarily available edge resources for processing and storing data [9]. A distributed cloud architecture called Nebula was proposed by M. Ryden *et al.* in response to the ineffectiveness of distributed applications with high data throughput [9]. Other research have looked at volunteer-based edge cloud services [10]. Utilizing cloud-centered technology, enabled hardware platforms from several vendors offer unified services for Internet of Things applications.

By implementing the MapReduce architecture, they were able to further confirm Nebula's resilience to multiple errors. Other research use the volunteer approach to study the edge cloud platform using the home server as its foundation. They enable hardware platforms from various suppliers to offer unified services for Internet of Things Technology thanks to container technology. A distributed cloud architecture called Nebula was proposed in response to the ineffectiveness of distributed applications with high data throughput. Nebula employs voluntarily available edge resources for compute and data storage. By installing the MapReduce framework, they also confirmed Nebula's resistance to various errors.

The aforementioned projects have expanded the volunteer computing program's potential use cases. The nodes building the voluntary edge cloud, though, have various equities, resulting in a host-to-host setting. Designing a mechanism that inspires resource sharing and rewards is important to persuade various resource owners to share their resources while carefully maintaining the veracity of the data in such a decentralized system. In earlier studies, this issue has received little thought or attention.

3.3 Proposed System

The "voluntary edge cloud" constructs by allocating facilities like computing, capacity, and Internet donated by volunteer network nodes to deliver an interactive precise period.

The volunteer edge cloud primarily contains these three characteristics: contributing as edge nodes, IoT applications operate as consumers, and asset is created by divided-up nodes for volunteer work. This function allows for interactive real-time services (cloud computing features).

The recording of service provision and payment, the trustworthiness of the data, and system credibility are all challenges that are addressed by blockchain technology. Blockchain can be used to record contributions and charge for services because it is essentially a widely used ledger technology and has the property of automated payment. The users who make use of such resources include smart people, create a typical decentralized and distributed system (for providing data at the edge nodes) [18–25]. Many owners are helping to the development of volunteer edge cloud. Anyone has the capacity to commit malevolent acts for a variety of reasons—for instance, a malicious user continuously submits tasks to fill up the resources of the edge cloud, an edge node misrepresents its resource capacity to the scheduler in order to deceive it into accepting more jobs in exchange for rewards, etc. Malicious activity can be stopped with the aid of blockchain technology's tamper-proof and data-transparent characteristics.

Figure 3.1 gives the conceptual layout of the suggested volunteer edge cloud. The suggested architecture primarily consists of four elements: blockchain infrastructure, resource pools, providers, and consumers. Providers are network node devices whose resources are contributed to the edge cloud. They are owned by multiple parties and are located at the network's edge. They could be network server hardware like telecommunications gear, soft routers, gateways, or personal PCs. These resources have been designated by controllers as edge nodes, and they have been asked to join the cloud-based organization's resources in order to boost resource use and the rate of return on investment. In particular, sluggish terminal equipment that require edge cloud, such as mobile phones, automations, sensor nodes, and associated cars, are mostly used by consumers to access free edge cloud services. The resource pool serves as the central node of volunteer edge cloud, which also consists of a number of operational modules and a lookup controller in the information center. The pioneer is in charge of overseeing modules, obtaining requirements that are demanded, and coordinating occurrence, thus the location of the assets and the activities of both suppliers and customers. The exchange of messages of the aforementioned three features of components is handled by the blockchain infrastructure, which also maintains crucial data. Data reliability issues may inevitably arise when using several edge nodes. In order to achieve

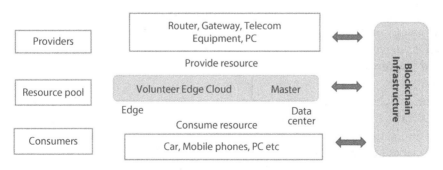

Figure 3.1 Use of blockchain technology in cloud computing.

this, the core business sense is carried out by the program on the chain, and blockchain techniques are utilized for carrying out assistance operation and message transmission. This allows the data to be publicly accessible and ultimately come to a contract. The decentralized nature of blockchain technology makes it ideally suited to address data protection issues in such distributed software.

The volunteer edge cloud's operational method looks like this: to begin with, edge nodes are those gadgets that are ready to provide their own resources. They unite the edge cloud resource pool of volunteer users and are managed by the master controller. They can also use the blockchain system to market their services. Afterward, the edge cloud controller receives a task request via the blockchain network when IoT devices need to do computational tasks.

The work is then started and scheduled to the relevant edge node by the edge cloud controller. When the task is finished, the service's quality is evaluated, and if the outcomes are trustworthy, payment is made. Appeals for the Internet of Things are supported by the service program now underway.

In order to establish the blockchain-based volunteer edge cloud, two tasks must be completed. The first is the development of a blockchain-wise contract that enables data trustworthiness and automatic transactions, and the second is the administration of edge nodes and the coordination of seek duties. Additionally, a web-based customer is created for job submissions from lowering the usage barrier.

3.3.1   Smart Contract

The primary duties of a smart contract on a blockchain are to load and certify sensitive data and workflow as well as to pay for services—for workflow, such as job requests, joining volunteer nodes, etc., and for data, such as node specs and a user's ownership score.

The smart contract built on Ethereum underpins programs and is open to the general public. This choice is supported by Ethereum network's size, thorough development documentation, and vibrant community. The smart contract defines three types of data structures—ClaimedNodeSpecs, TaskRequest, and Node—and each structure instance is mapped to a specific contract address. These plans are utilized to hold assets, modules that send access for the master to process them, and jobs that have not been begun after submission.

The contract and the client interact using the three features which are taskComplate, requestToJoin, and orderTask. The submission of tasks, the execution of tasks, and the request for a new node join are all performed using them. Every contract has a method that corresponds to an event, and that function emits an event log under the appropriate circumstances, communicating with the client asynchronously and permanently storing the event.As depicted in Figure 3.2, operation is carried out as containers, managed and scheduled by kubeedge, and communicated with the blockchain technology using an edge client.

Consumers submit queries to the blockchain application, keeps track of details, and uses an edge client to find transaction jobs. Tasks related to user requests are carried out by the edge hub and cloud according to their different architectures. The transaction is finished when the task is performed, and it is then added to the block.

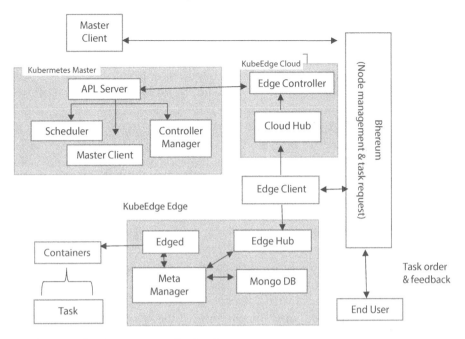

Figure 3.2 Elements of each component of KubeEdge.

3.3.2   Order Task Method

Smart contracts are the only means by which users can send requests for tasks to cloud. With the aid of Web3.js, an application for smart contract was established to make it easier for regular users. The orderTask method might be called by users by simply entering the necessary node specs and hitting a button. The task's resource requirements are automatically matched, and prices are provided for a variety of services from the pool of available resources.

3.3.3   KubeEdge

KubeEdge is the foundation for edge node management. Through the aid of this open-source edge cloud project, host nodes at the edge can now be managed, and containerized applications may be orchestrated. KubeEdge maintains the access of Kubernetes and creates a new analyst to take place of the original kubelet. Edge and Cloud are the two sections of KubeEdge. Figure 3.2 displays the elements of each component of KubeEdge. The development of a significant customer and an ultimate customer on cloud and modules separately, communicating with smart contracts, is required to incorporate smart contracts.

3.4   Implementation of Volunteer Edge Control

In order to validate the suggested architecture and further clarify the volunteer edge cloud's workflow, an IoT application–robot formation on the preceding volunteer edge cloud platform powered by blockchain has been installed.

3.4.1   Formation of a Cloud Environment

Currently, there are many domains where mobile robots are used extensively. Numerous scenarios call for the cooperative work of multiple robots. Robot systems are becoming twice as complicated and expensive due to the complexity of robot applications, which is raising the performance requirements on local processors and data interfaces. The idea of "cloud robots" has been advocated by the industry as a result. The typical framework, however suited for a small number of operations, does not allow applications for precise time control since the terminal's network performance to the data center is not adjustable. With edge cloud, centralized cloud computing capabilities are dispersed to the network's edge while providing the nearest processing power for IoT devices.

By running the software portion of the robot creating a task on the edge node, the software and hardware components of the robots may be separated. By eliminating the consideration of requirements for particular applications, sensor data reading and actuator control become the sole concerns for implementation, particularly the choice of devices. As a result, it is possible to significantly lower the hardware cost of robot systems, and the robot's versatility is also increased by the use of abstract and modular design strategies.

The robot task of formation based on the volunteer edge cloud is shown by its composition in Figure 3.3. A 4WD platform is used by the mobile robot, which also uses Raspberry Pi 3b and STM32 running ROS for its local processing capabilities (robot operating system). The LTE base stations known as edge nodes are software-defined. Stations consist of x86 computers, which may affix the volunteer edge cloud and give their unused processing

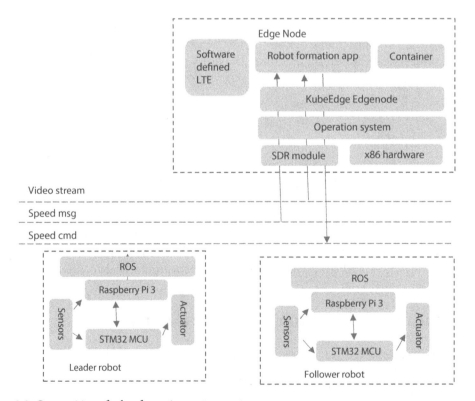

Figure 3.3 Composition of robot formation system.

power. The formation must be maintained by the application, which is operating on modules. Each robot transmits its speed to application, and a predecessor transmits a camera's information as well. Following computation, the Control App communicates to the follower the speed command that must be carried out in order to complete the subsequent control.

Hardware and software are separated in the edge computing mode, and the robot is only in charge of gathering sensor data and adjusting the actuator in accordance with commands. The application actually operates on modules and will bear majority of the computing work.

The Control App's program requires a lot of calculation. To get the correct following trajectory, the leader's track must first be determined using the robot movement model. Second, the follower's picture data must be analyzed instantly, and using a computational vision approach, the relative inaccuracy between the leader and the following is determined. The follower's speed command is calculated with the use of an algorithm iterative learning control in the final step.

The ROS framework, a robot domain-distributed meta-operating system or a middleware specifically designed for the development of robot software, serves as the foundation for the robot's software system, as was already indicated. A separate ROS Package called Control App is created, and a Docker image is created from it. In order to create an image containing the ROS Package that we created, we can build on the foundational image kinetic-ros-core-xenial that is provided by ROS. Through the web client created, we can be able to assign the work application from the modules to begin the program of robotics management on the modules. In the context of controlling robot formation, Figure 3.4 depicts the volunteer edge cloud's workflow.

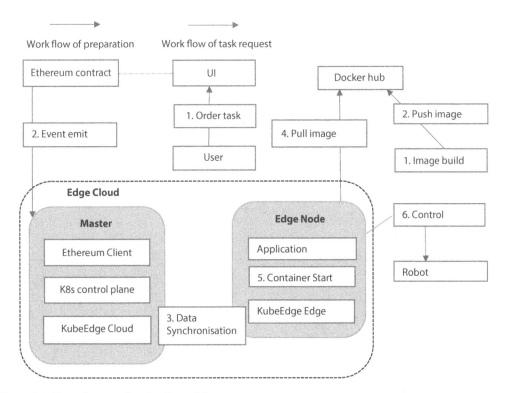

Figure 3.4 The volunteer edge cloud's workflow.

It should be noted that it depicts two different workflow types, namely, the task submission and the phase of preparation and execution process.

Workflow I: In the preliminary period, customers create a platform using pictures and upload the pictures.
Workflow II: Following are the stages in the phase of preparation and execution process:

Stage 1: Customer requests services run from smart contract and places their request
Stage 2: Test features before delivering them to the Kubernetes
Stage 3: The KubeEdge cloud component synchronizes commons to corresponding edge nodes once the module detects and really runs.
Stage 4: On the edge node, the KubeEdge can download the application picture from the picture database.
Stage 5: Kubedge initiates the application, which marks the official launch of the control program.
Stage 6: The edge node's control app establishes a connection and starts to request for transmitting at real time.

3.5   Result Analysis of Volunteer Edge Cloud

First, the investigation evaluated how quickly the subsequent control software would run on the robot's onboard computer and the edge node, respectively. Second, it disregarded the running efficiency and focused on the robot's power instead. Using the supply voltage as a gauge and the prevailing status in the two situations—application is decommissioned by a module and can regionally work on the robot computer—we can determine how much power the onboard computer uses.

The results from the two experiments are displayed in Figure 3.5. The time it takes for the control software to analyze a video frame and repeatedly determine a swift was calculated. The single-step calculation period on the edge node is about 30 ms; however, the calculation time on the device is over 400 ms, which is practical for a frequency of 5 Hz. The result

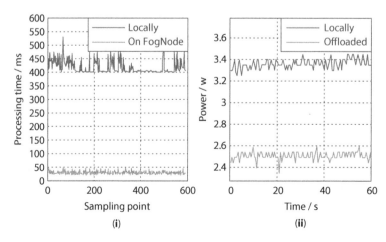

Figure 3.5 (i) The outcome obtained during the execution of the program. (ii) Power consumption of the onboard computer in two conditions.

for usage on the right demonstrates that the device's power consumption was lowered by 3.4 to 2.5 W, a reduction of approximately 25%, once application is offloaded from the device to the modules. The electricity saved is greater than what the experiment indicates since potent control processing unit (CPU) is required for a larger usage of electricity.

The next effect of robot formation is then put to the test. The test, which was conducted indoors in a space measuring approximately 8 × 6 m, used three robots. There are two different sorts of test scenarios: long-distance polyline tracking and formation tracking with initial mistakes. It represents the trajectory's beginning and conclusion (in terms of marking symbols). The solution performed as expected, according to the results. It is capable of fixing first mistakes. When moving over long distances, the maximum tracking error is 0.15 m, and the fault is 0.03 m.

3.6   Introducing Blockchain-Enabled Internet of Things Systems Using the Serverless Cloud Platform

The management of large-scale IoT systems has made use of cloud computing. IoT servers typically have to deal with a lot of requests from different devices, each of which is capable of sending a request at any time and from any location. In order to provide great scalability, steady performance, and cheap cost, IoT systems typically need the cloud. All of these traits are difficult for one cloud to have. First off: it is not at all feasible to retain the greatest task because quantity and frequency vary. When the task surpasses a cloud's volume, performance stability cannot be guaranteed. Secondly, the cost of various clouds might vary significantly and is subject to change. A straightforward way to lower the price is to select the least expensive cloud. Thirdly, distinct cloud vendors often offer a wide range of hardware and software characteristics. All these advantages cannot be benefited by using a single cloud.

A cross-cloud cooperation architecture is suggested by JointCloud computing. It presents an excellent opportunity to develop services by utilizing different clouds in a transparent manner to end customers. The current JointCloud system, however, continues to employ a typical virtualized computer illusion because inappropriate Internet of Things applications, for example—VMs, are too bulky to be moved between clouds. Here we present dependable serverless cloud services. The cloud execution design necessitates the implementation of an IoT server with numerous serverless services as opposed to the use of virtualized computers. The serverless platform will start a new instance of a function for each request made by a user. A great degree of scalability is achieved by adding extra instances when more requests are made. Each IoT device can establish a schedule strategy through HCloud that takes the required features, latency, cost, etc., into account. Anytime it calls, according to the regulations, it is allocated to the appropriate cloud.

The serverless computing must be modified for a JointCloud system, which is not simple to do. First, the services offer various cloud tasks. AliYun allows applications to return responses directly, but Lambda on AWS demands a callback mechanism. Second, it is challenging to effectively monitor a cloud's fluctuating status, of which HCloud needs to do the scheduling. Thirdly, the HCloud is in charge of gathering each cloud's status and scheduling serverless functions. In contrast, a hostile HCloud administrator might falsify and execute operations on an unsuitable cloud. To tackle all three of these issues, we designed HCloud. HCloud adapts a serverless task to various clouds in order to run it on them.

HCloud designates a cloud administrator for each cloud to keep track of its changing state. Each serverless function is scheduled on a distinct cloud by a cloud broker. Invoking the serverless function and retrieving are done for each client using a client library. We use a proof blockchain to document and confirm every cloud transaction status and the scheduling outcomes in order to require that HCloud must "correctly" carry out the scheduling.

In order to model the behaviors of various clouds, we put a prototype of HCloud into practice. With the help of these computers, the cloud administrator creates HCloud. It can alter device resources simulated for testing. We programmed using HCloud operations. The findings demonstrate that cloud can increase the throughput by an average of 25% and can do it more consistently.

3.7   Introducing Serverless Cloud Platforms

This section discusses few serverless cloud platforms for real world's applications as:

3.7.1   IoT Systems

The IoT system is evolving into a common infrastructure that may assist businesses in maximizing their competitive advantage and capturing new opportunities. An IoT system, from the standpoint of networking, is a network of related "things" that may each be uniquely named, offer particular assistance, and interact *via* established rules. RFID tags, sensors, smart devices, embedded systems, actuators, sensor networks, etc., are examples of "objects". The required functionality for each device in an IoT system are provided by the IoT cloud. Theoretically, a cloud may support an infinite number of IoT devices by providing storage, computing, and networking resources.

3.7.2   JointCloud

Cloud companies like AWS, Azure, Alibaba, and IBM are multiplying as cloud computing technology advances. Researchers developed JointCloud computing, which combines many clouds, to benefit from various clouds. Any feature of a different cloud can be accessed through a JointCloud platform. Any combination of public or private clouds may make up the JointCloud platform. Additionally, a mix of both public and private clouds may be present. Multiple clouds are crudely pieced together by existing JointCloud systems. As a result, they make an effort to maintain the majority of cloud computing characteristics including unified network layer, active motion, and hard disks.

3.7.3   Computing Without Servers

Computing without servers is referred as function and as service. Users can post operational activities, service giver handle development, congestion management, and measuring. The technique involving placing a code into use can be made simpler from the user's point of view with serverless computing. The developer is not informed of scaling or capacity planning. The programmer also does not think regarding the maintenance of a virtualized computer. Cost also depends on the real sources that a software uses.

3.7.4   Oracle and Blockchain Technology

Peer-to-peer network's participants maintain a decentralized, trustless ledger using blockchain technology. The platform's condition is arranged in blocks that are listed in order and can be detectable, and each computation time is limited and verified using a user, also called builders. Byzantine fault tolerance is included into the blockchain technology. Anyone can join a protocol on a public blockchain (like those used by Bitcoin and Ethereum), as there are no admission requirements. In contrast, a trusted coordinator and auditor is often established on a permissioned blockchain (such as Quorum) that has stringent access controls and involves a small number of identifiable players. Practical Byzantine Fault Tolerance and other effective consensus algorithms are frequently adopted by permissioned blockchain.

Blockchain, on the other hand, is a de-analyzing and presenting complex system, so dangerous actions such as wireless I/O are prohibited. Blockchain is unable to successfully authenticate the input data. In a verifiable manner, Database (Oracle) is a kind of data input service that feeds blockchain with information from the outside world. Decentralized oracles and centralized oracles are the two main types of oracle solutions that are now available.

3.8   Serverless Cloud Platform System Design

This section discusses few serverless cloud platform with their respective design in detail as:

3.8.1   Aim and Constraints

For IoT systems, Cloud aims to offer reliable services for numerous HCloud. The developers of applications can concentrate on a particular logic: HCloud handles the scheduling and operations across many clouds. HCloud faces the following three difficulties: (1) What should be done about the incompatibility caused by various serverless clouds' heterogeneous implementations? (2) How can I schedule each cloud while also determining how its resources are being used in real time? (3) How can one stop a rogue HCloud administrator from misrepresenting a cloud's condition and planning a client invocation to the wrong cloud?

Before offering developers with uniform interfaces, HCloud analyzes the currently available serverless APIs. After that, we employ numerous cloud administrators, and cloud agents track each cloud's current condition and carry out scheduling in accordance with the user-specified schedule rules. In order to enable the customer to audit the scheduling outcome, we employ and observe blockchain for logging and validate the status that the HCloud has uploaded.

3.8.2   Goals and Challenges

A single serverless platform that works with several clouds is called HCloud. As users, you must just compensate the HCloud maintainer, who also provides an accounting approach. Additionally, the maintenance pays the public clouds. We designate a cloud manager for each cloud to keep an eye on its current status, including its pricing and resource usage. The serverless cloud is managed in the meantime by the cloud manager. After that, a central agent arranges and retrieves the current situation of all cloud administrators. Each client collaborates using agents to set a policy and activates a cloud broker using a client library.

We shall introduce HCloud's function interfaces and sharing of data technique in the sections that follow. Following that, we will provide the client library, cloud manager, and cloud brokers detailed designs. Last but not least, we demonstrate how a hostile HCloud administrator cannot fake the cloud status by using witness blockchain.

3.8.3 HCloud Connections

The serverless function must be accessible across many clouds with different interfaces. In order to provide uniform interfaces, HCloud initially categorizes serverless interfaces into three kinds. After that, we offer a translation technique for using various clouds to run serverless functions created with HCloud interfaces (refer to Figure 3.6). The serverless function developer frequently has access to a variety of interfaces from several cloud vendors. It is categorized into three groups as follows:

- **Invoking and Returning:** Accessing serverless functions requires sending an HTTP request and getting an HTTP response. To parse parameters and return values, many clouds offer a variety of interfaces. There are various APIs offered by AWS and AliYun.
- **API Interface:** Various clouds offer APIs gaining access for their resources. AWS, for instance, permits functions such as access and storage.
- **Coding languages and runtime constraints:** Various clouds provide various functions and various programming languages.

With the unified interfaces offered by HCloud, the function arguments flow through the user inputs. The response is immediately provided in the interim. Currently, offers to APIs for storage purposes are controlled by the run-time API.

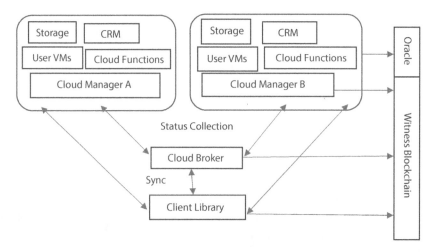

Figure 3.6 HCloud virtual view.

FUNCTION TRANSLATION: HCloud must be in the updated version in order for it to run on a particular serverless cloud. We implement HCloud interfaces using the cloud interfaces. At the moment, HCloud can only write the function using the serverless cloud that supports Python.

We propose HCloud protocols to allow the activation of the serverless function on numerous HCloud techniques that are recommended to promote the execution of the serverless feature across a variety. Creating an interface baseline for serverless computing, however, is a preferable solution. We believe that the standard might be defined by further extending the HCloud interfaces.

3.8.4   Data Sharing Platform

Processing might lead to certain platform data remaining, giving the subsequent functions access to such data. In HCloud, there are various clouds, and each one has its own storage. It is being operated as various clouds; the first function may be storing the data there. Given that HCloud lets a customer pick a cloud service to execute a function, one option is to require the creator to specifically indicate the dependency of function provided by the cloud and make its functions work together in all instances. In addition, it offers high storage to resolve the issues. GPFS is used for storage implementation.

3.8.5   Cloud Manager

Each cloud is given a cloud manager by HCloud who is responsible for building a serverless platform, scheduling the serverless function, and keeping track of the cloud's health. The cloud manager's design is depicted in Figure 3.7. The administrator will give a calling function to respond to the request. We offer native mode and container mode as our two execution options. A worker VM implements the preceding one. For each instance of a function, the worker constructs a container. Any cloud, even those that do not support the serverless architecture, can be used with the container mode and built using the latter's inherent serverless platform. The HCloud API was used to construct the serverless function when a function is pushed to the cloud and used in the application build.

A scheduler is also used by the administrator to manage and organize all user requests. It begins rather fast and charges you only when you invoke its pricing model. In essence, native mode will be used to launch the serverless function. The container mode will be less expensive when there are numerous user requests—for instance, AWS Lambda costs 0.20 USD for every one million queries. Think about a serverless operation that lasts for 1 s. Three million invocations cost $25.60 for a client. The storage of 2GB, however, costs just $0.0084 per hour. It will only cost $7 to process three million inquiries. The scheduler will launch agent and container mode process queries when it notices a high workload. The scheduler additionally watches.

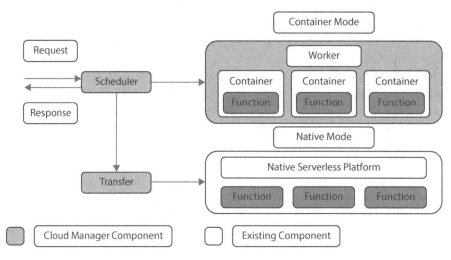

Figure 3.7 Architecture of cloud manager.

3.8.6   The Agent

Serverless function and statuses are gathered by the cloud broker. The broker then gives the client the option to establish a scheduling policy before deciding to process customer queries.

Progress: Both state and modules must be gathered by the cloud broker. The preceding was synchronized using HCloud. It is up to date for the available version. The agent offers function deployment and management. The broker will roll out any improvements made by a developer to function.

Cloud Scheduling: After compiling all of the cloud statistics, the cloud broker can select the best cloud. Figure 3.8 illustrates how HCloud enables various clients to establish their own schedule policies. Client C requests that the broker choose the least expensive cloud. Clients A and B are both interested in calling the cloud from the closest location. The JointCloud environment drastically changes the network latency depending on how far the client is from the cloud. Less than 30 ms constitutes the smallest latency, while less than 100 ms constitutes the longest for completion. The broker might determine the quickest path by calculating the length from the customer.

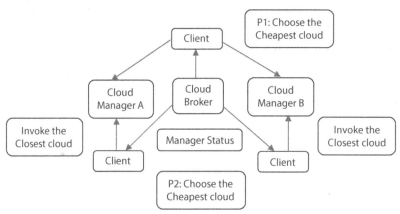

Figure 3.8 Policies for scheduling.

However, once the developer updated the function, there is a problem. A cloud might not finish deploying the new service right away. The client could still make a request to the cloud using the outdated function since she is unaware that it has been updated. The client is prompted by HCloud to provide the function's version information. The cloud broker before can provide the version number. The client must check by calling to a task that will establish the error and will receive a platform that contains the requested operation.

3.8.7   Client Library

The operations are as follows:

- **Implementation**: Serverless function in HCloud can be updated and deployed thanks to the library.
- **Cloud Selection**: A customer may insert the operations. In the meantime, the cloud broker periodically provides the chosen cloud to the library.
- **Function Invocation**: A customer can access operation from a chosen cloud with the aid of the library.
- **Schedule Auditing**: A client can use HCloud to confirm that a cloud was chosen based on its actual state and not a phoney one. The library offers the client interfaces for auditing.

3.8.8   Witness Blockchain

Risk brought: The customer must have confidence in the platform's ability to schedule tasks honestly and in accordance with the customer. In real-world circumstances, the relationship between various cloud service providers upholds the competitiveness. They all want to cling onto their advantages and maintain a strong position during the scheduling process so that they can profit more from the sale of additional computing resources. As a result, cloud service providers have a tremendous incentive to influence HCloud's actions and extract schedule favoritism. Consider this:

- Cloud service providers may bribe the broker in order to work together, and they may secretly alter functionality. Additionally, the agent presents the customers with a modified policy based on a bid that favors the highest bidder.
- As managers run privileges, they might persuade the agent to take biased conclusions.
- Might currently alter the cost in order to entice agents with alluring prices, lure them into using their services over time, and then return the prices to their original levels before to ensure benefits.

Reliable: Platform status will not altered, and the agent accurately executes scheduling in accordance with the schedule policy. Because it consistently offers better usable performance for massive computing than public blockchain, we chose this for creating blockchain.
   The witness blockchain architecture:

- **Submission Situation**: Uploading the cloud status to the witness blockchain is necessary every time a manager synchronizes instances with an agent.

A hacked controller might (1) publish the fabricated situation, (2) fail to publish the situation, or (3) publish the true situation to synchronize the agent and the fabricated module. Status verification can stop the first harmful activity, while schedule logging and auditing can stop the last two.

- **Collection of Public Data**: The uploaded condition must match the cloud's publicly available information—for instance, the price that is uploaded must match the price that the cloud has published. Public data is required by the witness blockchain in order to validate the submitted status. A closed blockchain, however, is unable to access external data. We use database for gathering people's information in order to address this issue.
- **Status Verification**: Might verify that the uploaded state corresponds to the public information after receiving the latter. On the witness blockchain, a smart contract is used to carry out the verification. The verified status should be the sole one used for schedule tracking and accounting.
- **Schedule Logging**: The scheduling log should be uploaded to the blockchain every time an agent executes operations. The schedule policy, schedule result, and cloud status utilized in scheduling are all included in the log.
- **Schedule Auditing**: Every time a customer gets from scheduling analysis from agent, the customer cloud use witness blockchain to audit the outcome. The client can confirm three things using the scheduling log: (1) that the agent utilizes the right cloud results, (2) that the right schedule rule is being used, and (3) that the scheduling is being done appropriately.

In last, several interesting work on blockchain in useful sectors/ domains like cyber security, cloud computing can be found in [16–24].

3.9 Evaluation of HCloud

To conduct the evaluation, we put an HCloud prototype into practice. To simulate three clouds, we utilized three computers. The 8-core Intel, Eight GB memory, and 256GB SSD are all present in every PC. Another computer that has 4-core Intel, Eight GB of memory, and 256GB SSD powers a client. An H3C 240 Gbps switch connects all of the devices.

Run two tests as part of the assessment. In order to demonstrate how HCloud improves performance, we first adjust the control processing unit utilization rates of various platforms and select the one with the greatest control processing unit utilization rate. Second, we adjust the price and examine to lower the price.

3.9.1 CPU Utilization

In order to simulate the performance variations of a cloud, we vary the control processing unit usage in this test. We employ three operations to simulate the variability of the control processing unit utilization rates:

- **Sine:** A sine curve can be seen in the rate wave. It frequently goes up and down.
- **Linear:** The rate of free CPU usage increases and decreases linearly.
- **Stable:** The percentage of free CPU time is a constant figure.

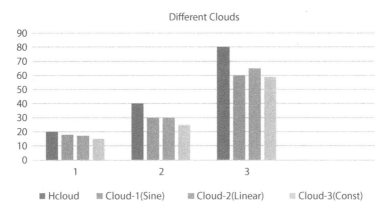

Figure 3.9 Throughput of different clouds and HCloud.

The cloud management is set up to update us on developments. In the meantime, each control processing unit utilization rate gradually changes based on one of the aforementioned strategies. The variation occurs more frequently and is smaller in the real world. The output of employing the first step is called the trial. The output from the platform is then measured for throughput. HCloud will have a better throughput as can be seen in Figure 3.9.

3.9.2   Cost Analysis

We examine the cost-saving benefits of HCloud for the user. Similar to the last test, this one also assumes that each public cloud's cost swings, with each wave of fluctuation resembling a different function.

- **Sine:** A sine curve can be seen in the rate wave. It frequently goes up and down.
- **Linear:** The rate of free CPU usage increases and decreases linearly.
- **Stable:** The percentage of the control processing unit time was a constant figure.

The cloud management is set up to update us every 15 s, employing particular modules that require 2 s. Examining the resources for making the HCloud platform for a single cloud, it turns out that using HCloud typically costs less than using a single cloud.

3.10   HCloud-Related Works

This section discusses HCloud ad its related work in detail as:

3.10.1   Serverless

Several use cases have made use of serverless computing. For the optimization of machine learning and linear algebra, PyWren leverages AWS Lambda services. Using a serverless infrastructure, Werner et al. suggest implementing distributed matrix multiplication. This method has also been used to migrate MapReduce and Spark to serverless versions. A real-world programmer has many options; all their components work together and communicate while it is running. In just a few minutes, ExCamera analyzes a structure–task for generating operations for video encoding. Sprocket, a system for quickly processing videos, is built on the mu framework and enables creators to write a number of subsequent functions. It focuses on an IoT use case, which also needs a sophisticated Internet of Things platform to support all Internet of Things devices. It may allocate operations across many platforms in the meanwhile to reap their full advantages.

3.10.2   Efficiency

Most operations were implemented inside either containers or virtual machines. It is the goal of some research to speed up how serverless functions start up. If the workload being observed is based on Node.js, OpenWhisk is able to pre-launch Node.js containers. A similar strategy is used by SOCK for Python functions. Pocket uses multistorage, including secondary storage devices, to enhance the efficiency. According to the characteristics of serverless operations and the state of resource utilizations, Pocket suggests that the administrator appropriately structures the reallocation. The main purpose of Crail is to exchange and store massive amounts of transitory data. However, it strives for minimal latency and a wide bandwidth. These improvements can be combined with the HCloud design.

3.11   Conclusion

The technologies of blockchain and IoT can be merged in various ways. Since the integration of these technologies will enhance business models, products, and services, one can contend that a convergence of these advances will occur. Such commercial models could be broadly used for any autonomous agents, including sensors, vehicles, equipment, trucks, cameras, and other IoT devices. The creation of these business models and the digital transformation of industrial enterprises will be fueled by convergence. The use of these technologies by executives will help them achieve significant efficiency improvements. A new era of digitization will be paved by blockchain technology and IoT. This chapter examines the difficulties of IoT applications, proposes a structure of module and standard cloud computing, and introduces a blockchain platform to address problems with operation payments and information authenticity decentralized environments. Systems built on KubeEdge and Ethereum were created. In addition, we built a robot formation application to serve as a demonstration, showing how edge cloud technology may simplify the IoT terminal hardware, increase the application flexibility, and charge for services in order to promote greater resource sharing. This can be a model for a commercial operation for, for example, the traditional network providers to offer cloud employing requirements scattered throughout their system nodes and network nodes for customers.

This chapter shows that serverless cloud has been created, a dependable serverless platform that uses blockchain technology. Each IoT administrator can be deployed with various operations thanks to HCloud. After then, HCloud will distribute these tasks among many clouds in order to achieve high scalability, consistent performance, cheap cost, a variety of functionalities, and other goals. To do this, we first offer standardized interfaces for implementing the serverless function and a transformation technique for running the function across several clouds. Each cloud is given a cloud manager to collect module information; the central operations between modules are based on rules. Using witness blockchain to verify a module's behavior in order to make sure that HCloud always executes the scheduling appropriately, we put the HCloud prototype into practice and evaluate it by simulating the actions of various clouds. HCloud can assist a client that wishes to establish the platform with maximum control processing unit utilization rate in proving 25% performance.

References

1. Fellows, W., *A sea of change - migrating workloads and applications to the cloud*, BrightTALK, 12-Sep-2018. https://www.brighttalk.com/webcast/10363/318591

2. Columbus, L., *83% of enterprise workloads will be in the cloud by 2020*, Forbes, 25-Jan-2018.

3. Armbrust, M., Fox, A., Griffith, R., Joseph, A.D., Zaharia, M., A view of cloud computing. *Commun. ACM*, 53, 4, 50–58, 2010.

4. Chiang, M. and Zhang, T., Fog and IoT: An overview of research opportunities. *IEEE Internet Things J.*, 3, 6, 854– 864, 2016.

5. Liu, S., Engineering autonomous vehicles and robots: The DragonFly modular-based approach, p. 3, Wiley-IEEE Press, Hoboken, 2020. https://ieeexplore.ieee.org/book/9063369

6. BONIC technical documentation. https://github.com/BOINC/boinc-devdoc/wiki; https://boinc.berkeley.edu/trac/wiki/ProjectMain

7. Fedak, G., Germain, C., Neri, V., Cappello, F., XtremWeb: A generic global computing system. Proceedings First IEEE/ACM International Symposium on Cluster Computing and the Grid.

8. Khan, A.M. and Freitag, F., On edge cloud service provision with distributed home servers. *2017 IEEE International Conference on Cloud Computing Technology and Science (CloudCom)*, 2017.

9. Ryden, M., Oh, K., Chandra, A., Weissman, J., Nebula: Distributed edge cloud for data intensive computing. *2014 IEEE International Conference on Cloud Engineering*, 2014.

10. Mengistu, T.M., Alahmadi, A.M., Alsenani, Y., Albuali, A., Che, D., cuCloud: Volunteer Computing as a Service (VCaaS) System. In: Luo, M., Zhang, LJ. (eds), Cloud Computing – CLOUD 2018. CLOUD 2018. Lecture Notes in Computer Science, 10967, 2018. Springer, Cham. https://doi.org/10.1007/978-3-319-94295-7_17

11. Lutz, M., Verbeek, C., Schlegel, C., Towards a robot fleet for intra-logistic tasks: Combining free robot navigation with multi-robot coordination at bottlenecks, in: *2016 IEEE 21st International Conference on Emerging Technologies and Factory Automation (ETFA)*, Berlin, Germany, pp. 1-4, 2016.

12. Zhaohui, D., Min, W., Xin, C., Multi-robot cooperative transportation using formation control, in: *2008 27th Chinese Control Conference*, Kunming, China, pp. 346-350, 2008.

13. Miratabzadeh, S.A., Gallardo, N., Gamez, N., Haradi, K., Puthussery, A.R., Rad, P., Jamshidi, M., Cloud robotics: A software architecture: For heterogeneous large-scale autonomous robots. *2016 World Automation Congress (WAC)*, 1–6, 2016.

14. Tyagi, A. K. (Ed.). Handbook of research on quantum computing for smart environments. IGI Global, 2023. https://doi.org/10.4018/978-1-6684-6697-1

15. Lv, M.-M., Li, X.-D., Xiao, T.-F., Iterative learning control for linear time-variant continuous systems with iteration-varying initial conditions and iteration-varying reference trajectories. *IEEE ICCA 2010*, Xiamen, China, pp. 235-240, 2010.

16. Tyagi, A.K, Chapter 2 - Decentralized everything: Practical use of blockchain technology in future applications, in: *Distributed Computing to Blockchain*, Rajiv Pandey, Sam Goundar,

Shahnaz Fatima (eds.) Academic Press, Pages 19-38, 2023, ISBN 9780323961462, https://doi.org/10.1016/B978-0-323-96146-2.00010-3.

17. Tyagi, A.K., Dananjayan S., Agarwal D., Thariq Ahmed H.F. Blockchain internet of things applications: Opportunities and challenges for industry 4.0 and society 5.0. *Sensors,* 23, 2, 947, 2023.

18. Rekha G., Tyagi A.K., Anuradha N., Integration of fog computing and internet of things: An useful overview, in: *Proceedings of ICRIC 2019. Lecture Notes in Electrical Engineering,* Singh P., Kar A., Singh Y., Kolekar M., Tanwar S. (eds.), vol 597. Springer, Cham. https://doi.org/10.1007/978-3-030-29407-6_8

19. Sheth, H.S.K., Tyagi, A.K., Mobile cloud computing: Issues, applications and scope in COVID-19, in: *Intelligent Systems Design and Applications. ISDA 2021. Lecture Notes in Networks and Systems,* Abraham, A., Gandhi, N., Hanne, T., Hong, TP., Nogueira Rios, T., Ding, W. (eds.), vol 418. Springer, Cham, 2022. https://doi.org/10.1007/978-3-030-96308-8_55

20. Nair, M.M., Kumari, S., Tyagi, A.K., Internet of things, cyber physical system, and data analytics: Open questions, future perspectives, and research areas, in: *Proceedings of the Second International Conference on Information Management and Machine Intelligence. Lecture Notes in Networks and Systems,* Goyal D., Gupta A.K., Piuri V., Ganzha M., Paprzycki M. (eds.), vol 166, 2021, Springer, Singapore. https://doi.org/10.1007/978-981-15-9689-6_36

21. Deshmukh, A., Patil, D., Tyagi, A.K., Arumugam S. S, and Arumugam, Recent trends on blockchain for internet of things based applications: Open issues and future trends, in: *Proceedings of the 2022 Fourteenth International Conference on Contemporary Computing (IC3-2022). Association for Computing Machinery,* New York, NY, USA, 484–492, 2022. https://doi.org/10.1145/3549206.3549289

22 Tyagi, A. K.,Chandrasekaran, S., Sreenath, N., Blockchain technology – A new technology for creating distributed and trusted computing environment, in: *2022 International Conference on Applied Artificial Intelligence and Computing (ICAAIC),* pp. 1348-1354, 2022.

23. Tibrewal, I., Srivastava, M., Tyagi, A.K., Blockchain technology for securing cyber-infrastructure and internet of things networks, in: *Intelligent Interactive Multimedia Systems for e-Healthcare Applications,* Tyagi A.K., Abraham A., Kaklauskas A. (eds). Springer, Singapore, 2022. https://doi.org/10.1007/978-981-16-6542-4_1

24. Tyagi, A. K., Fernandez, T. F., Aswathy, S. U., Blockchain and Aadhaar based electronic voting system, in: *2020 4th International Conference on Electronics, Communication and Aerospace Technology (ICECA),* Coimbatore, pp. 498-504, 2020.

25. Shah, H., Shah, D., Jadav, N.K., Gupta, R., Tanwar, S., Alfarraj, O., Tolba, A., Raboaca, M.S., Marina, V., Deep leaming-based malicious smart contract and intrusion detection system for IoT environment. *Mathematics,* 11, 418, 2023. https://doi.org/10.3390/mathl 1020418

4

Artificial Intelligence–Blockchain-Enabled–Internet of Things-Based Cloud Applications for Next-Generation Society

V. Hemamalini[1], Anand Kumar Mishra[2], Amit Kumar Tyagi[3]* and Vijayalakshmi Kakulapati[4]

[1]Department of Networking and Communications, School of Computing, SRM Institute of Science and Technology, Chennai, India
[2]Computer Science and Engineering, NIIT University, Neemrana, Rajasthan, India
[3]Department of Fashion Technology, National Institute of Fashion Technology, New Delhi, Delhi, India
[4]Sreenidhi Institute of Science and Technology, Yamnampet, Ghatkesar, Hyderabad, Telangana, India

Abstract

Artificial intelligence (AI), blockchain technology, and Internet of Things (IoT) are three of the most rapidly evolving technologies in the current era. The integration of these technologies can provide significant benefits to cloud-based environments by enhancing security, privacy, and data management. This paper proposes an architecture that combines AI, blockchain, and IoT in a cloud-based environment. The proposed architecture provides a secure and reliable platform for data exchange and analysis, enabling the development of smart applications that can improve the efficiency, productivity, and quality of life. The architecture's core components are the IoT sensors, AI algorithms, and blockchain technology, which ensure data security and privacy, immutability, and transparency. The proposed architecture can be used in various applications, such as healthcare, logistics, and smart cities. In summary, this chapter provides an overview of the benefits and challenges associated with the integration of AI, blockchain, and IoT and proposes a novel architecture that can leverage these technologies to improve cloud-based environments' efficiency and security. This research work will discuss about futuristic technology and their role in respective fields in detail.

Keywords: Artificial intelligence, blockchain, Internet of Things (IoT)-based cloud applications, next-generation society

4.1 Introduction

We need to explain each term in detail (before moving further):

- Artificial Intelligence: Artificial intelligence (AI) refers to the development of computer systems that can perform tasks that typically require human intelligence, such as visual perception, speech recognition, decision-making, and

---

*Corresponding author: amitkrtyagi025@gmail.com

Amit Kumar Tyagi (ed.) Automated Secure Computing for Next-Generation Systems, (65–82) © 2024 Scrivener Publishing LLC

language translation. AI involves the use of algorithms and statistical models to enable machines to learn from data and improve their performance over time. The goal of AI is to create intelligent machines that can solve complex problems and make decisions that are at least as good as, if not better than, those made by humans. AI has numerous applications in various fields, including healthcare, finance, education, transportation, and entertainment. Some of the popular applications of AI include virtual assistants like Siri and Alexa, self-driving cars, image and speech recognition software, fraud detection systems, and personalized marketing. AI is a rapidly evolving field, and recent advancements in deep learning, natural language processing, and computer vision have greatly expanded the capabilities of AI systems [1]. However, the development of AI also raises ethical and societal concerns, including the impact on employment, privacy, and bias. As such, there is a growing need for responsible AI development and governance to ensure that AI benefits society as a whole.

- Blockchain: Blockchain is a decentralized, distributed ledger technology that enables secure, transparent, and tamper-proof recording of transactions and data across a network of computers [2]. In a blockchain, data is stored in a series of blocks that are linked together using cryptographic techniques, creating an unchangeable and permanent record of each transaction or data point. One of the main features of blockchain technology is its security. Since the data in a blockchain is distributed across multiple computers, it is difficult for any one party to tamper with the data without the consensus of the other parties in the network [3]. This makes blockchain ideal for applications that require high levels of security, such as financial transactions, supply chain management, and healthcare data management. Another key feature of blockchain is its transparency. Since all the transactions and data recorded on a blockchain are visible to all the participants in the network, there is no need for a central authority to manage the transactions. This makes blockchain a highly democratic and decentralized technology, with the potential to disrupt traditional models of governance and control.

    Note that blockchain has numerous applications in various industries, including finance, healthcare, logistics, and energy [4]. Some of the popular applications of blockchain include cryptocurrency transactions, digital identity management, smart contracts, and secure data sharing.

    Despite its many benefits, blockchain technology is still in the early stages of development and faces a number of challenges, including scalability, interoperability, and regulatory uncertainty. As such, there is a need for ongoing research and development to address these challenges and fully realize the potential of blockchain technology.

- Internet of Things-based Cloud Applications: Internet of Things (IoT)-based cloud applications refer to the integration of IoT devices with cloud computing technology to enable the storage, processing, and analysis of data generated by these devices. IoT devices, such as sensors and actuators, collect data on various physical phenomena, such as temperature, humidity, and motion, and transmit this data to the cloud for further analysis. Cloud computing provides a scalable and flexible platform for storing and processing large amounts of data generated by IoT devices [5]. This enables organizations to leverage the data collected from IoT devices to gain insights into various aspects of their operations, such as energy consumption, inventory management, and customer behavior.

IoT-based cloud applications have numerous benefits, including increased operational efficiency, improved decision-making, and enhanced customer experience—for example, a manufacturing company could use IoT devices to monitor the performance of its machines and send data to the cloud for real-time analysis. Based on this data, the company could identify areas for optimization and implement changes to improve the efficiency of its operations.

Another example is a smart home system that integrates IoT devices with cloud-based applications to control various aspects of the home, such as lighting, temperature, and security. The system could use data collected from sensors to adjust the temperature based on the occupancy of the room or turn off lights when no one is in the room, resulting in energy savings and improved convenience for the homeowner.

However, the use of IoT-based cloud applications also raises concerns about data privacy and security. The large amounts of data generated by IoT devices are often sensitive in nature, and organizations must take steps to protect this data from unauthorized access and cyber threats [6]. Hence, IoT-based cloud applications have the potential to transform various industries and improve the way we live and work. However, it is important to carefully consider the benefits and risks associated with this technology and implement appropriate safeguards to ensure its safe and responsible use.

- Cloud-Based IoT Applications: Cloud-based IoT applications refer to software programs that enable the management and analysis of data from internet of things (IoT) devices through cloud computing platforms. These applications typically collect data from sensors, devices, and other sources, process and analyze it in real time, and provide insights that can be used to improve business operations, optimize performance, and drive innovation.

Cloud-based IoT applications provide several advantages over traditional on-premises solutions, including scalability, flexibility, and cost-effectiveness. With cloud-based solutions, organizations can easily scale up or down their IoT infrastructure as needed without having to invest in expensive hardware or software [7]. They can also take advantage of the latest advancements in IoT technology, such as machine learning and artificial intelligence, to gain deeper insights and improve decision-making.

Cloud-based IoT applications also enable organizations to store and process large volumes of data, which is critical for IoT applications that generate massive amounts of data in real time. Cloud platforms provide a cost-effective way to store and process this data without requiring organizations to invest in expensive hardware or software.

Hence, cloud-based IoT applications offer a powerful set of tools for managing and analyzing IoT data and are becoming increasingly popular among organizations that are looking to leverage the benefits of IoT technology to drive innovation and improve business operations.

- Next-Generation Society: The next-generation society refers to a future society that is expected to emerge as a result of rapid advancements in technology, shifting demographics, and changing social norms. It is a society that is more connected, more diverse, and more technologically advanced than ever before and is characterized by a range of new opportunities and challenges. One of the key drivers of the next-generation society is technology, particularly digital technology. The widespread adoption of technologies such as artificial intelligence, blockchain, and IoT is expected to transform many aspects of our lives, from the way we work and communicate to the way we access healthcare and education [8]. Demographic shifts are also expected to play a significant role in shaping the next-generation society—for example, the aging of populations in many developed countries is likely to lead to an increased demand for healthcare and social services, while the growth of younger populations in many developing countries is likely to drive economic growth and innovation.

  Changing social norms are also expected to have a significant impact on the next-generation society—for example, the growing awareness of issues such as climate change and social inequality is likely to lead to an increased demand for sustainable and equitable solutions.

  In summary, the next-generation society represents a new era of social and technological transformation and presents both opportunities and challenges for individuals, businesses, and governments around the world.

- Society 5.0: Society 5.0 is a concept that originated in Japan and is seen as the next stage of human evolution. It refers to a society that is characterized by the integration of cyber and physical systems or what is known as the "cyber-physical system". The aim of Society 5.0 is to leverage advanced technologies such as artificial intelligence, robotics, and IoT to create a human-centric society that is sustainable, inclusive, and innovative. In Society 5.0, digital technologies are used to solve social problems and improve the quality of life for people [9]—for example, advanced healthcare systems that use AI and remote monitoring can help to improve healthcare outcomes and reduce costs. Smart transportation systems can reduce traffic congestion and improve safety, while smart energy systems can increase energy efficiency and reduce carbon emissions.

  The Society 5.0 concept is driven by a strong sense of social responsibility, with the aim of using technology to create a better society for all. It is seen as a solution to the challenges facing modern societies, such as an aging population, climate change, and inequality. Hence, Society 5.0 represents a new approach to society that is characterized by the integration of digital and physical systems to create a sustainable, inclusive, and innovative society that prioritizes the needs of its citizens.

- Industry 5.0: Industry 5.0 is a concept that builds on the principles of Industry 4.0 and extends it further by emphasizing the importance of human skills and creativity in the manufacturing process. It is also known as "human-centric manufacturing". Industry 5.0 focuses on a collaborative approach that brings together advanced technologies such as artificial intelligence, robotics, and IoT with human expertise, creativity, and problem-solving skills [10]. It aims to create a manufacturing environment that is more flexible, adaptable, and responsive to customer needs. One of the key aspects of Industry 5.0 is the concept of "co-creation", which involves a collaborative approach between humans and machines to design and produce products [11]. This means that machines and robots are not just tools to automate the manufacturing process but are also active participants in the creative process, working alongside humans to develop innovative solutions.

Industry 5.0 also emphasizes the importance of sustainability and social responsibility in the manufacturing process. This means that manufacturers need to consider the environmental impact of their operations and work to minimize waste, reduce energy consumption, and promote sustainable practices [12].

Hence, Industry 5.0 represents a new approach to manufacturing that prioritizes human skills and creativity, collaboration between humans and machines, and sustainability. It is expected to lead to more efficient, innovative, and responsible manufacturing practices that benefit both businesses and society as a whole.

In last, this chapter is summarized in 12 (twelve) sections.

4.2   Background Work

Imran Ahmed *et al.* aims to examine the convergence of blockchain technology and artificial intelligence, a unique driver towards technological transformation in intelligent and sustainable IoT applications [13]. The system provides digital analytics and saves results in decentralized cloud repositories through blockchain technology to promote various applications. The significant contributions and rapid developments of advanced artificial intelligence-based technologies and approaches, like machine learning and deep learning, which are applied for extracting accurate information from extensive data, perform a potential role in IoT applications. Thus, artificial intelligence and blockchain technology convergence revolutionizes smart city infrastructures to establish sustainable ecosystems for IoT applications.

Sushil Kumar Singh *et al.* investigated to design and develop an IoT architecture with blockchain and AI to support an effective big data analysis. In this paper, we propose a blockchain-enabled intelligent IoT architecture with artificial intelligence that provides an efficient way of converging blockchain and AI for IoT with current state-of-the-art techniques and applications [14]. In qualitative evaluation, we describe how to use AI and blockchain in IoT applications with "AI-driven blockchain" and "blockchain-driven AI". In quantitative analysis, we present a performance evaluation of the Block IoT Intelligence architecture to compare existing research on device, fog, edge, and cloud intelligence according to some parameters such as accuracy, latency, security and privacy, computational complexity, and energy cost in IoT applications.

Philipp Sandner *et al.* studied the autonomous agents (i.e., sensors, cars, machines, trucks, cameras, and other IoT devices) which will, in the future, act as own profit centers that (1) have a digital twin leveraging IoT, (2) send and receive money leveraging blockchain technology on their own, and (3) autonomously make decisions as independent economic agents leveraging AI and data analytics [15]. Blockchain technology, combined with IoT and AI, will pave the way to a new age of digitization. Over the last decade, blockchain technology has improved considerably. Historically, for example, the main critiques about blockchain technology were its limited scalability and inefficiencies. The General Data Protection Regulation's (GDPR) right for data to be forgotten and the integration with legacy systems are examples of such issues.

Meghna Manoj Nair *et al.* investigated the significant advances in information and communication technologies. The IoT has undergone remarkable developments in recent years, reshaping each field of human society, including finance, healthcare, transportation, education, and entertainment [16]. Despite the potential for prompting core technological innovation and industrial transformation, blockchain has several pain points in terms of power consumption, data redundancy, detection of unusual behaviors, efficiency of smart contracts, and the management of blockchain. Benefiting from its success in a number of different fields, AI can provide attractive solutions to improve the performance of blockchains, enabling the blockchain to be more secure, more reliable, and more efficient. However, the research on intelligent blockchain still is in its infancy, with many problems to be solved.

Sukhpal Singh Gill *et al.* proposed that cloud computing plays a critical role in modern society and enables a range of applications from infrastructure to social media. Enabling these systems are a cohort of conceptual technologies synthesized to meet the demands of evolving computing applications. In this study, we aim to explore how three emerging paradigms(blockchain, IoT, and artificial intelligence) will influence future cloud computing systems. Finally, we proposed a conceptual model for cloud futurology to explore the influence of emerging paradigms and technologies on the evolution of cloud computing. In this review paper, we have presented the systematic review of computing paradigms and technologies and the influence of the triumvirate (blockchain, IoT, and artificial intelligence) to the evolution of cloud computing [17].

Houshyar Honar Pajooh *et al.* [18] investigated the 6G-enabled IoT technology that provides a platform for information collection and processing at high speed and with low latency. This paper is dedicated to discussing the advantages, challenges, and future research directions of integrating 6G-enabled IoT and blockchain technology for various applications such as smart homes, smart cities, healthcare, supply chain, vehicle automation, etc. The benefits of blockchain-enabled IoT systems should be studied carefully to eliminate the risk of implementation failures in different scenarios. The benefits of 6G-enabled IoT and blockchain, potential use cases, and the challenges associated with this merger are presented in detail in this article.

Dinh C. Nguyen *et al.* studied blockchain with its decentralized, transparent and secure nature; it has emerged as a disruptive technology for the next generation of numerous industrial applications. One of them is Cloud of Things which is enabled by the combination of cloud computing and Internet of Things. In this context, blockchain provides innovative solutions to address the challenges in Cloud of Things in terms of decentralization, data privacy, and network security, while Cloud of Things offer elasticity and scalability functionalities to improve the efficiency of blockchain operations [19]. Therefore, a novel paradigm of blockchain and Cloud of Things integration, called BCoT, has been widely regarded as a promising enabler for a wide range of application scenarios.

Simanta Shekhar Sarmah *et al.* investigated the blockchain technology which is a recent and eminent financial technology that completely transforms business transactions. It is a decentralized network that supports and employs a variety of cryptography models. This robust and flexible secured transaction is being integrated with another eminent computing paradigm—cloud computing. The main aim of this integrated system is to ensure and enhance the trust between the data server, the data users, and the data security [20]. The review states that the study on blockchain-based cloud systems is still in the development process. Access control is one of the core issues faced by the researchers. In view of rewarding the data, the communication between multi-party computations disrupts the networks as well as unexpected financial loss.

Tanweer Alam *et al.* [21] studied the smart city which is an urbanization region that collects data using several digital and physical devices. The information collected from such devices is used efficiently to manage revenues, resources, assets, etc., while the information obtained from such devices is utilized to boost performance throughout the city. Cloud-based IoT applications could help smart cities that contain information gathered from citizens, devices, homes, and other things. This information is processed and analyzed to monitor and manage transportation networks, electric utilities, resource management, water supply systems, waste management, crime detection, security mechanisms, proficiency, digital library, healthcare facilities, and other opportunities. The author also covered IoT and cloud convergence, cloud-based IoT solutions, and cloud-based IoT applications for smart cities.

Baha Rababah *et al.* found that increasing the implication of growing data generated by the IoT brings the focus toward extracting knowledge from the raw data derived from sensors. In the current cloud computing architecture, all the IoT raw data are transmitted to the cloud for processing, storage, and controlling things [22]. This aims to bring the attention of IoT specialists to distributed intelligence and its role to deduce current IoT challenges such as availability, mobility, energy efficiency, security, scalability, interoperability, and reliability. Distributed intelligence in IoT plays an important role to support the exact communication and processing functions to be offered at the exact place at a certain time.

4.3 Motivation

We are writing this chapters on this emerging topic because of its necessity in near future. Hence,

- This paper aims to address the challenges and opportunities posed by the convergence of four transformative technologies—AI, blockchain, IoT, and cloud computing—and their potential to create a new value and enable novel applications for the next-generation society.
- This work helps to explore the current state of the art in these technologies and their integration and to highlight the potential benefits, such as increased security, transparency, efficiency, and automation, that can be achieved through their use in cloud-based applications.
- The paper also aims to identify the key research challenges and open issues that need to be addressed in order to fully realize the potential of these technologies in the context of the next-generation society.

- The paper seeks to stimulate further research and development in this area and to provide guidance and insights for practitioners and researchers alike.

4.4   Existing Innovations in the Current Society

There are numerous innovations that exist in our current society, and here are just a few examples:

- Artificial Intelligence: AI is revolutionizing the way we interact with technology and has applications in various fields, including healthcare, finance, and transportation. It is being used for everything—from diagnosing medical conditions to optimizing supply chains [23].
- 3D Printing: 3D printing technology has made it possible to create complex objects using a variety of materials—from plastics to metals. This technology has applications in industries such as healthcare, aerospace, and architecture [24].
- Renewable Energy: Renewable energy sources such as solar, wind, and hydropower are becoming more affordable and accessible, helping to reduce our dependence on fossil fuels and combat climate change [25].
- Electric Vehicles: Electric vehicles are becoming increasingly popular as a more environmentally friendly alternative to traditional gas-powered cars [26]. They are also becoming more affordable and practical, with longer ranges and faster charging times.
- Blockchain: Blockchain technology is being used for secure and transparent transactions in various industries, including finance, healthcare, and supply chain management. It has the potential to revolutionize the way we handle data and conduct transactions [27].
- Virtual and Augmented Reality: VR and AR technologies are being used in industries such as gaming, education, and healthcare to create immersive experiences and improve learning outcomes [28].
- Biotechnology: Biotechnology is being used to develop new treatments for diseases, improve crop yields, and create sustainable materials [29]. It has the potential to transform various industries and improve our quality of life.

These are the few examples of the many innovations that exist in our current society. As technology continues to advance, we can expect to see even more exciting and impactful innovations emerge in the future.

4.5   Expected Innovations in the Next-Generation Society

There are several expected innovations that could shape the next-generation society. Here are some of the most notable ones:

- Internet of Things: IoT will continue to grow and connect everything around us, from our homes to our cities to our vehicles [30]. This technology will enable better automation, real-time data analysis, and more personalized experiences.

- 5G Networks: 5G networks are expected to provide ultra-fast, low-latency connectivity that will power the next generation of technologies, such as augmented and virtual reality, smart cities, and autonomous vehicles [31].
- Artificial Intelligence: AI will become even more advanced and ubiquitous in the next-generation society. It will continue to transform various industries, such as healthcare, finance, and transportation, by improving decision-making, automation, and efficiency [32].
- Quantum Computing: Quantum computing has the potential to revolutionize the way we process information and solve complex problems. It could lead to breakthroughs in various fields, such as drug discovery, finance, and cryptography [33].
- Smart Cities: Smart cities will become more widespread and sophisticated, leveraging IoT, AI, and other technologies to improve sustainability, efficiency, and livability [34].
- Robotics: Robotics will become more advanced and versatile, with applications in various industries, such as healthcare, manufacturing, and agriculture. Robots will be used to perform tasks that are dangerous, difficult, or tedious for humans [35].
- Biotechnology: Biotechnology will continue to advance, with new discoveries and innovations in areas such as gene editing, regenerative medicine, and synthetic biology [36].

Hence, the next-generation society is expected to be characterized by advanced technologies that enable better connectivity, automation, and efficiency while also promoting sustainability, inclusivity, and well-being. These innovations will have a profound impact on how we live, work, and interact with each other and our environment.

4.6   An Environment with Artificial Intelligence–Blockchain-Enabled–Internet of Things-Based Cloud Applications

An environment with artificial intelligence–blockchain-enabled–IoT-based cloud applications would be a highly advanced and interconnected system that could transform various industries and improve efficiency, security, and transparency. Here are the ways on how each of these technologies could contribute to such an environment:

- Artificial Intelligence: AI algorithms could be used to analyze vast amounts of data generated by IoT devices and cloud applications [37]. This analysis could help organizations make better decisions, optimize operations, and improve customer experiences.
- Blockchain: Blockchain technology could provide secure and transparent transactions and data sharing between IoT devices and cloud applications. It could also enable secure digital identity management, smart contracts, and decentralized data storage [38].

- Internet of Things: IoT devices could generate real-time data that could be analyzed by AI algorithms and stored on the blockchain for secure and transparent access. These devices could be used for various applications, such as remote monitoring and control, predictive maintenance, and asset tracking [39].
- Cloud Applications: Cloud applications could provide a centralized platform for data analysis, processing, and storage. They could be used for various applications, such as data analytics, machine learning, and business intelligence [40].

AI, blockchain, IoT, and cloud applications could together enable organizations to achieve greater efficiency, security, and transparency. This environment could be used for various applications, such as supply chain management, healthcare, finance, and smart cities. It could also improve collaboration between organizations and promote innovation by enabling data sharing and analysis. Hence, an environment with AI, blockchain, IoT, and cloud applications would be a highly advanced and interconnected system that could transform various industries and improve efficiency, security, and transparency.

4.7   Open Issues in Artificial Intelligence–Blockchain-Enabled–Internet of Things-Based Cloud Applications

There are several open issues in the intersection of artificial intelligence, blockchain, IoT, and Cloud applications. Here are a few:

- Scalability: One of the primary challenges in blockchain-enabled IoT systems is scalability. As the number of IoT devices increases, the blockchain network becomes more crowded, and the system becomes slow and inefficient. Researchers are exploring different approaches, such as sharding and sidechains, to address this issue [41].
- Security and Privacy: With the increasing number of IoT devices connected to the cloud, security and privacy have become a significant concern. The blockchain can help provide security through its distributed and decentralized nature, but there is still a need for better security and privacy mechanisms, such as encryption and access control [42].
- Interoperability: The lack of standardization and interoperability among different IoT devices and cloud platforms can pose a significant challenge [43]. Blockchain can help create a more standardized ecosystem, but more work needs to be done in this area.
- Data Management: The massive amount of data generated by IoT devices can be difficult to manage and analyze. AI can help process and analyze this data, but there is a need for more efficient and scalable data storage and retrieval mechanisms [44].
- Energy Efficiency: IoT devices consume a lot of energy, and this can be a significant challenge for blockchain-enabled IoT systems. Research is ongoing

to develop more energy-efficient IoT devices and blockchain consensus algorithms [45].

- Governance and Regulation: The integration of AI, blockchain, IoT, and cloud technologies raises new governance and regulatory challenges. There is a need for clear guidelines and regulations to ensure that these technologies are used ethically and in compliance with privacy and security laws [46].

In summary, the integration of AI, blockchain, IoT, and cloud technologies has enormous potential to transform the way we live and work. However, several open issues need to be addressed to realize the full potential of these technologies. Ongoing research and collaboration among industry, academia, and government can help address these challenges and create a more secure, efficient, and sustainable ecosystem.

4.8   Research Challenges in Artificial Intelligence–Blockchain-Enabled–Internet of Things-Based Cloud Applications

The intersection of artificial intelligence, blockchain, Internet of Things, and cloud applications poses several research challenges. Here are some of the most critical research challenges in this area:

- Integration of AI With Blockchain and IoT: One of the main research challenges is to integrate AI with blockchain and IoT technologies effectively. AI can help process and analyze the vast amount of data generated by IoT devices, but integrating AI algorithms into blockchain-enabled IoT systems can be challenging [47].
- Blockchain-Based Consensus Algorithms: Another significant research challenge is to develop more efficient and scalable consensus algorithms for blockchain-enabled IoT systems. The current consensus algorithms used in blockchain technology, such as proof-of-work and proof-of-stake, are not well suited for IoT devices due to their high energy consumption and scalability issues [48].
- Security and Privacy: Security and privacy are crucial research challenges in the context of AI, blockchain, IoT, and cloud applications. Blockchain can provide a more secure and decentralized infrastructure, but more research is needed to develop effective security and privacy mechanisms for these systems [49].
- Data Management and Analytics: The massive amount of data generated by IoT devices requires efficient and scalable data management and analytics solutions [50]. Researchers need to develop more effective data processing and analysis methods that can handle the large volume, variety, and velocity of IoT data.
- Interoperability: The lack of standardization and interoperability among different IoT devices and cloud platforms is a significant research challenge [51]. Blockchain technology can help create a more standardized ecosystem, but more research is needed to develop interoperability standards and protocols.

- Energy Efficiency: Energy efficiency is a crucial research challenge in blockchain-enabled IoT systems [52]. Researchers need to develop more energy-efficient IoT devices and blockchain consensus algorithms to reduce energy consumption and improve the sustainability of these systems.
- Governance and Regulation: The integration of AI, blockchain, IoT, and cloud technologies raises new governance and regulatory challenges [53]. Researchers need to study the ethical, legal, and social implications of these technologies and develop clear guidelines and regulations to ensure their ethical and responsible use.

In summary, the integration of AI, blockchain, IoT, and cloud technologies presents several research challenges that require multidisciplinary collaboration among researchers, industry, and government. Addressing these challenges can help realize the full potential of these technologies to transform the way we live and work.

4.9   Legal Challenges in Artificial Intelligence–Blockchain-Enabled–Internet of Things-Based Cloud Applications

The integration of AI, blockchain, IoT, and cloud applications poses several legal challenges. Here are some of the most critical legal challenges in this area:

- Data Protection and Privacy: One of the most significant legal challenges in AI, blockchain, IoT, and cloud applications is data protection and privacy [54]. With the vast amount of data generated by IoT devices, it is essential to ensure that personal data is collected and processed in compliance with privacy laws such as the GDPR.
- Intellectual Property: Intellectual property rights are another legal challenge in this area. With the rapid development of AI algorithms and IoT devices, it is essential to ensure that intellectual property rights are respected and protected [55]. Blockchain technology can provide a secure and decentralized infrastructure for managing intellectual property rights, but more research is needed in this area.
- Liability and Accountability: Another legal challenge is determining liability and accountability for damages caused by AI, blockchain, IoT, and cloud applications. With the increasing use of autonomous systems, it can be challenging to assign responsibility when things go wrong. There is a need for clear legal frameworks to ensure accountability and liability for these technologies [56].
- Standards and Regulations: The integration of AI, blockchain, IoT, and cloud technologies raises new governance and regulatory challenges. There is a need for clear guidelines and regulations to ensure that these technologies are used ethically and in compliance with privacy and security laws. Standardization is also critical to ensure interoperability among different IoT devices and cloud platforms [57].

- Cybersecurity and Cybercrime: The integration of these technologies also raises concerns about cybersecurity and cybercrime. Blockchain can provide a more secure infrastructure, but it is not foolproof, and vulnerabilities still exist. There is a need for clear legal frameworks to address cybersecurity and cybercrime issues in AI, blockchain, IoT, and cloud applications [58].

In summary, the integration of AI, blockchain, IoT, and cloud technologies presents several legal challenges that require careful consideration by policymakers, regulators, and legal professionals. Addressing these challenges can help ensure that these technologies are used ethically and responsibly and contribute to the development of a more secure, efficient, and sustainable ecosystem.

4.10 Future Research Opportunities Towards Artificial Intelligence–Blockchain-Enabled–Internet of Things-Based Cloud Applications

Artificial intelligence, blockchain, and IoT are three of the most promising and transformative technologies that are shaping the future of various industries. The convergence of these technologies has the potential to create a new paradigm of intelligent, decentralized, and secure cloud applications that can drive innovation and growth in various sectors. Here are some future research opportunities towards AI–blockchain-enabled IoT-based cloud applications:

- AI–Blockchain-Enabled IoT-Based Supply Chain Management: The integration of AI, blockchain, and IoT can improve the visibility and transparency of supply chain processes, thereby enhancing efficiency, reducing costs, and mitigating risks [59]. Researchers can explore the use of machine learning algorithms and smart contracts to optimize supply chain operations and automate contract execution, payment, and settlement processes.
- AI–Blockchain-Enabled IoT-Based Healthcare: The use of AI, blockchain, and IoT can revolutionize the healthcare industry by providing real-time patient monitoring, personalized treatments, and secure data sharing [60]. Researchers can investigate the use of AI-powered predictive analytics and blockchain-enabled secure data sharing to improve the accuracy and speed of diagnosis, treatment, and disease prevention.
- AI–Blockchain-Enabled IoT-Based Energy Management: The integration of AI, blockchain, and IoT can enable the development of smart energy management systems that can optimize energy consumption, reduce costs, and enhance sustainability [61]. Researchers can explore the use of AI-powered predictive analytics and smart contracts to manage energy demand and supply, facilitate peer-to-peer energy trading, and promote the use of renewable energy sources.
- AI–Blockchain-Enabled IoT-Based Smart Cities: The convergence of AI, blockchain, and IoT can enable the development of smart cities that can

improve the quality of life, enhance sustainability, and promote economic growth [62]. Researchers can investigate the use of AI-powered predictive analytics and blockchain-enabled secure data sharing to optimize urban planning, traffic management, public safety, and environmental monitoring.
- AI–Blockchain-Enabled IoT-based agriculture: The use of AI, blockchain, and IoT can transform the agriculture industry by providing real-time monitoring of crops, soil, and weather conditions and enabling precision agriculture. Researchers can explore the use of AI-powered predictive analytics and blockchain-enabled secure data sharing to optimize crop yields, reduce costs, and enhance sustainability [62–66].

In summary, the integration of AI, blockchain, and IoT has the potential to create new opportunities for research and innovation in various industries. By leveraging these technologies, researchers can develop intelligent, decentralized, and secure cloud applications that can improve efficiency, reduce costs, and enhance sustainability.

4.11   An Open Discussion

As an open discussion, one of the primary benefits of combining these three technologies is that it enables the development of highly secure and decentralized cloud applications. By leveraging blockchain's immutable ledger and smart contract functionality, organizations can create highly secure and transparent data storage and transaction systems. This can provide benefits such as enhanced data privacy and security as well as streamlined and automated processes for contract execution and payment settlement. Additionally, by combining IoT with AI and blockchain, organizations can create highly intelligent systems that can automate decision-making and optimize resource utilization—for example, in smart cities, intelligent traffic management systems can use real-time data from IoT sensors to optimize traffic flow and reduce congestion. Similarly, in agriculture, smart irrigation systems can use real-time weather and soil data from IoT sensors to optimize watering schedules and conserve water resources. However, there are also potential challenges and limitations to consider when combining these technologies. One of the primary challenges is interoperability, as different devices and systems may use different protocols and standards for data exchange. Additionally, there are concerns around data privacy and security, as IoT devices may collect sensitive data that could be vulnerable to cyberattacks. Finally, there is the challenge of scalability, as the large volumes of data generated by IoT devices can strain cloud infrastructure and require complex data management strategies.

Hence, the combination of AI, blockchain, and IoT has the potential to transform a wide range of industries, from supply chain management and healthcare to energy management and agriculture. However, realizing this potential will require careful planning, collaboration, and investment in developing the necessary infrastructure and standards.

4.12 Conclusion

As discussed above, the convergence of artificial intelligence, blockchain, and Internet of Things has the potential to create a new paradigm of intelligent, secure, and decentralized cloud applications. By leveraging these technologies, organizations can create highly intelligent and efficient systems that can automate decision-making, optimize resource utilization, and enhance data privacy and security. However, realizing this potential will require addressing various challenges such as interoperability, data privacy, security, and scalability. Additionally, developing the necessary infrastructure and standards will require collaboration between industry, academia, and government. Despite these challenges, the opportunities presented by AI–blockchain-enabled IoT-based cloud environment are vast and can transform a wide range of industries—from supply chain management and healthcare to smart cities and agriculture. By embracing this convergence and investing in research and innovation, organizations can create a more efficient, sustainable, and secure future.

References

1. Kaul, V., Enslin, S., Gross, S.A., History of artificial intelligence in medicine. *Gastrointestinal Endosc.*, 92, 4, 807–812, 2020.
2. Jain, A., Tripathi, A.K., Chandra, N., Ponnusamy, C., Smart contract enabled online examination system based in blockchain network, in: *2021 International Conference on Computer Communication and Informatics (ICCCI)*, pp. 1–7, IEEE, 2021.
3. Yu, B., Wright, J., Nepal, S., Zhu, L., Liu, J., Ranjan, R., IoTChain: Establishing trust in the Internet of Things ecosystem using blockchain. *IEEE Cloud Comput.*, 5, 4, 12–23, 2018.
4. Al-Jaroodi, J. and Mohamed, N., Industrial applications of blockchain, in: *2019 IEEE 9th Annual Computing and Communication Workshop and Conference (CCWC)*, pp. 0550–0555, IEEE, 2019.
5. Fortino, G., Pathan, M., Di Fatta, G., Bodycloud: Integration of cloud computing and body sensor networks, in: *4th IEEE International Conference on Cloud Computing Technology and Science Proceedings*, pp. 851–856, IEEE, 2012.
6. Kimani, K., Oduol, V., Langat, K., Cyber security challenges for IoT-based smart grid networks. *Int. J. Crit. Infrastructure Prot.*, 25, 36–49, 2019.
7. Alenezi, M., Almustafa, K., Meerja, K.A., Cloud based SDN and NFV architectures for IoT infrastructure. *Egyptian Inf. J.*, 20, 1, 1–10, 2019.
8. Bublitz, F.M., Oetomo, A., Sahu, K.S., Kuang, A., Fadrique, L.X., Velmovitsky, P.E., Nobrega, R.M., Morita, P.P., Disruptive technologies for environment and health research: An overview of artificial intelligence, blockchain, and Internet of Things. *Int. J. Environ. Res. Public Health*, 16, 20, 3847, 2019.
9. Sá, M.J., Santos, A.I., Serpa, S., Ferreira, C.M., Digital literacy in digital Society 5.0. *Acad. J. Interdiscip. Stud.*, 10, 2, 1–9, 2021.
10. Al Mubarak, M. Sustainably developing in a digital world: Harnessing artificial intelligence to meet the imperatives of work-based learning in Industry 5.0, *Development and Learning in Organizations*, 37. 3, 18–20.2023. https://doi.org/10.1108/DLO-04-2022-0063
11. Carayannis, E.G., Morawska-Jancelewicz, J., The futures of Europe: Society 5.0 and Industry 5.0 as driving forces of future universities. *J. Knowl. Econ.*, 13, 3445–3471, 2022. https://doi.org/10.1007/s13132-021-00854-2

12. Zizic, M.C., Mladineo, M., Gjeldum, N., Celent, L., From Industry 4.0 towards Industry 5.0: A review and analysis of paradigm shift for the people, organization and technology. *Energies*, 15, 14, 5221, 2022.

13. Ahmed, I., Zhang, Y., Jeon, G., Lin, W., Khosravi, M.R., Qi, L., A blockchain- and artificial intelligence-enabled smart IoT framework for sustainable city. *Int. J. Intell. Syst.*, 2022. https://doi.org/10.1002/int.22852 Available at: https://onlinelibrary.wiley.com/doi/abs/10.1002/int.22852

14. Singh, S.K., Rathore, S., Park, J.H., Block IoT intelligence: A blockchain-enabled intelligent IoT architecture with artificial intelligence. *Future Gener. Comput. Syst.*, 721–743, 2020. https://doi.org/10.1016/j.future.2019.09.002

15. Sandner, P., Gross, J., Richter, R., Convergence of blockchain, IoT, and AI. *Blockchain Sci.*, 3, 2020. ttps://doi.org/10.3389/fbloc.2020.522600

16. Nair, M.M., Tyagi, A. K., Chapter 11 - AI, IoT, blockchain, and cloud computing: The necessity of the future, Rajiv Pandey, Sam Goundar, Shahnaz Fatima (eds.), *Distributed Computing to Blockchain*, 189–206, Academic Press, 2023, ISBN 9780323961462, https://doi.org/10.1016/B978-0-323-96146-2.00001-2

17. Gill, S.S., Tuli, S., Xu, M., Singh, I., Singh, K.V., Transformative effects of IoT, blockchain and artificial intelligence on cloud computing: Evolution, vision, trends and open challenges. *Internet of Things* 8, 100118, December 2019. https://doi.org/10.1016/j.iot.2019.100118

18. Pajooh, H.H., Demidenko, S., Aslam, S., Harris, M., Blockchain and 6G-enabled IoT. *Inventions*, 7, 109, 2022. https://doi.org/10.3390/inventions7040109

19. Nguyen, D.C., Pathirana, P.N., Ding, M., Seneviratne, A., Integration of blockchain and cloud of things: Architecture, applications and challenges, in: *IEEE Communications Surveys & Tutorials*, 22, 4, 2521–2549, Fourthquarter 2020.

20. Sarmah, S.S., Application of block chain in cloud computing. *Int. J. Innov. Technol. Exploring Eng.*, 8, 12, 2019.

21. Alam, T. Cloud-Based IoT applications and their roles in smart cities. *Smart Cities*, 4, 1196–1219, 2021. https://doi.org/10.3390/smartcities4030064

22. Rababah, B., Alam, T., Eskicioglu, R., The next generation Internet of Things architecture towards distributed intelligence: Reviews, applications, and research challenges. *SSRN Electronic J.*, 12, April –June 2020. Available at: https://jtec.utem.edu.my/jtec/article/view/5535/3932

23. Shahrubudin, N., Te Chuan, L., Ramlan, R.J.P.M., An overview on 3D printing technology: Technological, materials, and applications. *Procedia Manuf.*, 35, 1286–1296, 2019.

24. Rabbi, M.F., Popp, J., Máté, D., Kovács, S., Energy security and energy transition to achieve carbon neutrality. *Energies*, 15, 21, 8126, 2022.

25. Adhikari, M.; Ghimire, L.P.; Kim, Y.; Aryal, P.; Khadka, S.B. Identification and analysis of barriers against electric vehicle use. *Sustainability*, 12, 4850, 2020. https://doi.org/10.3390/su12124850

26. Idrees, S.M., Nowostawski, M., Jameel, R., Mourya, A.K., Security aspects of blockchain technology intended for industrial applications. *Electronics*, 10, 8, 951, 2021.

27. Dhar, P., Rocks, T., Samarasinghe, R.M., Stephenson, G., Smith, C., Augmented reality in medical education: Students' experiences and learning outcomes. *Med. Educ. Online*, 26, 1, 1953953, 2021.

28. Prasad, R., Kumar, V., Prasad, K.S., Nanotechnology in sustainable agriculture: Present concerns and future aspects. *Afr. J. Biotechnol.*, 13, 6, 705–713, 2014.

29. Mohanty, S.P., Choppali, U., Kougianos, E., Everything you wanted to know about smart cities: The Internet of Things is the backbone. *IEEE Consum. Electron. Mag.*, 5, 3, 60–70, 2016.

30. Onwuegbuzie, I.U. and Ajibade, S.M., 5G: Next generation mobile wireless technology for a fast pacing world. *J. Pure Appl. Sci. (JPAS)*, 1, 1, 1–9, 2022.

31. Gubbi, J., Buyya, R., Marusic, S., Palaniswami, M., Internet of Things (IoT): A vision, architectural elements, and future directions. *Future Generation Comput. Syst.*, 29, 7, 1645–1660, 2013.

32. Gill, S.S., Kumar, A., Singh, H., Singh, M., Kaur, K., Usman, M., Buyya, R., Quantum computing: A taxonomy, systematic review and future directions. *Softw.: Pract. Experience*, 52, 1, 66–114, 2022.

33. Allam, Z. and Dhunny, Z.A., On big data, artificial intelligence and smart cities. *Cities*, 89, 80–91, 2019.

34. Javaid, M., Haleem, A., Singh, P.R., Suman, R., Substantial capabilities of robotics in enhancing Industry 4.0 implementation. *Cogn. Robotics*, 1, 58–75, 2021.

35. Katz, L., Chen, Y.Y., Gonzalez, R., Peterson, T.C., Zhao, H., Baltz, R.H., Synthetic biology advances and applications in the biotechnology industry: A perspective. *J. Ind. Microbiol. Biotechnol.*, 45, 7, 449–461, 2018.

36. Mishra, S. and Tyagi, A.K., Emerging trends and techniques in machine learning and internet of things-based cloud applications, in: *Handbook of Research of Internet of Things and Cyber-Physical Systems*, pp. 149–167, 2022.

37. Rahman, M.A., Rashid, M.M., Hossain, M.S., Hassanain, E., Alhamid, M.F., Guizani, M., Blockchain and IoT-based cognitive edge framework for sharing economy services in a smart city. *IEEE Access*, 7, 18611–18621, 2019.

38. Gupta, R., Kumari, A., Tanwar, S., Fusion of blockchain and artificial intelligence for secure drone networking underlying 5G communications. *Trans. Emerging Telecommun. Technol.*, 32, 1, e4176, 2021.

39. Larson, D. and Chang, V., A review and future direction of agile, business intelligence, analytics and data science. *Int. J. Inf. Manag.*, 36, 5, 700–710, 2016.

40. Rejeb, A., Keogh, J.G., Treiblmaier, H., Leveraging the internet of things and blockchain technology in supply chain management. *Future Internet*, 11, 7, 161, 2019.

41. Liu, Y., Zhang, J., Zhan, J., Privacy protection for fog computing and the internet of things data based on blockchain. *Cluster Comput.*, 24, 1331–1345, 2021.

42. Zhang, Z., Wu, C., Cheung, D.W., A survey on cloud interoperability: Taxonomies, standards, and practice. *ACM Sigmetrics Perform. Eval. Rev.*, 40, 4, 13–22, 2013.

43. Do, J., Ferreira, V.C., Bobarshad, H., Torabzadehkashi, M., Rezaei, S., Heydarigorji, A., Souza, D. *et al.*, Cost-effective, energy-efficient, and scalable storage computing for large-scale AI applications. *ACM Trans. Storage (TOS)*, 16, 4, 1–37, 2020.

44. Xu, X., Zhao, H., Yao, H., Wang, S., A blockchain-enabled energy-efficient data collection system for UAV-assisted IoT. *IEEE Internet Things J.*, 8, 4, 2431–2443, 2020.

45. Tang, Y., Xiong, J., Becerril-Arreola, R., Iyer, L., Ethics of blockchain: A framework of technology, applications, impacts, and research directions. *Inf. Technol. & People*, 33, 2, 602–632, 2020.

46. Singh, S.K., Rathore, S., Park, J.H., Block IOT intelligence: A blockchain-enabled intelligent IoT architecture with artificial intelligence. *Future Generation Comput. Syst.*, 110, 721–743, 2020.

47. Yang, F., Zhou, W., Wu, Q., Long, R., Xiong, N.N., Zhou, M., Delegated proof of stake with downgrade: A secure and efficient blockchain consensus algorithm with downgrade mechanism. *IEEE Access*, 7, 118541–118555, 2019.

48. Salah, K., Rehman, M.H.U., Nizamuddin, N., Al-Fuqaha, A., Blockchain for AI: Review and open research challenges. *IEEE Access*, 7, 10127–10149, 2019.

49. Patel, J., An effective and scalable data modeling for enterprise big data platform, in: *2019 IEEE International Conference on Big Data (Big Data)*, IEEE, pp. 2691–2697, 2019.

50. Zeid, A., Sundaram, S., Moghaddam, M., Kamarthi, S., Marion, T., Interoperability in smart manufacturing: Research challenges. *Machines*, 7, 2, 21, 2019.

51. Singh, S.K., Pan, Y., Park, J.H., Blockchain-enabled secure framework for energy-efficient smart parking in sustainable city environment. *Sustain. Cities Soc.*, 76, 103364, 2022.

52. Gill, S.S., Tuli, S., Xu, M., Singh, I., Singh, K.V., Lindsay, D., Tuli, S. *et al.*, Transformative effects of IoT, blockchain and artificial intelligence on cloud computing: Evolution, vision, trends and open challenges. *Internet Things*, 8, 100118, 2019.

53. Sivan, R. and Zukarnain, Z.A., Security and privacy in cloud-based e-health system. *Symmetry*, 13, 5, 742, 2021.

54. Gerke S, Minssen T, Cohen G. Ethical and legal challenges of artificial intelligence-driven healthcare. *Artificial Intelligence in Healthcare*, 295–336, 2020.

55. Fosch-Villaronga, E. and Millard, C., Cloud robotics law and regulation: Challenges in the governance of complex and dynamic cyber–physical ecosystems. *Robotics Autonomous Syst.*, 119, 77–91, 2019.

56. Tang, Y., Xiong, J., Becerril-Arreola, R., Iyer, L., Ethics of blockchain: A framework of technology, applications, impacts, and research directions. *Inf. Technol. & People*, 33, 2, 602–632, 2020.

57. Lewis, T.G., *Critical infrastructure protection in homeland security: Defending a networked nation*, John Wiley & Sons, 2019. ISBN: 978-1-119-61453-1.

58. Min, H., Blockchain technology for enhancing supply chain resilience. *Bus. Horizons*, 62, 1, 35–45, 2019.

59. Hathaliya, J., Sharma, P., Tanwar, S., Gupta, R., Blockchain-based remote patient monitoring in Healthcare 4.0, in: *2019 IEEE 9th International Conference on Advanced Computing (IACC)*, pp. 87–91, IEEE, 2019.

60. Sharma, P.K., Kumar, N., Park, J.H., Blockchain technology toward green IoT: Opportunities and challenges. *IEEE Network*, 34, 4, 263–269, 2020.

61. Singh, S., Sharma, P.K., Yoon, B., Shojafar, M., Cho, G.H., Ra, I.H., Convergence of blockchain and artificial intelligence in IoT network for the sustainable smart city. *Sustain. Cities Soc.*, 63, 102364, 2020.

62. Javaid, M., Haleem, A., Khan, I.H., Suman, R., Understanding the potential applications of artificial intelligence in agriculture sector. *Adv. Agrochem*, 2, 1, 15–30, 2023. https://doi.org/10.1016/j.aac.2022.10.001

63. Mishra S. and Tyagi A.K., The role of machine learning techniques in internet of things-based cloud applications, in: *Artificial Intelligence-based Internet of Things Systems*, S. Pal, D. De, R. Buyya (eds.), Internet of Things (Technology, Communications and Computing), Springer, Cham., 2022, https://doi.org/10.1007/978-3-030-87059-1_4.

64. Nair, M.M. and Tyagi, A. K., Chapter 11 - AI, IoT, blockchain, and cloud computing: The necessity of the future, in: *Distributed Computing to Blockchain*, R. Pandey, S. Goundar, S. Fatima (eds.), Academic Press, pp. 189–206, 2023, https://doi.org/10.1016/B978-0-323-96146-2.00001-2.

65. Tyagi, A. K., Chapter 2 - Decentralized everything: Practical use of blockchain technology in future applications, in: *Distributed Computing to Blockchain*, R. Pandey, S. Goundar, S. Fatima (eds.), Academic Press, pp. 19–38, 2023, https://doi.org/10.1016/B978-0-323-96146-2.00010-3.

66. Nair, M.M. and Tyagi, A. K., Blockchain technology for next-generation society: current trends and future opportunities for smart era, in: *Blockchain Technology for Secure Social Media Computing*, 2023. DOI: 10.1049/PBSE019E_ch11.

5

Artificial Intelligence for Cyber Security: Current Trends and Future Challenges

Meghna Manoj Nair[1]*, Atharva Deshmukh[2] and Amit Kumar Tyagi[3]

[1]Tandon School of Engineering, New York University, New York, USA
[2]Department of Computer Engineering, Terna Engineering College, Navi Mumbai, Maharashtra, India
[3]Department of Fashion Technology, National Institute of Fashion Technology, New Delhi, Delhi, India

Abstract

Artificial intelligence (AI) has helped industries and society today to become modern and more productive. Using the Internet of Things (IoT), we can sense and transfer data through the Internet from one device to another and can perform/do tasks efficiently AI use today has been increased from one application to many, i.e., from the agriculture sector to weather prediction. In agriculture, the quality of soil and crop growing or crop cutting, etc., work can be performed with the help of AI; similarly in weather prediction, the situation of upcoming days can be identified, and AI can help in reducing causalities. Note that AI is more useful with IoT/smart devices. Around the world, when these sectors use IoT in their work, several cyber-attacks or vulnerabilities are mitigated. which addresses the need to prevent, detect, and recover from any failure of systems. Such attacks need to be detected so quickly, but human/skilled professionals take a lot of time to trace and track or recover from such cyber-attacks. Thus, in the near future, we predict what will happen when AI will help professionals to trace and track cyber-attacks and avoid many huge losses. Identifying spam mail, junk mails, etc., is an example of machine learning. Hence, cyber security is the need of the hour because it is the need of every industry/business, especially critical businesses or sectors like healthcare. We are looking forward to providing innovative solutions to avoid such attacks or vulnerabilities by mitigation on a public network/infrastructure using artificial intelligence. We discuss about AI and its importance in intrusion detection/vulnerability detection (benefits, pitfalls, future uses), etc.

Keywords: Computer network security, information security, cyber security, application security, artificial intelligence-based cyber security

5.1 Introduction: Security and Its Types

The technologically fast-moving world has led to the development of various new technologies and virtual advancements, and this has resulted in many users and customers sacrificing

---

*Corresponding author: mnairmeghna@gmail.com

Amit Kumar Tyagi (ed.) Automated Secure Computing for Next-Generation Systems, (83–114) © 2024 Scrivener Publishing LLC

their security through online presence. Security and privacy are two of the most important aspects of the current world because nearly all activities, actions, and communications take place through the online medium. This indicates that large volumes of data pertaining to the users are available online. There are different types of security like information security, computer network security, cyber security, web services security, software coding security, etc. [1]. Many startups and businesses have completely digitalized their work culture especially amidst the pandemic, and the online mode of recording, tracking, storing data, etc., has been on an exponential rise. However, cyber-attacks, data breaches, data leakages, etc., are quite common and lead to personal and confidential data being exposed to malicious users who can use the data for various crude reasons. It is of utmost importance to identify and recognize the various cyber-attack techniques and to develop systemic solutions that would safeguard and protect the system holistically from further cyber-attacks. Computer security, cyber security, and information technology security come under computer security and networks. The Internet and wireless network standards like Bluetooth and Wireless networks (IEEE 802.11) are being used lesser due to the growth of smartphones/computer device/other smart devices that use Internet to make a quick communication [2].

Cyber security is also one of the major challenges in the contemporary world. We examine the security threats identified in government sites, big companies, and other public documents from websites and databases to determine the threats faced by cloud consumers. Threats to computer security are of adverse effects and often take up a plethora of disguise forms and end up exploiting the target user. Computer security mainly deals with safeguarding and protecting the computer machines and devices from possible cyber-attacks, viruses, malware, thefts, and any sort of unauthorized usage. There are plenty of users who get their systems hacked, and this number has been on the rise almost every day. This is due to the absence of proper defense mechanisms and strategies incorporated into the computer. Computer security comes to the rescue and ensures that the systems are majorly guaranteed safety and security precautionary measures by ensuring that the privacy, integrity, and accessibility of computers and their stored data are properly secured with a multilayer firewall. There are many methods, software, and techniques involved to protect system security, guard computing resources, protect data integrity, restrict access to authorized users, and retain data confidentiality. Antivirus and firewall are some of the efficient security systems available to entitle users with computer security [3].

A few basic steps which every user can take up to avoid cyber-attacks from their end could be the following:

- Users should never type down their passwords in plain text files or spreadsheets.
- Always avoid saving passwords on the Internet browser.
- Ensure that the passwords used are complex and not easy to guess.
- Try to maintain a separate password for every different account.
- Always maintain a two-factor authentication wherever possible.

There are different types of securities, and it is essential to know the importance and necessity of each type [4]. Some of the major types of securities are discussed below:

- Critical Infrastructure Security: This type of security bounds the cyber physical systems for various societies belonging to different fraternities like that of hospitals, water purification, traffic signals, shopping malls, electricity grid, etc. The companies which are responsible for this type of security must work and offer services rigorously to comprehend the possible defaults in the infrastructure and improvise them. This security type is extremely vital and important for the safety and privacy of society and hence needs to be maintained well. There are organizations that may not completely utilize a critical infrastructure but rely on it for complementing their business. These organizations must develop a strategic contingency place by evaluating and analyzing how any type of external attack on critical infrastructural frameworks could pose an adverse effect [5].

- Application Security: This security type contains software and hardware techniques to handle any form of bullying or malicious behavior during the curation of the application. In fact, attacks on applications are much easier than that on networks requiring a heavy and extensive security layer in the applications during the development of the same. Encryption, firewalls, anti-virus, malware detectors, etc., are some of the methods which can be used for securing applications as they ensure that unauthorized access is prohibited. Furthermore, companies can also detect observant data assets and shield them through precise application security processes attached to these data sets [6].

- Network Security: This type of security ensures that the internal networks being developed are safe and sound from any malicious attack. It takes care of the internal networks by safeguarding the infrastructure and other attachments to it. Strong passwords, login and authentication, application security strategies, etc., are some of the ways in which network security can be implemented [7].

5.1.1   Human Aspects of Information Security

Information security mainly highlights the various processes and techniques which are designed for protecting and safeguarding printed, electronic, digital, or any other type of highly confidential and private information or data from unauthorized access and malicious attacks. When looking at it from a human aspect, there are a few key features that represent information security as given below [8]:

- Security: Information is an important aspect that is to be secured by an organization. Protecting the information through organizational controls and technological aspects plays an important role in information security. People's interaction is closely related to technological and organizational control aspects [9].

- Information security technology alone cannot keep the safety of information in organizations. Human interactions along with organizational controls are needed to make information secure [9].

- Safety of information comes all the way down to the awareness, behavior, and abilities of the people in the organization. People in an organization lead the position in reaching protection, and elements like lack of relevant sources, blended with unreasonable demands from safety technology, can affect the security capability.

There are various types of security threats to organizations, of which some of the familiar ones include computer viruses, spyware, worms, denial of services attacks, SQL injection, etc.

Organization of the work: This work is organizsed in 16 sections, which can be found or explained in Figure 5.1.

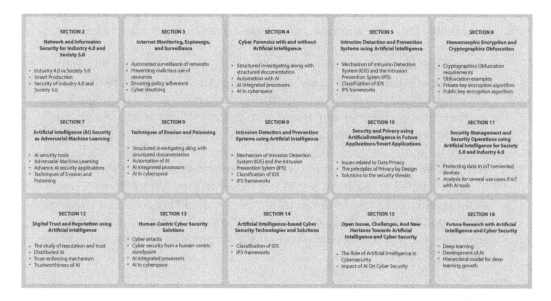

Figure 5.1 Explanation of this work.

5.2   Network and Information Security for Industry 4.0 and Society 5.0

The core of Industry Vision 4.0 is in the Internet of Things and the Internet of Things. Computers and operating systems will come together, mainly based on cyber–physical production systems that include communications, IT, data, and physical objects and where these systems transform traditional plants into smart firms [10].

a) Industrial revolution 1.0—machines and utilization of machines
b) Industrial revolution 2.0—mass production (volume)
c) Industrial revolution 3.0—employing automation
d) Industrial revolution 4.0—cyber–physical system (machine talking to machine)

Today Indian manufacturing companies are heading towards Industry 4.0. The Indian manufacturing companies prepare for high-value manufacturing. There should be a dual automation strategy:

- One in technology and the other in choosing the right partner
- Connect all existing automation sources to a single source

Industry 4.0 emphasizes the idea of digital integration consistently and changing the economic rules of the sector. Smart production combines knowledge, technology, and people to bring about a rapid change in the development of manufacturing industries [11]. It has features like:

- The changes focus more on the product life cycle rather than on the production process.
- On the basis of small production, a company can build a good product.
- For a smart productive leader, we will make decisions based on knowledge, not just based on experience.

Knowledge/skills management:

- Bring new talented resources
- Maintain and train resources where skills development is possible
- Continued awareness and strengthening of the use of the latest technology

On another side, Society 5.0 is a people-centered society that balances economic development and the resolution of social problems through a system that integrates a wide range of communication and physical space [12]. Society 5.0 was nominated for the 5th Science and Technology Basic Plan as the future society of Japan should aspire. It follows the hunting community (Social 1.0), the agricultural community (Society 2.0), the industrial community (Society 3.0), and the knowledge society (Society 4.0). In the information society (Society 4.0), shared knowledge and information sharing were inadequate, and collaboration was difficult. Social (new) change in Social 5.0 will extend to a forward-looking society that reduces the existing sense of standing, a society with respectful members, past generations, and a society in which each individual can lead an active and happy life. Society 5.0 achieves a high level of interaction between cyberspace (virtual space) and virtual space (real space) [13].

In the past information society (Society 4.0), people would have been able to access cloud (information) services online through the Internet and search for, retrieve, and analyze data. In Social 5.0, a large amount of information from the nerves in body space is collected in cyber space. In cyber space, this big data is analyzed by artificial intelligence (AI), and the results of the analysis are returned to humans in the physical space in various ways, and the analysis results are fed back to humans in the physical space in various forms. Japan aims to be the first country in the world to achieve a socially focused society (Social 5.0) where anyone can enjoy a high standard of living full of vigoro It aims to achieve this by incorporating advanced technologies in various industries and social services and encouraging innovation to create new value. Figure 5.2 describes the major and essential elements of Society 5.0 which revolve around comfort, vitality, and high-quality lives.

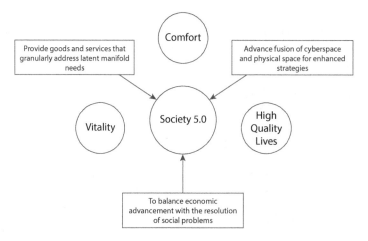

Figure 5.2 Various elements and components of Society 5.0.

5.2.1   Industry 4.0 vs Society 5.0

Industry 4.0, also known as digitalization in industry, makes different promises to enterprises, whereas Society 5.0, which merges cyber and physical technologies for individual or collective usage, makes numerous promises to humanity. Few Points over Industry 4.0 and Society 5.0 are:

- Industry 4.0 emphasizes how to get the job done, while Society 5.0 emphasizes how we can use someone's hourly work to get the job done [14].
- Industry 4.0 emphasizes the efficiency of automated equipment, while Society 5.0 emphasizes the function of recognizing the knowledge of the worker with the help of smart devices.
- Industry 4.0 is about computer communication by all means, while Society 5.0 is designed to harmonize work with the help of smart devices to benefit employees [15].

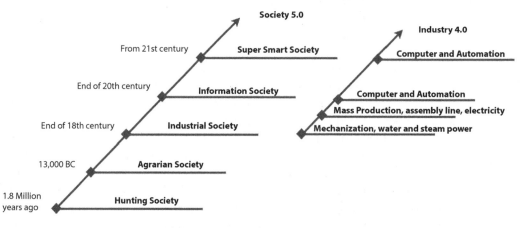

Figure 5.3 Evolution of Society 5.0 and Industry 4.0.

Basically and concisely, in Industry 4.0, the production of knowledge and ingenuity is done by people with the help of technology. In Social 5.0, a generation of knowledge and intelligence will emerge from machines with artificial intelligence in human performance. Advances in the definition of technology (artificial intelligence, big data, robotics, deep learning, and machine learning) create a new era of automation, which includes human skills, including cognitive skills, and the development of Organization 5.0. Figure 5.3 describes the evolutions of societies and industries over millions of years to finally reach a modern Society 5.0 and Industry 4.0 [16].

5.2.2   Industry 4.0 to Society 5.0

The progression from Industry 4.0 to Society 5.0 has some notable features such as the journey from AI to enterprise AI [16] as

a)   Society 5.0 is not limited to digital production but is being digitized at all levels of the Japanese society to address key issues such as staff shortages and older workers.

b)   Industry 4.0 has so far focused on AI to solve many technical challenges such as speech preferences, natural language processing, and negotiating AIs. The journey to the AI business will require the use of AI to solve real sector problems—this is still a small growth, and the discovery is not available.

5.3   Internet Monitoring, Espionage, and Surveillance

There are plenty of methods, algorithms, and techniques used for the surveillance of networks and web traffic, and this is a crucial component as it helps the governments and agencies in controlling and gaining authoritative power over the various illicit happenings which take place via the Internet. Monitoring and tracking the data, Internet traffic, and user activity cover a major portion of surveillance in this field. In the USA, a number of laws and policies have been enforced, which implies that all sorts of phone calls and Internet traffic are to be made available for real-time supervision by government agencies [17]. Packet sniffing is one of the activities which focus on supervising data and related traffic on a certain network, wherein the data sent between various network nodes are called packets, and a certain packet capture node would intercept and monitor these packets to analyze for any possible threats or maliciousness. This is because it is impossible to sniff through each of the generated packets manually due to the massive number of packets being generated. This definitely calls for automated and computer-based Internet surveillance in order to filter out and report suspicious packets to investigators for further analysis. The Information Awareness Office, NSA, FBI, etc., are a few of the companies which spent billions of dollars on advancing and enhancing their system of packet sniffing [18].

The data gathered and collected from surveillance activities in the corporate field is majorly utilized for marketing and is even sold to other corporations for profit [19]. However, this data also forms a major part of the data collection process by the government agencies which is, in turn, used for business intelligence and analysis so as to provide services that are catered to the needs of the user. One important component of prevention is establishing the business purposes of monitoring, which may include the following:

- Preventing the Malicious Use of Resources: Companies and agencies can monitor and ensure that the data is not used for malicious or personal reasons, and with the help of employee performance monitoring, all unnecessary traffic and congestion on the network and overconsumption of network bandwidth can be reduced.
- Ensuring Policy Adherence: Through online and network surveillance, employees can be monitored and supervised to keep track of adherence to the policies being enforced for a better work environment.
- Preventing Lawsuits: Firms, organizations, and institutions can be held responsible for any sort of racism or discrimination and harassment of employees in the workspace. They can also be ticketed for cases that involve employees distributing copyrighted materials through various connections and networks.
- Safeguarding Records: As per the legislature, it is essential that companies and organizations protect and secure the personal information and data they have access to by monitoring and safeguarding it from malicious use of personal information, spam, and virus.
- Safeguarding Company Assets: Protecting and shielding the assets, intellectual properties, business strategies, and techniques is one of the major concerns. Easing the process of data transmission and storage makes the need to supervise the actions of employees imperative.
- The protection of intellectual property, trade secrets, and business strategies is a major concern. The ease of information transmission and storage makes it imperative to monitor employee actions as part of a broader policy.

One of the other major components of prevention is determining and analyzing who owns the technology resources. The ownership details of the company's networks, servers, computers, files, information, etc., need to be explicitly stated and mentioned, and proper distinction between the employee's personal devices should be limited. Intelligence and information collection is a major part of national security, and cyber espionage deals with various activities which involve penetrating computer systems, networks, and other software applications used by adversaries and attackers so as to extract information and details which are relevant. Even though states and countries have been conducting espionage and collecting intelligence before the full-fledged development of the Internet, over the last few years, the availability of cyber exploitation has expanded these activities for sure on a massive scale. Over the years, state-sponsored surveillance and spy work have transformed and revolutionized into technologies that incorporate extensive strategies and techniques. Electronic surveillance for foreign monitoring, anticipating attacks and malicious encounters, etc., are a few of the activities done so far. However, a good deal of cyber sleuthing involves economic matters, sometimes extending to include intellectual property theft, and is undertaken by states or their proxies to secure a comparative economic advantage in trade negotiations, other deals, or for particular companies.

5.4   Cyber Forensics with Artificial Intelligence and without Artificial Intelligence

Computer forensics focuses on the application of inquiry and investigation-related techniques to collect data and relevant information from certain computational devices so as to present them suitably before the court [20]. The main aim of computer forensics is to carry out an organized and structured investigation process while in parallel following a structured documented chain of all proofs and evidence to trace out the actual reason for the happening of an illicit event. The investigators involved in this field follow a standard set of procedures and utilize various proprietary software and application to examine and study the digital copy of all collected shreds of evidence and scrounge for any hidden folders or files and unallocated disk space for any skeptical deleted files or data. Any evidence found on the digital copy is then stored and documented in the report and verified for further legal measures. Computer forensics today has become its own area of scientific expertise, with accompanying coursework and certification [21].

The cyber security personnel put together their expertise and strategies to put a halt to the atrocious battle against hackers, crackers, and cybercriminals by leveraging various technologies and their advantages. Over the last few years, these investigators have been extensively using artificial intelligence and machine learning which are extremely powerful and have brought about a strong turnover in the field of cyber security. As per the survey conducted by the Deloitte State of AI, approximately 63% of the companies and organizations incorporate machine learning in their businesses. Capgemini has reported that some of the most popular applications are network security but along with artificial intelligence being used for improving protocol-related developments like data security, endpoint security, and identity and access management to name a few. It is observed that the majority of the companies believe that they will not be able to retaliate back to cyber-attacks after a certain point due to the large influx of such attacks. In fact, it is not even easy for a large, highly skilled cyber security team to handle such a large influx of cyber-attacks on their framework, and they are hence relying heavily on AI and ML for advanced methodologies and methods [22].

The government of the US has been actively involved in this field, too, and organizations like the National Science and Technology Council (NSTC) Machine Learning and Artificial Intelligence Subcommittee have been analyzing the possible challenges and hurdles involved in the field of cyber AI. However, various guidelines and surveys have portrayed that those investments in integrating AI should enhance and advance both theoretically and practically, which should be sufficient enough for securing a strong training strategy alongside the development of defensive models and verification of system robustness and privacy. NSTC has worked on and revealed a plethora of cyber AI strategies and methodologies, including those of monitoring networks for the detection of spurious and malicious activities, identifying code vulnerabilities, etc. The incorporation of AI in these solutions ensures that the analyses are obtained with ease and speed—much faster than human analysts— and given how fast cyber-attacks can penetrate infrastructure, analysis and response should take place within seconds, not days or weeks [23].

One of the major components when it comes to digital forensics is the use of the right algorithms to analyze and interpret the vast amount of data that is acquired from various gadgets and sensors. AI would be a great option for automating the majority of the processes and generating results with speed and accuracy, which would otherwise take long if done manually. In fact, AI is one of the other tools in the box which help various law and rule enforcement institutions scrounge through the data for gaining deeper insights as they are capable of incorporating functionalities and models which can help in spotting, detecting, and recognizing elements in images and video feeds, identifying common elements in communication, location, etc., and based on its past experience, it can make educated guesses on predictions and other incidents. However, one hindrance amidst all these developments is the trust factor in digital evidence for criminal and related investigations [24]. With rapid advancements and developments in AI and other technologies, digital shreds of evidence curated using AI take time to be accepted as the judges and jury members need to connect with the essence of AI. Considering the fact that plain human logic on various issues and decisions can itself be debated at the grassroot level, it is highly essential that those AI functions are capable of generating results that are fully litigated. AI is a tool, but it is not an investigator. We are far away from that if we ever get there at all. Thus, while it is important to understand and harness this tool, it is equally not to conflate AI as analogous to an investigator. The main task of AI is to offload and ease out work from the physical human engineers in cyberspace in order to deal with the depth and details of various activities that may be difficult to handle physically. Further advances and enhancements in ML indicate a faster pace toward automation, and systems can easily adapt to threats and detect bottlenecks that arise.

Some of the pressing needs and requirements for cyber security using AI tools and platforms are discussed below. Handling massive volumes of data is a major task because humans often tend to mishandle the data and feel overwhelmed. The AI-integrated processors can ensure that the software and other applications are able to zip through and process huge data chunks within shorter periods of time and list the problems and anomalies on the fly. One of the other needs is picking out possible threat needles from large cyber haystacks [25]. Cyber-attackers and criminals mostly find it easy to plunge into the system and are found waiting for the right moment to launch their attack. With leading AI technologies, the systems will be able to identify and notify the entry of any unauthorized access into the system, thus preventing the attack. Acceleration of detection of various problems and speeding up the response time is one of the other improvisations that AI can bring. In fact, AI is extremely essential in cyberspace because it is the root key and the sword needed to fight the cyber-attackers as they have already gotten there and are extensively utilizing AI techniques and strategies for their benefit. Furthermore, AI provides the extra push and support needed for cyber security workers and investigators, extracting the best out of them at all times.

5.5 Intrusion Detection and Prevention Systems Using Artificial Intelligence

The two major devices included in the intrusion detection and prevention system (IDP) are the intrusion detection system (IDS) and the intrusion prevention system (IPS). IDS is responsible for overlooking the attacks and traffic likely to be incoming, and IPS is useful in deploying necessary protocols after the attack to prevent its recurrence [26]. It also has a mechanism that involves warning the security workers and employees about possible incoming threats and attacks to stipulate necessary action being taken at the right time. IDS uses intrusion signals and related patterns which are streams of bytes in order to interpret and analyze the traffic in the concerned network and to identify any possible abnormalities, and it also uses the previously known signals if attacks of a similar range are occurring again. One slight bottleneck of the signature-based IDS is that it keeps a track of the previous attacks in order to detect possible future attacks, and there are chances that a new pattern of attack may go unnoticed. In order to combat this issue, most of the IDPs make use of the anomaly detection technique wherein the detectors use comparisons among the network activities in order to identify the presence of any malicious activities within the network [27].

Some new methods use AI and ML to detect and prevent attacks, but sometimes it can cause false positives which are allowed activities taken as malicious by the AI. One of the main advantages of anomaly-based detection is that it can even detect zero-day attacks. Zero-day attacks are the attacks that happen as a result of a vulnerability in the software even before deployment. The developer may not know about the vulnerability but the attacker uses this as a way to intrude. A typical IDS cannot detect zero-day attacks but anomaly-based ones can. Nowadays, an IDS uses both anomaly-based and signature-based types to detect attacks to use the advantages of both systems. The main goal of the attacker is to gather information about the network and then try to take advantage of it. Intrusion detection is used to check if there are any possible vulnerabilities that are being exploited [28]. The classification of IDS can now be explained into five types:

- Network IDS (NIDS): In NIDS, an IDS is deployed in the network at certain points to check for network traffic for unwanted or abnormal activity. When an anomaly is discovered, then an alert is sent to the security team to stop the attack.
- Host IDS (HIDS): HIDS is deployed on the host machine or a network device and keeps track of the packets traveling to and for that machine only. It also looks over important system files and checks if there are any changes in them, and if there are, an alert is sent to the security team.
- Protocol-Based IDS (PIDS): PIDS is deployed in the server, and it checks if the protocol used by the server is not being exploited. If it is, then an alert is sent.
- Application Protocol-Based IDS (APIDS): AIPDS is deployed over a group of servers and is used to track database protocol exploits—for example, exploiting data going to and for the database and changing or interfering with it.
- Hybrid IDS (HIDS): HIDS is when two or more of the above-mentioned systems are used together to detect intrusions.

IPS frameworks are systems that have access to all packets and data stores where they are deployed, either in the form of NIPS or HIPS, where NIPS tends to have a much larger and holistic view of the full network. NIPS can also be executed or deployed inline within the network or offline to the network in the form of a passive member which gets packets from a TAP network or a certain port [29]. For detection purposes, signature- or anomaly-based methods can be employed, and predefined signatures are patterns and interpretations of popular attacks which occur in the network. IPSs usually compare the flow of packets with the signature to check for possible matches in pattern, while anomaly-based IPS utilizes heuristics to identify threats, like for comparing a sample of traffic with respect to a known baseline.

5.6   Homomorphic Encryption and Cryptographic Obfuscation

The basic definition is it allows the computation of encrypted data without ever decrypting it. In encryption, we make use of keys (public or private keys) to encrypt and decrypt data, but in obfuscation we do not make use of keys. Here the human-understandable and readable strings are converted to strings that are less comprehensible like reversing the order of characters or making ANSI-encoded or ASCII [30]. An obfuscation O of a function F should satisfy two requirements—If we take obfuscation as (O) of a function (F), it must satisfy two requirements:

- Firstly, O should be such that it can be used to calculate F.
- Secondly, O should have the hiding feature where it does not reveal anything related to F that otherwise cannot be gathered from the oracle access to F.

It has broadly two points [31]:

a.   Consider an encryption strategy of a secret key encryption technique that can undergo obfuscation. The output must lead to a highly secure public key encryption scheme.
b.   A function of uniform and even random points can undergo obfuscation as per the above-mentioned definition with the help of one-way permutation.

Some examples which show obfuscation are as follows:

a.   Suppose a software vendor wants to sell products such that the user would not know the internal implementation completely and he only knows the main functionality, but there are hardware substitutes also, and the only way to execute this is to obfuscate the code that is to make the code incomprehensible.
b.   There is a username and password giving query. Verification will be based on whether the user correctly enters the password, which can be done by storing all passwords on the computer machine. This works, but a smart user can learn all passwords with just a read-only process. Therefore, we can store it in terms of hashes (images of the password under a one-way function).

For this to be achieved, let $H(p1)$ be a hash function for every user password $p1$. Let the password entered by the user be $p2$, then verification of $p2$ with $p1$ is done by comparing $H(p1)$ and $H(p2)$. The one-wayness of H gives surety that $p1$ is not found even when $H(p1)$ becomes known.

In previous times, initially implemented is obfuscation VBB (virtual black box used). VBB is basically a cryptography procedure to encrypt a circuit while maintaining its full input/output functionality, but the group of Barak et al. showed that a general obfuscator that obfuscates classical circuits into classical circuits cannot exist, and they only brought the concept of indistinguishability and obfuscation which is used in simulation and probabilistic functions. The main visions of obfuscation include taking arbitrary programs and obfuscating them into byte codes (example: Java program converted into obfuscated Java byte code and to deploy byte code on VM; example: run obfuscated byte code on JVM) [32]. Simply said, we obfuscate the encryption algorithm for a private key, and the result we got will be a public key. Then, a public key will allow encrypting of messages.

A. Private Key Encryption:

 i. Firstly, we will generate the keys using the key generation algorithm (K). Let kt be the set of all keys K on security parameter k.
 ii. Then, we will use encryption algorithm E which will help in encrypting a message M, and it produces a ciphertext as C, such that $E(K, M) \to C$.
 iii. Then, we will use a decryption algorithm D which will help in decrypting a ciphertext C to a message M, such that $D(K, C) \to M$.

B. Public Key Encryption:
It is almost the same as the private key encryption scheme except that this encryption is done by a public key and decryption is done by a private key.

 i. There is also a key generation algorithm (let it be k2); it also generates a key pair (pk, sk) unlike the private key where pk = public key and sk = private key, such that $k2(\text{€}) \to (pk, sk)$.
 ii. Then, we will use encryption algorithm E2 which will help in encrypting a message M, and it produces a ciphertext as C, such that $K2 (pk, M) \to C$.
 iii. Then, we will use a decryption algorithm D2 which will help in decrypting a ciphertext C to a message M, such that $D2(sk, C) \to M$.

5.7 Artificial Intelligence Security as Adversarial Machine Learning

Artificial intelligence is defined as machines that perform "intelligent" or "intelligent" things on their own without human guidance. As such, AI security involves using AI to identify and stop cyber threats with less human intervention than expected or as required by traditional security measures. AI security tools are often used to identify "good" compared with "bad" by comparing business behavior across the environment with those in the same area. This process enables the system to automatically read and flag changes [33, 34]. Often referred to as uncontrolled reading or "life pattern" of learning, this approach leads to a myriad of false and bad things. Advanced AI security applications can go beyond identifying positive or negative behaviors by analyzing more information and helping to integrate related activities that may reflect suspicious behavior. In this way, AI security behaves in the same way as a highly competent and very powerful human analyst. Recovery has been a historic challenge for many SOCs. Speaking of labor alone, the proposed talent gap in the cyber security industry is expected to find 3.5 million unfilled jobs by 2021. While some say AI equipment can or will fill this gap, a daunting solution is to adopt AI security tools that increase the workload of existing employees. This can greatly free up short-term resources by cutting down on the time needed to hunt down threats and alert warnings or consolidation, for example. Cyber security employees are able to focus on other important tasks that can be automated with AI [35].

A type of machine learning (ML) that is capable of manipulating the models by providing deceptive or false inputs to them is called adversarial machine learning. Many such strategies and techniques in the field of ML have emerged, which mainly focus on certain problem sets wherein the data used for training and testing are generated from the same statistical distribution. The usage of such models might lead to opponents providing details that disrupt the root mathematical logic involved [36]. This data can even be divided and grouped to reap the maximum benefits and weaknesses of the results. One of the best ways to dwell deeper into any particular field is to consider the plethora of available examples pertaining to that field like spam filtering, computer security attacks, hacking malware code into network packets, etc. In the intelligent transportation sector, many such possibilities exist as well. In fact, investigators and researchers are finding ways to interfere with the appearance of a stop sign that a private vehicle has set as a junction or speed limit. Opposing attacks on the neural network can allow the attacker to install algorithms on the target system. Investigators can also create opposing audio input to hide commands from intelligent assistants in sound that looks good [37].

A few of the major strategies involved include techniques of evasion and poisoning. Evasion correlates to escape attacks which are one of the most common attacks that spammers and hackers try to evade detection and identification by inserting bogus content and data where samples are traded to avoid detection legally. One of the best examples of evading is spam-related images where the spam-intended content is embedded along with an attached image to avoid analyzing and parsing through text with anti-spam filters. Poisoning, on the other hand, involves an essence of toxicity which is a counterproductive measure of training data. ML systems can be retrained or further trained using the data that has been collected throughout the operation—for example, access systems (as IDSs) are trained many a time using the same data. Attackers can poison the data by inducing bad and bogus samples during their operations that tend to interfere with retraining [38].

5.8 Post-Quantum Cryptography

In order to understand post-quantum cryptography, one must first understand what cryptography is and the current state of cryptography. According to [39], cryptography is the study of secure communication techniques that allow only the sender and intended recipient of a message to view its contents. Cryptography, as a concept, has been part of history for a long time. In today's time, cryptography is done on computers as we primarily send and receive messages through the use of computers. Emails, text messages, voice messages, and video calls are all communication techniques that we use as mentioned in the definition by

Kaspersky. The amount of security that current cryptographical techniques offer depends on the amount of computational power available to crack particular difficult problems such as integer factorization or the discrete log problem. The issue that we will face in the future is that of increased computational power, especially as a result of the maturing of quantum computing [40]. The computational power of such computers will deem the current cryptographical techniques that we use insecure. Hence, in order to secure data in the future, we need more complex cryptographical techniques, i.e., post-quantum cryptography. In short, according to CSRC: "The goal of post-quantum cryptography (also called quantum-resistant cryptography) is to develop cryptographic systems that are secure against both quantum and classical computers and can interoperate with existing communications protocols and networks."

A quantum computer has very high computational power and could, therefore, reverse-engineer through trapdoor functions much faster than regular computers, but why do quantum computers have higher computational power compared with the conventional computers of today? In order to understand this, we must go back to the fundamental make-up of conventional and quantum computers. As we have all learned in our smaller classes, the conventional computers of today use the system of bits. Conventional computers can only understand 0s and 1s. Every form of the medium that we consume through a computer comes from a series of 0s and 1s—let it be movies, podcasts, word documents, and websites. All of these come from a series of 0s and 1s [41]. On the other hand, quantum computers use the concept of qubits. These qubits can represent numerous possible states of 1 and 0 at the same time through a phenomenon in quantum physics known as super-position. They also have the power to influence one another at a distance through another phenomenon in quantum physics known as entanglement. These phenomena in quantum physics are outside the scope of this article. In this article, we only need to understand what this gives rise to. Qubits can lead to giant leaps in computing power. "A quantum machine with 300 qubits could represent more values than there are atoms in the observable universe". This amazing statistic itself shows that such a quantum computer would be more than capable of cracking the RSA 2048-bit implementation key.

In the current scenario, post-quantum cryptography research is, for the large part, focused on six different approaches as follows:

a) Lattice-Based Cryptography: According to an NYU paper[5]: "Lattice-based cryptographic constructions hold a great promise for post-quantum cryptography, as they enjoy very strong security proofs based on worst-case hardness, relatively efficient implementations, as well as great simplicity. In addition, lattice-based cryptography is believed to be secure against quantum computers". There are various approaches used in lattice-based cryptography. Some of these approaches are learning with errors, ring learning with errors, ring learning with errors key exchange, and so on [42].

b) Multivariate Cryptography: This technique integrates cryptographic frameworks and systemic models like rainbow plots which depend on the need to understand and analyze the multivariate situations. Various trials and research to develop secure and safe multivariate encryption have failed, but plans and systems like rainbow plots could be a revolutionary model [43].

c) Hash-Based Cryptography: This incorporates cryptographic frameworks like Lamport signatures and consequently the Merkle signature plot and the more up to date XMSS and SPHINCS plans. Hash-based advanced marks were created in the last part of the 1970s by Ralph Merkle and have been concentrated since the time as a fascinating choice for number-hypothetical computerized marks like RSA and DSA. Their essential downside is that, for any hash-based public key, there is a breaking point on the measure of marks which will be marked utilizing the comparing set of individual keys. This one downside resulted in the overall lack of interest in this type of cryptography. However, with the need for new and enhanced cryptography in the years to come, thanks to the computing power of quantum computers, interest has been revived [44].

d) Code-Based Cryptography: This technique is responsible for integrating cryptographic frameworks which take in codes capable of error correction and are quite similar to McEliece and Niederreiter calculations for encryption purposes. It basically includes the various cryptosystems which majorly depend on coding hardness for security. It usually finds its applications in public key decryption schemes, digital signs, etc. [45].

e) Supersingular Elliptic Curve Isogeny Cryptography: This technique relies on super-singular elliptic bends and super-singular isogeny charts to maintain the necessary level of secrecy. This framework also extracts benefits from the arithmetical background of the elliptic bends to generate keys similar to those of Diffie Hellman which would be strong enough to take up the direct quantum computational space. Since it works fundamentally the same as the existing Diffie–Hellman usage, it offers forward secrecy which is seen as significant both to stop mass observation by governments and, additionally, to make preparations for the trade-off of long-term keys through fallacies [46].

f) Symmetric Key Quantum Resistance: This framework is really suitable when using keys of quite a massive size as it works with ease. Key monitoring systems and models that use this technique instead of public key cryptographic methods lean towards Kerberos. Given that such a system will be crucial enough to be deployed worldwide, a few analysts suggest the extended utilization of Kerberos-like symmetric key administration as a productive method to get post-quantum cryptography today [47].

5.9   Security and Privacy in Online Social Networks and Other Sectors

Online social networks (OSNs) are a perpetual presence in the present individual and professional existence. They have quickly developed into a wide network and offer clients an assortment of advantages. Be that as it may, they additionally bring new dangers and privacy issues to the network. Tragically, there are assailants that endeavor to uncover OSN clients' private data or conceal the data that the client wants to impart to different clients.

This article talks about the privacy and security issues that developed so far in OSNs. We present a scientific categorization of privacy and security attacks in OSNs and different ways to help the user overcome it [49].

User-created content on social media may incorporate users' experiences, viewpoints, and information. Furthermore, it might incorporate private information—for instance, name, sexual orientation, area, and private photographs or videos. Online-shared data is electronically stored; therefore, it is permanent, replicable, and could be shared. OSN clients face the difficulties of dealing with their social character while bargaining for their social security [49]. Social media platforms are used to such a large extent that the number of users has reached a total of 2.95 billion by 2020, which is approximately one-third of the worldwide population. These dangers can be classified into classic and modern threats. Classic dangers are online dangers that make OSN clients powerless, yet additionally other online clients also who do not utilize any OSN. The second kind of danger is present-day dangers, which are identified with OSN clients only as OSN infrastructure that can compromise user privacy and security.

Over the years, with enhancement on the Internet, classic threats have always been an issue, which mainly include malware, phishing, spam, cross-site scripting, etc. Both businesses and scientists have tended to these threats through OSNs. The main motive of using these threats is to extract the personal information/data from clients which are further sent and transmitted over OSNs to harass the target users and to further spread the data to the user's friend circle and family circle. Malware is one of the classic threats which represents maliciousness in programming and is capable of intruding into software applications and developed with the aim of logging into a person's computer to get hold of their personal information and data. Malware attacks on social network frameworks are much easier and simpler when compared with online services because of the complex structure involved in OSN [50]. Phishing is one of the other classic attacks which is more of a deceitful attack wherein the attacker gets his hands on the target user's private data by tricking the user to believe that the attacker is a reliable third-party application. One of the other common and classic threats is spam attacks where spam refers to undesirable messages or posts. These messages or spam content usually contain advertisements or harmful links which further lead to phishing or other malicious destinations.

5.10   Security and Privacy Using Artificial Intelligence in Future Applications/Smart Applications

In this world full of issues, one of the issues which have been gaining the most importance is the issue of data privacy. It has been regarded as the most important issue of the next decade. The term "data privacy" means keeping the private data of an individual safe from the destructive hands of hackers or cybercriminals. It has become one of the major concerns in the field of cyber security. Before buying different types of electronics items, people make a list of all the features and services which they want to have in those products, and "data privacy" has become an important feature in that list [51]. Many companies have used the concept of data privacy as their unique selling point for increasing their sales—for example, the famous Apple Company is advertising its product as the best in the race of keeping data private. Data privacy has gained such huge popularity because of legislation like the European Union's General Data Protection Regulation (GDPR) and the California Consumer Privacy Act (CCPA). All the companies, researchers, and developers have been instructed to follow the guidelines specified by these legislations, but these guidelines are not very clear and are a complex set of new rules which are still a work in progress, especially in the case of CCPA. CCPA which gives the consumers the power or control over their personal information is used in the online network [52].

As a result, all the companies, researchers, and developers are trying hard to keep up with the new set of rules. In the case of GDPR, privacy by design has become its integral part, and it is predicted that it will gain more popularity in the coming years. The concept of privacy by design was developed by Ann Cavoukin, Information and Privacy Commissioner, Ontario, Canada, back in the 1990s. She developed this concept in view of addressing the ever-growing and systemic effects of information and communication technologies. Privacy by design gives us the view that privacy should not be acquired only by following regulatory frameworks but should become the default mode of operation for any organization. It extends to applications like IT systems, accountable business practices, physical design, and networked infrastructure [53].

The principles of privacy by design must be applied to all types of personal information and most importantly to sensitive data like medical reports and financial status data. Its main objective is to ensure that a person has control over his/her own personal data. By using the privacy-preserving techniques, the legislation seems less daunting and so does ensuring data security which is very important in maintaining the user's trust. AI, being one of the technologies gaining rapid popularity over the years, resonates with the simulation of human intelligence in systems and machines which are capable of executing tasks and activities just like humans. The striking feature of AI is its ability to rationalize and make decisions that ensure efficient actions. Weak AI is simple and is single-task-oriented, while strong AI performs tasks that are more complex and human-like. The main or central issue to training and testing the AI models which are specifically designed for sensitive data like healthcare and financial data is data privacy, but presently we do not have any perfect guidelines or notes on how to achieve perfect privacy preservation using AI. The discussion or learning on these topics has given us four pillars that are required to achieve perfect privacy preservation using AI. The research in the field of privacy preservation using machine learning is quickly growing. There are four main pillars of privacy preservation in the field of machine learning including the following [54]:

- Training Data Privacy: This ensures that no sort of malicious and harmful node or individual will be able to pose an adverse effect on the data training.
- Input Privacy: This technique makes sure that the input data and information of the user cannot be observed or extracted by anyone else, including those of the model creator.
- Output Privacy: This guarantees that the output of the model is not clearly visible to people, except for the user whose data is currently being processed.
- Model Privacy: This technique ensures that the model can never be stolen or replicated by unauthorized or illicit people.

Note that pillars 1 to 3 are responsible for protecting the user's privacy, and pillar 4 is meant for protecting the model creator. The data given as input by the user and the model outputs based on those input data should not be visible or accessible to anybody except the user. Preserving data privacy is beneficial not only to the users but also to the companies who are involved in the processing of this sensitive information. Privacy is linked directly and strongly with security. Proper security means that data leaks are less likely to occur, which leads to an ideal scenario where there is no loss of user trust as well as no fines for improper data management. Here now some possible solutions to the security threats can be included as follows:

- Homomorphic Encryption—This type of encryption helps in performing some of the non-polynomial actions and operations on the encrypted data [31]. In machine learning, this ideally points to having the same training and inference being performed on the data which is encrypted and has been incorporated in Naïve Bayes, Logistic Regression, Random Forests, etc.
- Secure Multiparty Computation (MPC)—The main motive of this technique is that, in the case where there's no trust between the communicating parties, the input will be converted into illogical data which, on evaluation by a function, would give illogical output due to the illogical input data. There are quite a few tasks that cannot be carried out using machine learning because of the absence of the necessary data required to train the classification and generative models [56]. It is not because the data is not available but because the data is sensitive and personal, which means that it cannot be shared or sometimes even collected.
- Federated Learning—This basically refers to machine learning that happens on-device. It can be made completely private especially when it is combined and merged with various private training and MPC models for better security [55].

5.11 Security Management and Security Operations Using Artificial Intelligence for Society 5.0 and Industry 4.0

In today's world, there are new operational risks for the fourth industrial revolution in the field of smart manufacturers and also in the field of digital supply networks in the cyber world. The modern nature of this cyber world thus brings in more chances of cyber-attacks, and they have more effect than before, but there may be chances that the manufacturers and their supply networks in this interconnected chain may not be prepared for the risks and need an update in the field of security. In the age of Industry 4.0, for cyber risks to be properly addressed, its strategies should include properties like security, resilience, and also vigilance which are also integrated fully into informational technology and organizational strategy from the beginning. The use of malware in the industry has set a prominent record in history—for example in 2009, malware "Stuxnet" was introduced in a nuclear enrichment plant via a flash drive, and it changed the speed of centrifuges in the plant, which resulted in them spinning out of control. This can be an example of the fact that the battle is unbalanced between the organizations and the attackers because the attackers just need to pinpoint the most fragile part of the software, and the organizations have to protect them. Thus, it is a better idea to implement cyber security as an integral part of the design, operations, and strategy from the beginning of any newly connected Industry 4.0 system. As a new age of industry emerges, the risks from cyber-attackers also increase and thus should be managed and mitigated. The connectivity of smart industry and machinery has increased, and this change is known as Industry 4.0. It comprises a new age of manufacturing and smart innovation in products and is highly efficient than before. The services, networks, and use of technologies that are automated enable advanced manufacturing and thus also increase digital capabilities, but like this, all bring in a threat from the attackers. We need to have a fully integrated approach to cyber risks and make the system safe.

5.11.1   Implementation on the Internet of Things and Protecting Data in IoT Connected Devices

As a very important part of Industry 4.0, IoT devices can also fall prey to cyber-attackers, the vast amount of data created and stored by any IoT device can be very critical to any Industry 4.0. For the process of this data and maximum benefit from it, modern industries also use machine learning algorithms, and based on those computations, real-time calculations are produced, but all these may refer to the fact that the sensitive data is not limited to process sensor information but also to manufacturers' intellectual property rights and other privacy regulations based on the amount of information collected. Thus, for such cases, proper security regulations and better procedures need to be adopted. As more IoT devices are connected day by day, the cloud storage for these must be protected by using strong encryption, machine learning, and artificial intelligence solutions which should be able to detect and apply responsive steps to protect the data. Thus, artificial intelligence comes in handy in Industry 4.0 as a usable cyber security system. Table 5.1 gives a comprehensive approach to this title.

Table 5.1 Analysis of several use cases of IoT with AI tools.

SDG goal	Use cases	AI tools	Impact
Goal 1: No poverty	Sustainability	Sensors	Feeding an algo with day and night satellite images to regions
Goal 2: Zero hunger	Farmwave	Image processing	Farmwave provides image processing to detect plant growth
Goal 3: Good health	Google Deep Mind Health	Machine learning	Deepmind AI system can recommend doctors to patients
Goal 4: Quality education	Liulishuo	Machine learning	Adaptive language learning experience offered by Liulishuo

(Continued)

Table 5.1 Analysis of several use cases of IoT with AI tools. (*Continued*)

SDG goal	Use cases	AI tools	Impact
Goal 5: Gender equality	Textio	Natural language processing	Textio helped increase 80% job for women in Australia
Goal 6: Clean water sanitation	Emagin	Sensors	Emagin supports progressing water facilities to save expenditure
Goal 7: Affordable energy	Ecoisme: Smart Home App	Natural language processing	This provides with electricity bill forecast using AI algorithms
Goal 8: Industry, innovation, and infrastructure	Parc	Machine learning	Parc uses AI techniques to enhance user experience in field

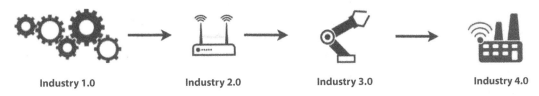

| Industry 1.0 | Industry 2.0 | Industry 3.0 | Industry 4.0 |

Figure 5.4 Progression of cyber and physical threats for each industrial revolution.

Note that Industrial 1.0 (in the 18th century) revolution represents mechanization, stream power, and water power, and Industry 2.0 (in the 19th century) revolution represents the mass production of good, items, assembly line, and electricity generation. Furthermore, Industry 3.0 (in the 20th century) evolution represents computer and automation. Lastly, Industry 4.0 (today's era) evolution represents cyber-physical systems (CPSs) (refer to Figure 5.4). Thus, in today's era, we may face many serious cyber-attacks on such CPSs.

5.12   Digital Trust and Reputation Using Artificial Intelligence

Building trust has always been one of the main objectives of human beings, and we as humans tend to trust anyone slowly, be it an animal or another fellow human being. As far as reputation is concerned, all animals need that either to prove that they are more dominant or for any other reason. However, we as humans take it as a state of living in the society so formed by human beings and are also treated according to reputation most of the time. This has been examined and applied in many studies from several areas, each from a different standpoint. These are the perfect examples of efforts taken towards understanding how humans develop trust and reputation and whether they are interlinked or not. This is about human trust and trusting fellow human beings and respecting their reputation. There is now another new type of object which is becoming more and more integrated into our lives, which is automated machines and the use of AI. However, in this review, we will concentrate on another subject in which the study of reputation and trust has been more important in recent years. We are talking about distributed AI. The multi-agent system paradigm and the remarkable expansion of e-commerce have both resulted in a significant surge in attention in reputation and trust in this field. In the field of information and technology, the study of reputation and trust has several applications. Intelligent software agents employ all of these multi-agent systems as a tool for finding reliable partners to make a decision. To avoid frauds and cheaters, nowadays electronic markets rely on reputation as an incentive mechanism, deterrent, and trust-enforcing mechanism. Although the research of computational reputation and trust models is relatively new, many alternative approaches have emerged in recent years. Nowadays real engines of the AI and ML models have been embedded in numerous products and services. We believe that a shift to a phronetic paradigm that focuses on the ethical challenges that arise from the conceptualization and implementation of AI in order to create practical suggestions is today's need. AI is a multidisciplinary effort to create robots that make decisions, and also learn from them, and eventually evolve intelligently in their surroundings. The decisions that these models make can be the result of the learning process. Machines are technical artifacts that are made up of both hardware and software components. The capability of AI to endow goods and services with "cognitive functions" with the ability to propose judgments and learn from the digital data is driving increased interest in the fields of AI such as financial services, healthcare, retail, and marketing. The ability of AI to offer results such as aiding financial development and cost reductions or even outperforming human specialists in computer vision tasks has encouraged their adoption in modern cultures. ML blends algorithmic science and statistical modeling to develop computer systems that can automatically make predictions and recommendations and also support decision-making by learning inductively from the incoming data, which is a critical component of AI's effectiveness and success.

Reputation and trust may be studied from a variety of angles and applied to a variety of scenarios. This complicates the categorization of reputation and trust models. In this part, we suggest criteria for categorizing current computational reputation and trust models into a logical landscape. As previously said, we concentrate on computational models. As a result, the categorization dimensions were chosen based on the unique properties of these models and the environment in which they must evolve.

In summary, AI is a phenomenon that affects societies, individuals, and businesses. The capacity of ensembles of ML algorithms and models to accomplish complicated tasks as well as help in decision-making would boost AI adoption in a variety of sectors. As a result, it is important to talk about the dynamics and nature of trust in the context of human interactions with AI, including an emphasis on trustworthy AI qualities. Researchers say that a trust model that grows over time should be adopted, which could be used for both human–AI and human–human connections that combine cognitive and noncognitive theories of trust. The trustworthiness of AI might be either absolute or relative. The creation of AIs does not have a valid normative objective of relative trustworthiness. Those who use the idea of trustworthy AI to signify a moral purpose must define trustworthiness cautiously.

5.13   Human-Centric Cyber Security Solutions

The safeguarding of systems connected to the Internet, such as software, hardware, and data associated with them, from cyber-attacks is known as cyber security. Individuals and businesses utilize the method to prevent illegal access to data centers and hardware connected to these digital systems. It is an area where individuals and enterprises are investing a lot of money. According to reports, over $1 lakh crore has been spent on cyber security during the last 7 years; however, there is still a 95% success rate for the hackers and attackers. Despite boosting spending by about 10% year over year, enterprises have witnessed an increase in security breaches. Our study aims to expose these shortcomings and examine cyber security from a human-centric standpoint. The fundamental task ahead of us is to develop a cyberspace governance framework that effectively meets human rights rules.

The emergence of cyberspace has had an influence on practically every element of human existence during the last two decades. The expansion of cyberspace's range, speed, and volume of communications has had an undeniable impact on how societies communicate, businesses serve the market, and individuals are governed. The cyber sector is likewise posing an increasing variety of security issues. Cyber-attacks constitute a threat to critical national infrastructure, while cyber espionage and criminality pose a threat to the global economy.

The examples above highlight the relevance of cyberspace for national security and how it is becoming increasingly important. As a result, governments have designated cyberspace as a new area of combat in their security doctrines and military. As a result, the attention of cyber security must move away from the safeguarding of essential information infrastructure and towards the protection of human rights in cyberspace. Digital human rights abuse data privacy and Internet freedom and all these must be addressed through a human-centric approach. The things we need to focus on are as follows:

- The current approach, which views cyber security as a national security concern and points out its flaws. The focus of the essay is on cyberspace's militarization and the paradoxes of the so-called cyber security conundrum.
- The second issue is the need for a different perspective on cyber security, one that prioritizes human rights. People's rights should be safeguarded both online and offline according to this idea.

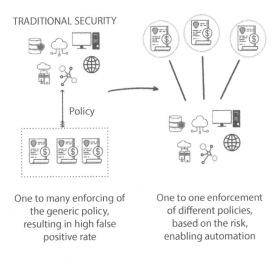

Figure 5.5 Traditional security vs cloud-based security.

- The lack of a cyberspace governance framework as well as doubts over whether the suggested governance models can protect human rights in cyberspace.

Hence, Figure 5.5 depicts traditional security vs cloud-based security in brief.

5.14   Artificial Intelligence-Based Cyber Security Technologies and Solutions

In today's era, a world cannot be imagined without the Internet. Although the Internet has made many things easier, at the same time it has posed many security risks, too, if not used in a proper way. Thus, it is important to know about the possible threats, challenges, and risks of working on the Internet to ensure personal safety and information security. Thus, we will talk about the possible risks and threats on the Internet and the safety measures to avoid them.

Cyber-safety is the responsible use of the Internet to protect the security and safety of personal information while not endangering the information of others.
Artificial Intelligence: AI is the study of how to make computers do the things which at present humans can do better. It is a grand project to build non-human intelligence. Some of the examples of AI are as follows:

- DECISION MAKING: self-driving (autonomous) vehicles.
- IMAGE RECOGNITION: Google photos.
- SOUND RECOGNITION: labeling of bird sounds.

Machine Learning: Newer security methods that use AI algorithms to identify odd network behavior are being developed. Machine learning is used by AI to find differences and similarities in data collection as well as flag any abnormalities associated with that data.
Machine Learning in Cyber Security: To handle such a wide range of difficulties in computer security, a variety of machine learning algorithms has been effectively used. Machine learning has a wide range of applications in cyber security:

- Detection of Phishing: It is aimed at stealing personal sensitive information.
- Network Intrusion Detection: These systems are being used to detect hostile networks that compromise a network's systems. Because of its unknown threats, many systems rely on machine learning approaches.
- Testing Protocol Implementation: It is a novel learning-based technique to test protocol implementation security characteristics automatically and systematically.
- Cryptography: Cryptography is the technique of storing and transferring data in a certain format such that only those who need it may read and interpret it.

- Spam Detection in a Social Network: As soon as an online communication medium gets widespread, spam becomes an issue. Spams are unsolicited messages that contain harmful content.

In summary, machine learning's capacity to adapt quickly to changing and complicated conditions has aided its development as a key instrument in computer security. AI and machine learning are powerful techniques that may be used in a variety of security situations.

5.15   Open Issues, Challenges, and New Horizons Towards Artificial Intelligence and Cyber Security

Minsky and McCarthy defined AI as a work carried out by a computer that, if carried out by a person, would need a high level of intellect. To make an accurate choice, we will need a collection of data on all of our behavioral characteristics. Thinking, manipulation, thinking, planning, and problem-solving are the behavioral traits in question.

5.15.1   An Overview of Cyber-Security

Cyber security refers to the procedures and technologies that are used to protect data and our network from illegal access. Military groups, governments, and corporations all acquire, store, and analyze vast amounts of data or information on the systems, making cyber security critical. A significant portion of this data is sensitive; it is mostly personal details or some kind of financial data or other types of data to which unlawful access or disclosure might have substantial effects and issues for the people as a whole. Organizations communicate a vast volume of information to various systems all across the world. This data, which is kept in systems, is frequently attacked and retrieved without difficulty. This will result in issues beyond our wildest dreams. We have seen a number of examples of information theft in recent years, all of which were caused by the organization's own lack of cyber security procedures. Data thefts of this size are prevented by cyber security. As a result, it aids a person's privacy.

5.15.2   The Role of Artificial Intelligence in Cyber Security

Many businesses are still experimenting with manual attempts to blend internal security findings and contextualize them with external threat information, while cybercriminals are investing in automation to launch attacks. With the current security mechanisms in place, it can take a long time to detect breaches, and attackers will use weaknesses to penetrate systems and harvest data during this age. To address these issues, a number of firms are looking at incorporating AI into their routine cyber risk operations. New flaws and weaknesses may be promptly found and investigated using AI to help minimize future cyber-attacks. It is the ability to reduce the amount of stress placed on humans. They are notified whenever an incursion is discovered and when their assistance is needed.

5.15.3   AI Is Continually Made Smarter

A good analogy is to acknowledge the most basic professionals who work for our company. If we hire this talent to train our AI and ML systems, the AI will be as intelligent as our top staff. Now, if we spend the time to train our AI and ML systems alongside our best employees, the end result will be an answer that is as intelligent as the brains of all these people combined. In recent years, the debate between ML and AI has been a hot subject.

5.15.4   AI Never Misses a Day of Work

The advantage of artificial intelligence in cyber security is that it does not take vacations or become fatigued after long periods of constant labor. As a result, we will infer that AI aids in doing tasks with maximum efficiency, at the utmost feasible pace, and with the most basic quality goods. Although preventing cyber threats and, as a result, avoiding attacks is ideal, it is practically impossible to prevent these situations from occurring. Once they have, a timely response is critical in reducing the damage inflicted by the attack as well as recovering from its repercussions. A rapid answer might be programmed into the mechanism of a "thinking machine".

5.15.5   AI Swiftly Spots the Threats

There are algorithms for detecting possible attacks which should be implemented in real time to provide a moment-by-moment reaction to an attack. Most security algorithms have limited scope, and they are frequently unable to keep up with the rapid invention and mutation of new attack vectors. ML algorithms included in an intelligent security system have shown a great ability to detect and respond to risks as they arise, even dynamic dangers. These intelligent security systems could also require the ability to continuously learn, observe existing streams of information, and eventually help in predicting future dangers and suitable solutions.

5.15.6   Impact of AI on Cyber Security

The impact of AI on cyber security can be included as:

- Increases the Resistance's Size: AI has the ability to increase a system's overall resilience against continuing threats. If a business communicates and transfers data using a range of hardware devices such as mobile devices and computers, the chances of a cyber-attack to steal data from these systems are rather considerable.
- Capable of Dealing With Any Incoming Threat: Machine-driven mechanisms powered by artificial intelligence are frequently used to fight every incoming danger and take countermeasures immediately. The influence of artificial intelligence on cyber security has been recognized in a number of ways.
- Developing a Threat–Response Strategy That Is Effective: In most security setups, real-time threat response is impeded by speed and, in some cases, the changing nature of the attack itself. As a result, a large amount of knowledge must be examined in order to construct a reaction and sketch out a proper approach.

5.15.7   AI in Cyber Security Case Study

The White House issued a study in October 2016 titled "Preparing for the Longer Term of AI". This study discussed the AI management tactics that we should always employ. Events were held so that more people debate and discuss these new technologies as well as become more aware of them and technological advances may emerge. It was observed that such conferences are really beneficial, as the people who were previously unaware of these new technologies now have a thorough understanding of them. This also resulted in a slew of practical AI applications that are being hailed as our planet's future. We do not know what the future holds for technology because it is so young. Some scientists or researchers have no clue what issues could arise in the future or how they will deal with them or they are just being ignorant. Even after the world has been seeing countless examples of the use of AI in cyber security, there is still a lot of misinformation. AI will require some high-tech supervision in the future to ensure that it accomplishes the positive duties it was designed to do and does not become a weapon of devastation. Artificial intelligence should be designed in such a way that it is vulnerable to cyber threats.

5.16   Future Research with Artificial Intelligence and Cyber Security

From a technological standpoint, advances at below the three levels are likely to accelerate the development of AI: the first level is a system–AI-enabled physical equipment, and systems are known as systems; the second level is AI behavior patterns, also known as algorithms; and the last level is interactions between AI and external environments, referred to as interfaces. Modern artificial intelligence mostly rely on computing equipment represented by computer systems at the platform level. A typical computer's core central processing unit is mostly employed for general purposes or day-to-day computing operations. Although these CPUs are compatible with all of the clever tasks that AI is faced with, they performs poorly. The creation of high-performance AI platforms is now becoming fashionable or trendy. New and intelligent AI processing technologies, like GPU, have been developed by NVIDIA, Google, Intel, and other well-known businesses. In the coming years, GPU will take the position of the CPU, and then future artificial intelligence would eventually have to deal with a variety of sophisticated adversaries.

Deep learning is a key driver of AI research; however, it is presently mostly concentrated on data processing, with less emphasis paid towards the development of intelligent capabilities like logical and memory reasoning as well as storing and anticipating information sequences. It is vital to forecast and retain material that comprises sequences of information when faced with difficult real-world activities. The use of a hierarchical model as part of the deep learning growth process not only has excellent expressive capacity but is also easier to examine conceptually. Furthermore, we must create a deep learning model that is appropriate for solving certain challenges.

When it comes to AI, there is a slew of difficulties to contend with, and every company will want robust AI solutions to deploy it. There are legal and ethical considerations to consider, such as who would be held accountable for the activities of an autonomous machine that chooses its own course of action. However, given the numerous benefits it provides,

AI in cyber security appears to have a bright future. We may have to wait for a few years, if not decades, to see how it affects the world in the following days.

Furthermore, in [57–65], readers/researchers can find out more details on cyber-attacks/attacks on cyber physical systems. Researchers can also find useful research issues and challenges on various interesting and emerging technologies to do work on in the near future.

5.17 Conclusion

Cyber-attacks are a serious concern that will undoubtedly intensify and become more sophisticated in the future years. As a result, we must be prepared and make use of new technology tools such as cyber security with AI to secure sensitive and critical data at all levels, from individuals to businesses to governments and the countries, from cyber-attacks. In this sense, countries all over the world must implement initiatives to raise knowledge about emerging technologies and provide financial assistance towards R&D in these fields. Since AI has significant promise in the cyber security area, it is critical for researchers and practitioners to grasp the present state-of-the-art and the problems that come with it.

However, in regards to cyber security, users might still always be the weakest link. Although AI may substantially help in reducing cyber-attacks by using machine-to-machine data learning, a single reckless user might inflict serious harm to the entire system, and no one can forecast this. Prior to actually implementing any new technology, IT security managers must be aware of different ways to adapt and utilize new technology with ease. In this paper, we have discussed different cyber security attacks and the ways to mitigate them. We have also discussed the significant role of AI in cyber security and how AI can automate and keep learning with the use of ML in such a way as to reduce cyber-attacks without much human interference.

References

1. Moura, J. and Serrão, C., Security and privacy issues of big data, in: *Handbook of Research on Trends and Future Directions in Big Data and Web Intelligence*, pp. 20–52, IGI Global, 2015. Available at: https://www.igi-global.com/chapter/security-and-privacy-issues-of-big-data/137016

2. Stellios, I., Kotzanikolaou, P., Psarakis, M., Alcaraz, C., Lopez, J., A survey of IoT-enabled cyberattacks: Assessing attack paths to critical infrastructures and services. *IEEE Commun. Surv. & Tutorials*, 20, 4, 3453–3495, 2018.

3. Nachenberg, C., Computer virus-antivirus coevolution. *Commun. ACM*, 40, 1, 46–51, 1997.

4. Shukla, V., Tyagi, A. K., Role of artificial intelligence in cyber security: A useful overview, in: *Information Security Practices for the Internet of Things, 5G, and Next-Generation Wireless Networks*.

5. Hurst, W., Merabti, M., Fergus, P., A survey of critical infrastructure security, in: *International Conference on Critical Infrastructure Protection*, pp. 127–138, Springer, Berlin, Heidelberg, 2014, March.

6. Balapour, A., Nikkhah, H.R., Sabherwal, R., Mobile application security: Role of perceived privacy as the predictor of security perceptions. *Int. J. Inf. Manag.*, 52, 102063, 2020.

7. Sengupta, S., Chowdhary, A., Sabur, A., Alshamrani, A., Huang, D., Kambhampati, S., A survey of moving target defenses for network security. *IEEE Commun. Surv. & Tutorials*, 22, 3, 1909–1941, 2020.

8. Wiley, A., McCormac, A., Calic, D., More than the individual: Examining the relationship between culture and information security awareness. *Comput. & Secur.*, 88, 101640, 2020.

9. Da Veiga, A., Astakhova, L.V., Botha, A., Herselman, M., Defining organisational information security culture—Perspectives from academia and industry. *Comput. & Secur.*, 92, 101713, 2020.

10. Pereira, A.G., Lima, T.M., Santos, F.C., Industry 4.0 and Society 5.0: Opportunities and threats. *Int. J. Recent Technol. Eng.*, 8, 5, 3305–3308, 2020.

11. Sołtysik-Piorunkiewicz, A. and Zdonek, I., How Society 5.0 and Industry 4.0 ideas shape the open data performance expectancy. *Sustainability*, 13, 2, 917, 2021.

12. Bag, S., Gupta, S., Kumar, S., Industry 4.0 adoption and 10R advance manufacturing capabilities for sustainable development. *Int. J. Prod. Econ.*, 231, 107844, 2021.

13. Zengin, Y., Naktiyok, S., Kaygın, E., Kavak, O., Topçuoğlu, E., An investigation upon Industry 4.0 and Society 5.0 within the context of sustainable development goals. *Sustainability*, 13, 5, 2682, 2021.

14. Potočan, V., Mulej, M. and Nedelko, Z., Society 5.0: Balancing of Industry 4.0, economic advancement and social problems, *Kybernetes*, 50, 3, 794–811, 2021.. https://doi.org/10.1108/K-12-2019-0858.

15. Fatorachian, H. and Kazemi, H., Impact of Industry 4.0 on supply chain performance. *Prod. Plann. & Control*, 32, 1, 63–81, 2021.

16. Polat, L. and Erkollar, A. Industry 4.0 vs. Society 5.0, in: *The International Symposium for Production Research*, pp. 333–345, Springer, Cham, 2020, September.

17. Al-Dhief, F.T., Latiff, N.M.A.A., Malik, N.N.N.A., Salim, N.S., Baki, M.M., Albadr, M.A.A., Mohammed, M.A., A survey of voice pathology surveillance systems based on Internet of Things and machine learning algorithms. *IEEE Access*, 8, 64514–64533, 2020.

18. Deng, X., Jiang, Y., Yang, L.T., Yi, L., Chen, J., Liu, Y., Li, X., Learning-automata-based confident information coverage barriers for smart ocean Internet of Things. *IEEE Internet Things J.*, 7, 10, 9919–9929, 2020.

19. Jiang, H., Tsohou, A., Siponen, M., Li, Y., Examining the side effects of organizational internet monitoring on employees. *Internet Research*, 30, 6, 1613–1630, 2021. https://doi.org/10.1108/intr-08-2019-0360

20. Jarrett, A. and Choo, K.K.R., The impact of automation and artificial intelligence on digital forensics. *Wiley Interdiscip. Reviews: Forensic Sci.*, 3, 6, e1418, 2021.

21. Sarker, I.H., Furhad, M.H., Nowrozy, R., Ai-driven cybersecurity: An overview, security intelligence modeling and research directions. *SN Comput. Sci.*, 2, 3, 1–18, 2021.

22. Formosa, P., Wilson, M., Richards, D., A principlist framework for cybersecurity ethics. *Comput. Secur.*, 109, 102382, 2021.

23. McDaniel, P., Launchbury, J., Martin, B., Wang, C., Kautz, H., Artificial intelligence and cyber security: Opportunities and challenges technical workshop summary report. in: *Networking & Information Technology Research Devevelopment Subcommittee and the Machine Learning & Artificial Intelligence Subcommittee of the National Science & Technology Council*, 2020. Available at: https://www.nitrd.gov/pubs/AI-CS-Tech-Summary-2020.pdf.

24. Kumar, G., Saha, R., Lal, C., Conti, M., Internet-of-Forensic (IoF): A blockchain based digital forensics framework for IoT applications. *Future Gen. Comput. Syst.*, 120, 13–25, 2021.

25. Bowman, B. and Huang, H.H., Towards next-generation cybersecurity with graph AI. *ACM SIGOPS Operating Syst. Rev.*, 55, 1, 61–67, 2021.

26. Amit, K.T., Rekha, G., Shabnam, K., Applications of blockchain technologies in digital forensic and threat hunting, in: *Recent Trends in Blockchain for Information Systems Security and Privacy*, CRC Press, 2021.

27. Quincozes, S.E., Albuquerque, C., Passos, D., Mossé, D., A survey on intrusion detection and prevention systems in digital substations. *Comput. Networks*, 184, 107679, 2021.

28. Girdler, T. and Vassilakis, V.G., Implementing an intrusion detection and prevention system using software-defined networking: Defending against ARP spoofing attacks and blacklisted MAC addresses. *Comput. & Electr. Eng.*, 90, 106990, 2021.

29. Singh, A., Nagar, J., Sharma, S., Kotiyal, V., A gaussian process regression approach to predict the k-barrier coverage probability for intrusion detection in wireless sensor networks. *Expert Syst. Appl.*, 172, 114603, 2021.

30. Viand, A., Jattke, P., Hithnawi, A., SoK: Fully homomorphic encryption compilers, in: *2021 IEEE Symposium on Security and Privacy (SP)*, IEEE, pp. 1092–1108, 2021, May.

31. Yousuf, H., Lahzi, M., Salloum, S.A., Shaalan, K., Systematic review on fully homomorphic encryption scheme and its application, in: *Recent Advances in Intelligent Systems and Smart Applications*, pp. 537–551, 2021.

32. Alagic, G., Brakerski, Z., Dulek, Y., Schaffner, C., Impossibility of quantum virtual black-box obfuscation of classical circuits, in: *Annual International Cryptology Conference*, pp. 497–525, Springer, Cham, 2021, August.

33. Li, B., Feng, Y., Xiong, Z., Yang, W., Liu, G., Research on AI security enhanced encryption algorithm of autonomous IoT systems. *Inf. Sci.*, 575, 379–398, 2021.

34. Sarker, I.H., Furhad, M.H., Nowrozy, R., AI-driven cybersecurity: An overview, security intelligence modeling and research directions. *SN Comput. Sci.*, 2, 3, 1–18, 2021.

35. Oseni, A., Moustafa, N., Janicke, H., Liu, P., Tari, Z., Vasilakos, A., Security and privacy for artificial intelligence: Opportunities and challenges. *arXiv preprint*, 2021, arXiv:2102.04661. https://doi.org/10.48550/arXiv.2102.04661.

36. Moustafa, N., A new distributed architecture for evaluating AI-based security systems at the edge: Network TON_IoT datasets. *Sustain. Cities Soc.*, 72, 102994, 2021.

37. Schmidt, E., Work, B., Catz, S., Chien, S., Darby, C., Ford, K., Griffiths, J.M., Horvitz, E., Jassy, A., Mark, W., Matheny, J., National security commission on artificial intelligence (AI), National Security Commission on Artificial Intelligence, 2021. https://www.nscai.gov/wp-content/uploads/2021/03/Full-Report-Digital-1.pdf.

38. Lv, Z., Qiao, L., Kumar Singh, A., Wang, Q., AI-empowered IoT security for smart cities. *ACM Trans. Internet Technol.*, 21, 4, 1–21, 2021.

39. Mardon, A., Barara, G., Chana, I., Di Martino, A., Falade, I., Harun, R., Hauser, A., Johnson, J., Li, A., Pham, J., Varghese, N., *Cryptography*, 2021.

40. Fritzmann, T., Van Beirendonck, M., Roy, D.B., Karl, P., Schamberger, T., Verbauwhede, I., Sigl, G., Masked accelerators and instruction set extensions for post-quantum cryptography. *IACR Transactions on Cryptographic Hardware and Embedded Systems*, 2022, 1, 414–460, 2021.

41. Wang, L.J., Zhang, K.Y., Wang, J.Y., Cheng, J., Yang, Y.H., Tang, S.B., Yan, D., Tang, Y.L., Liu, Z., Yu, Y., Zhang, Q., Experimental authentication of quantum key distribution with post-quantum cryptography. *NPJ Quantum Inf.*, 7, 1, 1–7, 2021.

42. Bhasin, S., D'Anvers, J.P., Heinz, D., Pöppelmann, T., Van Beirendonck, M., Attacking and defending masked polynomial comparison for lattice-based cryptography. *IACR Trans. Cryptographic Hardware Embedded Syst.*, 334–359, 2021. Available at: https://eprint.iacr.org/2021/104.pdf

43. Øygarden, M., Smith-Tone, D., Verbel, J., On the effect of projection on rank attacks in multivariate cryptography, in: *International Conference on Post-Quantum Cryptography*, pp. 98–113, Springer, Cham, 2021, July.

44. Wang, J., Zhu, Y., Maqbool, S., An efficient hash-based authenticated key agreement scheme for multi-server architecture resilient to key compromise impersonation. *Digital Commun. Networks*, 7, 1, 140–150, 2021.

45. Thiers, J.P. and Freudenberger, J., Generalized concatenated codes over Gaussian and Eisenstein integers for code-based cryptography. *Cryptography*, 5, 4, 33, 2021.

46. Nieminen, R., Supersingular elliptic curve isogeny cryptography, 2016. Available at: https://math.colorado.edu/~saar7867/What_Is_Seminar_Talk_10_21_21.pdf.

47. Mashatan, A. and Heintzman, D., The complex path to quantum resistance: Is your organization prepared? *Queue*, 19, 2, 65–92, 2021.

48. Jain, A.K., Sahoo, S.R., Kaubiyal, J. Online social networks security and privacy: Comprehensive review and analysis. *Complex Intell. Syst.*, 7, 2157–2177, 2021. https://doi.org/10.1007/s40747-021-00409-7

49. Voloch, N., Gal-Oz, N., Gudes, E., A trust based privacy providing model for online social networks. *Online Soc. Networks Media*, 24, 100138, 2021.

50. Nair, M. M. and Tyagi, A. K,, Privacy: History, statistics, policy, laws, preservation and threat analysis. *J. Inf. Secur. Appl.* 16, 1, 24–34. 11p, 2021.

51. Oseni, A., Moustafa, N., Janicke, H., Liu, P., Tari, Z., Vasilakos, A., Security and privacy for artificial intelligence: Opportunities and challenges. *arXiv preprint*, 2021, arXiv:2102.04661. Available at: https://doi.org/10.48550/arXiv.2102.04661.

52. Siriwardhana, Y., Porambage, P., Liyanage, M., Ylianttila, M. AI and 6G security: Opportunities and challenges, in: *2021 Joint European Conference on Networks and Communications & 6G Summit (EuCNC/6G Summit)*, pp. 616–621, IEEE, 2021, June.

53. Deebak, B.D. and Fadi, A.T., Privacy-preserving in smart contracts using blockchain and artificial intelligence for cyber risk measurements. *J. Inf. Secur. Appl.*, 58, 102749, 2021.

54. Jhanjhi, N.Z., Humayun, M., Almuayqil, S.N., Cyber security and privacy issues in industrial internet of things. *Comput. Syst. Sci. Eng.*, 37, 3, 361–380, 2021.

55. Nguyen, D.C., Ding, M., Pathirana, P.N., Seneviratne, A., Li, J., Poor, H.V., Federated learning for Internet of Things: A comprehensive survey. *IEEE Commun. Surv. & Tutorials*, 23, 3, Third quarter 2021.

56. Makri, E., Rotaru, D., Vercauteren, F., Wagh, S., Rabbit: Efficient comparison for secure multi-party computation, in: *International Conference on Financial Cryptography and Data Security*, pp. 249–270, Springer, Berlin, Heidelberg, 2021, March. Available at: https://eprint.iacr.org/2021/119.pdf

57. Nair, M.M., Tyagi, A.K., Sreenath, N., The future with Industry 4.0 at the core of Society 5.0: Open issues, future opportunities and challenges. *2021 International Conference on Computer Communication and Informatics (ICCCI)*, pp. 1–7, 2021.

58. Tyagi, A.K., Fernandez, T.F., Mishra, S., Kumari, S., Intelligent automation systems at the core of industry 4.0, in: *Intelligent Systems Design and Applications. ISDA 2020*, Advances in Intelligent Systems and Computing, A. Abraham, V. Piuri, N. Gandhi, P. Siarry, A. Kaklauskas, A. Madureira (eds.), vol. 1351, Springer, Cham, 2021, https://doi.org/10.1007/978-3-030-71187-0_1.

59. Goyal, D. and Tyagi, A., A look at top 35 problems in the computer science field for the next decade, 2020 Available at: https://www.taylorfrancis.com/chapters/edit/10.1201/9781003052098-40/look-top-35-problems-computer-science-field-next-decade-deepti-goyal-amit-kumar-tyagi.

60. Varsha, R., Nair, S.M., Tyagi, A.K., Aswathy, S.U., RadhaKrishnan, R., The future with advanced analytics: A sequential analysis of the disruptive technology's scope, in: *Hybrid Intelligent Systems. HIS 2020*, Advances in Intelligent Systems and Computing, A. Abraham, T. Hanne, O. Castillo, N. Gandhi, T. Nogueira Rios, T.P. Hong (eds.), vol. 1375, Springer, Cham, 2021, https://doi.org/10.1007/978-3-030-73050-5_56.

61. Tyagi, A.K., Nair, M.M., Niladhuri, S., Abraham, A., Security, privacy research issues in various computing platforms: A survey and the road ahead. *J. Inf. Assurance & Secur.*, 15, 1, 1–16, 16p, 2020.
62. Tyagi, A.K. and Aghila, G., A wide scale survey on Botnet. *Int. J. Comput. Appl.*, 34, 9, 9–22, November 2011.
63. Tyagi, A.K., Article: Cyber physical systems (CPSs) – Opportunities and challenges for improving cyber security. *Int. J. Comput. Appl.*, 137, 14, 19–27, March 2016. Published by Foundation of Computer Science (FCS), NY, USA.
64. Rekha, G., Malik, S., Tyagi, A.K., Nair, M.M., Intrusion detection in cyber security: Role of machine learning and data mining in cyber security. *Adv. Sci. Technol. Eng. Syst. J.*, 5, 3, 72–81, 2020.
65. Tyagi, A.K. and Sreenath, N., Cyber physical systems: Analyses, challenges and possible solutions. *Internet Things Cyber-Physical Syst.*, 1, 22–33, 2021. https://doi.org/10.1016/j.iotcps.2021.12.002.

Part 2
METHODS AND TECHNIQUES

6

An Automatic Artificial Intelligence System for Malware Detection

Ahmad Moawad[1]*, Ahmed Ismail Ebada[2], A.A. El-Harby[1] and Aya M. Al-Zoghby[1]

[1]Department of Computer Science, Faculty of Computers and Artificial Intelligence, Damietta, Egypt
[2]Department of Information Systems, Faculty of Computers and Artificial Intelligence, Damietta, Egypt

Abstract

One of the major issues in computer system security is detecting malware threats before they spread. The continuous development of malware makes it challenging to detect malware with traditional anti-malware software, which relies on the signature database. As new malware samples increase daily, standard malware detection tools become less effective; thus, the AI method is required to detect and prevent malware spread. Machine learning and deep learning methods have promising results and can handle malware by identifying patterns in malware samples and detecting similar malware. The analysis process is essential for identifying the malware and its outcome with patterns or features that are used in the detection process. Malware analyses are static, dynamic, hybrid, and memory-based; all of them have pros and cons. Applying the outcome from the analysis process by employing machine learning and deep learning provides good and accurate results, is quick, is less costly, is independent from the reverse engineers, and offers promising detection solutions to safeguard individuals and governments. This chapter covers the following: malware types, the structure of binary executables, malware analysis and detection, obfuscation, malware detection with application of AI, the open issues and challenges, and discussion and conclusion.

Keywords: Malware, malware analysis, malware detection, obfuscation, deep learning, machine learning, automatic

6.1 Introduction

The fast expansion of malware on the Internet per day makes it one of the most challenging tasks in computer security. The malware word came from "malicious software", which indicates any unwanted actions, usually without the user's knowledge or permission. Malware is an umbrella that describes any malicious program or code harmful to systems [1]; malware is essential in any cybercrime attack. Malware attacks are increasing and targeting different types of victims, including individuals, companies, and governments; the attacks

---

*Corresponding author: ahmad.moawad@outlook.com

Amit Kumar Tyagi (ed.) Automated Secure Computing for Next-Generation Systems, (117–138) © 2024 Scrivener Publishing LLC

could even target critical systems like power stations. Norton labs [2] reported 9 million threats, on average, every day, and according to Kaspersky, in 2022, the estimation of cyber-crime attacks that use malware is 400,000 every day [3]. The malware's effects depend on the attack type and the targeted victims. The effectiveness could be cost, recovery, or even business loss by losing the system's reputation. According to Meterpreter, the estimation of global ransomware damage costs 20 billion US dollars (USD). Kaspersky also reported that enterprises lose half a million USD, on average, from a security breach [4, 5].

Malware has different types, like viruses, worms, Trojans, ransomware, botnets, adware, spyware, rootkits, file-less malware, etc. [6, 7]. The malware attacks' purposes may differ from stealing, damaging, spying, allowing remote access, etc. The development of malware is increasing from simple to advanced persistence threats; one of the complex malwares which use a modularity mechanism is Trickbot [8]. Each module does a specific task; this malware does not require installing all modules to run; instead it is integrated with the downloaded module. The Trickbot module came in dynamic link library (DLL) format. After infection, the payload connects to command and control servers and tries to install the modules. This malware targets finance organizations. Traditional malware detection methods are less effective, and malware easily bypasses the detection process. Traditional anti-malware tools cannot detect new malware variants and are less effective with zero-day malware. Generating new malware variants is easy; it can be performed with different techniques like changing some bytes at the beginning or end of the malware files, obfuscation techniques, and packers. Because malware technologies constantly evolve, traditional anti-malware software that relies on database signatures to identify malware by looking up malicious patterns cannot detect unknown and novel malware [9]. Traditional dynamic, static, or hybrid (static and dynamic) analysis techniques still also need to be improved; they are time-consuming and require domain expertise (malware analysts and reverse engineers).

Artificial intelligence (AI) is beneficial in various techniques today, like healthcare, medicine, self-driving cars, etc. It is not just task automation but understanding and making decisions. AI has different subfields, and it intends to make the machine learn and solve problems; there are two main subfields, machine learning (ML) and deep learning (DL). Recently, these two approaches have become popularly used in malware detection.

The results will help anti-virus developers and cyber security specialists create solutions against malware based on facts and safeguard the Internet from bad actors. In order to develop technology and help choose the finest malware-fighting solutions, this article will show the variations in malware detection techniques, highlighting their strengths and limitations.

Organization of the Chapter

The rest of the chapter is outlined as follows: Section 6.2 shows the malware types, Section 6.3 shows the structure of binary executable files, Section 6.4 outlines the malware analysis and detection, Section 6.5 shows the obfuscation techniques, Section 6.6 discusses malware detection with applying AI, Section 6.7 shows the open issues and challenges, and, finally, Section 6.8 is the concluding chapter.

6.2   Malware Types

Malware has different types, and each type has different groups consisting of families based on their actions and characteristics. The malware could share other characteristics from different types to perform sophisticated and effective attacks. Following is a summary of the important malware types (see Table 6.1):

Table 6.1 Summary of malware types.

Viruses	Like biological viruses, computer viruses also need a host to operate, and the victim starts them by launching and double-clicking an executable file. Companion, prepending, and post-pending viruses are some self-replicating, host-dependent viruses. In order to protect themselves, viruses can employ several strategies, including encryption, polymorphism, and metamorphism. The term polymorphism means that the malicious code can modify its appearance to evade detection, through a process known as polymorphism, without altering its core functionality, while metamorphism is the term for the process by which a virus alters its functioning as it spreads [10].
Worms	Worms, unlike viruses, are host-independent and self-replicating. They can rapidly grow and disrupt network or email systems. Morris created Worms as a student project in 1988 to count the number of computers in the network by replicating the code from one computer to another. The concept is then used in the attacks [9, 11].
Trojan	The Trojan or Trojan horse is a program that impersonates as a legitimate software and conceals its true purpose. It allows remote access to the computer system and executes actions designed to steal, destroy, or disrupt data once installed without the user's knowledge. It does not self-replicate, unlike viruses [12, 13].
Ransomware	Ransomware, also known as crypto-malware, is a type of malware that encrypts data and prevents the victim from using the operating system until the victim pays the attacker a ransom to regain access. To conceal their identity, attackers have recently begun using bitcoin to receive money rather than through traditional bank transactions.
Botnet	Bots, spiders, web bots, and crawls are examples of Internet robots. Once installed on the victim's device, the bots can collect data and passwords. A botnet malware controls many computers and infected systems; attackers can use these powerful computers to launch DDoS attacks against specific servers (DDoS).
Spyware	It saves a user's login information, such as usernames and passwords, or collects sensitive data. Keyloggers are types of spyware that record keystrokes on the keyboard and steal login information.

(Continued)

Table 6.1 Summary of malware types. (*Continued*)

Rootkits	Rootkits are a type of malware that allows the hacker to gain remote access and control of the victim's device without the victim's knowledge. This type of malware is intended to remain undetected for an extended period of time while causing various types of damage. Once an attacker gains access to computers, they can steal data or use the victim's device to carry out a criminal act, such as using a computer as part of a botnet to launch a distributed DDoS attack.
Microsoft Office documents	Employing the Visual Basic (VBA) macros means that, when the victim opens the document and clicks on enable macros, this allows the code to be executed and perform different tasks, like downloading a payload, known as a multi-stage attack.
Crypto-mining	Due to the increasing income of cryptocurrency, this malware exploits the victim's resources, such as processors, graphics cards, and network bandwidth, for illicit crypto-mining [14].
File-less malware	The name implies that this malware does not need to be downloaded or installed and instead exploits operating system applications. When a victim clicks on a specific link, for example, memory is loaded, allowing the attacker to load codes that remotely capture the victim's data.
Adware	It contains advertisements and constantly displays unwanted advertisements. It gathers information about a user's online browsing history in order to target advertisements. The most common reason for Adware is to collect user data in order to earn advertising revenue [15].

The actual attack could combine or mix various types of malware to perform the attack effectively—for example, by combining Trojans, worms, and viruses. The multi-stage attack has been widespread recently, which starts with social engineering by employing links or email. The links target malicious websites, and emails may contain links or malicious documents like office documents or portable document format (PDF) files. The reason behind using Office or PDF documents is the facility of VBA macros feature in Office documents, which intended to use automated tasks by applying the macros. A PDF document consists of multiple objects and XML and has the ability to analyze the JavaScript code. By employing VBA or JavaScript, the attack, after entering the victim's device and triggering the document by opening it, could install the payload, install the malware, and run it. Once the malware is running, it starts the actions designed to be performed. It applies a persistence mechanism, which allows the malware program to run with the system startup, like using registry keys, task scheduler, etc. Recently, we noticed some critical attacks in reputation companies by tricking the internal employee with effective social engineering, which allows the attacker to enter the internal company or, worst, when the company is a third-party company like a monitoring company which is used by the government agency. Figure 6.1 shows the multi-stage cybercrime attack.

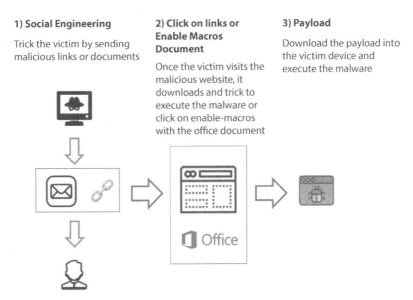

1) Social Engineering

Trick the victim by sending malicious links or documents

2) Click on links or Enable Macros Document

Once the victim visits the malicious website, it downloads and trick to execute the malware or click on enable-macros with the office document

3) Payload

Download the payload into the victim device and execute the malware

Figure 6.1 Multi-stage cybercrime attacks.

6.3   Structure Format of Binary Executable Files

Understanding the format of binary executable files is essential in developing the detection solution or framework. The executable file has a specific format according to the different operating systems (OS). This structure is important as it allows the OS loader to load from the disk into memory and execute the code instructions. There are different structures for different OS—for example, Windows has Portable Executable (PE), Linux has Executable and Linkable Format (ELF), MacOS has Mach-O, and Android has Android Package Kit or Android Application Package (APK). In general, the executable has a header and sections. The header contains information about the code and targets running, whether it is a 32/64 or x86/x64 machine, and how to load the code by the loader, while the sections have different purposes.

In order to apply AI techniques to detect malware, it is good and common to understand the underlying binary files and use the appropriate features. The AI techniques rely on the features which are extracted from the binary files—for example, some studies use the byte sequences of a binary file, strings extracted from the binary, operation code (opcode), which is the assembly instruction, headers, etc. In addition to the binary format, understanding the basic of the underlying OS is also important. We will start with the basic of each binary file format and the details related to each executable format. In PE, there are file headers, optional headers, offset, raw data, entry points, data directories, etc. These details are out of the scope of this chapter.

Windows is the most prevalent OS in the world, and it is not surprising that most malwares are written for it [16]. PE is the Windows binary format that is used in EXE, DLL, and OLE files. This format contains the following important structure: header and sections (Figure 6.2). When the executable file is executed, the Windows loader first reads the

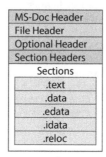

Figure 6.2 Windows PE format.

program's head to determine its specifications, such as whether it is 16-bit, 32-bit, or 64-bit, how to address the program into memory, where the entry point's start address is, which system modules should be loaded, etc. Table 6.2 shows the different sections and descriptions of the PE file format [17, 18].

Linux malware is less common in contrast to Windows malware. Linux also has ELF format for the executable file. ELF has a similarity with PE (Figure 6.3) with headers and sections [18, 19].

Like Windows OS, the Android is vulnerable to malwares. In total, 3.25 million malicious Android apps have been found in 2016. In other words, this means a new malware app per 10 seconds [20, 21]. The Android uses Dalvik virtual machine, which is the android virtual machine optimized for mobile devices. The Android OS uses the APK format which has the following features: AndroidManifest.xml, classes.dex, res, Meta-INF directory, Assets, and Lib (Figure 6.4) and Table 6.3 is a summary description of the APK format [22, 23].

Table 6.2 PE format description.

Header	Description
DOS header	Represents a file's binary
PE signature	Represents a file's modern binary
Optional header	Contains execution information
Data directories	Points to extra data structures like import, export, etc.
Section table	Defines how the file is loaded into memory
Section	**Description**
.text	Contains executable code
.data	Globally accessed and initialized data
.idata	Import functions information
.edata	Export functions information
.rsrc	Resources which are needed by the program, like icons, images, etc.

Figure 6.3 Linux ELF format.

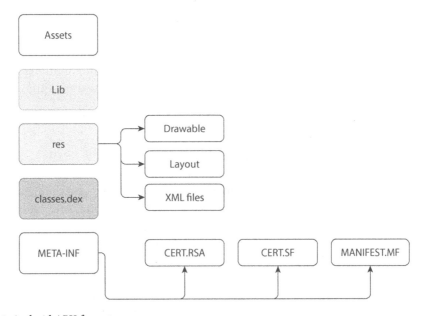

Figure 6.4 Android APK format.

The linking procedure and the manner in which libraries are imported are two binary format considerations. The three types of linking are static, dynamic, and runtime. Static linking entails including all referenced modules in the executable file, linking them after compilation, and loading them when the main module is loaded. The code referred to by dynamic linking can be separated from the executable file. The directed modules are loaded alongside the executable when the operating system loads the program. Before the program begins, all modules are loaded into memory, and resolve is performed to provide the called modules-load address or entry point address to the calling module. Runtime linking is the

Table 6.3 APK format description.

File	Description
AndroidManifest.xml	Contains essential information about build tools, Android OS, Google play, permissions, app components like (activities, services, broadcast), hardware and software required [22]
classes.dex	Contains the Java libraries that the application uses
res	Contains drawable, layout, and xml files
Meta-INF directory	Has a folder that contains the manifest information and other metadata about the java package carried by the jar file
Assets	Contains any images, icons, fonts, etc.
Lib	Contains any library which is used in the app

executable use of the APIs provided by the OS or through a library to load a DLL when the code needs it and performs the symbol resolution. The majority of malicious software prefers runtime and dynamic linking.

We introduced the fundamentals of binary format files; however, many details surrounding this topic—such as relative virtual address, image base, the concept of raw and offset, how to convert the address between disk and random access memory (RAM), and so on—are beyond the scope of this chapter. However, we recommend that you understand these concepts which will help you select the appropriate and effective features with AI detection techniques.

6.4   Malware Analysis and Detection

Malware analysis entails understanding how it operates, behaves, and defines its characteristics. The analysis results in the development of effective anti-malware tools to defend against malware attacks or to remove malware from infected machines. There are various types of analysis, all of which attempt to explain how the malware works. There are four types: static, dynamic, hybrid, and memory analyses (see Table 6.4).

- Static analysis
  Static analysis involves extracting different patterns/features from the malware, such as opcode n-grams, opcode frequency, control flow graph, PE header, strings, API calls, and entropy, without running it. The malware extraction patterns/features could be extracted at the byte level or by converting the binary file into an assembly code using a disassembler such as interactive disassembler (IDA), Radare2, Binary Ninja, OllyDbg, WinDbg, and so on. Once the malware is in assembly format, different features could be extracted, like opcode n-grams, opcode frequency, and strings. Features extracted from the byte level include PE header, strings, and API calls in case the malware uses dynamic linking. Figure 6.5 illustrates the reverse process of converting the binary file into an assembly code using IDA. Static analysis

Figure 6.5 Reverse process using IDA disassembler.

is fast and provides good accuracy, but it has low accuracy with obfuscated malware and relies on domain experts, which could be a long analysis process depending on the complexity of the malware [24].

- Dynamic analysis

  Dynamic analysis or behavior analysis is studying the malware while running it inside an isolated and safe environment like a virtual machine or emulator. The changes made by the malware are captured and analyzed or even used to generate the signature for the malware based on the behavior. The malware could perform changes like process and associated threads, files, network connections, registry, event scheduler, etc. Different tools could be used to monitor and capture the changes, like process monitor, process hacker, Regshot, FakeNet, Cuckoo, emulators, etc. [20]. The benefits of dynamic analysis are to overcome static analysis weaknesses like obfuscated malware. Still their weakness is that malware could identify it as running inside a fake environment and terminate, change, or hide its real behavior. Some techniques used by the malware are monitoring the mouse speed, searching for common registry keys and files, and installing programs for VMware and VirtualBox. Figure 6.6 shows the dynamic process.

  One approach which is used with other studies is by using Cuckoo to capture and monitor the behavior of the malware. Cuckoo is powerful, too, and provides a set of APIs that you define with a Python code to determine which to monitor, like process ID, DLL invocation, network traffic, memory dump, etc. [25]. Some studies used AI top clustering in understanding the invoked DLLs with each malware family. Other studies try to extract signatures for the behavior of the malware based on the DLLs and network traffic. However, Cuckoo sandbox is a powerful tool, but it could be easily escaped by the malware by changing its behavior upon detecting that it is running inside the Cuckoo.

- Hybrid analysis

  The hybrid analysis involves static and dynamic analyses to improve the overall accuracy. First, it scans the malware to look for any signature or any other static analysis procedure; then, it performs the dynamic analysis to look up the malware behaviors. However, the hybrid could improve the accuracy and provide a shortcut when stuck in static analysis by performing dynamic analysis and *vice versa*. It could suffer from its weakness of them [13].

- Memory analysis

  Memory analysis has gained popularity recently due to its accuracy and low false-positive rates. This analysis has the ability to detect obfuscated and

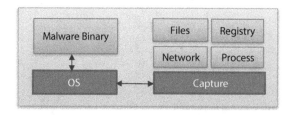

Figure 6.6 Dynamic analysis of malware inside a controlled environment.

Table 6.4 Summary of the malware analysis.

Analysis type	Pros	Cons
Static analysis	- Fast - Safe	- Difficult or unable to detect obfuscated malware - Difficult or unable to detect packed malware - Rely on reverse engineer - Time-consuming
Dynamic analysis	- Identify the obfuscated malware - Identify the packed malware	- Malware escape (can detect that it is running inside an isolated environment) - Time-consuming
Hybrid analysis	- Both from static and dynamic analyses	- Both from static and dynamic analyses
Memory analysis	- Identify the obfuscated malware - Identify the packed malware	- Malware escape (can detect that it is running inside an isolated environment)

unknown malware by looking for a memory region that is used by the malware code. Memory analysis consists of two stages: (1) memory acquisition, which takes an image of the memory with tools like Memdump, Lime, etc., and (2) memory analysis which examines the memory image for threats' persistence using tools like Volatility, etc. The analysis involves examining the process and associated threads, system API calls, kernel hooks, and network. However, this analysis is good by providing a good result in detection, but the authors of malware can add memory acquisition failure to make the memory acquisition fail [24, 25].

Malware detection techniques are required to protect computers and systems from malware by determining whether or not a piece of software or a file contains malware [26, 27]. There are different techniques, including signature-based, heuristic-based, specification-based, and visual-based detections (see Table 6.5).

- Signature-based
  Most antivirus software relies on a signature-based approach to detect malware. This method involves extracting a unique signature from a file that contains malware, and using it to recognize similar files. The antivirus program

Table 6.5 Summary of the malware detection.

Detection type	Pros	Cons

Signature-based	- Fast
	- Safe
	- Capture known
	  malware
		- Difficult or unable to detect
		  obfuscated malware
		- Difficult or unable to detect
		  packed malware

Heuristic-based	- Identify the obfuscated
	  malware
	- Identify the packed
	  malware
		- Use the system resources
		  intensively

Specification-based	- Low false-positive	- High false-negative

thoroughly examines each file and generates its own set of signatures, which are then compared to a database of known malware signatures. This constant monitoring and scanning of network traffic and file contents helps identify files that match any of the signatures in the database. Upon finding such a match, the antivirus program flags the file as a threat and prevents it from executing actions. To keep up with emerging threats, antivirus vendors regularly update their signature databases whenever new malware is discovered. This technique excels at swiftly detecting familiar malware. However, it does have a weakness in that attackers can alter the malware signature, thus evading detection. By changing the malware's signature, antivirus tools become incapable of catching unknown malware that lacks a signature in their database [27, 28].

• Heuristic-based
  Heuristic-based, anomaly-based, or behavior-based detection malware monitors the system's behavior and saves the behavior information into records

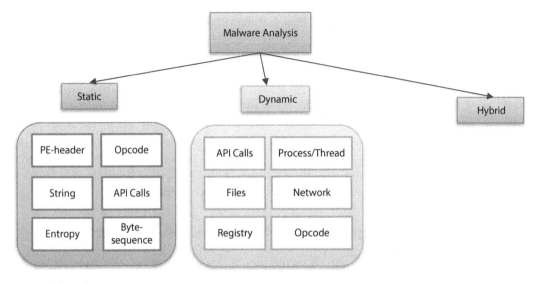

Figure 6.7 Malware analysis hierarchy.

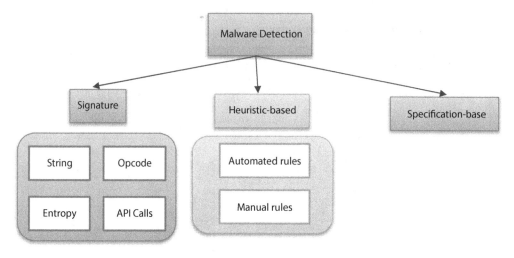

Figure 6.8 Malware detection hierarchy.

to be validated in case of any attack. This detection technique involves three main components: (1) data collection, which collects the data from the system, (2) interpretation algorithm, which interprets and converts the data from the data collections, and (3) matching algorithm, which matches the behavior signature with the converted data. The benefits of this technique are the ability to detect known and unknown malware. In contrast, the disadvantage is using system resources intensively, CPU and RAM, in addition to a high false-positive rate [27].

- Specification-based
  Specification-based detection malware looks for the applications' specification and determines if the application runs normally or otherwise. This technique deviates from heuristic-based detection, and the difference between them is that heuristic-based detection uses ML to determine the legitimate application. In contrast, the specification examines the behaviors stated in the application specification. It also differs from heuristic-based detection because it has lower false-positive and high false-negative rates.

Malware analysis and detection are correlated, and the outcome of the analysis process could be used in malware detection. Several methods have been introduced to detect malware; however, the most effective today is by using AI techniques. The following is the structure hierarchy of malware analysis and malware detection. The detection of the malware could use combined different features to effectively detect the malware and lower the positive rate as the malware develops and mature; hence, it requires a good detection mechanism that is able to detect and stop the malware from spreading. The following figures (Figures 6.7 and 6.8) show the malware analysis and detection techniques.

6.5   Malware Techniques to Evade Analysis and Detection

Malware authors employ a variety of techniques to avoid detection. Obfuscation, static anti-analysis, and dynamic anti-analysis are all techniques. The process of making something difficult or meaningless is referred to as obfuscation. It was initially designed to protect intellectual property by making reverse engineering difficult. Businesses or developers can use this strategy to protect their products from being reverse-engineered and to be aware of how the software or product is made. This technique is used in the creation of malware in order to avoid detection. However, malware authors can use obfuscation techniques to convert a malware code into a new distinct version while retaining its normal functionality.

- Dead code insertion
  Dead code is a code that has been inserted but has no impact on the program's functionality, like inserting a series of *NOP* meaningless instructions or unreachable instructions. The inserted code may confuse the analysis step and trick the signature-based detection [29, 30].
  1. NOP instruction stands for no operation, and it is a one-byte instruction that does nothing in the assembly code. The NOP could be used when the code needs to be patched or when dealing with memory issues. In the context of malware, this instruction could be inserted randomly in different parts of the code, having no effect on the functionality but allowing the malware to avoid detection by producing a new signature. Table 6.6 shows an example of inserting NOPs.
  2. Unreachable instructions by using conditional jump, and the condition will never happen—in other words, unreachable code (see Table 6.7).

Table 6.6 An example of inserting a series of NOP.

Before	After

```mov eax, 0x0A```
```mov ebx, eax```
```   xor ecx, ecx```
	```nop```
	```mov eax, 0x04```
	```nop```
	```mov ebx, eax```
	```xor ecx, ecx```
	``` nop```

Table 6.7 An example of unreachable instructions.

Before	After

```xor eax, eax```
```xor ebx, ebx```
```mov eax, 0x0A```
```mov ebx, 0x0B```
```add eax, ebx```
	```xor eax, eax```
	```xor ebx, ebx```
	```mov eax, 0x0A```
	```mov ebx, 0x0B```
	```cmp ecx, ebx```
	```jne reachable```
	```mov ecx, ebx```
	```add ebx, 0x0C```
	```reachable:```
	``` add eax, ebx```

Table 6.8 An example of instruction reordering.

Before	After
`xor eax, eax`	`xor ebx, ebx`
`xor ebx, ebx`	`xor eax, eax`
`mov eax, 0x0A`	`mov ebx, 0xB`
`mov ebx, 0xB`	`mov eax, 0x0A`
`add eax, ebx`	`add eax, ebx`

Table 6.9 An example of register reassignment.

Before	After
`xor eax, eax`	`xor ecx, ecx`
`xor ebx, ebx`	`xor edx, edx`
`mov eax, 0x0A`	`mov ecx, 0x0A`
`mov ebx, 0xB`	`mov edx, 0xB`
`add eax, ebx`	`add ecx, edx`

3. Meaningless instructions by canceling their effects like add ebx, 0xA, then sub ebx, 0xA; another example: inc ecx then dec ecx. The output of these instructions has no effect on the registers.

- Instruction reordering
  Changing the order of the instructions in which it does not affect the execution or change the behavior. Changing the instruction sequence may be useful with the detection techniques which rely on the instructions' orders (see Table 6.8).
- Register reassignment
  Register reassignment or register renaming is a technique that changes the register assignment by using unused registers and replacing them (see Table 6.9).

In addition to those mentioned above, there are subroutine reordering, XOR encryption, base64 encoding, string obfuscation, code format, etc. [27]. The anti-dynamic methods include detecting debuggers and virtual environments. Once the malware detects that it runs inside a fake or isolated environment, it terminates, hides, or changes its behavior to appear like a legitimate program. The code packer is another technique that is used to compress the source code to make it smaller. In order to execute the program, you need to unpack the code (examples of packers are XPS, UPACK, etc.). The intended usage of the packer is to minimize the size of the executable by using compression algorithms.

6.6   Malware Detection With Applying AI

"A major thrust in algorithmic development is the design of algorithmic models to solve increasingly complex problems. The term intelligence means the ability to comprehend to understand from experience." [31].

Artificial intelligence "is the study of intelligent agents, any device that perceives its environment and takes actions that maximize its chance of success at some goal." This happens by making the machines able to solve problems and provide a high level of reasoning and decision-making rather than only automating the tasks. AI intends to allow the machine to mimic the human brain by learning, solving complex problems, and making decisions. AI applications are increasing more and more common, from decision-making to auto pilot, self-driving cars, robots, medical assistants, etc. [32].

Machine learning is a subset of AI; it is a set of algorithms that allow machines to learn on their own by providing data, and they can figure out and identify patterns in the data. There were two types of machine learning: (1) supervised learning and (2) unsupervised learning. Supervised learning includes a dataset with labels, which allows the algorithm to train from the label in the training dataset and then predict the correct label in the test dataset; classification and regression are examples of supervised learning. Classification tasks include supplying a set of images and having the model predict what the correct image label is, whereas regression tasks include predicting the house price. Unsupervised learning happens by providing dataset without labels and grouping the dataset into groups or clusters based on the similarity between the datasets. An example of unsupervised learning is clustering human faces. Some of the famous classifications in ML are decision tree, K-nearest neighbor (KNN), support vector machine (SVM), random forest, etc.

Deep learning is a subset of ML that mimics the human brain cell mechanism by providing layers of neurons or nodes connected with each other to map the input to the output. The more hidden layers are inserted between the input and the output, the more complex the model and the more training time. Each neuron in the hidden layer has an activation function, which is responsible for triggering or firing the neuron or not, depending on the incoming weight or strength. There are multiple activation functions that exist, like linear activation functions and non-linear activation functions (Sigmoid, SoftMax, ReLU, PReLU, Tanh, etc.). An example of DL is convolution neural networks (CNN), which trains with a dataset of labeled images and predicts the label of the images, like VGG16, VGG19, ResNet-50, Inception V3, etc. [33–36].

As previously stated, the number of new malware is increasing every day, and providing a valid and accurate solution capable of dealing with large amounts of malware is required to protect computer systems. ML and DL offer a good solution for dealing with many malware samples while maintaining high accuracy (Figure 6.9). Different features could be used with

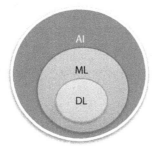

Figure 6.9 Difference between AI, ML, and DL.

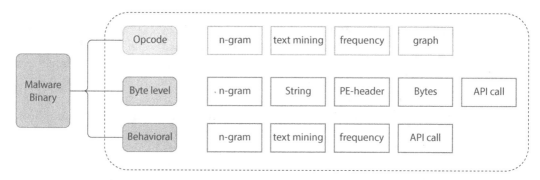

Figure 6.10 Different features of extraction form static or dynamic malware.

ML (Figure 6.10), such as opcode n-gram, opcode frequency, byte plot, PE header, behavior logs, etc. Security researchers use different features and models to improve security solutions with valid and more accurate AI models. As the feature is important, we will discuss them to connect the components. The feature could be based on opcode (like n-gram, text mining, opcode frequency, graph-based, and word-embedded) or byte level (byte n-grams, strings, PE headers, and API calls). These features could be represented as numeric vectors or image-based and then passed to the model (see Table 6.10). Figure 6.11 shows as summary of the feature engineering steps.

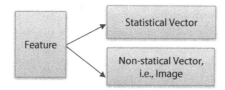

Figure 6.11 Feature representation.

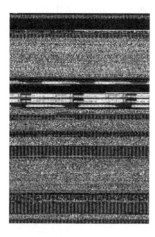

Figure 6.12 Malware binary image.

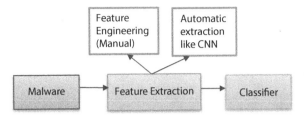

Figure 6.13 General architecture of AI malware detection.

Once the features are extracted, they can pass to the ML or DL classifier to classify and detect the malware—for example, a feature of the opcode frequency vector is passed to the SVM to classify the executable file into malware or benign. Another example is using the n-gram of the opcode with KNN. One of the improvements to using DL models in detecting malware is using visual image representation of the features with CNN [33–36], which is used to extract features from the image and then pass to the activation function of the output layer. Image malware is a popular topic in security research due to its accuracy and ability to determine unknown or obfuscated malware. It uses the byte level of the malware file and converts it to an image by grouping every byte, converting it to a corresponding value between 0 and 255, constructing the image pixel by pixel, and passing the generated images into the CNN to extract features and classify the malware. The visual image intends that any changes in the byte code will be reflected in the generated images. Figure 6.12 illustrates the visual image representation of the malware binary. Figure 6.13 represents the general architecture of developing ML and DL models for malware detection.

The following Table 6.10 summarizes the feature extraction and classifier techniques which are used in different studies. The term of the vector is intentionally mentioned as

Table 6.10 Summary of feature representation, extraction, and classification.

Feature representation	Image (2D vector)	Vector (1D)
Feature extraction	- CNN - SURF - SIFT - GIST - GLCM - Local binary pattern - Gabor descriptor	- Statistical (opcode)
Classifier	- SoftMax or any activation function - KNN - SVM - Decision tree - Random forest - XGBoost	- SoftMax or any activation function - KNN - SVM - Decision tree - Random forest - XGBoost

Table 6.11 Summary of AI studies for malware detection.

Method	AI type	Feature	Feature extraction	Classifier
Nataraj *et al.* [37]	ML	Byte plot image	GIST	KNN
LMP-KNN [38]	ML	Byte plot image	Local binary pattern	KNN
IMCEC [39]	DL	Byte plot image	Fine-tuned VGG16, ResNet-50	SoftMax
DTMIC [40]	DL	Byte plot image	Fine-tuned VGG16	SoftMax
MTL [41]	DL	Byte plot image	Custom CNN	PReLU
Opcode frequency + SVM [42]	ML	Opcode frequency	Disassembler + instruction counter	SVM, decision tree, boost, random forest
Opcode + transformer [43]	NLP + ML	Opcode	Disassembler	KNN + SVM
Opcode + SVM [44]	ML	Opcode	Disassembler	SVM

image because we mean that the vector could be opcode frequency while the image is a 2D grayscale image.

The following Table 6.11 summarizes the AI studies to detect malware by applying different features, feature extractions, and classifiers.

6.7   Open Issues and Challenges

Malware detection continues to be improved, but a gap between the detection solution and state-of-the-art malware is presented in the following open issues and challenges which needed to be investigated. The old solution of detecting malware has become less effective and makes it easy to escape the malware. These are the open issues and challenges which should be taken into consideration in future studies when designing a solution for detection.

- Cross-Operating System Detection
  Developing a model capable of detecting different malware formats which target different operating systems like Linux, Windows, MacOS, Android, and iOS is needed to provide good flexibility and apply the technique with different malware formats. The majority of the study models handle Windows

malware (such that Windows is the most malware-targeted system), and fewer studies target cross-platforms. The reason for this is to apply the detection technique with different OS and boost the model.

- Zero-Day Vulnerability
  Zero-day malware is dangerous, and until now there is no effective solution for them as they exploit unknown vulnerabilities. ML and DL could improve, handle, or minimize the risk by applying appropriate feature engineering or combining different techniques to overcome the whole gap between detection and zero-day malware.
- Dataset
  Different studies use different datasets, which makes it difficult to assist the superiority of the models. A balanced dataset is recommended between the malware and benign. Some studies take an old dataset and ignore the new malware samples, while others depend on the new malware samples and ignore the older malware samples. A balanced dataset with old and new malware and benign samples is recommended in order to train and evaluate the AI model effectively and accurately [45].
- Packers
  Packed malware is hard to detect unless it is unpacked by dynamic analysis. An AI model that is able to detect the packed malware will be helpful in the area of malware detection. There are lots of packers that are open-source and close-source; each has its own code, and evading the packer step will be a good step in detecting the malware [46–49].

6.8 Discussion and Conclusion

This chapter has presented information on the current technical status of malware, including malware analysis techniques, detection approaches, techniques to evade analysis and detection, and the era of AI with malware. The exponential growth of malware daily and year after year makes handling significantly tricky for traditional methods. Hence, ML and DL help in detecting malware effectively. However, a balanced dataset is essential to train a good model which provides real accuracy in the real world. While these models do not apply to real-life solutions, we do not have a measurement to evaluate the model's accuracy in real solutions. We recommend using a hybrid model which uses a different set of features and implements client–server architecture. Using a different set of features can be a good improvement to the model's accuracy. Another recommendation is to use an ensemble network which improves the overall accuracy.

Since malware threats are increasing, much new malware necessitates the development of a new technique for fast detection and detection in less time. As demonstrated in this chapter, traditional anti-malware software is increasingly incapable of detecting unknown malware. As a result, the use of ML and DL in malware detection, which can handle the challenges posed by massive amounts of imbalanced network data and malware mutations, has recently gained popularity. This is because it is more accurate and takes less time to detect. Future research that analytically examines available malware detection techniques is recommended to help advance cybersecurity ahead of malware's emergence.

References

1. Malwarebytes, Malware. Available online: https://www.malwarebytes.com/malware, last accessed 2022.
2. Norton Labs. Available online: https://www.nortonlifelock.com/blogs/norton-labs/july-2021-consumer-cyber-safety-pulse-report, last accessed 2021.
3. Kaspersky. Available online: https://www.kaspersky.com/about/press releases/2022_cyber-criminals-attack-users-with-400000-new-malicious-files-daily—that-is-5-more-than-in-2021.
4. Meterpreter. Available online: https://meterpreter.org/in-2031-global-losses-caused-by-ransomware-will-exceed-265-billion.
5. Kaspersky. Available online: https://media.kaspersky.com/pdf/it-risks-survey-report-cost-of-security-breaches.pdf.
6. Landage, J. and Wankhade, M.P., Malware and malware detection techniques: A survey. *Int. J. Eng. Res.*, 2, 12, 61–68, 2013.
7. Sihwail, R., Omar, K., Ariffin, K.Z., A survey on malware analysis techniques: Static, dynamic, hybrid and memory analysis. *Int. J. Adv. Sci. Eng. Inf. Technol.*, 8, 4-2, 1662–1671, 2018.
8. Malwarebytes. Available online: https://www.malwarebytes.com/trickbothttps://www.malwarebytes.com/trickbot.
9. Zolkipli, M.F. and Jantan, A., An approach for malware behavior identification and classification, in: *2011 3rd International Conference on Computer Research and Development*, vol. 1, pp. 191–194, IEEE, 2011, March.
10. Ec-council. Available online: https://codered.eccouncil.org/courseVideo/malware-analysis-fundamentals.
11. Cisco. Available online: https://www.cisco.com/c/en/us/products/security/what-is-a-worm.html#~is-a-worm-a-virus.
12. Razaque, A., Amsaad, F., Hariri, S., Almasri, M., Rizvi, S.S., Frej, M.B.H., Enhanced grey risk assessment model for support of cloud service provider. *IEEE Access*, 8, 80812–80826, 2020.
13. Webb, J., Ahmad, A., Maynard, S.B., Shanks, G., A situation awareness model for information security risk management. *Comput. & Secur.*, 44, 1–15, 2014.
14. Zimba, A., Wang, Z., Mulenga, M., Odongo, N.H., Crypto mining attacks in information systems: An emerging threat to cyber security. *J. Comput. Inf. Syst.*, 60, 4, 297–308, 2020.
15. Norton, What is adware. Available: https://us.norton.com/internetsecurity-emerging-threats-what-is-grayware-adware-and-madware.html.
16. Kleymenov, A. and Thabet, A., *Mastering malware analysis: The complete malware d and IoT attacks*, Packt Publishing Ltd, Birmingham B3 2PB, United Kingdom, 2022.
17. Microsoft. Available online: https://learn.microsoft.com/en-us/windows/win32/debug/pe-format
18. Wang, T.Y., Wu, C.H., Hsieh, C.C., Detecting unknown malicious executables using portable executable headers, in: *2009 Fifth International Joint Conference on INC, IMS and IDC*, pp. 278–284, IEEE, 2009, August.
19. Linuxhint. Available online: https://linuxhint.com/understanding_elf_file_format.
20. Kalysch, A., *Android Application Hardening: Attack Surface Reduction and IP Protection Mechanisms*, Friedrich-Alexander-Universitaet, Erlangen-Nuernberg (Germany), 2020.
21. Seneviratne, S., Shariffdeen, R., Rasnayaka, S., Kasthuriarachchi, N., Self-supervised vision transformers for malware detection. *IEEE Access*, 10, 103121–103135, 2022.

22. Developer android. Available online: https://developer.android.com/guide/topics/manifest/manifest-intro.

23. Oo, W.K.K., Koide, H., Sakurai, K., Analyzing the effect of moving target defense for a web system. *Int. J. Networking Comput.*, 9, 2, 188–200, 2019.

24. Bhatt, M.S., Patel, H., Kariya, S., A survey permission based mobile malware detection. *Int. J. Comput. Technol. Appl.*, 6, 852–856, 2015.

25. Menezes, F.S., Jancy, F., Baji, H.S., Malware detection and analysis. *IJAsRSCT*, 2, 2581–9429, 2022.

26. Talukder, S., Tools and techniques for malware detection and analysis. arXiv preprint, pp. 2002.06819, 2020.

27. Saeed, I.A., Selamat, A., Abuagoub, A.M., A survey on malware and malware detection systems. *Int. J. Comput. Appl.*, 67, 16, 2013.

28. Tahir, R., A study on malware and malware detection techniques. *Int. J. Educ. Manag. Eng.*, 8, 2, 20, 2018.

29. Brezinski, K. and Ferens, K., Metamorphic malware and obfuscation -a survey of techniques. *Variants Gen. Kits*, 2021.

30. Techopedia. Available online: https://www.techopedia.com/definition/11989/no-operation-nop.

31. Engelbrecht, A.P., *Computational intelligence: An introduction*, John Wiley & Sons, 2007.

32. Ongsulee, P., Artificial intelligence, machine learning and deep learning, in: *2017 15th International Conference on ICT and Knowledge Engineering (ICT&KE)*, pp. 1–6, IEEE, 2017, November.

33. Jogin, M., Madhulika, M.S., Divya, G.D., Meghana, R.K., Apoorva, S., Feature extraction using convolution neural networks (CNN) and deep learning, in: *2018 3rd IEEE International Conference on Recent Trends in Electronics, Information & Communication Technology (RTEICT)*, pp. 2319–2323, IEEE, 2018, May.

34. Tekerek, A. and Yapici, M.M., A novel malware classification and augmentation model based on convolutional neural network. *Comput. & Secur.*, 112, 102515, 2022.

35. Zhuang, F., Qi, Z., Duan, K., Xi, D., Zhu, Y., Zhu, H., He, Q., A comprehensive survey on transfer learning. *Proc. IEEE*, 109, 1, 43–76, 2020.

36. Tammina, S., Transfer learning using vgg-16 with deep convolutional neural network for classifying images. *Int. J. Sci. Res. Publications (IJSRP)*, 9, 10, 143–150, 2019.

37. Nataraj, L., Karthikeyan, S., Jacob, G., Manjunath, B.S., alware images: Visualization and automatic classification, in: *Proceedings of the 8th International Symposium on Visualization for Cyber Security*, pp. 1–7, 2011, July.

38. Hashemi, H. and Hamzeh, A., Visual malware detection using local malicious pattern. *J. Comput. Virol. Hacking Techniques*, 15, 1–14, 2019.

39. Vasan, D., Alazab, M., Wassan, S., Safaei, B., Zheng, Q., Image-based malware classification using ensemble of CNN architectures (IMCEC). *Comput. & Secur.*, 92, 101748, 2020.

40. Kumar, S. and Janet, B., DTMIC: Deep transfer learning for malware image classification. *J. Inf. Secur. Appl.*, 64, 103063, 2022.

41. Bensaoud, A. and Kalita, J., Deep multi-task learning for malware image classification. *J. Inf. Secur. Appl.*, 64, 103057, 2022.

42. Yewale, A. and Singh, M., Malware detection based on opcode frequency, in: *2016 International Conference on Advanced Communication Control and Computing Technologies (ICACCCT)*, pp. 646–649, IEEE, 2016, May.

43. Kale, A.S., Pandya, V., Di Troia, F., Stamp, M., Malware classification with Word2Vec, HMM2Vec, BERT, and ELMo. *J. Comput. Virol. Hacking Techniques*, 19, 1–16, 2022.

44. Manavi, F. and Hamzeh, A., A new method for malware detection using opcode visualization, in: *2017 Artificial Intelligence and Signal Processing Conference (AISP)*, 96–102, IEEE, 2017, October.

45. Aboaoja, F.A., Zainal, A., Ghaleb, F.A., Al-rimy, B.A.S., Eisa, T.A.E., Elnour, A.A.H., Malware detection issues, challenges, and future directions: A survey. *Appl. Sci.*, 12, 17, 8482, 2022.

46. Yan, W., Zhang, Z., Ansari, N., Revealing packed malware. *IEEE Secur. & PrivaCy*, 6, 5, 65–69, 2008.

47. O'Kane, P., Sezer, S., McLaughlin, K., Obfuscation: The hidden malware. *IEEE Secur. & Privacy*, 9, 41–47, 2011.

48. Li, X., Shan, Z., Liu, F., Chen, Y., Hou, Y., A consistently-executing graph-based approach for malware packer identification. *IEEE Access*, 7, 51620–51629, 2019.

49. Mohanta, A. and Saldanha, A., *Malware analysis and detection engineering: A comprehensive approach to detect and analyze modern malware*, Apress, New York, NY, USA, 2020.

7

Early Detection of Darknet Traffic in Internet of Things Applications

Ambika N.

St. Francis College, Department of Computer Science & Applications, Bangalore, India

Abstract

A darknet IDS system that employs supervised machine learning identifies common Internet of Things (IoT) cyber attacks' darknet activities in the work. Using a pipeline of pre-processing stages that begin with the data accumulation process, characteristic commerce is the choice, management, and alteration of fresh information into properties. These are fed into the machine learning procedures for further computation, exercise, authentication, and forecast. The CSV version of the CIC-DarkNet-2020 database is initially available. The platform developed by MATLAB processes it. It gains a deeper understanding of the dataset using exploratory data analysis and performs essential data curation tasks. By envisaging the info sessions' histograms to obtain additional visions into the categories and characteristics, this procedure finishes an initial improvement procedure of the database by validating for misplaced facts and obtaining appropriate substitutions for the missing records. The CIC-DarkNet-2020 dataset's most influential features are extracted using the coefficient score method to find the best features for exercise and confirm the knowledge representations later. Detail points are rescaled using normalization to maintain the same range and significance. The process of transforming unconditional statistics into arithmetic facts that machine learning techniques can process is known as label encoding. By haphazardly reorganising information from a database, the shambling procedure is a pre-processing procedure carried out over the knowledge examples. It produces a novel planning for the database that can be used securely for machine learning evaluation and exercise without the classifier being prejudiced toward any of the primary courses. It carried out a k-fold cross-endorsement procedure with five distinct folds. The suggestion cuts down the steps by speeding the process by 24%. It uses a sample dataset collected from various sources. This dataset consists of a set mapping the intention of the malicious content to its behavior. This dataset is mapped to draw out the outcome of the collected darknet dataset.

Keywords: Darknet, cyber attack, speed, intrusion detection, traffic analysis

7.1 Introduction

Society has become digital through online communication, socialization, education, and business. There are numerous attacks on the darknet. One-third of the world's Internet is

---

Email: ambika.nagaraj76@gmail.com; ORCID: 0000-0003-4452-5514

Amit Kumar Tyagi (ed.) Automated Secure Computing for Next-Generation Systems, (139–154) © 2024 Scrivener Publishing LLC

used by darknet projects, which monitor various cyber threat [1] activities. Traffic that targets advertised but unoccupied IP addresses is referred to as darknet [2] data. Since these network addresses have never been used, they characterize a brand-novel server that have never exchanged messages with other gadgets for malicious or legitimate reasons. Through these unused IP addresses, these darknet-based surveillance organizations are intended to entice or trick assailants for intellect assembly. A darknet [3] is an excellent way to conclude numerous web-scale penetrating actions. Figure 7.1 represents the same.

The darknet is a subdivision of the deep net. It accesses only programs like the Tor browser, but search engines cannot detect it. Tor allows clients to conceal their identities by routing the traffic of the systems. It cannot trace it back to the users who sent it. Tor has set up "relays" on computers to reposition information from one tier to another as it travels through its underpasses worldwide. Between the relays, the encoded data is kept. After passing through three relays, Tor traffic is routed to its final destination. While sustaining perfect ahead secretiveness among the devices and Tor's confidential assistance, this mechanism frequently communicates via consensus (Tor nodes) managed by volunteers worldwide. It mimics the regular gridlock of the hypertext transfer algorithm safety procedure, making it extremely difficult for even encountered web creators or critics to detect Tor channels. Statistically analyzing and identifying differences in the safe Sockets tier algorithm is one effective strategy for detecting Tor traffic. SSL encrypts data with both symmetric and public keys. Every SSL connection begins with the host and user exchanging messages until a protected association is established. It uses public-key encryption, and the server can confirm its individualism to the customer through a handshake. The client and server can then collaborate to make a symmetric credential used to encode and decrypt the facts they exchange quickly. It uses an arbitrary algorithmically developed discipline that alters approximately every 3 min, and the customer causes a self-signed SSL. As a result, Tor sessions on cyberspace combined with HTTPS traffic can be identified by a statistical analysis of network traffic based on the particulars and attributes of SSL.

The method [5] is semiautomated. It combines human domain expertise with various information collection and analysis forms. The approach uses knowledge origins, accumulation processes, filtering, and examination to help mortal researchers obtain dark web cleverness [6, 7]. Many online services for terrorism-related information make up information sources. Some of these are easy to find. Computerized search, browsing, and harvesting

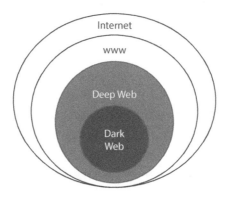

Figure 7.1 The association between cyberspace, deep net, and dark web [4].

details from recognized authorities are made conceivable by collection methods. Sifting through the data collected and removing results that are not relevant are done when filtering, but this requires knowledge of both the domain and the language. Data analysis aids in identifying trends and validating hypotheses by providing insights into the data.

It gathered the study's data [8] in two stages. For a month, we gathered as many hidden service addresses as possible as the first step. Link-Grabber, a Python-based specialized web crawler, was used to accomplish this. It used the SOCKS proxy to connect the crawler to the Internet via the Tor network. After it had gathered these onion addresses, we used Content-Grabber, a different customized crawler. The opening page markup (HTML) of each hidden service that this crawler discovered was downloaded and stored locally. It is helpful to identify content hosted by secret services to ascertain the characteristics of the dark cyberspace. Examining the content of each hidden service and classifying that information are part of this classification. It discovered hidden services that did not fit into any particular category during the classification process, so it removed them.

An extensive, heterogeneous text corpus from the d2web is analyzed in the recommendation [9] using Latent Dirichlet Allocation (LDA). The Beta Process HMM (BP-HMM) is a hidden Markov model that is not parametric. Every forum is characterized by a multivariate period sequence using a BP-HMM and the topics discovered by LDA as variables. The general conditions between platforms, where each state is distributed over themes, are then found using this BP-HMM. It makes it easier to keep track of discussions in various forums and find unusual behavior or significant events. It can also use this strategy to locate mediums applicable to a particular topic, i.e., environments or epochs within settings where clients converse about complex subjects, such as hacking strategies and cybersecurity-linked problems. It also organizes conferences into meaningful groups using this method. It used posts on 80 D2web forums covering exploits and hacking techniques, marketing pharmaceutical and non-prescription medications, and constructing bogus IDs to test this framework.

TrafficAnalysis Profile feature vectors [10] of 27 dimensions are created from the grid containers shipped from a sub-area to a darknet. Following that, a hierarchical grouping procedure is carried out to generate collections for distinct hostile manners. During the surveillance stage, a subnet's malevolent movements are analyzed from the nearest TAP characteristic bunch. After that, these TAP feature clusters are displayed in real time on the suggested monitoring method for each subnet. It uses the darknet pack dataset gathered by the National Institute of Information and Communications Technology in Tokyo, Japan, from February 1 through February 28, 2014. The darknet packets collected by the utilized darknet sensor had a total of 303,733,994 IP addresses. In the experiments, the sub-web disguise is considered to be /16 for convenience's sake; the proposed system simultaneously monitors 65,536 subnets.

There are three main parts to the transmission knowledge-based cross-lingual Internet danger discovery outline [11]. It includes cross-lingual cyber risk finding and assessment, bilingual testbed generation, and data collection and preparation Deepdotweb.com was the basis for identifying seven English DNMs and one Russian DNM. Each DNM was traversed by a web spider that avoided anti-crawling measures to extract all product descriptions. In an interactive dataset, 95,095 invention explanations were gathered and analyzed. It arbitrarily tested the creation detailing in each linguistic by conserving the proportion of web to non-Internet products. It found 2,373 creation schedules, counting 1,821 English and 552

Russian products. The resulting BiLSTM can be collective among two systems exercise in a diverse linguistic to detention the hidden states common to both languages. A monolingual architecture features joint learning of a common representation from two English classification tasks, which inspires the approach. It created CL-LSTM to detect Russian cyber threats. This architecture consists of three layers. In step 1, two linguistic-specific LSTM sheets interpret the standard representation for threat detection in Russian and English separately. A language-independent shared BiLSTM layer also simultaneously captures the English and Russian terms. Step 2 involves feeding language-specific layers the concealed condition vectors generated by the communal tier at each period phase. In step 3, each language's lesson tags for the goods is forecast separately.

It [12] made use of the most recent dataset that Matsushita had provided. There was a total of 30 recordings used in the experiment. The dataset is set up to choose the details from the start, central, and finish for each image. The text of those data was excluded from the importance of the other knowledge. It made three different images that were different from one another because of their backgrounds. For each stage, there are 1,005 images with induced dopamine release. The first partitioning technique was used on the image's y-axis from pixel 320 to 520, consequential in an 875×200-pixel image. Patch extraction methods extract 200×200 patches from the common release area manually and automatically. A publication highest location used to eliminate physical reinforcements is included in the dataset and designated as the core of the image. It used the MATLAB image processing objects' Image Data-Store component to import the collected images. It used Image Resizing and JPG image extension during the pre-processing phase to reduce each appearance to $256 \times 256 \times 3$. Target encoding uses binary to encode the two categories. At each training epoch, a shuffling operation is used to achieve a stochastic re-circulation of the copies' database to guarantee an equitable distribution of the image categories. It uses a variety of twin processes, such as accidental duplicate distorting, harvesting, shade transformation, artificial sound, and fake fuzziness, for data enhancement and database expansion. It uses the k-fold cross-authentication mechanism, and database allocation divides the knowledge set into drill and challenging datasets. It can use the darknet network to train and validate the resulting pre-processed images.

The previous research's [13] intention was to advance a darknet intrusion detection system that uses supervised machine learning to identify the darknet activities of common IoT cyber attacks. Characteristic business is the assortment, management, and alteration of fresh information into characteristics that can be input into engine-learning procedure for supplementary calibration, drill, authentication, and forecast. It is done through a pipeline of pre-processing stages that begin with the data accumulation process. The CIC-DarkNet-2020 database CSV version is initially available. It is processed by the platform that MATLAB developed. It uses exploratory data analysis to increase a profounder thoughtful of the database and performs essential data curation tasks. This procedure finishes an initial augmentation of the dataset by examination for lost details and giving appropriate replacements for the missing records by visualizing the dataset classes' histograms to gain additional insight into the categories and structures. The coefficient score method is used to extract the essential elements from the CIC-DarkNet-2020 dataset so that it can use the best features later to train and validate learning models. Normalization is used to rescale data points so that the range and the significance stay the same. Label encoding converts categorical data into numerical data that machine learning methods can process.

The shuffling process is a pre-processing step that takes place over a dataset's rows (samples) and involves rearranging data from that dataset at random. It creates a novel arrangement for the dataset that is safe for machine learning examination and exercise without causing the classifier to be biased toward any primary programs. It used five distinct folds in the k-fold cross-authentication process.

The suggestion cuts down the steps by speeding the process by 24%. It uses a sample dataset collected from various sources. This dataset consists of set mapping the intention of the malicious content to its behavior. This dataset is mapped to draw out the outcome of the collected darknet dataset.

The work is separated into six parts. Literature review trails the overview section. The proposal is elaborated in Section 7.3. The work is analyzed in Section 7.4. Section 7.5 briefs the future work. The work is concluded in Section 7.6.

7.2   Literature Survey

An operational system [14] for gathering web danger astuteness from numerous communal podia on the Internet, particularly darknet and deep net sites, is the aim of this work. It makes use of both supervised and semi-supervised approaches. The well-recognized organization methods Naive Bayes, random forest, support vector machine, and logistic regression are all examples of the administered methods. It uses expert-labeled datasets and machine learning to identify appropriate goods and themes from marketplaces and opportunities. It considers 10 markets for our learning model's training and testing. The research found 16 zero-day exploits in the market data over 4 weeks. Zero-day achievements make usage of exposures that the retailer is ignorant of. A vulnerability in Android devices' web page rendering is affected by the Android WebView zero-day. Devices with Android 4.3 Jelly Bean or earlier operating systems are affected. A reinforcement was unconfined in Android KitKat 4.4 and Lollipop 5.0 following the initial posting of this zero-day, requiring devices to upgrade their operating systems.

Worms, DOS attacks, backdoors, DDoS attacks, RDoS attacks, spam, and malicious content are all detected by the proposed work [15]. TF-IDF is used with a light gradient-enhanced engine knowledge procedure to produce the concluding characteristic of administered info after a darknet stream of traffic information is collected from authoritative data sources and cleaned and pre-processed using data mining methods. Using a credential and hash price created by the TOR directory with communication nodes, the data travels from the browser to the dark web router, concealing its identity and rendering it anonymous. It traces host-generating dark web crime and malicious behavior. The gridlock details are examined. It is valuable data, and the designs are investigated for supplementary enterprise growth. Pre-processing, attribute removal, collection, and arrangement are the phases. Knowledge pre-processing is the chief step in transforming formless details into structured data. In vector interstellar prototypical text and text mining, the frequently used weighting technique for analyzing features is TF-IDF. Quantifying a word's significance across the entire corpus is a solid strategy. It eliminates a tendency toward lengthy documents. The term frequency is only determined concerning the many times that a term seems to occur in the document. It is typically standardized in a particular quadrant between 0 and 1. Accentuation is removed from all text during tokenization to build the

TF-IDF list of terms. The first two letters of the term frequency indicate its significance if it occurs more frequently in a document. The additional evaluation established that when the period is significant in specific credentials, the TF becomes higher. The entire preparation dataset is used to evaluate the weighted value.

DeepImage [16] is a novel method that employs characteristic assortment to select the essential structures in a gray picture before feeding it to a two-dimensional convolutional neuronic system to identify a darknet gridlock. The datasets ISCXVPN2016 and ISCXTor2017 are utilized. The darknet dataset combined these datasets to create a brand-new traffic dataset with two layers. The darknet database's first layer is usually designated for presenting a steady traffic. The next tier is the darknet representing anonymized traffic about the darknet's hidden services. For labeling at the second layer, it divided the streaming traffic into eight categories based on audio and video. There is a total of 158,659 records in the darknet dataset. There are 24,311 darknet samples and 134,348 benign samples. Audio-streaming has the most samples in this dataset at 13,284, while the P2P protocol has the fewest instances. When choosing the finest attribute to notice and illustrate darknet circulation, feature extraction plays a crucial role. It involves two steps: pre-processing—a labeled darknet dataset to recognize goal tags and extract characteristics. It utilizes an additional trees classifier to rank features, selecting the attribute collection with the uppermost position standards by sorting them in descending order of importance for each node in the forest of trees. CICFlowMeter is employed to obtain 80 web traffic features from the database during the data pre-processing phase. Target labels are given to all activity traffic recorded in the dataset to create a feature vector. Before going on to the ensemble model, the selected features are used in the following step to create a two-dimensional image vector and mathematically encrypt destined tags. Utilizing Scikit-Learn, it implemented the proposed system in Python with Keras and TensorFlow. Experiments are carried out on the Ubuntu server with 50 CPUs and 500 GB of RAM.

The proposed approach [17] uses an Internet crawler and other alike dark web information gathering tools to collect datasets. The wok utilized a profitable instrument, Sixgill, for this experiment. It used critical posts as accurate knowledge and non-critical posts as improper knowledge after assembling the forwarding information. It did it physically. As pre-processing steps, it carried out expression tokenization, noise elimination, standardization, curtailing, and stop word calibration. The process of separating individual words is known as word tokenization. The term "noise removal" refers to eliminating pointless typescripts from the text, such as parentheses and numbers. Engine education is carried out based on the attribute content that have been obtained through the use of doc2vec and natural language processing. The learning phase of machine learning produces a prototypical text, and the assessment stage assesses the model's performance. doc2vec's feature values are learned and used to create a model during the learning stage with training statistics. The model's operation is evaluated using evaluation data during the evaluation phase. The data are separated into evaluation and training data to measure the model's generalization performance for unseen data. Anonymous data from the dark web are added to the model after the generalization performance is guaranteed.

The work [18] discusses the problems with getting information from the dark web for web safety astuteness resolutions. The theoretical prototypical of the acumen sequence serves as a vital source of inspiration for the phases of the process. BlackWidow plans to examine the text of these environments once it has established a foothold to automate the acquisition of additional relations and talks to other goals in subsequent iterations. All stages are completely automated after the planning and requirements stage. The raw data collection and anonymous forum access are the focus of the collection phase over Tor. Using Docker containers, Tor to admittance concealed facilities, and VPNs for standard deep web sites creates anonymous gateways to the identified forums. It used the node.js headless Chrome browser puppeteer as a crawler within the Docker vessels to collect the forum content and metadata. The processing phase involves:

- interpreting the text into English,
- parsing the collected raw HTML data, and
- removing the objects of attention sto input into an information chart.

The idea [19] is a structure to gather the URLs of malevolent websites on the dark cyber. Using VirusTotal and the Gred engine, the suggestion evaluates malicious URLs and automatically crawls shady websites. We developed a Python 3.6 crawler for collecting HTML content by crawling the website in the Tor network with seed URLs from the association gathering. Additionally, it generated the HTML request using the Python library AIOHTTP. AIOHTTP is a library that works with ASYNCIO, a Python 3 asynchronous I/O library. As a method for predicting the wickedness of removed URLs from gathered HTML text, it uses the VirusTotal and Gred engines. VirusTotal is an Internet facility that can run 66 discovery machines for files and URLs using blacklist-based classifiers and antivirus software. SecureBrain Corporation developed the Gred motor, an Internet provision that can identify phishing and tampering websites for HTML content and their degree of malignancy. The Tor crawler saves the HTML it finds in the dark web database, extracting links to the surface and saving their URLs in the link database. A URL is sent to VirusTotal, and a collection of HTML is sent to the Gred machine. It determines the amount of malevolence of the portal listed in this dataset. Once a month, the Tor network is crawled, and the collected HTML content's malignity is evaluated.

The characteristic is mined from the composed mails using doc2vec in this study's algorithm [20]. The extracted features are then subjected to deep clustering, an engine-education technique that gathers clustering and an auto-encrypter. A web crawler, for example, is used to gather data that specializes in dark web data collection. It used 850 forum mails relevant to virus bids and 850 posts not associated with malicious propositions as the exercise information for the experiment. The info gathering was done with a tool called Sixgill. As part of pre-processing, stop words, tokenization, noise removal, standardization, stopping, and others are used. Deep clustering on the features is carried out following the completion of natural linguistic calculation and by extracting the features using doc2vec. The autoencoder receives the features obtained by doc2vec first. The autoencoder's encoder output is then divided into clusters using K-means. After training, the clustering result is used to evaluate each group based on the proportion of serious posts to other mails in each collection. As unseen data, the afresh gathered dark Internet mail served as our model's contribution. doc2vec is used to perform natural linguistic calibration on the composed information to obtain the characteristics. The components are fed into the model as input, and the gathered mails are sorted into bunch.

The recommendation [21] suggests concealing one or more classes by employing arithmetical facts of the knowledge set to obscure particular information attributes. The

CIC-Darknet2020 dataset combines two Academia of New Brunswick public datasets. It has associations with the ISCXT or 2016 and ISCXVPN2016 datasets, which use Wireshark and TCPdump to record real-time traffic. These traffic samples generate features for the CIC-Darknet2020 dataset using CICFlowMeter. Each CIC-Darknet2020 model is made up of traffic features that have been extracted in this way from sessions that capture raw traffic packets. There are 158,659 hierarchically labeled samples in CIC-Darknet2020. Tor, VPN, and non-VPN are the labels for the top-level traffic category. These subcategories are sound streaming, perusing, talk, email, record move, P2P, video-web-based, and VOIP. After this pre-processing step, it has 72 features altogether. The classifiers perform better when the IP data is taken, according to initial examinations conducted on the database with and without these IP octet characteristics. To generate new samples, SMOTE linearly interpolates between feature values. Python is used to code all of the experiments. Scikit-learn runs most of the experiments except for the Tensorflow and Keras collections, which are used to examine CNN and AC-GAN. The Imblearn collection is employed to analyze SMOTE to stabilize the database. Scikit-learn is used to implement the majority of the experiments.

The work [22] gathered traffic from sensors on the darknet and mined attributes from the gridlock to identify designs that identify multiple terrorizations. The darknet gridlock features utilized to exercise machine learning segregators serve as the foundation for the structure. Gridlock creation and gathering, characteristic mining, knowledge set computation, and classifier construction are just a few of the framework's many modules. An idea drift detector, which measures the magnitude of drift by comparing performance to a threshold, is also included in the framework. SURFnet, a group that provides high-superiority web amenities to all Dutch instructive and investigate organizations, collected the darknet feeds. A darknet sensing device that tracks gridlock going to their unallocated address area gathered the feeds. It guards against adversarial feed poisoning. The address domain employed to gather the input is kept private. The study mined characteristics from the PCAP records following the collection of the darknet traffic. It trained the ML model, and the dataset was pre-processed using the Microsoft Azure ML podium. It classified the dataset as either malicious or normal for each instance. It cleaned up the missing values in the data. It carried out experiments by combining various ML algorithms and feature scaling methods. The concept drift detector analyzes the new dataset to determine the magnitude of the drift.

An essential first stage to letting down the cost of humanoid management in cyber danger intelligence organizations is made possible by the proposed method [23]. It provides a writing classification methodology with TSVM as an underlying semi-supervised labeling method because of its success in semi-supervised learning. This algorithm can then counterpart innovative managed text classification methods to increase the effectiveness of automated cyber threat detection. Based on the linguistic and organizational features of text in the DNM knowledge set, it developed two heuristic functions. Nine darknet areas were found, including the maximum prevalent domain during this study. Deepdotweb.com, a trustworthy darknet news, picked the demands from the best ones. There were seven of these domains in English. A cyber crawler was created and run for the breadth-first traversal of the onion links. There are several ways by which the crawler can get around darknet marketplace's anti-crawling measures. Parsing extracts product descriptions, vendor descriptions, and vendor reviews from the DNM web pages stored in the file system.

They propose a deep learning-based general strategy [24] for identifying and classifying darknet traffic. It performs data pre-processing and examines the cutting-edge complex dataset, which contains a wealth of information about darknet traffic. It discusses various feature selection methods to select the best darknet traffic detection and classification features. Decision tree, gradient boosting, random forest regressor, and extreme gradient boosting (XGB) engine knowledge algorithms that are used to fine-tune the performance of selected features. Convolution-gradient recurrent unit and modified convolution-long short-term memory deep learning methods are then used to identify network traffic better.

The suggestion [25] exemplifies a smart organization based on Scrapy and engine education capable of identifying and evaluating minute subcategories of services containing malicious content. Researchers can quickly and effortlessly obtain the range of Tor darknet websites and categorize websites into unidentified categories thanks to this. The Tor darknet content is primarily detected and pre-processed by the edge computing module. Due to the enormous amounts of info produced by the web of object strategies, old-style stockpile systems experience latency and bandwidth congestion. It will upload the contents to a classifier following pre-processing, relieving the training module of the burden of data processing and the transmission network. The data are divided into two sets—one for training and one for testing—and these sets are used to train the classifier. The results are displayed utilizing the output module. The crawler begins collecting data and transmits it to the classifier for analysis when unknown URLs are entered. The system will show a performance report and the classifier's results.

A framework [26] based on machine learning is recommended for identifying measures by portraying gridlock changing across numerous period sequences created from fresh transmission administered by the Corsaro programming set. It abstracts attacks' signs from time-sequence figures, which can disclose talented ages for using raw packet traces to investigate an attack further.

7.3   Proposed Work

The previous research's [13] intention was to advance a darknet intrusion detection system that uses supervised machine learning to identify the darknet activities of common IoT [27] cyber attacks. Characteristic business is the assortment, management, and alteration of fresh information into characteristics that can be input into engine-learning procedure for supplementary calibration, drill, authentication, and forecast. It is done through a pipeline of pre-processing stages that begin with the data accumulation process. The CIC-DarkNet-2020 database CSV version is initially available. It is processed by the platform that MATLAB developed. It uses exploratory data analysis to increase a profounder thoughtful of the database and performs essential data curation tasks. This procedure finishes an initial augmentation of the dataset by examination for lost details and giving appropriate replacements for the missing records by visualizing the dataset classes' histograms to gain additional insight into the categories and structures. The coefficient score method is used to extract the essential elements from the CIC-DarkNet-2020 dataset so that it can use the best features later to train and validate learning models. Normalization is used to rescale data points so that the range and significance stay the same. Label encoding converts categorical data into numerical data that machine learning methods can process. The shuffling process is a pre-processing step that takes place over a dataset's rows (samples) and involves rearranging data from that dataset at random. It creates a novel arrangement for

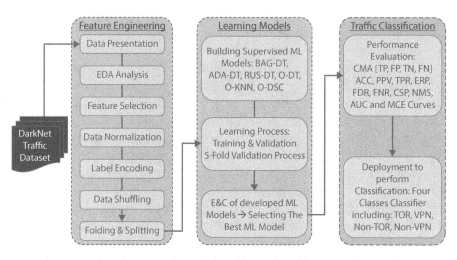

Figure 7.2 Darknet-IDS of IoT (DTDS-IoT) network traffic via ML techniques [13].

the dataset that is safe for machine learning examination and exercise without causing the classifier to be biased toward any primary programs. It used five distinct folds in the k-fold cross-authentication process. The authors divided the data by 70% for training and 30% for validation to guarantee the proposed predictive models' high level of assurance. The knowledge procedure is known as the exercise of iteratively applying procedure representations to information to enable a machine, like a system, to learn concealed designs that it can use to create forecasts. The misperception matrix, which lists the number of true-positive foretold examples, true-negative indicated models, false-positive forecast trials, and false-negative forecast models, is an investigation that is part of the traffic classification unit. There was a total of 141,530 records of system gridlock in the CIC-DarkNet-2020 dataset, with benign traffic accounting for 11,7219 and darknet traffic accounting for 24,311. Figure 7.2 portrays the same.

7.3.1   Drawback

With the increasing variation in data, the knowledge set also increases. It decreases the search speed and adopts accurate methods to take precise action.

- Data Presentation—The extracted dataset is utilized in appropriate software to analyze the malicious content in it. R programming is used in the study. Kaggle dataset is utilized in the recommendation.
- Sample Dataset—Different datasets are collected from various sources along with its behavior. A sample knowledge set mapping the behavior against the amount of malicious intention is prepared.
- Data Reconstruction—The obtained dataset is reconstructed by mapping the behavior of the same with the knowledge set. This makes the set of malicious datasets spread in the particular region.

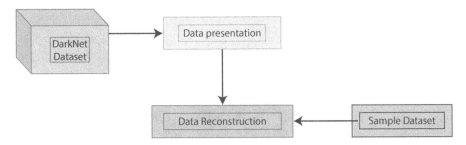

Figure 7.3 Proposed work.

Learning models and traffic classification utilization are similar to the previous work. Figure 7.3 presents the same.

7.4   Analysis of the Work

The work is examined using R-Programming. Table 7.1 shows the set of parameters used in the recommendation.

SPEED—The previous research's [13] intention was to advance a darknet intrusion detection system that uses supervised machine learning to identify the darknet activities of common IoT [27, 28] cyber attacks. Characteristic business is the assortment, management, and alteration of fresh information into characteristics that can be input into engine-learning procedure for supplementary calibration, drill, authentication, and forecast. It is done through a pipeline of pre-processing stages that begin with the data accumulation process. The CIC-DarkNet-2020 database CSV version is initially available. It is processed by the platform that MATLAB developed. It uses exploratory data analysis to increase a profounder thoughtful of the database and performs essential data curation tasks. This procedure finishes an initial augmentation of the dataset by examination for lost details and giving appropriate replacements for the missing records by visualizing the dataset classes'

Table 7.1 Parameters used in the work.

Parameters	Explanation
Number of darknet datasets	16,238
Number of sample datasets used	100
Set of cases considered a) above malignant b) average c) below malignant	 45 30 25

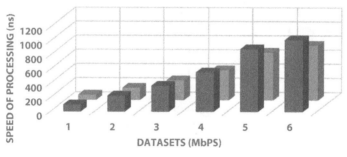

Figure 7.4 Comparison of the speed of two suggestions.

histograms to gain additional insight into the categories and structures. The coefficient score method is used to extract the essential elements from the CIC-DarkNet-2020 dataset so that it can use the best features later to train and validate learning models. Normalization is used to rescale data points so that the range and significance stay the same. Label encoding converts categorical data into numerical data that machine learning methods can process. The shuffling process is a pre-processing step that takes place over a dataset's rows (samples) and involves rearranging data from that dataset at random. It creates a novel arrangement for the dataset that is safe for machine learning examination and exercise without causing the classifier to be biased toward any primary programs. It used five distinct folds in the k-fold cross-authentication process. The authors divided the data by 70% for training and 30% for validation to guarantee the proposed predictive models' high level of assurance. The knowledge procedure is known as the exercise of iteratively applying procedure representations to information to enable a machine, like a system, to learn concealed designs that it can use to create forecasts.

The suggestion cuts down the steps by speeding the process by 24%. The same is represented in Figure 7.4. It uses a sample dataset collected from various sources. This dataset consists of a set mapping the intention of the malicious content to its behavior. This dataset is mapped to draw out the outcome of the collected darknet dataset.

7.5   Future Work

The threat posed by cybercrime to the digital world is on the rise. Defenders are attempting to adapt to attackers' evolving tactics to counterattack effectively. Cybercriminals are driven by their desire to constantly develop novel strategies for avoiding detection, defense, and disruption by law enforcement. Each cybercrime business's revenue is inversely proportional to its capacity for uninterrupted operation and maximum potency. Cybercriminals can use their resources privately or offer them to potential customers as a product or service for a fee called cybercrime-as-a-service.

"Dark web" mentions to an encoded Internet system that it can only access with specialized software. Peer-to-peer networks and private networks are two possible configurations for the dark web. These networks route gridlock using the encoding tier to ensure client secrecy. The Dark Web domain frequently substitutes the usage of novel area tags to prevent regulatory agencies from being traceable. These new domain names are much faster than regular websites on the superficial cyber and can be moved or locked at any period. Supervisors cannot obtain the factual uniqueness and site of both gatherings involved in the data discussion nor can they monitor routing information.

- It provides practical sustenance for dark cyber client management. De-anonymization methods necessitate customer device detection, content examination, trailing, and aligning. Anonymity enhancement technology necessitates gridlock concealment and other augmentation knowledge sub-missions that are more sophisticated and intelligent, making it more challenging to analyze dark web traffic.
- Large-scale mechanical gathering is possible from the dark web and the surface web. The valuable information in the Tor dark web data is extracted using various methods, including template extraction, semantic artificial intelligence extraction, knowledge graph extraction, and extensive data extraction. This results in updated, high-coverage, and highly usable Tor dark web data.

7.6   Conclusion

The web's scope is expanding. Content that has been deliberately hidden can be found in the dark web, which is the deep web's farthest reaches. It is possible to access the dark web for genuine drives and to hide illegal or malevolent activity. The use of the dark web for illegal activities has piqued the interest of government officials and policymakers. The term "dark web" refers to hidden websites on the Internet that require specialized software to access.

The previous research's intention was to advance a darknet intrusion detection system that uses supervised machine learning to identify the darknet activities of common IoT cyber attacks. Characteristic business is the assortment, management, and alteration of fresh information into characteristics that can be input into engine-learning procedure for supplementary calibration, drill, authentication, and forecast. It is done through a pipeline of pre-processing stages that begin with the data accumulation process. The CIC-DarkNet-2020 database CSV version is initially available. It is processed by the platform that MATLAB developed. It uses exploratory data analysis to increase a profounder thoughtful of the database and performs essential data curation tasks. This procedure finishes an initial augmentation of the dataset by examination for lost details and giving appropriate replacements for the missing records by visualizing the dataset classes' histograms to gain additional insight into the categories and structures. The coefficient score method is used to extract the essential elements from the CIC-DarkNet-2020 dataset so that it can use the best features later to train and validate learning models. Normalization is used to rescale data points so that the range and significance stay the same. Label encoding converts categorical data into numerical data that machine learning methods can process. The shuffling process is a pre-processing step that takes place over a dataset's rows (samples) and involves rearranging data from that dataset at random. It creates a novel arrangement for the dataset that is safe for machine learning examination and exercise without causing the classifier to be biased toward any primary programs. It used five distinct folds in the k-fold cross-authentication process. The authors divided the data by 70% for training and 30% for validation to guarantee the proposed predictive models' high level of assurance. The knowledge procedure is known as the exercise of iteratively applying procedure representations to information to enable a machine, like a system, to learn concealed designs that it can use to create forecasts. The suggestion cuts down the steps by speeding the process by 24%. It uses a sample dataset collected from various sources. This dataset consists of a set mapping the intention of the malicious content to its behavior. This dataset is mapped to draw out the outcome of the collected darknet dataset.

References

1. Ambika, N., Precise risk assessment and management, in: *Cyber-Physical Systems: Foundations and Techniques*, pp. 63–83, Wiley, Canada, 2022.
2. Fachkha, C. and Debbabi, M., Darknet as a source of cyber intelligence: Survey, taxonomy, and characterization. *IEEE Commun. Surv. & Tutorials*, 18, 2, 1197–1227, 2015.
3. Ambika, N., Minimum prediction error at an early stage in darknet analysis, in: *Dark Web Pattern Recognition and Crime Analysis Using Machine Intelligence*, pp. 18–30, IGI Global, US, 2022.
4. Demertzis, K., Tsiknas, K., Takezis, D., Skianis, C., Iliadis, L., Darknet traffic big-data analysis and network management for real-time automating of the malicious intent detection process by a weight agnostic neural networks framework. *Electronics*, 10, 7, 781, 2021.
5. Chen, H., Chung, W., Qin, J., Reid, E., Sageman, M., Weimann, G., Uncovering the dark web: A case study of Jihad on the web. *J. Am. Soc. Inf. Sci. Technol.*, 59, 8, 1347–1359, 2008.
6. Chen, H., IEDs in the Dark web: Genre classification of improvised explosive device web pages, in: *IEEE International Conference on Intelligence and Security Informatics*, Taipei, Taiwan, 2008.
7. Samtani, S., Li, W., Benjamin, V., Chen, H., Informing cyber threat intelligence through dark web situational awareness: The AZSecure hacker assets portal. *Digital Threats: Res. Pract. (DTRAP)*, 2, 4, 1–10, 2021.
8. Faizan, M. and Khan, R.A., Exploring and analyzing the dark web: A new alchemy. *First Monday, Chicago*, 2021, 1–5, 2019.
9. Tavabi, N., Bartley, N., Abeliuk, A., Soni, S., Ferrara, E., Lerman, K., Characterizing activity on the deep and dark web, in, *Characterizing Activity on the Deep and Dark Web*, San Francisco ACM, USA, 2019.
10. Nishikaze, H., Ozawa, S., Kitazono, J., Ban, T., Nakazato, J., Shimamura, J., Large-scale monitoring for cyber attacks by using cluster information on darknet traffic features, in: *INNS Conference on Big Data*, San Francisco, Elsevier, CA, USA, 2015.
11. Ebrahimi, M., Surdeanu, M., Samtani, S., Chen, H., Detecting cyber threats in non-english dark net markets: A cross-lingual transfer learning approach, in: *International Conference on Intelligence and Security Informatics (ISI)*, Miami, FL, USA, 2018.
12. Al-Haija, Q.A., Smadi, M., Al-Bataineh, O.M., Identifying phasic dopamine releases using DarkNet-19 convolutional neural network, in: *International IOT, Electronics and Mechatronics Conference (IEMTRONICS)*, Toronto, ON, Canada, 2021.
13. Abu Al-Haija, Q., Krichen, M., Abu Elhaija, W., Machine-learning-based darknet traffic detection system for iot applications. *Electronics*, 11, 4, 556, 2022.
14. Nunes, E., Diab, A., Gunn, A., Marin, E., Mishra, V., Paliath, V., Robertson, J., Shakarian, J., Thart, A., Shakarian, P., Darknet and deepnet mining for proactive cybersecurity threat intelligence, in: *IEEE Conference on Intelligence and Security Informatics (ISI)*, Tucson, AZ, USA, 2016.

15. Rawat, R., Mahor, V., Chirgaiya, S., Shaw, R.N., Ghosh, A., Analysis of darknet traffic for criminal activities detection using TF-IDF and light gradient boosted machine learning algorithm, in: *Innovations in Electrical and Electronic Engineering*, pp. 671–681, Springer, Singapore, 2021.

16. Habibi Lashkari, A., Kaur, G., Rahali, A., DIDarknet: A contemporary approach to detect and characterize the darknet traffic using deep image learning, in: *10th International Conference on Communication and Network Security*, ACM, Tokyo Japan, 2020.

17. Kadoguchi, M., Hayashi, S., Hashimoto, M., Otsuka, A., Exploring the dark web for cyber threat intelligence using machine leaning, in: *International Conference on Intelligence and Security Informatics (ISI)*, Shenzhen, China, 2019.

18. Schäfer, M., Fuchs, M., Strohmeier, M., Engel, M., Liechti, M., Lenders, V., BlackWidow: Monitoring the dark web for cyber security information, in: *11th International Conference on Cyber Conflict (CyCon)*, Tallinn, Estonia, 2019.

19. Ma, H., Cao, J., Mi, B., Huang, D., Liu, Y., Zhang, Z., Dark web traffic detection method based on deep learning, in: *10th Data Driven Control and Learning Systems Conference (DDCLS)*, Suzhou, China, 2021.

20. Kadoguchi, M., Kobayashi, H., Hayashi, S., Otsuka, A., Hashimoto, M., Deep self-supervised clustering of the dark web for cyber threat intelligence, in: *International Conference on Intelligence and Security Informatics (ISI)*, Arlington, VA, USA, 2020.

21. Rust-Nguyen, N., Sharma, S., Stamp, M., Darknet traffic classification and adversarial attacks using machine learning. *Comput. & Secur.*, 127, 103098, 2023.

22. Kumar, S., Vranken, H., van Dijk, J., Hamalainen, T., Deep in the dark: A novel threat detection system using darknet traffic, in: *International Conference on Big Data (Big Data)*, Los Angeles, CA, USA, 2019.

23. Ebrahimi, M., N, J.F., Jr, Chen, H., Semi-supervised cyber threat identification in dark net markets: A transductive and deep learning approach. *J. Manag. Inf. Syst.*, 37, 3, 694–722, 2020.

24. Sarwar, M.B., Hanif, M.K., Talib, R., Younas, M., Sarwar, M.U., DarkDetect: Darknet traffic detection and categorization using modified convolution-long short-term memory. *IEEE Access*, 9, 113705–113713, 2021.

25. Li, R., Chen, S., Yang, J., Luo, E., Edge-based detection and classification of malicious contents in tor darknet using machine learning. *Mobile Inf. Syst.*, 2021, 1–13, 2021.

26. Gao, M. and Mok, R.K., A scalable network event detection framework for darknet traffic, in: *22nd ACM Internet Measurement Conference*, France, 2022.

27. Nagaraj, A., *Introduction to sensors in IoT and cloud computing applications*, Bentham Science Publishers, UAE, 2021.

28. Nagaraj, A., Adapting blockchain for energy constrained IoT in healthcare environment, in: *Sustainable and Advanced Applications of Blockchain in Smart Computational Technologie*, p. 103, CRC Press, Boca Raton, Florida, 2022.

8

A Novel and Efficient Approach to Detect Vehicle Insurance Claim Fraud Using Machine Learning Techniques

Anand Kumar Mishra[1]*, **V. Hemamalini**[2], **Amit Kumar Tyagi**[3], **Piyali Saha**[4] **and Abirami A.**[5]

[1]Computer Science and Engineering, NIIT University, Neemrana, Rajasthan, India
[2]Department of Networking and Communications, School of Computing, SRM Institute of Science and Technology, Chennai, India
[3]Department of Fashion Technology, National Institute of Fashion Technology, New Delhi, Delhi India
[4]School of Computer Science and Engineering, Vellore Institute of Technology, Chennai, Tamil Nadu, India
[5]Department of Information Technology, Bannari Amman Institute of Technology, Sathyamangalam, Erode, Tamil Nadu, India

Abstract

The past few years have seen an increase in fraud cases for all types of claims at insurance companies operating as commercial enterprises. Since the amount fraudulently claimed is quite large and could result in serious issues, in addition to the government, other entities are working to identify and curtail such activity. Related frauds happened in all insurance claim industries with great severity, including insurance claims for the automobile sector, which is a scam that is prominently and regularly claimed and which may be accomplished by making fraudulent accident claims. Hence, in order to identify fraud and inflated claim amounts, we plan to construct a project that uses data from insurance claim sets. In order to construct a model to label and classify claims, the project uses machine learning methods. Additionally, it will also be using a confusion matrix to compare all machine learning methods for classification in terms of soft accuracy, precision, recall, etc.

Keywords: Machine learning, fraud detection, insurance, supervised learning

8.1 Introduction

Insurance fraud is an extremely old problem, and some preventative measures date back to the Middle Ages. At that period, breaching moral laws may result in severe penalties. The cargo of a merchant ship that was recovered in Jascoyne Bay in the 15th century was later revealed to have stones despite the shipping policy stating textiles. The consequence for insurance fraud in 1570 was taken after an insurance broker and the captain were both

Corresponding author: anandr.mishra13@gmail.com

Amit Kumar Tyagi (ed.) *Automated Secure Computing for Next-Generation Systems*, (155–176) © 2024 Scrivener Publishing LLC

found guilty and given death penalty. In the event of deception, the Prague and Antwerp Statutes of 1598 stipulated physical and monetary penalties for the captains of navigators and holders of documents. The fraud may occur within or externally. The fraudulent conduct causes insurance firms to focus on two issues: the evaluation of fraud and the impact of fraud on premium costs. The goal of this research is to create a model that can identify a fraudulent vehicle insurance. Since fraudulent insurance claims are substantially less common than legitimate insurance claims, machine learning fraud detection faces a difficulty. Due to the wide range of fraud schemes and the generally low ratio of discovered fraud in ordinary samples, detecting insurance fraud is a challenging task [1]. While developing detection algorithms, it is important to balance the expense of erroneous alerts against the expense of loss avoidance. Loss control units can now operate in additional areas owing to machine learning techniques that increase forecast accuracy. The term "insurance fraud" refers to a range of unethical actions that a person may commit in order to win an insurance company's favor [2]. This could involve planning the incident, creating the details, identifying important people and the issue's cause, and, finally, exaggerating the incident's scope.

8.2   Literature Survey

The authors of [3] used fuzzy thinking to better detect fraud by structuring the fuzzy rules. The training dataset will be made subject to fuzzy rule-based techniques. This approach will be used for higher efficiency and enormous datasets, which depends on the level of fraud and authenticity found. The primary drawback of this approach is that it entails a lot of human interaction. In [4], the author identifies the fraud cases. This research does an exploratory survey by examining various supervised as well as unsupervised classification approaches. They have taken into account three different categories or approaches:

- The supervised learning, which uses techniques like random forest, deep neural networks, Naive Bayes, etc.
- The hybrid learning that contains the NN model.
- The unsupervised learning that comprises KNN, Autoencoder, etc. Their findings demonstrate that supervised learners do markedly better than other types of learners. In [5], the author employs the nearest neighbors method and the statistical method to identify fraud cases, and this paper goes into great detail about each of these techniques. They compared the SVM approach to the methodology used in this research and discovered that the nearest neighbors method outperforms both the SVM and the interquartile range (statistical method) in terms of performance.

In [6], the author uses three algorithms to analyze and forecast fraud patterns from data: Bayesian network, C4.5, and decision tree-based algorithm. Naive Bayesian visualization, decision tree visualization, and rule-based classification will all help this model for prediction. They studied the recall, accuracy, and precision matrices for the models. This will be more effective than class skew because it will be a consistent performance matrix in several important functional areas of insurance fraud detection.

The authors of [7] suggested that iterative dichotomizer 3 (ID3), J48, and Naive Bayes be used in distinct approaches for the detection of health fraud. Based on the poll, it was determined that ID3 had 100% accuracy, whereas J48 had less accuracy. It was also determined that a decision tree was superior to the other two algorithms.

By retaining the interoperability property, a way to improve the performance of an analytical model is proposed by [8]. They suggest many techniques related to data engineering. This process of data engineering has been divided into many feature and instance engineering steps. They show the improvement in the results of these steps for popular analytical models on a real payment transaction data set.

The survey's results reveal that supervised learning is superior to unsupervised learning and that decision trees are the best classification algorithms. However, using decision trees has the major drawback of performing well with smaller datasets but performing poorly with larger datasets. As a result, the Naive Bayes algorithm is used in the proposed system, which performs well with both smaller and larger datasets.

8.3   Implementation and Analysis

8.3.1   Dataset Description

The dataset was generated via the Oracle database. The dataset contains facts/information about both the consumer and also the insurance policy [10]. It also contains information regarding the incident that served as the basis for the claims. Together with policy information, this data comprises vehicle datasets (attributes, model, accident information, type, tenure, etc.). The objective is to assess whether or not a claim application is fraudulent. The dataset used for our study has 15,420 instances overall and more than 30 attributes.

8.3.2   Methodology

In this project, first we have imported the required libraries like numpy, pandas, etc., and then we imported our dataset and displayed it for better understanding (refer Figure 8.1).

	A	B	C	D	E	F	G	H	I	J	K	L	M	N	O	P	Q	R	S	T	U	V	W
335	Jun	4	Wednesda	VW	Urban	Friday	Jun		4	Male	Single	55	Policy Hol Sedan - All Sedan	more than	0	334	11	400		3	more than more than none
336	Mar	5	Thursday	Honda	Urban	Thursday	Mar		5	Male	Married	27	Policy Hol Sedan - Co Sedan	30000 to 3	0	335	9	400		4	more than more than more tha
337	Aug	4	Tuesday	Toyota	Urban	Monday	Aug		5	Female	Married	29	Policy Hol Sedan - Co Sedan	20000 to 2	0	336	14	400		2	more than more than none
338	Aug	2	Saturday	Honda	Urban	Wednesda	Aug		3	Male	Single	25	Policy Hol Sport - Col Sport	more than	0	337	9	400		1	more than more than none
339	Apr	3	Monday	Toyota	Urban	Monday	Apr		3	Male	Married	38	Policy Hol Sedan - Lie Sport	more than	0	338	11	400		2	more than more than none
340	Apr	3	Monday	Toyota	Urban	Tuesday	Apr		4	Male	Married	26	Policy Hol Sedan - Co Sedan	30000 to 3	0	339	12	400		4	more than more than none
341	Feb	4	Wednesda	Pontiac	Urban	Tuesday	Mar		1	Male	Married	56	Policy Hol Sedan - All Sedan	less than 2	0	340	6	400		4	more than more than
342	Feb	4	Tuesday	Pontiac	Urban	Friday	Feb		4	Male	Married	47	Third Party Sedan - Co Sedan	more than	0	341	3	400		2	more than more than 2 to 4
343	Sep	4	Sunday	Toyota	Urban	Tuesday	Oct		2	Male	Married	29	Policy Hol Sedan - Co Sedan	30000 to 3	0	342	4	700		3	more than more than none
344	Jul	2	Tuesday	Honda	Urban	Tuesday	Jul		2	Male	Single	31	Policy Hol Sedan - Lie Sport	20000 to 2	0	343	4	400		1	more than more than
345	Jan	4	Thursday	Honda	Urban	Friday	Jan		4	Male	Married	46	Third Party Sedan - Lie Sport	20000 to 2	0	344	13	400		1	more than more than 2 to 4
346	Sep	4	Monday	Chevrolet	Urban	Wednesda	Sep		4	Male	Married	80	Policy Hol Sedan - All Sedan	20000 to 2	0	345	5	400		2	more than more than
347	Sep	3	Monday	Pontiac	Urban	Thursday	Sep		4	Male	Single	30	Policy Hol Sedan - Co Sedan	20000 to 2	0	346	4	400		3	more than more than
348	Aug	5	Tuesday	Ford	Rural	Thursday	Sep		1	Male	Married	51	Policy Hol Sedan - All Sedan	40000 to 5	0	347	10	400		2	more than more than
349	Mar	3	Friday	Chevrolet	Rural	Wednesda	Mar		4	Male	Married	80	Policy Hol Sedan - All Sedan	30000 to 3	0	348	5	400		3	more than more than none
350	Mar	3	Saturday	Honda	Urban	Thursday	Mar		4	Male	Single	0	Policy Hol Sedan - All Sedan	more than	0	349	6	400		2	more than more than
351	Nov	1	Friday	VW	Urban	Friday	Nov		2	Male	Married	52	Policy Hol Sedan - All Sedan	more than	0	350	1	400		1	more than more than
352	Nov	1	Friday	VW	Urban	Friday	Nov		1	Male	Married	36	Policy Hol Sedan - Lie Sport	20000 to 2	0	351	6	400		2	more than more than 2 to 4
353	Sep	5	Thursday	Honda	Urban	Wednesda	Oct		1	Male	Married	67	Third Party Sedan - All Sedan	20000 to 2	0	352	7	400		2	more than more than 2 to 4
354	Sep	1	Sunday	Pontiac	Urban	Wednesda	Oct		2	Female	Single	58	Policy Hol Sedan - Lie Sport	20000 to 2	0	353	15	400		2	more than more than none
355	Mar	2	Wednesda	Toyota	Urban	Monday	Mar		2	Female	Single	31	Policy Hol Sedan - Co Sedan	20000 to 2	0	354	11	400		4	more than more than
356	Mar	2	Tuesday	Chevrolet	Urban	Wednesda	Sep		2	Male	Married	50	Third Party Sedan - All Sedan	20000 to 2	0	355	10	400		2	more than more than 2 to 4
357	Mar	2	Tuesday	Pontiac	Urban	Monday	Mar		3	Male	Married	50	Third Party Sedan - All Sedan	30000 to 3	0	356	7	400		4	more than more than
358	Aug	2	Wednesda	Chevrolet	Urban	Thursday	Jan		2	Female	Married	55	Policy Hol Sedan - Lie Sport	20000 to 2	0	357	8	400		2	more than more than none
359	Mar	1	Friday	Toyota	Rural	Sunday	Mar		1	Male	Married	36	Policy Hol Sedan - All Sedan	less than 2	0	358	14	500		4	more than more than none
360	Mar	1	Tuesday	VW	Urban	Wednesda	Aug		1	Male	Single	31	Policy Hol Sedan - Co Sedan	more than	0	359	8	400		4	more than more than none
361	Sep	1	Monday	Honda	Urban	Thursday	Sep		2	Male	Single	23	Policy Hol Sedan - Co Sedan	20000 to 2	0	360	13	400		3	more than more than none
362	Jan	1	Monday	Mazda	Urban	Tuesday	Jan		1	Male	Married	34	Third Party Sedan - Co Sedan	20000 to 2	0	361	14	400		3	more than more than none
363	Nov	3	Saturday	Pontiac	Urban	Monday	Nov		3	Male	Married	30	Policy Hol Sedan - Co Sedan	30000 to 3	0	362	1	400		4	more than more than none

Figure 8.1 Dataset.

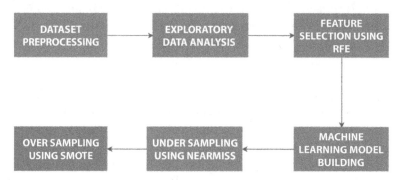

Figure 8.2 Methodology.

Then, we checked for missing data values, and it turned out that there are no missing values. Then, we checked for the data types of our attributes and looked into our target variable, from which we found out that our dataset is an imbalanced dataset. Then, we did some exploratory data analysis like checking for correlation and relation between different attributes using different types of charts and graphs. After this, we encoded our categorical variables using a label encoder like day of week, sex, etc., and then we implemented feature selection using recursive feature elimination (RFE) [9]. After this, we built machine learning models like KNN, decision tree classifier, and random forest. Since our f1 score was very poor, we had to go with undersampling or oversampling. Thus, we first implemented undersampling using near-miss algorithm. Still the f1 score was not improved for a satisfactory level. Thus, we carried on with oversampling using smote, and then the f1 scores improved in a great amount.

Figure 8.2 depicts that, first, we have performed pre-processing steps, and then on the pre-processed data we performed exploratory data analysis on our dataset followed by feature selection using RFE and applied some ML model followed by undersampling using "near-miss" and then the SMOTE oversampling technique.

A. Recursive feature elimination

Recursive feature elimination, a mechanism for selecting a subset of features, excludes the weakest feature (or features) from a model until the necessary number of features is reached.

B. Near-miss algorithm

A method known as "near-miss" [10] can help to balance an imbalanced dataset. It falls into the realm of undersampling algorithms and is a useful method for balancing the data. The method accomplishes this through examining at the class's distribution and picking samples at random from the bigger group. If two points in the distribution that fall into separate classes are quite similar to one another, this method eliminates the data point from the bigger class in an attempt to equalize the distribution.

C. SMOTE: Synthetic minority oversampling technique

SMOTE [11] is an oversampling method that uses fictional samples to symbolize the minority group. This approach minimizes the overfitting issue driven by random oversampling. By interpolating between the positive examples that are grouped together, it relies on the feature set to produce new instances.

D. KNN classifier

K-nearest neighbor is one of the most basic supervised learning-based strategies for machine learning. Assuming that the new instance and the prior instances are comparable, the K-NN algorithm allocates the new instance in the group that is most similar to the existing groups. The K-NN algorithm classifies new input based on similarity and preserves all available information. This indicates that new data can be accurately and quickly labeled using the K-NN approach. Although the K-NN technique is frequently utilized for classification jobs, it may also be used for regression.

The algorithm used here is defined as follows:

- Step 1: to choose the number of K neighbors.
- Step 2: Compute the Euclidean distance between K number of neighbors.
- Step 3: Based on the determined Euclidean distance, select the K nearest neighbors.
- Step 4: Count the number of data points in each category among these k neighbors.
- Step 5: Put the new data points to the category where the neighbor count is highest.
- Step 6: Our model is finished.

Figure 8.3 shows an example of the K-NN classifier approach.

E. Decision tree classifier

Decision tree analysis is a predictive modeling approach that can be applied in a variety of ways. An algorithmic approach can segment the dataset in numerous ways based on various criteria and be used to generate decision trees. Decision trees are the group of supervised algorithms' most advanced algorithms.

Both classification and regression issues can be solved with them. The two main parts of a tree are its decision nodes, which divide the data, and its leaves, which store the outcomes. An illustration of a binary tree that uses a person's age, eating habits, and activity level to determine how fit they are is provided below.

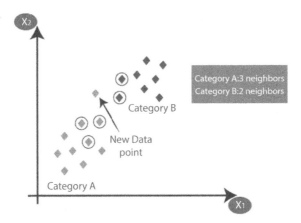

Figure 8.3 K-NN.

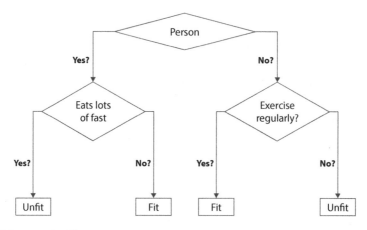

Figure 8.4 Decision tree classifier.

The question is a decision node in the decision tree shown in Figure 8.4, and the results are leaves. The next two decision trees are of the following categories.

- Classification decision tree: In these decision trees, the decision variable is categorical. A classification decision tree is shown in Figure 8.4.
- Regression decision trees —Decision variables are continuous in regression decision trees.

F. Random forest classifier

- Instead of relying on a single decision tree, the random forest takes the prediction from each tree and bases its prediction of the final output on the

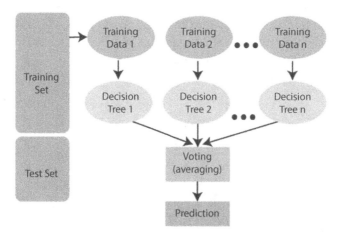

Figure 8.5 Random forest classifier.

majority votes of predictions. The greater number of trees in the forest leads to higher accuracy and prevents the problem of overfitting.

- The random forest algorithm's operation is illustrated in the diagram in Figure 8.5. Random forest runs on two stages: the first involves merging N decision trees to build the random forest, and the second involves making predictions for each tree that was produced in the first stage.

8.3.3   Checking for Missing Values

Figure 8.6 shows that the attributes in the dataset do not have any null values.

Figure 8.7 shows the information about the DataFrame. The information contains the number of columns, column labels, column data types, memory usage, range index, and the number of cells in each column (non-null values).

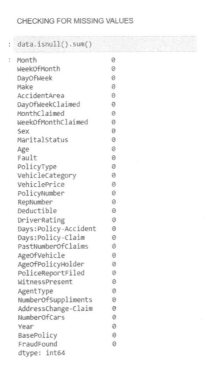

Figure 8.6 Checking for missing values.

```
data.info()

<class 'pandas.core.frame.DataFrame'>
RangeIndex: 15420 entries, 0 to 15419
Data columns (total 33 columns):
 #   Column              Non-Null Count  Dtype
---  ------              --------------  -----
 0   Month               15420 non-null  object
 1   WeekOfMonth         15420 non-null  int64
 2   DayOfWeek           15420 non-null  object
 3   Make                15420 non-null  object
 4   AccidentArea        15420 non-null  object
 5   DayOfWeekClaimed    15420 non-null  object
 6   MonthClaimed        15420 non-null  object
 7   WeekOfMonthClaimed  15420 non-null  int64
 8   Sex                 15420 non-null  object
 9   MaritalStatus       15420 non-null  object
 10  Age                 15420 non-null  int64
 11  Fault               15420 non-null  object
 12  PolicyType          15420 non-null  object
 13  VehicleCategory     15420 non-null  object
 14  VehiclePrice        15420 non-null  object
 15  PolicyNumber        15420 non-null  int64
 16  RepNumber           15420 non-null  int64
 17  Deductible          15420 non-null  int64
 18  DriverRating        15420 non-null  int64
 19  Days:Policy-Accident 15420 non-null object
 20  Days:Policy-Claim   15420 non-null  object
 21  PastNumberOfClaims  15420 non-null  object
 22  AgeOfVehicle        15420 non-null  object
 23  AgeOfPolicyHolder   15420 non-null  object
 24  PoliceReportFiled   15420 non-null  object
 25  WitnessPresent      15420 non-null  object
 26  AgentType           15420 non-null  object
 27  NumberOfSuppliments 15420 non-null  object
 28  AddressChange-Claim 15420 non-null  object
 29  NumberOfCars        15420 non-null  object
 30  Year                15420 non-null  int64
 31  BasePolicy          15420 non-null  object
 32  FraudFound          15420 non-null  object
dtypes: int64(8), object(25)
memory usage: 3.9+ MB
```

Figure 8.7 Information about the dataset.

8.3.4   Exploratory Data Analysis

A) Fraud vs Not fraud

Figure 8.8 shows the proportion of fraud (6%) and not fraud (94%) in the dataset.

```
import matplotlib.pyplot as plt
plt.figure(figsize=(10,8))
plt.pie(data.FraudFound.value_counts().values,labels=data.FraudFound.value_counts().index, autopct='%.0f%%')
plt.title("Fraud Type")
plt.show()
```

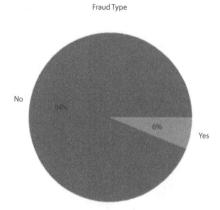

c

Figure 8.8 Fraud type.

B) Count of genders

Figure 8.9 depicts the count along with the comparison of sex for the female and male genders. It is clearly seen that there is a high number of male individuals, i.e., 13,000 and very less count of the female gender, i.e., 2,420 only in the dataset.

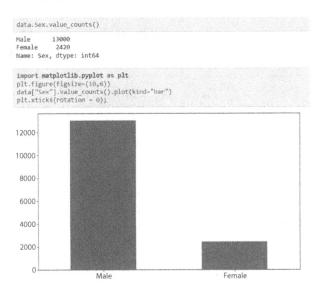

Figure 8.9 Count for each sex attribute.

C) Count of urban vs Rural accident areas

Figure 8.10 depicts the count along with the comparison of accident area for the urban and rural areas. It is clearly seen that urban areas have a higher number of accidents (13,822) compared with that of rural areas (1,598).

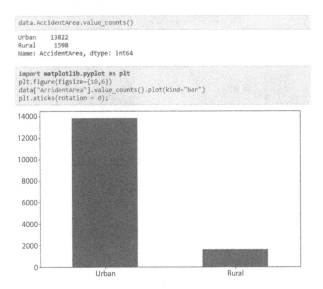

Figure 8.10 Accident area.

D) Age of the vehicle

Figure 8.11 shows a list of the number of vehicles with different ages based on after their purchase. It clearly shows that vehicles that have been bought at least 7 years back have higher counts (5,807) compared with the newly bought cars (2, 3, and 4 years back, etc.).

E) Correlation

Figure 8.12 shows that the policy number and year attributes are highly correlated. It implies multi-collinearity because their correlation value of 0.94 is greater than 0.5.

```
data.AgeOfVehicle.value_counts()
```

```
7 years        5807
more than 7    3981
6 years        3448
5 years        1357
new             373
4 years         229
3 years         152
2 years          73
Name: AgeOfVehicle, dtype: int64
```

Figure 8.11 Counts of vehicle according to age.

```
import matplotlib.pyplot as plt
import seaborn as sns
plt.figure(figsize = (25, 16))
corr = data.corr()
sns.heatmap(data = corr, annot = True, fmt = '.2g', linewidth = 1)
plt.show()
```

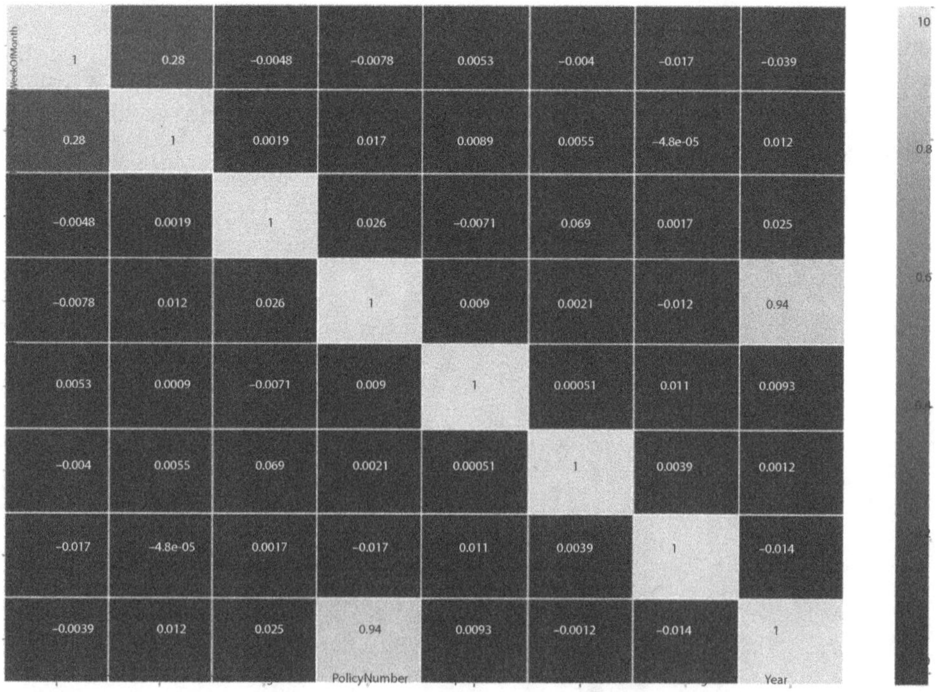

we can see policy number and year are highly correlated

Figure 8.12 Heat map of the correlation matrix.

Figure 8.13 shows the different counts of fault insurance claim from the policy holder and third party. It shows that 11,230 policy holders have fault insurance claims and 4,190 third party.

Figure 8.14 shows the fraud frequency according to gender, such that male gender has the highest fraud count compared with the female gender.

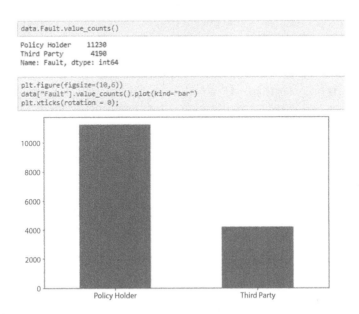

Figure 8.13 Fault.

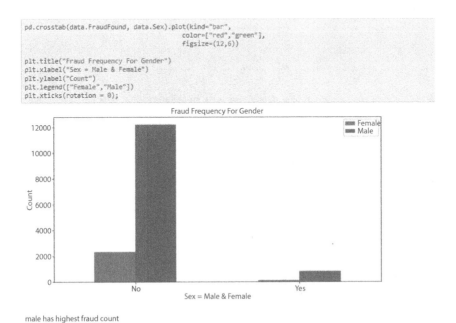

male has highest fraud count

Figure 8.14 Fraud frequency for gender.

In Figure 8.15, we turned all the categorical object values to numeric values to make the data transformation process easier.

Figure 8.16 shows a data frame of selected features which were obtained after applying feature selection using RFE. It has eliminated the weak features from the model that has resulted false by applying fit.support_.

Figure 8.17 shows a dataset that consists of attributes like month, day of week, make, accident area, month claimed, sex, marital status, age, fault, policy type, etc.

Figure 8.18 shows a correlation matrix where it shows that month and month claimed are highly correlated, which means that they show multi-collinearity.

Figure 8.19 depicts the model building for our dataset. Firstly, we had divided our dataset into two: test and train. After that, we trained the dataset using KNN and got a KNN score of 0.9234. It also shows the performance matrix for the model trained, which gives us the precision, recall, f1-score, support score, and accuracy as shown in Figure 8.19.

ENCODING CATEGORICAL VALUES

```
from sklearn.preprocessing import LabelEncoder
```

```
le = LabelEncoder()
cols = data.select_dtypes('object').columns
data[cols]= data[cols].apply(le.fit_transform)
```

```
data.head(5)
```

	Month	WeekOfMonth	DayOfWeek	Make	AccidentArea	DayOfWeekClaimed	MonthClaimed	WeekOfMonthClaimed	Sex	MaritalStatus	...	AgeOfPolicyHolder
0	2	5	6	6	1	8	5	1	0	2	...	3
1	4	3	6	6	1	2	5	4	1	2	...	4
2	10	5	0	6	1	5	10	2	1	1	...	6
3	6	2	2	17	0	1	6	1	1	1	...	7
4	4	5	1	6	1	8	4	2	0	2	...	4

5 rows × 33 columns

```
data['Year'] = le.fit_transform(data.Year)
```

```
data.head(5)
```

	Month	WeekOfMonth	DayOfWeek	Make	AccidentArea	DayOfWeekClaimed	MonthClaimed	WeekOfMonthClaimed	Sex	MaritalStatus	...	AgeOfPolicyHolder
0	2	5	6	6	1	8	5	1	0	2	...	3
1	4	3	6	6	1	2	5	4	1	2	...	4
2	10	5	0	6	1	5	10	2	1	1	...	6
3	6	2	2	17	0	1	6	1	1	1	...	7
4	4	5	1	6	1	8	4	2	0	2	...	4

5 rows × 33 columns

```
data.describe()
```

Figure 8.15 Data encodings.

FEAUTRE SELECTION USING RFE

```
Y = data['FraudFound']
X = data.drop(['FraudFound'], axis=1)
```

```
from sklearn.feature_selection import RFE
from sklearn.ensemble import AdaBoostClassifier
```

```
model=AdaBoostClassifier(random_state=0, n_estimators=100)
rfe = RFE(model,n_features_to_select=20,step=1)
fit = rfe.fit(X, Y)
print("Num Features: %s" % (fit.n_features_))
print("Selected Features: %s" % (fit.support_))
print("Feature Ranking: %s" % (fit.ranking_))
```

```
Num Features: 20
Selected Features: [ True False  True  True  True False  True False  True  True  True  True
  True False False  True  True  True False  True  True  True  True False
 False False  True  True  True False False False]
Feature Ranking: [ 1  3  1  1  1  4  1  7  1  1  1  1  1  9  2  1  1  1 13  1  1  1  1 12
  8 10  1  1  1 11  6  5]
```

```
from numpy import array
features = array(X.columns)
print("All features:")
print(features)
filter = rfe.support_

print("Selected features:")
print(features[filter])
```

```
All features:
['Month' 'WeekOfMonth' 'DayOfWeek' 'Make' 'AccidentArea'
 'DayOfWeekClaimed' 'MonthClaimed' 'WeekOfMonthClaimed' 'Sex'
 'MaritalStatus' 'Age' 'Fault' 'PolicyType' 'VehicleCategory'
 'VehiclePrice' 'PolicyNumber' 'RepNumber' 'Deductible' 'DriverRating'
 'Days:Policy-Accident' 'Days:Policy-Claim' 'PastNumberOfClaims'
 'AgeOfVehicle' 'AgeOfPolicyHolder' 'PoliceReportFiled' 'WitnessPresent'
 'AgentType' 'NumberOfSuppliments' 'AddressChange-Claim' 'NumberOfCars'
 'Year' 'BasePolicy']
Selected features:
['Month' 'DayOfWeek' 'Make' 'AccidentArea' 'MonthClaimed' 'Sex'
 'MaritalStatus' 'Age' 'Fault' 'PolicyType' 'PolicyNumber' 'RepNumber'
 'Deductible' 'Days:Policy-Accident' 'Days:Policy-Claim'
 'PastNumberOfClaims' 'AgeOfVehicle' 'AgentType' 'NumberOfSuppliments'
 'AddressChange-Claim']
```

Figure 8.16 Feature selection using RFE.

Month and month claimed are highly correlated

martial status and age are negatively correlated

```
data_new.head(5)
```

	Month	DayOfWeek	Make	AccidentArea	MonthClaimed	Sex	MaritalStatus	Age	Fault	PolicyType	...	RepNumber	Deductible	Days:Policy-Accident	Days:Policy-Claim
0	2	6	6	1	5	0	2	21	0	5	...	12	300	3	2
1	4	6	6	1	5	1	2	34	0	4	...	15	400	3	2
2	10	0	6	1	10	1	1	47	0	4	...	7	400	3	2
3	6	2	17	0	6	1	1	65	1	2	...	4	400	3	2
4	4	1	6	1	4	0	2	27	1	4	...	3	400	3	2

5 rows × 21 columns

Figure 8.17 Head of the new dataset.

NEW DATA AFTER FEAUTURE SELECTION

```
data_new=data[['Month','DayOfWeek','Make','AccidentArea','MonthClaimed','Sex',
  'MaritalStatus','Age','Fault','PolicyType','PolicyNumber','RepNumber',
  'Deductible','Days:Policy-Accident','Days:Policy-Claim',
  'PastNumberOfClaims','AgeOfVehicle','AgentType','NumberOfSuppliments',
  'AddressChange-Claim','FraudFound']]
```

CORRELATION

```python
import matplotlib.pyplot as plt
import seaborn as sns
plt.figure(figsize = (25, 16))
corr = data_new.corr()
sns.heatmap(data = corr, annot = True, fmt = '.2g', linewidth = 1)
plt.show()
```

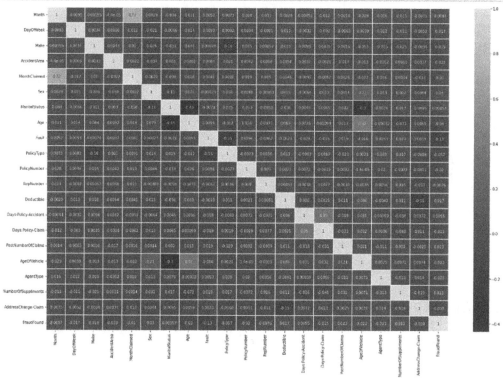

Figure 8.18 New data correlation matrix.

MODEL BUILDING

```
from sklearn.metrics import confusion_matrix
from sklearn.metrics import precision_score
from sklearn.metrics import recall_score
from sklearn.model_selection import train_test_split
```

TRAIN TEST SPLIT

```
y = data_new['FraudFound']
x = data_new.drop(['FraudFound'], axis=1)

x_train, x_test, y_train, y_test = train_test_split(x, y, test_size=0.20, random_state=42)
```

KNN

```
from sklearn import neighbors
```

```
print("KNN Score :")
KNNClassifier = neighbors.KNeighborsClassifier(n_neighbors=3, weights='distance')
KNNClassifier.fit(X=x_train,y=y_train)
KNNClassifier.score(x_test,y_test)
```

```
KNN Score :
```

```
0.9234760051880675
```

```
KNN_y_predicted = KNNClassifier.predict(x_test)
class_names = np.unique(np.array(y_test))
confusion_matrix(y_test, KNN_y_predicted)
```

```
array([[2842,   45],
       [ 191,    6]])
```

```
from sklearn.metrics import classification_report
from sklearn.model_selection import cross_val_score
print(classification_report(y_test, KNN_y_predicted))
scores = cross_val_score(KNNClassifier, x, y, cv=10, scoring='f1')
knn_f1 = scores.mean()
print('f1: %0.2f' % knn_f1)
```

```
              precision    recall  f1-score   support

           0       0.94      0.98      0.96      2887
           1       0.12      0.03      0.05       197

    accuracy                           0.92      3084
   macro avg       0.53      0.51      0.50      3084
weighted avg       0.88      0.92      0.90      3084
```

```
f1: 0.06
```

Figure 8.19 Model building using KNN.

Here we have trained the dataset using a decision tree and got a score of 0.9088. It also shows the performance matrix for the model trained, which gives us the precision, recall, f1-score, support score, and accuracy as shown in Figure 8.20.

Here we have trained the dataset using random forest and got a score of 0.9381. It also shows the performance matrix for the model trained, which gives us the precision, recall, f1-score, support score, and accuracy as shown in Figure 8.21.

We have done undersampling on our dataset using near-miss and then trained the undersampled data on different machine learning algorithms like KNN and random forest as shown in Figure 8.22.

We have done oversampling on our dataset using SMOTE and then trained the oversampled data on different machine learning algorithms like KNN and random forest as shown in Figure 8.23.

DECISION TREE

```
|: from sklearn import tree
   DTClassifier = tree.DecisionTreeClassifier()
   DTClassifier.fit(x_train, y_train)

   print("Decision Tree Score :")
   DTClassifier.score(x_test,y_test)
```

Decision Tree Score :

```
|: 0.9088845654993515
```

```
|: DT_y_predicted = DTClassifier.predict(x_test)
   class_names = np.unique(np.array(y_test))
   confusion_matrix(y_test, DT_y_predicted)
```

```
|: array([[2743,  144],
          [ 137,   60]])
```

```
|: from sklearn.metrics import classification_report
   from sklearn.model_selection import cross_val_score
   print(classification_report(y_test, DT_y_predicted))
   scores1 = cross_val_score(DTClassifier, x, y, cv=10, scoring='f1')
   DT_f1 = scores1.mean()
   print('f1: %0.2f' % DT_f1)
```

```
               precision   recall  f1-score   support

           0        0.95     0.95      0.95      2887
           1        0.29     0.30      0.30       197

    accuracy                           0.91      3084
   macro avg        0.62     0.63      0.63      3084
weighted avg        0.91     0.91      0.91      3084

f1: 0.16
```

Figure 8.20 Model building using decision tree.

RANDOM FOREST

```
from sklearn import ensemble
RFTClassifier = ensemble.RandomForestClassifier()
RFTClassifier.fit(x_train, y_train)

print("Random forest Score :")
RFTClassifier.score(x_test,y_test)
```

Random forest Score :

```
0.9380674448767834
```

```
RFT_y_predicted = RFTClassifier.predict(x_test)
class_names = np.unique(np.array(y_test))
confusion_matrix(y_test, RFT_y_predicted)
```

```
array([[2887,    0],
       [ 191,    6]])
```

```
print(classification_report(y_test, RFT_y_predicted))
scores2 = cross_val_score(RFTClassifier, x, y, cv=10, scoring='f1')
RFT_f1 = scores2.mean()
print('f1: %0.2f' % RFT_f1)
```

```
               precision   recall  f1-score   support

           0        0.94     1.00      0.97      2887
           1        1.00     0.03      0.06       197

    accuracy                           0.94      3084
   macro avg        0.97     0.52      0.51      3084
weighted avg        0.94     0.94      0.91      3084

f1: 0.05
```

as we can see we have poor f1 scores due to imblanced dataset so we can go with over sampling and under sampling

Figure 8.21 Model building using random forest.

UNDER SAMPLING USING NEARMISS

```
import imblearn
from imblearn.under_sampling import NearMiss
nm = NearMiss()
x_nm, y_nm = nm.fit_resample(x, y)
```

```
x_nm.shape
```

```
(1846, 20)
```

```
y_nm.shape
```

```
(1846,)
```

```
x_train1, x_test1, y_train1, y_test1 = train_test_split(x_nm, y_nm, test_size=0.20, random_state=12)
```

KNN UNDER SAMPLING

```
from sklearn import neighbors
print("KNN Score :")
KNNClassifier1 = neighbors.KNeighborsClassifier(n_neighbors=3, weights='distance')
KNNClassifier1.fit(X=x_train1,y=y_train1)
KNNClassifier1.score(x_test1,y_test1)
```

```
KNN Score :
```

```
0.5945945945945946
```

```
KNN_y_predicted1 = KNNClassifier1.predict(x_test1)
class_names = np.unique(np.array(y_test1))
confusion_matrix(y_test1, KNN_y_predicted1)
```

```
array([[141,  52],
       [ 98,  79]])
```

```
from sklearn.metrics import classification_report
from sklearn.model_selection import cross_val_score
print(classification_report(y_test1, KNN_y_predicted1))
scores4 = cross_val_score(KNNClassifier1, x_nm, y_nm, cv=10, scoring='f1')
knn_f11 = scores4.mean()
print('f1: %0.2f' % knn_f11)
```

```
              precision    recall  f1-score   support

           0       0.59      0.73      0.65       193
           1       0.60      0.45      0.51       177

    accuracy                           0.59       370
   macro avg       0.60      0.59      0.58       370
weighted avg       0.60      0.59      0.59       370
```

```
f1: 0.04
```

RANDOM FOREST UNDER SAMPLING

```
from sklearn import ensemble
RFTClassifier1 = ensemble.RandomForestClassifier()
RFTClassifier1.fit(x_train1, y_train1)

print("Random forest Score :")
RFTClassifier1.score(x_test1,y_test1)
```

```
Random forest Score :
```

```
0.827027027027027
```

```
RFT_y_predicted1 = RFTClassifier1.predict(x_test1)
class_names = np.unique(np.array(y_test1))
confusion_matrix(y_test1, RFT_y_predicted1)
```

```
array([[136,  57],
       [  7, 170]])
```

```
print(classification_report(y_test1, RFT_y_predicted1))
scores5 = cross_val_score(RFTClassifier1, x_nm, y_nm, cv=10, scoring='f1')
RFT_f11 = scores5.mean()
print('f1: %0.2f' % RFT_f11)
```

```
              precision    recall  f1-score   support

           0       0.95      0.70      0.81       193
           1       0.75      0.96      0.84       177

    accuracy                           0.83       370
   macro avg       0.85      0.83      0.83       370
weighted avg       0.85      0.83      0.82       370
```

```
f1: 0.50
```

Figure 8.22 Undersampling.

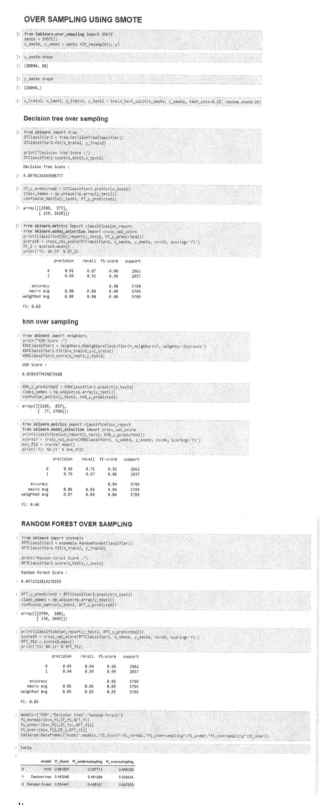

Figure 8.23 Oversampling.

We have compared the f1_score for normal, undersampled, and oversampled dataset using KNN, decision tree, and random forest, and we have observed that these machine learning models are giving better f1_score on oversampled data than normal and under-sampled, which are 0.658, 0.29, and 0.887, as shown in Figure 8.24.

We have compared all the f1_score for normal, undersampled, and oversampled datasets using KNN, decision tree, and random forest using a bar chart, and we can easily observe that the oversampled data is giving the best results on trained models, out of which random forest is performing best in all these three trained models as shown in Figure 8.25.

In last, the readers/researchers are recommended to read articles [12–18] to secure the systems against such frauds/third party attacks.

```
models=["KNN","Decision tree","Random Forest"]
f1_normal=[knn_f1,DT_f1,RFT_f1]
f1_under=[knn_f11,DT_fsc,RFT_f11]
f1_over=[knn_f12,DT_2,RFT_f12]
table=pd.DataFrame({"model":models,"f1_Score":f1_normal,"f1_undersampling":f1_under,"f1_oversampling":f1_over})
```

```
table
```

	model	f1_Score	f1_undersampling	f1_oversampling
0	KNN	0.061603	0.037713	0.668228
1	Decision tree	0.162040	0.461208	0.829338
2	Random Forest	0.054441	0.495197	0.887828

Figure 8.24 Comparison of f1_score.

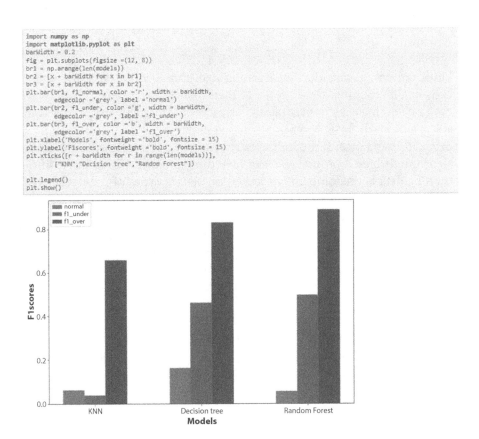

Figure 8.25 Bar chart comparing the f1_score.

8.4 Conclusion

Finding an insurance fraud is a difficult endeavor; from the start, this industry has struggled with issues related to false insurance claims. The proposed approach attempts to provide a system that can identify potential frauds with the highest degree of accuracy. The proposed methodology determines if the insurance being claimed is "fraud" or "genuine", helping insurance firms in identifying frauds more quickly and accurately.

8.4.1 Future Work

It is possible to enhance the system to identify massive insurance fraud. The framework may be enhanced through the introduction of a report module. If the individual in charge clicks the report button anytime the report is fraud, a detailed analysis must be submitted to the local police station. Users will be able to offer comments using the feedback module to rectify any issues, and the report module would demand that a thorough report be submitted to the nearby police station anytime the output is detected.

8.4.2 Limitations

Machine learning has proven to be a powerful tool for detecting and preventing fraud in the vehicle insurance industry. However, there are also several limitations to consider, including the following:

- Limited training data: Machine learning algorithms require large amounts of high-quality training data to learn to identify fraud accurately. However, in the case of vehicle insurance fraud, there may be limited historical data available, particularly for new types of fraud or emerging fraud patterns.
- Biased training data: If the training data used to train the machine learning algorithm is biased, it may result in biased predictions—for example, if the training data is predominantly focused on certain types of fraud, the algorithm may miss other types of fraud that are less common but still important.
- Limited feature sets: Machine learning algorithms rely on a set of features or variables to detect fraud. However, if the feature set is limited or not well defined, it can lead to inaccuracies in fraud detection—for example, if the algorithm only looks at the age of the driver and the make and model of the vehicle, it may miss other important factors that contribute to fraud, such as driving history or location.
- Lack of interpretability: Machine learning algorithms are often considered "black boxes" because they are difficult to interpret and understand. This lack of interpretability can make it challenging for insurers to explain to customers why a particular decision was made, which can lead to trust issues and potentially legal challenges.

- Adversarial attacks: Fraudsters can attempt to evade detection by manipulating or tampering with the data used to train the machine learning algorithm. Adversarial attacks can result in false positives or false negatives, which can have significant consequences for insurers and customers alike.

In summary, machine learning is a valuable tool for detecting and preventing fraud in the vehicle insurance industry. However, insurers should be aware of these limitations and take steps to mitigate them to ensure accurate and reliable fraud detection.

References

1. Leite, R.A., Gschwandtner, T., Miksch, S., Gstrein, E., Kuntner, J., Visual analytics for event detection: Focusing on fraud. *Visual Inf.*, 2, 4, 198–212, 2018, https://doi.org/10.1016/j.visinf.2018.11.001.
2. Modic, D., Palomäki, J., Drosinou, M., Laakasuo, M., The dark triad and willingness to commit insurance fraud. *Cogent Psychol.*, 5, 1, 2018.
3. Supraja, K. and Saritha, S.J., Robust fuzzy rule based technique to detect frauds in vehicle insurance, in: *2017 International Conference on Energy, Communication, Data Analytics and Soft Computing (ICECDS)*, pp. 3734–3739, Chennai, India, 2017.
4. Bauder, R.A. and Khoshgoftaar, T.M., Medicare fraud detection using machine learning methods, in: *16th IEEE International Conference on Machine Learning and Applications (ICMLA)*, pp. 858–865, Cancun, Mexico, 2017.
5. Badriyah, T., Rahmaniah, L., Syarif, I., Nearest neighbour and statistics method based for detecting fraud in auto insurance, in: *International Conference on Applied Engineering (ICAE)*, 2018, pp. 1–5, Batam, Indonesia, 2018.
6. Simmachan, T., Manopa, W., Neamhom, P., Poothong, A., Phaphan, W., Detecting fraudulent claims in automobile insurance policies by data mining techniques. *Thailand Statistician*, 21, 3, 552–568, 2023. Retrieved from https://ph02.tci-thaijo.org/index.php/thaistat/article/view/250065.
7. Pal, R. and Pal, S., Application of data mining techniques in health fraud detection, 3, 5, 129–137, October 2015.
8. Baesens, B., Höppner, S., Verdonck, T., Data engineering for fraud detection. *Decis. Support Syst.*, 12, 113492, 2021 Jan.
9. Zeng, X., Chen, Y.W., Tao, C., Feature selection using recursive feature elimination for handwritten digit recognition. *2009 Fifth International Conference on Intelligent Information Hiding and Multimedia Signal Processing*, Kyoto, Japan, pp. 1205–1208, 2009.
10. Improving imbalanced classification using near-miss instances. *Expert Syst. Appl.*, 201, 117130, 2022.
11. Chawla, N.V., Bowyer, K.W., Hall, L.O., Kegelmeyer, W.P., SMOTE: synthetic minority over-sampling technique. *J. Artif. Int. Res.*, 16, 1, 321–357, 2002, January 2002.
12. Sai, G.H., Tyagi, A.K., Sreenath, N., Biometric security in internet of things based system against identity theft attacks, in: *2023 International Conference on Computer Communication and Informatics (ICCCI)*, pp. 1–7, Coimbatore, India, 2023.
13. Deshmukh, A., Patil, D.S., Soni, G., Tyagi, A.K., Cyber security: New realities for industry 4.0 and society 5.0, in: *Handbook of Research on Quantum Computing for Smart Environments*, A. Tyagi (Ed.), pp. 299–325, IGI Global, 2023. https://doi.org/10.4018/978-1-6684-6697-1.ch017.

14. Erondu, U.I., Asani, E.O., Arowolo, M.O., Tyagi, A.K., Adebayo, N., An encryption and decryption model for data security using vigenere with advanced encryption standard, in: *Using Multimedia Systems, Tools, and Technologies for Smart Healthcare Services*. A. Tyagi (Ed.), pp. 141–159, IGI Global, 2023. https://doi.org/10.4018/978-1-6684-5741-2.ch009.

15. Tyagi AK, Dananjayan S, Agarwal D, Thariq Ahmed HF. Blockchain—Internet of Things applications: Opportunities and challenges for industry 4.0 and society 5.0. *Sensors*, 2023, 23, 2, 947, 2023. https://doi.org/10.3390/s23020947.

16. Tyagi, A.K, Chapter 2 - Decentralized everything: Practical use of blockchain technology in future applications, in: *Distributed Computing to Blockchain*, Pandey, R., Goundar, S., Fatima, S., (Eds.), Academic Press, 19–38, 2023, ISBN 9780323961462, https://doi.org/10.1016/B978-0-323-96146-2.00010-3.

17. Nair, M.M., Tyagi, A.K., Blockchain technology for next-generation society: Current trends and future opportunities for smart era, in: *Blockchain Technology for Secure Social Media Computing*, 2023.

18. Tyagi, A.K., Chandrasekaran, S., Sreenath, N., Blockchain Technology:– A new technology for creating distributed and trusted computing environment, *2022 International Conference on Applied Artificial Intelligence and Computing (ICAAIC)*, 1348–1354, 2022.

9

Automated Secure Computing for Fraud Detection in Financial Transactions

Kuldeep Singh[1]*, Prasanna Kolar[2], Rebecca Abraham[3], Vedantam Seetharam[1], Sireesha Nanduri[1] and Divyesh Kumar[1]

[1]Faculty of Management Studies, CMS Business School JAIN (Deemed to be) University, Bangalore, India
[2]Department of Agriculture Koneru Lakshmaiah Educational Foundation, Vijaywada, India
[3]Finance and Economics, Nova South-eastern University, Florida, United States

Abstract

In today's society, financial fraud is a severe and ongoing issue. Automatic fraud detection devices have been developed to assist in addressing this problem; but, in order to secure against cyber attacks by malicious players, these systems must be designed with security in mind. An automated secure computing system for fraud detection in financial transactions is suggested in this research. The technology is intended to process and analyze transaction data securely, find abnormalities, and send out notifications for possibly fraudulent activities. In order to safeguard against cyber attacks, the study suggests that the system should include a number of security mechanisms, such as encryption, data obfuscation, and access limits. The suggested approach is based on prior observations in research studies related to fraudulent transactions while maintaining a high standard of security. This study illustrates the viability and efficiency of automated secure computing for financial transaction fraud detection.

Keywords: Automated secure computing, fraud detection, financial transaction

9.1 Introduction

For decades, financial fraud has been a constant issue for both people and businesses [1, 2]. Figure 9.1 provides a listing of the different types of financial fraud. Fraudsters have modified their approaches and methods to take advantage of the new possibilities provided by digital channels as technology has developed, but still new tools and techniques for identifying and combating fraud have also been made available by technology [3, 4]. Financial fraud found previously led to lost savings or retirement assets, identity theft, ruined credit ratings, and other personal consequences for an individual. Financial fraud, as found in research, has put organizations at risk for lost sales, harm to their reputations,

---

*Corresponding author: kuldeepsinghcsr@gmail.com

Amit Kumar Tyagi (ed.) *Automated Secure Computing for Next-Generation Systems*, (177–190) © 2024 Scrivener Publishing LLC

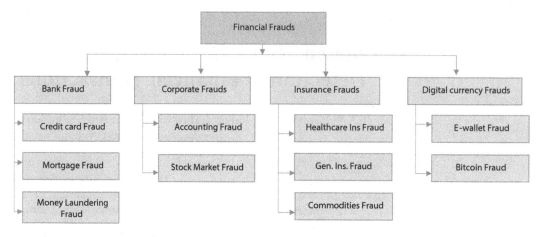

Figure 9.1 Types of financial frauds.

and legal trouble [5]. New tools and techniques for identifying and combating financial fraud have been made possible by technology, such as the following: (a) Large volumes of data can also be analyzed using data analytics techniques to find patterns and abnormalities that could be signs of fraud. To find a probable fraud, these techniques could be used to examine transaction data, social media data, and other information sources; (b) Data analysis using artificial intelligence (AI) is mostly used to spot trends in the data that developed at some point to fraud. Moreover, AI is used to create prediction models that identify and stop fraud before it happens; (c) The development of a tamper-proof digital ledger that is normally used to record financial transactions can be made using blockchain technology. More security and transparency might result, making it more difficult for scammers to pull off their scams; (d) The identification of anyone accessing bank accounts should be confirmed via biometric verification, such as fingerprint scanning or face recognition (see Figure 9.2). This definitely aid in reducing the risk of fraud and identity theft; (e) Large volumes of data are better used to analyze, using machine learning algorithms, and find trends that point to a fraud. Moreover, prediction models that are able to identify and stop fraud before it happens were found to be created using machine learning; (f) Real-time financial transaction monitoring and anomaly detection

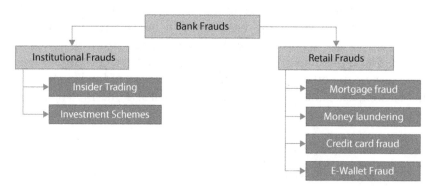

Figure 9.2 Types of bank frauds.

are mostly done with the use of fraud detection software. It is also possible to utilize this program to provide warnings for possibly fraudulent activities [5–7].

The process of automating the secure processing of data and the analysis of that data to find fraud in financial transactions is known as automated secure computing [4, 5]. With a quick reaction to any abnormal transactions, this method assists in real-time detection and prevention of fraudulent conduct. Real-time monitoring of financial transactions by automated secure computing enables it to spot fraudulent conduct as it takes place. Real-time monitoring makes it possible to react quickly to any questionable transactions, thus halting future fraud. Automatic secure computing employs data encryption methods to prevent unauthorized individuals from accessing private financial information.

Its encryption minimizes the possibility of fraud and data breaches by guaranteeing the security of any data that the system collects and analyzes [7, 8]. Automatic secure computing also analyzes transaction data and seeks for irregularities that could point to a fraudulent conduct. These algorithms are able to spot patterns and trends in the data, enabling the system to swiftly and precisely identify a fraudulent behavior. In essence, machine learning techniques are used in automated secure computing to continuously enhance its fraud detection skills. The system is constantly up to date and efficient thanks to these algorithms, which develop learning from historical data to discover new patterns and trends that can suggest fraud [9, 10]. Figure 9.3 shows the co-concurrence of keywords associated with fraud detection.

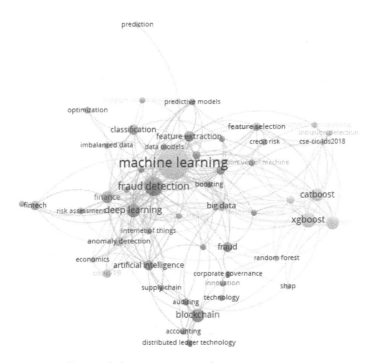

Figure 9.3 Co-occurrence of keywords (source: Vos-viewer).

9.2   Historical Perspective

With the emergence of automated fraud detection technologies in the early 2000s, automated secure computing started to take shape [5, 6]. Financial institutions were able to react fast and stop more losses because to their systems' use of algorithms to recognize and flag questionable transactions in real time. The importance of automated secure computing has increased along with the amount and complexity of financial transactions [11, 12].

However, when it comes to identifying financial fraud, automated secure computing is still relatively new [13, 14], yet the emergence of safe systems and automated computing dated to the early decades of computers in the middle of the twentieth century. Security in computing became in relevance in the 1970s. It became vital to create secure systems that could shield sensitive data from unwanted access with the advent of multi-user systems and the need for data sharing between users [14–16]. As a result, security solutions like firewalls, access restrictions, and encryption were created and are still in use today. Financial transactions started to shift online in the 1990s as the Internet and e-commerce expanded, and new security risks appeared. Financial institutions started using more advanced security measures, such as SSL encryption and two-factor authentication, to combat these threats [17–20]. Automated fraud detection systems, which employed algorithms to spot and report questionable transactions, were more prevalent in the early 2000s [3–6]. These technologies have the ability to spot fraud in real time, giving financial institutions the opportunity to act immediately and stop additional losses. Automated secure computing is becoming a crucial component of the financial sector for fraud detection in financial transactions [21–24]. Financial institutions are now able to identify and prevent fraud more successfully than ever before because of the use of advanced algorithms, machine learning, and data analysis. The importance of automated secure computing has increased along with the amount and complexity of financial transactions [12, 25, 26].

We conducted an extensive search and analysis of all pertinent published research on automated secure computing and financial fraud detection studies as part of this study's review procedure. This literature analysis for automated secure computing included discovering and assessing the most current relevant research papers, examining them, and

Table 9.1 Keyword search in Web of Science and Google Scholar.

Number	Keywords	Web of Science title/topic	Google Scholar all in title/all
1	Automated secure computing	1/227	284/830,000
2	Financial frauds	232/1,697	238/222,000
3	Machine learning and financial frauds	14/164	6/45,400
4	Technology and financial frauds	1/169	2/136,000
5	Automated secure computing and financial frauds	0/1	0/23,500

presenting the major results in a systematic and unbiased way. It was developed with the use of the Google Scholar and Web of Science search engines.

It is recognized in Table 9.1 that less research has been conducted in automated secure computing for fraud detection in financial transactions. The research is chiefly current. Furthermore, we used Vos-viewer to know the co-occurrence of a keyword structure. Vos-viewer presents bibliometric data using a range of algorithms and methods. The relationships between various nodes in a network are visualized in this study by grouping together related important keywords (see Figure 9.2).

9.3   Previous Models for Fraud Detection in Financial Transactions

9.3.1   CatBoost

Yandex, a Russian multinational firm that specializes in Internet-related services and goods, developed the machine learning algorithm CatBoost [27]. CatBoost, which is designed to handle categorical data, has grown in popularity recently because of its great performance, simplicity of use, and capacity for handling huge datasets. Decision trees are the basis for CatBoost, a gradient boosting method [28, 29]. Many weak learners (decision trees) are combined using the machine learning approach known as gradient boosting to produce a strong prediction. Adding decision trees to the model repeatedly and fixing the flaws in earlier trees is how the method works [30, 31].

CatBoost is a well-liked option for machine learning tasks due to a number of additional capabilities [32, 33]—for instance, it has a built-in feature selection algorithm that has to choose the model's most crucial characteristics on its own. This can lower the chance of overfitting and make the model easier to understand [31, 32, 34]. CatBoost also comes with a collection of hyperparameters that have been adjusted to enhance its performance for a particular job or dataset. For financial transactions, we mostly use CatBoost to create a model that examines financial transactions and looks for trends that could point to fraud. The CatBoost model is taught to detect shady transactions in real time by training it on past data. A model that analyzes credit card transactions to detect fraud can be created using CatBoost [35]. The program is able to spot transactions that are probably fraudulent by examining trends in transaction data, such as location and time of day.

9.3.2   XGBoost

A structured data handling machine learning technique, XGBoost has been used in a variety of tasks, including picture identification, natural language processing, and financial fraud detection [36, 37]. XGBoost is an ensemble learning method that generates forecasts using a variety of decision trees. It is based on the gradient boosting framework, which makes a final prediction by combining the predictions of many weak learners (in this instance, decision trees). In contrast to previous gradient boosting techniques, XGBoost makes use of a more sophisticated gradient descent technique dubbed "regularized gradient boosting", which aids in reducing overfitting and enhancing model accuracy [38, 39]. Together with its gradient descent technique, XGBoost includes a number of other crucial characteristics that make it well liked among machine learning professionals—for instance, it enables parallel processing, handles missing data, and has a built-in method for categorical data management. This potent machine learning method is perfect to detect financial fraud [40]. A model that analyzes financial transactions to find trends that point to fraud was found to be created using XGBoost [41–43]. The model was used to catch and to recognize suspicious transactions in real time by being trained on past data. Using XGBoost, one may create a model that examines consumer behavior to spot suspicious activities—for instance, the model is eligible to provide an alert to the user if a consumer makes abrupt, substantial withdrawals or purchases that are out of the ordinary [38–40].

9.3.3 LightGBM

A gradient boosting framework called LightGBM is intended to be quick, effective, and scalable. Similar to XGBoost and CatBoost, it was created by Microsoft and is based on the gradient boosting technique [43, 44]. LightGBM combines the predictions of several decision trees to provide a final prediction, similar to other gradient boosting methods [45]; yet, instead of the conventional "level-wise" growth utilized by other algorithms, it employs a special strategy dubbed "leaf-wise" growth. With less nodes needed to construct deeper trees, this method enables LightGBM to achieve higher accuracy and less overfitting [46]. In addition to its leaf-wise development strategy, LightGBM includes a number of other critical components that contribute to its speed and efficiency—for instance, it is able to handle big datasets, supports both CPU and GPU processing, and has a built-in approach for dealing with categorical characteristics. LightGBM is a versatile machine learning framework that is mostly used in several tasks. It has been used, for instance, in image identification, natural language processing, and financial fraud detection [47, 48].

A strong machine learning framework, LightGBM has been very successfully used in the detection of financial fraud. It is well suited to address the issues of fraud detection because to its distinctive characteristics, which include its economical memory consumption, support for categorical data, and built-in regularization approaches [44–46]. Dealing with unbalanced datasets, where the number of fraudulent transactions is much lower than the number of valid transactions, is one of the difficulties in detecting financial fraud. By using a method known as "weighted sampling", which provides greater weight to the minority class (fraudulent transactions) during training, LightGBM assists in resolving this issue. This process makes the possibility of false positives lower while enhancing the model's capacity to identify fraud [47, 48].

9.4 Proposed Model Based on Automated Secure Computing

Machine learning and encryption are used in the promising field of automated secure computing (ASC), which offers safe and private calculations [49, 50]. Financial fraud detection is only one of its many possible uses. We will go through how ASC can be utilized to create a safe and private fraud detection system in this suggested approach.

(i)   Data Preprocessing: The data are preprocessed in this stage to eliminate any noise or discrepancies. For the machine learning model, the data can also be standardized or modified [51, 52].

b)   Feature Selection: To be employed in the model, relevant characteristics are chosen in this stage. The chosen characteristics should have a strong correlation with fraudulent activity but no correlation with honest behavior [53–55]. The ASC model is developed during this phase using the chosen characteristics. Both a machine learning component and a cryptography component are included in the ASC model [8]. Although the cryptography component is in charge of assuring the data's confidentiality and privacy, the machine learning component is in charge of training the model using the chosen features [39, 56, 57].

c)   Evaluation: Using relevant measures, such as accuracy, precision, recall, and F1 score, the model's performance is assessed in this stage [58]. To make sure that the model can be applied to novel and unheard-of scenarios, assessment should be done on both the training and testing datasets [59, 60].

d)   Deployment: In this last stage, the model is set up in a safe environment under strict supervision [61]. The implementation should contain the necessary security safeguards, including audits, data encryption, and access restrictions [62, 63].

Using ASC for financial fraud detection has a number of benefits, one of which is that it offers a high degree of protection and anonymity [64–66] (see Figure 9.3). Before being utilized in the machine learning model, the data is secured to make sure that no unauthorized individuals can access it or alter it. Given the involvement of sensitive financial data in financial fraud detection, this is especially crucial. A number of recommendations have been released by the Reserve Bank of India to help stop and identify financial transaction scams.

Financial organizations should use a thorough Know Your Customer (KYC) procedure to confirm the legitimacy of deals and the identification of clients. This entails gathering identification and address documentation as well as running background checks and risk analyses (Source RBI master direction, 2022a).

Banking organizations should have sufficient anti-money laundering policies and processes in place to stop the funding of terrorism and money laundering. This entails carrying out client due diligence, keeping an eye on transactions, and alerting the authorities to any suspect activity (Source RBI master direction, 2022b).

To spot and stop fake activities, financial organizations should have effective fraud monitoring and detection tools in place. This involves examining trends and abnormalities in transaction data using artificial intelligence and machine learning technologies (Source RBI master direction, 2022c).

To evaluate and reduce risks associated with financial transaction scams, financial organizations should have a thorough risk management strategy in place. Internal investigations, frequent risk evaluations, and continuous tracking of important risk markers are all part of this (Source RBI master direction, 2022d).

Financial organizations are required by the Prevention of Money Laundering Act and other related statutes to disclose any suspect transactions or operations to the appropriate officials, including the Financial Intelligence Unit (Source RBI master direction, 2022e).

9.5 Discussion

Popular machine learning techniques include CatBoost, XGBoost, and LightGBM, which are applied to supervised learning tasks like categorization, regression, and scoring. Due to their ability to quickly find trends and abnormalities in huge databases, these algorithms are frequently used in financial transaction fraud detection. Mainly, decision trees are the basic learning in CatBoost, an open-source toolkit for gradient boosting. It is renowned for having a strong grasp of categorical characteristics, which is advantageous in financial operations where there may be a variety of categorical factors, such as transaction type or vendor categorization. Considering that fake transactions are typically irregular occurrences, CatBoost also includes built-in techniques for handling skewed datasets. Another well-liked gradient boosting tool that makes use of decision trees as basis of learning found in previous studies is XGBoost. It is well adapted for big databases because of its quickness and flexibility. Additionally, XGBoost has built-in ways for dealing with absent data, which is helpful in financial deals as missing data can be a frequent problem. A gradient boosting library called LightGBM was also designed to be quicker and more effective than other well-known gradient boosting libraries. It accomplishes this by calculating gradients using a histogram-based method, which provides for more effective memory utilization and quicker calculation. LightGBM, like XGBoost, excels at managing big databases and has techniques for dealing with lost data integrated right in.

As per this study's proposed model (see Figure 9.4), ASC employs hardware-based security methods to safeguard confidential data and calculations. In order to safeguard confidential financial data and stop illegal access to the data, ASC can be used in fraud identification in financial operations. ASC can also be used to guarantee the security and authenticity of the machine learning models used for fraud identification. Overall, CatBoost, XGBoost, and LightGBM are well-known machine learning algorithms used in financial transaction scam detection because of their capacity to spot trends and abnormalities in huge datasets. However, sensitive data can be safeguarded through automated secure computing that can guarantee the security of the machine learning models used for fraud detection.

In addition to technology, there are other strategies for avoiding and identifying fraudulent behavior, including the following: (a) An organization's internal controls in terms of policies and practices set in place to guarantee that financial operations are carried out in an open and responsible manner. By ensuring that there are checks and balances in place to identify and discourage fraudulent behavior, strong internal controls can help avoid a fraudulent activity; (b) Employee education on financial fraud threats, as well as how to spot and report suspect behavior, can actually prevent fraud from happening. Staff members should receive training on how to spot fraud like odd transactions, unexplained disparities, and behavioral changes; (c) Background checks on potential workers and suppliers can aid in preventing deception by revealing those who have a past of dishonesty or illegal activity; (d) Financial activities should be regularly audited and monitored to spot suspect behavior and stop scams. Internal or external accountants can conduct an audit, reviewing

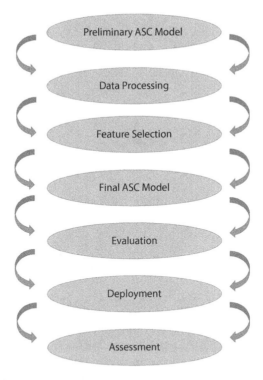

Figure 9.4 Proposed model.

financial records, paperwork, and procedures to look for irregularities or mistakes; (e) Working together with law enforcement can aid in the detection and prevention of financial scams. Law enforcement organizations can offer direction and experience in spotting and looking into fake activity. They can also help in getting money that has been taken back.

9.6   Conclusion

Machine learning is becoming a crucial weapon in the fight against financial fraud. With considerable success, many machine learning algorithms have been employed to identify financial fraud, including CatBoost, XGBoost, and LightGBM [67–70]. Each algorithm has advantages and disadvantages, and the best algorithm will be chosen based on the application's particular needs. The security and privacy issues of applying machine learning models for financial fraud detection must also be taken into account. Machine learning and encryption are used in the promising area of ASC to produce calculations that are safe and maintain anonymity. ASC can help preserve private bank information while still delivering precise fraud detection findings. Overall, detecting financial fraud is a crucial duty in the financial sector, and machine learning algorithms and approaches have significantly increased this capability. The creation of safe and privacy-preserving machine learning models, like those built on ASC, may significantly boost the potency and reliability of systems that identify financial fraud. As technology develops, a number of new technologies, including artificial intelligence and machine learning, blockchain technology, the Internet of Things (IoT), biometric authentication, and quantum computing, can be employed to identify and avoid financial fraud. These and other new technologies, as well as continuing improvements in established technologies, are likely to play a role in the future of financial scam identification and avoidance.

References

1. Zhu, X. *et al.*, Intelligent financial fraud detection practices in post-pandemic era. *Innovation*, 2, 4, 1–11, 2021.
2. Al-Hashedi, K.G. and Magalingam, P., Financial fraud detection applying data mining techniques: A comprehensive review from 2009 to 2019. *Comput. Sci. Rev.*, 40, 713–715, 2021.
3. Kadoya, Y., Khan, M.S.R., Narumoto, J., Watanabe, S., Who is next? A study on victims of financial fraud in Japan. *Front. Psychol.*, 12, 1–13, 2021.
4. West, J. and Bhattacharya, M., Intelligent financial fraud detection: A comprehensive review. *Comput. Secur.*, 57, 47–66, 2016.
5. Reurink, A., Financial fraud: A literature review. *J. Econ. Surv.*, 32, 8–15, 5, 2018.
6. Karpoff, J.M., The future of financial fraud. *J. Corp. Finance*, 66, 713–715, 2021.
7. Ngai, E.W.T., Hu, Y., Wong, Y.H., Chen, Y., Sun, X., The application of data mining techniques in financial fraud detection: A classification framework and an academic review of literature. *Decis. Support Syst.*, 50, 3, 495–502, 2011.
8. Kalejahi, B.K., Eminov, R., Guliyev, A., Using blockchain technology in mobile network to create decentralized home location registry (HLR). *Comput. Syst. Sci. Eng.*, 39, 2, 287–296, 2021.
9. Kim, M., Yu, S., Lee, J., Park, Y., Park, Y., Design of secure protocol for cloud-assisted electronic health record system using blockchain. *Sensors (Switzerland)*, 20, 10, 2–21, 2020.
10. Elhoseny, M., Abbas, H., Hassanien, A.E., Muhammad, K., Kumar Sangaiah, A., Secure automated forensic investigation for sustainable critical infrastructures compliant with green computing requirements. *IEEE Trans. Sustain. Comput.*, 5, 2, 174–191, 2020.
11. Kim, H., Kang, E., Broman, D., Lee, E.A., Resilient authentication and authorization for the internet of things (IoT) using edge computing. *ACM Trans. Internet Things*, 1, 1, 1–27, 2020.
12. Dhaya, R. and Kanthavel, R., Dynamic automated infrastructure for efficient cloud data centre. *Comput., Mater. Continua*, 71, 1, 1625–1639, 2022.
13. Mallika, R., Fraud detection using supervised learning algorithms. *IJARCCE*, 6, 6, 6–10, 2017.
14. Sharma, V., Pandey, B., Kumar, V., Importance of big data in financial fraud detection. *Int. J. Autom. Logistics*, 2, 4, 332–348, 2016.
15. West, J., Bhattacharya, M., Islam, R., Intelligent financial fraud detection practices: An investigation, in: *Lecture Notes of the Institute for Computer Sciences, Social-Informatics and Telecommunications Engineering, LNICST*, 2015.
16. Ye, C., Li, Y., He, B., Li, Z., Sun, J., GPU-accelerated Graph Label propagation for real-time fraud detection, in: *Proceedings of the ACM SIGMOD International Conference on Management of Data*, 2021.
17. Gallo, C., The forex market in practice: A computing approach for automated trading strategies. *Int. J. Econ. Manag. Sci.*, 03, 01, 1–9, 2014.
18. Wang, W., Xu, Y., Du, C., Chen, Y., Wang, Y., Wen, H., Data set and evaluation of automated construction of financial knowledge graph. *Data Intell.*, 3, 3, 418–443, 2021.
19. López-Vizcaíno, M.F. *et al.*, IEEE transactions on affective computing manuscript ID 1 approaches to automated detection of cyberbullying: A survey. *IEEE Access*, 8, 3, 1–25, 2020.
20. Lee, S., Tariq, S., Shin, Y., Woo, S.S., Detecting handcrafted facial image manipulations and GAN-generated facial images using Shallow-FakeFaceNet. *Appl. Soft Comput.*, 105, 1–16, 2021.

21. Alrabiah, A., Optimal regulation of banking system's advanced credit risk management by unified computational representation of business processes across the entire banking system. *Cogent Econ. Finance*, 6, 1, 2–22, 2018.

22. Stojanović, B., Hofer-Schmitz, K., Kleb, U., APT datasets and attack modeling for automated detection methods: A review. *Comput. Secur.*, 92, 1–19, 2020.

23. Steinhubl, S.R., Muse, E.D., Topol, E.J., The emerging field of mobile health. *Sci. Trans. Med.*, 7, 283, 8–12, 2015.

24. Banwo, A., Artificial intelligence and financial services: Regulatory tracking and change management. *J. Securities Oper. & Custody*, 10, 4, 354–365, 2018.

25. Wazid, M., Das, A.K., Kumar, N., v. Vasilakos, A., Design of secure key management and user authentication scheme for fog computing services. *Future Gen. Comput. Syst.*, 91, 475–492, 2019.

26. Brito, A. *et al.*, Secure end-to-end processing of smart metering data. *J. Cloud Comput.*, 8, 1, 1–13, 2019.

27. Hancock, J.T. and Khoshgoftaar, T.M., CatBoost for big data: An interdisciplinary review. *J. Big Data*, 7, 1, 1–45, 2020.

28. Luo, M. *et al.*, Combination of feature selection and catboost for prediction: The first application to the estimation of aboveground biomass. *Forests*, 12, 2, 2–21, 2021.

29. Liu, W. *et al.*, A semi-supervised tri-catboost method for driving style recognition. *Symmetry (Basel)*, 12, 3, 1–18, 2020.

30. Bentéjac, C., Csörgő, A., Martínez-Muñoz, G., A comparative analysis of gradient boosting algorithms. *Artif. Intell. Rev.*, 54, 3, 1937–1967, 2021.

31. Ben Jabeur, S., Gharib, C., Mefteh-Wali, S., Ben Arfi, W., CatBoost model and artificial intelligence techniques for corporate failure prediction. *Technol. Forecast Soc. Change*, 166, 2–10, 2021.

32. Huang, G. *et al.*, Evaluation of CatBoost method for prediction of reference evapotranspiration in humid regions. *J. Hydrol (Amst)*, 574, 1029–1041, 2019.

33. Shahriar, S.A. *et al.*, Potential of arima-ann, arima-svm, dt and catboost for atmospheric pm2.5 forecasting in bangladesh. *Atmos. (Basel)*, 12, 1, 1–12, 2021.

34. Ibrahim, A.A., Ridwan, R.L., Muhammed, M.M., Abdulaziz, R.O., Saheed, G.A., Comparison of the catboost classifier with other machine learning methods. *Int. J. Adv. Comput. Sci. Appl.*, 11, 11, 1–11, 2020.

35. Barua, S., Gavandi, D., Sangle, P., Shinde, L., Ramteke, J., Swindle: Predicting the probability of loan defaults using CatBoost algorithm, in: *Proceedings - 5th International Conference on Computing Methodologies and Communication, ICCMC 2021*, 2021.

36. Li, Y., Stasinakis, C., Yeo, W.M., A Hybrid XGBoost-MLP model for credit risk assessment on digital supply chain finance. *Forecasting*, 4, 1, 184–207, 2022.

37. Kim, H., Mean-variance portfolio optimization with stock return prediction using xgboost. *Econ. Comput. Econ Cybern. Stud. Res.*, 55, 4, 5–17, 2021.

38. Gao, J., Sun, W., Sui, X., Research on default prediction for credit card users based on XGBoost-LSTM model. *Discrete Dyn. Nat. Soc.*, 2021, 1–13, 2021.

39. Fang, W., Li, X., Zhou, P., Yan, J., Jiang, D., Zhou, T., Deep learning anti-fraud model for internet loan: Where we are going. *IEEE Access*, 9, 9777–9784, 2021.

40. Kim, S., Ku, S., Chang, W., Chang, W., Chang, W., Song, J.W., Predicting the direction of US stock prices using effective transfer entropy and machine learning techniques. *IEEE Access*, 8, 111660–111682, 2020.

41. Patil, H., Sharma, S., Raja, L., Study of impact of COVID-19 on different age groups using machine learning classifiers. *J. Interdiscip. Math.*, 24, 2, 479–487, 2021.

42. Simon Yange, T., Ojochogwu Egbunu, C., Adeiza Rufai, M., Onyekwere, O., Abiodun Abdulrahman, A., Abdulkadri, I., Using prescriptive analytics for the determination of optimal crop yield. *Int. J. Data Sci. Anal.*, 6, 3, 72–82, 2020.

43. Ilyas, S., Zia, S., Butt, U.M., Letchmunan, S., Unnisa, Z., Predicting the future transaction from large and imbalanced banking dataset. *Int. J. Adv. Comput. Sci. Appl.*, 11, 1, 273–286, 2020.

44. Nguyen, D.T. and Lee, S., LightGBM-based ransomware detection using API call sequences. *Int. J. Adv. Comput. Sci. Appl.*, 12, 10, 138–146, 2021.

45. Machado, M.R., Karray, S., de Sousa, I.T., LightGBM: An effective decision tree gradient boosting method to predict customer loyalty in the finance industry, in: *14th International Conference on Computer Science and Education, ICCSE 2019*, 2019.

46. Zhang, T. and Li, J., Credit risk control algorithm based on stacking ensemble learning, in: *Proceedings of 2021 IEEE International Conference on Power Electronics, Computer Applications, ICPECA 2021*, 2021.

47. Serengil, S.I., Imece, S., Tosun, U.G., Buyukbas, E.B., Koroglu, B., A comparative study of machine learning approaches for non performing loan prediction, in: *Proceedings - 6th International Conference on Computer Science and Engineering, UBMK 2021*, 2021.

48. Jian, C. and Yan, L.C., An empirical study on the stock prices moving trend based on DWT_LightGBM algorithm, in: *ISCIIA and ITCA 2018 - 8th International Symposium on Computational Intelligence and Industrial Applications and 12th China-Japan International Workshop on Information Technology and Control Applications*, 2018.

49. Garg, K., Nagpal, T., Luthra, S., A study of job satisfaction among managers in ICICI and HDFC Bank in Jalandhar. *Int. J. Appl. Bus. Econ. Res.*, 14, 7, 5255–5263, 2016.

50. Kekwaletswe, R.M. and Lesole, T., A framework for improving business intelligence through master data management. *J. South Afr. Bus. Res.*, 1–12, 2016.

51. Sachan, S., Almaghrabi, F., Yang, J.B., Xu, D.L., Evidential reasoning for preprocessing uncertain categorical data for trustworthy decisions: An application on healthcare and finance. *Expert Syst. Appl.*, 185, 1–45, 2021.

52. Huang, J., Chai, J., Cho, S., Deep learning in finance and banking: A literature review and classification. *Front. Bus. Res. China*, 14, 1, 1–10, 2020.

53. Farquad, M.A.H., Ravi, V., Raju, S.B., Analytical CRM in banking and finance using SVM: A modified active learning-based rule extraction approach. *Int. J. Electronic Cust. Relationship Manag.*, 6, 1, 48–73, 2012.

54. Sun, W. *et al.*, Semi-supervised anti-fraud models for cash pre-loan in internet consumer finance, in: *Proceedings - 2019 IEEE International Conference on Industrial Cyber Physical Systems, ICPS 2019*, 2019.

55. Zioviris, G., Kolomvatsos, K., Stamoulis, G., On the use of a sequential deep learning scheme for financial fraud detection, in: *Intelligent Computing - Proceedings of the 2021 Computing Conference*, 2021.

56. v. Parkale, Y., Buchake, M.D., Gaikwad, S.P., Gawade, M.R., Application of blockchain technology for 7/12 asset tracking system, in: *EAI/Springer Innovations in Communication and Computing*, 2022.

57. Sridevi, T., Mallikarjuna Rao, P., v. Ramaraju, P., Wireless sensor data mining for e-commerce applications. *Indonesian J. Electr. Eng. Comput. Sci.*, 14, 1, 903–911, 2019, doi: 10.11591/ijeecs.v14.i1.pp462-470.

58. Ampomah, E.K., Nyame, G., Qin, Z., Addo, P.C., Gyamfi, E.O., Gyan, M., Stock market prediction with gaussian naïve bayes machine learning algorithm. *Informatica (Slovenia)*, 45, 2, 1–8, 2021.

59. Simionescu, M., The evaluation of global accuracy of romanian inflation rate predictions using mahalanobis distance. *Manag. Dynamics Knowl. Econ.*, 3, 1, 133–149, 2015.

60. Basnet, M. and Ali, M.H., A Deep learning perspective on connected automated vehicle (CAV) cybersecurity and threat intelligence. arXiv.org, 6, 11, 1–18, 2021.

61. Aliapoulios, M., Ballard, C., Bhalerao, R., Lauinger, T., McCoy, D., Swiped: Analyzing ground-truth data of a marketplace for stolen debit and credit cards, in: *Proceedings of the 30th USENIX Security Symposium*, 2021.

62. Wang, Z. *et al.*, Could you describe the reason for the transfer?: A reinforcement learning based voice-enabled bot protecting customers from financial frauds, in: *International Conference on Information and Knowledge Management, Proceedings*, 2021.

63. I. Public. Neupane, A., Soar, J., Vaidya, K., Yong, J. *et al.*, Role of public e-procurement technology to reduce corruption in government procurement. *Crit. Perspect. Acct.*, 28, 2, 304–334, 2021.

64. Ammirato, S., Sofo, F., Felicetti, A.M., Raso, C., A methodology to support the adoption of IoT innovation and its application to the Italian bank branch security context. *Eur. J. Innov. Manag.*, 22, 1, 146–174, 2019.

65. Belás, J., Korauš, M., Kombo, F., Korauš, A., Electronic banking security and customer satisfaction in commercial banks. *J. Secur. Sustain. Issues*, 5, 3, 412–422, 2016.

66. Krishnamoorthy, B. and Shivkumar, A., Punjab national Bank: Implementing core banking solution. *Int. J. Services, Technol. Manag.*, 26, 6, 502–519, 2020.

67. Patil, C.S. and Pawar, K.N., A review on: Protocols and standards in different application areas of IOT. *Int. J. Adv. Res. Comput. Commun. Eng.*, 5, 2, 163–168, 2016.

68. Tiwari, T., Srivastava, A., Kumar, S., Adoption of digital payment methods in India. *Int. J. Electronic Finance*, 9, 3, 217–229, 2019.

69. Yamaoka, H., The future of central banking. *Acct., Econ. Law: A Convivium*, 13, 2, 103–132, 2019.

70. Naskar, D., Digital banking in india: The way ahead. *March Through Search*, VIII, 27, 54–64, 2021.

Additional Readings

RBI Master Direction on KYC (2022a): https://www.rbi.org.in/Scripts/NotificationUser.aspx?Id=11243&Mode=0

RBI Master Direction on AML/CFT (2022b): https://www.rbi.org.in/Scripts/NotificationUser.aspx?Id=11979&Mode=0

RBI Guidelines on Fraud Monitoring and Detection (2022c): https://www.rbi.org.in/Scripts/NotificationUser.aspx?Id=10011&Mode=0

RBI Guidelines on Risk Management (2022d): https://www.rbi.org.in/Scripts/NotificationUser.aspx?Id=10803&Mode=0

RBI Guidelines on Reporting of Frauds (2022e): https://www.rbi.org.in/Scripts/NotificationUser.aspx?Id=10149&Mode=0

10

Data Anonymization on Biometric Security Using Iris Recognition Technology

Aparna D. K.[1], Malarkodi M.[1], Lakshmanaprakash S.[1], Priya R. L.[2] and Ajay Nair[3]

[1]Department of Information Technology, Bannari Amman Institute of Technology, Erode, Tamil Nadu, India
[2]Department of Information Technology, Dept. of Computer Engineering, VESIT College, Maharashtra, India
[3]Bannari Amman Institute of Technology, Erode, India

Abstract

Our civilization has become increasingly reliant on technology. People all over the world are surrounded by smart devices, which begin with communication. Communication aided the development of gadgets such as automobiles, televisions, and other electronic equipment, all of which are now connected to the Internet. In addition, as technology advances, so does crime. The facial recognition security we provide in our mobile phones is probably not very much safer. The concept of facial recognition cannot afford that much security. This paper proposes biometric authentication by means of two-factor facial recognition. In addition to this, we can use iris scanning to make it much safer and secure. The advantages of iris scanning are that these structures do not change over time, and surgery cannot also modify the characteristics and appearance of their pattern. There is a large inter-class variability, such that there is a lot of difference even between the irises of twins. Technology has a tendency to fall short. To safeguard from such a type of problem, we can use two-factor authentication.

Keywords: Facial recognition, cyber security, data anonymization, two-factor authentication, iris scanner

10.1 Introduction

The word biometrics is the fusion of the Greek words bio and metrics. The word bio stands for life, and the word metrics stands for measurement. It is used to find a person's physical and behavioral features. Due to the sensitivity of case and precision, this technique is put forward on traditional methods like passwords and PIN numbers. It can be used as an identity or validation system, based on its architecture. This page explains what a biometric sensor is, the many types of biometric sensors, and how they work. Biometrics is a science

---

Corresponding author: abi.lecturer@gmail.com

Amit Kumar Tyagi (ed.) Automated Secure Computing for Next-Generation Systems, (191–204) © 2024 Scrivener Publishing LLC

that deals with the statistical study of biological properties in its strictest sense. As a result, biometric recognition of persons should be referred to as security applications that examine human traits for identity verification or identification. However, we shall refer to the "biometric recognition of humans" using the abbreviated word "biometrics". Biometric recognition is a potential security strategy that has several advantages over traditional methods that rely on something you have or something you know [1]. Any technology through which a technological system verifies the individuality of a human who looks to approach it is called authentication. The biometric authentication methods are a special type of security system that has a number of advantages over traditional approaches [2]. Some of the advantages are high assurance and security—a biometric identification which provides to "something an individual has", and it also gives hand to confirm an identification. It is not transferable—everybody has an ingress to a distinctive biometric set. Spoofing-proof biometrics are much harder to cheat, user-friendly, fast, and convenient. A face-recognizing technology can match a face from an image or a frame of a video opposed to a faces' database. This works by pointing and also estimating features of the face from a given picture or image, and it is being used to confirm the users through identity verification assistance. Related systems initially emerged in the 1960s as a kind of computer system application. Face recognition methods have been implemented on smart phones and in many kinds of technologies, like robotics, etc. The computerized face recognition methods are categorized as biometrics; hence, they necessitate the measurement of an individual's physical properties despite the fact that face recognition methods have little accuracy other than iris recognition and the fingerprint recognizing biometric technology [3, 4]. Governments and private organizations make use of face recognition systems all over the world these days. Its usefulness differs; some systems have been neglected because of their inefficacy. Facial recognition methods have been prohibited in several locations in the US due to these proclamations. The Meta organization has announced that it has planned to close down Facebook's face recognition method, removing the facial scanning data of over a billion users, in regard to growing societal domains. It would mark one of the supreme shifts in face recognition technology being used in recent memory. Identification of faces is a very hard pattern recognition problem in computing; however, the truth is that an individual can recognize faces without much effort. Face recognition technology leads to the detection of a 3D human face that differs from a look with lighting and facial emotions based on a two-dimensional photograph [5]. Face recognition methods undergo four steps to fulfill this algorithmic obstacle. The human face is initially split up from the image background using facial identification. The split-up facial picture is lined up in the next phase to account for the posture of the face, size of the image, and qualities of the photograph, like grayscale and lighting. The aim of the lineup method is to grant accurate face characteristic localization in the next stage, the extraction of facial features [1].

However, there are certain problems, too. There are drawbacks of unit potential to exploitation of face recognition methods as with any technology—like privacy threats, rights and private freedom violation , knowledge of potential stealing, and different criminal acts. There is additionally a chance of mistakes thanks to defects within the technology. The threat to a person's privacy could be an important drawback of facial recognition systems. People are hesitant to have their faces photographed and hold on to information for unknown future use. Lawbreakers will use face recognition methods to also commit crimes against unwitting victims. They will collect a person's personal info, together with mental image and video from a face scan, and hold on in the databases to defraud someone of their identity. Through this info, a stealer might dispose of the credit card and different debits or begin a bank account within the name of the victim. Other factors will have an effect on the ability of technology to acknowledge the faces of people, together with angles of the camera. Folks sporting impersonate or a bit dynamic looks will throw off face recognition technology, too. It has the potential to be grabbed. It is possible to get a fraudulent one. It is able to transfer it. Multiple identities can indeed be recognized for the same individual. It could be deduced or decoded. Passcodes that are tough to remember are difficult to come up with. It is possible to share it [6]. Multiple identities can be registered for the same person. A fraudulent one is issued in several instances. It cannot be replaced, and it cannot be kept a secret. It is unlikely to replicate a user's biometric information if it is taken. Data protection is concerned with protecting the data's confidentiality, security, and accessibility across all formats [7]. The need for a highly secure identification and personal verification technology is growing as the level of security drops and transaction fraud rises. Identification is necessary for secure operations. The modalities, like iris recognition or fingerprint, can be even used to distinguish identical twins; facial recognition method is not intrusive, can be obtained from afar, and does not necessitate a completely cooperative participant. Face recognition is becoming increasingly common in forensic applications, particularly when other biometric modalities are unavailable [2].

Face recognition is being used in the enforcement of law and by agencies of security all over the globe to identify crimes, and even when fingerprints or DNA traces are not left behind, unknown individuals are depicted in the act of committing crimes. Face recognition is also used in civil programs like driving license and passport issuance to identify fraud applications due to the fact that the face has long been accepted as an identification credential and because the capturing equipment is so readily available [8]. When using biometric technologies like these, it is important to keep in mind that misidentifications, on the other hand, must be kept away to reduce—or perhaps destroy—the risk of mistakenly accusing a blameless individual. The difficulty of the present algorithms in misidentifying people with the same facial structure and other marks on the face is so severe that certain driver licensing authorities have created additional procedures to detect potential matches against the other one. Furthermore, twins and monozygotic twins (identical twins) are bad case situations for face recognition because two independent people have a striking resemblance in looks.

If one topic is attempting to impersonate another, the two may look quite similar. It is critical to put existing face recognition algorithms to the test in the most difficult circumstances. If the algorithms can handle the hardest problems well enough, they should be able to tackle the easier issues as well. This problem can be given the solution of two-factor authentication which deals with both facial recognition and iris scanning [3].

Iris recognition refers to the extraction of biometric features from iris scans. Iris recognition, conjointly called identity verification, is a technique for taking a photo of a person's iris with a lot of contrast using visible and near-infrared light [9]. This is a form of technology of biometric that is just like process and biometric identification. Iris recognition method could be an identification mechanism that is novel and secure. AI can facilitate the usage of this technology in CCTV cameras, cell phones, and alternative access and other security controls, which will be as much useful. Biometric identification systems are likely to fail as a result of this identification. Because no two sets of iris are identical, iris recognition involves using the different iris patterns to distinguish one person from another. It is worth noting that the iris of the same person's left and right eyes can differ. As a result, it is a trustworthy biometric technology that may be used in a variety of settings. Biometric systems that can differentiate samples using separate unique traits are the best. It ensures that no two people with the same unique traits have a possibility of meeting. The developed technology extracts key traits from an iris and compares them with those from other people to see if they come from the same person.

The mathematical abstraction that accomplishes this is thoroughly discussed in the section on software implementation. To solve the problem, one must first get aware of biometric identification approaches that are biased in their usage of iris scans. It would be necessary to identify the key traits that contribute to iris uniqueness and distinguish one person from another. After that, software will be created and used to extract the features in question, primarily for identification purposes. Security issues will always be a top priority in organizations and businesses. Forgery and imposters never stop, and most have advanced to the point that they can breach and beat the majority of deployed systems. Iris comparisons for verification would be reliable because of their efficiency and originality, as their patterns differ from person to person. Other biometric techniques, such as fingerprint recognition, could be useful in authentication, albeit they are more easily falsified than the iris [8, 9]. The application sector is primarily interested in getting quick and precise results when verifying a subject's identity. This is an option provided by the iris scan technique, which takes only 10–15 s to extract and compare. Nothing can be left to chance in the age of technology, especially when it comes to combating fraud. Iris scans, when used correctly, can be a good alternative to most systems, especially those that are biometric in nature. Organizations will only spend significant costs during the installation and setup of the equipment but will save significantly in terms of security investment after that. This document would be extremely useful in assisting in the prevention of this problem where other efforts have failed.

10.2 Problems Faced in Facial Recognition

Like other technologies, facial recognition also has possible downsides, such as privacy dangers, rights abuses and private liberty, and potential knowledge, stealing, and other crime types. There are also possibilities to make mistakes. Because of faults in technology, individual privacy may be jeopardized. Face recognition technology has a significant disadvantage. People dislike having their face images taken and held in a database for unclear reasons or future use. Criminals will employ face recognition technologies to get around the law. Innocent victims are also victims of crimes. They will get personal information from people in addition to the video gathered from facial scans and mental imagery and keep track of you in databases in order to carry out identity theft. A data robber could utilize these details to get rid of credit cards and other cards. There are possibilities to create an account with the victim's name in the bank or make a list of the particular victim's personal information. Other elements will have an impact on the victim's identity exploitation considering the ability of technology to recognize a person's face combined with video camera technology [10]. Lighting levels, angles, and video or image quality are all factors to consider. People can dress in disguise. Their slightly dynamic appearance will also fool the face recognition software. It can be snatched. It is also feasible to obtain a forged one. It is accurate and will be able to transmit data. For the same person, multiple identities can be recognized. It is possible to deduce or decode it, so the passcodes must be difficult to crack. It is difficult to think of things to remember. Nonetheless, it is feasible to distribute it [4].

A forged one is issued on multiple occasions. It cannot be replaced, nor can it be kept hidden. It is true. If a user's biometric information is obtained, it is unlikely to be replicated. The term "protection" refers to safeguarding of the data's confidentiality, security, and integrity [11]. The requirement is high for extremely secure identification. As the level of security rises, so does personal verification technology. Transaction fraud is on the rise as the number of transactions declines. Secure transactions necessitate identification. Fingerprint or iris recognition are examples of modalities that can be used. Face recognition is non-intrusive, even when used to detect identical twins. In forensics, face recognition is becoming more widespread. When other biometric modalities are unavailable, this technology can be used in a variety of ways. Face recognition is used by many agencies—like law enforcement and security agencies—around the world to identify unfamiliar individuals and fraud depicted in photographs. Even fingerprints or DNA left behind in the act of committing violations were not forsaken. In civic programs such as driving, face recognition is also used because duplicate applications are detected during the issuance of licenses and passports. Because the face has long been considered as a form of identification, capturing equipment is very easy to come by [5]. When it comes to biometrics, it is crucial to remember that with technologies like this. Misidentifications, on the other hand, must be avoided in order to limit—or even eliminate—the risk of infection. The problem of current algorithms in misidentifying people with the same facial structure and other facial markings is so serious that certain driver licensing agencies have established additional methods to detect potential matches against the other. Furthermore, because two independent people have a significant likeness in appearance, twins and the identical twins are the worst-case scenarios for facial recognition. When one issue attempts to imitate another, the two may appear to be quite similar. Existing facial recognition algorithms must be put to the test in the most demanding situations. If the algorithms can handle the most difficult problems, they should be capable of solving the simpler problems as well. This difficulty can be solved by using two-factor authentication.

The performance of automated face recognition has been improved by university computer vision researchers and business product makers in a range of difficult face recognition methods tasks. Because of the human activities nowadays, in most of the real-world security situations, face recognition is required. In most real-world security situations, face recognition is required. In some cases, it is unclear if the employment of algorithms is appropriate (which enhances security) or it makes the situation more vulnerable. The genuine article face detection and identification technologies confront a hurdle which is the ability to deal with any situation in which there are multiple subjects that are uncooperative, and the purchase phase in its latter stages is unrestrained [6]. There are several things that contribute to this. There are two types of elements that cause diversity in facial appearance—these are the intrinsic factors and the extrinsic factors. Intrinsic factors are usually due to the physical or the external characteristics of a person's face, and they are even self-contained from the spectator's perspective. These variables can be further classified into two types—these are intrapersonal and interpersonal communication. Intrapersonal variables include the act of changing the appearance of a person's face. Age, for example, is a factor in determining whether or not two people are the same. The same is true for face expressions and accouterments (for example, facial hair, glasses, and cosmetics). However, interpersonal factors are to blame, which can be a result of the disparities in the facial appearance of a variety of persons, with some instances being ethnicity, as well as sexual category. The extrinsic factors lead to the face appearance to change over as a result of light contact with the face and the spectator. Illumination, position, imaging, and scale characteristics (for example, focus, resolution, noise, imaging, and so on) are all important considerations. The obstacles and the challenges that the system of face recognition may encounter in detecting the faces and recognizing the faces are listed below:

Occlusion—The word "occlusion" refers to an obstruction. Occlusion occurs when exactly the entire face was not accessible as the image's input required or the sequence of the image in a face recognition system. As illustrated in a graphic, it is one of the major obstacles of facial recognition. This is due to the existence of numerous occluding things on the face, such as spectacles, beards, and mustaches, and when a picture is acquired from a security camera, some areas of the face are missing. In real-world applications, it is not uncommon to see people chatting on a mobile phone, wearing spectacles, with scarves around the neck and hats on the head, or covering their faces with their hands for various reasons. Such an issue can have a significant concussion on the recognition system's categorization process [12].

Expressions—Our face is the most essential aspect for biometric technology, and it plays an important part in transmitting human identities and emotion, owing to its distinctive traits. The mood of humans varies as a result of various emotions, resulting in a variety of facial expressions. The facial expressions change as an outcome of make-up and hairstyle. Because of these variations in facial expressions, it becomes very hard for a facial recognition system to match or connect with the exact face contained in a database.

Illumination—Light fluctuations are referred to as illumination. Changes in illumination can also affect the total amplitude of the light from the object, which is reflected back, and also the shading and the shadow pattern shown in the picture. Indeed changing the illumination can produce larger visual variations than changing a face's identification or viewpoint. With changes in lighting conditions, the same person photographed with exactly the same camera and seen with virtually the same face expressions and stance might exist as significantly different. Face identification in changing lighting conditions is widely acknowledged as a difficult task for people and algorithms alike.

Locate the face automatically—In the system of facial recognition, the initial step is to locate or determine the face in a video or a picture. The position of the subject in an image series is not always feasible to predict. The position of the head remains unchanged. In a video surveillance system, for example, it is difficult to notice a system in a cluttered environment. There is always motion in a face. The second consideration is that, owing to the difficulty of the background, detection becomes more difficult.

Identify similar faces—Different people can have similar appearances, making it difficult for humans to distinguish them. As a result, a recognition system will have a tough time identifying them.

Low resolution—When the resolution of the face images is recognized to be less than 16 × 16, a low resolution issue emerges in the face recognition system. This issue arises in a variety of surveillance applications, including the small-scale standalone applications of cameras which are available in banks, supermarkets, CCTV cameras in public streets, and so on, where the pictures or images captured by surveillance cameras have an extremely small area of face and could not be provided with sufficient resolution for recognition of the face. The face region will be less than 16×16 because the particular person's face is not actually close to the camera. It contains very little information considering that practically all of the nuances are lost in such a low-resolution face picture. This can dramatically lower the recognition rate.

Pose—In the facial recognition technology, the position variations of a picture or an image is also a source of worry. The pose of the face changes when the spectator's viewing angle and head position changes. The identification of the input image is severely hampered by these changes in posture.

Aging—Because people's appearances are so similar, it is difficult for humans to distinguish between them. As a result, a recognition system will have a hard time recognizing them.

Other systematic problems—Humans find it difficult to distinguish between different persons because their appearances are so similar. As a result, they will be difficult to recognize by a recognition system [7].

10.3 Face Recognition

For a long time, human faces have been recognized as a reliable source of identification. Face recognition is a technique that uses a digital photograph of an individual's face to identify and verify them. Driver's license and passports, applications for duplicates, smartphones, screen locks, and national admission and exit utilizing face recognition technology are becoming increasingly frequent [8]. Face recognition systems have always faced significant hurdles as a result of the emergence of spoofing devices. The capacity to differentiate identical twins is one of these systems' key challenges. Even identical twins cannot be distinguished simply on their DNA [9]. Other biometrics, such as face recognition, fingerprint recognition, and iris recognition, are thus utilized to find them. The final aspect of the faces is remarkably the same, making it difficult to distinguish between identical twins simply based on their face picture [10]. According to Paone et al., identifying identical twins is substantially more difficult than identifying ordinary persons using seven of the best facial recognition algorithms, including three top MBE 2010 participants and four commercial algorithms.

Face recognition problems in identical twins should be investigated for the following reasons: First, boosting the accuracy of facial recognition methods for monozygotic twins can benefit regular people's face recognition. Because ordinary people's faces differ significantly from those of twins', ordinary people's faces are easier to recognize than those of twins. Another reason is that distinguishing a couple of monozygotic twins accurately is required for legal and safety concerns. The next factor is that the number of twin births is increasing, making the difficulty of determining their identification increasingly difficult to solve over time [11]. A normal face recognition set-up's main four components are acquisition of face, face detection, feature of classification, and extraction. In order to effectively recognize an individual, feature extraction is crucial. The term "feature extraction" refers to the process of taking out the correct, applicable, and crucial features that are hidden from a facial image. The method aids the system in ignoring faulty image information and speeding up the recognition process [11].

Face recognition will be improved by using features that have a higher degree of individual differentiation. The most prevalent extraction features for facial recognition are the discrete cosine transform (DCT), the linear discriminant analysis (LDA), and the principal component analysis (PCA). To learn a subspace, PCA and LDA utilize training data. The discrimination power analysis and the updated generation, the dynamic weighted discrimination power analysis (DWDPA), improves the recognition accuracy for photographs of regular people as well as other biometrics such as palm print images by increasing the discrimination power for the selected DCTs [12, 13].

When regular people's photos are used as inputs to the face recognition system, conventional face attributes can effectively reveal variations between individual faces because the database of regular people has a wide range of faces with evident differences. Due to the significant resemblance between face photos in particular databases, like identical twins, using traditional attributes to classify something could lead to a wrong classification. Here a couple of photos of monozygotic twins are sometimes more alike than the two images of a single person. As a result, removing traditional and generic facial traits has no influence on enhancing the accuracy of facial recognizing methods for monozygotic twins to assist the face recognition system in solving this challenge pleasantly.

The mismatching points are an appropriate portrayal of discrepancies between a couple of photos, while the matching points indicate similarities between two images. A face picture was also provided by its constituents, like the eyebrows, the mouth, the eyes, the nose, and also the curve of the face margin, using face recognition label detection (FLRD), which is a detection method of face region landmarks. The amount of mismatch points in each location identified the main distinguishing feature of each identical twin pair's face.

In recent years, crowdsourcing has aided in the resolution of numerous challenges in a variety of fields, ranging from company management to engineering [14].

How is it credited with being the first to scientifically introduce the crowdsourcing approach? Since the publication of Howe's work until now, the topic of crowdsourcing has always piqued people's curiosity [15]. To identify the optimal solution, this approach uses collective intelligence to give a solution to a problem or give an answer to a question. In this study, we also used collective intelligence to analyze the facial differences of monozygotic twins. In terms of human brain study, we created various questions to find the most distinguishable part in monozygotic twins' faces. For the right and good design of questions, various solutions were investigated. In the end, all the questions were posed in a couple of different ways: the non-biased and the prejudiced. When all of the users' replies to all of the questionnaires are added together, a region emerges as very distinct in the faces of monozygotic twins.

The research investigates the effectiveness of presenting the most distinguishing region in monozygotic twins' faces in fraudulently separating the monozygotic twins from the same individual by suggesting 12 traits. The M-SIFT algorithm's key points and face landmarks are used to obtain the features. The collection contains 650 photographs, including 290 shots of monozygotic twins (115 pairs) and 360 photos of normal people (120 people). According to the machine processing approach's results, the curve of the face is the most unique region in 65% of monozygotic twins' face photographs [16].

In addition, the curve of the face was selected as the most distinct location among the 35.5% of identical twins photographed by participants' responses to questionnaires. Finally, among the five regions of the human face, the face curve is identified as a significant area in distinguishing monozygotic twins. The proposed features retrieved from the facial curve region have a high accuracy, indicating that this area of historical significance is effective in distinguishing monozygotic twins.

10.4   The Important Aspects of Facial Recognition

Today's agencies of law enforcement rely heavily on face recognition databases. According to research provided by the Electronic Frontier Foundation, the arrestees' faces are compared with municipal, state, and federal facial recognition databases, agencies of law enforcement which frequently gather mugshots from individuals [17]. These mugshot databases can be used by law enforcement authorities to recognize individuals in images gathered from a number of different sources, including cameras of closed-circuit television, traffic cameras, social media, and images taken by cops themselves which are all used in this investigation. According to the Electronic Frontier Foundation, officers can capture photos of the drivers or the pedestrians and match them to faces in some databases of facial recognition using their cellphones, tablets, or other mobile devices. Face recognition databases are being frequently used by enforcement of law authorities. As stated by a study published by the Electronic Frontier Foundation, enforcement of law organizations often gathers mug shots from people who have been imprisoned and compare them to facial recognition databases at the local, state, and federal levels.

These mugshot databases can be used by law enforcement organizations to identify people in images from a variety of sources, including closed-circuit television cameras, traffic cameras, social media, and cop photos [15]. According to the Electronic Frontier Foundation, police officers can capture photos using their cellphones, tablets, or other mobile devices, and the drivers or the pedestrians compare their faces in one or more databases of facial recognition.

Face recognition is a type of biometric sort of technology that is being used to recognize human faces, as you may or may not be aware. It will validate an individual's identity by scanning their face. This might mean that a person cannot have several licenses of driver's or state identities, or that they cannot be found in a database of law enforcement. Face recognition is the most important component for intelligent vehicle applications in future, such as predicting if an individual is authorized to operate a motor vehicle. Many companies of security technology are working on a face recognition program of security that is accurate, rapid, and capable of validating and identifying a driver's identity even from outside of the car that he is driving [16].

Facial recognition systems are crucial for identifying undesirable suspects and drivers, but why is the technology's advancement so critical? During the development of this technology, many developers took shortcuts. Many developers utilize a web camera, which is low-cost to capture all photos as a limitation. These systems are made up of two distinct elements. Face detection comes first, followed by face recognition. Adjustment of lighting technologies could be used to help make these systems show better results. Identification and categorization are two purposes of facial recognition. Identification is accomplished by comparing live or recorded digital footage to photos stored in a database. The consequences of facial recognition grow more far-reaching when such information is "categorized". Without the assistance of a person, technology may automatically sort people into categories based on recognizable characteristics such as age, gender, weight, or even inferred sexual orientation [18].

By comparing photographs to the "statistical representation of the average of that category", the system classifies people into categories. Facial recognition technology opens the door to biometric mass surveillance if it becomes widely available. This is because facial recognition capabilities may be added to CCTV and other cameras, which are pervasive in public and private settings. Law enforcement and private actors are already using facial recognition technology at a variety of locations, such as schools and train stations. What is worrying though is that, without our awareness or consent, our photos are often uploaded to facial recognition databases—for example, Clearview AI, a US technology company, recently revealed that it scrubbed more than three billion images of faces from social media sites like Twitter, YouTube, and Facebook and sold our data to the government and private companies in exchange for payments. Such very private information is presently being used in law enforcement to make police judgments, and it may be used in the future by public or commercial organizations to make choices about your suitability for a job, a university course or loans, international travel, or festival admittance [17].

Police personnel benefit from mobile facial recognition programs because they can identify people shortly in their area from a safer distance. It can assist them by offering background on who they're working with and whether they should move cautiously. If an officer pulled over a needed drug trafficker or murderer during a regular traffic stop, the officer will be alerted right away that the suspect is wanted. They could request assistance from here. Gatekeeper's DriverCam is one type of face recognition system that could be utilized in this situation [19]. This face-recognizing camera scans and checks in with a database for the information in a matter of seconds. Using face recognition technology, law enforcement agencies can sometimes identify children even if they have been missing for years. These law agencies are able to employ facial recognition to identify the criminals. Airports all over the world employ the face recognition method to identify criminals and threats when they enter the airports or seek to board an aircraft. Other than retailers, facial recognition can boost the security and safety of locations like banks and airports. It has been a common element of screening of airport security for years. This software has aided in the identification of criminals and threats to planes and its passengers much like this has aided in the identification of crooks who enter stores. According to the US Customs and Border Protection, facial recognition will be employed on 97% of foreign visitors by 2023. One more advantage is that the technology could undertake the border inspections much more quickly and precisely than humans—for example, banks use a software to prevent a crime by detecting persons who have been charged with crimes previously and telling the banks so that they could pay special attention to an individual's business in the bank [18]. Retailers can employ face recognition to help customers check out more quickly. Instead of forcing the consumers to pay with credit or cash, stores might employ face recognition to immediately charge the things to their bank accounts. While the most obvious advantages of facial recognition are the ability to identify and locate missing people and criminals, they provide ease also. Completing either credit or cash purchases at businesses, face recognition systems may recognize the face and bill the goods to your account. It was used more frequently during the pandemic for security and convenience as well as to help manage the reduced customer-to-staff ratio. Businesses expect the technology to be utilized in the future to recognize and market to loyal club members—for example, fingerprinting requires a large number of resources than face recognition. It does not include direct human interaction or physical contact. Despite this, businesses use artificial intelligence to automate and streamline this process [20, 21]. When we unlock smartphones and doors, withdraw an amount from an automated teller machine, or perform other operations that require a password, key, or PIN, the number of touch points is reduced. You may use facial recognition of your cloud storage to tag photos. It makes it very comfortable to conduct, search, and share the photos. This is used to make Facebook tag suggestions also [19].

10.5   Proposed Methodology

Iris scanning, which is also known as the iris recognition, is actually the process by which a high-contrast snapshot of a person's iris is taken using visible and near-infrared light. Iris recognition is also one of the types of biometric technology that is almost similar to fingerprinting and face recognition. Advocates of iris scanning technology claim that it allows officers to compare the suspects' iris scans with the database of photos in addition to determining or confirming the identification of the subject. They also argue that iris scanning is faster and much more accurate than other fingerprint scans because it is much easier to impersonate or change one person's fingers than it is to change the eyes. Iris scanning raises serious issues related to civil privacy and liberty. It is possible to scan the irises from afar or even while a person moving, thus implying that data might be acquired privately, beyond the acknowledgement or the agreement of the users. There are several security vulnerabilities as well: apart from a renewed credit card number, if the database of biometric data is stolen or hacked, getting a new set of eyes is not straightforward. In addition, third-party companies regularly acquire and maintain iris biometrics, which aggravates the security-related problem.

Iris scanning is one of the techniques to determine the extraordinary patterns in people's irises or the colored circles in people's eyes. The iris recognition scanners actually function by directing the invisible infrared lights on the iris to pick up the unique patterns which are not visible to the human eye. The eyelashes, the eyelids, and the specular reflections, which often block the sections or parts of the iris, are actually determined by iris scanners and are also closed out by it [22]. The final outcome is a cluster of pixels that are strictly adhered to the iris. Following that, the lines and the colors of the eyes are studied in order to generate a specific pattern that is characterized by the iris. This certain pattern is digitized and compared with the recorded templates in the database for verification (one-to-one matching pattern) or identification (one-to-many matching pattern).

The iris is the visible body part that may be assessed remotely using the vision system of a machine for automated iris recognition.

A.   Optics, statistical inference, pattern recognition, and computer vision are all used in iris pinpointing technologies.

B.   The spatial patterns which are visible in the human iris are extremely unique and vary with each individual.

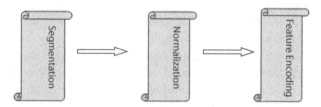

Figure 10.1 Different steps in iris recognition.

The system has been built up by several subdomain systems, in which each one of them will correlate to a different step of the iris recognition process. These are the stages illustrated in Figure 10.1.

Iris recognition starts with isolating the exact iris region in the digitized eye image. To approximate the iris region, we can utilize two circles: one by the iris or sclera boundary and another for the iris or pupils boundary. The image quality of the ocular pictures determines the success of segmentation. The outside radius of the iris patterns can be determined by using the pupil's center. The inner and the outer edges of the iris are located by employing the Canny edge detector to find the edge picture [23].

10.6   Results and Discussion

Because it is extremely dependable and accurate, iris recognition technology is the preferred method for the enforcement of law and border control. However, because of its hardware requirements, it is far less extensively employed for consumer-facing use cases than other modalities such as face and voice recognition [22]. The iris scanners identify and exclude eyelids, eyelashes, and also specular reflections that frequently obstruct the parts of the iris. Then, the final outcome is a gathering of pixels which includes the iris only. Moreover, the eye colors and lines are observed in a sequence to build a design of bits which encode the data in the iris. Iris biometrics provides several different advantages when used for identification and authentication. These are some of them [23]:

- There is no physical contact when scanning.
- Accurately matching performance.
- It is possible to photograph it even from a distance.

10.7   Conclusion

In the field of biometrics for human identification, iris recognition is gaining popularity. We began by discussing two iris recognition techniques: Gabor wavelet-based iris encoding and the use of correlation filters. Although these algorithms perform well for properly acquired iris images, the identification rates decline in more realistic acquisition situations when elements such as gaze angle, specular reflections, occlusions, and deformations alter the image appearance. The use of Bayesian graphical models is one technique to match such difficult images. Local deformations and occlusions can be accommodated in these models, and a match score which takes both occlusions and deformations into consideration can be calculated. The pictures are separated into non-overlapping patches, and the patch cross-correlations can also be employed as the input models. The model learns parameters using cross-correlation peak values and peak positions. The model can be used to generate a match score for a probing image and a template image once the model's parameters have been estimated. For a reasonably simple iris image database and a more difficult ocular image database, we showed matching results. This paper covers the study of an iris, a thorough account on how the iris has become a biometric property, and the general foundation for the iris recognition systems that are now in use. The primary goal of this project is to create a timeline of various iris recognition systems. Formulated on this viewpoint, it can be argued that most of the iris recognition research is more or less comparable, but attention has primarily been on four important areas: iris segmentation, normalization (which includes the removal of noise), feature extraction, and template classification of iris. The researchers are focused on building the algorithms for all the four primary areas from 1993 to 2002, and they were also interested in creating systems of their own. Much research on the segmentation stage, which entails iris segmenting and decreasing the presence of noise in it, took place between 2003 and 2009. The majority of the research work between 2007 and 2012 focused on building new feature extraction methods and improving the iris classification. Until 2006, the majority of the research was focused on developing new filters and image processing algorithms to improve the system's accuracy. However, in 2006, this sector saw a significant transformation, with researchers implementing machine learning methods for improving system accuracy. The attention has now shifted to multimodal biometric approaches. Following the timeline review, a full examination of multiple publicly available iris databases is presented. Based on this research, it is concluded that, despite the fact that this field has witnessed enormous progress over the last two decades, there are still more domain areas in which this iris technology may be applied by tweaking a few more ways. Many powerful iris recognition systems will be developed spontaneously and can also be deployed in a variety of domain areas like security systems in borders, immigration checking systems, and access control systems both to the devices and the premises as well as in time and attendance maintenance systems in the coming decade.

References

1. Murukesh, C., Thanushkodi, K., Preethi, P., Mohamed, F., Multimodal biometric authentication system based on score-level fusion of palmprint and finger vein. *Adv. Intell. Syst. Comput.*, 324, 551–560, 2015.
2. Kuznetsov, A.A., Legal basis of biometric methods of identity authentication, in: *Economics Law Innovaion*, pp. 85–90, 2021.
3. Kintonova, A., Povkhan, I., Gabdreshov, G., Improvement of iris recognition technology for biometric identification of a person. *East.-Eur. J. Enterp. Technol.*, 6, 60–69, 2022.
4. Kant, J., Jaffery, Z., Singh, L., A short review on machine learning techniques used for fingerprint. 2020.
5. Dong, Y., 3D face recognition neural network for digital human resource management. *Sci. Programming*, 6544282, 2022.
6. Cain, A. and Still, J., Graphical authentication passcode memorability: Context, length, and number. *Proc. Hum. Factors Ergon. Soc. Annu. Meeting*, 63, 447–451, 2019.

7. Aval, R., Fatemeh, S., Baigi, M., Sarbaz, M., Kimiafar, K., Mousavi, F., Security, privacy, and confidentiality in electronic prescribing systems: A review study, 10, 2022.

8. Alketbi, S. and Saif, A., Dual recovery of DNA and fingerprints using minitapes. *J. Forensic Sci. Criminal Inves.*, 16, 001–004, 2022.

9. Nguyen, K., Proença, H., Alonso-Fernandez, F., Deep learning for iris recognition: A survey, 2022.

10. Agrawal, P., Smart surveillance system using face tracking. *Int. J. Res. Appl. Sci. Eng. Technol.*, 9, 2613–2617, 2021.

11. Kasten, A., *Secure semantic web data management: Confidentiality, integrity, and compliant-availability in open and distributed networks*, Vom Promotionsausschuss des Fachbereichs 4: Informatik der Universität Koblenz-Landau zur Verleihung des akademischen Grades Doktor der Naturwissenschaften (Dr. rer. nat.) genehmigte.

12. Pandiaraj, A., Prakash, S.L., Kanna, P.R., Effective heart disease prediction using hybrid-machine learning. *2021 Third International Conference on Intelligent Communication Technologies and Virtual Mobile Networks (ICICV)*, Tirunelveli, India, pp. 731–738, 2021.

13. Singh, K. and Parihar, A., Illumination estimation for nature preserving low-light image enhancement. *Visual Comput.*, 2023.

14. Chiranjeevi, S. and Das, P., *15 Detection of augmented facial landmarks-based face swapping*, 2023.

15. Clarke, K., Barari, A., Hogue, A., Dubrowski, A., Using a delphi method approach to select theoretical underpinnings of crowdsourcing and rank their application to a crowdsourcing app. *Simul. Healthc. J. Soc. Simul. Healthc.*, 2023.

16. Vinusha, S. and Shanthi, S., Monozygotic twin face recognition: An in-depth analysis and plausible improvements. *Image Vision Comput.*, 116, 104331, 2021.

17. Shree, M., Dev, A., Mohapatra, A., Review on facial recognition system: Past, present, and future, 2023.

18. Mao, J., Zhao, G., Chang, Y., Yin, X., Peng, X., Xu, R., Hierarchical Bayesian theme models for multipose facial expression recognition. *IEEE Trans. Multimed.*, 19, 861–873, 2017.

19. Zulfiqar, M., Syed, F., Khan, M.J., Khurshid, K., Deep face recognition for biometric authentication, in: *2019 International Conference on Electrical, Communication, and Computer Engineering (ICECCE)*, pp. 1–6, Swat, Pakistan, 2019.

20. Pandiaraj, A., Venkatesan, R., Manochitra, S., Lakshmanaprakash, S., Neural network based approach on sentimental analysis using herb. *2022 4th International Conference on Smart Systems and Inventive Technology (ICSSIT)*, Tirunelveli, India, pp. 1092–1100, 2022.

21. Abirami, A. and Palanikumar, S., Proactive network packet classification using artificial intelligence, in: *Artificial Intelligence for Cyber Security: Methods, Issues and Possible Horizons or Opportunities*, Studies in Computational Intelligence, S. Misra, and A. Kumar Tyagi (eds.), vol. 972, Springer, Cham, 2021, https://doi.org/10.1007/978-3-030-72236-4_7.

22. Jayasinghe, D., Abeysinghe, C., Opanayaka, R., Dinalankara, D., Silva, B., Wijesinghe, R., Wijenayake, U., Minimizing the effect of specular reflection on object detection and pose estimation of bin picking systems using deep learning. *Machines*, 11, 91, 2023.

23. Vemuru, K., Implementation of the canny edge detector using a spiking neural network. *Future Internet*, 14, 371, 2022.

11

Analysis of Data Anonymization Techniques in Biometric Authentication System

Harini S.[1]*, Dharshini R.[2], Agalya N.[2], Priya R. L.[3] and Ajay Nair[3]

[1]Department of Artificial Intelligence and Data Science, Bannari Amman Institute of Technology, Sathyamangalam, Tamil Nadu, India
[2]Department of Information Technology, Bannari Amman Institute of Technology, Sathyamangalam, Erode, Tamil Nadu, India
[3]Department of Computer Engineering, VESIT College, Maharashtra, India

Abstract

In today's smart era, recent advances in digital world technologies paved a way to sneak, access, and analyze sensitive personal data like bank transfer details, medical records, and social media activities. This may result in data breach and privacy violations. As a result, the protection of data and privacy management nowadays has become a hard challenge. Many solutions for securing data have been offered as of today, such as biometric authentication systems that use the palm vein throughout the authentication process. Furthermore, by adopting data anonymization techniques, the database records can be rendered anonymous, ensuring that the data is properly protected. It does not, however, provide the essential capacity for data protection against attackers. There is a risk of data/information being leaked to the unauthenticated population. Attackers can manipulate the user's unique authentication identity for stealing data. To overcome this risk, this paper proposes a biometric authentication system by means of retinal recognition, which makes it hard for the attackers to crack it. While comparing palm vein authentication with retinal recognition, retinal recognition stands out as a superior technology—high accuracy, advanced technique, and better positioned for future development in biometric authentication. Furthermore, this paper discusses the implementation of data anonymization techniques in the biometric authentication database records, which makes the data highly impossible to access.

Keywords: Anonymization, privacy, biometrics, authentication, retinal

11.1 Introduction

Data storage plays a mandatory role in this modern era. As every person needs to store their personal data or important data, they use the Internet as a way to store it. Hence, the Internet became a part of our life, but the data stored in it can be violated using various ways. Storing data with advanced privacy techniques is needed to make sure that our data

---

*Corresponding author: harini.ad21@bitsathy.ac.in

Amit Kumar Tyagi (ed.) Automated Secure Computing for Next-Generation Systems, (205–222) © 2024 Scrivener Publishing LLC

cannot be violated. Thus, the Internet of Things (IoT) enables the development or deployment of smart devices to solve the challenges and issues faced in the real world. The high pace of adoption of IoT technologies can make people's lives easier, but users' data must be adequately protected [1]. One of the major difficulties faced is violation of data. It is the real-time crisis in which data is violated and used for some other purposes without the authentication of the person who owns the data. This makes the data in dire need to be secured and protected with more techniques and also with the implementation of IoT. The implementation of IoT can make sure that the data is stored in an effective manner. In the coming years, every organization and company will be expected to increase their personal data security [2]. The data of a user plays a mandatory part in a company or organization, as a person working in the company will have a unique ID. This ID can be linked to other companies for various purposes, which can be traceable actively [3]. Now, without the knowledge of that person, by using the ID, someone can violate the personal data of that particular person. Here comes the problem of data breaching. This has been a major problem for the past decades but is still not solved by any enhanced methods. Thus, the demand for data security is always a top priority as the whole modern world is now using the Internet as a major part of their life.

Data anonymization is used to rectify this crisis. Here the data of the person or an organization is encrypted or modified to a non-understandable source which can only be known by a particular person or organization. This makes the data protected and known only by certain persons. The data stored using data anonymization cannot be violated in an easy way. It requires a certain process to violate that particular data. Thus, storing data by data anonymization can be more effective and helpful for its security. Data anonymization uses certain techniques to store a particular data like encryption of that data and using different symbols or letters instead of the real data, thus making it secure [4]. These methods are used to safeguard sensitive data while also ensuring data utility [5]. As a result, recognizing the true data becomes more difficult. Moreover, the attacker would have a difficult time identifying the data because he just gets the equivalence class and no other information [6]. Even though data is more secure using modern technologies, it can also be violated, which underscores the demand for enhanced security of data and privacy. The implemented program must meet the needs of clients, such as data storage, individual administration, and public insights, as well as approval of information sharing with other members or organizations. Therefore, there is always a proposal of new methods and ideas on how to store data securely.

There are three types of privacy: policy, personal, and corporate. Privacy, statistics, and encryption are three terms that come to mind while thinking about privacy [7]. Thus, biometric cryptography is one of the emerging techniques that can be used for data privacy. Biometric encryption enjoys comparable benefits and drawbacks as customary biometric acknowledgment for client verification. What is more—ID: helpfully, a client generally conveys his biometrics with him; thus, he cannot neglect or render his encryption keys. Be that as it may, the encryption framework should simultaneously adapt to changing keys since biometrics are intrinsically "boisterous". Biometric technology employs a variety of techniques, including palmprint, palm vein, fingerprint, and iris recognition. There has been a surge in interest in using biometrics as keys to encrypt private information during the last decade. During the authentication procedure, the existing system of storing data uses biometric authentication methods of palm vein. This procedure ensures that the data is stored in a secure manner. This method uses the pseudonym creation technique to stored data anonymous, ensuring that the information is truly secure. Unauthorized parties will not be able to access the data using this method. This data is fully unique and can be used in digital locks and security apps with restricted access. This system's registration process entails entering biometric attributes, preprocessing, feature extraction, and, lastly, storing the extracted features. This is one of the most effective strategies for storing data. Every solution offered, however, has some limits. The data can also be tampered with a little effort or by knowing the person's palm vein.

Therefore, there is still a need for an efficient and more secure protection of data in the upcoming years. As the protection of data increases, the violation of privacy is also gradually increasing. This reduces the confidentiality of the users in storing data. Thus, the demand for increased protection rises, so even more advanced techniques are needed to secure data. However, the above mentioned existing system has certain limitations in storing and protecting data. We need to have an alternative and effective way to store and protect data to improve the privacy and confidentiality of users. Therefore, this study discusses the protection of data using data anonymization and the techniques implemented in the biometric authentication method by means of retinal scanning. Here retinal scanning makes the data protected in an authenticated way where a third party cannot gain access to that data. The data will be more secure by using this method. The data anonymization techniques help us make the data encrypted and stored; this will also make it hard for the third party to violate that data. This method requires more effort to violate the data; thus, it can ensure security to that data. The data stored by this method is comparatively more secure than by the other methods. The biometric traits will always be unique and the retinal scanning of a person cannot be known by the attacker. so even though it is known, it also requires certain efforts to get the data as it is stored by using data anonymization techniques. Thus, this method provides more security to a user's personal data from the attacker.

Here the techniques implemented in data anonymization and its analysis are discussed, and the main concepts of retinal scanning by means of biometric authentication method are also elaborately discussed. The combination of data anonymization techniques in the biometric authentication system of retinal scanning is explained, and its properties are also discussed.

11.2 Literature Survey

Data anonymization and biometric authentication have evolved to a greater position these years. It came across a lot of process and evolution to reach almost an effective level of storing data securely. Data anonymization has certain techniques like generalization, suppression, distortion, swapping, and masking, which are implemented to secure data in an easy manner. Every technique has certain strengths and weaknesses which were analyzed and explained by many researchers. Thus, the strength of each technique is implemented by many people in their ideas on how to secure data. The weaknesses are also being rectified by certain researchers. Hence, the concept of securing data has a lot of demand in this new era, and the techniques of preserving data, without any weaknesses, should be increased [8].

The concept of using data anonymization techniques was implemented for the reason of privacy-preserving data publishing as most of the anonymization algorithms that were traditionally used were rarely used for the social network (SN) data. Thus, in order to safeguard the SN data, data anonymization and de-anonymization procedures were applied. As the research on SN data increases, there is still a need for a newer method to secure data. [11].

In this fast-growing era, many techniques and systems were developed and used to secure data in an efficient manner. Thus, one of the developing technologies is using biometric systems everywhere for certain purposes. Hence, this system is also used for securing data.

The first and foremost concept of authenticating fingerprints was developed and used for securing data. This method serves better than using passwords and PINs as it is robust and authentic, but this method has certain limitations like false rejection rate (FRR) and false acceptance rate (FAR). Therefore, fingerprint authentication needs certain improvements in the enhancement process of fingerprint and a better identification algorithm without FRR and FAR [12]. The implementation of data anonymization techniques in fingerprint authentication systems paved a way to secure the data for some time as every human being has a different fingerprint pattern, and it gives high accuracy for authentication. Then, the anonymization techniques were also implemented in the fingerprint, which enables the data to be stored securely. The duplication of fingerprints can be done easily, thus making a third party gain access to the data in a faster way [13].

Then, the concept of palmprint authentication was introduced [14]. This method gives a higher recognition rate and low cost of acquisition equipment than fingerprint authentication. It is one of the best methods in biometric authentication. However, this method also deals with the same limitation like fingerprint authentication as the palmprint can also be duplicated [15]. Then, the concept of palmprint authentication with the implementation of data anonymization techniques was introduced. This gives a wider area than fingerprint authentication. This method also performs in a similar manner to fingerprint authentication as the system takes both the outer patterns of the finger and the palm. Here also the techniques of data anonymization were implemented to secure data.

Table 11.1 Advantages and disadvantages of the previously existing systems.

Previous systems	Advantages	Disadvantages
Data anonymization techniques	Efficient and easy to use	Can be easily identified by a third party
Anonymization techniques for privacy-preserving data publishing	New techniques were implemented	Sn data needs a new method to be secure
Password authentication	Unique id for each person	Can be easily leaked
Fingerprint authentication	Robust and reliable	FAR and FRR
Anonymization techniques in fingerprint authentication	High accuracy	Duplication
Palmprint authentication	Higher recognition rate	Duplication
Anonymization techniques in palmprint authentication	Wider area	Duplication and can leave the palmprint anywhere

As both fingerprint authentication and palmprint authentication were similar, the technique has the same limitations in terms of duplicating the palmprint and gaining access to the data by a third party [13].

Thus, the limitations of these previous methods gave way to newer concepts in biometric authentication retina, and iris scanning [16]. The important limitations are given in Table 11.1. Data anonymization is also implemented in all these biometric authentication systems, and the existing system and the proposed plan are discussed in the following sections.

11.3 Existing Survey

There are lots of existing systems by which to store data in an efficient manner. As the ideas are innovative and creative, the data can be stored in many ways, and it also can be protected. As technology develops, the problem also arises; so, even though the existing system increases, still the violation also takes place. Data is becoming increasingly large, and it is necessary to share it with others for various purposes. As a result, there is a danger of data breach. The suggested and developed methods should become increasingly efficient and protective when they are implemented in various locations. As a result, de-identification, privacy-preserving aggregation, and operations on encrypted data are currently the three widely used approaches [17]. As a result, the existing system uses biometric authentication since it is more successful in dealing with this real-time situation.

11.3.1 Biometrics Technology

The modern world necessitates data sharing at all times. Almost all businesses and organizations must store massive amounts of data in a safe and secure manner. The difficulty of obtaining someone's personal data without their knowledge is constantly there in this digital era. This makes the user lose their hope on data security. Thus, there should always be new ways to solve this problem. This issue can be solved by biometric technology which comes into the concept of data protection in a secure way [18]. Biometric technology identifies and verifies the individuals through their biometric traits and allows access to their data. Here the verification process validates the user who he or she claims to be [19]. This is a one-to-one process where the individual's trait and the biometric profile matches accordingly. Thus, nowadays biometric technology is blooming in the concept of data security [20]. Biometric systems also have various methods to store the data, like using an individual's fingerprint, palm, iris, and retina. As some of these biometrics will be unique even for twins, thus storing data using such methods can be more effective and secure. Here we can use biometric cryptography to secure the data, where biometric scanning takes the print of a particular part, and using data anonymization we can encrypt that data to make it secure and private.

11.3.2 Palm Vein Authentication

Fingerprint authentication and palmprint authentication fails to secure data in an efficient manner as it has certain limitations. Thus, the palm vein authentication concept takes place to secure data properly. Since the problem of violation of data is still increasing, this method of palm vein authentication has become more popular and been more

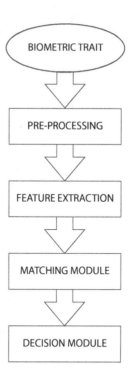

Figure 11.1 Process involved.

effective in storing the data properly and protectively. This is also due to the need to store vast volumes of data for a variety of purposes. This method can be used for a variety of authentication and privacy protection purposes, such as entering an ATM or logging onto a computer system. Palm veins have a number of properties that remain consistent throughout an individual's lifespan—qualities that are difficult to change or mimic [21]. Palm vein authentication compares the pattern of veins in the palm of the individual being authenticated (which show as blue lines) to a pattern stored in a database. Each person's vascular patterns are distinct; even identical twins have diverse patterns. As a result, it distinguishes this procedure from others. The process flow is illustrated in Figure 11.1.

11.3.3   Methods of Palm Vein Authentication

Palm vein authentication involves certain methods to make the data more protective. As it is an existing and popular method of data privacy, it requires a combination of new and old techniques of data anonymization, and the plan comes into effect with great output. The palm vein scanner first captures a picture of the palm vein [13]. Figure 11.2 shows the vein images. The palm vein has certain characteristics, as can be seen in Figure 11.3. Then, in order to improve the quality of the vein image, it is filtered using the median filter method, which may remove noise and is combined with contrast-limited adaptive histogram equalization. The image border is detected using the Canny edge detector [22] after the filtering procedure. Figure 11.4 shows the result of the Canny detector. It is used to find out more about the vein pattern. It undergoes three phases to get the clear boundary [13].

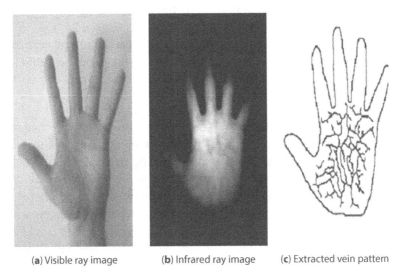

(a) Visible ray image   (b) Infrared ray image   (c) Extracted vein pattern

Figure 11.2 Features on a palm vein [13].

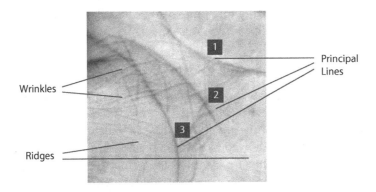

Figure 11.3 Palmprint features [13].

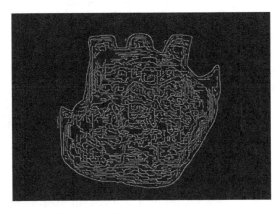

Figure 11.4 Result of using a Canny detector [13].

Phase 1: The original image's Gaussian smoothing filtration must be done in such a way that the phase shift of an image particle does not impair rim recognition.

Phase 2: In order to determine the gradients in 45°, 135°, horizontal, and vertical directions, Sobel operators are used in multiple directions with the spots to be measured.

Phase 3: High and low thresholds are used to identify edges. This makes possible the identification of the boundary of the fuzzy region.

Following all of the processes, the Harris Stephens method was proposed for recognizing the corner point and was implemented to the extracted picture feature. The window averaging function was used to control the image during this operation. The blood vessel architecture can be efficiently investigated and traced using the process described above. Then, there is the idea of storing data through data anonymization, where a public key can validate the signature of an anonymous sender who verified a message with his or her own private key [13]. There is also the idea of transforming the biometrics key to a master key, which will make the data even more secure. Pseudonyms are created using two partial pseudonyms, the first of which is produced from characteristic keys and the second of which is formed from random user ID numbers. The two partial pseudonyms will then be combined to form the final pseudonym [13]. These are the steps taken to protect data using palm vein authentication, pseudonym procedures, and data anonymization. There are numerous advantages to utilizing this strategy to protect data [13]. As a result, this procedure is quite popular and widely used because the palm vein cannot be readily harmed.

11.3.4 Limitations of the Existing System

Even though new and modern concepts arise, there will always be certain limitations which, in turn, requires even more effective methods to protect data. Now, in this modern era, everyone is in need of a more effective method to store data. Palm vein authentication proves almost so good to secure data in this modern world, but it has certain limitations which need to be solved—for example, if someone identifies the palmprint of the person, then he can easily use it and get the data. Even if the palmprint is encrypted, it can be easily decrypted by using modern technology. If the attacker gets the two partial pseudonyms, he can easily find the final pseudonym and gain access to the data. Then, there is also the limitation that if the attacker gains access to the palm vein and gets the data, he can also encrypt the palm vein to another code and thus make it impossible for the owner to open the data until he finds the encrypted code by the attacker. If the owner cannot identify the code, he can totally lose his data, and the attacker will use the data for his own purposes. This can be the biggest limitation of using palm vein authentication. Then, if the palm vein of the person is affected naturally by some disease, he also cannot use it until it has healed. It is also costly compared with the other forms of biometric authentication and involves a lot of processing time to secure the data. If a mistake is made while doing any of the methods, then it can totally collapse and lead to loss of data. Thus, it should be done carefully with precision and care.

11.4 Proposed System

As we can see, there are many new techniques available in the modern world to secure our data and keep such private, yet there are some breaches happening and hackers thinking of how to get their hands on our confidential data and make them profitable. This situation cannot be totally prevented, yet it can be reduced by implementing more security measures to keep our data secure. As discussed above, this paper provides a new idea regarding the prevention of someone illegally using our data and how to make our data more secure. The overall view of the plan is to secure data with the biometric authentication system. This plan may be an old idea, but here is where data anonymization comes into the part. The patterns from a biometric scan can be converted into a code and be encrypted by the data anonymization techniques and can be stored securely in the database. The biometric characteristics of every human being differ from each other and are unique in different aspects. Not even twins share the same biometric traits [13]. A special device is used to capture the unique traits in an accurate way with the help of sensors and transform the data into machine codes. The data obtained by this method are more secure and unique, which proves its uses in data protection and security systems [13].

Here the biometric system refers to the retinal scan of the eye. The patterns of the retina (blood capillaries) are captured by a retinal scanner and converted into a machine-readable code and will be stored in the database. There will be three steps through which the data can be secured: (i) scanning the retina of the eye, (ii) converting the scanned patterns into the machine-understandable code, and (iii) applying the techniques of data anonymization. Through these steps, our data can be secured, and although not quite completely, it will still be harder to crack by an anonymous user.

11.4.1   Biometric System

In the modern era, there are many applications where users need to share their sensitive data and exchange confidential information. A lot of companies and organizations usually need to store a large amount of their customers' sensitive information like bank details, medical records, and some confidential data [13]. With large amounts of data stored in their database, this makes the company a vulnerable platform for the hackers to access the data illegally for their own purpose. There are many strategies used by the companies to hide their data and protect them such as encrypting the data or by generating a private key or using biometric technique. Biometric systems usually play a vital role in the protection of data from any risks. Biometric systems scan and verify the similarities in the scanned pattern, and the patterns are stored in the database of the server. Biometric systems usually identify the individuals through behavioral biometrics—i.e., handwriting and signature—and physical biometrics—i.e. palmprint, palm vein, fingerprint, voice, and iris [13]. Biometric factors have properties such as universality, permanence, uniqueness, collectability, acceptability, performance, and circumvention. The identification process happens by way of searching and comparing the unknown and known traits of the biometric patterns of the scanned data with the existing data of biometric traits stored in the database.

The proposed plan suggests the scanning of retinal images and uses data anonymization techniques to make them private and protected. The retina—i.e., blood capillaries inside the eye—is scanned using a special type of a retinal scanner. People usually confuse the iris with the retina and think that both are the same. The distinction between the iris and the retina is depicted in Figure 11.5. The fundamental distinction between the iris and the retina is that the iris is the colored portion of the eye that surrounds the pupil. It is a muscular tissue that controls the size of the pupil and how much light gets into your eye. The retina is indeed

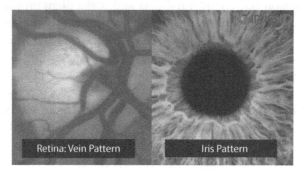

Retina: Vein Pattern   Iris Pattern

Figure 11.5 Difference between a retina (left) and an iris (right).

a part of the eye which is not visible to the naked eye. It is a thin nerve tissue layer that extends all along the back of the eyeball, closer to the optic nerve. Iris scans are 70 times less authentic than retinal scans. Iris scans take photographs of the iris from a distance, whereas retinal scan photographs the iris by placing the person's eye closer to an eyepiece.

The retinal scanner device is used to capture the unique characteristics of the human retina precisely and search the database for the perfect match. Prior to this, the biometric patterns should be scanned and registered in the database before the process of comparing. It involves certain steps to be performed. It involves scanning the biometric traits, extraction of unique features, and finally storing the extracted feature, which is then followed by the comparison process. The comparison process involves the scanning of biometric traits, identification of regions of uniqueness, extraction of the unique data, comparing the extracted data and finding the exact match, and decision making. Since the palm vein is in the internal region of the body, it can only be scanned via a HD camera within a close range as ambient light would interfere with recognition. As a replacement for palm vein (due to its drawbacks), retinal scan, which has some advantages over palm vein, is proposed. The data indicates that the retina cannot be damaged easily. Usually, it only gets damaged due to aging and damaging light. Therefore, it can be considered as a high-security technique which provides reliability. It has grown only in recent times and is the most applicable technique for high security issues since data protection has become more important in companies and organizations. It finds its applications in privacy purposes like computer system logins, ATM system access, access to medical data, etc. Its popularity is also due to its uniqueness and differentiating characteristics. It is believed that the uniqueness and the reliability of the retinal pattern provides a precise and secure tool. The retina has unique characteristics which cannot be altered or faked easily. According to the result, the retina stands a high chance in securing data using biometric technology and has a false rate that is less than 2%.

Retinal scans are being used to characterize an individual's distinct retinal patterns. The blood vessels in the retina absorb the light more effectively than the encircling healthy cells and can be easily recognized with the use of correct lighting. Following the capture of a retinal image by the scanner, specialized software combines the retinal blood vessel network's unique qualities into a template. A high-quality image is required for retina scan procedures, and the software will just not allow the user to enroll or verify until it can capture one. The retina template is usually one of the tiniest of any biometric device. A retina scan is a particularly solid approach for identification because it is extremely accurate and challenging to spoof. However, the technology has a number of flaws, including time-consuming image acquisition and restricted consumer uses.

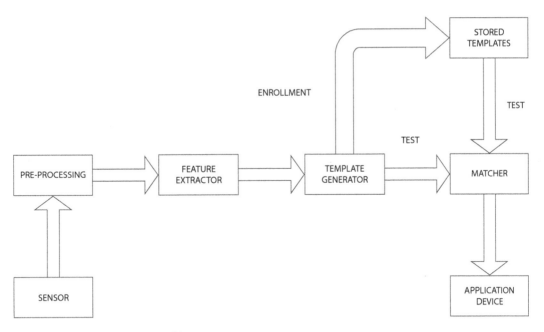

Figure 11.6 Biometric system architecture.

Due to the necessity of continually obtaining photos, which can be difficult for users, registering in a retinal scanning biometrics system is typically time-consuming. A listed user can be recognized in minutes using a retinal scan once the consumer has become acclimated to the method.

Retinal scanning technology has strong matching abilities, and it is typically configured to do one-to-many validations against a user database. However, because acquiring high-quality images is so challenging, it sometimes takes several attempts to get it to the stage where a match can be made. While the methods themselves are robust, providing enough data for matching to occur can be a tough procedure. A user may be incorrectly rejected in many circumstances due to an inability to supply sufficient data to construct a match template. The quantity of reflection fluctuates during the scan as retinal blood vessels absorb more log-energy infrared radiation than the rest of the eye. Variation patterns are transformed to software code and kept in a database. The process is depicted in Figure 11.6.

11.4.2   Data Processing Technique

The scanned biometric traits are preprocessed and are converted into machine-readable binary codes, i.e., zeros and ones. It undergoes certain processes including capturing the unique traits precisely, processing the image, extracting the needed patterns, and converting the patterns into binary digits. It involves a slow and steady process which needs to be done carefully. Even slight changes made in the process can result in the collapse of scanned traits and make the data inaccessible even by its owner. The converted binary digits are then made anonymous using the data anonymization techniques using certain functions and methods.

(i)   The retinal veins are first captured using the retinal scanner. The patterns are captured by passing an infrared light into the eye which highlights the retinal vein, and then the image is sent to the next process.

(ii)   The next step involves image processing which removes the unwanted veins from the pattern. Only the unique characteristics are taken into account. This process involves noise removal and returning the required unique pattern. It needs to be filtered with a filtering tool in order to have a high-quality pattern. The filtering tool should exclude the eye lashes, rheum, eye discharge, exfoliated skin cells, oil, tears, and mucus produced during sleep. The edges are cut out, and the blurred patterns are removed as shown in Figure 11.7. The boundaries are smoothed and produce a clear pattern and high-quality image of the extracted pattern.

(iii)   The extracted patterns are now converted into binary code using a special algorithm. This algorithm suggests that the main and unique veins alone get converted into binary bits. The binary digits consist of random 25 bits. Every time it scans a biometric trait, it generates unique binary digits which will never be repeated. These unique 25 bits are converted into a hexadecimal number using the binary conversion method which acts as a set of

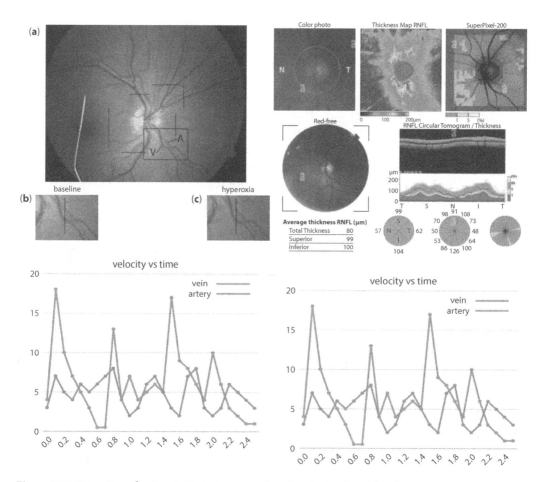

Figure 11.7 Extraction of unique traits, noise removal, and capturing the main vein.

Table 11.2 Selected 25 elements from the unique vein patterns.

0.689361840	0.5639254992	0.673925582	0.579255896	0.786936588
0.548295620	0.6791658397	0.673955746	0	0.673629879
0	0.7934175991	0.673956486	0.638951756	0.769367899
0.578194658	0.6792557815	0	0	0.768302660
0.658301589	0	0.254875964	0.673956289	0

Table 11.3 Set of a generated master key (hexadecimal numbers).

```
1 0 1 1 0
1 1 1 1 1
1 1 0 1 1 -----> 9A449F A986DE 69DBE0D
0 1 1 1 0
0 1 1 0 1
```

master keys to protect the data. The master keys are a group of hexadecimal numbers which are then hidden by the process of data anonymization technique. This process is presented in Tables 11.2 and 11.3.

11.4.3   Data-Preserving Approach

This chapter suggests an idea of implementing data anonymization techniques to preserve data in order to reduce the vulnerability of illegal breaching. There are many anonymization techniques, but certain suitable techniques are used to make the data anonymous. Let us consider the following set of master keys of an individual to apply certain techniques (the data is shown in the Table 11.4).

11.4.3.1   Generalization

Generalization is the process of substituting a less particular but semantically coherent value for the original value. This method is used at the basic level, in which some original values are kept but with more confusion. This will make it more difficult for the intruder to infer confidential material. However, not all characteristics can be generalized. Given the above-mentioned data set, it can be generalized into a certain range as shown. After generalization, a single data set of master keys is separated into two keys each. This is shown in Table 11.4.

Table 11.4 Generated master key after generalization.

Generated master key	Master key after generalization
9A449F	9A449A - 9A449F
A986DE	A986DA - A986DE
69DBE0D	69DBE0A - 69DBE0D

11.4.3.2   Suppression

Suppression is the process of removing an entire section of data (column or tuple) from a data set by altering the value to a meaningless value. Suppressions, on the other hand, hide information by eliminating records from the original data, which are fully eliminated from the output. This approach works on columns or tuples, hiding them when they are not in use. The anonymized data after suppression is shown in Table 11.5.

11.4.3.3   Swapping

Swapping is the process of randomly reordering variables within each case. The element name can be used to jumble data inside the same attribute in this case. This method cannot be used for all qualities because the study results may not be reliable. The likelihood of getting the same result as the original value owing to the randomization procedure is the major concern in this technique. The result after swapping is given in Table 11.6.

11.4.3.4   Masking

Masking is a technique for altering characters in the chosen component(s) to a specific character, therefore rendering the variable unusable. Any number from 1 to 9 will be swapped

Table 11.5 Master key after suppression.

Generated master key	Master key after suppression
9A449A	9#44&A
9A449F	&A44#F
A986DA	A#8&DA
A986DE	&98#DE
69DBE0A	69&B#0A
69DBE0D	6#DB&0D

Table 11.6 Master key after swapping.

Generated master key	Master key after swapping
9#44&A	A#9#44&
&A44#F	F4#A4&
A#8&DA	D8#A&A
&98#DE	E9&8#D
69&B#0A	0#6&B9A
6#DB&0D	D&0B#6D

Table 11.7 Master key after masking.

Generated master key	Master key after masking
A#9#44&	Z#1#11&
F4#A4&	Z1#Z1&
D8#A&A	Z1#Z&Z
E9&8#D	Z1&1#Z
0#6&B9A	0#1&Z1Z
D&0B#6D	Z&0Z#1D

with 1, and any lowercase letter a–z will be swapped with z as well as any uppercase letter A–Z with Z. The true version will be kept for the initial character, number 0, and special character. The issue with masking is that it requires more resources to check and change the value, but the data is ultimately useless for research. Instead of masking, we can employ suppression, which does not check the value but instead changes all of the values to some symbols, producing the same effect as masking but with greater efficiency. The data after the anonymization is shown in Table 11.7.

11.5   Implementation of AI

This paper suggests an AI algorithm to keep data more private and secure. AI is one of the most rapidly growing technologies in recent years. This algorithm should be able to keep track of the changes made in the original key and should be able to reprocess it. It then combines the generated master key into a single FINAL key as depicted in Table 11.8. The algorithm plans on repeating the data anonymization techniques applied in the master key randomly and produces a new key over an interval of time [22]. Once the anonymized techniques are applied to the master key, the generated master key will have a set of unique elements. After a certain period of time, i.e., once a month, these unique elements will go through the data anonymization techniques randomly and repeat all the processes and produce another unique and new key. This will be the FINAL key which will only match the retinal pattern of the owner. The time period can be set by the owner as of his wish. This algorithm will be more effective and makes the data more anonymous and secure as of now because no one can predict the FINAL key as it changes itself over an interval of time.

Table 11.8 FINAL key generated by the anonymization technique.

```
Z#1#11&
Z1#Z1&
Z1#Z&Z ------- > Z#1#11&Z1#Z1&Z1#Z&ZZ1&1#Z0#1&Z1ZZ&0Z#1D
Z1&1#Z
0#1&Z1Z
Z&0Z#1D
```

Once the owner scans his retina, it is compared with the already available retinal patterns in the database and checks for a match. If it matches, no problem. The confidential files can be accessed by the owner. If it mismatches, the files can only be accessed through the FINAL key which is the owner's biometric trait. No other methods will work. This makes the data nearly impossible to hack and the FINAL key impossible guess. It will not completely prevent the illegal user from accessing our data, but it will surely make it harder for them to crack as there are some drawbacks in this technique. If the hacker gains access to the main server where the database records are stored, he is able to collapse the stored biometric data and make the file useless to the owner. This will be the main drawback of this technique which can be rectified in a future work.

11.6   Limitations and Future Works

In this real world, there is always a development of new technologies for various purposes. Even though these new developments solve most of the real-time problems, there are still certain problems which can be identified by the hackers, and they will use it for their own purpose. This proposed plan also has some problems which need to be rectified in the future. The common problem in retinal scanning is that the retina can be affected by certain diseases which will make it hard to gain access to the data. Aging plays a major defect in retinal scanning as it causes changes in the retina. Therefore, retinal scanning can be used up to a certain age limit while the retina does not get affected yet by any infections. If a person has diabetes, he cannot use this method to secure data as diabetes can cause the development of abnormal capillaries which can break and bleed, thus affecting the retinal scan. Then, retinal scanning can also become a problem to those who have a family history of retinal diseases. Thus, a healthy retina is needed to use this type of authentication system as it is used to secure some kind of private data. The problem is that taking the picture of retinal veins needs more work to be performed, and it should be done correctly as the retinal vein pictures are taken by bringing the person's eyes nearer to the camera. This method causes fear in people as the infrared light is directly passed through the eyes to capture retinal veins, which can also affect the retina if more infrared light is passed or continuously passed to get the clear image. This may be one of the major disadvantages in using retinal scanning to secure data. Unfortunately, if eye or eye vision is lost in exposure to hazardous acids or an unexpected accident, the retina will get damaged. Thus, it will be harder for them to access their own data. However, this can be rectified by using the master key concept. The master key concept still needs to be experimented and worked on in the future in order to get an effective output. Retinal scanning is somewhat slower compared with other scanning methods because more time is taken for scanning the retina, and the process involved is also more complicated when compared with the other systems. The process involved many steps toward getting a clear vision of the retina while avoiding the rheum and other particles in eyes. This takes more time, and this is one of the major defects in regard to following this system. It is one of the costliest methods of biometric authentication as it requires more steps of work, and the picture quality should be more precise and clearer; thus, more machinery is needed to acquire high-quality images. Nonetheless, everyone cannot afford much for this retinal scanning, so this is one of the major drawbacks of using this system.

Many future works have to be done to solve these problems and make this method more reliable and affordable as well as to make more use of this system.

11.7   Conclusion

In this modern era, every company and organization expects to store data in a secure way. To have such data stored securely, they came into the concept of biometric techniques and data anonymization concepts. There are many studies and ideas to complement each and every concept to secure data in a highly orderly manner. The loopholes of each concept are still being rectified, and new effective methods are proposed. In such a way, here the new concept of proposing a method of using biometric authentication by means of retinal scanning is implemented, and their data is encrypted and implemented by data anonymization techniques which will make such users' data more secure. Here retinal scanning acts as a unique method to secure data as everyone has a unique trait of their respective retina—even twins; so, it serves as a great method to secure data. Thus, applying anonymization techniques in retinal scanning makes the data even more protected and safe. Even so, it acts as a new concept of protecting data. Here we are implementing AI, which makes the data more and more protected so that the attacker cannot even get a clue of the data. Thus, it proves to be the best method to secure data in this modern era. After all the limitations of the previous works and methods, here comes the idea of implementing all the concepts together just to protect and secure data even more. As the demand on securing data increases, the method of protecting data also increases—thus paving the way for new concepts and ideas in this technical era. This method can act as a solution for many systems to secure data.

References

1. Garg, V., Cybersecurity and data privacy, in: *Computer Security and Reliability*, pp. 1, 2023.
2. Shrestha, N.M., Alsadoon, A., Prasad, P.W.C., Hourany, L., Elchouemi, A., Enhanced E-health framework for security and privacy in healthcare system, in: *Proc. 6th Int. Conf. Digit. Inf. Process. Commun. (ICDIPC)*, pp. 75–79, Apr. 2016.
3. Camenisch, J. and Lehmann, A., (Un)linkable pseudonyms for governmental databases, in: *Proc. 22nd ACM SIGSAC Conf. Comput. Commun.Secur. (CCS)*, pp. 1467–1479, 2015.
4. Muntés-Mulero, V., and Nin, J. Privacy and anonymization for very large datasets. *Proceeding 18th ACM Conf. Inf. Knowl. Manag. CIKM '09*, pp. 2117–2118, 2009.
5. Priya, R.L., Abirami, A., Desai, N., Machine learning-based emerging technologies in the post pandemic scenario, in: *Artificial Intelligence and Machine Learning Methods in COVID-19 and Related Health Diseases*, Studies in Computational Intelligence, vol. 1023, V. Chang, H. Kaur, S.J. Fong (eds.), Springer, Cham, 2022, https://doi.org/10.1007/978-3-031-04597-4_3.
6. Sweeney, L., K-anonymity: A model for protecting privacy. *Int. J. Uncertainty, Fuzziness Knowl.-Based Syst.*, 10, 5, 557–570, 2002.
7. Xu, J., Yang, G., Chen, Z., Wang, Q., A survey on the privacy preserving data aggregation in wireless sensor networks. *China Commun.*, 12, 5, 162–180, May 2015.
8. Murthy, S., Abu Bakar, A., Abdul Rahim, F., Ramli, R., A comparative study of data anonymization techniques. *2019 IEEE 5th Intl. Conference on Big Data Security on Cloud (BigDataSecurity)*,

IEEE Intl. Conference on High Performance and Smart Computing, (HPSC) and IEEE Intl. Conference on Intelligent Data and Security (IDS), pp. 306–309, 2019.

9. Kaur, P.C., Ghorpade, T., Mane, V., Analysis of data security by using anonymization techniques. *2016 6th International Conference - Cloud System and Big Data Engineering (Confluence)*, pp. 287–293, 2016.

10. Goswami, P. and Madan, S., Privacy preserving data publishing and data anonymization approaches: A review. in: *2017 International Conference on Computing, Communication and Automation (ICCCA)*, pp. 139–142, 2017.

11. Majeed, A. and Lee, S., Anonymization techniques for privacy preserving data publishing: A comprehensive survey. *IEEE Access*, 9, 8512–8545, 2021.

12. Hemalatha, S., A systematic review on Fingerprint based biometric authentication system. *2020 International Conference on Emerging Trends in Information Technology and Engineering (IC-ETITE)*, pp. 1–4, 2020.

13. Abd Razak, S., Mohd Nazari, N.H., Al-Dhaqm, A., Data anonymization using pseudonym system to preserve data privacy. *IEEE Access*, 8, 43256–43264, 2020.

14. Leng, L. *et al.*, Dynamic weighted discrimination power analysis in DCT domain for face and palmprint recognition, in: *2010 International Conference on Information and Communication Technology Convergence (ICTC)*, IEEE, 2010.

15. Wang, J., Zhang, X., Gong, W., Xu, X., A summary of palmprint recognition technology. *2019 4th International Conference on Control, Robotics and Cybernetics (CRC)*, pp. 91–97, 2019.

16. Westmoreland, B., Lemp, M., Snell, R., *Clinical anatomy of the eye*, 2nd edition, Blackwell Science Inc., Oxford, 1998.

17. Burke, J., Deborah, E., Hansen, M., Parker, A., Nithya, R.A., Reddy, S., Srivastava, M.B. Participatory sensing, in: *Workshop on World-Sensor-Web (WSW '06): Mobile Device Centric Sensor Networks and Applications*, pp. 117–134, 2006.

18. Verma, I. and Jain, S.K., Biometrics security system: A review of multi-modal biometrics based techniques for generating crypto-key, in: *Proc. 2nd Int. Conf. Comput. Sustain. Global Develop*, INDIACom, pp. 1189–1192, 2015.

19. Oloyede, M.O. and Hancke, G.P., Unimodal and multimodal biometric sensing systems: A review. *IEEE Access*, 4, 7532–7555, 2016.

20. Paone, J.R., Flynn, P.J., Philips, P.J., Bowyer, K.W., Bruegge, R.W.V., Grother, P.J., Quinn, G.W., Pruitt, M.T., Grant, J.M., Double trouble: Differentiating identical twins by face recognition. *IEEE Trans. Inf. Forensics Secur.*, 9, 2, 285–295, 2014.

21. Wu, K.-S., Lee, J.-C., Lo, T.-M., Chang, K.-C., Chang, C.-P., A secure palm vein recognition system. *J. Syst. Softw.*, 86, 11, 2870–2876, Nov. 2013.

22. Pandiaraj, A., Prakash, S.L., Kanna, P.R., Effective heart disease prediction using hybrid machine learning. *2021 Third International Conference on Intelligent Communication Technologies and Virtual Mobile Networks (ICICV)*, Tirunelveli, India, pp. 731–738, 2021.

Part 3
APPLICATIONS

12

Detection of Bank Fraud Using Machine Learning Techniques

Kalyani G.[1], Anand Kumar Mishra[2], Diya Harish[1], Amit Kumar Tyagi[3]*, Sajidha S. A.[1] and Shashank Pandey[1]

[1]School of Computer Science and Engineering, Vellore Institute of Technology, Chennai, Tamil Nadu, India
[2]Computer Science and Engineering, NIIT University, Neemrana, Rajasthan, India
[3]Department of Fashion Technology, National Institute of Fashion Technology, New Delhi, Delhi India

Abstract
In this digitally advanced age, the number and types of frauds happening around has also increased exponentially. The one place which people trust their money and other precious belongings to be with is the bank. These days, bank fraud, too, has been rising to an extent that it is high time that we understand the need for its early detection and prediction. Bank fraud refers to the use of illegal means to obtain the money, property, or other belongings of another individual or institution by some individuals who pose themselves as a bank or another financial institution. Most often, bank fraud is considered to be a criminal offense, but sometimes it also applies to actions that employ a scheme, and hence it is categorized as a white-collar crime, too. This project aims to detect fraudulent transactions from the banksim dataset. The utilization of machine learning (ML) in the finance industry can enhance the efficiency of bank transactions. This study showcases the ability of various regression models to predict insurance costs. A comparison of the results of the various models will be done—for example, random forest and various other regression and classification algorithms. The issues and frauds regarding the transactions associated with the banking field have been of utmost concern as these are quite high in spite of keeping the best of security systems. This project aims to determine the personal factors of an individual account that lead to bank frauds using various ML algorithms and take decisions on where and how much to invest or deposit.

Keywords: Machine learning, fraud detection, security, privacy, online transactions

12.1 Introduction

The banking industry is made up of interconnected financial institutions, called banks, that provide individuals with the ability to store and use their money. Customers have the option of opening accounts for various purposes, such as saving or investing their money. By providing resources for transactions and investments, the banking industry contributes to the

---

*Corresponding author: amitkrtyagi025@gmail.com

Amit Kumar Tyagi (ed.) *Automated Secure Computing for Next-Generation Systems*, (225–242) © 2024 Scrivener Publishing LLC

economy. One way in which banks achieve this is by creating and allocating loans to applicants for things like purchasing real estate, starting a business, or paying for college. There are various types of banks, such as commercial, investment, retail, and central banks. Bank fraud is defined by the Reserve Bank of India as "a deliberate act of omission or commission by any person, carried out in the course of a banking transaction or in the books of accounts maintained manually or under computer system in banks, resulting into wrongful gain to any person for a temporary period or otherwise, with or without any monetary loss to the bank" [1]. Bank fraud has led to a loss of billions of rupees in the Indian banking sector, resulting in a loss of 1,134.4 ""crores rupees in 2005 alone, which is 2.5 times greater than the previous year's losses, thus shattering the investors' confidence.

A transaction can be classified as fraudulent or not based on the personal histories and details of the account that does the transaction. An individual account's details like customer ID, age, transaction amount, and the category of payment can be used to find out or predict whether the transaction is a fraud or not.

12.2   Literature Review

A book [2] mentions about several causes of fraud in the banking industry. These include inadequate supervision by top management; faulty incentive mechanisms for employees; collusion between staff, corporate borrowers, and third-party agencies; a weak regulatory system; lack of appropriate tools and technologies for early detection of fraud signals; lack of awareness among bank employees and customers; and lack of coordination among different banks in India and abroad. The study emphasizes the critical role played by financial institutions in facilitating the process of intermediation but also notes that fraud is a significant problem faced by these institutions. Calderon and Green (1994) conducted a study of 114 actual cases of corporate fraud and found that limited separation of duties, false documentation, and inadequate or non-existent control accounted for 60% of the fraud cases, with professional and managerial employees involved in 45% of the cases. They recommended the establishment of robust prevention systems based on fundamental principles of good internal control and the existence of strong internal audit departments with sufficient resources to handle increased responsibilities.

According to a study conducted by [2] on the causes and prevention of fraud in the banking industry, it was found that while the banking sector is generally well regulated and supervised, it still faces various problems and challenges in terms of ethical practices. Similarly, in the book by [3], the authors show the literature from the 18th century on banking highlights related to various types of fraud, such as loan disbursement fraud, accounting fraud, clerical fraud, and corruption. One example of bank failure due to mismanagement and credit fraud is the failure of the Presidency Bank of Bombay in 1890. Unfortunately, the current situation is even worse as Indian banks lost 410 billion in the financial year 2017–2018, which is 72% higher than that of the previous financial year, and more than 5,000 instances of bank fraud have shaken the Indian financial system. With technology, banking fraud has become larger than ever, with 18% of young Indians facing banking fraud challenges.

As stated in legal definitions, fraud refers to the intentional deception for the purpose of gaining unlawful advantages [4]. It is considered a significant challenge for governments, and if not detected or prevented effectively, it can lead to the dissolution of an organization or even the economy. One of the major challenges faced by regulatory organizations is the poor response from victim organizations due to several factors [5]. Bank fraud is a form of financial fraud that should be distinguished from bank robbery. Bank fraud can be defined as the utilization of illicit means to acquire assets held by a financial institution or to acquire the assets of an individual, organization, or public by using a financial institution.

[6] explained in their research on electronic banking fraud that an effective security system must be capable of withstanding external attacks; otherwise, fraudsters may render the system inoperative through attacks. Therefore, it is essential that electronic banking applications possess a certain level of security intelligence and be able to defend themselves against external attacks.

In [7], it is stated that bank fraud involves the use of deceptive methods to obtain illegal money and financial assets held or owned by a financial institution.

In today's world, misappropriation can occur in numerous ways, often complicated by factors such as the use of unauthorized methods or jurisdictional issues. Fraudulent actions can escalate into serious offenses, such as theft, burglary, and robbery, carried out in a professional and premeditated manner, either as part of an organized crime or a white-collar crime. Any enterprise dealing with significant financial assets is highly susceptible to fraud, and this vulnerability is even more pronounced for those heavily indebted to large banks. Enterprises that handle large amounts of financial assets are particularly vulnerable to fraud, and this risk is even greater for those who are heavily indebted to banks. Therefore, it is evident that the incidence of banking fraud is increasing rapidly.

12.3   Problem Description

Bank fraud is a type of fraud that occurs through banks, which many people may not be aware of as they are not directly involved in it. However, by trusting their money with banks, people may inadvertently become victims of fraud. While it may not be possible to completely eliminate the risk of fraud, various measures can be taken to reduce the chances of it occurring. Several measures can be taken to prevent fraud, such as engaging internal audit specialists in prevention efforts, educating consumers on fraud prevention, strengthening legal requirements, utilizing data analytics technology, following best practices for fraud mitigation, and implementing multipoint inspections. When fraud occurs, it can result in the loss of money that belongs to someone other than the bank. This can lead to the bank's liquidation and a significant reduction in patronage in the banking sector. Fraud also affects management policies and necessitates costly maintenance of check and control systems. Therefore, bankers must be vigilant in detecting, costing, and preventing fraud to mitigate its impact.

In this project, we use the banksim dataset from Kaggle [8] along with features from various other references to perform the data analysis using Python language. The project aims to determine the factors that lead to bank fraud using various ML algorithms and hence help to make decisions on the right details to provide the banks with.

The banking industry serves as a driving force for economic growth and is equipped to perform duties that ultimately benefit several interest groups, including the industrial and agricultural sectors, individual customers, as well as the government or public sector.

12.4   Implementation and Analysis

12.4.1   Workflow

Figure 12.1 depicts that, first, we have performed exploratory data analysis on our banksim dataset, followed by data preprocessing and then SMOTE oversampling technique; then, finally we have built a model using various ML algorithms.

12.4.2   Dataset

The dataset used in this project is from Kaggle, and it contains almost five lakh records with 10 columns including step, customer ID, age, gender, zipcode, merchant, merchantzip, category, amount, and fraud or not.

Figure 12.2 depicts the banksim dataset and oversampling techniques that can be done on it to make the dataset more balanced and equal.

12.4.3   Methodology

Step 1: Exploratory Data Analysis
At the beginning, we perform exploratory data analysis on the banksim dataset to discover patterns, detect anomalies, verify hypotheses, and validate assumptions using summary statistics and visual representations.

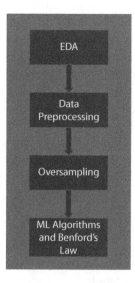

Figure 12.1 Workflow of the project.

step	customer	age	gender	zipcodeOri	merchant	zipMercha	category	amount	fraud
0	'C1093826	'4'	'M'	'28007'	'M348934(	'28007'	'es_transp	4.55	0
0	'C3529681	'2'	'M'	'28007'	'M348934(	'28007'	'es_transp	39.68	0
0	'C2054744	'4'	'F'	'28007'	'M182307.	'28007'	'es_transp	26.89	0
0	'C1760612	'3'	'M'	'28007'	'M348934(	'28007'	'es_transp	17.25	0
0	'C7575037	'5'	'M'	'28007'	'M348934(	'28007'	'es_transp	35.72	0
0	'C1315400	'3'	'F'	'28007'	'M348934(	'28007'	'es_transp	25.81	0
0	'C7651552	'1'	'F'	'28007'	'M348934(	'28007'	'es_transp	9.1	0
0	'C2025312	'4'	'F'	'28007'	'M348934(	'28007'	'es_transp	21.17	0
0	'C1058451	'3'	'M'	'28007'	'M348934(	'28007'	'es_transp	32.4	0
0	'C3985825	'5'	'F'	'28007'	'M348934(	'28007'	'es_transp	35.4	0
0	'C9870774	'4'	'F'	'28007'	'M348934(	'28007'	'es_transp	14.95	0
0	'C1551465	'1'	'M'	'28007'	'M182307.	'28007'	'es_transp	1.51	0
0	'C6236014	'3'	'M'	'28007'	'M500398.	'28007'	'es_health	68.79	0
0	'C1865204	'5'	'M'	'28007'	'M182307.	'28007'	'es_transp	20.32	0
0	'C4902384	'3'	'M'	'28007'	'M348934(	'28007'	'es_transp	13.56	0
0	'C1940169	'3'	'F'	'28007'	'M348934(	'28007'	'es_transp	30.19	0
0	'C1207205	'4'	'M'	'28007'	'M182307.	'28007'	'es_transp	17.54	0
0	'C8349637	'5'	'F'	'28007'	'M348934(	'28007'	'es_transp	40.69	0
0	'C1897705	'2'	'M'	'28007'	'M348934(	'28007'	'es_transp	21.21	0
0	'C1245391	'2'	'F'	'28007'	'M348934(	'28007'	'es_transp	10.09	0
0	'C1687101	'2'	'F'	'28007'	'M348934(	'28007'	'es_transp	19.31	0
0	'C1695454	'2'	'M'	'28007'	'M348934(	'28007'	'es_transp	44.22	0

Figure 12.2 Banksim dataset.

Reading our dataset: The dataset consists of attributes like customer ID, their age, gender, zipcode, category, amount, and fraud (indicates whether the data contains fraud or not) as we can see in Figure 12.3.

We created two data frames as shown in Figure 12.4—one with fraudulent data and the other with non-fraudulent data. It was found that, out of 587,443 samples in the dataset, only 7,200 contained fraudulent data.f percent of fraudulent data.

Figure 12.5 shows the percent of fraudulent data in each category. Categories like transportation, food, and contents were found to have 0% fraud. The leisure and travel category was found to have the highest percentage of frauds.

Figure 12.6 shows a boxplot for the amount spent in each category.

Figure 12.7 presents the correlation matrix using a heat map. The darker shade represents the positively correlated data, and the lighter shade represents negative correlation.

In Figure 12.8, the red color in the histogram represents the nonfraudulent payments, and the blue shade represents the fraudulent data. We can see in the histogram above that the fraudulent transactions are less in count but more in amount.

```
df.head()
```

	step	customer	age	gender	zipcodeOri	merchant	zipMerchant	category	amount	fraud
0	0	'C1093826151'	'4'	'M'	'28007'	'M348934600'	'28007'	'es_transportation'	4.55	0
1	0	'C352968107'	'2'	'M'	'28007'	'M348934600'	'28007'	'es_transportation'	39.68	0
2	0	'C2054744914'	'4'	'F'	'28007'	'M1823072687'	'28007'	'es_transportation'	26.89	0
3	0	'C1760612790'	'3'	'M'	'28007'	'M348934600'	'28007'	'es_transportation'	17.25	0
4	0	'C757503768'	'5'	'M'	'28007'	'M348934600'	'28007'	'es_transportation'	35.72	0

Figure 12.3 Head of dataset.

```
# Create two dataframes with fraud and non-fraud data
df_fraud = df.loc[df.fraud == 1]
df_non_fraud = df.loc[df.fraud == 0]

sns.countplot(x="fraud",data=df)
plt.title("Count of Fraudulent Payments")
plt.show()
print("Number of normal examples: ",df_non_fraud.fraud.count())
print("Number of fradulent examples: ",df_fraud.fraud.count())
#print(data.fraud.value_counts()) # does the same thing above
```

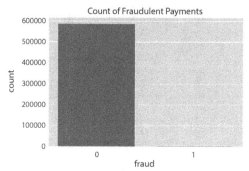

Number of normal examples: 587443
Number of fraudulent examples: 7200

Figure 12.4 Data frames created.

category	Fraudulent	Non-Fraudulent	Percent(%)
'es_transportation'	NaN	26.958187	0.000000
'es_food'	NaN	37.070405	0.000000
'es_hyper'	169.255429	40.037145	4.591669
'es_barsandrestaurants'	164.092667	41.145997	1.882944
'es_contents'	NaN	44.547571	0.000000
'es_wellnessandbeauty'	229.422535	57.320219	4.759380
'es_fashion'	247.008190	62.347674	1.797335
'es_leisure'	300.286878	73.230400	94.989980
'es_otherservices'	316.469605	75.685497	25.000000
'es_sportsandtoys'	345.366811	88.502738	49.525237
'es_tech'	415.274114	99.924638	6.666667
'es_health'	407.031338	103.737228	10.512614
'es_hotelservices'	421.823339	106.548545	31.422018
'es_home'	457.484834	113.338409	15.206445
'es_travel'	2660.802872	669.025533	79.395604

Figure 12.5 Fraudulent data in the dataset.

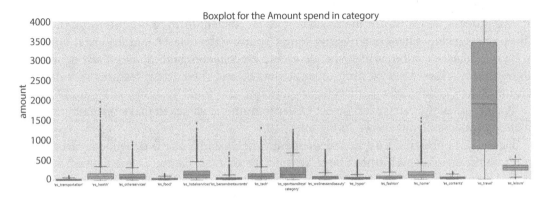

Figure 12.6 Boxplot.

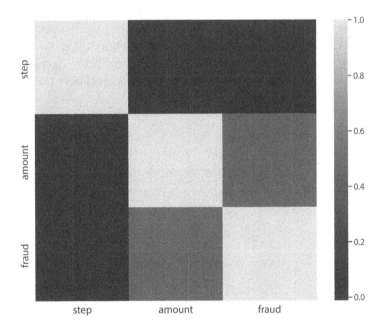

Figure 12.7 Heat map of the correlation matrix.

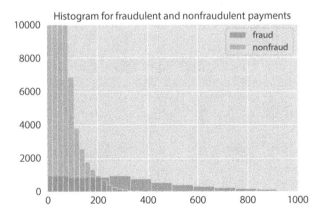

Figure 12.8 Histogram of fraudulent and non-fraudulent payments.

Step 2: Data Preprocessing

In this process, we transform the raw data into an efficient form in order to train the data. The process includes handling missing values, splitting the dataset, and feature scaling.

In our dataset, attributes like zipcodeori and zipcodemerchant do not really contribute to our model. Therefore, we drop those attributes, and the current features include step, customer, age, gender, merchant, category, amount, and fraud as shown in Figure 12.9.

We turned all the categorical object values to numeric values to make the data transformation process easier as shown in Figure 12.10.

Figure 12.11 presents X as the independent variable and Y as the dependent variable.

From the analysis performed above, we inferred that our dataset is imbalanced. So as to balance the dataset, we used a technique of oversampling with SMOTE.

Step 3: Oversampling with SMOTE

A method of oversampling called synthetic minority oversampling [9] creates artificial samples specifically for minority classes. The technique begins by selecting random data from the minority class and identifying its k-nearest neighbors. The synthetic data is created by combining the random data with the k-nearest neighbors selected at random. The process is repeated until the minority class and the majority class have the same proportion.

Data pre processing

```
[ ] print("Unique zipCodeOri values: ",df.zipcodeOri.nunique())
    print("Unique zipMerchant values: ",df.zipMerchant.nunique())
    # dropping zipcodeori and zipMerchant since they have only one unique value
    data_reduced = df.drop(['zipcodeOri','zipMerchant'],axis=1)

    Unique zipCodeOri values:  1
    Unique zipMerchant values:  1
```

```
    data_reduced.columns

    Index(['step', 'customer', 'age', 'gender', 'merchant', 'category', 'amount',
           'fraud'],
          dtype='object')
```

Figure 12.9 Data preprocessing.

```
    # turning object columns type to categorical for easing the transformation process
    col_categorical = data_reduced.select_dtypes(include= ['object']).columns
    for col in col_categorical:
        data_reduced[col] = data_reduced[col].astype('category')
    # categorical values ==> numeric values
    data_reduced[col_categorical] = data_reduced[col_categorical].apply(lambda x: x.cat.codes)
    data_reduced.head(5)
```

	step	customer	age	gender	merchant	category	amount	fraud
0	0	210	4	2	30	12	4.55	0
1	0	2753	2	2	30	12	39.68	0
2	0	2285	4	1	18	12	26.89	0
3	0	1650	3	2	30	12	17.25	0
4	0	3585	5	2	30	12	35.72	0

Figure 12.10 Data transformation.

```
X = data_reduced.drop(['fraud'],axis=1)
y = df['fraud']
print(X.head(),"\n")
print(y.head())
```

```
   step  customer  age  gender  merchant  category  amount
0     0       210    4       2        30        12    4.55
1     0      2753    2       2        30        12   39.68
2     0      2285    4       1        18        12   26.89
3     0      1650    3       2        30        12   17.25
4     0      3585    5       2        30        12   35.72

0    0
1    0
2    0
3    0
4    0
Name: fraud, dtype: int64
```

```
[ ]  y[y==1].count()
```

```
     7200
```

Figure 12.11 Dependent and independent variables.

Since fraudulent data are in the minority class while non-fraudulent data are in the majority class, oversampling using SMOTE is used to balance the dataset; we use oversampling with SMOTE.

Here a function for displaying the ROC AUC curve [10] has been defined. The categorization performance can be shown well visually with the help of Figure 12.12. It was discovered that the base accuracy score is 98%. Given the low fraud percentage in this dataset and most others, our accuracy would be close to 99%. Even though our accuracy is quite good,

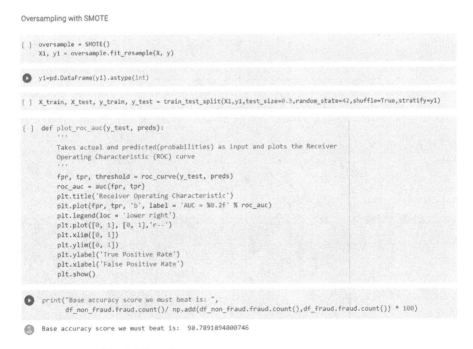

Figure 12.12 Function of the ROC AUC curve.

we are not finding out any fraud; hence, the classifier is useless. Therefore, the minimum threshold for a good base accuracy score in fraud detection should be higher than simply predicting all transactions as non-fraudulent.

Step 4: Building The Model Using Various Machine Learning Algorithms

According to how its neighbor is classified, the k-nearest neighbors classifier classifies the data point. In the KNN [11] procedure, we categorize any incoming fraudulent transaction by finding the location that is the closest to the new fraudulent transaction.

Figure 12.13 depicts an ROC curve presenting the performance of K-nearest neighbors which shows an AUC of 1 and represents the classification report in which we got the precision, recall, f1-score, and support score for our model.

The random forest classifier [12] is a collection of independent decision trees, known as an ensemble. Each tree in the random forest produces a class prediction, and the class with the highest number of votes is predicted by our model.

Figure 12.14 depicts an ROC curve presenting the performance of a random forest classifier which shows an AUC of 1 and represents the classification report in which we got the precision, recall, f1-score, and support score for our model.

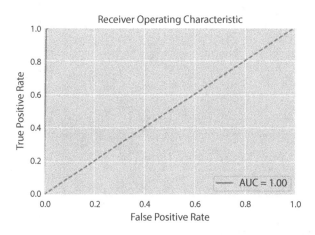

```
print("Classification Report for K-Nearest Neighbours: \n", classification_report(y_test, y_pred))
print("Confusion Matrix of K-Nearest Neigbours: \n", confusion_matrix(y_test,y_pred))
plot_roc_auc(y_test, knn.predict_proba(X_test)[:,1])
```

```
Classification Report for K-Nearest Neighbours:
              precision    recall  f1-score   support

           0       1.00      0.98      0.99    176233
           1       0.98      1.00      0.99    176233

    accuracy                           0.99    352466
   macro avg       0.99      0.99      0.99    352466
weighted avg       0.99      0.99      0.99    352466

Confusion Matrix of K-Nearest Neigbours:
 [[171966   4267]
 [   362 175871]]
```

Figure 12.13 Classification report and ROC curve for KNN performance.

Random forest

```
[ ]  rf_clf = RandomForestClassifier(n_estimators=100,max_depth=8,random_state=42,
                                      verbose=1,class_weight="balanced")


     rf_clf.fit(X_train,y_train)
     y_pred = rf_clf.predict(X_test)
```

```
/usr/local/lib/python3.7/dist-packages/ipykernel_launcher.py:4: DataConversionWarning: A column-vector y was passed when a 1d array was expected.
  after removing the cwd from sys.path.
[Parallel(n_jobs=1)]: Using backend SequentialBackend with 1 concurrent workers.
[Parallel(n_jobs=1)]: Done 100 out of 100 | elapsed:  1.3min finished
[Parallel(n_jobs=1)]: Using backend SequentialBackend with 1 concurrent workers.
[Parallel(n_jobs=1)]: Done 100 out of 100 | elapsed:   2.9s finished
```

```
print("Classification Report for Random Forest Classifier: \n", classification_report(y_test, y_pred))
print("Confusion Matrix of Random Forest Classifier: \n", confusion_matrix(y_test,y_pred))
plot_roc_auc(y_test, rf_clf.predict_proba(X_test)[:,1])
```

```
Classification Report for Random Forest Classifier:
               precision    recall  f1-score   support

           0       0.99      0.97      0.98    176233
           1       0.97      0.99      0.98    176233

    accuracy                           0.98    352466
   macro avg       0.98      0.98      0.98    352466
weighted avg       0.98      0.98      0.98    352466

Confusion Matrix of Random Forest Classifier:
 [[170116   6117]
 [  1029 175204]]
[Parallel(n_jobs=1)]: Using backend SequentialBackend with 1 concurrent workers.
[Parallel(n_jobs=1)]: Done 100 out of 100 | elapsed:   2.9s finished
```

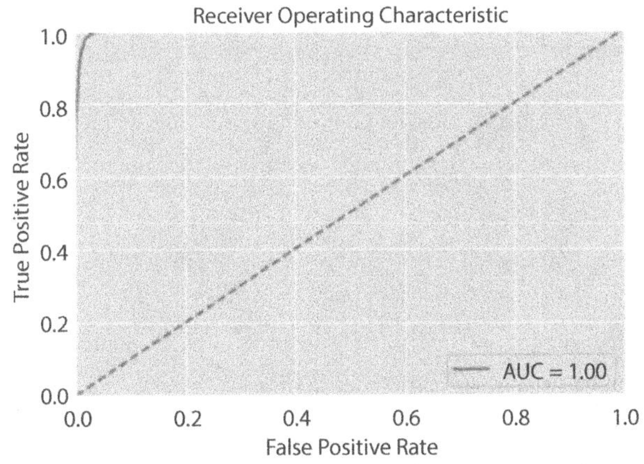

Figure 12.14 Classification report and ROC curve for random forest classifier.

For identifying fraudulent transactions and determining the correctness of those transactions, we used the random forest algorithm.

The approach utilized in this involves supervised learning and employs decision trees for classification of the dataset, which is followed by the generation of a confusion matrix.

XGBoost Classifier

In addition to returning an XGBoost Classifier [13] object that we can use to evaluate how effectively the model generalizes, XGBoost iterates through all potential estimators and prints the parameters used for the one that performs best.

XGBoost

```
[ ] XGBoost_CLF = xgb.XGBClassifier(max_depth=6, learning_rate=0.05, n_estimators=400,
                                    objective="binary:hinge", booster='gbtree',
                                    n_jobs=-1, nthread=None, gamma=0, min_child_weight=1, max_delta_step=0,
                                    subsample=1, colsample_bytree=1, colsample_bylevel=1, reg_alpha=0, reg_lambda=1,
                                    scale_pos_weight=1, base_score=0.5, random_state=42)

    XGBoost_CLF.fit(X_train,y_train)

    y_pred = XGBoost_CLF.predict(X_test)
```

```
print("Classification Report for XGBoost: \n", classification_report(y_test, y_pred))
print("Confusion Matrix of XGBoost: \n", confusion_matrix(y_test,y_pred))
plot_roc_auc(y_test, XGBoost_CLF.predict_proba(X_test)[:,1])
```

```
Classification Report for XGBoost:
              precision    recall  f1-score   support

           0       1.00      0.99      0.99    176233
           1       0.99      1.00      0.99    176233

    accuracy                           0.99    352466
   macro avg       0.99      0.99      0.99    352466
weighted avg       0.99      0.99      0.99    352466

Confusion Matrix of XGBoost:
[[174028   2205]
 [   780 175453]]
```

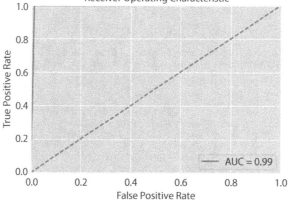

Figure 12.15 Classification report and ROC curve for XGBoost.

Figure 12.15 depicts an ROC curve presenting the performance of XGBoost which shows an AUC of 0.99 and represents the classification report in which we got the precision, recall, f1-score, and support score for our model.

Decision tree

The simplest and most often used classification algorithm is the decision tree. The decision tree is a commonly used and straightforward classification algorithm that considers all available features in the data to create a model and identify the essential features. Additionally, decision tree techniques can be used to determine the importance of feature metrics, providing an added benefit.

Figure 12.16 depicts an ROC curve presenting the performance of a decision tree classifier which shows an AUC of 0.99 and represents the classification report in which we got the precision, recall, f1-score, and support score for our model.

```
def decision_tree_classification(X_train, y_train, X_test, y_test):
    # initialize object for DecisionTreeClassifier class
    dt_classifier = DecisionTreeClassifier()
    # train model by using fit method
    print("Model training starts.......")
    dt_classifier.fit(X_train, y_train.values.ravel())
    print("Model training completed")
    acc_score = dt_classifier.score(X_test, y_test)
    print(f'Accuracy of model on test dataset :- {acc_score}')
    # predict result using test dataset
    y_pred = dt_classifier.predict(X_test)
    # confusion matrix
    print(f"Confusion Matrix :- \n {confusion_matrix(y_test, y_pred)}")
    # classification report for f1-score
    print(f"Classification Report :- \n {classification_report(y_test, y_pred)}")
    plot_roc_auc(y_test, dt_classifier.predict_proba(X_test)[:,1])
```

```
decision_tree_classification(X_train, y_train, X_test, y_test)
```

```
Model training starts........
Model training completed
Accuracy of model on test dataset :- 0.9934178048379134
Confusion Matrix :-
 [[174702   1531]
 [   789 175444]]
Classification Report :-
              precision    recall  f1-score   support

           0       1.00      0.99      0.99    176233
           1       0.99      1.00      0.99    176233

    accuracy                           0.99    352466
   macro avg       0.99      0.99      0.99    352466
weighted avg       0.99      0.99      0.99    352466
```

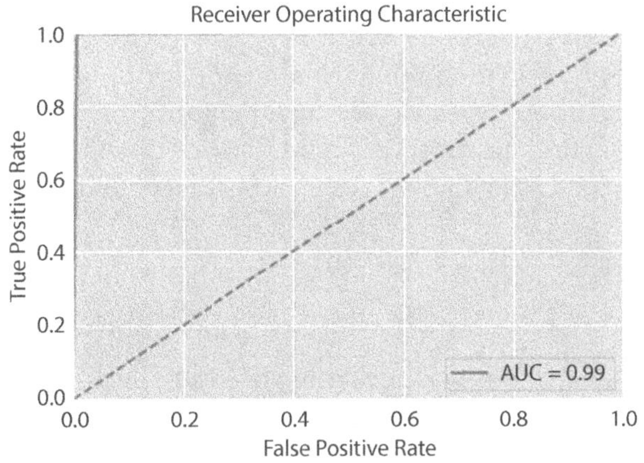

Figure 12.16 Classification report and ROC curve for decision tree classifier.

Step 5: Applying Benford's Law

Benford's Law [14], also known as the Law of First Digits or the Phenomenon of Significant Digits, is a phenomenon which states that the initial digits in a numerical dataset that are not distributed uniformly (or numerals, to be precise) in a sequence of records follow a specific distribution pattern. Recently established statistical methods underpin the application of Benford's Law to detect financial fraud by analyzing the frequencies of naturally occurring numbers. Despite its significance in fraud detection,

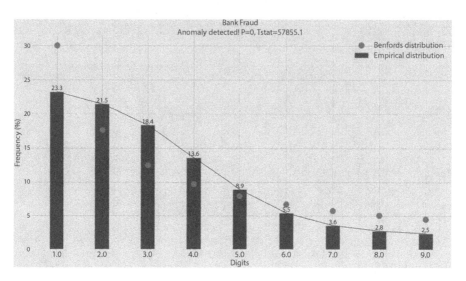

Figure 12.17 Benford's Law and empirical distribution.

many financial experts remain oblivious to the existence of Benford's Law and its optimal utilization.

Benford's Law tests are applied by fraud investigators to natural numbers, such as payment amounts. According to the hypothesis, if a fraudster wants to get away with submitting fake invoices for payment, he would not submit ones for $100 or $200; he will instead go huge and submit ones for $900 or $800.

We applied Benford's Law on the amount column of our dataset.

The red dot in Figure 12.17 represents the actual Benford's distribution, and the bar indicates the distribution of our dataset. It was found that our distribution slightly varies from the actual distribution, indicating that the data has very less fraud.

12.5   Results

- We generated new minority classes using oversampling using SMOTE.
- The model was built using classification algorithms like KNN, random forest, decision tree, and XGBoost.

12.6   Conclusion

There are many ways to automate the identification of fraudulent behavior, including rule-based methods and machine learning. The latter method employed by this repository is to categorize fraudulent transactions. The dataset comprises of payments made by various consumers over a period of time in varying amounts and was generated synthetically. Machine learning, as a part of computational intelligence, has the ability to solve diverse problems across various applications and systems. However, detecting the existence of fraudulent data remains a challenge in society that requires further investigation and enhancement. In this chapter, by using a set of ML algorithms and with the help of Benford's Law, a computational intelligence approach is applied to detect fraud in bank payments. The dataset known as banksim was acquired from the KAGGLE repository and used for training and testing various classification models such as KNN, random forest, decision tree, and XGBoost (refer Table 12.1 to Table 12.3 for more details). These models followed a sequence of steps

Table 12.1 Classification report for k-nearest neighbors.

	Precision	Recall	f1-score	Support
0	1	0.98	0.99	176233
1	0.98	1	0.99	176233
Micro average	0.99	0.99	0.99	352466
Macro average	0.99	0.99	0.99	352466
Weighted average	0.99	0.99	0.99	352466

Table 12.2 Classification report for random forest classifier.

	Precision	Recall	f1-score	Support
0	1	0.97	0.98	176233
1	0.97	1	0.98	176233
Micro average	0.98	0.98	0.98	352466
Macro average	0.99	0.98	0.98	352466
Weighted average	0.99	0.98	0.98	352466

Table 12.3 Classification report for XGBoost.

	Precision	Recall	f1-score	Support
0	1	1	1	176233
1	1	1	1	176233
Micro average	1	1	1	352466
Macro average	1	1	1	352466
Weighted average	1	1	1	352466

including pre-processing, data splitting, classification, and evaluation. For this work, we endeavored to detect fraud in bank payment data, and our classifiers yielded impressive outcomes. To tackle the issue of an imbalanced class in the fraudulent dataset, we utilized the SMOTE oversampling technique to generate more instances of the minority class.

The process was then followed by applying Benford's Law on the amount's column. The resultant outcome revealed that there is only a slight deviation from that of the original Benford distribution.

12.7   Future Works

From the detection of frauds made above, our future work shall include building a simulation model between a client and a merchant. Simulation modeling refers to the dominant modeling method for analyzing complex adaptive systems. These models specifically take into account how the system's constituent people behave. These agents are able to adjust to system changes by adopting new behaviors when their surroundings change. The two agents can be a client and a merchant. Banks need to lead the fight against financial crime by developing new ways to detect fraudulent techniques that may not have been previously thought of, and this can be achieved through effective training in simulated environments [15–18]. By enabling banks to outsmart their own detection systems, they could gain an advantage over fraudsters and potentially win the battle against financial crime.

References

1. Patel, J., An empirical study of technological frauds in banks. *Int. J. Innov. Res. Multidiscip. Field*, 4, 9, September 2018.
2. Vigneshwaran, T.V. and Yokesh, M., A study on causes and prevention of frauds in banking industry. *Int. J. Pure Appl. Math.*, 12, 5, 311–321, 2018.
3. Thangam, M. and Bhavin, P., Banking frauds in India: A case analysis. *J. Emerging Technol. Innov. Res.*, 6, 1, 29–35, 2019.
4. Abiola, I. and Oyewole, A.T., Internal control system on fraud detection: Nigeria experience. *J. Acct. Finance*, 13, 5, 141–152, 2013.
5. Singh, C., Pattanayak, D., Dixit, D., Antony, K., Agarwala, M., Kant, R., Mukunda, S. *et al.*, Frauds in the Indian banking industry. *IIM Bangalore Res. Paper*, 505, 2016. https://www.iimb.ac.in/sites/default/files/2018-07/WP_No._505.pdf
6. Eneji, S.E., Angib, M.U., Ibe, W.E., Ekwegh, K.C., A study of electronic banking fraud, fraud detection and control. *Int. J. Innovative Sci. Res. Technol.*, 4, 3, 708–711, 2019.
7. Khan, Z.A., Fraudulent practices in banking institutions: Legal issues and challenges.
8. Lopez-Rojas, E.A. and Axelsson, S., BankSim: A bank payment simulation for fraud detection research. *26th European Modeling and Simulation Symposium, EMSS 2014*, 2014.
9. Chawla, N.V., Bowyer, K.W., Hall, L.O., Kegelmeyer, W.P., SMOTE: Synthetic minority over-sampling technique. *J. Artif. Intell. Res.*, 16, 321–357, 2002.
10. Bradley, A.P., The use of the area under the ROC curve in the evaluation of machine learning algorithms. *Pattern Recognition*, 30, 7, 1145–1159, 1997.

11. Guo, G., Wang, H., Bell, D., Bi, Y., Greer, K., KNN model-based approach in classification, in: *On The Move to Meaningful Internet Systems 2003: CoopIS, DOA, and ODBASE: OTM Confederated International Conferences, CoopIS, DOA, and ODBASE 2003*, Springer, Catania, Sicily, Italy, November 3–7, 2003, Proceedings, pp. 986–996, Berlin Heidelberg, 2003.

12. Breiman, L., Random forests. *Mach. Learn.*, 45, 5–32, 2001, https://doi.org/10.1023/A:1010933404324.

13. Chen, T. and Guestrin, C., Xgboost: A scalable tree boosting system, in: *Proceedings of the 22nd ACM SIGKDD International Conference on Knowledge Discovery and Data Mining*, pp. 785–794, 2016.

14. Hill, T.P., The significant-digit phenomenon. *Am. Math. Monthly*, 102, 4, 322–327, 1995.

15. Tyagi, A.K., Bansal, R., Anshu, Dananjayan, S. A step-to-step guide to write a quality research article, in: *Intelligent Systems Design and Applications, ISDA 2022*. Abraham, A., Pllana, S., Casalino, G., Ma, K., Bajaj, A. (eds), vol. 717, Lecture Notes in Networks and Systems, Springer, Cham, 2023, https://doi.org/10.1007/978-3-031-35510-3_36.

16. Deshmukh, A., Patil, D.S., Soni, G., Tyagi, A.K., Cyber security: New realities for Industry 4.0 and Society 5.0, in: *Handbook of Research on Quantum Computing for Smart Environments*, Tyagi, A. (ed.), pp. 299–325, IGI Global, 2023, https://doi.org/10.4018/978-1-6684-6697-1.ch017.

17. Tyagi, A.K., Analysis of security and privacy aspects of blockchain technologies from smart era' perspective: The challenges and a way forward, in: *Recent Trends in Blockchain for Information Systems Security and Privacy*, CRC Press, 2021.

18. Sai, G.H., Tyagi, A.K., Sreenath, N., Biometric security in Internet of Things based system against identity theft attacks, *2023 International Conference on Computer Communication and Informatics (ICCCI)*, Coimbatore, India, pp. 1–7, 2023.

13

An Internet of Things-Integrated Home Automation with Smart Security System

Md. Sayeduzzaman[1]*, Touhidul Hasan[2], Adel A. Nasser[3] and Akashdeep Negi[4]

[1]*Department of Electrical Engineering, American International University Bangladesh, Dhaka, Bangladesh*
[2]*Department of Computer Science & Engineering, American International University Bangladesh, Dhaka, Bangladesh*
[3]*Department of Information Systems and Computer Science, Faculty of Sciences, Sa'adah University, Sa'adah, Yemen*
[4]*Department of Mechanical Engineering, Graphic Era (Deemed to be University), Clement Town Dehradun, India*

Abstract

The Internet of Things (IoT) is a cutting-edge technology in today's transformative age of Industry 4.0. While the IoT and its applications are expanding and improving, there is still opportunity for growth in the areas of social support and technological progress. The IoT-integrated smart home system is increasing in popularity every day since it helps to minimize human workload and makes life easier. The system must be updated and restored since it increases home security and safety while facilitating daily life. The automatic and electronic management of domestic tasks, activities, and equipment is known as home automation. The most advanced technology of the current generation is found in Android devices. Therefore, an IoT-integrated home automation with smart security system has been implemented to enable us to control, monitor, and provide a smart security system that may serve as an example of the advancement of IoT technology with just the assistance of a smartphone. The system connects electrical devices via hardware, connection, and software interfaces to construct an automated house with smart security. This prototype will benefit the elderly, children, and those with disabilities. It will also provide a security system to aid everyone using it. This prototype intends to modernize IoT security with a smart door lock system, CCTV monitoring at the door, and gas or fire detection by alerting the homeowner. A voice-activated home automation system allows users to control various electronic devices. It helps the 21st century, also known as the "Industry 4.0" era, which conceptualizes the rapid change in technology, industries, and societal patterns and processes that occurred in the 21st century due to increasing interconnection and smart automation, and provides security by detecting an unplanned activity. Measures that can be taken by a store owner to deter a fraudulent activity include an electronic door lock system with a six-digit keypad which allows for safety and notifies the owner when someone or something approaches. Through the Internet, it enables remote device monitoring. The user can find and shut

---

*Corresponding author: sayedz.shuvo@gmail.com

Amit Kumar Tyagi (ed.) *Automated Secure Computing for Next-Generation Systems*, (243–274) © 2024 Scrivener Publishing LLC

down the devices while away to reduce energy usage and management. This prototype had micro-controller-based smart security and automated home support with various sensors.

Keywords: Internet of Things, intelligent security system, home automation, prevention of theft, detection of gas and fire, smart SMS alert

13.1 Introduction

The rapid transformations in the 21st century's technological landscape, economic sectors, and social structures and rituals as a result of improved communication and Smart automation have led to the term "Industry 4.0" being used to characterize this period. The proliferation of connected devices is partly responsible for this dramatic shift. Everyone nowadays acknowledges that the Internet is essential to modern living. There has been a breakthrough in the evolution of technology for automated and smart devices. It is common knowledge that the transformation has advanced much and is almost at its peak of modernity, but it is also common knowledge that every industry has to keep evolving. The lives of ordinary people have been entwined with inventiveness. Impacting all facets of life, it has boosted communication, travel, anticipation, and news. It has also contributed to the expansion of other markets. One of the most widely used mobile devices is the smartphone.

The Internet is another component that contributes significantly to modern life. Using a smartphone with Internet is the key to successfully navigating the world of digital machines. With the help of these two microcontrollers equipped with various sensors, home automation becomes feasible, making it possible to provide a simpler and safer lifestyle for its inhabitants. Looking back a few years, we can see that the home typically uses various appliances such as washing machines, water heaters, and hair dryers. Every day, most homes in the west, but not all households in Bangladesh, use these tools to assist with their housework. These kinds of systems could be regarded as pioneering efforts in home automation. With a button on a smartphone, we can now turn on electronics such as televisions, lamps, fans, refrigerators, and more. This prototype entails the development of a user-friendly and cost-effective home automation tool and security system. The Android operating system powers the majority of smartphones on the market today and has quickly risen to become the most popular choice among people. Because of this, the Android smartphone has become an essential part of modern life. With the assistance of this itty-bitty device, it is feasible to automate tasks around the house. We can now manage a home computer remotely using our mobile phones due to the explosive expansion of Internet-based correspondence. The explosive growth of wireless connectivity compelled us to use cell phones to control a home computer from a remote location. There is no specific definition of embedded systems. Embedded systems is an alternative term for computer-controlled devices. With improved technology and software, cable telephones have proven that they can become vital to the customers' daily lives. To begin with, there are programs for wireless proxy servers; personal computers have been accessible to consumers for the past 3 years.

Artificial intelligence manages electrical equipment. Take, for example, the Amazon Echo—the most recent technological advancement is a human-friendly interactive robot for Rovio, Roomba, etc. In a few applications, high technology is not tied. The automatic device represents the next stage of technological advancement. As a result, the need for electronic devices that can do automated tasks is increasing. Home automation and an intelligent security system are necessary to overcome this obstacle. The major role of this prototype is to enable remote house control and security system monitoring. As a result of this project, smart home automation with a security system was enhanced for the following reasons:

- To monitor and control home appliances from a distance.
- To conserve time and use energy effectively.
- To monitor the camera-equipped security system.
- To create and deploy a user-friendly, secure, and cost-effective home automation system.

A. Motivation

To get around the Covid-19 problem, Sayeduzzaman M. *et al.* [1] built a disinfection fog machine, which evaporates disinfectant liquids as fog, and published their findings in a publication that is now part of the World Health Organization's database. Due to their efforts, the frequency of COVID-19 cases decreased, and they were rewarded socially. It inspires researchers to design a proof-of-concept Internet-of-Things-based smart home equipped with a security system, which will have far-reaching social repercussions and significantly contribute to the advancement of automation technology. The system's management and monitoring features are built with the Arduino IDE [2]. To further secure the home, this prototype uses an automated door lock that can only be opened with a manual keypad entry and pin code. It is also Inspired by the film "Iron Man". Jarvis is an artificial intelligence-based program that gives and receives instructions from Iron Man to help him carry out his duties. It was portrayed as a computer-generated butler who could listen to music and communicate. He could also reveal who is at the door. In actuality, this program has created a fictional figure. His great analysis inspired this prototype of home automation with a security system. We anticipate that most homes will be smart. This strategy provides a small improvement in smartphones, TVs, watches, coolers, washing machines, and garages, leading to smart homes in nearly every home. Thus, almost every home will be smart and self-sufficient.

B. Problem Statement

Home automation provides household appliances with convenience and ease of usage. Home automation is a modern way of life that allows people to monitor their entire home, from a television to a smartphone. Home automation gives a contemporary lifestyle. It also promotes confidence and decreases energy use. Having or gaining access to such an integrated system would be prohibitively expensive. It explains the lack of demand and interest in home automation, exacerbated by the complexity of installation and configuration, and if made available to the public, it would be affordable and simple to use in homes, offices, and schools. In other words, a device change is necessary to reduce the cost of adopting home automation in households. This prototype, however, offers a cost-effective and user-friendly home automation and smart security system that enables persons with impairments or the elderly to accomplish their goals with a single click.

C. Proposed System

This microcontroller- and sensor-based wireless home appliance control system comprises the following:

- NodeMCU, a Wi-Fi-integrated module, allows Android phones to control and monitor associated loads using the Blynk application.
- The GSM module notifies the owner of a fire, a gas leak, and an item or human movement at the front entrance.
- Temperature and gas sensors detect toxic fire, gas, and smoke.
- A light-dependent resistor (LDR) is installed in front of the house for security reasons. This device automatically turns on just before dusk.
- These devices can be remotely monitored using a smartphone, the Internet, and a NodeMCU web server to maintain front door security.
- A keypad module with a 16 × 2 LCD module is being used.
- A surveillance camera module is used to monitor security equipment.
- A voice-activated, automatic, and remote system is installed.
- Finally, an Android application monitors all devices through Android smartphones.

D. System Requirements
- Hardware
  - NodeMCU ESP8266 V3.0 and an Arduino Uno microcontroller.
  - Relay module for connecting NodeMCU to electrical appliances.
  - Wi-Fi is connected to NodeMCU
  - Smartphone with minimum Android version.
  - ESP32 camera module, DHT11, and other security monitoring sensors.
  - Keypad module, electronic door lock, LCD, and so forth.
- Software
  - The server and device programs are programmed using Arduino IDE.
  - The server-side program was written using Blynk IDE.
  - Google Assistant is voice-controlled with IFTTT.
  - Internet assistant giving voice to the server's choice to activate the Blynk application's integration with the AdaFruit web server to control household appliances and provide alerts when an incident occurs.

Organization of the Chapter

These are the main points of the remaining chapters. The entire research's examination of the literature is presented in Section 13.2, the methodology is shown in Section 13.3, and the research's overall analysis is presented in Section 13.4. The project's implementation is shown in Section 13.5, and the research's findings and data analysis are shown in Section 13.6. Section 13.7 brings the research to a conclusion.

13.2   Literature Review

Life is more enlightened and easier in the age of the Internet. Due to the Internet, we now have incredible, never-before-seen options that tie us to automated smart devices. The rapid expansion of the Internet inspired the creation of automatic intelligent machines, which reduce machine risk and human engagement. On a global scale, attempts are being made to absorb the power of computers or electrical systems to minimize energy waste drastically. The right goal for an automated system, which can be used reliably, securely, and without human intervention, may be attained through effective energy management. The Internet of Things (IoT) curriculum is rather comprehensive. In IoT, home automation is one of the most fascinating and well-studied topics. Because of this home automation program, our technological market is working toward lowering the overall power consumption levels. On the subject of these concerns, numerous research articles and Internet projects have developed compelling ideas for protecting our energy system. Their contributions, in terms of their thoughts and labor, have broadened the scope of our investigation. This academic work aims to achieve that end. Home automation, appliances, home energy management systems, smart security, and smart appliance scheduling were just some of the many uses and research highlighted in these articles and publications on IoT. The information offered here can help in drawing conclusions from this study and deciding on an energy-efficient method of project management.

A. IoT and Home Automation Systems

Several research publications briefly depicted the IoT's enormous chamber to demonstrate its principle. The advantages of home automation include convenient mobile device integration, cheaper installation costs, system stability, easy extension, and aesthetic usage. We need things like cameras, magnetic doors, and automated lighting to automate our homes. In 2016, S. Bharat *et al.* published a special issue of the International Journal of Computer Technology and Research (IJCTR) titled "Internet of Things: Home Automation", which discussed various hardware and software-based applications and components, such as RFID and wireless sensor networks [3]. IoT-based smart device IT and control technologies are used to automate chores and activities for the nuclear family. Domotics refers to the automation and intelligence of the domestic environment [4]. Automating your home's lighting, heating, ventilation, and air conditioning (HVAC) as well as your other appliances and structures may improve your quality of life in a number of ways. Although the concept of automating one's home is not new, no one has yet come up with a winning strategy. Home automation systems have come a long way from their labor-saving beginnings to become useful aids for the elderly and the disabled in their everyday lives and in the usage of home appliances [5]. To keep tabs on a propelled cell or network traveler program using methods, it may also provide a remote link to home mechanical congregations or the automation system by phone line, remote transmission, or the Internet. Using Wi-Fi technology and a NodeMCU, you can build a reliable, affordable, and straightforward system for automating your home's functions. The recommended setup consists of an Arduino NodeMCU ESP8266-based smartphone app, a board, a relay module, sensors, and a security camera. NodeMCU ESP8266 links the Arduino board to electronic devices in the house using a relay. Using the smartphone app, smartphones may engage in serial communication with NodeMCU and Arduino boards. Sensors and machinery can be operated from a distance. Most of today's home automation systems are aimed at the elderly and the disabled who use them to monitor their children via security cameras or for other purposes. This gadget may be managed remotely from home, office, or anywhere using a cloud-connected mobile app. Thus, the smartphone may control the complete equipment from home and the cloud.

Google Assistant connects the voice-controlled automation cloud. Google Assistant links the voice automation cloud.

B. Home Energy Management System

We must consider our house and building's IoT management structure to improve IoT use. Power-efficient and user-friendly systems perform better. Numerous solutions for minimizing power loss are proposed on a regular basis by researchers and students, but none have been shown to be effective without further testing. The "HEMS—House Energy Management System" research by Junyon Kim illustrated [6] the core features of a modern smart home. LED, closed-circuit television, speakers, infrared (IR) sensors, ultrasonic (US) sensors, cellphones, and devices for networking inside and outside the home were used to demonstrate a home automation management system. To write our thesis, we looked for the most effective strategy for minimizing energy waste. In their essay "IoT Based Smart Security and Home Automation System" for the International Conference on Computing, Communication, and Automation, Ravi Kodali *et al.* presented a smart home automation system that is both easy to use and reliable, thanks to the use of a microcontroller [7]. An energy management system for the house is necessary for starting up and making a better project output, but more accurate and conditional output data is required. As an example, the cost of running a computer or other electronic device during peak hours is significantly higher than the cost of running it at other times. The research suggested installing motion sensors in homes to automatically turn lights on and off as well as recommended that customers manually take action after reading the peak hour pricing. The purpose of this article is to provide a brief overview of the project's overall objective: reducing energy waste through the use of more effective automated applications. It resulted in an increase in demand for workers skilled in energy-efficient automation [8].

C. Smart Home Security System

Previous designs for Internet of Things-enabled home security systems have been presented. Touhidul Hasan *et al.* [9] developed an automated smoke and fire security alert system for IoT-based smart homes. A multi-part home automation system is discussed. The prototype had automatic gas detection, a door lock system, and a smart smoke and fire warning system. The prototype was constructed using open-source software and inexpensive components. This work makes use of a qToggle system based on ESP8285 and ESP8285 to link sensors to actuators [10]. The microcontroller unit (MCU) has a Wi-Fi connection. Kodali *et al.* [11] described the TI-CC3200 Launch Pad. They used an Android app to track environmental conditions like humidity and mobility in a cheap WI-FI-based automation system. Gupta and Chhabra [12] developed a cheap ethernet-based smart home system that keeps tabs on things like energy use, intruders, smoke, and temperature. The cloud, a firewall-protected fog, and a security analysis engine all came together to form a sophisticated home architecture. The "Design and Implementation of an Internet of Things-Based Smart Home Security System" [13] was written by Mohammad Asadul Hoque *et al.* They used inexpensive smart devices including door sensors, infrared motion detectors, thermometers, smoke alarms, and webcams.

13.3   Methodology and Working Procedure with Diagrams

A. Introduction

Internet-connected devices are referred to as IoT. Computers are sensors and actuators with a processing unit, storage, and software. They also have a wireless communications interface. It enables items to connect to the Internet and connects devices to humans. RFID, sensor, and intelligence are IoT's core technologies. IoT networks are built on RFID. IoT's processing and communication capabilities and specific technologies allow the combination of various elements to work as an automated unit while allowing for the easy addition and removal of components with minimal effect, making it stable but versatile to adapt to environmental and user preferences. This work aims to create a flexible, economically smart system that remotely saves home machines. The Web app manages support. Controlled monitoring and remote management solutions meet our bit-by-bit proximity requirements and conserve electricity distribution. This endeavor intends to produce a modernized notoriety that saves via IoT-supported fantastic residences from the skilled world. IoT technology lets consumers use a PC or phone to check the status of many devices across the network. Figure 13.1 represents this endeavor. We can monitor the gadgets and get sensor data in web applications. Arduino solves this problem by talking to sensors.

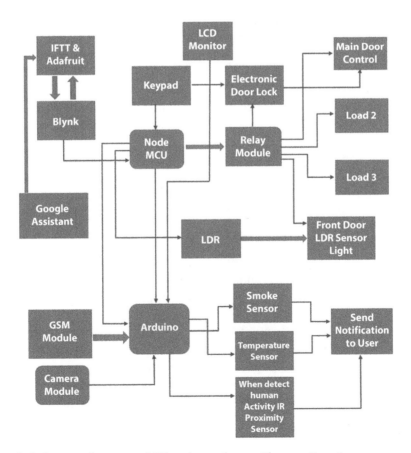

Figure 13.1 Block diagram of an a smart IoT-based smart home with a security system.

B. Project Features

- Main door control
- Intelligent notification system
- CCTV monitoring
- Automated light and door control
- Fire, smoke, and toxic gas detectors emit audible alarms
- Light intensity control

C. Proposed Working Prototype

- As a Smart Security System
  Putting an infrared (IR) sensor on a building's construction process reveals the aforementioned flaw shift. This icon monitors the effectiveness of the input signal to the miniaturized enhancement controller. Sending an email to the occupant's PDA (whose e-mail address is specified by the program) with the subject "There is an intruder in the room" triggers the camera module to take a picture and send it to the occupant, who may or may not be present in the home at the time. The gatecrasher instructs the owner to switch on the lights and fans by pressing "1" on his convenient keypad. Unless the proprietor learns that his building is uninsured, he may contact the police department by short message service to explain his dilemma [14].
- As an Automated Smart Home With Security
  Under home hutomation, all electrical equipment can be monitored through wireless connection from a noteworthy isolation. They are tracking lights and fans via the Internet at this moment of exploration. Because of whether Wi-Fi is not available, they will go to 3G or 4G organizations and operate on the network. It will encourage us to work towards a noteworthy separation of our home appliances [15]. It will help the obstructed and established people unproblematically manage their home mechanical assemblies.

D. Methodology

Home automation is a network of hardware, communication, and electrical interfaces that lets common devices talk to each other over the Internet. Every system has sensors and Wi-Fi, so you can control it with your phone or tablet from anywhere in the world. It lets you turn on the lights, lock the front door, and turn off the heat from anywhere. A home automation system is made up of three main parts: sensors, controllers, and actuators. Changes in motion, temperature, and light can be picked up by sensors. Then, in the future, home automation systems will change these settings based on what you tell them to do. Devices like computers, tablets, and smartphones can be used as controllers to send and receive information about the status of electronic apps in your home. Actuators can be light switches, motors, or motorized valves, and they control the system or feature that the system is controlling. They are designed to be operated via remote control. It refers to wireless home gadgets, such as smart thermostats, that consumers install in order to collect data and send orders over the Internet via a remote control. Home automation systems and Internet of Things technologies are also used. Wireless home automation is enabled through the installation of low-power communication devices, such as light sensors that detect the rising sun and swiftly send signals to turn off the front light. As previously stated, the development of several wireless protocols for a home automation system has begun. Alternatively, the walls of the house are demolished and rebuilt. None of these alternatives appeared to be the greatest. You now have more options, which is a great development. Everything will soon work digitally in protecting your house.

E. Working Diagram and Procedure

Smart IoT-dependent NodeMCU, Arduino UNO, an electronic door lock, ESP camera module, LDR, gas, fire, and PIR sensors were used to construct a smart home with an intelligent security system. NodeMCU manages the 5V DC-powered system powered by an adapter. The automated front door utilized a proximity sensor for motion detection. The fitted electronic door lock automatically or remotely unlocks the door when the user confirms their identity by being notified and viewing the front view through the hidden CCTV camera. The functional block diagram of a smart home is IoT-based. Three modes of operation are possible for an IoT-integrated home automation and security system: (i) automatically, (ii) remotely by a user, as depicted in Figure 13.2, and (iii) via a voice command, as depicted in Figure 13.3.

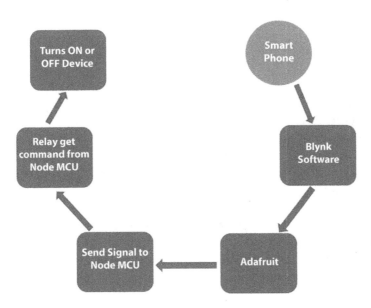

Figure 13.2 Remote-controlled operation.

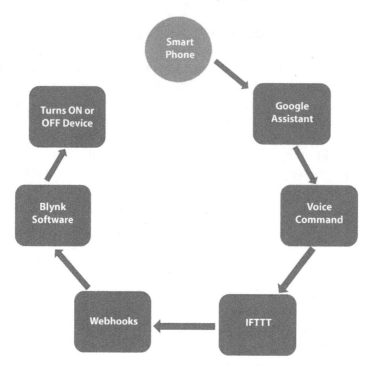

Figure 13.3 Voice-controlled operation.

13.4   Research Analysis

The research prototype analysis is presented in the following three sections.

A. Swot Analysis
The SWOT analysis evaluates the project's strengths, weaknesses, opportunities, and threats to enhance its success.

- Project strengths define its originality and novelty.
- Cost-effective.
- This project is more affordable than Alexa, Google Home, Amazon, etc.
- This system should be used by a non-professional in a certain way and configured without a control screen. The method's cleverness makes even a definite shape theoretically possible.
- Energy efficient.
- It remotely turns off lights and other electronics using sensors (LDR and ultrasonic sensors) and Google Assistant.
- Anti-theft mechanism implies multiple sensors that trigger the alert. Fire, gas, and temperature sensors activate alarms.

- Weaknesses
  Project weaknesses, like strengths, are intrinsic. Therefore, the focus is on people, resources, systems, and procedures. Identifying bad habits might help in overcoming difficulties.
  - Security
    Because the network uses Internet, the protection is inadequate. Since researchers did not use Internet authentication, the gadget is vulnerable.
  - Massive Investment
    Because home automation systems lack Wi-Fi backup routers, the network goes down. Otherwise, home automation would cost hundreds of thousands of dollars. A simple single-family home management system might be expensive. Overpriced devices, sensors, and smart home components should be avoided.
  - Data Challenges
    When no Wi-Fi backup router is attached to the PC for home automation, the network thus goes down without Internet.
  - Make People Lazy
    Remote controllability would make active individuals lazy.
- Opportunities
  Opportunities exist outside the scope of your project and necessitate a forward-looking mindset so that your invention or market position may improve.
  - AI-Based IoT Smart Home
    The addition of AI would improve the future. Awaiting you are houses managed by AI. IoT enables gadgets to "learn" from your actions and provide relevant data. Your preferences, routines, and habits will adjust the settings automatically.
  - Good Investment Chances in the Future
    Smart homes revolutionized electronics. Seven billion IoT devices are connected, excluding smartphones, tablets, and laptops. The IoT growth will disrupt all businesses. By 2026, the IoT sector might reach $3 trillion [16]. Our project is highly investable.
- Threats
  Google Home and Alexa are popular IoT-based smart home devices, but many others exist. Since it is for education and personal use, this project does not provide business issues. No marketing campaign is needed; but because the product is cheaper than Google Home, Alexa, and other Smart Home gadgets, it may disrupt the IoT industry.

B. Pest Analysis

PEST analyses help organizations discover, assess, coordinate, and monitor the macroeconomic variables affecting their industry. Opportunities and challenges are determined by political, economic, social, and technological forces. Analytical outcomes guide strategic planning and market research.

- Political Factors
  Changes in an organization's structure may be brought about through political pressure. Under this are foreign exchange policies, tax policies, export limitations, environmental laws, copyright laws, consumer protection laws, grant and program funding, administration, corruption, firm management, and international exchange policies, among other things. In other words, it is a fantastic method for improving one's standard of living. There are no unauthorized sensors or equipment used in our process [17].
- Economic Factors
  Economic aggregates include market expansion, seasonality, foreign currency rates, international commerce, labor costs, customer disposable income, unemployment, inflation, interest rates, loan supply, tax policy, raw material prices, etc.
  - Financially Accessible
    This project makes use of low-cost NodeMCU, Arduino microprocessors, sensors, and relay modules.
  - Double-Digit Growth Capability
    The growth of the smart home market is due to the increasing popularity of items like smart speakers, smart appliances, lighting control systems, home healthcare products, smart furniture, smart kitchens, and HVAC control solutions. From 2015 through 2020, the market for home automation around the world is expected to grow at a double-digit rate. In the years between 2018 and 2024, the smart home market is expected to grow by 12.02%, thus reaching $1,514.3 billion.
  - Raw Material
    The cost of the raw materials is relatively low, and they are readily available.
- Social Factors
  Your company and field are not immune to the effects of societal shifts. Factors such as population growth/demographics, immigration/emigration, household size/structure, standard of living, etc., also play a role.
  - Specific Markets
    All but the most specialized market can buy IoT-based smart homes for the elderly, disabled, and children.
  - Better Tomorrow
    Together as a community of smart home adopters, one can make a difference however little. People can together create a world where everyone may live longer, have healthier lives, and contribute to a brighter future for all of humanity. It is incredible that, with a click of a button, we can connect and monitor our home appliances from anywhere in the globe. The most exciting prospect, though, is the opportunity to conserve energy and reduce carbon emissions by shutting off unused lights and using machinery during off-peak hours.

- Effects
  It is possible that living in a smart house may make its inhabitants sluggish and uninterested in socialism. That would cause a major upheaval in the community.
- Technological Factors
  Technological advancements have altered the production, distribution, and advertising processes. These pertain to things like telecom networks, tech-policy, consumer access, competitive technology and growth, inventions, robots, research and innovation, IP protection, technological potential, etc.
  - Innovative Technology
    Technology wants this project because it focuses on wireless infrastructure and integrated devices which are the products of current technologies.
  - AI for Future Improvements
    AI will make it better. Coming soon are homes with AI control. IoT enables apps to "learn" about human experience and provide accurate perspectives. Your preferences, routines, and habits will change regularly.
  - Health Issue
    Wi-Fi radiation is harmless; thus, it does not harm people's health.

C. Theoretical Analysis

- IoT
  The Internet of Things is a network of interconnected devices that includes the objects that we use every day. These gadgets are web-enabled feature sensors and can be communicated with and controlled remotely. Thanks to IoT, "smart" devices can communicate with humans and other IoT-enabled gadgets through the web. Smart homes are a good example of the Internet of Things. Thermostats, doorbells, smoke detectors, and security alarms that can connect to the Internet function as nodes in a network where information is exchanged. Through a mobile app or online interface, users may perform actions such as changing the thermostat or opening a door remotely. Here is how IoT works:
  - Sensors are a type of hardware that may be added to a device in order to gather information or data.
  - The sensors collect data, which is subsequently transmitted digitally and analyzed by application.
  - After the information has been analyzed, the software sends it to users via their choice of app or website.
  - WSN
    Wireless sensor network (WSN) technology is used ad hoc to monitor many wireless sensors' physical and environmental systems. WSN uses sensor nodes with processors to regulate and monitor the environment in a field. They handle WSN data for the base station. Internet data sharing connects the WSN system base station.

13.5   Establishment of the Prototype

A. Introduction

This section details the project's implementation, including the components utilized. This chapter explains why each component model was chosen for the desired result. This chapter also explains the switching control scheme choice and also details the project implementation procedure.

B. Hardware Implementation

The assembly of required hardware is a crucial aspect of any undertaking. Therefore, each project component was evaluated and examined before being implemented with care. This project involved installing an automatic door, a remote-controlled door, and a light-dependent resistor.

C. Equipment Used

- **ESP32 Camera:** The ESP32-CAM camera module, as shown in Figure 13.4, is a wireless camera development board that comes relatively cheap. Building IP camera projects with multiple resolutions can be helpful when it comes to video streaming. The PCB antenna for the ESP32-CAM is incorporated into the device itself. The ESP32-CAM is a fully functional microcontroller device that also includes a micro-SD card and a real-life video camera that has been configured. It is highly suited for IoT devices requiring specialized capabilities such as image detection and recognition because of its low cost and simplicity of operation.
- **PIR Sensor:** Electronic devices that generate infrared light to detect certain features of their environment are called infrared sensors, and one such system is seen in Figure 13.5. Infrared sensing equipment is illustrative of this kind of technology. An infrared camera can record thermal imagery and detect movements. Unlike active infrared sensors, which also generate radiation, passive infrared sensors just detect it.
- **Relay Module:** In Figure 13.6, we see how the four-channel relay module may be used to regulate not only high voltage but also high current loads,

Figure 13.4 ESP32 cam [18].

Figure 13.5 PIR sensor [19].

Figure 13.6 Relay module [20].

including motors, solenoid switches, lights, and AC loads. It is compatible with a wide range of microcontrollers including Arduino and PIC. Moreover, it has a light-emitting diode (LED) that shows the current status of the relay.

- **Keypad:** As may be seen in Figure 13.7, one of the most widespread forms of input is a typical microprocessor keyboard. Pressing a key on a keypad wired in the familiar X–Y switch matrix normally makes a connection between the corresponding rows and columns.
- **LCD:** Liquid crystal displays, as shown in Figure 13.8, are quite common and widely utilized to display information such as sensor data from the project.
- **Electronic Door Lock:** Electronic door locks, such as the one depicted in Figure 13.9, can be used instead of traditional locks and keys to provide convenient home automation capabilities such as remote locking and unlocking.

Figure 13.7 Keypad [21].

Figure 13.8 LCD display [22].

Figure 13.9 Electric door lock [23].

Figure 13.10 DHT11 sensor [24].

Most people associate electronic door locks with cars, but many modern home security companies sell them.

- **DHT11 Sensor:** The DHT11, as shown in Figure 13.10, is a simple digital temperature and humidity sensor available at an affordable price. A digital signal is transmitted to the data pin from the sensor, which uses a thermistor and an air humidity sensor (no analog input pins needed).

- **GSM Module:** Through the GSM library, as shown in Figure 13.11, an Arduino board equipped with a GSM shield can connect, send, and receive text messages and make voice calls. Additionally, the GSM shield enables the Arduino board to send and receive voice calls. When used with Arduino Uno, the shield will be ready to use right out of the box.

- **Smoke and Gas Sensor:** Figure 13.12 shows that a significant amount of gas is produced during a fire. As a result of the sensor's detection, the power source is activated. Carbon monoxide can be identified if it is present. It is possible to make the case for both smoke and gas detectors simultaneously.

Figure 13.11 GSM module [25].

Figure 13.12 Smoke and gas sensor [26].

Figure 13.13 Flame sensor [27].

- **Flame Sensor:** The grove-flame sensor, shown in Figure 13.13, can detect flames and other light sources with wavelengths between 750 and 1,500 nm.

D. Major Implementation Equipment

- **Arduino Uno:** The ATmega328P chip used in Arduino Uno serves as its basis (see Figure 13.14). This board has a USB connector, power jack, ICSP header, reset button, and 14 digital I/O pins. Overall, you will find six analog inputs. It includes everything required to operate a microcontroller. Connect it to a computer or power supply to get started. When things go wrong with your

Figure 13.14 Arduino UNO [28].

Arduino Uno project, you would not break the bank replacing it. This is in contrast to more costly boards like the Raspberry Pi, STM, etc.

- **ESP8266:** In Figure 13.15, we see that the ESP8266 WIFI Module is a system-on-a-chip that includes a TCP/IP protocol stack. It allows a microcontroller to connect to any available Wi-Fi network. The ESP8266's built-in Wi-Fi networking capabilities allow it to either host a running program or download one from another application processor.
- **Resistor:** A resistor is a type of passive electrical component, as shown in Figure 13.16, that consists of two terminals and functions as an element of a circuit by implementing electrical resistance.

Figure 13.15 ESP8266 [29].

Figure 13.16 Resistor [30].

- **LED Light:** As can be seen in Figure 13.17, loads stand in for the light emitted by a light-emitting diode when a current flow travels through it.
- **Holder:** The light can be set using the holder, as shown in Figure 13.18.
- **Jumper and Electric Wire:** As can be seen in the connection in Figure 13.19, a wire is employed in the component process.

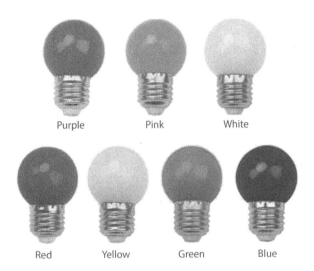

| Purple | Pink | White |

| Red | Yellow | Green | Blue |

Figure 13.17 LED light [31].

Figure 13.18 Holder [32].

Figure 13.19 Jumper and electric wire [33].

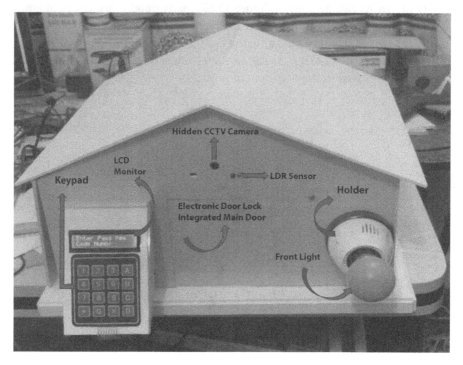

Figure 13.20 Implemented hardware of the prototype.

E. Implementation of The Prototype

The implementation stage is the most important part of the research. The first step in the implementation process was to develop an implementation idea, which resulted in the hardware shown in Figure 13.20. Because it comes with a single integrated Wi-Fi system, NodeMCU is utilized for mobile wireless control on a global scale. Arduino IDE was used for the programming of Arduino Uno in the past [34].

F. Implementation of A Main Door

A door can be controlled by a person or a machine using a remote. A computer or a mobile device can be used to control it. Although it is nearly identical to an automatic door, the main difference is that it requires human or mechanical control [35]. When a person or object approaches the front door, when motion is detected by the PIR sensor, the owner is alerted that there is someone (or something) at the door. To control an electronic door lock that requires a PIN code of six digits, the PIR sensor is wired directly to NodeMCU. In order to unlock and lock this door, you can use your mobile device. A hidden CCTV camera installed above the entrance allows for constant monitoring of the lobby.

G. Implementation of LDR Sensor Light

Light-sensitive gadgets contain light-dependent resistors. When light bounces off the LDR, the resistance modifies. LDRs exhibit a strong resistance in low-light environments compared with weak resistance in bright environments [36]. The LDR generates an analog voltage proportional to the light beam when connected to Vcc. Thus, LDR voltage increases along with changes in light intensity. A NodeMCU pin receives the LDR's analog voltage.

H. Sensor Implementation and Sending Notifications to the User in Case of Accidents

The user is quickly alerted if there is a fire, gas leak, or theft from the front door using the prototype over the Adafruit web server. This prototype included a covert CCTV camera module and safety features for the keypad, gas, and fire. It was created for a safe and wholesome life.

I. IFTTT Implementation for Voice Command

IFTTT is the greatest platform for working with Google Assistant on the web and in Blynk apps. IFTTT can offer services through Google Assistant and webhooks to finish the work.

For Turning on a Device

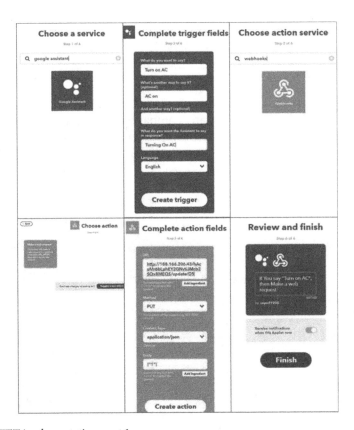

Figure 13.21 IFTTT implementation, part 1.

For Turning Off A Device

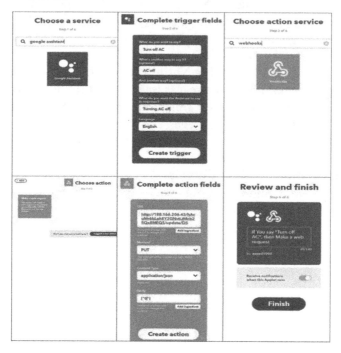

Figure 13.22 IFTTT implementation, part 2.

The same approach can be used with any compatible device. The only place to be modified is the URL section after step 5, where D5 is the GPIO PIN of NodeMCU. The corresponding PIN should be located somewhere. As can be seen in Figure 13.21 and Figure 13.22, the body portion of step 5 accepts the values 0 and 1, respectively, to turn the device on and off.

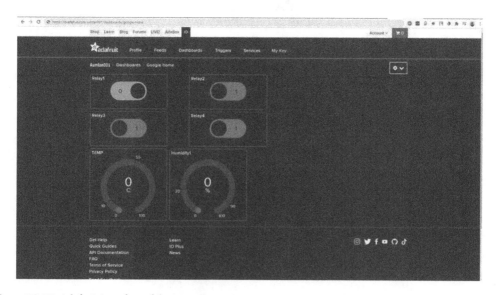

Figure 13.23 Adafruit interface of the prototype.

J. Adafruit Implementation for Remote-Controlled Operation

The Blynk apps and web server will make it possible for the security system in the smart home to function. Adafruit offers the best functioning platform for remotely triggering loads. When it notices a problem with a smart home or smart security system, it can also provide services via a web server to alert the customers. The Adafruit web server's user interface is shown in Figure 13.23.

13.6   Results and Discussions

A. Introduction

The outcomes of the project are discussed in this chapter. The data findings have been examined using the appropriate tables, and simulation has been provided for every project phase. In conclusion, an observation is made on the whole effort.

B. Data Findings

- Recorded LDR Sensor Data
  Collection of data was performed throughout the course of 24 h based on the light levels. The values of LDR are shown (in Table 13.1) to be greater during the day and lower throughout the night (in addition, see also Figure 13.24).

Table 13.1 LDR light intensity data.

Time	Intensity of sunlight	LED light state
6:00	35	ON
7:00	40	ON
8:00	55	OFF
9:00	70	OFF
10:00	85	OFF
11:00	102	OFF
12:00	125	OFF
13:00	120	OFF
14:00	103	OFF
15:00	70	OFF

(Continued)

Table 13.1 LDR light intensity data. (*Continued*)

Time	Intensity of sunlight	LED light state
16:00	65	OFF
17:00	45	OFF
18:00	40	ON
19:00	35	ON
20:00	31	ON
21:00	29	ON
22:00	25	ON
23:00	21	ON
0:00	19	ON
1:00	19	ON
2:00	17	ON
3:00	15	ON
4:00	13	ON
5:00	25	ON
6:00	40	ON

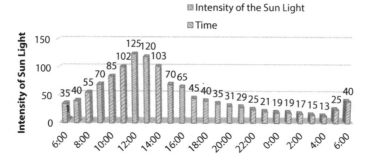

RECORDED LDR SENSOR DATA

Figure 13.24 Graphical form of the light intensity worktime.

- Relay Operational Data
  Table 13.2 demonstrates that the relay needs a continuous 5 V to operate.
- Electronic Automatic Door Lock Operational Data
  Based on the information in Table 13.3, one may be certain that the door lock will open within half a second and close itself after 5 s.
- Fire Sensor Operational Data
  According to Table 13.4, if the temperature in the home increases to above 80°Celsius, the fire sensor will signal the homeowner. The simple observation of a temperature rise will trigger an alert.

Table 13.2 Supply voltage of the relay module.

Supply voltage	Load state
2.5 V	OFF
3.5 V	OFF
4.5 V	OFF
5 V	ON
5.5 V	OFF
6 V	OFF

Table 13.3 Electronic door lock operational data.

Observation	Time (seconds)	Load state
01	0.0	OFF
02	0.5	ON
03	1.5	ON
04	3.5	ON
05	5	OFF

Table 13.4 Fire sensor operational data.

Temperature (°C)	Alarm
70	OFF
75	OFF
80	ON
90	ON
100	ON
105	ON

Table 13.5 Smoke sensor data.

Smoke sensor observation	Amount of smoke (cm³)	Alarm
01	100	OFF
02	150	OFF
03	200	ON
04	300	ON
05	195	OFF

- Smoke Sensor
  Table 13.5 shows that it detects the gas density and warns the user by emitting an alarm when the potentially hazardous gas density is greater than 200 cm³.

C. Results and Discussions

Analyzing all the data and graph charts, we can see that the smart home device can provide better efficiency. All the sensors work properly and give a better response. In the project, a better output is obtained.

D. Observations

Using Blynk and Google Assistant with the aid of IFTTT, all loads were observed through their connections as per load. Here load 1 is connected with a LED bulb, which is turned on and off manually by Blynk App by pressing the ON and OFF buttons. Based on the observation recorded 10 times, it may infer that the command was carried out after the phrase "OK, Google" was stated. As can be seen in Figure 13.25, the instruction to turn on the light was given first, and then the reaction time was noted. The light was subsequently told to be turned off. On average, it takes 4.5 s to switch on a light and 4.7 s to turn it off.

Table 13.6 presents an additional finding on voice command interoperability with Google Assistant. It was decided to listen to and record the voices of 10 different people to evaluate how well their voice instructions worked together on time. The experiment allows us to draw some conclusions. According to the findings, there is 0.10% probability that Google Assistant can discern the difference between two voices. Because it can only hear the pre-programmed speech, the prototype is safer.

E. Summary

The necessary graph, data analysis, and schematic diagram were presented in this chapter, and the results were compared and discussed. Analyzing the data led to the discovery and correction of several errors in the data that had previously been reported. The data must be processed on multiple occasions before it is possible to obtain the needed results. Finally, some summaries of the entire study were made available to the public.

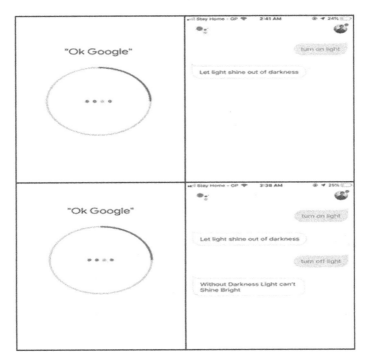

Figure 13.25 Google Assistant with the aid of IFTTT.

Table 13.6 Google Assistant voice command compatibility.

Voice of persons randomly checked	Is the voice working?
1	No
2	No
3	No
4	No
5	Yes
6	No
7	No
8	No
9	No
10	No

13.7 Conclusions

A. Summary of Findings

The research team behind this project set out to create a home automation system and smart home security system that would provide homeowners access to trustworthy Internet of Things-based home automation. We looked at every facet of this project. Once the task has been completed, it is time to collect the required equipment. This project was divided into three parts, each treated as an independent endeavor until it was finally brought together to form the whole. They were built with NODE MCU, Arduino UNO, and various other components, and then they were programmed and connected to the different parts of the design [37].

B. The Novelty of the Work

The methodology was based on this research work. However, it was not original. As an alternative, the topology for multilevel automation has been covered in some earlier scholarly papers. This project's originality comes from using Google Assistant and numerous sensor types, which develops a novel idea with several advantages over the conventional systems utilized in this home automation framework. Most home automation systems can manage high electricity levels even when not in use, which is a known fact. This inefficiency raises the price of solar projects, making them barely profitable. This research aims to enhance automation systems that use little power. In essence, it is an entirely new online architecture that will provide people the confidence that they need to make sensible and secure life decisions.

C. Limitations of the Work

Despite hitting the target, this project still had a lot of restrictions. A major issue or disadvantage of a smart home network is price. Many businesses offer the smart home system, which is very expensive. A smart home network must have access to the Internet. As a result, we must rely on the Internet, which is somewhat concerning for our nation. If the smart home system has issues, we cannot call a handyperson or someone nearby to fix or handle the bug. We will have to rely on the professionals. You can only get the help that you need from the company's experts.

D. Ethical Concerns

This project's primary goal is to create an IoT-based smart home that uses technology to provide a simple and comfortable way of life. The main guidelines that we follow for this project are to make it affordable and useful for most people and help them comprehend the smart home system. This project allows us to understand and utilize smart home technology [38]. In just a few short years, there have been significant changes in the demand for IoT applications.

The market has expanded to include entrepreneurs who work together to create mobile technology-specific ecosystems that enable interoperability between Internet of Things apps. The idea of domestic automations would have formerly looked weird and unrealistic, but as our gadgets get smarter and more money is poured into developing IoT consumer products, we will probably see more innovation in the market due to increasing competition. We want to make our idea simpler and more affordable for the long-term benefit of the people and the planet.

Acknowledgment

The authors would like to take this opporunity to express their gratitude to the Almighty as well as their own mothers and fathers. We would like to thank Dr. Carmen Z. Lamagna, the Electrical and Electronics Engineering Department and the Computer Science and Engineering Department at the American International University—Bangladesh, and the Mechanical Engineering Department at Graphic Era (Deemed to be a University) for their support and encouragement. My sincere gratitude goes out to Mr. Adel A. Nasser for the unwavering assistance and direction he has provided.

References

1. Sayeduzzaman, M., Borno, M.I., Islam, M., Howlader, S., A design of an IoT-based Smart home with auto-sanitization system, in: *Smart Trends in Computing and Communications,* Lecture Notes in Networks and Systems, vol. 286, Y.D. Zhang, T. Senjyu, C. So-In, A. Joshi (eds.), Springer, Singapore, 2022.
2. Kumari, S. and Mehta, M., Knowledge about indoor plants by homemakers in Hisar City. *Indian J. Health Wellbeing,* 12, 1, 33, 33–39, 2021.
3. Bharath, S., Pasha, M.Y., Deepth, J., IoTHome automation. *Int. J. Comput. Technol. Res.,* 5, 4–6, 2017, April.
4. Kodali, R.K., Jain, V., Bose, S., Boppana, L., IoT based smart security and home automation system, in: *2016 International Conference on Computing, Communication and Automation (ICCCA),* IEEE, pp. 1286–1289, 2016, April.
5. Li, B. and Yu, J., Research and application on the smart home based on component technologies and Internet of Things. *Procedia Eng.,* 15, 2087–2092, 2011.
6. Kim, J., HEMS (home energy management system) base on the IoT smart home. *Contemp. Eng. Sci.,* 9, 1, 21–28, 2016.
7. Kodali, R.K., Jain, V., Bose, S., Boppana, L., IoT based smart security and home automation system, in: *2016 International Conference on Computing, Communication and Automation (ICCCA),* IEEE, pp. 1286–1289, 2016, April.
8. Haque, K.F., Saqib, N., Rahman, M.S., An optimized stand-alone green hybrid grid system for an offshore Island, Saint Martin, Bangladesh, in: *2019 International Conference on Energy and Power Engineering (ICEPE),* IEEE, pp. 1–5, 2019, March, 2019.
9. Hasan, T., Abrar, M.A., Saimon, M.Z.R., Sayeduzzaman, M., Islam, M.S., Constructing an integrated IoT-based smart home with an automated fire and smoke security alert system. *Malaysian J. Sci. Adv. Technol.,* 3, 1, 1–10, Jan. 2023.
10. Abhay, K.R., IoT based smart home: Security aspects and security architecture. *IoT Based Smart Home: Security Aspects and Security Architecture,* IEEE Conference Publication | IEEE Xplore, 2020, ieeexplore.ieee.org/document/9115737.
11. Kodali, R.K., Jain, V., Bose, S., Boppana, L., IoT based smart security and home automation system. *2016 International Conference on Computing, Communication and Automation (ICCCA),* Noida, IEEE, India, pp. 1286–1289, 2016.

12. Gupta, P. and Chhabra, J., IoT based smart home design using power and security management. *2016 International Conference on Innovation and Challenges in Cyber Security (ICICCS-INBUSH)*, IEEE, Noida, India, 2016.

13. Hoque, M.A. and Davidson, C., Design and implementation of an IoT-based smart home security system. *Int. J. Networked Distributed Comput.*, 7, 2, 85–92, 2019.

14. Digital Trends, The best home security systems in 2020 | digital trends, 2020. Available at: https://www.digitaltrends.com/home/best-home-security-systems/ Accessed 14 March 2020.

15. Davies, E. and Anireh, V., Design and implementation of smart home system using internet of things. *Adv. Multidiscip. & Sci. Res. J. Publication*, 7, 1, 33–42, 2019.

16. RS Web Solutions, Smart homes - is it the future of home automation?, 2020. Available at: <https://www.rswebsols.com/tutorials/technology/smart-homes-future-home-automation> Accessed 10 February 2020.

17. Markskilton.com. 2020. Available at: <https://www.markskilton.com/single-post/2016/10/27/Impact-of-IoT-on-political-systems> Accessed 11 February 2020.

18. Hamza, I., How to make smart home automation system using ESP32 module?, Appuals.com, 5 Oct. 2019, appuals.com/how-to-make-smart-home-automation-system-using-esp32-module.

19. IR Sensor working principal and applications - robocraze. *Robocraze*, 20 June 2022. robocraze.com/blogs/post/ir-sensor-working.

20. What is a power relay module | relay modules. *GEP Power Products*. www.geppowerproducts.com/standard-products/power-distribution-fuse-relay-holders-fuse-blocks/relay-modules. Accessed 21 Jan. 2023.

21. What is keypad? - definition from techopedia. Techopedia.com, www.techopedia.com/definition/7940/keypad. Accessed 21 Jan. 2023.

22. *Liquid Crystal Display | Electronics*, Encyclopedia Britannica, www.britannica.com/technology/liquid-crystal-display. Accessed 21 Jan. 2023.

23. Quality electronic door locks, fingerprint door lock factory, electronic door locks manufacturer, fingerprint door lock from china. *Guangzhou Light Source Electron. Technol. Limited.* www.electronicdoor-locks.com/index.php. Accessed 21 Jan. 2023.

24. DHT11–temperature and humidity sensor. *Components101.* components101.com/sensors/dht11-temperature-sensor. Accessed 21 Jan. 2023.

25. What Is GSM (Global System for Mobile Communication)? *Mobile Comput.*, 1 Mar. 2021. www.techtarget.com/searchmobilecomputing/definition/GSM.

26. Centre, scottish sensory. https://www.ssc.education.ed.ac.uk/BSL/physics/smokegassensord.html. www.ssc.education.ed.ac.uk/BSL/physics/smokegassensord.html. Accessed 21 Jan. 2023.

27. Agarwal, T., flame sensor: Working, types, and its applications. *ElProCus - Electronic Projects Eng. Students*, 19 Aug. 2019, www.elprocus.com/flame-sensor-working-and-its-applications.

28. "What Is Arduino Uno?" What Is Arduino Uno?, 6 Sept. 2001, www.flyrobo.in/blog/what-is-arduino-uno.

29. "ESP8266 Wi-Fi MCU I Espressif Systems." ESP8266 Wi-Fi MCU I Espressif Systems. www.espressif.com/en/products/socs/esp8266. Accessed 21 Jan. 2023.

30. How do resistors work? What's inside a resistor?, in: *Explain That Stuff*, 16 Aug. 2008, www.explainthatstuff.com/resistors.html.

31. Learn about LED lighting, in: *Learn About LED Lighting*, ENERGY STAR, www.energystar.gov/products/lighting_fans/light_bulbs/learn_about_led_bulbs. Accessed 21 Jan. 2023.

32. Lamp-holder — Definition, examples, related words and more at Wordnik. Wordnik.com, www.wordnik.com/words/lamp-holder. Accessed 21 Jan. 2023.

33. How to make jumper wires - dummies, in: *How to Make Jumper Wires - Dummies*, www.dummies.com/article/technology/electronics/general-electronics/how-to-make-jumper-wires-138049. Accessed 21 Jan. 2023.

34. Robo India, Tutorials || Learn Arduino || Robotics, in: *Blynk For Nodemcu - Introduction - Robo India || Tutorials || Learn Arduino || Robotics*, 2020, Available at: <https://roboindia.com/tutorials/blynk-introduction-nodemcu/> Accessed 9 March 2020.

35. Creativitybuzz.org. 2020. Available at: <https://www.creativitybuzz.org/make-remote-control-door-lock/> Accessed 13 March 2020.

36. Lepcha, T., Street light automation using LDR and arduino. *Int. J. Res. Appl. Sci. Eng. Technol.*, 7, 6, 1196–1199, 2019.

37. UKEssays.comonline. A review: IoT based smart home, 2020. Available at: <https://www.ukessays.com/essays/information-technology/a-review-iot-based-smart-home.php> Accessed 2 April 2020.

38. Medium, The ethics of smart home tech. online, 2020. Available at: <https://medium.com/@ryan.c.laux/its-no-secret-that-when-it-comes-to-the-ethics-of-the-internet-of-things-there-can-certainly-a-ea79d73e41f7> Accessed 7 April 2020.

14

An Automated Home Security System Using Secure Message Queue Telemetry Transport Protocol

P. Rukmani*, S. Graceline Jasmine, M. Vergin Raja Sarobin, L. Jani Anbarasi
and Soumitro Datta

School of Computer Science and Engineering, Vellore Institute of Technology, Chennai, India

Abstract

Homeowners can set, monitor, and operate their security system remotely or through an in-home interface, providing both home safety and protection as well as adding a potential burglar deterrent. An automated home security system's purpose is to keep houses safe from sophisticated burglars. Individual device-level security is also necessary to ensure total protection. In its implementation, the Internet of Things devices are passive infrared (PIR) sensors that detect human movement and include multiple surveillance technologies to automatically monitor a dwelling. When PIR sensors detect a movement, the security devices go into active mode. When motion is detected in a room, facial recognition cameras begin recording the activity. The other devices remain idle throughout, resulting in a cost-effective and data-rich solution. The devices' isolation during that idle state, as well as the advanced encryption standard encryption of any/all payload, keeps them secure. The automated security system employs the secure message queue telemetry transport protocol to protect transferred device-based payload to and from the network.

Keywords: Home security, MQTT, IoT, PIR sensor, AES

14.1 Introduction

Home automation solutions are a relatively new sector of research that has yet to be fully integrated into our everyday lives [1]. This is because the construction of a suitable smart home system is covered in many distinct research and technical areas. The cost of a smart home remains a major impediment to the widespread adoption of smart home technologies. The higher installation cost is attributable to the fact that technologies have advanced greatly since most homes were built. This means that most residences were built prior to this equipment being accessible [2], thus posing a challenge for home automation commercialization. Smart home solutions, on the other hand, will become a reasonable investment as new homes are created as technology advances and become more inexpensive. Home automation in the future will likely focus on merging home gadgets and even appliances to

---

Corresponding author: rukmani.p@vit.ac.in

Amit Kumar Tyagi (ed.) Automated Secure Computing for Next-Generation Systems, (275–294) © 2024 Scrivener Publishing LLC

improve personalization, security, and usability in the home [3]. The first reason to install a home security system is to protect your family and your belongings. A home burglary occurs every 13 s, four times per minute, 240 times per hour, and approximately 6,000 times per day. We have addressed how frequently, how, and where burglaries occur around your home in the most recent home burglary report as well as why home security is so vital. You can view all of the statistics by checking. Installing a home security system allows you to secure your home and assets as well as your family against potential burglary.

Unfaithful domestic servants have also been involved in a number of cases of domestic robbery. This trend has been on the rise for a few years, and it mostly targets the elderly, single women, varied families, and children. Domestic robbery is the term used to describe a situation wherein a domestic assistant steals things from a home. Domestic help has become an important element of any household these days, with many families providing refuge to maids and slaves. Because the assistant spends the entire day and night in a particular household, he or she is familiar with how the home operates as well as the advantages and disadvantages of the family's lifestyle. In other circumstances, a domestic help may be a co-conspirator in the crime, and a simple security system may be ineffective. In these situations, a high number of objects are vulnerable to theft (Figure 14.1). Both of these problems can be readily solved with the creative method, which was the driving force behind this research.

A smart home security (SHS) system is presented as a solution that can prevent intruders with exceptional accuracy. The method presented in this paper helps prevent illegal access by utilizing security features such as motion detection and facial recognition. The primary goal of this SHS system is to provide an Internet of Things (IoT)-enabled secure application for home monitoring that is also resistant to hackers. To establish a fully secure system, IoT hardware and device endpoints must be securely protected. Advanced encryption standard (AES), a powerful and lightweight encryption algorithm, can be used to encrypt and protect inputs and responses from eavesdropping.

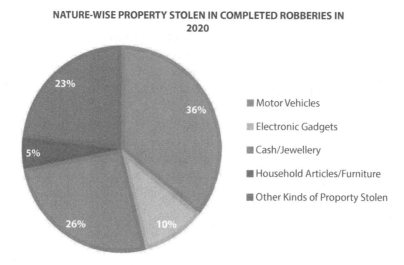

Figure 14.1 Nature-Wise property stolen in completed robberies in 2020 [4].

ORGANIZATION OF THE CHAPTER

The rest of this chapter is outlined as follows: Section 14.2 shows the related works, Section 14.3 outlines the proposed methodology, Section 14.4 presents the result analysis, and, finally, Section 14.5 provides the conclusion of this chapter.

14.2   Related Works

This section details the related research work implanted using passive infrared (PIR) security systems and message queue telemetry transport (MQTT) security.

14.2.1   PIR Home Security Solutions

Kodali *et al.* [4] have described a model consisting of TI-CC3200 Launchpad and a microcontroller unit (MCU) which is battery-powered with a built-in Wi-Fi connection as a lucrative wireless security and automation system for homes. The PIR sensors are installed at building entrances and linked to a digital input–output pin on an MCU. The Wi-Fi-capable MCU is programmed using the Energia Integrated Development Environment (IDE). The configuration devised allows mobile handsets with no Internet access to receive security alerts and operate IoT devices connected to the microcontroller.

Tanwar *et al.* [5] describe a significantly low-cost security system with a regular email notification system. A PIR device and a Raspberry Pi MCU are included in the configuration. USB ports and general purpose input/output pins are used to connect surveillance cameras and PIR sensor systems to the Raspberry Pi. The technique assumes that all homes have Internet connectivity and uses it to deliver real-time e-mails to residents. To detect motion, the system's motion detection circuitry compares signal inputs from PIR sensors to previous values. The security camera takes a photo when the current and previous signals diverge, which is maintained on the Raspberry Pi for a brief period before being relayed to the resident.

14.2.2   Solutions for MQTT Security

To enhance the MQTT security, Bali [6] proposes a minimalist authentication technique centered around a chaotic algorithm that integrates self-key authentication with block cypher; data protection was proven after the simulation.

Bhawiyuga [7] provides a token-based MQTT protocol verification idea for limited devices, which included four components as follows: publisher, MQTT broker, subscriber, and token authenticator.

L. Bisne *et al.* [8] suggest a hybrid MQTT security mechanism relying on attribute-based cryptography and AES S-boxes. Because the approach is based on public key as well as secret key encryption, the subscriber must perform double-decoding, which makes the system more complicated.

M. Singh [9] and others introduce the "SPublish" secured publish command for (MQTT, MQTT-SN), which encrypts data with lightweight elliptic curve cryptography and a collection of attribute-based encryption (ABE) policies, including the key policy KP-ABE and the ciphertext policy CP-ABE. The major disadvantage of employing ABE is that using CP-ABE adds unnecessary overhead.

To secure the transit of distributed communications between the participants of the MQTT protocol, Mektoubi's [10] proposal is to use a certification authority to issue a certificate and a private key to a MQTT topic that is broadcast for authorized clients.

14.2.3   Solutions for Home Automation

The mobile home automation shows which devices are ZigBee-enabled [11, 12]. With the use of IOT, which allows us to link non-smart gadgets to the Internet, we can turn them into smart devices. It transforms a regular home into a smart home and provides an efficient system to operate household products. The camera installation in the home which can be traced via cyberspace can help boost security. Users may also find their homes and operate the appliances from away. This will save both energy and money spent on power.

14.3   Proposed Solution

The proposed solution comprises four different components which are described further in detail in this section. Message transmission via the MQTT protocol aids the components to achieve this interconnection.

14.3.1   Technological Decisions

A. Message Transfer Protocol

The message transfer protocol between multiple modules is decided to be MQTT. It was chosen because it secures the delivery of messages. Some IoT gadgets are mobile, while others are powered by batteries. In some circumstances and for some purposes, this can cause the IoT connectivity to become unstable. MQTT's lightweight protocol is significantly better suited to these devices than HTTP protocols. This is due to the fact that an HTTP protocol header is normally approximately 8,000 bytes long, whereas the MQTT protocol is only 2 bytes long and contains only a few lines of code. While HTTP protocols have their usefulness in IoT—particularly in fields like 3D printing—they are typically regarded as inadequate for the majority of IoT devices.

B. Application Framework

The Node.js Framework is ideal for this application. To begin with, any IoT device is always dealing with dynamically changing data. This necessitates the use of a framework capable of handling real-time applications and large data flows.

Node.js is based on Google's V8 JS engine, which is extremely powerful and scalable. Node.js is the most popular framework for real-time apps and platforms because of this functionality. Constantly changing data is also not a problem for it. MQTT, a publish–subscribe-based messaging protocol, is widely used in IoT applications. This protocol, in turn, employs WebSocket for transport and encapsulation. Both MQTT and WebSocket have a lot of support and are simple to use with Node.js.

C. Encryption Method

The encryption of the message payload is done with AES. AES has shown to be a dependable and effective way of protecting sensitive information over time. A robust security algorithm may be implemented in both hardware and software, which is one of the main advantages of adopting AES. Because of its lengthier key widths, it is resilient to hacking efforts (128, 192, and 256 bits). It is a free and open-source program. Because AES is royalty-free, it is extensively applied in the public and private sectors equally. AES is the most widely used security technology today, as shown in Figure 14.2, with applications starting from encrypted data storage to wireless communications.

D. OpenCV

In the realm of computer vision, Open-Source Computer Vision (OpenCV) is a well-known C/C++ package. Despite being built in C/C++, it has been successfully implemented in Python and Java. It is one of the most powerful libraries for working with photos and image databases. It makes tasks like feature extraction and manipulation a lot easier.

E. Face Recognition

The world's slightest face recognition public library permits one to distinguish and manipulate faces from Python or the command line. Built with deep learning and dlib's advanced

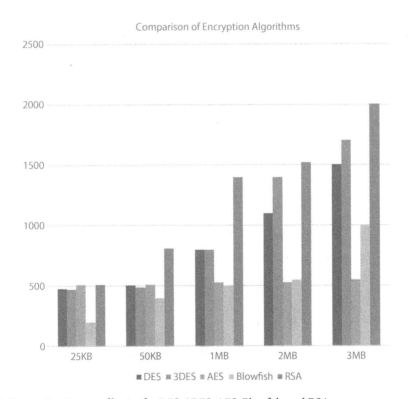

Figure 14.2 Encryption time vs. file size for DES, 3DES, AES, Blowfish, and RSA.

face recognition, with the labeled faces in the wild benchmark, the model has 99.38% accuracy rate.

14.3.2   Hardware Decision

A. Microcontroller Unit

The Amica NodeMCU ESP8266 is the cheapest option among these MCUs that satisfies the use case. The prototyping board for open-source designs is existing for NodeMCU. The name "NodeMCU" is a mixture of the words "node" and "MCU" (micro-controller unit), as shown in Figure 14.3 and Figure 14.4. The word "NodeMCU" denotes the firmware rather than the development kits that can go with it. The firmware and the prototyping board designs are both from a free source. The scripting language Lua is used by the firmware. Espressif Non-OS SDK was used to create the firmware for ESP8266 and is based on the eLua project. Many open-source projects are used, including lua-cjson [9] and SPIFFS [10]. The components important to their project must be selected by the users, and firmware is constructed and tailored to their needs because of resource limits. Support for the 32-bit ESP32 has been included as well. The Arduino IDE can be used to program the NodeMCU. The prototyping board for open-source designs is existing for NodeMCU as shown in Table 14.1.

Figure 14.3 NodeMCU (top view).

Figure 14.4 NodeMCU (PIN view).

Table 14.1 Comparison of the different MCUs that can be used for implementation.

Board	Specs	Features	Price
Teensy 3.6	256 kB RAM, 1 MB flash storage, 4 kB EEPROM, 180-MHz Cortex M4F	Teensyduino-Arduino IDE, SD card reader	4,599/-
Launchpad MSP430	32 kB Program FRAM, 4 kB RAM, 24-MHz MSP430	Energy Trace Technology - low power, Energia, onboard buttons two and LED, Booster Pack	1194/-
Amica NodeMCU Esp8266	80 MHz, 64 kB SRAM, 4 MB flash storage	External QSPI flash, compatible with Arduino IDE, Wi-Fi	209/-
Particle Photon	120-MHz ARM Cortex M3, 128 kB RAM, 1 MB flash storage	Device Cloud, SDKs for mobile and ParticleJS, 18 GPIO, plenty of references and guides	NA
Seeeduino Nano	16 MHz, 2 kB SRAM, 32 kB flash storage	Fully compatible with Arduino Nano, additional Grove 12C connector, USB type C, compact	NA
ESP8266	32 KiB instruction RAM 32 KiB instruction cache RAM	Wifi Module, needs to be attached with Arduino Board for usage	117/-

B. PIR Sensor

PIRs are constructed using a pyroelectric sensor (Figure 14.5; shown as a round metal ampule with a middle rectangular crystal) that could perceive infrared radiation levels. All things emit a small quantity of low-level radiation, and the hotter something is, the more radiation it releases. A sensor for motion detection is actually separated into two sections

Figure 14.5 PIR sensor PIN view (left); PIR sensor top view (right).

in order to distinguish mobility from average IR levels. The two parts have been wired such that they abandon one another. The outcome also will swing to maximum or low if any one part gets more or less IR radiation than the other.

PIR sensors are idyllic for numerous basic projects or items that require identifying whether a person has left or entered an area or is approaching. They consume very less power and cost, are somewhat durable, have a wide lens range, and are simple to use. PIRs will not inform you how many individuals there are in the vicinity or how near they are to the sensor.

14.3.3   Module Overview

A. Node-Red Edge Control Module

This module is made up of controls as shown in Figure 14.6. The main purpose here is to retrieve and read the response from a simple two-state sensor that can only be operated via MQTT from the outside. MQTT payloads of switch state and PIR state are acknowledged. All other payloads are disregarded, and inputs are turned case-insensitive using a service node. As a result, errors during setup will have no impact on this controller. The sensor responds to the signal by changing its state and publishing the new state. The program then calculates the response that it must provide, according to the various scenarios, and sends an MQTT message in response. AES encryption of the information is also handled by this module. This AES encryption makes sure that the payloads from the PIR devices are not vulnerable to any MITM eavesdropping.

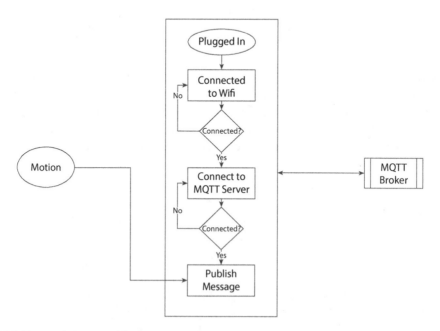

Figure 14.6 Proposed system architecture.

B. Interactive User Interface and Control System Module

The user interfaces for controlling the home automation system (Figure 14.7) from outside the home. It also shows the room where the burglar was discovered (when lockdown mode is activated). The lockdown mode is activated by pressing the "leave home" button. When you click Arrive Home, it will be turned off. There is also an added weather monitoring component in this system, which will assist the user in his everyday life by reminding him to bring an umbrella if there is prediction of a rain. The camera is connected with face recognition and further to the implementation via REST. If an abnormality or break-in is detected by the program, the user can go to the camera module page. Face recognition allows you to see who is present.

C. Hardware Module

This module contains a PIR sensor connected to NodeMCU and programmed accordingly to detect and respond to any motion detected as shown in Figure 14.8. This PIR and NodeMCU module are made encrypted using the AES Middleware Security. Payloads are encrypted and are dispatched securely over MQTT.

D. Security Middleware

The most important asset of this implementation is this security module. AES in counter configuration will be used to encode and decode data payload sent via MQTT as well as to preserve device payload. CTR (short for counter) is a common AES block encryption algorithm mode that enables all stages to be performed simultaneously. Both counter and output feedback (OFB) entail XORing a succession of pad vectors containing plaintext and ciphertext units, which are 128-bit units created by breaking the plaintext. It functions as shown in Figure 14.9.

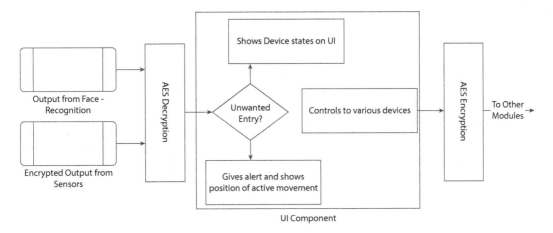

Figure 14.7 Workflow of the UI and control system.

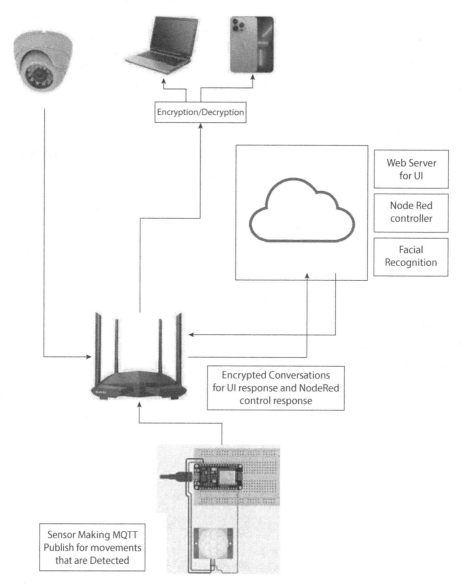

Figure 14.8 Workflow of the hardware module.

E. Facial Recognition

The procedure of face recognition has been applied to discover features in an image that are exclusively determined. In utmost circumstances, the facial images have already been scaled, cropped, and transformed to grayscale. Face detection, feature extraction, and face recognition are the three phases involved in face recognition. OpenCV is a C++-based open-source library. It comprises the execution of several computer vision techniques and deep neural networks. Face recognition is performed using these two packages in conjunction with flask (as shown in Figure 14.10). The response on this module is again encrypted using the security module and made available within the project through a MQTT message.

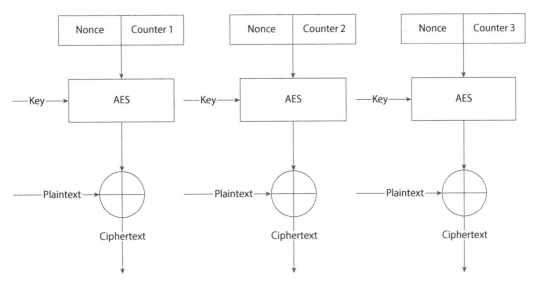

Figure 14.9 AES security workflow.

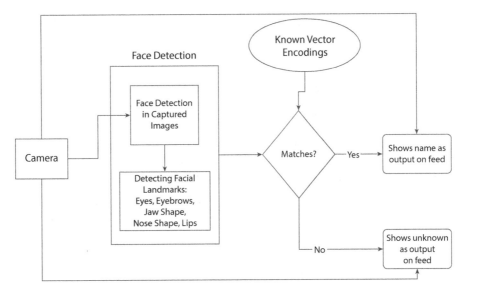

Figure 14.10 Facial recognition workflow.

14.4 Implementation

A. Agile Methodology for Software Development

According to the Agile philosophy, Agile adheres to four principles:

- Individuals and communications come first, followed by procedures and technology means.

- Software that is operational and functional as well as extensive certification and documentation.
- Maintaining a close relationship with users and consumers rather than relying on contract diplomacy.
- Adapting to changes rather than sticking to a rigid plan.

Consumers, not paper certifications, are the focus of the Agile methodology. In Agile, tasks and objectives are separated into "client stories", and the working team strategizes for the tasks ahead and predicts the total project time. A story could be non-coding—like research, exploration, and design—or coding—like code rewriting and new feature and element development. Throughout each sprint, the team collaborates extensively and decides on the tasks to be performed. In order to come up with a more thorough strategy for what everyone is doing, the team will hold a daily scrum meeting or use Kanban to discuss "what they did yesterday", "what they are about to do today", and "any blockers". Topics such as "what went well", "what we did that went wrong", and "how will we improve" may be discussed. This system aids in the provision of maintenance.

B. Face Recognition Model Development

A face dataset script takes frames from a video feed for this facial recognition. It is vital to have an image dataset of the known faces for this facial recognition. Face detection is performed on this feed. If the camera feed frames are recognized, it will record them and save them in a dataset. The face trainer script is then executed on the dataset; it trains and saves the model as a YML file. The model will build bounding boxes for various parts of the face, including lips, eyes, nose, and brows, based on the photographs in the dataset. These are then vector-encoded and saved in a YML file to be used later. Using the facial encodings of the person available to us and matching them with the encoding acquired from the camera feed, we can easily identify the people in this application. This feed also had to work on the online interface. In order to accomplish this, the flask framework is used. The processed frames returned via Facial Recognizer are translated to frame bytes and rendered live.

a. Prepare the dataset

Two directories were made: one for training and the other for testing. Use the dataset OpenCV script to capture photographs of myself and saved them to our "train" directory. Make sure that the photographs you have chosen adequately depict the traits of the face for the classifier. Let us take a picture of myself and save it to our "test" directory to test the model.

Use the Face Recognition library's face detection feature to ensure that the images saved as dataset are suitable for model training. This ensures that the image is legible by the algorithm and that the face can be distinguished for vector encoding.

b. Training the model

- First, import the modules that you will need.
- The library for face recognition comprises implementations of different services that will aid in the face recognition process.

- Create two lists to keep track of the names of the photos (people) and their facial encodings.
- A vector value reflecting critical dimensions among the defining aspects of a face, such as the remoteness among the eyes, the breadth of the forehead, and so on, is known as face encoding.
- We cycle through each image in our train directory, extracting the person's name, calculating the face encoding vector, and storing the data in the appropriate lists.

c. Testing the model

- As previously stated, our test dataset only has one image that contains all of the people.
- Using the cv2 imread () method, read the test image.
- Face locations () is a method in the Face Recognition library that traces the coordinates (right, left, top, and bottom of all faces spotted in the image. We can simply find the face encodings using those location values.
- We get over each of the face positions and their encoding in the image in a loop. We then compare the encoding of this to the face encodings in the "train" dataset.
- Next, we calculate the face distance, which is the similarity between the test image's encoding and that of the train images. Now, we take the lowest valued distance from it, which indicates that this face in the test image belongs to one of the people in the training dataset.
- Now, using the cv2 module's functions, a rectangle is drawn with the coordinates of the face location.

C. Node Red Controller Flow

Various function nodes are added with the intention of restricting unwanted access to the equipment as shown in Figure 14.11. The system is also set up to send an alert to the user when terrible weather conditions are present so that the user is aware of the situation while out. The user will be notified via email along with text messages on their phone. Two state variables "sw" and "pir" are accessed for usage in the flow. "sw" represents the switch state, and "pir" represents the PIR sensor state. The resultant state is stored in the variable "res". If PIR is high and SW is on, the resultant variable is set to true; otherwise, it is set to false. The code includes a check to distinguish between genuine and fraudulent messages. The MQTT topic, which is also encrypted and decrypted, is analyzed to determine the room name from which the messages are published. The message will not be processed further if both the switch and sensor MQTT messages do not have the same room name and "control" keyword.

D. Hardware Module

For this module, NodeMCU, PIR sensors, and jumper wires were used. The input from PIR sensor will be read by NodeMCU. The security module used here is responsible to provide a further robust encryption of the responses. Over the Wi-Fi, then, this encrypted signal will be transmitted over secure MQTT.

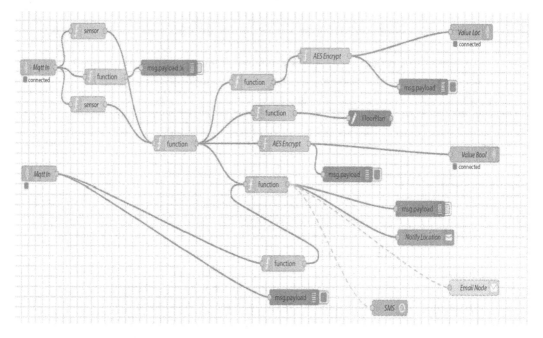

Figure 14.11 Node-Red flow for the controller module.

E. Interactive UI

An interactive UI was created using NodeJS and EJS, and the following objectives were required to be achieved by the UI. The UI should allow users to control the home automation system remotely as well as display the room in which a burglar has been identified, which is updated on a regular basis as an MQTT message received via the Node-Red controller (when lockdown mode is activated). The lockdown mode is activated by pressing the "leave home" button. The weather monitoring feature is also an addition to the proposed solution, and it will assist the user in his everyday life by reminding him to bring an umbrella if it is projected to rain. All encrypted payloads received here are decrypted at the application level. This payload is then visible in this well-presented user interface.

F. Encryption/Decryption Using AES

About 98% of all IoT system traffic is unprotected, exposing private and sensitive data across the network [12]. As a result, minimal payload encryption, when used in conjunction with other security best practices, aids in the protection of the surveillance system. The AES encryption of messages to and from different modules is handled by Algorithm 1 as described in the following.

To use AES-CTR, we need plaintext (PT) to be divided into blocks of 128 bits or less. The encryptor handles this process as shown in Equation 14.1.

$$PT = PT\,[1]\,PT\,[2]\,...\,PT[n] \tag{14.1}$$

To generate the ciphertext, each PT block is XORed with a block of the key stream. The encryption of AES considers each counter block results in 128 bits of key stream. The nonce value is set by the most noteworthy 96 bits of the counter block, which is 32 bits, followed by the per-packet IV value, which is 64 bits. One is initially set to the least significant 32 bits of the counter block. The counter value is increased by 1 to generate subsequent counter blocks, each resulting in another 128 bits of key stream. The algorithm of encryption of the n plaintext blocks can be summarized as Algorithm 14.1.

Algorithm 14.1: AES Encryption CTR mode of Operation	
1:	CTRBLK: = NONCE ‖IV‖ ONE
2:	FOR i: = 1 to n-1 DO
3:	⎸CT[i] XOR AES(CTRBLK)
4:	⎸CTRBLK: = CTRBLK + 1
5:	END
6:	CT[n]: = PT[n] XOR TRUNC(AES(CTRBLK))
AES encryption with the fresh key is performed by the AES () function	

The TRUNC () function truncates the output of the AES encrypt operation to the same length as the final plaintext block, thus returning the most significant bits.

This algorithm proves very efficient throughout our implementation because it has a small, encrypted payload size and is noticeably efficient while transmitting over MQTT.

The MQTT message is encrypted before transmission using the symmetric key described in this section. The text is first transformed to bytes and then encrypted with aesCtr, an AES container that operates in the CTR mode. The length of the encrypted bytes is then reduced by converting them to hexadecimal. Finally, this takes the place of the msg.payload variable.

The above-mentioned code blocks in Node-Red control home automation and help preserve electricity and data storage by preventing the cameras from producing a video feed when they are turned off. This workflow changes in lockdown mode, and the function responsible for recording the Boolean value after interpreting the sensor response is now tied to the lockdown mode function.

G. Lockdown Mode Function

The switch and PIR response are used to generate an alert message in this case. This alert message includes the room name in its text and is displayed in the UI or in the message/ email notification as part of the alert. This feature, which sends out alarms, aids in the detection of a burglar within the property. The MQTT communications help in providing a real-time update of the room where the thief is present.

The camera module's built-in facial recognition feature can be utilized to determine who is in the room. There may be instances where house assistance has inadvertently triggered an alert, in which case the situation can be double-checked using a camera. Because the user's location will be revealed, the Node-Red controller can also assist the user in providing more information to the authorities regarding the burglar's possible getaway. Because the camera only begins recording after the PIR detects a movement in the room, the camera feed will be precise and brief. As a result, authorities will not have to go through hours of footage to find the active burglary tape.

14.5   Results

The client will be able to see who is at their entrance gates using facial recognition-enabled video surveillance (as shown in Figure 14.12) and will be warned when someone lingers outside the gate (as given in Figure 14.13). The software can also be configured to send a text message to the consumer in addition to delivering notifications from any control unit if the user wants. If the system is in lockdown mode and a burglar enters the premises and the user has configured the system to notify him, the alarms will be instantly triggered.

In addition, surveillance cameras with face identification are put on the walls of every room in the house, as well as the exterior, to provide additional protection. If users want confidentiality, they can simply switch off the webcam. The server must then be modified to allow for bulk data retention and video/audio streaming. The possibility of discovering subjects will be determined using infrared motion sensors mounted on walls.

As shown in Figure 14.14, the current solution comprises a camera system that monitors the main entrance and may be updated to keep track of who has entered and left the property, at what time, and whether or not somebody is currently present. Video surveillance, which may be placed in numerous locations throughout the house, is an important part of home surveillance. These webcams can be designed to notify the user via text message or other ways when someone is observed in the area. All cameras will be set to operate only when another sensor is activated in order to maintain them in "sleep mode" and prevent them from wasting energy observing nothing of importance.

The working of AES security middleware is also shown in the UI (Figure 14.15), demonstrating how all payloads transported over secure MQTT are encrypted and protected. PIR sensors trigger the inactive device state, which disconnects them from the main network. This security module on top ensures that, once the devices are reconnected, the data is kept safe and encrypted.

Figure 14.12 Facial recognition working on top of the video feed.

Figure 14.13 The user is notified via email about the unknown entries into the residence.

Figure 14.14 Working UI showing the hardware's detection of motion.

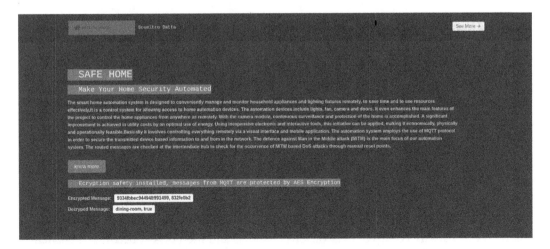

Figure 14.15 Presentation of the functioning of the security module.

The solution would help save a lot of electricity, lowering electricity costs while also lessening the negative influence on the environment.

Others may be satisfied with a simple sound alert system, while some will not be satisfied until their home is cleaner and safer than anybody else's. For those searching for a simple security setting, the device has protections, and for those wanting for more, it may feature greater security measures. By using video monitoring, the customer will be able to observe if a person is at their door and will be notified if someone waits outside the door. If the user desires, the system could also be designed to send text messages to the user in addition to sending information to the user from any configuration unit. The alerts will be triggered if the device is in lockdown mode and an intruder enters the building, but the user has enabled the system to warn, and he is encountered.

In addition, video cameras with facial recognition are mounted on the walls in all of the house's rooms and exterior to give extra protection for the solution. Users can, however, simply turn off the camera if they want privacy. The server will then need to be updated to enable for mass storage and streaming of audio and video. Infrared motion sensors on walls will be used to determine the likelihood of discovering subjects. Light sensors can be used to track the intensity of light throughout the day and adjust the lighting in the room accordingly.

The current function includes a security camera to track the main entrance, which can be updated to keep track of who has entered and left the house, at what time, and whether or not someone is currently present in the house. Surveillance cameras installed in various positions around the home are a vital piece of security. These cameras can be programmed to alert the user when someone is spotted in the vicinity and to notify the user through text message or other means. All cameras will be configured to activate only when another sensor is engaged in order to keep them in "sleep mode" in order to save electricity and avoid the cameras from spending unnecessary amounts of power with respect to observing nothing of significance. Another security feature for these cameras is the ability to wake them up and monitor them from a central control point, i.e., the 0user interface. These elements have been enabled for usage in order to develop an ecosystem that can replace the conventional alarm system that many houses have.

14.6   Conclusion and Future Work

The proposed model is executed, and it can be used in homes to increase the level of home security. There were a few challenges that were uncovered during this execution. The NodeMCU can be connected to and used with Arduino IDE. Unlike Arduino, it does not connect immediately and does not come with its own IDE for programming. As a result, the on-connection driver must be loaded according to the instructions on the chip's back. It is critical to keep the mode of operation, counter of AES, and key set in the application during AES encryption all the same while configuring the AES encryption/decryption. If any of these factors are incorrect, the application may not function properly.

The MQTT messages that were received will be lost in interpretation. Different IoT modules, such as the PIR module, the Camera and Face Recognition module, and the REST-based UI module, are connected via various channels and methods. It becomes a challenge to integrate them all while simultaneously maintaining the data integrity and security across the entire implementation. The MQTT transmission was used to connect the PIR sensors to the Node-Red controller in this scenario, and MQTT was also utilized to publish messages to the Web UI. Between this link, data loss and man-in-the-middle cyberattacks are possible, thus we need to defend ourselves using Payload encryption. Face recognition was also run as a script on a separate framework and connected to the main app over REST. Although the solution fits many of the customer's needs, it also has the advantage of being able to be used without a computer. In the future, this work will be upgraded to be used as a mobile application with better usability. The UI also will be improved with more customizations.

References

1. Ragmahale, R., A literature survey on smart home automation security. *International Journal of Computer Networks and Communications Security (IJCNCS)*, 6, 1, 1–8, 2018.
2. Chang, S. and Nam, K., Smart home adoption: The impact of user characteristics and differences in perception of benefits. *Buildings*, 11, 393, 2021, https://doi.org/10.3390/buildings11090393.
3. M., A. and Davidson, C., Design and implementation of an IoT-based smart Home Security System. *Int. J. Networked Distributed Comput.*, 7, 2, 85, 2019, https://doi.org/10.2991/ijndc.k.190326.004 CRB data for 2020 of City-Wise, Nature-Wise, Property stolen and Recovered. https://ncrb.gov.in/sites/default/files/crime_in_india_table_additional_table_chapter_reports/023%20City-wise%20Naturewise%20Property%20Stolen%20and%20Recovered%20during%202020.xlsx.
4. Kodali, R.K., Jain, V., Bose, S., Boppana, L., IoT based smart security and home automation System. *2016 International Conference on Computing, Communication and Automation (ICCCA)*, IEEE, Noida, India, 2016.
5. Tanwar, S., Patel, P., Patel, K., Tyagi, S., Kumar, N., Obaidat, M.S., An advanced internet of thing based security alert system for smart home. *2017 International Conference on Computer, Information and Telecommunication Systems (CITS)*, IEEE, Dalian, China, 2017.
6. Bali, R.S., Jaafar, F., Zavarasky, P., Lightweight authentication for MQTT to improve the security of IoT communication, in: *Proceedings of the3rd International Conference on Cryptography, Security and Privacy (ICCSP '19)*, Association for Computing Machinery, New York, NY, USA, pp. 6–12, 2019.
7. Bhawiyuga, Data, M., Warda, A., Architectural design of token based authentication of MQTT protocol in constrained IoT device, in: *2017 11th International Conference on Telecommunication Systems Services and Applications (TSSA)*, pp. 1–4, 2017.
8. Bisne, L. and Parmar, M., Composite secure MQTT for Internet of Things using ABE and dynamic S-box AES, in: *2017 Innovations in Power and Advanced Computing Technologies (i-PACT)*, pp. 1–5, 2017.
9. Singh, M., Rajan, M.A., Shivraj, V.L., Balamuralidhar, P., Secure MQTT for Internet of Things (IoT). *Présenté à 2015 Fifth International Conference on Communication Systems and Network Technologies*, 2015.
10. Mektoubi, Hassani, H.L., Belhadaoui, H., Rifi, M., Zakari, A., New approach for securing communication over MQTT protocol A comparaison between RSA and Elliptic Curve, in: *2016 Third International Conference on Systems of Collaboration (SysCo)*, pp. 1–6, 2016.
11. Omar, Y.A., Goyal, S.B., Varadarajan, V., Apply blockchain technology for security of IoT devices. *2021 Emerging Trends in Industry 4.0 (ETI 4.0)*, pp. 1–6, 2021.
12. Albagul, A., Efheij, H., Muhammad, M., Telemetry home automation based on ZigBee. *Libyan International Conference on Electrical Engineering and Technologies (LICEET)*, pp. 3–7, March 2018.

15

Machine Learning-Based Solutions for Internet of Things-Based Applications

Varsha Bhatia[1]* and Bhavesh Bhatia[2]

[1]Department of Computer Science Engineering, DPG Institute of Technology and Management, Gurugram (Haryana), India
[2]Department of Computer Science, University of Western Ontario London, London, Ontario, Canada

Abstract

The growth of Internet-connected sensory devices, known as the Internet of Things (IoT), has led to the development of a range of services and applications across various sectors, including infrastructure, retail, transportation, and personal healthcare. Machine learning (ML) allows the IoT to extract meaningful information from an enormous amount of data. ML plays a vital role in coping with the growing demands of future IoT systems for businesses, governments, and individual users. The primary goal of IoT is to sense the physical environment and use intelligent methods for automated decision making as humans will do. This chapter will explore the various applications of IoT where machine learning helps to create intelligent systems as well as the potential future of IoT and machine learning and how these technologies can contribute to the development of communication devices. This chapter will consider the taxonomy of machine learning algorithms that can be applied to IoT and the ways in which machine learning can be used in IoT applications. This chapter will also discuss machine learning algorithms, IoT challenges, and emerging trends to make our societies more prosperous and sustainable.

Keywords: Machine learning, Internet of Things, IoT ecosystem, IoT applications, supervised learning, unsupervised learning, reinforcement learning

15.1 Introduction

The Internet has become widely available and is having a significant impact on people's lives, but this is just the beginning. A new era is thriving where many more devices will be connected to the Internet; these devices can collect and transmit data. The data collected from these devices can provide relevant information about the physical environment where these devices are deployed. These tiny devices are called Internet of Things (IoT) devices. By definition, the Internet of Things is simply an interaction between the physical and digital worlds [1]. The IoT refers to the network of interconnected physical devices deployed inside

---

Corresponding author: varsha.bhatia.in@gmail.com

Amit Kumar Tyagi (ed.) *Automated Secure Computing for Next-Generation Systems*, (295–318) © 2024 Scrivener Publishing LLC

buildings, vehicles, and other items embedded with electronics, software, sensors, and connectivity which enable these objects to collect and transmit data. These physical devices are embedded with sensors and actuators that allow them to collect and transmit data, enabling the creation of smart and connected systems [2]. The IoT allows for the automation and remote operation of a specific routine task and can lead to improved efficiency and convenience in various industries such as transportation, healthcare, and manufacturing.

The Internet has transformed from just a network of computers to a network of various interconnected devices known as the Internet of Things. Nowadays, devices of all sizes and functions, from smartphones to vehicles, industrial systems, cameras, toys, buildings, and home appliances, can share information over the Internet and perform tasks like smart reorganization, tracing, positioning, control, real-time monitoring, and process control.

In recent years, the number of Internet-capable devices has dramatically increased, with the consumer electronics field witnessing the most significant impact, particularly in the revolution of smartphones and growing interest in wearable devices. The movement towards integrating the digital and physical worlds has gone beyond just connecting people.

This chapter provides an overview of machine learning (ML) for IoT solutions. It starts by defining IoT and its significance and explains how ML is used in IoT solutions. The chapter then covers the different types of ML algorithms used in IoT, including supervised, unsupervised, and reinforcement learning, and examines the various applications of ML in IoT. The chapter concludes by addressing the challenges and limitations of ML for IoT solutions and highlights future directions for research and development in this field.

15.2   IoT Ecosystem

As the IoT continues to expand its reach in terms of the number of devices and functions it can run, it offers a virtually limitless supply of opportunities for businesses and research. An IoT ecosystem is a network of interconnected devices, sensors, and other hardware, software, and systems that work together to enable the IoT to function effectively. It includes all of the components that are required to enable IoT devices to collect, process, and transmit data as well as the applications and services that make use of that data.

The main components of an IoT ecosystem are discussed below.

15.2.1   IoT Devices

These are the physical devices or "things" that make up the IoT, such as sensors, cameras, and other connected devices.

15.2.2   IoT Gateways

These devices act as a bridge between the physical devices and the rest of the ecosystem, allowing them to communicate with other devices and systems. IoT gateways are an essential component of an IoT ecosystem; they connect devices to the cloud and provide security, protocol conversion, and local intelligence. They can be software- or hardware-based, and they come in different form factors, depending on the use case.

15.2.3   IoT Platforms

These are the software platforms that enable the management and administration of IoT devices and gateways. They handle tasks such as device provisioning, configuration, and data management. Some examples of popular IoT platforms include AWS IoT, Azure IoT, Google Cloud IoT, IBM Watson IoT, Thing Worx, Losant, *etc.* [3]. These are just a few examples of the many IoT platforms available on the market today. Each platform may have its own set of features and capabilities, and the best choice of IoT platform will depend on the specific requirements of your project.

15.2.4   IoT Applications

These are the applications and services that make use of the data generated by IoT devices. They can include applications for monitoring, control, and automation of various aspects of the physical world.

15.2.5   IoT Connectivity

This includes the communication protocols, networks, and infrastructure required to connect IoT devices and gateways to the rest of the ecosystem. IoT connectivity refers to the various technologies and protocols that are used to connect IoT devices to the Internet and to each other. Some of the most common types of IoT connectivity include Wi-Fi, Bluetooth, Zigbee, Z-Wave, LoRaWAN, cellular, NB-IoT, ethernet, 5G, etc. [4]. These are just a few examples of the many connectivity options available for IoT devices. The best choice of connectivity technology will depend on the specific requirements of your project, such as the range, power consumption, data rate, security, and cost.

15.2.6   Analytics and Data Management

These are the tools and systems that are used to process, analyze, and store the data generated by IoT devices.

15.2.7   Security and Privacy

These are the measures and technologies that are used to secure the IoT ecosystem, including encryption, authentication, and access control. The main issues related to IoT security are encryption, privacy, and information security. A secure connection must be established between devices, and the exchange of secret keys must be protected to prevent information theft. To address privacy concerns, the current IT technology mechanisms can be modified and expanded to resolve common issues such as malicious software deployment and DDoS attacks on IoT applications [5]. Overall, the emphasis is on ensuring that the necessary security measures are in place to protect the privacy and security of information transmitted over the IoT network.

15.2.8   Infrastructure

In order to maintain quality of service (QOS) requirement and to manage massive IoT device data, IoT infrastructure plays the role of key facilitators. Physical infrastructures like Edge IT systems, data center, cloud, and network are necessary for IoT to work. Edge IT systems form a distributed network, which supports faster insights, enhanced response times, and enhanced bandwidth availability. Edge IT systems make this possible by positioning the enterprise applications closer to data sources such as IoT devices or on-site servers. The components of the IoT ecosystem are not fixed; new technologies and advancements are adding new components and expanding the capabilities of existing ones.

15.3   Importance of Data in IoT Applications

15.3.1   Data Gathered from IoT Applications

Data from the IoT is generated by the sensors and devices that make up the IoT ecosystem. This data can come in many forms, including the following:

- Sensor data: This is data generated by the sensors embedded in IoT devices, such as temperature, humidity, or motion sensors.
- Location data: This is data generated by GPS or other location-based sensors, such as the location of a vehicle or the location of a package in transit.
- Usage data: This is data generated by the usage of an IoT device, such as the number of times a washing machine is used or the amount of energy consumed by a smart thermostat.
- Image and video data: This is data generated by cameras and other imaging devices, such as security cameras or drones.
- Audio data: This is data generated by microphones and other audio devices, such as voice commands or ambient noise levels.

The data generated by the IoT can be used for a wide range of purposes, including monitoring and control, predictive maintenance, and analytics.

15.3.2   Quality of an IoT Application

The desired quality of an IoT application is a combination of several factors that ensure that the application is reliable, secure, and user-friendly. Reliability is an essential characteristic of IoT applications as it ensures that the application will function as intended and provide accurate results. This can be achieved by implementing robust testing and quality assurance processes to ensure that the application is free from bugs, errors, and other issues that could impact its performance.

Security is another important aspect of IoT applications as it ensures that the data collected and transmitted by the application is protected from unauthorized access, manipulation, and breaches [6]. This can be achieved by implementing robust security measures such as encryption, authentication, and access control to protect the data and devices.

User-friendliness is another important characteristic of IoT applications. It ensures that the application is easy to use and intuitive and provides a smooth user experience. This can be achieved by following user-centered design principles, providing clear and concise instructions, and incorporating features such as real-time feedback and error handling to make the application more user-friendly. In addition, scalability and interoperability are also important characteristics of IoT applications. Scalability ensures that the application can handle increasing numbers of devices, users, and data, while interoperability ensures that the application can communicate and interact with other systems and devices [6].

Overall, the desired quality of an IoT application is a combination of reliability, security, user-friendliness, scalability, and interoperability. By ensuring that these characteristics are met, organizations can provide a high-quality IoT experience to users while ensuring that the data and devices are protected and that the application is easy to use and efficient.

15.3.3   Effective IoT Data Utilization

Effective use of data collected from IoT devices is crucial for organizations to gain insights and make informed decisions. The data collected from IoT devices can be used for various purposes such as monitoring and control, predictive maintenance, and analytics [6]. One of the most important aspects of effectively using IoT data is to process and analyze it in real time to gain insights that can be used to improve operations, increase efficiency, and reduce costs. Organizations can use advanced analytics techniques such as machine learning and artificial intelligence to process and analyze the data in real time and identify patterns, trends, and anomalies. Data analysis mechanisms should always use the most suitable approach for the given data and use case. However, selecting the proper algorithm can be challenging as there are a plethora of algorithms and techniques available, each with its own strengths and weaknesses.

15.4   Machine Learning

ML is a subset of artificial intelligence that involves developing algorithms that can learn from data and improve their performance over time. Integrating ML with IoT holds the potential to transform many industries by providing advanced and efficient solutions for a wide range of real-life applications.

Studies have been conducted to compare different ML algorithms and classifiers, but most are use-case specific and do not provide insights into the most suitable algorithm for diverse scenarios. ML for IoT solutions is a rapidly growing field that involves using ML algorithms to analyze and extract insights from the vast amounts of data generated by IoT devices. This leads to improved performance and functionality of IoT systems, such as predictive maintenance, smart home automation, and traffic management, resulting in cost savings, increased efficiency, and improved user experiences.

ML can be applied to IoT solutions at three levels: device/edge, fog node, and cloud node. The choice of level depends on the use-case-specific requirement, with edge and fog computing being useful for IoT applications that require real-time actions. Edge computing processes data closer to the device, reducing the time required for data to travel, while fog computing involves a more centralized approach with data being processed at intermediate

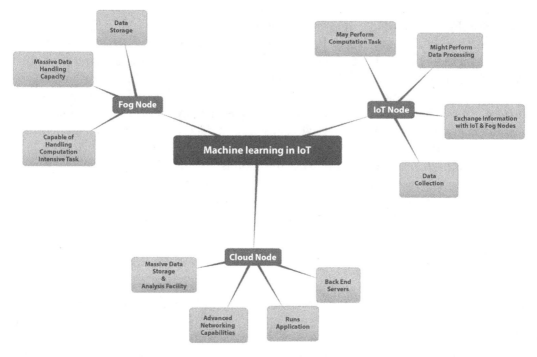

Figure 15.1 Implementing machine learning in IoT-based solutions.

edge devices. The role of ML algorithms at fog nodes and cloud nodes is to improve the efficiency and accuracy of data processing, decision-making, and resource management.

However, implementing ML for IoT solutions faces challenges, including data collection, management, and privacy and selecting and tuning appropriate ML algorithms. Despite these challenges, the potential benefits of ML for IoT solutions make it a promising area of research and development as depicted in Figure 15.1.

In machine learning for IoT, three main types of algorithms are used: supervised learning, unsupervised learning, and reinforcement learning.

15.4.1   Supervised Learning

Supervised Learning is a widely used machine learning technique. It infers a function using labeled training data and a set of training examples. The labeled training data consists of input–output pairs, where the inputs are the data's features and the outputs are the corresponding labels. The aim of supervised learning is to find a function that maps inputs to outputs based on the training data. During training, the algorithm learns from the labeled data by adjusting its parameters to reduce the difference between the predicted outputs and the actual outputs. Once training is complete, the algorithm can make predictions on new data by applying the learned function to the inputs. The predictions will be more accurate as the training data becomes more diverse and high-quality [7]. Supervised learning is a task-driven approach used when specific goals are identified to be achieved from a set of inputs. These goals can be various tasks, such as classification, regression, or prediction—for instance, a supervised learning algorithm can predict whether a device will fail or not based on its sensor data. The algorithm is trained using labeled data, with the sensor data provided along with the failure or non-failure status of the device. Once trained, the algorithm can predict the failure status of new devices based on their sensor data.

15.4.2 Unsupervised Learning

Unsupervised learning analyzes unlabeled datasets without human intervention to extract information from the data [8]. It is a data-driven process where the algorithm extracts information from the data without prior knowledge of the desired output [9]. This technique is widely used for tasks such as clustering, density estimation, feature learning, dimensionality reduction, finding association rules, and anomaly detection.

Clustering groups similar data points together by finding patterns in the data. It is useful for image segmentation, customer segmentation, and anomaly detection. Density estimation estimates the probability density function of a random variable and finds the underlying probability distribution of a dataset. Feature learning learns a feature representation of the data and extracts important features from the data. Dimensionality reduction reduces the number of features in a dataset to simplify it and make it easier to work with. Finding association rules identifies relationships between variables in a dataset and is useful for market basket analysis and anomaly detection. Anomaly detection finds outliers or anomalies in a dataset for tasks such as fraud detection, intrusion detection, and monitoring of sensor data.

In conclusion, unsupervised learning is a valuable machine learning technique that enables the extraction of information from unlabeled datasets without human interference.

15.4.3 Reinforcement Learning

Reinforcement learning (RL) is a type of machine learning that focuses on training agents to make decisions in an environment by learning from the consequences of their actions. The agent learns to take actions that lead to positive outcomes, such as receiving rewards, while avoiding actions that lead to negative outcomes, such as penalties. RL is commonly used in applications where the decision-making process is sequential and the agent's actions have an impact on the future state of the environment. The RL process can be broken down into three main components: the agent, the environment, and the reward signal. The agent is the entity that makes decisions and interacts with the environment. The environment is the system that the agent operates in, and it provides the agent with information about its state. The reward signal is a scalar value that the agent receives after taking an action, which indicates how well the action was performed. One of the most popular RL algorithms is Q-Learning [8]. It is an off-policy algorithm that uses a Q-table to store the expected reward for each state–action pair. The agent learns to select the action that leads to the highest expected reward. Another popular algorithm is state–action–reward–state–action (SARSA) [10] which is an on-policy algorithm that uses the Q-table to update the action-value function. It takes into account the next action that the agent will take rather than the action that leads to the highest expected reward. Another popular RL algorithm is the policy gradient methods [11]. It optimizes the policy function directly rather than the value function. This is useful when the action space is continuous and the value function is difficult to estimate. In summary, reinforcement learning is a type of machine learning that focuses on training agents to make decisions in an environment by learning from the consequences of their actions. Some of the popular algorithms are Q-Learning, SARSA, and policy gradient methods. It is worth noting that these types of algorithms can also be combined in various ways to achieve more complex and robust solutions, such as semi-supervised learning and deep reinforcement learning.

15.5   Machine Learning Algorithms

Here are a few examples of ML algorithms that can be used for predictive maintenance in smart cities along with a brief description and pseudo-code for each algorithm:

15.5.1   k-Nearest Neighbors

k-nearest neighbors (KNN) is a non-parametric machine learning algorithm that is commonly used for classification tasks. It works by taking in a new data point and identifying the k number of training instances in the dataset that are closest to it. The class of the new data point is then determined by the majority vote of its k-nearest neighbors. This approach does not require any assumptions about the underlying distribution of the data, and the model can be created simply by storing the training instances in memory [12]. The number of nearest neighbors, k, is typically determined through a process of experimentation and cross-validation. The study [13] compared the performance of three non-parametric classifiers—random forest (RF), KNN, and support vector machine (SVM) for land use/cover classification using Sentinel-2 image data from the Red River Delta in Vietnam. The study area of 30 × 30 km² with six land use/cover types was classified using 14 different training sample sizes ranging from 50 to over 1,250 pixels/class, both balanced and imbalanced. The results showed a high overall accuracy (OA) ranging from 90% to 95%. Among the three classifiers, SVM had the highest OA with the least sensitivity to the training sample size, followed by RF and KNN.

15.5.2   Logistic Regression

Logistic regression (LR) is a statistical method that is commonly used for binary classification problems, where the goal is to predict one of two possible outcomes. It does this by using a logistic function to model the relationship between the input variables and the binary dependent variable. In the simplest form, the logistic function separates the training data into two categories, "0" and "1", which corresponds to the Bernoulli distribution [14]. When there are more than two possible outcomes, a variation of LR called multinomial logistic regression can be used. In general, LR is used to estimate the parameters of a logistic model which is a form of binary regression. In the paper of [15], an IoT-powered smart bin that uses machine and deep learning models to efficiently manage garbage disposal and forecast air pollutants in the surrounding environment is proposed. The smart bin is connected to a Google cloud server which performs the necessary computations to predict the bin's status and air quality based on real-time data. The traditional models (k-nearest neighbors and logistic regression) are compared with a non-traditional [long short-term memory (LSTM) network-based] deep learning algorithm to generate alerts for bin status and CO pollutant levels. The logistic regression and kNN algorithms have a recall of 79% and 83%, respectively, in real-time testing for bin status prediction. On the other hand, the accuracy of the modified LSTM and simple LSTM models for predicting future gas concentration is 90% and 88%, respectively.

15.5.3   Decision Tree

Decision tree is a type of a supervised machine learning algorithm that can be used for both classification and regression tasks. The algorithm constructs a tree-like model of decisions and their possible consequences. Each internal node of the tree represents a "test" on an attribute, each branch represents the outcome of the test, and each leaf node represents a class label or a value. The topmost node in the decision tree is known as the root node. The decision tree algorithm starts at the root node and traverses the tree by making a decision at each internal node based on the input features until it reaches a leaf node which contains the prediction or decision [16]. The decision tree algorithm is easy to understand and interpret, and it is useful for both categorical and numerical input and output variables.

15.5.4   Random Forest

Leo Breiman developed the RF algorithm, a machine learning method that builds a group of decision trees by randomly selecting samples from the training data. At each split, it randomly chooses a subset of features instead of considering all of them, a process known as random feature selection. The algorithm then combines the predictions of each tree in the ensemble through majority vote (for classification) or averaging (for regression) to make the final prediction [17]. In short, RF combines multiple decision tree predictions and takes the average to make a final prediction.

15.5.5   Support Vector Machines

SVMs use supervised learning to perform classification or regression tasks by finding a hyper plane that best separates different classes of data points. SVMs aim to maximize the margin or the distance between the boundary and the closest data points of each class by identifying the boundary that best separates the data. The data points closest to the boundary are known as support vectors and play a crucial role in determining the boundary's position. SVMs can handle non-linearly separable data by applying a kernel trick that maps the data into a higher-dimensional space where a linear boundary can be found [18]. Despite its ability to handle high-dimensional and complex data, SVMs can be sensitive to the choice of kernel and parameters, so it is important to choose an appropriate kernel for each specific application.

15.5.6   Artificial Neural Networks

Artificial neural networks (ANNs) are machine learning algorithms modeled after the human brain's structure and function. They consist of layers of interconnected "neurons" that receive and transmit information. Input information enters the input layer, gets processed by one or more hidden layers, and finally outputs at the output layer. To train ANNs, the back propagation algorithm is used, a supervised learning method that calculates the gradient of the error function with respect to the weights of the network by propagating the error from the output layer to the input layer. ANNs are effective for solving complex, non-linear problems, such as image and speech recognition, natural language processing, and prediction [19]. However, their results can be difficult to interpret, and their architecture must be chosen carefully for the specific application. Some common types of ANNs include feed forward neural networks, recurrent neural networks, and convolutional neural networks.

15.5.7   Long Short-Term Memory

LSTM is a type of recurrent neural network (RNN) architecture that specializes in handling sequential data with long-term dependencies. Unlike traditional RNNs, LSTMs have a memory cell that stores information for a longer period, enabling the network to use past events so as to make better predictions [20].

LSTMs control the flow of information into and out of the memory cell through three gates—an input gate, an output gate, and a forget gate—that allow the network to selectively remember or forget information. LSTMs are widely used in natural language processing, speech recognition, and time series prediction tasks that require the ability to remember past events for accurate predictions.

Table 15.1 summarizes the various machine learning algorithms used in IoT solutions, highlighting the learning type, advantages, disadvantages, and problem statement for each algorithm. This information serves as an overview of recent developments in the field and can help make informed decisions about the best algorithms for specific IoT applications—for example, it provides insight into algorithms that are suited for prediction tasks or real-time data processing and highlights the limitations and trade-offs of each approach.

15.6   Applications of Machine Learning in IoT

15.6.1   Smart City

A smart city is a concept that aims to use technology and data to improve the quality of life for citizens, enhance sustainability, and increase efficiency in the use of resources. Smart cities employ a wide range of technologies such as the Internet of Things, big data, cloud computing, and artificial intelligence (AI) to collect and analyze data from various sources such as sensors, cameras, and mobile devices. This data is then used to make informed decisions, optimize resources, and improve the delivery of services.

One of the main trends in smart cities is the increasing use of IoT technology to connect and monitor various city systems such as transportation, energy, and waste management. This allows cities to gather data on these systems in real time, which can be used to optimize their performance, reduce costs, and improve the delivery of services. ML algorithms can be used to predict energy usage patterns and optimize the operation of smart grids

Another important area where ML is being used in smart cities is in the field of public safety. ML algorithms can be used to analyze data from cameras and other sensors to detect and predict criminal activity, which can help to improve public safety and reduce the

Table 15.1 Machine learning algorithms in Internet of Things.

Machine learning algorithm	Learning technique	Description	Nature of the problem statement	Output result type	Advantages	Disadvantages	Area of applications	References
Support vector machine	Supervised	A method for classification and regression that finds a boundary that maximizes the margin between different classes	Classification and regression	Categorical or continuous	Can handle non-linearly separable data, efficient for high-dimensional data, robust against overfitting	Can be sensitive to the choice of kernel and parameters, not suitable for large datasets, computationally intensive	Image classification, text categorization, bioinformatics	[21]
Bayesian learning	Supervised	A method of statistical inference that uses Bayes' theorem to update the probability of a hypothesis as more evidence or information becomes available	Classification and regression	Categorical or continuous	Provides a principled way to incorporate prior knowledge, handles missing data and uncertain inputs, efficient for low-dimensional data	Assumes that all variables are independent, can be computationally intensive for large datasets, sensitive to prior choices	Natural language processing, computer vision, bioinformatics	[22, 23]
Naïve Bayes	Supervised	A simple probabilistic classifier based on applying Bayes' theorem with strong (naïve) independence assumptions between the features	Classification	Categorical	Simple and efficient, works well with high-dimensional data, robust to irrelevant features	Assumes independence between features, can perform poorly with correlated features	Text classification, spam filtering, sentiment analysis	[24]

(Continued)

Table 15.1 Machine learning algorithms in Internet of Things. (*Continued*)

Machine learning algorithm	Learning technique	Description	Nature of the problem statement	Output result type	Advantages	Disadvantages	Area of applications	References
K-nearest neighbors	Supervised	A method for classification and regression that assigns an instance to the class or value of the majority of its k-nearest neighbors	Classification and regression	Categorical or continuous	Simple and intuitive, works well with small and high-dimensional data, can handle non-linearly separable data	Can be computationally intensive for large datasets, sensitive to the choice of k and distance metric, can be sensitive to irrelevant features and noise	Image classification, text categorization, anomaly detection	[12]
Backpropagation	Supervised	A method for training feed forward artificial neural networks by minimizing the error between the network's output and the desired output through gradient descent	Classification and regression	Categorical or continuous	Can model non-linear and complex relationships, can handle large and high-dimensional data, can learn from end-to-end data	Can be sensitive to the choice of architecture and parameters, can be computationally intensive, can be prone to overfitting and local minima	Image classification, speech recognition, natural language processing	[25]
K-means clustering	Unsupervised	A method for partitioning a dataset into k clusters based on the mean distance to the centroid of each cluster	Clustering	None	Simple and efficient, works well with small and high-dimensional data, can handle non-linearly separable data	Can be sensitive to the choice of k and initialization, can be sensitive to the scale and noise of the data, can be sensitive to the outliers	Image segmentation, text mining, customer segmentation	[26]

(*Continued*)

Table 15.1 Machine learning algorithms in Internet of Things. (*Continued*)

Machine learning algorithm	Learning technique	Description	Nature of the problem statement	Output result type	Advantages	Disadvantages	Area of applications	References
Logistic regression	Supervised	A method for classification that models the probability of the target variable as a function of the input variables through a logistic function	Classification	Categorical	Simple and efficient, works well with small and high-dimensional data, can handle missing data and categorical variables	Assumes linearity and independence between features, can be sensitive to outliers and multicollinearity, can be prone to overfitting		[14]
Decision tree	Supervised	Splits data based on a certain parameter; makes predictions or classifications by recursively splitting the data based on feature values	Classification and regression	Categorical or continuous	Suitable for both classification and regression, easy to interpret and handle categorical and quantitative values, fills missing values with most probable value	Prone to overfitting, unstable, locally optimal solution	Predicting the future use of library books, tumor prognosis problems	[17, 27]
Random forest	Ensemble	Uses multiple decision trees to make a final prediction	Classification and regression	Categorical or continuous	Reduces overfitting, high performance	Prone to overfitting, unstable, locally optimal solution	Predicting the future use of library books, tumor prognosis problems	[17, 28]
LSTM	Recurrent neural network	Used for sequential data, such as time series or natural language processing	Time series forecasting, natural language processing	Continuous	Good performance on sequential data, ability to handle long-term dependencies	Requires a lot of data, computationally expensive	Time series forecasting, natural language processing	[20]

crime rate. In addition, ML can also be used for the prediction and optimization of resource allocation—for example in waste management, ML algorithms can be used to predict waste collection patterns and optimize the routes of waste collection vehicles to reduce costs and improve the efficiency of the service.

This chapter presented a model that utilizes public data from urban sensing systems to predict the air quality index (AQI) in all regions of Shenyang [28]. The model uses AQI data from 11 air quality monitoring stations, meteorological data from weather stations, road information, real-time traffic status from Baidu Map and Google Maps, and point of interest distributions from Baidu Map and Google Maps. The random forest algorithm was used to predict AQI for all uncovered regions in the downtown area, resulting in an overall precision of 81% for AQI prediction. The results of the algorithm were found to be superior to those of other algorithms such as naive Bayes, logistic regression, single decision tree, and ANN.

This chapter [29] examined the use of machine learning techniques to locate leaks in a water distribution network by creating hydraulic zones and using sensors to measure water supply variations and pressure. The collected data was then used to train machine learning models. The study evaluated the performance of six different machine learning methods in the water distribution network of a university campus using data generated by EPANET software. The results showed that the supervised methods, particularly logistic regression and random forest, as well as artificial neural network, performed well. However, the unsupervised methods had a difficulty in localizing leaks due to overlapping clusters. The study then applied the findings to offline water supply flow data to locate the leaks in the university campus, providing some indications on where the leaks were likely located.

A simulation and prediction sample of the electrical energy consumption of buildings using the new algorithm models was presented [30]. The proposed hybrid ARIMA-GBRT model and GBRT model are compared with other prediction models found in literature, and it was found that the proposed models have a better performance. The analysis of the results shows that the proposed models have lower values for the RMSE and MAE indices, indicating that the forecasting performance of the proposed models is more accurate. Additionally, the proposed models are also more efficient in terms of computational speed. The proposed models for forecasting electrical energy consumption can be used to design building HVAC systems by accurately estimating the energy consumption and allocating it in an optimal way. These models can also be used to optimize the cost of electrical energy consumption in buildings.

In conclusion, machine learning is playing a crucial role in smart cities. It enables cities to analyze large amounts of data and make predictions about future events, which can help to optimize the resources and improve the delivery of services.

15.6.2 Smart Agriculture

Smart agriculture is the use of technology and data-driven approaches to improve the efficiency and sustainability of agricultural practices. Machine learning can be used to analyze large amounts of data from various sources such as sensors, drones, and weather stations to make predictions about crop yields, weather patterns, and soil conditions. One of the main areas where machine learning is being used in smart agriculture is crop yield prediction. ML algorithms can be used to analyze data from various sources such as weather data, soil data, and satellite imagery to make predictions about crop yields. This can help farmers to optimize their crop management practices and improve the efficiency of their operations.

Another important area where machine learning is being used in smart agriculture is precision farming. ML algorithms can be used to analyze data from sensors and drones to make predictions about soil conditions, crop health, and weather patterns. This can help farmers to optimize their resource use, such as fertilizer and water, and reduce their environmental impact.

A system has been developed to optimize crop irrigation by using decision tree learning algorithms to analyze real-time data on soil moisture, temperature, and humidity sensors [31]. The system was trained using a dataset provided, and the output was a yes/no decision on whether or not to water the crops. This decision was then sent to the farmer via email, allowing them to make informed decisions on water usage and avoiding unnecessary wastage.

This project created a platform called "smart tillage" that allows farmers to rent and lease equipment [32]. It also utilized a machine learning model using decision trees, which are well suited for tool and equipment rental. The goal is to improve the farmers' quality of life by reducing labor-intensive tasks. This thesis focuses on smart farming through equipment sharing and leasing. The proposed tasks that employ various machine learning techniques were developed through exploratory and experimental work.

Another area where machine learning is playing a key role is in precision livestock farming. ML can be used to monitor and predict the health status of the livestock and to optimize the feeding and housing conditions. In conclusion, machine learning is becoming increasingly important in the field of smart agriculture. It enables farmers and agribusinesses to analyze large amounts of data and make predictions about crop yields, weather patterns, and soil conditions, which can help to optimize agricultural practices and improve the efficiency and sustainability of agricultural operations.

15.6.3 Smart Transportation

IoT and ML have the potential to revolutionize the transportation industry by providing new and innovative ways to improve efficiency, safety, and convenience for both passengers and transportation providers. IoT technology enables the collection of real-time data from various sources such as vehicles, traffic lights, and sensors. This data can be used to improve traffic flow, optimize routes, and reduce congestion—for example, by using traffic sensor data and GPS information, smart transportation systems can adjust traffic lights to reduce wait times and improve traffic flow. Additionally, IoT-enabled vehicles can communicate with each other and with traffic management systems to improve safety and reduce accidents.

Machine learning can be used to analyze the large amounts of data collected by IoT devices and make predictions, identify patterns, and make decisions—for example, ML algorithms can be used to predict traffic congestion, forecast demand for transportation services, and optimize routes for vehicles. Furthermore, machine learning can be used to detect anomalies and predict equipment failures, which can help prevent breakdowns and reduce maintenance costs.

This chapter [33] presents a method for reducing traffic congestion at six signalized junctions in Shiraz City by using the multi-agent reinforcement learning (MARL) algorithm to adjust traffic signals in real time. Real-world traffic data was obtained from the city's transportation and municipality organization, and the method was tested in both simulated and real-world scenarios. The results indicate that the MARL approach, when combined with data from IoT sensors, leads to a decrease in average queue length and waiting time at intersections compared with the traditional fixed-time scheduling method currently in use in Shiraz. The fingerprint method was used to improve cooperation between intersections, and the results were most significant during peak traffic hours. The goal of the work [34] was to accurately classify the availability of on-street parking on a segment level using a cyber-physical system developed to generate realistic data about cruising and parking events in the San Giovanni City area of Rome. To achieve this, a large amount of data was generated, and preprocessing steps were applied to create a training dataset for machine learning models. These steps included map matching techniques, identifying 10 features and 761 segment samples. Four machine learning models were then trained and tested on the dataset, and all performed well in both the training and testing phases.

In summary, the combination of IoT and ML in smart transportation can help improve efficiency, safety, and convenience for passengers while also reducing the costs and increasing the revenue for transportation providers. By leveraging the vast amounts of data generated by IoT devices, transportation providers can make data-driven decisions and improve their operations.

15.6.4   Smart Grid

The transformation of traditional power systems into an intelligent grid, known as a "smart grid", is achieved through the use of an intelligent information and communication architecture, advanced design methods, and automation. This new and advanced energy system integrates traditional energy systems with information networks that have the capability to perform computational, communicative, and control operations [35]. To establish a smart grid, the renewable and conventional energy producers, grid management, energy storage facilities, and electricity consumers must be interconnected through a cyber–physical system.

The integration of advanced metering infrastructure, control technologies, and communication technologies in the smart grid is allowing for the collection of vast amounts of data about the electric power grid operations. This data is high-dimensional, which means that it has many features, and multi-type, which means that it comes from different sources and in different forms. The traditional modeling, optimization, and control technologies have limitations in processing and making sense of this data [36].

ML algorithms can be used to analyze large amounts of data generated by the smart grid, make predictions, and identify patterns—for example, ML can be used to capture customer consumption patterns, forecast energy demand, predict equipment failures, and optimize the operation of distributed energy resources. Reinforcement learning can be used to make energy dispatch decisions and activate demand management signals in order to balance the power supply and the demand [37].

Smart grids were developed for efficient energy management and have advantages for both consumers and utility companies by decreasing energy waste, expenses, and peak energy demands. Additionally, they promote the use of clean, renewable energy sources to ensure sustainability and minimize the negative impact on the environment [38].

15.6.5   Application in Supply Chain Management

Supply chain management solutions provide configurable processes that encompass all aspects of supply chain operations, from the acquisition of raw materials to the sale of the finished product. These solutions offer a comprehensive approach to managing the flow of goods, services, and information across the entire supply chain. They are designed to automate and optimize different processes such as sourcing, procurement, production, logistics, and distribution [39].

Supplier selection is a crucial activity in the purchasing function and has a significant impact on time, cost, and quality [40]. The selection process can be challenging, as it involves evaluating multiple competing factors and finding the right balance among them. ML algorithms have better performance than traditional MCDM techniques in handling large and complex data. ML techniques such as DT and SVM as supervised learning techniques and Q-learning as a reinforcement learning technique have been applied by researchers to solve the supplier selection problem [40]. These algorithms can be used to analyze data and make predictions on supplier performance and, thus, aid decision-makers in making informed decisions.

15.6.6   Application in Wearable

The widespread use of wearable devices has led to a continuous stream of personal data being generated. These devices are capable of capturing and storing large amounts of real-time data that covers multiple aspects of health. The data collected by wearable devices is unique in terms of the types and timing of data being collected. They tend to capture information on daily physical activities and certain biometrics that are not typically available through traditional health data sources such as electronic medical records or registry data [41]. Moreover, these data capture information for a large time duration, which can be used to improve clinical research quality.

Early seizure detection is crucial for timely care. A review of various seizure types and wearable detection devices is discussed in [42]. The study with the largest sample size (135 participants) was conducted by [43], utilizing the Embrace Empatica watch [44] equipped with an accelerometer and electrodermal activity sensors. In [45], various motion, dexterity, and sleep features were recorded using inertial measurement unit sensors on the chest, wrist, and ankle to link these measures to neurological impairments in multiple sclerosis. A recent survey suggests that patients are willing to share personal health data obtained from wearable devices to improve the efficiency of decision support system.

15.6.7   Applications in Smart Factories

Smart factories, also known as Industry 4.0, are factories that are equipped with advanced technologies such as IoT, big data, and automation. These technologies enable the collection of large amounts of data from various sources such as machines, sensors, and workers. This data can be used to improve production processes, reduce downtime, and increase efficiency.

ML algorithms can be used to predict equipment failures, optimize production schedules, and improve quality control [46]. Additionally, ML can be used to develop intelligent

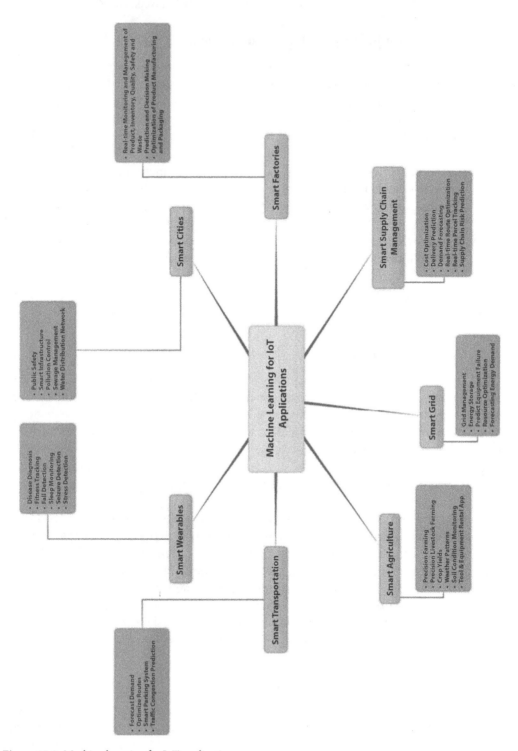

Figure 15.2 Machine learning for IoT applications.

control systems that can adapt to changes in the factory and make real-time decisions to improve efficiency. The work used 11 ML algorithms to predict lead time in a semiconductor facility using 2 years of historical data from the manufacturing execution system (MES) [51]. The best prediction given by RF algorithm and ANN had the weakest performance. The work developed a risk prediction framework for supply chain risk management in aerospace manufacturing using 36,677 product deliveries from MES over 6 years [47]. They used SVM and DT binary classifiers to predict future delivery delays, with SVM having higher precision and recall compared with DT.

In summary, the combination of ML and smart factories can lead to significant improvements in efficiency, productivity, and quality in the manufacturing industry. ML can be used to analyze the data generated by smart factories and make predictions, identify patterns, and make decisions. This can help improve production processes, reduce downtime, and increase efficiency.

The applications of machine learning in IoT are visualized in Figure 15.2, which presents a summary of how machine learning is utilized in IoT systems. This figure provides a comprehensive overview of the various ways in which machine learning is employed in IoT, helping to demonstrate the wide range of applications and benefits that it offers. This could include things such as predictive maintenance, improved decision-making processes, and increased efficiency in data analysis and processing. Overall, the summary in Figure 15.2 serves as an effective tool for understanding the impact and importance of machine learning in the context of IoT.

15.7   Challenges of Implementing ML for IoT Solutions

Using ML for IoT solutions poses several challenges and limitations. These are described in the following paragraphs.

15.7.1   Privacy and Security

IoT is vulnerable to cyber attacks due to its decentralized edge devices connecting to various devices. There is a lack of universal standards for authentication and authorization of IoT devices [48], making it easy for attackers to exploit vulnerabilities. To address security issues, IoT systems must implement robust security measures at all levels, including encryption and secure communication protocols. Strong security policies and procedures are also important to respond to and recover from security breaches.

15.7.2   Scalability

Implementing ML in IoT applications poses scalability challenges when the number of connected devices and data they generate becomes too large for the system to handle. One major issue is the limited resources of IoT devices, making it difficult to run complex ML algorithms [49]. To address scalability, it is important to use distributed architectures and lightweight algorithms.

15.7.3   Lack of Data

ML algorithms often require significant amounts of data, and obtaining additional data is the most favorable solution.

15.7.4   Data Quality

Ensuring data quality is important for ML models to generalize well to unseen data. Poor quality of training data or lack of diverse data can cause overfitting and limit the model's capabilities.

15.7.5   Interpretability

Interpretability is crucial for ML models to be understood and used by humans. Most state-of-the-art ML algorithms like deep learning are difficult to interpret, making it difficult for practitioners to understand how the model is making predictions and identify errors or biases [50]. Hence, interpretability is a key quality to prioritize for ML methods to be successful in real-world applications.

15.8   Emerging Trends in IoT

The IoT is rapidly evolving, and there are several emerging trends that are shaping its future development.

15.8.1   Edge Computing

The increasing volume of data generated by IoT devices is leading to the development of edge computing, which reduces latency by allowing data processing and analysis to be performed closer to source of the data.

15.8.2   5G and IoT

Owing to the inclusion of 5G networks, it is possible to have more reliable and faster connectivity for IoT devices, thus paving the way for new and innovative applications.

15.8.3   Artificial Intelligence and Machine Learning

The integration of AI and ML into IoT systems is enabling devices to make intelligent decisions based on the data that they collect, thus leading to improved efficiency and automation.

15.8.4   Security

As IoT devices become more widespread, security remains a key concern, and there is a growing focus on developing secure and trusted IoT solutions that protect sensitive data and prevent cyber attacks.

15.8.5   Blockchain

The use of blockchain technology in IoT is gaining traction and is being explored as a way to secure and validate data transactions between IoT devices.

15.8.6   IoT and Cloud Computing

The increasing utilization of IoT in the cloud has fueled the growth and deployment of scalable IoT applications and business models. IoT and cloud computing have become closely linked technologies for the future Internet. The convergence of IoT and cloud computing has brought numerous benefits.

These trends are shaping the future development of IoT and are likely to have a significant impact on the way we live and work.

15.9   Conclusion

ML is now an integral part of IoT solutions, owing to its ability to analyze and interpret vast amount of data gathered from IoT devices. ML algorithms use this gathered data for pattern recognition, prediction, and decision making for IoT solutions. In this work, the IoT ecosystem and importance of data management in IoT solutions are discussed. In addition, an overview of some common ML algorithms and their advantages and disadvantage are discussed. The work presents some recent literature comprising ML algorithms that are used for IoT solutions in various domains. The study emphasizes on the need for further research in the area of security, data management, and privacy of IoT-based solutions.

References

1. Asghari, P., Rahmani, A.M., Javadi, H.H.S., Internet of Things applications: A systematic review. *Comput. Netw.*, 148, 241–261, 2019, https://doi.org/10.1016/j.comnet.2018.12.008.
2. Mahdavinejad, M.S., Rezvan, M., Barekatain, M., Adibi, P., Barnaghi, P., Sheth, A.P., Machine learning for internet of things data analysis: A survey. *Digit. Commun. Netw.*, 4, 161–175, 2018, https://doi.org/10.1016/j.dcan.2017.10.002.
3. Inc, G, *Global Industrial IoT Platforms Reviews 2023*, Gartner Peer Insights, https://www.gartner.com/market/global-industrial-iot-platforms, Stamford, CT, USA, last accessed 2023/01/30, 2023.
4. Gerber, A. and Romeo, J., Connecting all the things in the Internet of Things - IBM developer, 2017, https://developer.ibm.com/articles/iot-lp101-connectivity-network-protocols/, last accessed 2023/01/30.
5. Rekha, S., Lingala, T., Renikunta, S., Gangula, R., Study of security issues and solutions in internet of things (IoT). *Mater. Today Proc.*, 80, 3554–3559, 2021, https://doi.org/10.1016/j.matpr.2021.07.295.
6. Internet of things is a revolutionary approach for future technology enhancement: A review. *J. Big Data*, 6, 111, 1–21, 2019 | Full Text, https://journalofbigdata.springeropen.com/articles/10.1186/s40537-019-0268-2, last accessed 2023/01/18.

7. Bian, J., Arafat, A.A., Xiong, H., Li, J., Li, L., Chen, H., Wang, J., Dou, D., Guo, Z., Machine learning in real-time internet of things (IoT) systems: A survey. *IEEE Internet Things J.*, 9, 8364–8386, 2022, https://doi.org/10.1109/JIOT.2022.3161050.

8. Watkins, C., Learning from delayed rewards, Thesis, Cambridge, 80, Part 9, 3554–3559, 1989.

9. Han, J., Pei, J., Tong, H., *Data mining: Concepts and techniques*, Morgan Kaufmann, Burlington, Massachusetts, 6, 1–21, 111, 2019, 2022.

10. Sutton, R.S. and Barto, A.G., *Reinforcement learning: An introduction*, The MIT Press, Cambridge, Massachusetts, London, UK, 2018.

11. Williams, R.J., Simple statistical gradient-following algorithms for connectionist reinforcement learning. *Mach. Learn.*, 8, 229–256, 1992.

12. Uddin, S., Haque, I., Lu, H., Moni, M.A., Gide, E., Comparative performance analysis of k-nearest neighbour (KNN) algorithm and its different variants for disease prediction. *Sci. Rep.*, 6256, 12, 1–11, 2022, https://doi.org/10.1038/s41598-022-10358-x.

13. Thanh Noi, P. and Kappas, M., Comparison of random Forest, k-nearest Neighbor, and Support Vector Machine Classifiers for Land Cover Classification using sentinel-2 imagery. *Sensors*, 18, 18, 2018, https://doi.org/10.3390/s18010018.

14. Freedman, D., *Statistical models: Theory and practice*, Cambridge University Press, Cambridge CB2 8BS UK, 2005, https://doi.org/10.1017/CBO9781139165495.

15. Hussain, A., Draz, U., Ali, T., Tariq, S., Irfan, M., Glowacz, A., Daviu, J.A.A., Yasin, S., Rahman, S., Waste management and prediction of air pollutants using IoT and machine learning approach. *Energies*, 3930, 13, 1–22, 2020, https://doi.org/10.3390/en13153930.

16. Ray, S., A quick review of machine learning algorithms, in: *2019 International Conference on Machine Learning, Big Data, Cloud and Parallel Computing (COMITCon)*, pp. 35–39, 2019, https://doi.org/10.1109/COMITCon.2019.8862451.

17. Ali, J., Khan, R., Ahmad, N., Maqsood, I., Random forests and decision trees. *Int. J. Comput. Sci. Issues (IJCSI)*, 9, 272–278, 2012.

18. Nayak, J., Naik, B., Behera, Prof. Dr. H., A comprehensive survey on support vector machine in data mining tasks: Applications & challenges. *Int. J. Database Theory Appl.*, 8, 169–186, 2015, https://doi.org/10.14257/ijdta.2015.8.1.18.

19. Sharkawy, A.-N., Principle of neural network and its main types: Review. *J. Adv. Appl. Comput. Math.*, 7, 8–19, 2020, https://doi.org/10.15377/2409-5761.2020.07.2.

20. Staudemeyer, R. and Morris, E., Understanding LSTM -- A tutorial into long short-term memory recurrent neural networks, arXiv preprint:1909.09586, 2019.

21. Ma, Y. and Guo, G., *Support vector machines applications*, Springer, New York, 2014, https://doi.org/10.1007/978-3-319-02300-7.

22. Schmidhuber, J., Deep learning in neural networks: An overview. *Neural Netw.*, 61, 85–117, 2015, https://doi.org/10.1016/j.neunet.2014.09.003.

23. Friedman, N., Geiger, D., Goldszmidt, M., Bayesian network classifiers. *Mach. Learn.*, 29, 131–163, 1997, https://doi.org/10.1023/a:1007465528199.

24. Zhang, W. and Gao, F., An improvement to naive bayes for text classification. *Procedia Eng.*, 15, 2160–2164, 2011, https://doi.org/10.1016/j.proeng.2011.08.404.

25. Li, J., Cheng, J., Shi, J., Huang, F., Brief introduction of back propagation (BP) neural network algorithm and its improvement, in: *Advances in Computer Science and Information Engineering*, D. Jin, and S. Lin (eds.), pp. 553–558, Springer, Berlin, Heidelberg, 2012, https://doi.org/10.1007/978-3-642-30223-7_87.

26. Na, S., Xumin, L., Yong, G.: Research on k-means clustering algorithm: An improved k-means clustering algorithm, in: *2010 Third International Symposium on Intelligent Information Technology and Security Informatics*, pp. 63–67, 2010, https://doi.org/10.1109/IITSI.2010.74.

27. Ray, S., A quick review of machine learning algorithms, in: *International Conference on Machine Learning, Big Data, Cloud and Parallel Computing (COMITCon)*, IEEE, Faridabad, India, pp. 35–39, 2019.

28. Yu, R., Yang, Y., Yang, L., Han, G., Move, O.A., RAQ–A random forest approach for predicting air quality in urban sensing systems. *Sensors*, 16, 86, 2016, https://doi.org/10.3390/s16010086.

29. Mashhadi, N., Shahrour, I., Attoue, N., El Khattabi, J., Aljer, A., Use of machine learning for leak detection and localization in water distribution systems. *Smart Cities*, 4, 1293–1315, 2021, https://doi.org/10.3390/smartcities4040069.

30. Nie, P., Roccotelli, M., Fanti, M.P., Ming, Z., Li, Z., Prediction of home energy consumption based on gradient boosting regression tree. *Energy Rep.*, 7, 1246–1255, 2021, https://doi.org/10.1016/j.egyr.2021.02.006.

31. Abraham, G., R., R., Nithya, M.: Smart agriculture based on IoT and machine learning, in: *2021 5th International Conference on Computing Methodologies and Communication (ICCMC)*, pp. 414–419, 2021, https://doi.org/10.1109/ICCMC51019.2021.9418392.

32. Rakhra, M., Sanober, S., Quadri, N.N., Verma, N., Ray, S., Asenso, E., Implementing machine learning for smart farming to forecast farmers' interest in hiring equipment. *J. Food Qual.*, 2022, e4721547, 2022, https://doi.org/10.1155/2022/4721547.

33. Damadam, S., Zourbakhsh, M., Javidan, R., Faroughi, A., An intelligent IoT based traffic light management system: Deep reinforcement learning. *Smart Cities*, 5, 1293–1311, 2022, https://doi.org/10.3390/smartcities5040066.

34. Bassetti, E., Berti, A., Bisante, A., Magnante, A., Panizzi, E., Exploiting user behavior to predict parking availability through machine learning. *Smart Cities*, 5, 1243–1266, 2022, https://doi.org/10.3390/smartcities5040064.

35. Bhatia, V., Kumawat, S., Jaglan, V., Overview of role of internet of things and cyber physical systems in various applications, in: *Handbook of Research of Internet of Things and Cyber-Physical Systems*, Presented at the June 9 2022.

36. Omitaomu, O.A. and Niu, H., Artificial intelligence techniques in smart grid: A survey. *Smart Cities*, 4, 548–568, 2021, https://doi.org/10.3390/smartcities4020029.

37. Azad, S., Sabrina, F., Wasimi, S., Transformation of smart grid using machine learning, in: *2019 29th Australasian Universities Power Engineering Conference (AUPEC)*, pp. 1–6, 2019, https://doi.org/10.1109/AUPEC48547.2019.211809.

38. Silva, B.N., Khan, M., Han, K., Futuristic sustainable energy management in smart environments: A review of peak load shaving and demand response strategies, challenges, and opportunities. *Sustainability*, 12, 5561, 2020, https://doi.org/10.3390/su12145561.

39. Bastas, A. and Liyanage, K., Sustainable supply chain quality management: A systematic review. *J. Clean. Prod.*, 181, 726–744, 2018, https://doi.org/10.1016/j.jclepro.2018.01.110.

40. Tirkolaee, E.B., Sadeghi, S., Mooseloo, F.M., Vandchali, H.R., Aeini, S., Application of machine learning in supply chain management: A comprehensive overview of the main areas. *Math. Probl. Eng.*, 2021, e1476043, 2021, https://doi.org/10.1155/2021/1476043.

41. Chan, M., Estève, D., Fourniols, J.-Y., Escriba, C., Campo, E., Smart wearable systems: Current status and future challenges. *Artif. Intell. Med.*, 56, 137–156, 2012, https://doi.org/10.1016/j.artmed.2012.09.003.

42. Rukasha, T., Woolley, S.I., Kyriacou, T., Collins, T., Evaluation of wearable electronics for epilepsy: A systematic review. *Electronics*, 9, 968, 2020, https://doi.org/10.3390/electronics9060968.

43. Regalia, G., Onorati, F., Lai, M., Caborni, C., Picard, R.W., Multimodal wrist-worn devices for seizure detection and advancing research: Focus on the empatica wristbands. *Epilepsy Res.*, 153, 79–82, 2019, https://doi.org/10.1016/j.eplepsyres.2019.02.007.

44. Onorati, F., Regalia, G., Caborni, C., LaFrance, W.C., Blum, A.S., Bidwell, J., De Liso, P., El Atrache, R., Loddenkemper, T., Mohammadpour-Touserkani, F., Sarkis, R.A., Friedman, D.,

Jeschke, J., Picard, R., Prospective study of a multimodal convulsive seizure detection wearable system on pediatric and adult patients in the epilepsy monitoring unit. *Front. Neurol.*, 12, 724904, 2021, https://doi.org/10.3389/fneur.2021.724904.

45. Quantifying neurologic disease using biosensor measurements in-clinic and in free-living settings in multiple sclerosis. *NPJ Digit. Med.* 2, Part - 1, 1–8, 123, 2019, https://www.nature.com/articles/s41746-019-0197-7, last accessed 2023/01/30.

46. Kotsiopoulos, T., Sarigiannidis, P., Ioannidis, D., Tzovaras, D., Machine learning and deep learning in smart manufacturing: The smart grid paradigm. *Comput. Sci. Rev.*, 40, 1–25, 2020, https://doi.org/10.1016/j.cosrev.2020.100341.

47. Baryannis, G., Dani, S., Antoniou, G., Predicting supply chain risks using machine learning: The trade-off between performance and interpretability. *Future Gener. Comput. Syst.*, 101, 993–1004, 2019, https://doi.org/10.1016/j.future.2019.07.059.

48. Bzai, J., Alam, F., Dhafer, A., Bojović, M., Altowaijri, S.M., Niazi, I.K., Mehmood, R., Machine learning-enabled Internet of Things (IoT): Data, applications, and industry perspective. *Electronics*, 11, 2676, 2022, https://doi.org/10.3390/electronics11172676.

49. Arora, J., IoT and machine learning - A technological combination for smart application, in: Conference paper, in: *Conference Name -Proceedings of the 4th International Conference: Innovative Advancement in Engineering & Technology (IAET)*, 2020 https://doi.org/10.2139/ssrn.3548431.

50. Petch, J., Di, S., Nelson, W., Opening the black box: The promise and limitations of explainable machine learning in cardiology. *Can. J. Cardiol.*, 38, 204–213, 2022, https://doi.org/10.1016/j.cjca.2021.09.004.

51. Lingitz, L., Gallina, V., Ansari, F., Gyulai, D., Pfeiffer, A., Sihn, W., Monostori, L., Lead time prediction using machine learning algorithms: A case study by a semiconductor manufacturer. *Procedia CIRP*, 72, 1051–1056, 2018.

Machine Learning-Based Intelligent Power Systems

Kusumika Krori Dutta[1], S. Poornima[1]*, R. Subha[1], Lipika Deka[2] and Archit Kamath[3]

[1]Department of Electrical and Electronics Engineering, M S Ramaiah Institute of Technology,
Bangalore, India
[2]School of Computer Science and Informatics, De Montfort University, Leicester, UK
[3]Nanyang Technological University, Singapore, Singapore

Abstract

Machine learning (ML) plays a crucial role in power systems by providing advanced tools for data analysis, pattern recognition, and decision making. Some of the key applications of machine learning in power systems include load forecasting, predictive maintenance, load scheduling, state estimation, optimization, fault detection, energy management, power quality monitoring, etc. The researchers have used many classification and regression algorithms of ML towards developing a smart power system. Among all machine and deep learning methods, convolutional neural networks, support vector machines, recurrent neural network, K nearest neighbor, decision tree, etc., are widely used in various aspects of power systems. In this book chapter, various machine learning techniques are explained along with its implementations towards intelligent power systems. A case study on the fault detection of IEEE five-bus systems using different machine learning techniques is explained in greater detail.

Keywords: ML, DL, power systems, fault classification, KNN, RNN, SVM

16.1 Introduction

An intelligent power system is a power system equipped with advanced digital technology, such as smart sensors, communication networks, and control systems, to improve its performance, reliability, and efficiency. The aim is to optimize the generation, transmission, and distribution of electricity to meet changing demand patterns while maintaining stability and security. This can be achieved through field monitoring, control, and handling power system components, enabling the integration of multiple energy resources.

In Figure 16.1, which shows an intelligent power system [1], the smart grid has devices for monitoring and control which need to be seamlessly integrated in the operation of all stages of energy systems. On account of the variability of renewable energy, the mismatch between peak availability and consumption, energy storage technologies are emerging, which include nano gel batteries, new material-based batteries, magnetic energy storage, nano ultra/super capacitors, and flywheels. Transmission lines that adapt to dynamic

---
*Corresponding author: sripoorni@msrit.edu

Amit Kumar Tyagi (ed.) *Automated Secure Computing for Next-Generation Systems*, (319–344) © 2024 Scrivener Publishing LLC

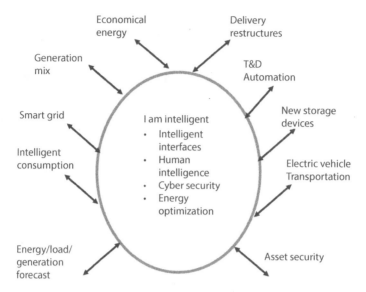

Figure 16.1 Intelligent power systems.

changes in load and emergencies along with continuity of service assure the reliability and standard quality of supply. The intelligent analytical tools are designed for dynamic optimal power flow, real-time stability assessment, robust state estimation, and reliability and restructuring simulation. With the help of state estimator sensors, phasor measurement units and communication technologies ensure the transmission functionality to be smart. Intelligent assets of transmission include the adaptability and robust predictability of generation and demand, a smart network, decision making, and reliability to resolve real-time changes in its use. At the low voltage distribution level, smart methodologies will have communication links between consumers and company, automation using smart meters, EMS components and AMI with self-learning capability, fault handling modules, voltage stability optimization and load balancing, programmed billing, system restoration and system restructuring, and online pricing. Demand-side management (DSM) and EMS modify the consumer demand to reduce the operating cost from generation to supply. DSM enables reduced emissions and less fuel consumption and costs, which contribute to the reliability of service. Smart buildings and appliances, plug-and-play, clean air requirements, two-way meters, and interfaces will be incorporated for good energy efficiency.

Machine learning-based intelligent power systems use advanced machine learning algorithms to improve the performance, efficiency, and reliability of power systems. Some of the key features of such systems include the following:

a) Real-time data analysis: Machine learning algorithms analyze large amounts of data from power system components and the grid to provide real-time insights that can support decision making.

b) Predictive maintenance: Machine learning algorithms can predict the failure of equipment and can hence trigger proactive maintenance and reduce the risk of unplanned outages.

c) Load forecasting: Machine learning algorithms can forecast a future electricity demand based on historical data, weather patterns, and other relevant factors, allowing better planning.

d) State estimation: Machine learning algorithms can estimate the state of the power system in real time, i.e., voltage levels and power flows at different points in the network.

e) Optimization: Machine learning algorithms can optimize energy management and control, including the scheduling of renewable energy sources, demand-side management, and the integration of energy storage systems.

f) Fault detection and diagnosis: Machine learning algorithms can detect and diagnose faults in power system components, such as transformers and generators, in real time.

g) Power quality monitoring: Machine learning algorithms can monitor power quality and detect problems, such as voltage dips, sags, and harmonics, allowing for the timely mitigation of their impacts.

h) Energy management: Machine learning algorithms can be used to optimize energy management and control, including the scheduling of multiple sources, demand-side management, and energy storage integration.

i) Anomaly detection: Machine learning algorithms can detect an abnormal behavior in the power system, such as cyber attacks or equipment malfunctions, allowing for prompt intervention and mitigation.

Overall, machine learning-based intelligent power systems can provide a more reliable, efficient, and sustainable energy delivery while reducing costs and improving grid stability.

16.2   Machine Learning Techniques

There are various machine learning techniques preferred for power systems as follows:

a) Regression Analysis: Predicts numerical outputs based on input variables, such as load forecasting or state estimation.

b) Decision Trees: A type of model that uses a tree-like graph to make decisions based on the input variables; used in fault diagnosis and predictive maintenance.

c) Artificial Neural Networks (ANNs): A type of model motivated by the biological structure and task of the human brain; used for a variety of applications, including load forecasting, state estimation, and fault diagnosis.

d) Support Vector Machines (SVMs): A type of model that uses linear or non-linear hyperplanes to separate data into different classes; used for fault detection and classification.

e) K-Nearest Neighbors (KNN): A type of model that classifies a data point based on the majority class of its neighbors; used in power quality monitoring.

f) Clustering Algorithms: A type of unsupervised learning algorithm that groups similar data points into clusters; used in energy management and demand-side management.

g) Reinforcement Learning: A type of model that learns from trial and error; used for optimal energy management and control.

These machine learning techniques can be combined and customized to meet the specific needs of power systems, leading to improved performance, reliability, and efficiency.

Deep learning (DL), a technique getting popularity in power systems, is basically a subset of machine learning that uses artificial neural networks with multiple hidden layers to model complex patterns and relationships in data. Some of the most common deep learning techniques used in power systems include the following:

a) Convolutional Neural Networks (CNNs): A type of DL algorithm commonly preferred for image recognition; used in monitoring and analyzing power system components and events.
b) Recurrent Neural Networks (RNNs): A type of DL algorithm that can handle sequences of data; used for load forecasting, state estimation, and fault diagnosis.
c) Long Short-Term Memory (LSTM) Networks: A type of DL-RNN that can better handle long-term dependencies in sequential data; used for load forecasting, state estimation, and fault diagnosis.
d) Autoencoders: A type of DL algorithm that can perform unsupervised feature learning and dimensionality reduction; used for anomaly detection and fault diagnosis.
e) Generative Adversarial Networks (GANs): A type of DL algorithm that can generate new data that resembles existing data; used in DSM and EMS.

With the help of ML and DL techniques, intelligent power systems can handle large amounts of data and make more accurate predictions and decisions, leading to improved reliability, efficiency, and stability. The relevant machine learning techniques are explained in the following sections.

16.2.1 Classification Algorithm

16.2.1.1 K-Nearest Neighbor

The KNN network assumes that similar data locate closer to each other in a plane, as depicted in Figure 16.2. It classifies the data points based on the values of "K" nearest neighbors. If the value of K is chosen as 1, the data point belongs to the closest neighbor class. In Figure 16.2, a blue hexagon is located between the concentrated circles representing sK = 3 and K = 5 neighbors. At K = 3, two green diamonds and one red star are nearer to the hexagon. For K = 5, three red stars and two green diamonds are present. Therefore, for K = 5, the test sample belongs to green and red class for K = 3 and 5, respectively. To avoid this, it is preferred to have K = 1 to have a better result, and the K values are also found based on Euclidean distance as in Equation 16.2.

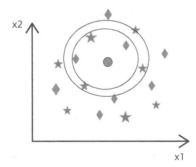

Figure 16.2 K-nearest neighbor algorithm.

The probability of a test input x is given as in Equation 16.1:

$$P(y = j \mid X = x) = \frac{1}{K} \sum_{i \in A} I(y^{(i)} = j)$$

(Eq. 16.1)

The distance is given as follows (where p = 2):

$$d(x, x') = \sqrt{(x_1 - y_1)^p + (x_2 - y_2)^p + \ldots + (x_N - y_N)^p}$$

(Eq. 16.2)

The performance is evaluated in terms of the Euclidean, Manhattan, and Minkowski metrics. The metric d(p, q) indicates the distance between points p and q as in Equations 16.3–16.5, respectively. Here n represents the dimensions of the train set, while p_i and q_i are the values of the i-th dimensions of data points p and q, respectively.

a) Euclidean metric

$$d(p, q) = \sqrt{\sum_i^n (p_i - q_i)^2}$$

(Eq. 16.3)

b) Manhattan metric

$$d(p, q) = \sum_i^n |p_i - q_i|$$

(Eq. 16.4)

c) Minkowski metric

$$d(p, q) = \left(\sum_i^n |x_i - y_i| \right)^{1/p}$$

(Eq. 16.5)

The merits of KNN can be identified as follows:

- simple implementation
- handles noisy data in a robust manner
- effective for massive data

The demerits of KNN algorithm include the following:

- The determination of the K value is difficult.
- More distance computations for every sample.
- The training sets need to be standardized.

16.2.1.2   Support Vector Machines

SVMs are used for classification, and support vector regression is used for regression problems. The hyper planes in 'n' dimensional space between classes, as shown in Figure 16.3, have a maximum distance between data points that is used to classify the data effectively. The 2D hyperplane equation is given in Equation 16.6:

$$H: \omega^T(x) + b = 0 \qquad \text{(Eq. 16.6)}$$

where w(x) and b represent the weight matrix and the intercept/bias, respectively.

Optimal w and b values are determined using the Lagrange method as given in Equation 16.7. The optimal value of weights w is derived with the known lambda as follows:

$$w = \sum_{i=1}^{l} \lambda_i y_i x_i \qquad \text{(Eq. 16.7)}$$

Types of SVMs:

1. Simple Linear SVM: Typically used for linear regression and classification problems (shown in Figure 16.3 and Figure 16.4)
2. Kernel SVM: Used for non-linear data. They are further subdivided into the following types:

   a. polynomial
   b. Gaussian radial basis function (RBF)
   c. Sigmoid
   d. Others: ANOVA radial basis, hyperbolic tangent, Laplace RBF

Simple Linear SVM: A simple SVM is used when data is linearly separable into classes using a straight line. Both classification and regression tasks can be performed.

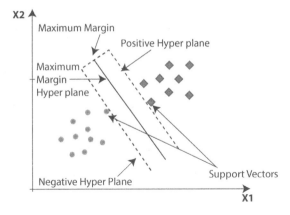

Figure 16.3 Support vector machine.

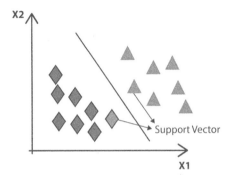

Figure 16.4 Linear SVM.

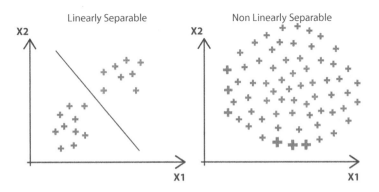

Figure 16.5 Kernel SVM.

Kernel SVM: Kernels are often used to classify non-linearly separable data, as observed in Figure 16.5. There exist several types of kernels, which can be selected based on the distribution of the input data.

a. Polynomial kernels fit a polynomial curve to appropriately separate the data.
b. Gaussian RBF is the kernel which measures both the similarity and the dissimilarity of data points by measuring the distance between them. The radius of influence is set using hyper parameters.
c. Sigmoid SVMs use the sigmoid as an activation function.

16.2.1.3   Decision Tree

Decision tree (DT) is a dominating ML algorithm which became familiar for its ability to handle continuous categorical data and interpret capacity and training speed. It is a hierarchical algorithm that begins with a root node and branches out into leaves based on the decision variable to categorize the data. In a DT, the decision and the leaf nodes, as depicted in Figure 16.6, decide based on the features extracted from the input data from simple yes/no questions.

The construction of a decision tree is carried out by computation of information gain or gini index. As the tree size increases, DTs tend to overfit and hence need pruning of unnecessary nodes to get the optimal tree.

16.2.1.4   Ensemble Boosted Trees

Boosting is an ensemble learning which combines and makes weak learners strong by reducing errors during training. Random sample data, which fits with a model, gets trained successively during boosting. Each successive model attempts to overcome the limitations of the past as the weak rules of the past are combined in every iteration to develop a single prediction rule.

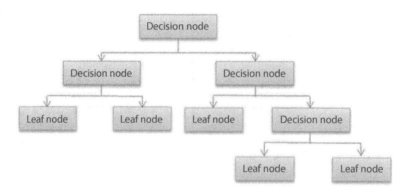

Figure 16.6 Structure of DT.

16.2.1.5 Random Forest

Random forest is an ensemble of non-related decision trees that performs better than the individual trees; hence, ensembling ensures the overall model performance.

16.2.1.6 Naïve Bayes

Naïve Bayes (NB) algorithm is a supervised learning probabilistic classifier based on Bayes theorem to perform quick binary as well as multiclass classification with the assumption that the features are interdependent. The Bayes theorem is given in Equation 16.8.

$$P(A \mid B) = (P(B \mid A)P(A))/P(B) \qquad \text{(Eq. 16.8)}$$

where $P(A \mid B)$ is called the posterior probability, $P(B \mid A)$ is called the likelihood probability, $P(A)$ is called the prior probability, and $P(B)$ is called the marginal probability. Depending on the distribution of data, a NB model can be classified as Gaussian, multinomial, and Bernoulli.

16.2.1.7 Logistic Regression

Logistic regression is a supervised network that classifies binary data by computing its probability. It uses a sigmoid activation function as defined in Equation 16.9 to map the predicted values to the probability values between 0 and 1.

$$f(x) = 1/(1 + e^{\wedge}(-x)) \qquad \text{(Eq. 16.9)}$$

This probability value is then mapped to a threshold discrete class as shown in Figure 16.7.

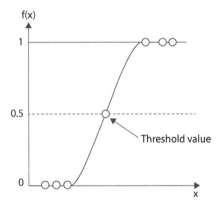

Figure 16.7 Sigmoid function used in LR.

16.2.2 Regression Analysis

16.2.2.1 Linear Regression

A regression network learns the association between a dependent variable and independent variables from the input–output pairs in the dataset used for training. The input–output relationships are related using linear predictor functions, in the case of linear regression, as shown in Equation 16.10 and as shown in Figure 16.8, where data is utilized to estimate unknown model parameters. The conditional mean (CM) of the response is assumed to be an affine function of explanatory variable values. Otherwise, any quantile like CM is utilized. As with any regression analysis, LR demands only the conditional probability distribution of the response for the given values of the predictors.

$$f(x) = w\,x + c \qquad\qquad \text{(Eq. 16.10)}$$

16.2.2.2 Regression Tree Ensemble

A decision tree is a non-parametric model that can be trained to predict the output by inferring easy decision rules with respect to training data. A DT used for regression is termed as a regression tree, and it can be seen as a piecewise constant approximation. Regression trees tend to overfit and do not generalize well on unseen data. A regression tree ensemble is a regression model built with multiple regression trees based on weight computations. Merging regression trees enhances the performance of the predictive model. Boosting is a type of learning in which the regression tree models are trained in a sequence, with each model trying to perform better than the previous model in the sequence.

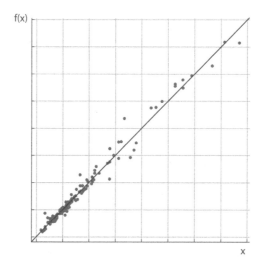

Figure 16.8 Linear regression model.

16.2.2.3   Elastic Net Regression

If the data holds many colinear properties, ridge regression (RR) technique is applied as those independent variables are highly correlated. Though the least square estimates are fair in collinearity, their variances cause a mismatch between the observed value and the actual value. RR reduces errors by biasing the regression estimates. Along with RR, the least absolute shrinkage and selection operator (LASSO) technique balances the absolute magnitude of the regression coefficient values to absolute zero using the proper variable selection. EN regression combines the RR and LASSO regression techniques for highly correlated data as it regularizes using penalties.

16.2.2.4   Gaussian Process Regression

The Gaussian process (GP) model has probabilistic-supervised network that can be preferred for regression as well as classification tasks. It is a probability distribution over possible functions that fit the training data following the Bayesian approach. The Gaussian process regression model is a nonparametric kernel-based model that uses the past value (kernel) to calculate posterior probability (predictions) using the training data and compute predictive posterior distribution on the testing data. It gives promising results on small datasets and provides uncertainty measures over predictions.

It is a stochastic, non-parametric, Bayesian approach to the regression process where an individual collection of random variables has a multivariate normal distribution. This process is getting popular in the field of machine learning as it can work on a small dataset and also provides uncertainty measurements on the predictions. Equations 16.11–16.13 show the Bayes' rule and prior Gaussian process, respectively, where p(w) represents prior distribution and p(w | y, X) represents the posterior distribution in Equation 16.11), f* and x* in Equation 16.12 represent the prediction label and test observation, respectively, and m(x) and k(x, x') are the mean and covariance functions in Equation 16.13.

$$p(w \mid y, X) = (p(y \mid X, w) \, p(w))/p(y \mid X) \qquad \text{(Eq. 16.11)}$$

$$p(f* \mid x*, y, X) = \int p(f* \mid x*, w) p(w \mid y, X) dw \qquad \text{(Eq. 16.12)}$$

$$f(x) \sim GP(m(x), k(x, x')) \qquad \text{(Eq. 16.13)}$$

16.2.2.5   Artificial Neural Networks

ANN is a promising model for mapping non-linear input–output pairs. The input layer, one or more hidden layers, and the output layer have weight-interconnected neurons, as shown in Figure 16.9, with an activation function. The neurons will be trained with appropriate input–output data sets such that they can interpolate any other similar data with high accuracy.

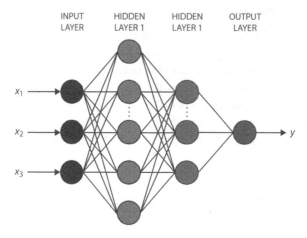

Figure 16.9 Structure of the feed forward neural network.

16.2.3   Deep Learning Techniques

16.2.3.1   Convolutional Neural Networks

Convolution is the distinguishing feature of a CNN. Its main parameter is a box of learnable filters (or kernels) with a small window size and strides through the full depth of the input data. The filter is applied on overlapping patches of the input data in both directions (left to right and top to bottom). This application results in element-wise multiplication between the filter with the input array, and their averaging gives out a single result per filter overlap region. This process is called convolution. The filter gets convolved multiple times across the input array, resulting in a smaller two-dimensional array as output. This output array represents some of the features of the input array in a smaller data space and is called a feature map.

Figure 16.10 represents the input image and filter/kernel which represents a filter of size 3×3; after the first convolution, the feature map is the sum of overlapping values as shown in Equation 16.14.

$$\text{Feature map} = (1 \times 2) + (4 \times 2) + (9 \times 3) + (-4 \times 2) + (7 \times 1) + (4 \times 4) + (2 \times 1) + (-5 \times 1) + (1 \times 2) = 51 \tag{Eq. 16.14}$$

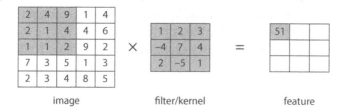

Figure 16.10 Feature map and convolution filter/kernel.

Typically, CNNs do not just use a single filter; they instead convolve the input data using multiple filters in parallel, thereby learning multiple features quickly. This makes the feature extraction of such models very rich and effective.

The activation function is a node that is put at the end of or in between activation in CNNs. The activation functions which are widely used in neural networks are rectified linear units (ReLU), hyperbolic tangent, etc. An activation example using ReLU is shown in Figure 16.3 and is defined by Equation 16.15.

$$f(x) = \max(0, x) \qquad\qquad (Eq.\ 16.15)$$

It replaces the negative values of the activation map with zeros as shown in Figure 16.11. This eases the decision function of the network without affecting the convolutional receptive fields.

Though convolution causes the compactness within the feature maps, pooling is responsible for the reduction in the dimensionality across such feature parameters. The principle behind pooling is that the rough relative location of a feature is more important than its exact location. During pooling, each feature map gets down-sampled independently, causing a reduction in their height and width but without affecting their depth. This step substantially reduces the size of the parameter space, thereby reducing the memory footprint of the model and the amount of computation required in the network. Hence, the training time shortens and prevents model overfitting. The most common pooling method is max pooling. Like a convolution filter, it has a window size and stride, which then slides across the data and extracts the max value within the pooling window.

Figure 16.12 shows the result of max pooling using a window size of 2 × 2 and stride of 2. Each color represents a different window. After a round of convolution and pooling (sometimes after multiple such rounds), the output will be pushed into a couple of fully connected neural network layers. However, the output of a convolution and pooling round is a 2D matrix, and a fully connected layer works on a 1D vector. Therefore, the output 2D matrix of the final pooling layer will need to be flattened to a 1D vector before entering a fully connected layer. Flattening is achieved by simple reshaping of the 2D matrix into a 1D vector as shown in Figure 16.13.

0.77	−0.11	0.11	0.33	0.55	−0.11	0.33
0.55	−0.11	0.33	0.77	−0.11	0.11	−0.11
−0.33	0.55	−0.11	0.33	0.77	−0.11	0.11
0.33	−0.77	0.55	−0.11	0.33	0.33	−0.77
0.77	−0.11	0.11	0.55	−0.11	0.33	0.55
−0.33	0.77	−0.11	0.11	0.55	−0.11	0.33
0.55	−0.11	0.33	0.77	−0.11	0.11	−0.33

0.77	0	0.11	0.33	0.55	0	0.33
0.55	0	0.33	0.77	0	0.11	0
−0.33	0.55	0	0.33	0.77	0	0.11
0.33	0	0.55	0	0.33	0.33	0
0.77	0	0.11	0.55	0	0.33	0.55
0	0.77	0	0.11	0.55	0	0.33
0.55	0	0.33	0.77	0	0.11	0

Figure 16.11 Activation function.

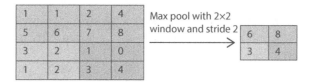

Figure 16.12 Max pooling.

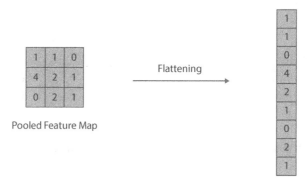

Figure 16.13 Pooling and flattening.

16.2.3.2 Recurrent Neural Networks

RNNs are mainly categorized based on input–output interconnection, and it has different architectural features. In this study, different types of architectural features have been considered. In this category, it mainly has three types: (i) simple RNN, (ii) LSTMs, and (iii) GRUs. Figure 16.14(a) shows the architecture of simple RNN and GRUs, respectively. Equation 16.16 and Equation 16.17 represents the computation of hidden layer and output layer vectors, respectively:

$$h_t = F(W_{ih}u_t + W_{hh}h_{t-1} + b_h) \qquad \text{(Eq. 16.16)}$$

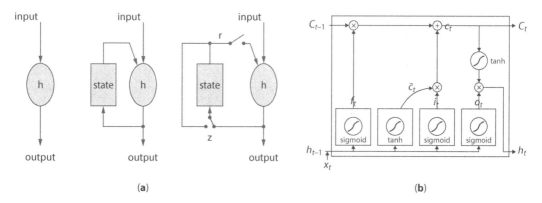

Figure 16.14 (a) Architecture of single neuron, simple RNN and GRU. (b) Architecture of a LSTM cell.

$$y_t = W_{ho} h_t + b_0 \qquad \text{(Eq. 16.17)}$$

where u represents input sequence $u = \{u_1, u_2, \ldots u_T\}$; h represents hidden vector sequence $h = \{h_1, h_2, \ldots h_T\}$; b, W, and F represent bias, weight matrix, and hidden layer activation function, respectively, and y represents output vector $y = \{y_1, y_2, \ldots y_T\}$, while t varies from 1 to T. Though in this example all the three layers are considered to have the same vector size, i.e., 1 to T, it is allowed to have a different number of neurons; so, a different vector size is possible.

Simple RNN is trained by back propagation through time (BPTT), and BPTT has issues of vanishing gradient in deeper layers, because of which simple RNN enables to train long sequences. To surmount from this, in place of an RNN cell, a gated cell is used as shown in Figure 16.14(a), which provides control on the information stored in memory.

Among the three, LSTM is the most advantageous architecture as (a) it can learn from raw time series data, (b) it can process data with long sequences (up to 200–400 steps), (c) it can handle sequences of different sizes without any pre-processing, and (d) it provides a solution to vanishing gradient problem. The main disadvantage of LSTM is its dependence on each neuron and each layer for the long term. The horizontal line shown in Figure 16.14(b) of the LSTM cell at the top side (Ct) represents the cell state, which plays a vital role in its architecture. LSTM prefers to remove or insert information into the cell state using three gates, and they are (a) forget gate, (b) gate with sigmoid layer, and (c) final output gate.

a) Forget Gate: This gate helps in removing information from the cell state.

$$h_t = \sigma\left(W_f \cdot [h_{t-1}, u_t] + b_f\right) \qquad \text{(Eq. 16.18)}$$

where σ represents the sigmoid function.

b) Gate With Sigmoid Layer: The main function of this gate is decision making about the weight updating sequence, and the storage of the new updated weight value is done at tanh by creating a vector. Equations 16.18, 16.19, and 16.20 represent the mathematical interpretation of this gate.

$$i_t = \sigma\left(W_i \cdot [h_{t-1}, u_t] + b_i\right) \qquad \text{(Eq. 16.19)}$$

$$\hat{C}_t = \tanh\left(W_c \cdot [h_{t-1}, u_t] + b_c\right) \qquad \text{(Eq. 16.20)}$$

Using Equations 16.16, 16.17, and 16.18, the cell state (Ct) is updated as shown in Equation 16.21.

$$C_t = h_t {}^* C_{t-1} + i_t {}^* \hat{C}_t \qquad \text{(Eq. 16.21)}$$

c) Final Output Gate: The output is calculated considering the updated cell state and sigmoidal activation layer, with this the gate selecting the final output among the cell states based on Equations 16.22 and 16.23.

$$O_t = \sigma\left(W_o \cdot [h_{t-1}, u_t] + b_o\right) \qquad \text{(Eq. 16.22)}$$

$$h_t = O_t * \tanh(C_t) \qquad \text{(Eq. 16.23)}$$

where σ logistic sigmoid function makes O_t in range $(0,1)$; tanh: hyperbolic tangent function ranges between -1 and 1; W_i's: weight matrix; h_{t-1} = past hidden state; b_i's: bias vector; and u_t = input vector.

In the case of GRUs, it uses one gate less in comparison to LSTMs; so, it is a little simpler architecture compared with LSTMs.

16.2.4 Reinforcement Learning

Reinforcement learning contradicts supervised and unsupervised learning as it neither uses labeled input data for training nor it requires to explicitly correct suboptimal actions. This type of learning is also known as neuro-dynamic programming or approximate dynamic programming. It is widely used in most of the online games like backgammon games, flappy birds, subway surfers, maze (as shown in Figure 16.15), etc. Because of the generality of reinforcement learning, it is also used in various fields like simulation-based optimization, swarm intelligence, multi-agent systems, statistics and genetic algorithms, etc.

16.3 Implementation of ML Techniques in Smart Power Systems

16.3.1 Fault Detection and Diagnosis

Power system analysis is a crucial approach for recognizing the short circuit currents caused by various faults, determining the location of the fault, calculating the under-rated power system devices, and sizing various distribution generation system components. Power system planning, protection, component selection, setup of relays, etc., and system dependability all require fault analysis. The equipment and conductors must be designed to resist the fault current. The single-phase equivalent circuit can easily perform the symmetrical fault analysis, which is necessary to determine the ratings and rupturing capability of the equipment connected to the power supply. Appropriate component modeling and fault analysis become essential for ensuring the safety and reliability of the system. Therefore, on a

Figure 16.15 Reinforcement learning process in a game theory.

power system network or electrical bus system, machine learning techniques are employed to automate the fault analysis process.

Research and development activities in power systems are facilitated by recent developments in machine learning in several fields. Fully convolutional networks were used to categorize failures in an IEEE 30-bus transmission system [2], while the topic of fault prediction using statistical and machine learning methods for improving software quality was covered in [3]. Hybrid authorization model for automatic fault detection in transmission lines, impedance variation distance calculation, and IOT-enabled DL and PMU data have been utilized to create a real-time hierarchical architecture for fault detection, categorization, and localization in HVDC point-to-point [4] and back-to-back [5] systems. Numerous modeling techniques are investigated in order to build a flexible system, including modulation of a multilevel inverter with a variable load, fault analysis by minimizing network downtime, and real-time voltage stability assessment using phasor measurement units and influence of synchro-phasor estimation algorithms [6]. Mathematical models are used to test the analysis of different fault kinds, and different ML and DL techniques are researched. RNN [7] and LSTM for load forecasting [8] are two methods that are most frequently utilized. The classification of process faults, multiple event detection and recognition through cluster-based sparse coding, the detection of false data injection attacks in smart islands, the detection and localization of events violating pre-defined ROCOF limits, the classification of PQ disturbances, microgrid faults, etc., are just a few applications where deep learning techniques are frequently used [9, 10].

16.3.2   Load Forecasting

Load forecasting predicts the power demands in short, medium, and long duration. A good forecasting prediction accounting for natural resources [11], electrical components (ventilating, heating, lighting, and air conditioning appliances), consumption history, and unplanned requirements will benefit both consumer and utility. A load forecasting task needs more variables along with curve fitting techniques. Due to massive data availability and prediction requirements, data analytics methods such as ML, ANN, genetic algorithms, fuzzy logic, and expert systems help engineers to focus toward edge devices. Conventional techniques also fail to handle random patterns which ML does in a better way. A well-trained ML model may fail with real time, whereas a simple model may give fair predictions. Regression algorithms of ML such as linear, Gaussian, support vector and elastic net, LSTM, etc., are preferred for predicting load and demands [12, 13]. The trained algorithm will be validated, and the least error can be measured through mean absolute percentage error as shown below.

$$M = \frac{100\%}{n} \sum_{k=1}^{n} \frac{|A_t - F_t|}{|A_t|} \qquad \text{(Eq. 16.24)}$$

Most of the ML networks are evaluated in terms of MAPE and mean square error. BPN predicts the heating load of buildings [14] along with limitation of having a vanishing gradient and an inadequate convergence. The LSTM model overcomes these drawbacks when predicting the day ahead demand using AMPds dataset [15]. When LSTM fails to handle different random patterns, SVM models are proposed for the same. The SVM models map the nonlinearity between weather and load consumption effectively and give better predictions.

16.3.3   Load Disaggregation

A range of techniques to be able to split the household energy consumption by individual appliances are broadly known as load disaggregation. The process of separating the individual power consumed by appliances from the total aggregate power is known as load disaggregation. A comprehensive overview of non-intrusive load monitoring and its related methods and techniques are used for disaggregated energy sensing as presented by [16]. This literature integrates the finding of several works and presents a unified theory on choosing a perfect load disaggregation algorithm. The authors of [17] have used the concept of particle filtering to estimate the status of an appliance in a household. In [18], a neural network-based disaggregation technique over data generated using Monte Carlo simulation is presented. The network used in this case was trained using radial basis function network with center updating principle. The drawback of this work is that the center updating will become computationally expensive and may yet, in time, cause instability in the solution obtained. In this work, supervised learning algorithms are used to perform load disaggregation as done for load forecasting. The disadvantage of this process is the need for re-sampling of the data after every iteration. This stage of the process can cause a loss of accuracy in prediction. Disaggregation can offer consumers greater visibility of where they are using the energy within the home and where the potential savings lie.

Machine learning models are trained to obtain the power consumed by the water heater, AC, and the washing machine from the total power value based on the appliance status and weather conditions. This stage is essential as it will give an idea as to the type of chore the user is performing at a particular hour of the day. As done for load forecasting, three regression models are developed to exclusively filter out the appliance-wise power from the total power. A set of regression algorithms is trained to take total power, temperature, humidity, and appliance status as inputs and predict the power consumed by the water heater, AC, and washing machine. To check the effectiveness of the proposed algorithms, cross-validation is performed as done before. However, it must be noted that the power consumed by the appliance becomes zero when the appliance is not being used. These zero entries hinder the use of MAPE as a suitable candidate for measuring error as in Equation 16.25. Hence, as a substitute, for disaggregation, we use the maximum absolute error as a measure of the performance of the algorithms.

$$E = \max\left(|A_t - F_t|\right) \text{ where } t = 1,2,3\ldots n \qquad \text{(Eq. 16.25)}$$

A_t represents the actual output, F_t the predicted output, and n the number of samples. The algorithm that produces the least maximum absolute error for a particular appliance is chosen to determine the power consumed by that appliance.

16.3.4 Scheduling of Load

To get power n financial benefits, electric loads are scheduled manually, semi-automatically, or automatically. Literature has worked on the load scheduling problem by only considering cost reduction or comfort maximization individually. Along with the value of lost load, cost minimization techniques are proposed [19, 20]. On the other side, considering energy cost as an objective function to be optimized by efficiently utilizing the available energy has been tried out. Whereas researchers also tried to minimize consumption cost by taking into account the user's convenience, mainly thermal comfort is considered as a metric of user's satisfaction [21]. A traveling salesman approach of performing grid-based load scheduling is carried out in [22]. This has been extended in [23] to schedule the HVAC loads in commercial buildings. However, the application of the traveling salesman approach can become quite complex when multiple constraints are considered. In addition, this sort of scheduling of the loads requires an iterative approach which can become computationally expensive.

A linear sorting algorithm is required for scheduling the loads, taking into account the comfort of the user in terms of the elasticity of the task that they are to perform. The drawback of this work is that the center updating will become computationally expensive and may yet, in time, cause instability in the solution obtained. In this work, supervised learning algorithms are used to perform load disaggregation as done for load forecasting.

In load scheduling, we use a time-varying tariff and the comfort level information of the user to optimally schedule the load. The linear sorting optimization algorithm is used to perform this task as it is computationally inexpensive. The implementation of this scheduling phase can be described in five steps:

a) From the predicted total power and disaggregated power, isolate the readings that can be subjected to load scheduling. This stage is done to cater to human comfort.

b) In the isolated data frame, arrange the power readings in either descending or ascending.

c) The time-varying tariff must be arranged in an order that opposes that of the power readings—however, not that the hour corresponding to the particular tariff rate must be kept intact.

d) Now pick a particular hour and its corresponding tariff. Based on its location in the data frame, pick a corresponding power reading and place it in a new data frame.

e) Sort the new data frame in ascending order of the hour and append the rest of the data frame that was initially removed.

It should be noted that the scheduling phase will be preceded by forecasting and disaggregation. Hence, the implementation of load scheduling, as in Figure 16.16, starts with train models for forecasting and disaggregation. Once this is done, the forecasting model must be placed first to take inputs from the dataset. The predicted output of this stage is then used to perform disaggregation of the loads. Finally, the outputs from both of these stages will be used for scheduling the loads as per the time-varying tariffs.

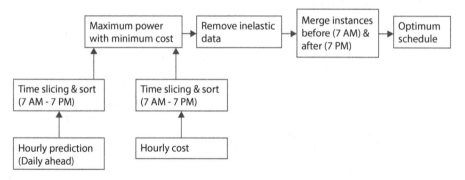

Figure 16.16 Optimal scheduling of load.

16.3.5   Energy Management

Advanced control centers use a software and hardware system for power system operation called energy management system (EMS). Over a common command and control system, the EMS has evolved over the half a century into complex systems using automation techniques and models. EMS monitors and manages power flows in the AC and DC transmission systems, whereas the distribution management system does the same in the low voltage distribution systems. The working group WG 13 for energy management system application program interface (EMS—API, CIM, IEC 61970) has been framed to monitor grid operations, frequency, reduce T&D losses, national security objectives, sharing of electricity with neighbor resources, and decrease fault duration and frequency.

Intelligent power systems have a good impact in terms of enhancement in renewable and/or conventional power generation, stability as well as energy consumption along with less carbon dioxide release and cost of energy. Power systems with multiple energy sources, various storage devices, uncontrollable/controllable loads, and grid interconnection work as a smart system to meet generation and load balance minute to minute. Forecasting, inclusion of advanced techniques, monitoring system performance, recovering from abnormal conditions, planned maintenance, and extensions are being modeled and implemented accurately using machine learning approaches.

Energy management involves challenges on sources of data collection, inefficient energy utilization, unplanned upgrading, unpredictable failures of equipment, and prolonged integration of data collected. Basic ANN models of feedforward and feedback networks have been upgraded into ML and DL models to handle the massive power system data. Energy management techniques are effectively handled by ML techniques in levels of battery storage, nano/micro power generation, limited controller size and design, switching device performance, etc. Intelligent systems employing ML as well as big data platforms extract features and make predictions to assist decision algorithms in the energy sector.

Appropriate ML techniques are being developed for the effective utilization of data and optimization methods involving them in providing control techniques. Energy management techniques are being researched or implemented in electric vehicles, residential loads (smart buildings), industrial loads, or smart cities. The various stages of energy management [24] shown in Figure 16.17 are handled by ML algorithms such as recursive partitioning and regression tree (Rpart) and RF methods, ANNs, RF, SVM, etc.

Figure 16.17 Processes involved in energy management.

16.3.6   Asset Monitoring

Intelligent power systems may employ a distributed acoustic sensing (DAS) system using fiber optic infrastructure to support its needs. DAS technology brings the opportunity to reuse this infrastructure by turning the fibers into distributed acoustic sensors to explore the multiple monitoring and security applications of this technology in high voltage systems [25]. DAS techniques enable the digitalization of physical asset management, and it is a lever towards a cost-effective maintenance in addition to the following:

a) Security: Detect unauthorized interventions when used in underground or submarine power lines by continuous and automated monitoring of assets.
b) Conductor and cable asset management
    i.   Predictive and condition maintenance helps to monitor the healthiness of the asset, monitor overhead lines to avoid any damages due to shorts, transients, and other environment conditions.
    ii. Patrolling services prevent unknown infringements like digging works in the workplaces.
    iii. Unlike geographical surveys for every 5 years, DAS are permanently monitoring the asset.
c) Future extensions: The DAS should have provision to monitor either conventional infrastructure or those enhanced with renewable energies.

Any abnormal event sensed by the fiber sensors installed along the fence and buried underground next to the inner perimeter activates the alarm when at least one sensor is activated. The sensor signal will be analyzed by different layers of ML techniques. The data processing unit detects and classifies the event in the following procedure:

1. Sensor signals are detected and needs to be conditioned. The raw data obtained from the sensor with time and space information could be a continuous signal that may be signal imposed with noise. The noise-filtered data reveals the anomalies by choosing a highly recommended adaptive threshold. The anomalies identified by unsupervised ML algorithms are considered as potential alarms. Some intrinsic characteristics of these alarms are processed as known patterns to be recognized and classified by the same ML architecture.
2. The potential alarms also provide important features like real intensity value, phase frequency window, multi-frequency data, etc., that can be registered as patterns and classified by ML techniques.

3. The logical gates employed under specific rules or conditions cut the false alarms.

4. The user gets alarms and handles the information with the help of SCADA, which controls cameras, actuators, drones, etc., or by any web application that stores them as patterns.

The familiar datasets such as KDDCup 1999, ISCX, UNSW-NB15, CICIDS, BATADAL, SWaT, and CTU-UNB datasets have foundation ML or DL algorithms like deep belief networks, autoencoders, CNN, and RNN to ensure intrusion detection in the SCADA system [26]. Hybrid detection systems, zero-knowledge proof, blockchain, graph, and privacy by design are also suggested along with the above-mentioned algorithm to face the real-time challenges.

16.4   Case Study

The health of the power system primarily depends on the current flowing in the buses [27]. During fault, the current surge may damage the equipment. The system parameters are

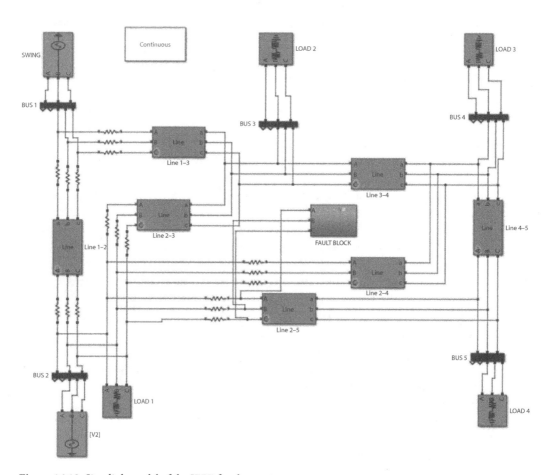

Figure 16.18 Simulink model of the IEEE five-bus system.

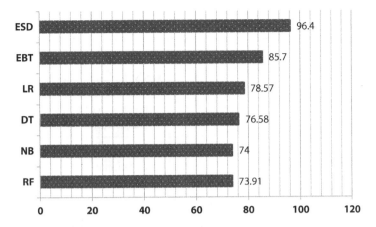

Figure 16.19 Accuracy performance of the various ML models.

monitored at all the five buses of the IEEE five-bus system modeled in Simulink as shown in Figure 16.18. The current values at 25%, 50%, 75%, and 100% of the rated voltage value are obtained with ±10% threshold. The threshold is very important as the model gives a robust determination of the state of the system despite a noise in the measurement of the current values at five buses. The measurement of voltage at bus 2 (namely, PV bus) and the bus currents at the five buses has been done under all states. A simple condition statement has been programmed to check the voltage and current values in the threshold limits to define the state of the system.

Random forests and naïve Bayes are less accurate as seen in Figure 16.19, as both usually perform well on a larger dataset. The decision tree performs less since the structure tends to overfit in comparison to other algorithms like RF and EBT. For an increase in one of the features, the entire dataset changes, and hence the system becomes deterministic and extremely greedy. Logistic regression has performed better by reducing overfitting using L2 regularization.

Boosted trees give good accuracy as the structure focuses on the whole dataset rather than on individual points. The ensemble subspace discriminant model classifies with an excellent accuracy of 96.4%, with the ability to perform well on a high-dimensional dataset and with few samples like the bus dataset.

16.5   Conclusion

The restructuring power system is being automated, smart, or getting intelligence. It would not have been possible without ML algorithms. ML techniques inherently adapt to the dynamic changes in a power system. Due to their adaptive, learning, and generous nature, many individual or combined ML models are being proposed to address various power system challenges. A few operations that require ML algorithms [28] are listed briefly in Table 16.1.

In this book chapter, the fundamental operations of power systems and various machine learning techniques, along with its role in making the system intelligent, are explained.

Table 16.1 ML algorithm for different applications.

Analysis	System	ML algorithms
Power flow analysis	IEEE standard buses, real-time bus data	CNN, KNN, SVM, reinforced learning, decision tree, extreme learning machine (ELM), XG Boost & Factorization machine FM
Power quality analysis	IEEE standard buses, real-time micro grid bus	SVM, ICA, CNN, RF, ANN, ELM, variational mode decomposition (VMD), GRU, DT, KNN
Demand/load forecasting	IEEE standard buses, real-time bus data of PV and wind generation, public datasets	LSTM, ELM, RF, tree structured self-organizing map (TS-SOM), SVM, ANN, CNN, PCA, reinforcement learning
Fault analysis	IEEE standard buses, real-time bus data	All supervised, unsupervised, and reinforced learning-type networks, instance-based networks, regression models, deep learning networks, dimension reduction, and kernel-based networks
State estimation	Nonlinear control systems, generation, battery storage	Recurrent neural networks, LSTM, hybrid models with extended Kalman filter

A study on fault detection is performed in IEEE five-bus systems using several machine learning techniques and is depicted in terms of performance, as explained in Section 16.3. Regularization and boosting techniques are also attempted to enhance ML performance. Hybrid models work more efficiently in the case of classification studies. The selection of hyper parameters, layers, performance evaluators, and enhancing techniques plays a vital role in ML algorithms employed in intelligent power systems.

Further Reading

In this chapter, several ML and DL techniques which can be implemented in various aspects of a power system are explained in detail. The techniques can be chosen according to the analysis to be done. The hybrid techniques perform better than individual networks as the dataset could be large for power systems. The case study described in this chapter can be explored further for a system having a greater number of buses. By handling various short-falls in power systems, DL and ML techniques will have a major contribution towards smart power system configurations.

References

1. Momoh, J.A., *Smart grid: Fundamentals of design and analysis*, Wiley, New Jersey USA. 2012.
2. Tikariha, A., Londhe, N.D., Bag, B., Raj, R., Classification of faults in an IEEE 30 bus transmission system using fully convolutional network. *Int. Trans. on Electrical Energy Syst.*, 31, 11, e13134, Oct, 2021, https://doi.org/10.1002/2050- 7038.13134.
3. Malhotra, R. and Jain, A., Fault prediction using statistical and machine learning methods for improving software quality. *J. Inf. Process. Syst.*, 8, 2, 241–262, 2012, 2012.
4. Manohar, P. and Dutta, K.K., Performance analysis of HVDC system including SCFCL. *National Power Engineering Conference (NPEC'10)*, Thiagarajar College of Engineering, Madurai, vol. 15, pp. 214–218, 2, 3 December 2010.
5. Manohar, P. and Dutta, K.K., Effect of SCFCL on the performance of BTB-HVDC system. *Int. conf on Electrical Energy Systems (ICEES-2011), SSN College of Engineering*, vol. 3-5, pp. 288–293, IEEE, Chennai, Jan 2011.
6. Shadi, M.R., Ameli, M.-T., Azad, S., A real-time hierarchical framework for fault detection, classification, and location in power systems using PMUs data and deep learning. *Int. J. of Electrical Power and Energy Syst.*, 134, 1–14, 2022.
7. Dutta, K.K., Poornima, S., Sharma, R., Nair, D., Ploeger, P.G., Applications of recurrent neural network: Overview and case studies, in: *Recurrent Neural Networks*, pp. 23–41, CRC Press, Boca Raton, June 2022.
8. Jahangir, H., Deep learning-based forecasting approach in smart grids with microclustering and bidirectional LSTM network. *IEEE Trans. on Ind. Elec.*, 68, 9, 8298–8309, Sept. 2021.
9. Dehghani, M., Kavousi-Fard, A., Dabbaghjamanesh, M., Avatefipour, O., Deep learning based method for false data injection attack detection in AC smart islands. *IET Gener. Transm. Distrib.*, 14, 24, 5756–65, 2020, https://doi.org/10.1049/gtd2. v14.2410.1049/iet-gtd.2020.0391.
10. Chowdhury, S.D., A novel data-driven method for detection and localization of power system events causing violation of pre-defined ROCOF limits. *Electr. Power Syst. Res.*, 192, 106895, 2021, 10.1016/j.epsr.2020.106895.
11. Ramakrishnan, C., Sridhar, S., Dutta, K.K., Karthick, R., Janamejaya, C., Deep feature selection for wind forecasting-I, in: *Artificial Intelligence for Renewable Energy Systems*, Wiley online Library, New Jersey, 07 February 2022, https://doi.org/10.1002/9781119761686.ch7.
12. Zou, H. and Hastie, T., Regularization and variable selection via the elastic net. *J. R. Stat. Soc. Series B (Stat. Methodol.)*, 67, 301–320, 2005, https://doi.org/10.1111/j.1467-9868.2005.00503.x.
13. Wang, J., An intuitive tutorial to Gaussian processes regression. *Preprint*, 2022, at http://arxiv.org/abs/2009.10862.
14. Kong, W., Dong, Z.Y., Hill, D.J., Luo, F., Xu, Y., Short-term residential load forecasting based on resident behavior learning. *IEEE Trans. Power Syst.*, 33, 1, 2018, 1087–1088, 2018.
15. Makonin, S., Popowich, F., Bartram, L., Gill, B., Bajić, I.V., AMPds: A public dataset for load disaggregation and eco-feedback research, in: *2013 IEEE Electrical Power & Energy Conference*, pp. 1–6, IEEE, 2013.
16. Zoha, A., Gluhak, A., Imran, M., Rajasegarar, S., Non-intrusive load monitoring approaches for disaggregated energy sensing: A survey. *Sensors*, 12, 12, 2012, 16838–16866, 2012.
17. Egarter, D., Bhuvana, V.P., Elmenreich, W., PALDi: Online load disaggregation via particle filtering. *IEEE Trans. Instrum. Meas.*, 64, 2, 2015, 467–477, 2015.
18. Xu, Y. and Milanović, J.V., Artificial-intelligence-based methodology for load disaggregation at the bulk supply point. *IEEE Trans. Power Syst.*, 30, 2, 2015, 795–803, 2015.
19. Rastegar, M., Fotuhi-Firuzabad, M., Zareipour, H., Home energy management incorporating operational priority of appliances. *Int. J. Electrical Power & Energy Syst.*, 74, 2016, 286–292, 2016, Project Report, ECE-674, GC Nikhitha Bonthala.

20. Shirazi, E. and Jadid, S., Optimal residential appliance scheduling under dynamic pricing scheme via HEMDAS. *Energy Buildings*, 93, 2015, 40–49, 2015.

21. Yu, D. and Robertazzi, T.G., Divisible load scheduling for grid computing, in: *Fifteenth IASTED International Conference on Parallel and Distributed Computing and Systems*, vol. 1, pp. 1–6, 2003.

22. Wang, L., Mathew, P., Pang, X., Uncertainties in energy consumption introduced by building operations and weather for a medium-size office building. *Energy Buildings*, 53, 2012, 152–158, 2012.

23. Yalcintas, M., Hagen, W.T., Kaya, A., An analysis of load reduction and load shifting techniques in commercial and industrial buildings under dynamic electricity pricing schedules. *Energy Buildings*, 88, 2015, 15–24, 2015.

24. Zekić-Sušac, M., Mitrović, S., Has, A., Machine learning based system for managing energy efficiency of public sector as an approach towards smart cities. *Int. J. Inf. Manag.*, 58, 102074, 1–12, 2021, https://doi.org/10.1016/j.ijinfomgt.2020.102074.

25. Kwik, S., Martinez, R., Preciaco, J., Sevillano, P., Subias, J., DAS Technology: An opportunity to use fibre optics for asset monitoring and security applications in electric power utilities. *CIGRE*, 1–15, 27 Jan 2023.

26. Balla, A., HadiHabaebi, M., Islam, M.R., Mubarak, S., Applications of deep learning algorithms for supervisory control and data acquisition intrusion detection system. *Cleaner Eng. Technol.*, 9, 1–10, 2022.

27. Poornima, S., Deep learning based fault identification of micro grid transformers, in: *Introduction to AI Techniques for Renewable Energy System*, 1st ed, CRC Press, Boca Raton, 2021.

28. Miraftabzadeh, S.M., Longo, M., Foiadelli, F., Pasetti, M., Igual, R., Advances in the application of machine learning techniques for power system analytics: A survey. *Energies*, 14, 4776, 2021, https://doi.org/10.3390/en14164776.

Part 4

FUTURE RESEARCH OPPORTUNITIES

17

Quantum Computation, Quantum Information, and Quantum Key Distribution

Mohanaprabhu D.[1], Monish Kanna S. P.[1], Jayasuriya J.[1], Lakshmanaprakash S.[1], Abirami A.[1] and Amit Kumar Tyagi[2]*

[1]Department of Information Technology, Bannari Amman Institute of Technology, Erode, Tamil Nadu, India
[2]Department of Fashion Technology, National Institute of Fashion Technology, New Delhi, Delhi, India

Abstract

The most advanced kind of computing, known as quantum computing, makes use of the laws of quantum physics to generate unmatched processing capacity while using less energy than traditional computers. Quantum computing integrates physics, mathematics, computer science, and information theory to reach exponential speed and efficiency above conventional computers by modifying the behavior of microscopic particles like electrons, atoms, and photons. This chapter gives an overview of the key ideas in quantum computing. It begins with a brief history of classical computing and some of its drawbacks before exploring how quantum computing functions and the quantum properties, such as superposition, entanglement, and interference, which give it its power. This study investigates the architecture, hardware, software, design, types, and algorithms uniquely required by quantum computers in order to understand the possibility of a viable quantum computer. It emphasizes the several ways by which quantum computing can have an influence on a variety of industries, including artificial intelligence, traffic optimization, health, and cyber security. The chapter ends with a summary of the benefits and drawbacks of quantum computers as well as the current state of this promising topic. While small-scale quantum computers are being built, it is crucial to understand the background and constraints of conventional computing in order to fully grasp the potential advantages and disadvantages of this new technology.

Keywords: Quantum computing, quantum mechanics, cyber security, artificial intelligence, emerging technology

17.1 Introduction

Quantum computing, a developing area of study, aims to create cutting-edge computational technology based on the laws of quantum physics. Quantum computing utilizes qubits [1], which may concurrently represent both states, as opposed to classical computing which uses bits to represent a binary 0 or 1. Superposition is a characteristic that allows

---

*Corresponding author: amitkrtyagi025@gmail.com

Amit Kumar Tyagi (ed.) *Automated Secure Computing for Next-Generation Systems*, (347–366) © 2024 Scrivener Publishing LLC

quantum computers to do some computations more quickly than conventional computers [2]. Numerous industries, including artificial intelligence, drug development, materials research, and encryption, stand to benefit from quantum computing. In this introduction to quantum computing, we will examine the fundamental ideas of quantum mechanics that form the basis of the technology and some of its most exciting uses. A basic theory in physics called quantum mechanics explains how matter and energy behave on the atomic and subatomic sizes. It is based on the wave–particle duality concept, which postulates that objects like photons and electrons may behave both like waves and like particles. A key concept in quantum physics is superposition, which defines a quantum system's capacity to exist in several states concurrently [3]. This enables a qubit, which is a quantum version of a classical bit, to simultaneously represent 0 and 1. Superposition's ability to do several calculations in parallel, which significantly speeds up some sorts of tasks, is what gives it its strength for quantum computing. Another key idea in quantum physics is called entanglement, which describes a phenomena in which two or more qubits become coupled in such a way that their states are dependent on one another. Because it can be used to develop quantum algorithms that are exponentially quicker than conventional ones, entanglement is a potent tool for quantum computing. The application of quantum mechanics' tenets for safe data transmission and processing is the main goal of the study of quantum information and key distribution. A crucial aspect of this research is quantum key distribution (QKD), which uses the special qualities of quantum systems to share cryptographic keys that cannot be intercepted or duplicated [4]. QKD has the potential to revolutionize cryptography by allowing for the safe transfer of data that is impenetrable to outsiders. This is due to the fact that any effort to measure or intercept the quantum information in motion would cause the qubits' states to change, making it impossible for the attacker to get a copy of the key. The concepts of quantum information and key distribution, including the idea of entanglement, a vital quantum mechanical phenomenon, are introduced in this article. QKD is based on the fact that entanglement allows for an entirely secure information transfer. The most popular way to implement QKD is through the BB84 protocol, which Charles Bennett and Gilles Brassard first presented in 1984. In this approach, Alice and Bob measure the polarization and phase of photons in order to produce a cryptographic key. QKD is regarded as entirely secure since any effort to intercept or quantify the photons being broadcast will result in an interference. This article serves as an excellent introduction to this fascinating area by giving an outline of the fundamentals of QKD and some of its possible applications. Why are those requirements? Quantum information and computation, particularly quantum key distribution, are developing quickly and have the potential to revolutionize how we handle and protect data. The goal of this essay is to explore the fundamental ideas of quantum physics that underlie these technologies and the special properties of quantum key distribution.

A branch of physics known as quantum mechanics explains how matter and energy behave at the atomic and subatomic scales [5]. It is built on a set of ideas that are fundamental to comprehending quantum computation and quantum information transfer and depart from those of classical physics. Entanglement is one of these concepts, which occurs when two or more particles are correlated to the point that their states are dependent on one another, allowing for the transfer of secure information. Another concept is superposition, which allows a quantum system to exist in numerous states at once and speeds up quantum computing exponentially. A contemporary method of computing known as quantum computing makes use of the quantum mechanical phenomenon to offer great processing capability and low energy use. Qubits, which may be in numerous states at once, are used in quantum computing to carry out computations. Qubits, which may exist in a superposition of states instead of the two states that bits can only have in traditional computing, allow for the simultaneous processing of numerous inputs. There are several designs for quantum computers, and their architecture is different from that of a conventional computer. One of the most popular designs is the gate-based approach, which manipulates qubits via quantum gates. The adiabatic model is a different architecture that makes advantage of quantum computing. A variety of methods, like Grover's algorithm for exploring unsorted databases and Shor's algorithm for factoring big numbers, have been created to make use of the particular features of qubits in quantum computing. The study of quantum information focuses on the safe transmission and processing of information using the concepts of quantum physics. A significant component of quantum information is QKD, which offers a brand-new technique for sending cryptographic keys that are impenetrable to intercept or copy. It is thought that QKD is completely safe since any effort to intercept or measure the quantum system would eventually result in changes that would notify the parties involved. QKD uses the characteristics of quantum systems to exchange keys securely. Finally, it should be noted that quantum computing and quantum information, such as quantum key distribution, have an enormous potential to revolutionize data processing and security. Realizing these technologies' full potential requires a thorough understanding of quantum mechanics' fundamental ideas as well as their distinctive characteristics. Quantum computers differ from conventional computers in a number of ways, including the following:

- Superposition: Quantum computers have the ability to live in several superpositions of states. This indicates that a qubit can be concurrently in the 0 and 1 states, allowing quantum computers to carry out many computations at once.
- Entanglement: In addition, quantum computers can get entangled [6]. This makes it possible to correlate two or more qubits such that, despite their distance from one another, their states are reliant on one another. Quantum computers can process information in a highly parallelized manner because of this characteristic.
- Quantum Gates: The building blocks of quantum circuits, which are utilized to carry out quantum calculations, are called quantum gates [7]. Although they work with qubits rather than bits, these gates are akin to conventional logic gates. The Pauli-X gate, Hadamard gate, and CNOT gate are a few examples of popular quantum gates.
- Quantum Algorithms: Programming for quantum computers is known as quantum algorithms. Shor's algorithm, which factors enormous numbers, and Grover's algorithm, which searches an unsorted database, are two examples of well-known quantum algorithms.
- Noise and Error Correction: Dealing with noise and mistakes is one of the main difficulties in quantum computing. The sensitive nature of quantum systems makes calculations susceptible to mistakes even from little disruptions. To find and fix the flaws in quantum calculations, researchers are creating error correction methods.

- Scalability: Scalability is a crucial factor since bigger quantum systems are needed when quantum computers are required to execute more complicated tasks. It can be difficult to create systems that are scalable and capable of carrying out useful calculations.
- Hardware Limitations: Hardware restrictions are still another crucial factor. The maximum number of qubits that may be employed in a calculation restricts the exponential speedup that quantum computers are capable of. The amount of qubits that may be employed in a calculation is being increased by researchers, but this needs major technological improvements.
- Quantum Supremacy: When a quantum computer can do a calculation better than a conventional computer, this is referred to as quantum supremacy. By completing a computation in 200 s that would have taken a conventional computer almost 10,000 years to complete, Google claimed to have attained quantum supremacy in 2019.

Applications: Numerous industries, including chemistry, materials science, encryption, and machine learning, stand to benefit from the development of quantum computers. The modeling of intricate chemical processes, the creation of novel materials, and the improvement of machine learning algorithms are all examples of applications for quantum computing. Do quantum computers have potential flaws? As a rapidly evolving technology, quantum computing has the potential to disrupt many industries. However, there are considerable obstacles that must be removed before quantum computers may be used effectively in practical settings. The following are some of the main challenges facing quantum computing:

- Fragility and Error Correction: Due to their extreme sensitivity to environmental noise and interference, quantum computers are susceptible to computing mistakes [9]. Thermal noise, quantum coherence, or other environmental conditions may cause these mistakes. It is essential for quantum computing to develop efficient techniques for error correction and fault tolerance, but this is still a difficult task.
- Scalability: Quantum computers need a lot of qubits in order to be useful for many applications (quantum bits). Quantum computers now have a finite number of qubits, which limits the amount of processing that they can perform. It is extremely difficult to develop techniques for increasing the number of qubits while preserving coherence and reducing mistakes.
- Limited Range of Applications: Quantum computing has a lot of potential for some applications, such as cryptography and optimization issues, but it is not a good solution for a lot of other issues. Finding new uses for quantum computers and creating new quantum algorithms are continuous challenges.
- High Cost: Building and maintaining quantum computers is costly, and their operation calls for specialized knowledge. As a result, quantum computing is still not widely available, and the expense of setting up and running a quantum computer is a major barrier to entry.
- Lack of Standardization: Since the area of quantum computing is still in its early stages, hardware, software, and algorithms are not yet standardized. This lack

of uniformity hinders advancement in the industry and makes it challenging to compare outcomes across different platforms. It will need continual research and development, partnership between academia and business, and a coordinated effort to improve the accessibility and practicality of quantum computing for a wider variety of applications for these obstacles to be overcome.

Would you want to know how this is being organized at work? Organizing the work of quantum computing is a complex undertaking that involves many different tasks, such as developing new hardware and algorithms as well as evaluating and enhancing existing systems. We shall examine several elements of arranging the work of quantum computing in this article as well as some of the difficulties that scientists and engineers face in this area.

- Equipment Development: Hardware development is one of the most important components of coordinating the work of quantum computing. The design and the construction of new systems that can enable quantum computing, such as quantum processors and quantum memory devices, are referred to as hardware development. Building quantum hardware can be done in a variety of ways, each of which has advantages and disadvantages.
- Superconducting Qubits: Using superconducting qubits is one of the most promising methods for creating quantum hardware. These superconducting circuits, which are generally chilled to 10 million Kelvin, are used to create the qubits. The comparatively lengthy coherence period of superconducting qubits makes them suited for quantum computing.
- Ions Trapped: This is a different method of developing a quantum circuitry. These systems work using ions that can be controlled by lasers and are maintained in place by electric and magnetic fields. Because they have a long coherence period, trapped ion systems are good candidates for some kinds of quantum calculations.
- Topological Qubits: Topological qubits are a third method for creating quantum electronics. The concepts of topology, which investigates the characteristics of things that are conserved through continuous deformations, serve as the foundation for these qubits. Although topological qubits are still in their infancy, they have the potential to be more durable than other kinds of qubits.
- Software Development: Organizing the work of quantum computing also include software development in addition to hardware development. The creation of new quantum-compatible algorithms is a component of quantum software development. Quantum algorithms come in a variety of forms, each with a unique combination of benefits and drawbacks.
- Quantum Simulation: Quantum simulation is one of the most exciting uses of quantum computing. Quantum simulation is the process of simulating the behavior of quantum systems, such as molecules or materials, using a quantum computer. For exploring the characteristics of complicated systems that are challenging to represent using conventional computers, quantum simulation is very helpful.

Quantum cryptography is another interesting area of use for quantum computers [8]. Quantum cryptography aims to develop impenetrable encryption protocols by applying the laws of quantum physics. These protocols are based on the fundamental aspects of quantum physics, including the entanglement and uncertainty principles. One further crucial aspect for quantum computing is optimization. Optimization issues that are challenging or impossible to address with conventional computers can be resolved using quantum computers. Numerous industries, including banking, logistics, and machine learning, experience optimization issues. Despite the potential of quantum computing, there are still a number of issues that need to be resolved before it can be used in practical ways for everyday tasks.

- Error Correction: Correcting errors is one of the biggest problems facing quantum computing. Environmental noise can skew calculations on quantum computers, which are quite vulnerable to it. The discipline is still working on developing efficient techniques for mistake correction and fault tolerance.
- Scalability: Scalability is one of the difficulties of quantum computing. For many applications, quantum computers require a large number of qubits. Quantum computers now have a finite number of qubits, which restricts the amount of processing that they can perform. It is extremely difficult to find ways to increase the quantity of qubits in a quantum computer while preserving coherence and reducing mistakes. Standardization is another difficulty with quantum computing [10]. Hardware, software, and algorithms are not yet standardized, which makes it challenging to compare the outcomes of various systems and impedes the field's advancement.

17.2   Literature Work

Due to the fact that quantum computing is a fast-developing discipline spanning physics, computer science, mathematics, and engineering, there is a substantial amount of literature and background research on the subject. The following sites give an overview of quantum computing and its underlying ideas:

- "Quantum Computation and Quantum Information" by Michael Nielsen and Isaac Chuang: This is a widely used textbook that provides a comprehensive introduction to quantum computing and quantum information theory [11].
- "Quantum Computing: A Gentle Introduction" by Eleanor G. Rieffel and Wolfgang H. Polak: This is a more accessible introduction to quantum computing that provides a gentle overview of the field [12].
- "Introduction to Quantum Mechanics" by David J. Griffiths: This is a classic textbook that covers the fundamentals of quantum mechanics, which is the foundation of quantum computing [13].
- "Quantum Computing for Computer Scientists" by Noson S. Yanofsky and Mirco A. Mannucci: This book provides an introduction to quantum computing from a computer science perspective [14].
- IBM Quantum Education: IBM has developed a comprehensive set of resources and tutorials to help users learn about quantum computing and programming on IBM's quantum computers [15].

- Quantum Open Source Foundation (QOSF): QOSF is a community-driven organization that provides resources and support for those interested in quantum computing, including an open-source library of quantum algorithms and software [16].

For individuals who are interested in learning more about quantum computing, there are a variety of materials accessible, including books, online courses, and research papers. It is a difficult yet fascinating area that might revolutionize computers as we know it.

17.3   Motivation Behind this Study

Quantum computing and quantum key distribution are two of the most exciting and rapidly developing fields of research in contemporary physics. Due to the huge potential influence that these technologies might have in areas like encryption, modeling, and optimization, there has been a large investment in research and development in these areas. Numerous aspects influence the study of quantum computing and quantum key distribution. In this article, we will look at the potential impact of these industries and discuss some of the key factors that are propelling them forward.

Cryptography: One of the primary motives for researching quantum computing and quantum key distribution is the potential influence that they may have on cryptography [17]. Traditional cryptography uses mathematical techniques that are difficult to crack in order to safeguard data. However, as computing power has increased, it has become easier to break many of these techniques via brute-force attacks.

This issue might be resolved via quantum computing. Quantum computers have the potential to solve some mathematical problems 10-fold more quickly than classical computers, including those involved in many popular encryption algorithms.

However, this also poses a substantial obstacle for the field of cryptography. Sensitive data may become exposed to attack if quantum computers are able to defeat several of the popular encryption techniques currently in use. This has increased the interest in creating new encryption methods that are immune to attacks using quantum computing.

One solution to this issue is quantum key distribution. Quantum key distribution uses the ideas of quantum physics to send secure information over a network in contrast to classical cryptography which depends on mathematical techniques to secure information. Entangled particles can be utilized to establish a shared secret key that is impenetrable to intercept and impossible to alter without being noticed.

Optimization and Simulation: The potential effects that quantum computing might have on simulation and optimization are a primary driving force behind the study of this technology. Due to the numerous variables involved, it is challenging to mimic many complicated systems using traditional computers, such as chemical processes and material properties.

Quantum computing has the ability to offer answers by imitating the behavior of quantum systems. The capacity of quantum computers to mimic the behavior of quantum systems is 10 times quicker than conventional computers has allowed for the simulation of complex systems that would ordinarily be difficult to model.

In a similar spirit, quantum computing may have a significant influence on optimization problems. It is difficult to utilize traditional computers to handle many real-world difficulties, including scheduling and route optimization, due to the enormous number of viable solutions.

By concurrently examining every conceivable answer using the concepts of quantum physics, quantum computing offers the possibility of finding solutions to these issues. Significant advancements in industries like logistics, transportation, and manufacturing may result from this.

Principles of Physics: One of the main forces behind the development of quantum computing and quantum key distribution is the potential to deepen our understanding of fundamental physics. Quantum mechanics is one of the most fundamental areas of physics, and studies of quantum systems have led to a number of important discoveries and advancements in our knowledge of the universe.

With the use of quantum computing and quantum key distribution, we can better understand quantum mechanics and investigate novel physics [18]. The creation of novel quantum technologies may potentially lead to new insights in other areas of physics, such as astrophysics and cosmology.

Business Quantum Computing Innovation: Entrepreneurship is essential for the commercialization of novel concepts and technologies. Entrepreneurs have a lot of space for creativity in the area of new goods and services in quantum computing. The creation of novel hardware components and software for quantum computers is only one of many instances [19].

The creation of innovative hardware components is one facet of quantum computing entrepreneurship. Specialized hardware elements needed for quantum computers are not yet commercially accessible. This comprises cryogenic systems, amplifiers, and qubits, the fundamental building blocks of quantum computers. It takes a lot of knowledge and resources to develop these components, making it the perfect sector for entrepreneurship.

Another area of quantum computing entrepreneurship is the development of software for them. To operate, quantum computers need specific software, and creating this software requires knowledge of quantum programming and algorithms. There are numerous options for business owners to create software for quantum computers, including creating brand-new quantum computer algorithms, improving already-existing quantum computer algorithms, and creating software tools for quantum computing [20].

The subject of quantum information and communication is open to entrepreneurship. The processing and transmission of information using the concepts of quantum physics is known as quantum information. This includes quantum cryptography, which uses concepts from quantum physics to secure communication. Entrepreneurs can develop novel quantum informational applications, quantum communication methods, and quantum cryptography protocols.

17.4   Existing Players in the Market

The rapidly evolving field of quantum computing has the potential to fundamentally transform how we approach complex problems. It is a multidisciplinary area that employs concepts from mathematics, computer science, and physics to create powerful machines that can handle and analyze enormous volumes of data much more quickly than ordinary computers. In this article, we will look at some of the major players in the quantum comput-ing market along with their products, services, and contributions to the industry.

IBM: IBM is one of the main rivals in the quantum computing sector [21]. Through sig-nificant expenditures in R&D, the company has achieved significant strides in the realm of quantum computing. IBM has created a variety of quantum computing systems, including the IBM Q System One, which has a processing capability of 20 qubits and is designed to operate at a temperature of 15 million Kelvin. The company also provides IBM Quantum Experience, a cloud-based tool that lets programmers experiment with quantum algo-rithms. IBM is also exploring the potential applications of quantum computing in sectors including finance, healthcare, and energy in cooperation with a number of other companies and organizations.

Microsoft: Microsoft is a key competitor in the quantum computing sector [22]. To help programmers design quantum applications, the company developed the Quantum Development Kit. Additionally, Microsoft has developed the Q# quantum programming language, allowing developers to write quantum programs using Visual Studio. The busi-ness is developing a full-stack quantum computing system, from hardware to software, and has developed Azure Quantum, a cloud-based platform that enables programmers to try out quantum algorithms on the cloud.

Google: In recent years, Google has made considerable strides in quantum computing [23]. The company built the 53-qubit Sycamore quantum computer and has achieved quantum supremacy, which means that it can solve problems that traditional computers cannot in a reasonable period of time. Google is also investigating the uses of quantum computing in artificial intelligence and machine learning. The company developed the Cirq quantum computing platform with the goal of helping programmers design quantum algorithms.

Rigetti Computing: The development of quantum computers is the focus of a new business named Rigetti Computing [24]. The company developed Forest, a cloud-based platform that provides developers with the resources that they need to construct quantum algorithms. The company has recently announced a 16-qubit quantum computer that cloud-based cod-ers may use. Rigetti Computing is working with several other companies and organizations to explore the potential applications of quantum computing in sectors including banking, materials research, and drug development.

D-Wave Systems: D-Wave Systems is a Canadian company that specializes in creating quantum computers. The company has developed the 2,000-qubit D-Wave 2000Q quan-tum computer which is meant for use in business. The company's cloud-based platform Leap provides developers with the tools that they need to design quantum algorithms [25]. D-Wave Systems is investigating the potential applications of quantum computing in sec-tors including finance, healthcare, and logistics in conjunction with a number of other com-panies and organizations.

Intel: Intel is a key competitor in the quantum computing sector. The company built Tangle Lake, a 49-qubit quantum computer, and is looking into how it may be used in machine learning and artificial intelligence [26]. Additionally, Intel is working with several other companies and organizations to explore the potential applications of quantum computing in fields including materials research and cryptography.

Alibaba: Alibaba, a Chinese company, has made large investments in quantum computing. The company has developed the Quantum Computing Cloud, a platform that runs on the cloud and provides programmers with the tools that they need to implement quantum algorithms. Alibaba is researching the use of quantum computing for machine learning and artificial intelligence.

17.5 Quantum Key Distribution

QKD can be discussed with following points:
ID Quantique: Swiss-based ID Quantique is a global leader in the distribution of quantum keys. A variety of QKD systems, including the QKD Plus, the Cerberis QKD, and the Clavis2, have been created by the business. Secure key exchange over fiber optic and free-space channels is made possible by these methods. Other quantum technologies, such as quantum sensors and quantum random number generators, have also been created by ID Quantique.

QuintessenceLabs: QuintessenceLabs is an Australian business that specializes in quantum cryptography and key distribution [27]. The business has created several secure key exchanges across fiber optic and free-space channels in QKD technologies, such as the qCrypt and the qStream. Other quantum technologies, such as quantum random number generators and quantum key management systems, have also been created by QuintessenceLabs.

Toshiba: During the early 2000s, Toshiba, a Japanese business, has been researching quantum key distribution. The business has created a number of secure key exchange through fiber optic channels known as QKD systems, such as the Quantum Key Distribution System. Other quantum technologies, such as quantum memories and quantum computers, are also being studied and developed by Toshiba.

17.6 Proposed Models for Quantum Computing

QUANTUM MACHINE LEARNING
In an emerging subject called quantum machine learning, machine learning and quantum computing are combined [27–31]. A proposed model for quantum machine learning typically involves the following steps:

- Data Encoding: The input data is encoded into quantum states that can be manipulated by quantum algorithms. This typically involves mapping the classical data to a set of qubits.
- Quantum Algorithm Design: A quantum algorithm is designed to perform the desired machine learning task. This method may be used to accelerate some calculations by making use of quantum superposition and entanglement.

- Quantum Circuit Construction: The quantum algorithm is implemented as a quantum circuit, which is a series of quantum gates that manipulate the input qubits to produce the desired output.
- Measurement: A classical outcome is obtained by measuring the quantum circuit's output and using it to inform additional analysis or decision-making.
- Classical Post-processing: Following the quantum measurement, the classical result is processed using traditional machine learning methods like clustering, classification, or regression.

The main objective of quantum machine learning is to use quantum computing to speed up traditional machine learning tasks like classification, clustering, and optimization. While there are many proposed models for quantum machine learning, the field is still in its early stages of development and faces significant technical challenges, such as improving the scalability and reliability of quantum hardware.

QUANTUM DEEP LEARNING

The goal of quantum deep learning is to use the strength of quantum computing in conjunction with deep learning methods to address challenging issues in speech recognition, natural language processing, and picture recognition. A proposed model for quantum deep learning typically involves the following steps:

- Data Encoding: The input data is encoded into quantum states that can be manipulated by quantum algorithms. This may involve encoding the input data into a quantum circuit or using a quantum embedding technique to map the data to a quantum state.
- Quantum Neural Network Design: A quantum neural network is designed to perform the desired deep learning task. It is possible that this network was created to maximize the performance of quantum phenomena like entanglement and superposition.
- Quantum Circuit Construction: The quantum neural network is implemented as a quantum circuit, which is a series of quantum gates that manipulate the input qubits to produce the desired output.
- Measurement: A classical outcome is obtained by measuring the quantum circuit's output and using it to inform additional analysis or decision-making.
- Classical Post-processing: Using conventional deep learning techniques like backpropagation and gradient descent, the classical result from the quantum measurement is post-processed.

The main objective of quantum deep learning is to use quantum computing to augment and speed up deep learning activities. While there are many proposed models for quantum deep learning, the field is still in its early stages of development and faces significant technical challenges, such as improving the scalability and reliability of quantum hardware and designing effective quantum neural network architectures.

1) DATA ENCODING

➢ Data encoding is the process of converting information from one format or representation to another, typically for the purpose of storage, transmission, or security. This entails taking the original data and translating it into a code or language that a computer or other device can understand.

➢ Binary encoding, which represents data using a sequence of 0s and 1s, and ASCII encoding, which utilizes a set of predefined codes to represent letters, numbers, and other characters, are two examples of different types of data encoding.

➢ Other common encoding methods include hexadecimal encoding, which uses a base-16 number system to represent data, and Unicode encoding, which can represent a vast range of characters from different languages and scripts.

➢ The purpose of data encoding is to ensure that data can be reliably stored, transmitted, and interpreted by different systems and devices. By converting data into a standardized format, it becomes easier to share and work with information across different platforms and applications.

2) QUANTUM ALGORITHM DESIGN

➢ Quantum algorithm design involves creating algorithms that can be executed on quantum computers. These algorithms are intended to address issues that are challenging or impractical for conventional computers by utilizing the special features of quantum computing, such as superposition and entanglement.

➢ Designing a quantum algorithm often entails a number of steps. Finding a problem that a quantum algorithm might be able to handle more quickly is the first step. This could include issues with simulation, optimization, or cryptography.

➢ The next step is for the designer of the quantum algorithm to create a quantum algorithm that can resolve the issue. This entails developing a set of instructions that can be carried out on a quantum computer utilizing mathematical techniques and concepts from quantum physics.

➢ Once the quantum algorithm has been developed, it needs to be tested and optimized. This involves simulating the algorithm on a classical computer to determine its performance characteristics and then making adjustments to improve its efficiency.

➢ Finally, quantum algorithm can be implemented on a quantum computer, and the results can be compared to those obtained from a classical simulation. This allows the algorithm designer to evaluate the effectiveness of the algorithm and make further adjustments if necessary.

➢ Numerous novel algorithms are being created in the active subject of quantum algorithm design that has the potential to transform industries including encryption, machine learning, and optimization.

3) QUANTUM CIRCUIT CONSTRUCTION

➤ Quantum circuit construction involves creating circuits that can be executed on quantum computers. Quantum gates, which are comparable to the classical logic gates used in digital circuits, are employed to build these circuits.

➤ Building a quantum circuit normally entails a number of steps. Finding the issue that a quantum circuit has to address is the first step. This could include problems in areas such as cryptography, optimization, or simulation.

➤ Next, the quantum circuit designer needs to select the appropriate set of quantum gates to use in the circuit. Different quantum gates can be used to perform different operations, such as single-qubit rotations, two-qubit entanglement, and measurements.

➤ Once the quantum gates have been selected, the designer can begin constructing the circuit by arranging the gates in a sequence that achieves the desired computation. The circuit can be represented graphically using a circuit diagram, with each gate represented by a symbol.

➤ After the circuit has been constructed, it needs to be optimized to improve its efficiency. Rearranging the gates to cut down on the number of operations needed or utilizing alternative gates to do the same computation more quickly can help with this.

➤ The quantum circuit may then be put into practice on a quantum computer, and the outcomes can be contrasted with those of a classical simulation. This allows the circuit designer to evaluate the effectiveness of the circuit and make further adjustments if necessary.

➤ Quantum circuit construction is a challenging task, as quantum gates can behave differently from classical gates due to the phenomenon of superposition and entanglement. Quantum circuits may be created to address issues that are beyond the scope of classical computers but with proper planning and optimization.

4) MEASUREMENTS

➤ Quantum machine learning methods must include measurement in order for them to provide output that is compatible with that of traditional computing. Measurements are frequently employed in quantum machine learning to extract information from the quantum state of a qubit or collection of qubits.

➤ In quantum machine learning, the qubits' quantum state is frequently changed by performing operations like rotations, entanglement, and superposition utilizing quantum gates. These techniques may be used to both compute on and encrypt classical data into a quantum state.

➤ The quantum state must be measured once the computation is finished in order to produce a classical result. When measuring using quantum machine learning, the qubit or qubits of interest are often subjected to a measurement gate. A qubit or qubits' quantum state is collapsed by the measurement gate into a classical state that may be read out and utilized as output.

➢ As the quantum state of the qubits before measurement is in a superposition of several states, the result of a measurement in quantum machine learning is probabilistic. The amplitudes of the associated quantum states in the superposition determine how likely it is that a certain classical state will be observed as a result of the measurement.

➢ Quantum machine learning frequently uses measurement to categorize data since the result of the measurement may be used to place a data point in a certain class. Because the results of the measurement may be utilized to direct the optimization process, it can also be used to optimize the parameters in quantum machine learning models.

➢ In general, measurement is a key component of quantum machine learning, enabling quantum computers to produce classical output that may be applied to forecast future events or direct actions.

5) CLASSIC POST-PROCESSING

➢ As it includes processing and interpreting the output from a quantum computer, traditional post-processing is a crucial part of quantum machine learning algorithms. In quantum machine learning, classical post-processing is necessary because the output obtained from a quantum computer is typically probabilistic and can be difficult to interpret directly.

➢ The output of a quantum computer after performing a quantum computation is generally a collection of probability amplitudes that depict the quantum state of the qubits. It is necessary to transform this quantum state into a classical output that may be applied to forecast future events or direct decision-making.

➢ In quantum machine learning, classical post-processing often entails applying conventional algorithms to evaluate and comprehend the results produced by the quantum computer. This can use methods like decision trees, support vector machines, and Bayesian inference.

➢ Post-selection, which is the act of rejecting or rerunning specific portions of the quantum computing to provide a more precise result, may also be a part of traditional post-processing. Post-selection is often necessary in quantum machine learning because the output obtained from a quantum computer is probabilistic and can be affected by errors and noise.

➢ Another important aspect of classical post-processing in quantum machine learning is error correction and fault tolerance. Quantum computers are susceptible to errors and noise, which can affect the accuracy of the output. Traditional post-processing methods can be applied to reduce these faults and increase the output's dependability.

➢ Generally speaking, classical post-processing is a crucial part of quantum machine learning algorithms because it enables the processing and interpretation of a quantum computer's output in a way that can be utilized to generate predictions or inform decision-making.

17.7   Simulation/Result

A set of probabilities corresponding to various potential measurements of the quantum state is the output of a quantum computing process. These probabilities are obtained by measuring the final quantum state of the qubits after the quantum computation has been performed. The probabilities are utilized to produce predictions or serve as a basis for decision-making and depend on the amplitudes of the associated quantum states in the superposition. Due to the probabilistic nature of quantum physics, which causes the same quantum computation to occasionally generate distinct outcomes, the output of quantum computation can be challenging to comprehend. However, some issues, including prime factorization and optimization issues, might be resolved by quantum computing far more quickly than by classical computing. Quantum computing has the ability to speed up problem solving and provide fresh perspectives in fields like chemistry, materials science, and cryptography. Quantum computing has the potential to transform computing and offer solutions to issues that are now insurmountable for conventional computers.

17.7.1   Issues and Challenges in Quantum Computing

Quantum computing research has the potential to fundamentally change how we process information today. Unlike classical computing, which utilizes binary digits or bits that can only take two values, quantum computing uses quantum bits or qubits, which may exist in a superposition of states and be entangled with one another (0 or 1). Quantum computers are especially useful for applications in modeling, optimization, and cryptography since they can do some tasks 10 times quicker than conventional computers. Despite its promise, quantum computing is still in its infancy and must overcome a number of challenges before it can be applied in practical settings. We will discuss some of the key problems with quantum computing in this essay.

Qubit Stability and Error Correction: One of the biggest challenges in quantum computing is qubit stability. Qubits are extremely sensitive to their surroundings and are readily decohered or disrupted by noise and other forms of interference. This is in contrast to conventional bits, which are rather stable and can be consistently stored and retrieved. This can cause errors in quantum calculations and make it difficult to execute complex algorithms.

To address this problem, researchers are developing error-correction algorithms that can detect and rectify qubit flaws. These codes encrypt data using multiple qubits in a way that enables the detection and correction of faults. These codes, however, are still in the experimental stage and need a lot of qubits to work properly.

Using topological qubits, which are shielded from noise and other disturbances by virtue of their distinctive topology, is another method for ensuring qubit stability. Topological qubits are still in the early phases of development and are now being studied by academics at Microsoft and other organizations.

Scalability: Scalability in quantum computing is a significant problem. Although several small-scale quantum computers with a few qubits have previously been constructed, it is difficult to scale up to systems with hundreds or thousands of qubits. This is because managing and controlling quantum systems become more difficult as the number of qubits rises due to the exponential growth of quantum systems' complexity.

Researchers are investigating various methods for scaling up quantum computers to address this problem. One method for developing fault-tolerant systems that can withstand faults in a lot of qubits is to employ quantum error correcting codes. An alternative approach called quantum annealing uses a quantum computer to locate a system's lowest energy state and resolve optimization problems.

Physical Implementation: The physical implementation of qubits presents another significant obstacle for quantum computing. Topological, trapped ion, and superconducting qubits are just a few examples of the several qubit types that may be used in quantum computers. Each of these qubit types has advantages and disadvantages, and researchers are currently working out the best ways to build extremely large quantum computers.

One of the most promising approaches is to use superconducting qubits, which are based on the superconductivity rules and are very easy to produce and maintain. Two examples of small-scale quantum computers that have already been built utilizing superconducting qubits are the IBM Q Experience and the Google Quantum AI lab. Scaling out to bigger systems with hundreds or thousands of qubits still presents a serious challenge.

Atomic Algorithms: Another challenge in quantum computing is the development of quantum algorithms that can utilize the unique capabilities of quantum computers. While a handful of quantum algorithms already exist, such as Grover's algorithm for database search and Shor's algorithm for factoring enormous numbers, many more algorithms must be developed in order to fully utilize the possibilities of quantum computers.

17.7.2 Issues in Quantum Key Distribution

Quantum key distribution, a cryptographic technique, enables the sharing of a secret key between two parties through an unsecure communication channel. The security of QKD may be impregnable even to an adversary with limitless computer power due to the principles of quantum physics. For applications like online banking, official communications, and military operations, QKD has the ability to change the encryption and provide secure communication channels. However, a lot of challenges and issues need to be overcome before QKD can be considered a viable technique. In this post, we will go through some of the main issues with quantum key distribution and discuss the research being done to address them.

Rate of Key Distribution: One of the trickiest difficulties in QKD is the key distribution rate. How rapidly the two parties can develop and exchange secret keys is constrained by the QKD system's speed and the efficiency of the key creation and detection procedures. Since QKD often has a significantly lower key distribution rate than traditional cryptography, this can restrict some of its practical uses.

To solve this issue, researchers are exploring ways to speed up the QKD key distribution. Using multiplexing, which enables the consolidation of several QKD channels into a single communication link, is one strategy. Using quicker detectors and better light sources is a different strategy that could speed up and improve the effectiveness of key generation.

Equipment Security: Device security presents another significant difficulty in QKD. The reliability of the equipment used to produce and detect the quantum signals is crucial to QKD systems. Any device breach, such as one caused by tampering or hacking, might put the QKD system's security at danger.

To address this issue, researchers are developing strategies to increase the security of QKD devices. To stop tampering, one strategy is to utilize tamper-evident packaging and physical security features like seals and alarms. Another strategy is to check the devices' integrity using device authentication methods like quantum fingerprinting.

Environmental Elements: Environmental elements that can contaminate the security of the QKD system and induce errors in the quantum signals include temperature changes and electromagnetic interference. These factors may also limit the functionality and range of the QKD system.

To get around this problem, researchers are developing strategies to decrease the influence of environmental factors on QKD. Utilizing active stabilization methods like temperature control and noise filtering is one way to maintain the QKD system's stability. A different approach is to use free-space QKD, which allows QKD signals to travel through the atmosphere while avoiding many of the environmental factors that hinder fiber-based QKD.

Cost: Cost is another issue that QKD faces. The use of QKD systems in commercial applications may be limited since they are currently significantly more expensive than conventional cryptography systems.

To circumvent this issue, researchers are developing strategies to reduce the cost of QKD systems. Using integrated photonics is one strategy that enables the fabrication of the QKD system using conventional semiconductor manufacturing techniques, hence lowering the system's cost and complexity. Using wavelength-division multiplexing is an alternative strategy that lowers the overall cost of the QKD system by combining numerous QKD channels into a single communication link.

QKD Over a Distance: Communication across vast distances is another difficulty in QKD. Because of communication channel losses and the influence of the environment, QKD systems perform worse across longer distances. The scope and the scalability of QKD systems are so constrained.

Researchers are creating methods to enable long-distance QKD to get around this problem. The use of quantum repeaters is one strategy that enables QKD signals to be amplified and re-transmitted over vast distances without jeopardizing the system's security. A different strategy is to utilize satellite-based QKD.

17.7.3 The Future Ahead With Quantum Computation, Quantum Information, and Quantum Key Distribution

The subject of quantum technology has made great strides in recent years, with various exciting developments in quantum computation, quantum information, and quantum key distribution. In this piece, we will discuss the future of these places and any potential societal effects.

The Quantum Computer: Quantum computation has the potential to drastically change how information is processed and complex problems are resolved. The most recent quantum computers are still in their infancy and have limited capabilities, but the potential for their development in the future is enormous.

> ➢ Quantum computers may be used in the realm of cryptography to break existing encryption techniques, which is one possible application for quantum computation. As a reaction to this danger, quantum-resistant encryption

methods that are impervious to attacks from quantum computers are being created.

➢ Quantum computers can also mimic complex systems that are beyond the capabilities of traditional computers, which is another application field for them. This might have a big influence on a lot of fields, such as materials science, drug discovery, and climate modeling.

Additionally, complex systems like energy grids, financial portfolios, and transportation networks might all be optimized using quantum computers. This might result in substantial increases in efficiency and cost savings.

Despite the potential benefits of quantum computing, a number of challenges need to be overcome before it can be applied to daily life. They encompass expanding to larger systems with thousands of qubits, creating error correction techniques, and enhancing qubit stability.

Quantum Information: Another area of quantum technology with a lot of room for advancement is quantum information. In this area, information is sent and processed using quantum mechanics.

One interesting quantum information application in the field of secure communication is QKD, which uses quantum information to transmit secret keys between two parties. Since QKD is based on concepts from quantum physics, it is secure from eavesdropper attacks.

Another use for them would be quantum sensors, which use quantum mechanics to measure physical variables like magnetic fields, gravity, and temperature with unprecedented accuracy. Quantum sensors may have significant implications for fields including geology, navigation, and medical imaging.

Quantum information may also be utilized to improve the performance of traditional communication systems by using quantum repeaters to extend the range of fiber optic communication networks.

Although there may be some benefits to quantum information, there are still many challenges to be overcome before this technology can be used in daily life. They include making quantum sensors more dependable and scalable as well as developing more efficient ways of handling and transmitting quantum information.

Distribution of Quantum Keys: QKD, a promising area of quantum technology, has the potential to fundamentally alter how secure data is sent. Since QKD is based on concepts from quantum physics, it is secure from eavesdropper attacks.

QKD uses quantum physics to create a shared secret key that two parties may use to encrypt and decode messages. Quantum states that have been sent back and forth between the two parties during generating the key are measured to form a shared bit string.

One of the numerous advantages of QKD over conventional encryption methods is that it is safe against attacks from quantum computers. However, there are still a few issues that need to be worked out before QKD can be considered an effective approach.

17.8   Conclusion

In summary, quantum computing has the potential to fundamentally alter how we approach challenging issues that are either impractical or impossible to tackle with conventional computers. Future models like quantum annealers and fault-tolerant quantum computers might lead to substantial developments in areas like artificial intelligence, materials research, and encryption. However, before quantum computing becomes a commonplace technology, there are still considerable obstacles to be solved. These difficulties include enhancing error correction methods, creating algorithms particularly for quantum computers, and creating more effective qubit technologies. Despite these difficulties, there has been substantial progress in the study of quantum computing, and this trend is likely to continue. Science and technology may see new discoveries that were previously unthinkable as quantum computers get more potent and more widely available.

References

1. Sharma, M., Choudhary, V., Bhatia, R., Malik, S., Raina, A., Khandelwal, H., Leveraging the power of quantum computing for breaking RSA encryption. *Cyber-Phys. Syst.*, 7, 1–20, 2020.

2. Perepechaenko, M. and Kuang, R., Quantum encryption of superposition states with quantum permutation pad in IBM quantum computers. *EPJ Quantum Technol.*, 10, 2023.

3. Ugwuishiwu, C., Orji, U., Ukwueze, O., Ogbobe, P., A review on the fundamental concepts of quantum elements, efficient quantum algorithms and quantum error correcting codes. *Int. J. Sci. & Technol. Res.*, 11, 1, 2022.

4. Begimbayeva, Y. and Zhaxalykov, T., Research of quantum key distribution protocols: BB84, B92, E91. *Sci. J. Astana IT Univ.*, 10, 4–14, 2022.

5. Sharma, A., *A textbook on modern quantum mechanics*, CRC Press, Boca Raton, 2021.

6. Romaniuk, R., Information quantum technologies. *Elektronika - Konstrukcje Technologie Zastosowania*, 62, 4–10, 2021.

7. Flarend, A. and Hilborn, B., *Quantum gates and quantum circuits*, Oxford University Press, Oxford, UK, 2022.

8. Subramani, S., Munuswamy, S., Arputharaj, K., Svn, S.K., Review of security methods based on classical cryptography and quantum cryptography, Shalini Subramani, Selvi Morcid Icon, Kannan A. & Santhosh Kumar Svn (eds.), *Cybern. Syst.*, 1–19, 11 Jan 2023.

9. Nilesh, K., Joshi, P., Panigrahi, P., Automated error correction in superdense coding, with implementation on superconducting quantum computer, 2022. Available at: https://arxiv.org/abs/2210.15161, https://doi.org/10.48550/arXiv.2210.15161.

10. Yang, H., Wang, J., Sun, X., Research on quantum computing standard system architecture and roadmap. *J. Phys. Conf. Ser.*, 2433, 012035, 2023.

11. Oskin, M., *Quantum computing-lecture notes*, Available at: https://arxiv.org/abs/1907.09415, 2023.

12. Sgarbas, K., Review of quantum computing: A gentle introduction by Eleanor Rieffel and Wolfgang Polak. *ACM SIGACT News*, 44, 31–35, 2013.

13. Griffiths, D. and Schroeter, D., *Introduction to quantum mechanics*, Cambridge University Press, Cambridge, 2018.

14. Yanofsky, N. and Mannucci, M., *Quantum computing for computer scientists*, 2008.

15. Maldonado-Romo, A. and Yeh, L., Quantum computing online workshops and hackathon for Spanish speakers: A case study, in: *2022 IEEE International Conference on Quantum Computing*

and Engineering (QCE), 2023. Available at arXiv:2302.12119, https://doi.org/10.48550/arXiv.2302.12119.

16. Myanmar, Myo & Foundation, Open. Open society foundations and myanmar. 2020. Available refer to https://www.opensocietyfoundations.org/newsroom/the-open-society-foundations-in-myanmar.

17. G., M. and Sivaram, R., CloudQKDP: Quantum key distribution protocol for cloud computing, in: *2016 International Conference on Information Communication and Embedded Systems (ICICES)*, Chennai, India, 2016. https://doi.org/10.1109/ICICES.2016.7518922 .

18. Soulas, A., On the measurement problems in (relativistic) quantum mechanics, 2023. Available at arXiv:2303.03465. https://doi.org/10.48550/arXiv.2303.03465.

19. Paul, S. and Mitra, A., A review on applications of quantum computing in machine learning technology, *Quantum Sci. Technol.*, 2022, http://dx.doi.org/10.4018/978-1-7998-9183-3.ch005.

20. Miranskyy, A., Using quantum computers to speed up dynamic testing of software, 2022. arXiv:2209.04860, https://doi.org/10.48550/arXiv.2209.04860

21. Sharma, S., Basnet, S., Khanal, R., Implementation of error correction on IBM quantum computing devices. *J. Nepal Phys. Soc.*, 8, 7–15, 2022. https://doi.org/10.1007/978-1-4842-7246-6.

22. Hooyberghs, J., Develop with the microsoft quantum development kit, 2022.

23. Duan, H., The principles, algorithms and state-of-art applications of quantum computing. *J. Phys. Conf. Ser.*, 2386, 012025, 2022.

24. Murali, P., Lao, L., Martonosi, M., Browne, D., Designing calibration and expressivity-efficient instruction sets for quantum computing, 2021, Available at IEEE Xplore. https://doi.org/10.48550/arXiv.2106.15490.

25. Grundy, Q., Imahori, D., Mahajan, S., Garner, G., Timothy, R., Sud, A., Soklaridis, S., Buchman, D., Cannabis companies and the sponsorship of scientific research: A cross-sectional Canadian case study. *PLoS One*, 18, e0280110, 2023.

26. Yahyavi, M., Jafarizadeh, M., Karimi, N., Heshmati, A., Quantum circuit for the direct measurement of the three-tangle of three-qubit states. *Prog. Theor. Exp. Phys.*, 2022, 2022.

27. Hogan, O., Charles, M., Kortt, M., The market's filthy lesson: Disruption for business and management education in australian public universities, 2023, http://dx.doi.org/10.1007/978-3-031-12725-0_12.

28. V., S.A., Soni, G., Tyagi, A.K., A review on recent trends in quantum computation technology, in: *Handbook of Research on Quantum Computing for Smart Environments*, A. Tyagi (Ed.), pp. 48–64, IGI Global, 2023, https://doi.org/10.4018/978-1-6684-6697-1.ch003.

29. P., S., Soni, G., Tyagi, A.K., Kakulapati, V., J. S., S.M., Singh, R.K., Quantum computing and the Qubit: The future of artificial intelligence, in: *Handbook of Research on Quantum Computing for Smart Environments*, A. Tyagi (Ed.), pp. 231–244, IGI Global, 2023, https://doi.org/10.4018/978-1-6684-6697-1.ch013.

30. Deshmukh, A., Patil, D.S., Soni, G., Tyagi, A.K., Cyber security: New realities for industry 4.0 and society 5.0, in: *Handbook of Research on Quantum Computing for Smart Environments*, A. Tyagi (Ed.), pp. 299–325, IGI Global, 2023, https://doi.org/10.4018/978-1-6684-6697-1.ch017.

31. Deshmukh, A., Patil, D.S., Pawar, P.D., Kumari, S., P., M., Recent trends for smart environments with AI and IoT-based technologies: A comprehensive review, in: *Handbook of Research on Quantum Computing for Smart Environments*, A. Tyagi (Ed.), pp. 435–452, IGI Global, 2023, https://doi.org/10.4018/978-1-6684-6697-1.ch023.

18

Quantum Computing, Qubits with Artificial Intelligence, and Blockchain Technologies: A Roadmap for the Future

Amit Kumar Tyagi[1]*, Anand Kumar Mishra[2], Aswathy S. U.[3] and Shabnam Kumari[4]

[1]Department of Fashion Technology, National Institute of Fashion Technology, New Delhi, Delhi, India
[2]Computer Science and Engineering, NIIT University, Neemrana, Rajasthan, India
[3]Department of Computer Science and Engineering, Marian Engineering College, Trivandrum, Kerala, India
[4]SRM Institute of Science and Technology, Chennai, Tamil Nadu, India

Abstract

Quantum computing is a rapidly evolving field of technology that has the potential to revolutionize traditional computing. It lies its foundation on that of quantum mechanics to execute computations that are much more efficient than traditional computation. The basic building block of quantum computing is the qubit, which can exist in multiple states at once, allowing for simultaneous calculations to take place. The combination of quantum computing with artificial intelligence (AI) has the potential to create powerful new applications in various domains, including the discovery of drugs, financial models, and sophisticated optimization problems. By leveraging the speed and efficiency of quantum computing, AI algorithms can be run faster and more accurately, leading to significant improvements in prediction accuracy and decision-making. Similarly, quantum computing has the potential to enhance the security and efficiency of blockchain technologies. By using the principles of quantum mechanics, it is possible to create more secure and efficient cryptographic algorithms, which can improve the security and privacy of blockchain networks. Additionally, quantum computing can be used to improve the scalability and efficiency of blockchain networks, allowing for faster and more efficient transaction processing. Hence, the combination of quantum computing with AI and blockchain technologies has the potential to create new opportunities for innovation and disruption across a wide range of industries. While the technology is still in its early stages, the potential benefits are significant, and continued research and development are likely to lead to further breakthroughs in the years to come. Hence, this chapter will discuss such topics in detail, which will help researchers find quality information regarding these emerging topics.

Keywords: Quantum computing, qubits, smart era, artificial intelligence and blockchain technologies

---

*Corresponding author: amitkrtyagi025@gmail.com

Amit Kumar Tyagi (ed.) *Automated Secure Computing for Next-Generation Systems*, (367–384) © 2024 Scrivener Publishing LLC

18.1 Introduction to Quantum Computing and Its Related Terms

Quantum computing is typically a form of computation that utilizes the foundation of quantum mechanics to execute computations. Instead of traditional binary computing, which relies on bits that have a value of 0 or 1, quantum bits are used in quantum computations (qubits) which can take both 0 and 1 values simultaneously. This allows quantum computers to perform certain calculations much faster than classical computers [1]. Here are some related terms in quantum computing [2]:

- Superposition: A qubit can be in a superposition of both 0 and 1 states simultaneously.
- Entanglement: Entanglement is a phenomenon where two qubits become connected and their states become correlated, even if they are physically far apart.
- Quantum gate: A quantum gate is a unitary operator that acts on one or more qubits to perform a quantum computation.
- Quantum algorithm: A quantum algorithm is a set of instructions that can be executed on a quantum computer to perform a specific calculation or solve a particular problem.
- Quantum supremacy: Quantum supremacy refers to the ability of a quantum computer to perform a calculation that would be impossible for a classical computer to perform in a reasonable amount of time.
- Quantum error correction: Quantum error correction is a set of techniques that can be used to protect quantum information from errors that may arise due to decoherence and other environmental factors.
- Quantum annealing: Quantum annealing is a type of quantum computing that is specifically designed to solve optimization problems.
- Quantum cryptography—the use of quantum mechanics to secure communication channels, making them resistant to eavesdropping.
- Quantum teleportation—a technique for transmitting quantum information over long distances without physically transmitting the quantum state itself.
- Quantum machine learning—the use of quantum computing to speed up machine learning algorithms, particularly in cases where large datasets are involved.
- Quantum key distribution: Quantum key distribution is a technique for secure communication that uses the principles of quantum mechanics to ensure that messages cannot be intercepted without being detected.

A few advantages of quantum computers in this smart era are as follows:

- Speed: Quantum computers can perform certain types of calculations much faster than classical computers, which is particularly useful for applications such as optimization and simulation.

- Security: Quantum computers are capable of tackling through various encryption algorithms which are used to protect information. It also has the potential to create and develop new secure encryption techniques.
- Machine learning: Quantum computers can potentially improve machine learning algorithms, allowing for faster and more accurate predictions.
- Complex problem solving: Quantum computers can potentially solve complex problems in fields such as chemistry, biology, and materials science by simulating complex systems at the quantum level.
- Real-time data processing: Quantum computers can process large amounts of data in real-time, which is particularly useful for applications such as real-time optimization and decision-making.

In summary, quantum computers have the potential to revolutionize many industries in this smart era, including finance, healthcare, and transportation [3]. As such, they are an important area of research and investment for governments and companies around the world. Each term related to quantum computing will then be discussed in the following subsections.

18.1.1 Quantum Computing

Quantum computing is a comprehensive technology that has the potential to compute and manipulate information through quantum mechanics. Unlike classical computers, which use bits that can be either 0 or 1, quantum computers use quantum bits (or qubits), which can exist in multiple states simultaneously. This allows quantum computers to perform certain tasks much faster than classical computers, especially for problems that involve a large amount of data or complex calculations—for example, quantum computers could potentially be used to break encryption algorithms, simulate complex chemical reactions, or optimize financial portfolios. However, quantum computing is still in its early stages of development, and there are significant challenges in building and operating quantum computers, including the need for extremely precise and stable control systems and the problem of quantum decoherence, which can cause errors in computations. Note that, despite these challenges, quantum computing has the potential to revolutionize many fields and industries, from cryptography and cybersecurity to drug discovery and materials science [4].

18.1.2 Qubits

Qubits, or quantum bits, are the basic building blocks of quantum computing. Unlike classical bits, which can have only two states (0 or 1), qubits can exist in multiple states simultaneously, a property known as superposition. In addition to superposition, qubits also exhibit another important property called entanglement, which means that the state of one qubit can be correlated with the state of another qubit, even if they are physically separated by a great distance. Superposition and entanglement together support quantum computers to compute and execute tasks and processes at a much faster speed than conventional systems even with massive data volume—for example, a quantum computer with just a few dozen qubits could ideally get through numerous encryption algorithms which are essential in securing online transactions in the current world. However, working with qubits is not easy, and there are many challenges in building and operating quantum computers. Qubits are very fragile, and they can be easily disturbed by their environment, leading to errors in computations. In addition, qubits require extremely precise and stable control systems to manipulate and measure their states. Hence, despite these challenges, qubits are a fundamental part of quantum computing, and they are the key to unlocking the potential of this revolutionary technology [5].

18.1.3   Quantum Computation

Quantum computation is a type of computation that uses quantum mechanical phenomena to perform calculations. Unlike classical computation where bits are either 0 or 1, quantum computation uses qubits, which can exist in superpositions of both 0 and 1 states. This enables quantum computers to perform certain calculations much faster than classical computers. Note that one of the key algorithms in quantum computation is Shor's algorithm, which can factor large numbers exponentially faster than any known classical algorithm. This has significant implications for cryptography, as many encryption algorithms rely on the difficulty of factoring large numbers [6]. Quantum computers can also be used for optimization problems, such as finding the shortest route between multiple points, with potentially significant applications in fields like logistics and transportation. Quantum computation also faces several challenges, including the difficulty of building stable and error-corrected qubits and the challenge of controlling and manipulating large numbers of qubits. However, significant progress has been made in recent years, with several companies and research institutions building quantum computers with increasing numbers of qubits and longer coherence times. Quantum computation has the potential to transform fields such as drug discovery, materials science, and machine learning by enabling calculations that are currently infeasible on classical computers. It is also important to throw light on the fact that not all issues can be solved at a faster rate through quantum computing. This would, hence, leave conventional computers a significant scope for competition.

18.1.4   Quantum Interference

Quantum interference is a phenomenon that occurs when two or more quantum states interfere with each other, resulting in a new state that is a combination of the original states. This interference can be constructive, where the new state has a greater probability of being measured than either of the original states, or destructive, where the new state has a lower probability of being measured—for example, double-slit experiment. In this experiment, a beam of particles, such as electrons or photons, is directed at a screen with two slits. When the particles pass through the slits, they interfere with each other and create an interference pattern on the screen. This pattern is caused by the constructive and destructive interference of the particles as they pass through the slits [7].

Another example of quantum interference is the quantum eraser experiment. In this experiment, a beam of entangled particles is directed at a double-slit apparatus, but a detector is placed in front of one of the slits to determine which path the particles take. This measurement collapses the wavefunction of the particles, and the interference pattern disappears. However, if a second detector is placed to detect which-path information after the particles have passed through the slits, the interference pattern reappears. This is because the second detector erases the which-path information, allowing the particles to interfere with each other once again. Note that quantum interference plays a crucial role in quantum computing, where quantum bits (qubits) can be in a superposition of states and can interfere with each other to perform computations much faster than classical computers.

18.1.5   Quantum Information

An area of study that focuses on transmission, processing, and storing data through quantum mechanical systems is called quantum information. The quantum information theory extends classical information theory by allowing quantum states to be used as information carriers, which can be in a superposition of multiple classical states and can exhibit entanglement, a unique quantum mechanical correlation between particles. Quantum information theory has led to the development of new types of information processing technologies, such as quantum computers, quantum cryptography, and quantum communication protocols. These technologies promise to revolutionize the way we process and secure information, offering much higher computational power and stronger encryption than classical methods. Quantum computers use quantum bits or qubits to perform computations using the principles of quantum mechanics. Because qubits can exist in superpositions of multiple states at once, quantum computers have the potential to solve certain problems much faster than classical computers. Quantum cryptography uses quantum states to secure communication channels against eavesdropping, while quantum communication protocols use quantum entanglement to transmit information over long distances with higher security than the classical methods [8].

In summary, quantum information theory represents a fundamental shift in the way we understand and use information and has the potential to transform fields such as cryptography, machine learning, and materials science.

18.1.6   Quantum Superposition

Quantum superposition is a fundamental concept in quantum mechanics, which refers to the ability of a quantum particle to exist in multiple states simultaneously. In classical physics, a particle can only be in one state at a time, but in the quantum world, a particle can be in a state of superposition where it exists in a combination of multiple states at the same time—for example, a photon of light can exist in a superposition of two polarization states, such as vertical and horizontal polarizations, at the same time. This means that when measured, the photon could be found to be polarized in either direction, and the probability of each outcome is determined by the wavefunction of the superposition. Another example is a quantum bit or qubit in a superposition of two basis states, typically denoted as $|0\rangle$ and $|1\rangle$. A qubit can be in a state of superposition where it exists as a linear combination of $|0\rangle$ and $|1\rangle$ states, such as $(|0\rangle + |1\rangle) / \sqrt{2}$. This superposition enables the faster execution of certain specific processes when compared with conventional and classic computers [9].

Hence, superposition is a crucial concept in quantum mechanics, and it plays a significant role in many quantum technologies, including quantum computing, quantum cryptography, and quantum sensing. It is also a fundamental feature of quantum entanglement, where two or more particles can be in a superposition state that is entangled, which means that the states of the particles are correlated in a way that cannot be explained by classical physics.

18.1.7 Quantum Mechanics

Quantum mechanics is a branch of physics that studies the behavior of matter and energy at the atomic and subatomic level. It was developed in the early 20th century to explain the peculiar behavior of particles at the atomic scale, such as electrons, protons, and photons. The principles of quantum mechanics are fundamentally different from those of classical mechanics, which describe the behavior of larger objects such as planets and cars. In quantum mechanics, particles do not have definite properties, such as position and momentum, until they are measured. Particles instead exist in a state of superposition, meaning that they exist in all possible states simultaneously until an observation forces them to "collapse" into one particular state. Quantum mechanics is often described as probabilistic, as the behavior of particles is described by probability distributions rather than exact values. This probabilistic nature has profound implications for how we understand the behavior of matter and energy at the atomic and subatomic level. Quantum mechanics has led to the development of many important technologies, including transistors, lasers, and MRI machines. It is also the foundation for emerging technologies such as quantum computing and quantum cryptography, which have the potential to revolutionize fields such as data processing and cybersecurity. Despite its many successes, quantum mechanics remains a challenging and mysterious field of study, and there are still many unanswered questions about the nature of quantum behavior [10].

18.1.8 Quantum Machine Learning

Quantum machine learning is a rapidly evolving interdisciplinary field that explores the intersection of quantum computing and machine learning. It aims to develop algorithms that leverage the unique properties of quantum systems to solve complex machine learning problems faster and more efficiently than classical computers. In classical machine learning, data is typically processed using algorithms that manipulate classical bits, which can exist in one of two states: 0 or 1. However, in quantum machine learning, data is processed using quantum bits or qubits, which can exist in multiple states simultaneously. This enables quantum computers to perform certain computations exponentially faster than classical computers. There are various approaches to quantum machine learning, including quantum-inspired classical algorithms, quantum-enhanced classical algorithms, and fully quantum algorithms. Some of the most promising applications of quantum machine learning include optimization, pattern recognition, and natural language processing [11]. However, quantum machine learning is still in its early stages, and there are many technical and practical challenges that need to be overcome before it can become a mainstream technology. Nonetheless, with the rapid advancement of both quantum computing and machine learning, it is an exciting area of research with great potential for future breakthroughs.

18.1.9   Quantum Deep Learning

Quantum deep learning is an emerging field that seeks to combine the power of quantum computing and deep learning, a subfield of machine learning that uses neural networks to analyze and learn from large datasets. The aim of quantum deep learning is to develop new algorithms that can process and analyze data exponentially faster than classical deep learning algorithms. Quantum deep learning offers a key advantage which basically translates to its leveraging capacity to perform operations on quantum data that is massive. Quantum deep learning algorithms use quantum circuits to manipulate quantum states and perform computations that are difficult or impossible to perform using classical computers. Some of the potential applications of quantum deep learning include quantum chemistry, materials science, and drug discovery, where the ability to simulate complex quantum systems could lead to significant advances in these fields [12]. However, quantum deep learning is still in its early stages of development, and there are many technical challenges that need to be addressed before it can become a practical technology—for example, quantum deep learning algorithms require large numbers of qubits, which are difficult to build and maintain, and the noise and errors inherent in quantum computing make it challenging to achieve high accuracy in computations. Nonetheless, researchers are making rapid progress in developing new quantum deep learning algorithms, and it is an exciting area of research with the potential to revolutionize many fields.

18.1.10   Importance of Quantum Computer in Today's Era

Quantum computers are a new kind of computer that use the principles of quantum mechanics to perform calculations. These computers essentially use qubits that complement the system in performing computations faster, and their potential lies in their ability to solve and perform tasks that are way beyond the reach of general computers—for example, quantum computers could be used to:

- Break encryption codes: Many of the encryption algorithms used to protect sensitive information today rely on the difficulty of factoring large numbers. Quantum computers could potentially factor large numbers much faster than classical computers, rendering many of these encryption algorithms useless.
- Optimize complex systems: Quantum computers could be used to optimize complex systems, such as the design of new drugs, the scheduling of transportation networks, and the management of supply chains.
- Simulate quantum systems: Quantum computers could be used to simulate complex quantum systems, such as chemical reactions or the behavior of materials at the quantum level, which is difficult or impossible to simulate with classical computers.
- Improve machine learning: Quantum computers could be used to improve machine learning algorithms, allowing for faster and more accurate predictions.

While quantum computers are still in the early stages of development, they have the potential to revolutionize many fields, including cybersecurity, finance, and scientific research. As such, they are an important area of research and investment for governments and companies around the world [3, 4].

18.1.11   Organization of this Work

This research work is organized into 10 main sections. Section 18.1 covers the introduction to quantum computing and describes all essential terms related to quantum computation. While Section 18.2 focuses on how quantum computation is different from security aspects, Section 18.3 highlights the use of AI and blockchain for quantum computing. Section 18.4 elucidates the process involved in building a quantum computer, while Sections 18.5 and 18.6 throw light on some of the issues in quantum computation. Section 18.7 focuses on some of the major challenges involved in implementing quantum computation-based models, and the paper concludes with Sections 18.8 and 18.9 that highlight the future opportunities of quantum computing and its integration with AI and blockchain, respectively. The paper is summarized and concluded with Section 18.10.

18.2   How Quantum Computing is Different from Security?

Quantum computing and security are two different concepts that are related in some ways, but they are not the same thing. As discussed above, quantum computing refers to the use of quantum mechanics to process information. Unlike classical computers, which use binary digits (bits) to represent information, quantum computers use quantum bits (qubits), which can exist in multiple states simultaneously. This allows quantum computers to perform certain types of calculations exponentially faster than classical computers, which has implications for a wide range of applications, including cryptography, machine learning, and scientific simulations.

Security, on the other hand, refers to the protection of information and systems from unauthorized access, use, disclosure, disruption, modification, or destruction. Security is a critical concern in many areas, including finance, healthcare, government, and national defense. In the context of computing, security involves protecting data, networks, and systems from various types of threats, including malware, hacking, and social engineering attacks.

While quantum computing has the potential to revolutionize many areas of science and technology, including cryptography, it also poses a significant security risk. Quantum computers could potentially break many of the encryption protocols that are currently used to secure sensitive information, such as credit card numbers, passwords, and government secrets. This has led to a significant effort to develop new cryptographic protocols that are resistant to attacks by quantum computers, known as post-quantum cryptography.

In summary, quantum computing and security are two different concepts that are related in some ways, but they address different aspects of information technology. While quantum computing has the potential to transform many areas of science and technology, it also poses a significant security risk that must be addressed through the development of new cryptographic protocols.

18.2.1   Quantum Computing vs Qubit vs Cryptography

Quantum computing, qubits, and cryptography are all related concepts in the context of information technology, but they address different aspects of computing and security.

- Quantum computing refers to the use of quantum mechanics to perform computations. Unlike classical computers, which use bits to represent information as 0s and 1s, quantum computers use qubits, which can exist in multiple states simultaneously. This property of qubits allows quantum computers to perform certain types of calculations much faster than classical computers, which has implications for many areas of science and technology.
- Qubits are the basic building blocks of quantum computers. They are the quantum analog of bits, and they can exist in multiple states simultaneously, a property known as superposition. This allows qubits to perform certain types of calculations much faster than classical bits. In addition to superposition, qubits also exhibit entanglement, which means that the state of one qubit can be correlated with the state of another qubit, even if they are physically separated.
- Cryptography, on the other hand, is the science of secure communication. It involves using mathematical algorithms and protocols to ensure the confidentiality, integrity, and authenticity of information transmitted over a network. Cryptography is used to secure a wide range of applications, including online banking, e-commerce, and government communications.

In the context of quantum computing, cryptography is a critical concern because quantum computers could potentially break many of the encryption protocols that are currently used to secure sensitive information. This has led to a significant effort to develop new cryptographic protocols that are resistant to attacks by quantum computers, which is known as post-quantum cryptography. In summary, quantum computing, qubits, and cryptography are all related concepts, but they address different aspects of computing and security. Quantum computing is the use of quantum mechanics to perform computations, qubits are the basic building blocks of quantum computers, and cryptography is the science of secure communication. The development of post-quantum cryptography is an important area of research in quantum computing, given the potential for quantum computers to break many of the encryption protocols currently used to secure sensitive information.

18.3   Artificial Intelligence—Blockchain-Based Quantum Computing?

Quantum computing, AI, and blockchain are being explored as drivers for business transformation and intelligent change by leading organizations.

18.3.1   How Artificial Intelligence is Related to Quantum Computing?

Artificial intelligence (AI) and quantum computing are two cutting-edge technologies that are related in several ways. Here are some examples:

- Faster Processing: Quantum computing has the potential to accelerate the processing power of AI algorithms significantly. This could lead to the development of more advanced AI models that can process vast amounts of data much faster than classical computers.
- Optimization Problems: Quantum computing can be used to solve optimization problems that are difficult for classical computers to solve. Many AI problems, such as training neural networks or optimizing decision-making processes, are also optimization problems that could be solved more efficiently with quantum computing.
- Improved Data Analytics: Quantum computing could help improve the accuracy of data analytics and machine learning models. By processing larger datasets and uncovering complex relationships between data points, quantum computing could lead to more accurate predictions and insights.
- Enhanced Security: Quantum computing could be used to improve the security of AI systems, particularly for data encryption and decryption. With the ability to break conventional encryption methods, quantum computing could also help develop new encryption methods that are more secure.
- Novel Algorithms: Quantum computing could enable the development of new algorithms and techniques that are not possible with classical computing. These novel algorithms could be used to enhance AI models, data analytics, and decision-making processes.

In summary, the integration of quantum computing and AI has the potential to unlock new capabilities and solve problems that are difficult or impossible with classical computing. As these technologies continue to evolve, we can expect to see more innovative applications, and use cases emerge in fields such as finance, healthcare, and cybersecurity.

18.3.2   How Blockchain is Related to Quantum Computing?

Blockchain and quantum computing are both rapidly developing fields in the realm of information technology, and they are related in several ways. As discussed in [13], blockchain is a decentralized digital ledger that is used to record and verify transactions across a network of computers. The transactions are recorded in blocks, which are linked together in a chain, hence the name "blockchain". The primary benefit of blockchain technology is that it allows for secure, transparent, and tamper-proof transactions without the need for a centralized authority or intermediary. Quantum computing, on the other hand, is a computing paradigm that uses quantum mechanical phenomena to process information. The relationship between blockchain and quantum computing arises primarily because of the potential for quantum computers to break the cryptographic algorithms that underpin many blockchain systems. The most commonly used cryptographic algorithms for blockchain are based on elliptic curve cryptography, which is vulnerable to attacks by quantum computers.

This means that, in theory, a sufficiently powerful quantum computer could break the encryption used to secure the blockchain and tamper with the transaction records.

To address this issue, researchers are developing new cryptographic protocols that are resistant to attacks by quantum computers, known as post-quantum cryptography. Post-quantum cryptography involves using different cryptographic algorithms that are believed to be secure even in the face of attacks by quantum computers. In summary, blockchain and quantum computing are related in the sense that quantum computing has the potential to break the cryptographic algorithms used to secure many blockchain systems. To address this issue, researchers are developing new post-quantum cryptographic protocols that are believed to be secure even in the face of attacks by quantum computers.

18.3.3   Artificial Intelligence-Based Quantum Computing

Artificial intelligence and quantum computing are both cutting-edge technologies that have the capability to bring about revolutionary changes in many domains of science and technology. AI-based quantum computing is an emerging field that combines these two technologies to create powerful new computing capabilities. Quantum computing is based on the principles of quantum mechanics, which allow quantum computers to perform certain calculations exponentially faster than classical computers [14]. On the contrary, AI consists of algorithms and machine learning strategies that enable computer systems to execute tasks which would otherwise necessitate human intervention. AI-based quantum computing is still in its early stages, but it has already shown promise in a number of areas. One potential application is in drug discovery, where quantum computers can be used to simulate the behavior of molecules, allowing scientists to identify potential new drugs more quickly and accurately. Another area where AI-based quantum computing could have a big impact is in optimization problems, such as logistics and supply chain management. Quantum computers can perform complex optimization calculations much faster than classical computers, and AI algorithms can be used to help identify the best solutions. Overall, the combination of AI and quantum computing has the potential to create new computing capabilities that are much more powerful than anything that currently exists. As the field continues to develop, we can expect to see many exciting new applications and breakthroughs in science and technology.

18.3.4   Artificial Intelligence—Blockchain-Based Quantum Computing

Artificial intelligence, blockchain, and quantum computing are all cutting-edge technologies with the potential to revolutionize the way we approach various problems in science and technology. AI and quantum computing have already been discussed in the previous answer, so I will focus on the combination of AI, blockchain, and quantum computing. Blockchain is a distributed ledger technology that enables secure and transparent peer-to-peer transactions without the need for intermediaries. The combination of blockchain with AI and quantum computing can create new opportunities for building secure and scalable decentralized applications. One potential application of AI–blockchain–quantum computing is in the field of finance, where quantum computers can be used to break the encryption of blockchain transactions. By using AI algorithms to detect suspicious behavior and blockchain to secure the transaction history, financial institutions can ensure the security of their transactions.

Another application is in the field of supply chain management, where blockchain can be used to create a transparent and immutable record of the entire supply chain, from the source of raw materials to the end product. Quantum computing can be used to optimize the supply chain by analyzing large amounts of data, and AI can be used to identify potential issues and recommend solutions. Overall, the combination of AI, blockchain, and quantum computing has the potential to create new opportunities for secure and scalable decentralized applications. As the field continues to develop, we can expect to see many exciting new applications and breakthroughs in science and technology [15].

18.4   Process to Build a Quantum Computer

Building a quantum computer is a highly complex and challenging process that involves several stages. Here are the basic steps involved in building a quantum computer:

- Choose a Quantum Computing Architecture: There are several different approaches to building a quantum computer, each with its advantages and challenges. Some of the popular quantum computing architectures include superconducting qubits, trapped ions, and topological qubits.
- Build a Quantum Processor: Once the architecture is chosen, the next step is to build a quantum processor, which is the heart of a quantum computer. A quantum processor is a complex device that contains qubits, which are the quantum equivalent of classical bits. The qubits must be highly isolated from the environment to prevent decoherence, which is a major challenge in quantum computing.
- Connect the Qubits: Once the qubits are built, the next step is to connect them in a way that enables quantum operations. This involves designing a quantum circuit, which is a series of operations performed on the qubits to perform a specific computation.
- Control and Readout: The quantum processor must be controlled and read out using sophisticated electronics and software. This requires specialized expertise in areas such as microwave engineering, cryogenics, and computer science.
- Error Correction: Finally, quantum computers are highly prone to errors due to decoherence and other factors. To overcome this challenge, error correction techniques are used to detect and correct errors in the quantum computation.

Hence, building a quantum computer is a highly interdisciplinary endeavor that requires expertise in a range of fields, including physics, engineering, and computer science [16]. The process is highly complex and challenging, but the potential benefits of quantum computing are vast, including breakthroughs in materials science, drug discovery, and cryptography.

18.5 Popular Issues with Quantum Computing in this Smart Era

Quantum computing is a rapidly developing field with the potential to revolutionize various aspects of modern technology. However, as with any emerging technology, there are several issues and challenges that need to be addressed before it can become a practical and useful tool in our smart era [10]. Some of the issues and challenges with quantum computing include the following:

- Hardware Development: The development of quantum computers is still in its early stages, and the current quantum computers are still relatively small and fragile. Scaling up quantum computers to larger sizes and improving their reliability and stability is a major challenge.
- Error Correction: Quantum computers are susceptible to errors due to the delicate nature of quantum states. Developing error correction techniques that can effectively detect and correct errors in a quantum system is crucial for building reliable quantum computers.
- Programming: Programming a quantum computer is a complex and difficult task, and there is currently a shortage of programmers with the necessary skills to work with quantum computers.
- Compatibility: Quantum computers are not compatible with classical computing systems, and developing software that can run on both classical and quantum systems is a significant challenge.
- Security: Several encryption algorithms can be easily broken by quantum computation. Developing quantum-safe encryption methods is therefore a critical challenge.
- Cost: Building and maintaining quantum computers is an expensive undertaking, and making quantum computing accessible and affordable to a wider audience will require a significant investment.

Hence, addressing these challenges will require collaboration between researchers, engineers, and policymakers as well as investment in research and development. Despite these challenges, quantum computing has the potential to revolutionize many fields, including cryptography, materials science, drug discovery, and machine learning.

18.6 Problems Faced with Artificial Intelligence–Blockchain-Based Quantum Computing

Artificial intelligence, blockchain, and quantum computing are three rapidly evolving technologies with enormous potential for transforming industries and societies. However, each of these technologies also presents its own set of challenges and issues [15]. Here are some of the problems faced with artificial intelligence–blockchain-based quantum computing:

- Data Privacy and Security: As AI systems generate and analyze large amounts of data, there is a growing concern about data privacy and security.

Blockchain-based solutions can provide decentralized and secure the storage and sharing of data, but they can be slow and resource-intensive. Quantum computing, on the other hand, could potentially break the current encryption methods and compromise data privacy and security.

- Bias and Ethics: AI systems can perpetuate biases and discrimination if not designed and trained properly. Blockchain technology can provide transparency and traceability to prevent tampering with data and algorithms, but it cannot eliminate bias and ethical issues. Quantum computing can also raise ethical concerns, such as the ability to crack passwords and access sensitive information.
- Scalability and Interoperability: AI systems require significant computing power and resources to operate effectively, and blockchain-based solutions can be slow and cumbersome. Quantum computing is still in its early stages and requires significant development to become scalable and interoperable.
- Regulation and Standards: As AI, blockchain, and quantum computing become more prevalent, there is a need for clear regulations and standards to ensure safety, privacy, and security. Governments and industry organizations are still developing the standards and guidelines for these technologies.
- Cost: AI, blockchain, and quantum computing require significant investments in research, development, and infrastructure. While these technologies can provide significant benefits, the high costs may limit their adoption and accessibility to smaller businesses and organizations.

In summary, while AI, blockchain, and quantum computing hold tremendous promise for transforming industries and societies, they also present significant challenges and issues that need to be addressed. By addressing these challenges, we can ensure that these technologies are used responsibly and ethically and that their benefits are realized by all.

18.7   Challenges with the Implementation of Quantum Computers in Today's Smart Era

Quantum computing has the potential to revolutionize many areas of technology and science, but there are several challenges that must be overcome before it can be implemented on a large scale in today's smart era [13]. Some of these challenges include the following:

- Complexity: Quantum computing is much more complex than classical computing, and it requires a completely different approach to software development, hardware design, and data processing. This complexity makes it challenging to build and maintain quantum computers.
- Error Correction: Quantum computers are inherently noisy, and the qubits that store quantum information are susceptible to errors. Therefore, error correction is critical to the success of quantum computing, but implementing effective error correction algorithms is a major challenge.

- Scalability: Building a quantum computer with just a few qubits is relatively straightforward, but scaling up to thousands or millions of qubits is a significant challenge. The current quantum computers are still in the early stages of development, and they have a long way to go before they can compete with classical computers in terms of speed and scalability.
- Integration with existing technology: Quantum computers will need to integrate with existing classical computing technology and infrastructure, which presents a number of challenges—for example, quantum algorithms that can work with classical data formats will need to be developed, and quantum networks will need to coexist with classical networks.
- Security: Quantum computers have the potential to break many of the cryptographic algorithms that are used to secure today's communications and transactions. Therefore, developing new quantum-resistant cryptographic algorithms is a critical challenge for the implementation of quantum computers in today's smart era.

In summary, the challenges with the implementation of quantum computers in today's smart era are significant, but they are not insurmountable. As researchers continue to develop new technologies and algorithms and as the field of quantum computing matures, we can expect to see significant progress in the coming years.

18.8   Future Research Opportunities with Quantum Computing

The field of quantum computing is evolving at rapid rates and is truly revolutionary [17, 18, 21, 22]. Some of the future research opportunities in quantum computing include the following:

- Quantum Algorithms: Developing new algorithms that can take advantage of the unique capabilities of quantum computers, such as the ability to perform certain types of calculations exponentially faster than classical computers.
- Quantum Machine Learning: Exploring the use of quantum computers to accelerate machine learning algorithms, which could lead to advances in fields such as drug discovery, financial modeling, and image and speech recognition.
- Quantum Cryptography: Investigating new cryptographic protocols that can take advantage of the inherent security properties of quantum mechanics, such as the ability to securely transmit information without the risk of interception or eavesdropping.
- Quantum Simulation: Using quantum computers to simulate complex physical systems, such as chemical reactions or materials properties, which could lead to advances in fields such as drug discovery, materials science, and renewable energy.
- Quantum Networking: Developing new networking protocols that can take advantage of the unique properties of quantum mechanics, such as the ability

to teleport quantum states, which could lead to advances in fields such as secure communication and distributed computing.

- Quantum Error Correction: Developing new techniques for error correction in quantum computers, which are highly susceptible to errors due to noise and other sources of interference.
- Quantum Sensors: Investigating the use of quantum sensors for applications such as precision measurement, medical diagnostics, and environmental monitoring.

Hence, the field of quantum computing is full of exciting research opportunities, and we can expect to see many new breakthroughs and discoveries in the years ahead.

18.9 Future Opportunities with Artificial Intelligence–Blockchain-Based Quantum Computing

Artificial intelligence, blockchain, and quantum computing are all rapidly advancing fields that are expected to have a significant impact on the future [19, 20, 24]. Let us explore the potential opportunities that may arise from the intersection of these three fields.

- Improved Machine Learning Models: Quantum computing has the potential to significantly enhance the processing capabilities of machine learning models. With quantum computing, AI models could process larger datasets, perform more complex calculations, and uncover insights that are not possible with classical computing.
- Secure and Transparent Data: Blockchain technology offers a secure and transparent way to store data [23]. By using blockchain-based AI systems, organizations can ensure that their data is secure, and they can track any changes to the data. This can be especially important in applications such as healthcare or finance where data privacy is crucial.
- Autonomous Decisions: AI algorithms can make decisions based on data analysis. By incorporating quantum computing, the decision-making process can be accelerated, allowing for near-real-time autonomous decisions.
- Fraud Detection: Combining blockchain and AI can enhance fraud detection in financial transactions. The transparency of blockchain technology can help identify fraudulent transactions, while AI algorithms can analyze the data to identify patterns of fraud.
- Supply Chain Management: Blockchain technology can be used to track the movement of goods throughout a supply chain. By integrating AI algorithms, the data can be analyzed to identify inefficiencies in the supply chain, which can be optimized for improved performance.
- Cybersecurity: Quantum computing can be used to enhance the security of blockchain-based systems [23]. By using quantum encryption, data can be protected against attacks from even the most advanced cybercriminals.

In summary, the integration of AI, blockchain, and quantum computing has the potential to revolutionize industries, from finance to healthcare and supply chain management to cybersecurity. The possibilities are endless, and it will be exciting to see how these technologies continue to evolve and shape the future. Further in [25], authors explain how the novel research can be published at reputed platforms and can be helpful for research/scientific community for further/future research.

18.10 Conclusion

The convergence of artificial intelligence, blockchain, and quantum computing has the potential to bring about a new era of technological innovation and advancement. This combination of cutting-edge technologies could lead to significant improvements in fields such as healthcare, finance, supply chain management, and cybersecurity. AI algorithms can process vast amounts of data to make autonomous decisions, while blockchain technology provides a secure and transparent way to store and track this data. Meanwhile, quantum computing can accelerate the processing power, making it possible to perform complex calculations that are not possible with classical computing. The possibilities for these technologies are limitless, and as they continue to evolve, we can expect to see even more significant advancements in the coming years. It is an exciting time to be a part of the technological revolution, and the future looks promising for those who are at the forefront of AI, blockchain, and quantum computing research and development.

References

1. Egger, D.J., Gambella, C., Marecek, J., McFaddin, S., Mevissen, M., Raymond, R., Simonetto, A., Woerner, S., Yndurain, E., Quantum computing for finance: State-of-the-art and future prospects. *IEEE Trans. Quantum Eng.*, 1, 1–24, 2020 Oct 13.

2. Cao, Y., Romero, J., Olson, J.P., Degroote, M., Johnson, P.D., Kieferová, M., Kivlichan, I.D., Menke, T., Peropadre, B., Sawaya, N.P., Sim, S., Quantum chemistry in the age of quantum computing. *Chem. Rev.*, 119, 19, 10856–915, 2019 Aug 30.

3. Gyongyosi, L. and Imre, S., A survey on quantum computing technology. *Comput. Sci. Rev.*, 31, 51–71, 2019, ISSN 1574-0137, https://doi.org/10.1016/j.cosrev.2018.11.002.

4. Wu, Y., Bao, W.S., Cao, S., Chen, F., Chen, M.C., Chen, X., Chung, T.H., Deng, H., Du, Y., Fan, D., Gong, M., Strong quantum computational advantage using a superconducting quantum processor. *Phys. Rev. Lett.*, 127, 18, 180501, 2021 Oct 25.

5. Henriet, L., Beguin, L., Signoles, A., Lahaye, T., Browaeys, A., Reymond, G.O., Jurczak, C., Quantum computing with neutral atoms. *Quantum*, 4, 327, 2020 Sep 21.

6. Gill, S.S., Xu, M., Ottaviani, C., Patros, P., Bahsoon, R., Shaghaghi, A., Golec, M., Stankovski, V., Wu, H., Abraham, A., Singh, M., AI for next generation computing: Emerging trends and future directions. *Internet Things*, 19, 100514, 2022 Aug 1.

7. Mezquita, Y., Alonso, R.S., Casado-Vara, R., Prieto, J., Corchado, J.M., A review of k-NN algorithm based on classical and quantum machine learning, in: *Distributed Computing and Artificial Intelligence, Special Sessions, 17th International Conference. DCAI 2020.* Advances in Intelligent Systems and Computing, Rodríguez González, S., *et al.*, vol. 1242, Springer, Cham, 2021. https://doi.org/10.1007/978-3-030-53829-3_20

8. Mangini, S., Tacchino, F., Gerace, D., Bajoni, D., Macchiavello, C., Quantum computing models for artificial neural networks. *Europhys. Lett.*, 134, 1, 10002, 2021 May 14.

9. Jazaeri, F., Beckers, A., Tajalli, A., Sallese, J.M., A review on quantum computing: From qubits to front-end electronics and cryogenic MOSFET physics, in: *2019 MIXDES-26th International Conference" Mixed Design of Integrated Circuits and Systems*, pp. 15–25, IEEE, 2019 Jun 27.

10. Huang, H.L., Wu, D., Fan, D., Zhu, X., Superconducting quantum computing: A review. *Sci. China Inf. Sci.*, 63, 1–32, 2020 Aug.

11. Bravyi, S., Dial, O., Gambetta, J.M., Gil, D., Nazario, Z., The future of quantum computing with superconducting qubits. *J. Appl. Phys.*, 132, 16, 160902, 2022 Oct 28.

12. Guillaud, J. and Mirrahimi, M., Repetition cat qubits for fault-tolerant quantum computation. *Phys. Rev. X*, 9, 4, 041053, 2019 Dec 12.

13. Fernandez-Carames, T.M. and Fraga-Lamas, P., Towards post-quantum blockchain: A review on blockchain cryptography resistant to quantum computing attacks. *IEEE Access.*, 8, 21091–116, 2020 Jan 23.

14. Khalid, Z.M. and Askar, S., Resistant Blockchain cryptography to quantum computing attacks. *Int. J. Sci. Bus.*, 5, 3, 116–25, 2021.

15. Cui, W., Dou, T., Yan, S., Threats and opportunities: Blockchain meets quantum computation, in: *2020 39th Chinese Control Conference (CCC)*, pp. 5822–5824, IEEE, 2020 Jul 27.

16. Martonosi, M. and Roetteler, M., Next steps in quantum computing: Computer science's role. *arXiv preprint*, 2019 Mar 25, Available at: https://arxiv.org/abs/1903.10541

17. Glover, F., Kochenberger, G., Du, Y., Quantum bridge analytics I: A tutorial on formulating and using QUBO models. *4OR*, 17, 335–71, 2019 Dec.

18. von Burg, V., Low, G.H., Häner, T., Steiger, D.S., Reiher, M., Roetteler, M., Troyer, M., Quantum computing enhanced computational catalysis. *Phys. Rev. Res.*, 3, 3, 033055, 2021 Jul 16.

19. Piattini, M., Peterssen, G., Pérez-Castillo, R., Quantum computing: A new software engineering golden age. *ACM SIGSOFT Softw. Eng. Notes*, 45, 3, 12–4, 2021 Oct 3.

20. Bertels, K.O., Sarkar, A., Hubregtsen, T., Serrao, M., Mouedenne, A.A., Yadav, A., Krol, A., Ashraf, I., Quantum computer architecture: Towards full-stack quantum accelerators, in: *2020 Design, Automation & Test in Europe Conference & Exhibition (DATE)* pp. 1–6, IEEE, 2020 Mar 9.

21. V., S.A., Soni, G., Tyagi, A.K., A review on recent trends in quantum computation technology, in: *Handbook of Research on Quantum Computing for Smart Environments*, A. Tyagi (Ed.), pp. 48–64, IGI Global, 2023, https://doi.org/10.4018/978-1-6684-6697-1.ch003.

22. P., S., Soni, G., Tyagi, A.K., Kakulapati, V., J. S., S.M., Singh, R.K., Quantum computing and the qubit: The future of artificial intelligence, in: *Handbook of Research on Quantum Computing for Smart Environments*, A. Tyagi (Ed.), pp. 231–244, IGI Global, 2023, https://doi.org/10.4018/978-1-6684-6697-1.ch013.

23. Deshmukh, A., Patil, D.S., Soni, G., Tyagi, A.K., Cyber security: New realities for Industry 4.0 and Society 5.0, in: *Handbook of Research on Quantum Computing for Smart Environments*, A. Tyagi (ed.), pp. 299–325, IGI Global, 2023, https://doi.org/10.4018/978-1-6684-6697-1.ch017.

24. Deshmukh, A., Patil, D.S., Pawar, P.D., Kumari, S., P., M., Recent trends for smart environments with AI and IoT-based technologies: A comprehensive review, in: *Handbook of Research on Quantum Computing for Smart Environments*, A. Tyagi (Ed.), pp. 435–452, IGI Global, 2023, https://doi.org/10.4018/978-1-6684-6697-1.ch023.

25. Tyagi, A.K., Bansal, R., Anshu, Dananjayan, S., A step-to-step guide to write a quality research article, in: *Intelligent Systems Design and Applications. ISDA 2022*. Lecture Notes in Networks and Systems, Abraham, A., Pllana, S., Casalino, G., Ma, K., Bajaj, A. (eds) vol. 717, Springer, Cham, 2023. https://doi.org/10.1007/978-3-031-35510-3_36

19

Qubits, Quantum Bits, and Quantum Computing: The Future of Computer Security System

Harini S.[1], Dharshini R.[2*], Praveen R.[2], Abirami A.[2], Lakshmanaprakash S.[2] and Amit Kumar Tyagi[3]

[1]Department of Artificial Intelligence and Data Science, Bannari Amman Institute of Technology, Sathyamangalam, Tamil Nadu, India
[2]Department of Information Technology, Bannari Amman Institute of Technology, Sathyamangalam, Tamil Nadu, India
[3]Department of Fashion Technology, National Institute of Fashion Technology, New Delhi, Delhi, India

Abstract

In this chapter, quantum computing is recognized as an emerging field that holds great promise for solving problems that are currently intractable for classical computers by controlling some sort of small computers. Here we present an intro to the application of quantum mechanics around us as well as some major ideas about quantum computing. Moreover, it will use qubits to preserve and process the data, and when used in tandem, they have so much more effective memory. They have the capacity to process exponentially large amounts of data and possess quantum properties like superposition, entanglement, and interface. In this abstract, we will provide an overview of the principles of quantum computing and the challenges associated with building qubits that are reliable and resistant to errors. We will discuss the different types of qubits that have been developed, including superconducting qubits, ion trap qubits, and topological qubits. We will also explore the different error correction techniques that have been proposed for mitigating the effects of errors in quantum computing systems. It is best to study the beginnings, potentials, and constraints of the current traditional computing before concentrating on the implications of the exploration of a general-purpose quantum computer and the potential of rapid technological advancement. This knowledge aids in our comprehension of potential obstacles to the creation of novel, cutting-edge technology. It will also provide us with information about the ongoing advancements in this area.

Keywords: Quantum computers, real-time systems, program processors, superposition, entanglement, interface, qubits

19.1 Introduction

Information [1]: The field is founded on the concepts of quantum mechanics, which explain how atomic and subatomic particles behave. We use quantum bits (qubits) in quantum computing, which can exist in several states at once, enabling parallel processing and

---
*Corresponding author: dharshinir.it21@bitsathy.ac.in

Amit Kumar Tyagi (ed.) Automated Secure Computing for Next-Generation Systems, (385–402) © 2024 Scrivener Publishing LLC

exponential speedup for some workloads, which control atom interactions and temporal evolution. Although the particulars of the quantum world may not be immediately apparent at first, applications of quantum computing can be found all around us, according to a closer examination. The foundation of quantum computation is Landauer's discovery that all information is inherently physical [1, 2]. A type of computation referred to as quantum computing modifies data using semiconducting phenomena like superposition as well as entanglement. Quantum computers utilize qubit, or qubits, which can exist in multiple states independently, differently from classical computers, which rely on bits which are limited to being in a 0 or 1 state. Redundancy involves duplicating or triplicating certain parts of a system in order to reduce the risk of errors or failures. Quantum computing has the potential to revolutionize many fields, including cryptography, drug discovery, materials science, and optimization—for example, quantum computers could be used to break modern encryption protocols, enabling secure communication that is currently impossible. They could also be used to simulate complex chemical reactions, leading to the discovery of new drugs and materials. Some of the most possible applications for quantum computing include optimizing complex systems, simulating the behavior of molecules and materials, and breaking encryption algorithms that are currently unbreakable by classical computers [3]. As has been emphasized, the very existence of atoms is entirely due to the certainties of quantum physics, including the Pauli exclusions theorem and stable and well-defined atomic energy levels, in contrast to the chaotic uncertainties of classical mechanics. The semiconductor industry, with its transistors and integrated circuits, and consequently the computer on which I am writing this lecture could not have evolved without our knowledge of the solid state from a quantum approach and the band theory of metals, semiconductors, and semiconductors. The same is true for quantum optics and lasers, which have given rise to a wide range of enterprises, including optical communications and music and video discs. As everything is fundamentally quantum mechanical, we may certainly picture storing information on quantum computers, as Feynman did in his seminal 1959 talk "Plenty of Room at the Bottom".

Individual Atoms or Electrons [3]: The Schroedinger equation, known as the "Newton's Law" of quantum mechanics, governs how these small particles evolve and interact instead of the Newton's Laws of classical physics [4]. At incredible velocities and sources of energy, we must use the Dirac equation and account for Einstein's theory of relativity, which makes assumptions about the formation of particle unpaired electrons and a relativistic mass increase. In fact, we now understand that even this is only a close estimate at typical speeds and energies. We can neglect these concerns and use the non-relativistic form of quantum physics, represented by Schroedinger's equation, for the preponderance of our everyday situations. As a result, we need to think about how the quantum nature of media influences information rather than merely seeing it as a collection of ones and zeros. While quantum computing is still in the early stages of development, ongoing research and development hold promise for unlocking the full potential of this exciting new field. In the following sections, we will explore the basic principles of quantum computing and the challenges that must be overcome to build more reliable and efficient quantum computers [5]. They employ their own quantum bits, commonly referred to as "qubits", to store and process the information in contrast to ordinary classical computers, which are based on classical computing and use binary bits 0 and 1 separately. Quantum computers are one way to describe this type of computation. In such tiny computers, transistors, logic gates, and integrated circuits cannot be used. It makes use of bits made of subatomic particles like atoms, electrons, photons, and ions as well as data about the spins and states of those particles. They can also be combined to make more combinations. As a result, they are more potent since they can efficiently utilize memory when operating in parallel. Quantum computers, which operate orders of magnitude more quickly than normal computers, are the only computing model that could defeat the Church–Turing theorem [6]. The microprocessor chip had doubled every year since its conception, according to Gordon Moore, an Intel co-founder, in 1965, and prices had dropped to 50%. What this is is described by Moore's Law. Because Moore's Law predicts that computers [7] will get smaller and more powerful over time, it is vital to understand. Even while this law is already slowing things down, traditional computers are no longer improving as quickly as they previously did.

According to Gordon Moore, a co-founder of Intel, a silicon microprocessor chip's transistor count increased annually, while its cost had reduced by half since it was created [3]. Understanding Moore's Law is crucial because it foretells a future in which computers will get smaller and more potent. Even while this law is already slowing things down, traditional computers are no longer improving as quickly as they previously did. Peter Shor showed in 1993 how quantum computers [8] may solve problems like this much faster—like in a couple of seconds—without overheating. He developed formulas to factor large numbers quickly. The likelihood of an atom's state before it is really known serves as the foundation for their calculations. They have the ability to process enormous amounts of data exponentially. It also demonstrates how a quantum computer in the real world could crack the codes used for encryption. Data and communications that are encrypted may no longer be confidential. The fact that quantum computers have significantly more advantages than disadvantages is also kept in mind. Nevertheless, further research is being pursued aimed at this clear indication for a bright future because they are still necessary.

19.2   Importance of Quantum Computing

Increased Computational Power: Quantum computers have the potential to solve complex problems much faster than classical computers, allowing for more efficient data analysis and processing. After processing in IBM's Deep Blue computer, chess champion Garry was defeated [9].

Improved Cryptography: Quantum computers can break many of the encryption methods used to secure communication and data storage, but they can also be used to create more secure encryption algorithms that are resistant to attacks from classical computers.

Advancement in Scientific Research: Quantum computing can provide new insights into the behavior of quantum systems, which could lead to significant advancements in fields such as chemistry, physics, and materials science.

Optimization: Quantum computers can perform optimization problems much faster than classical computers, which could lead to significant improvements in areas such as logistics, supply chain management, and transportation. There are some advantages of using quantum computing [3].

Machine Learning and Artificial Intelligence: Quantum computing has the potential to speed up the training of machine learning algorithms and improve their accuracy, enabling the development of more advanced AI systems.

Quantum Simulation: Quantum computers can simulate complex quantum systems, allowing scientists to explore new areas of research that were previously not possible with classical computers. Overall, quantum computing has the potential to revolutionize many industries and fields, providing new insights, solving problems faster, and improving efficiency and accuracy in various applications. This pace is projected to increase when additional research is used in practical contexts. This formerly outlandish idea is starting to look plausible despite the fact that practical devices remain years away. Quantum computing will enable a new wave of technological applications that aid in resolving some of the most pressing global problems of our day. Formerly unsearched effects of quantum theory can now be used as a resource in technologies with vast applications, such as secure communication networks, incredibly accurate sensors, the study of chemical reactions for medicine, innovative materials, and fundamentally new paradigms of computation. Global governments and corporations, such as Google, Microsoft, Intel, Toshiba, and IBM, have made substantial investments lately to tap into this potential. Although the development of quantum computing is impressive, the field still faces a number of challenges, including the challenges of building a large-scale quantum computer, building costs, and developing new quantum algorithms.

Artificial intelligence systems to get more intelligent every day. With little training, they are able to complete progressively difficult jobs. The diversity of scenarios to which contemporary AI systems can respond is constrained, and they are not as adaptable as they may be. Quantum computing has the potential to make AI systems smarter and more adaptable to various settings. To be able to respond correctly, this would require AI systems to assess a wide range of potential events and scenarios as well as their probability. AI systems will be able to make predictions even in scenarios with a large number of potential outcomes, thanks to quantum computing. It will also enable AI systems to learn more quickly.

19.3   Literature Survey

The most difficult of these new quantum-based technologies is the quantum computer, which is now under development. A scalable and universal quantum computer is built on the foundation of quick, repeatable, and controllable high-coherence quantum bits (qubits) [4]. Superposition and entanglement, two features of quantum physics, are used to improve information processing and simulation, which is a much-needed development. The exciting scientific discovery of the 20th century was quantum mechanics. This has been used to create a variety of modern electrical gadgets that have revolutionized technology, including lasers, MRIs, hard drives, and liquid crystal displays. Making even compact and more capable devices is the current challenge facing the information processing sector. The only option to continue advancing technology is to shrink the transistor to the size of an atom because the finest CPUs available today have approximately 14 billion transistors packed onto a chip. As matter gets closer to the nanoscale, the laws of quantum mechanics take over. At the quantum level, Moore's law appears to break down since qubit quality and needed error correction are now just as important as qubit count when it comes to computing. A literature survey on quantum computing would involve reviewing the current state of research in each of these areas as well as identifying key challenges and opportunities for future research. The industry is experimenting with the concept of a metric, recently presented by IBM as "quantum volume", that could be compared to Moore's law. Atomic matter presents a universe that is completely foreign to our senses, where atoms can cross obstacles and the act of looking at something can alter its state. By the 1920s, the formalism of quantum mechanics provided a satisfactory explanation for experiments exhibiting quantum behavior such as quantized photon energy (photoelectric effect), wave–particle duality (double-slit experiment), and electron spin (Stern–Gerlach experiment) [10]. Prior to the last few decades, many of the less logical predictions of quantum mechanics, such as quantum entanglement and measurement back-action, were untested. Even though our universe is made up entirely of quantum objects at the microscopic level, these items interact incoherently or at random. All of the quantum interactions are "smeared away" when we look at the macroscopic world more closely, leaving us with the well-known classical mechanics.

We must then manage our quantum systems to keep them from interacting inconsistently with the outside environment in order to exhibit quantum events (which includes ourselves as the classical observer) [5]. This has typically involved researching tiny items with little contact with the outside world, like individual atoms. Making small, isolated quantum systems, however, necessitates a trade-off because we experimentalists are firmly rooted in the classical world. If quantum systems are unable to answer our questions, they are of little service to humans. In the early to mid-1980s, researchers found macroscopic quantum coherent systems in Josephson tunnel junctions [11]. A 10 m × 10 m gadget with several regulated coupling lines to the outside world was shown to exhibit quantum behavior in these studies, a stunning finding given the system's abundance of atoms (Figure 19.1). This breakthrough sparked a series of studies that led to the realization of quantum systems at the millimeter and even centimeter scale in more subsequent experiments. With these bigger quantum devices, it is considerably simpler to regulate where quantum information goes and, more critically, does not go. It would also involve evaluating the strengths and weaknesses of existing approaches and identifying areas where new techniques or methodologies are needed. This offers scientists a unique chance to model quantum physics processes and evaluate the performance of potential quantum systems. Superposition, entanglement, and interference are the three most significant ideas in quantum physics.

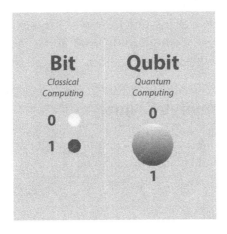

Figure 19.1 Bit vs. qubit.

Superposition makes it possible for a quantum qubit to exist in states other than the binary 1 or 0 [12].

The best comparison is the spinning of a coin as part of the state equation. Superposition is what gives active quantum computing its exponential growth in the amount of data that can be processed. Ten qubits can store 210 = 1,024 bits of data as opposed to one qubit's two (21) bits, yet entanglement is a strange concept that allows two qubits to remain synchronized even though they are thousands of miles apart. Superposition and entanglement are both involved in the well-known "Schrödinger's cat" thought experiment. Then, in this interference, the clashing of qubit states amplifies the right response while canceling out the wrong one. Interference, which is a very important part in the creation of many qubit supercomputers, is played by what is fundamentally a wave phenomenon. We might be capable of imitating and solving difficult issues effectively with a quantum processor if we have enough powerful, high-quality qubits. A single, widely used formula cannot completely describe the capabilities of a quantum processor. All that needs to be said is that the connectivity, quality level, and qubit count should all be as high as feasible. The number of logical qubits depends on the specific error correcting method used with the physical qubits. It is unrelated to the qubit quality in particular. Hence, the worse the qubit quality, the more error correction you might want to add. Thanks to this aspect of quality, we get at the concept of gate integrity. In quantum information theory, fidelity is a measure of how "close" two quantum states are to one another. It expresses the possibility that one state will be able to pass a test to establish its similarity to another. By examining the effects of the shape and power of the control pulses, we aim to determine whether the gate faithfulness is bound. If so, we must determine what is causing the restriction. Is it primarily brought on by the external devices or the behavior of the superconducting qubit itself? Qubits' existing capabilities enable us all to simulate with a degree of precision that is enough. With quantum computation, the requirements for error correction are a little higher [13]. Quantum computers are a truly revolutionary sort of computing device based on the ideas of quantum physics. They have the ability to solve problems that quickly scale up and are therefore impractical for ordinary computers to handle. To conduct research and address novel problems, real quantum computers are currently accessed over the cloud. The qubits themselves are incredibly robust and delicate at the same time. Contemporary superconducting qubits frequently lose their distinctive quantum properties within 100 microseconds, largely due to temperature fluctuations, vibrations, and the electromagnetic environment. To increase the reliability and sturdiness of quantum computers, it is vital to harmoniously combine multiple complementary technologies.

19.4   Quantum Computing Features

For doing specific computations, quantum computing makes use of quantum-mech phenomena like superposition and entanglement. Some of the key characteristics of quantum computing are as follows:

1. Superposition:

   a) In a classical computer, bits can only have two states: 0 or 1 (Figure 19.2). However, in a quantum computer, qubits (quantum bits) can be in a superposition of 0 and 1, allowing quantum computers to perform certain calculations exponentially faster than classical computers.

   b) Superposition is also used in quantum algorithms such as Shor's algorithm, which can efficiently factor large numbers, and Grover's algorithm, which can efficiently search through a database.

   c) This superposition of quantum states gives rise to a new, valid quantum state. In conventional computing, a bit can only be assigned a value of 0 or 1. In contrast, a qubit (quantum bit) allows for the simultaneous execution of several calculations since it can exist in a combination of both 0 and 1.

   d) Qubits can alternate between the fundamental states of 0 and 1. More precisely, in regard to a qubit's measurement, only observables may be measured.

   e) For instance, when a qubit is in a superposition state of equal weights, a measurement will have an equal probability of 50% of causing it to collapse to one of its two basis states, 0 or 1 (Figure 19.3). "0" is the condition that, when measured and subsequently collapsed, always returns the number 0. In a manner similar to this, 1 will always equal 1. Compared to the superposition of classical waves, it is fundamentally different.

   f) The superposition of classical waves and quantum states is fundamentally different from one another. Using n qubits, a quantum computer can be found in one of two superpositions, which range from 000...0 to 111...1. It can make n frequencies by playing n musical notes at n different frequencies.

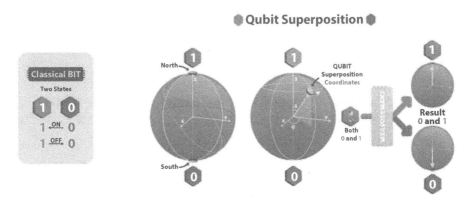

Figure 19.2 Superposition.

2. Entanglement:

   a) When two or more qubits become correlated, regardless of how far apart they are from one another, the state of one qubit influences the other qubits. This phenomenon is also called as quantum entanglement. This makes it possible for some computations to be completed more quickly than on conventional computers [7].

   b) The connection between two entangled qubits is distinct. The entanglement will be made clear by the measurements' findings. Each qubit's measurement results could come back as a 0 or a 1 [15].

   c) Yet the outcomes of the measurement of one qubit will always be connected with the outcomes of the measurement of the other qubit. An example of such states is the Bell states (Figure 19.3).

3. Quantum parallelism:

   a) With the use of quantum computing, certain algorithms can be created to carry out several calculations at once, enabling substantially faster processing of specific sorts of issues.

   b) Every input value to the function is connected with a matching output value in the first step of a quantum algorithm [8].

   c) Quantum parallelism is the foundation of several quantum algorithms. There are, however, a few significant restrictions that we must consider. Although they are superimposed in the output, the results we are interested in cannot be read directly. Any direct method of measuring will only give us one outcome, and the other three will be lost [15, 16].

   d) Hence, the final response that interests us must be read out using cunning tactics, some of which may not be computationally straightforward. Moreover, setting up the input state was simple in our example, but other problems may prevent it from being so. Whether or not using quantum parallelism will ultimately lead to speedups over classical alternatives depends on these restrictions (Figure 19.4).

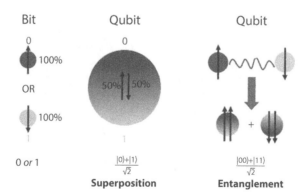

Figure 19.3 Entanglement.

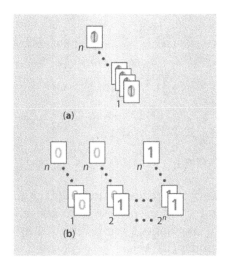

Figure 19.4 Parallelism.

4. Quantum interference:

a) Several quantum states can interact with one another in a phenomenon known as quantum interference, which can be either constructive or destructive (Figure 19.5). It will make it possible to do certain computations with great precision [9, 17].

b) One of the most important ideas in quantum computing is controlling the probability that a group of qubits will collapse into a particular measurement state. Quantum interference, a by-product of superposition, allows us to direct a qubit's measurement towards a certain state or group of states.

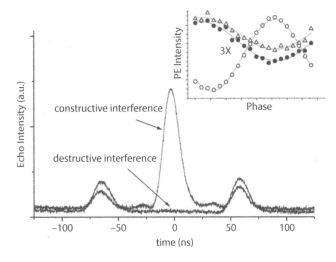

Figure 19.5 Interference.

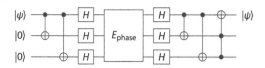

Figure 19.6 Error correction.

5. Quantum error correction:

   a) Due to issues like decoherence and noise, quantum computers are prone
      to errors by nature. However, these mistakes can be reduced, and the
      accuracy of the computations can be ensured by using quantum error
      correction techniques [10, 18].
   b) Traditional error correction employs redundancy. The simplest but least
      efficient tactic is the repetition code. The idea is to keep the information
      in multiple locations and utilize a majority vote if those copies subse-
      quently turn out to disagree.
   c) The three copied bits are the physical representation of the information
      (Figure 19.6), and decoding is the process of determining which logical
      state the physical state represents. Although QEC codes do not always
      correctly decode logical qubits, they reduce the impact of noise in a man-
      ner similar to classical error correction.

19.5   Quantum Algorithms

SHOR'S ALGORITHM:
The factorization of extremely large numbers is the main application of Shor's algorithm
[19], a highly effective quantum approach. Several banks and online accounts employ the
RSA public-key crypto system, which is subjected to factorization of enormous integers.
With Shor's method, calculating the period of a function can be done instead of factoring
large integers. A quantum computer calculates the period much faster than a classical computer. The Shor algorithm can be used to break the RSA public-key crypto system, endangering the security of organizations and websites that employ RSA.

The quantum processing component uses the superposition state and quantum interference to determine the co-prime integer n x that is chosen at random to be the period r of
the function, () mod an x n f an x = n, where x is the co-prime integer to be factored. The
classical section uses n gcd(x,n) = 1 n x and r from the quantum part to obtain a factor of n,
using a result from the classical number theory.

GROVER'S ALGORITHM:
Grover's algorithm, a quantum search algorithm, is another incredibly powerful quantum
algorithm. This method can be used to find data from a sizable set of unordered data [20].
Grover's algorithm has a time complexity of O, whereas the usual method has an O(N) time
complexity (N). This suggests that utilizing Grover's method to solve the same problem

will result in a far quicker solution than using the conventional methodology. Numerous applications of the Grover algorithm exist, including calculations in mathematics, password cracking, nuclear magnetic resonance, optics, and other domains.

PROPOSED SYSTEM:

There are many proposed systems in quantum computing, each with its own unique approach and potential applications. Quantum logic gates are fundamental building blocks used in quantum circuits to manipulate the quantum state of a system. Each of the bits 00, 01, 10, 11, and n can indicate two different states. The quantum computer, by using the quantum computing building blocks called "qubits", is represented in one-bit information which is a two-state system—for instance, in computational methods, an electron can be used as a qubit in place of an electrical signal [13]. The two possible states, 0 and 1, were depicted by the turn and turn states of an electron. In order to convey both states, a photon's horizontal and vertical polarization can be used as a qubit. The potential of one qubit to demonstrate the superposition of 0 and 1 states is a critical difference. When we depict 0 and 1 states as respective state vectors 0 and 1, we could really express such a superposition state as a linear combination of 0 and 1. The symbol $|a| = 2$ represents the possibility that the experiment on the qubit would end in 0. Moreover, they affirm that $|a|2 + |b|2 = 1$—for instance, we may write a superposition of two states as follows where the probability amplitudes a and b are equal to $(1/2)$: In this equation, $)= 1/2 | 0+1/2 | 1$, where $|0) = (1,0)$T and $|1) = (0,1)$T. When we measure a state of, for instance, $|1$, the condition will be detected as 0 with proportion $(1/2)2 = 12$ and as $|1)$ with chance $(1/2)2 = 12$. Two qubits can represent four states simultaneously since each qubit can only represent two states at once. As opposed to the four operations required by a conventional computer, we can get the outcome of four operations for four inputs by applying two qubits that are the superposition of the 0 and 1 states as that of the operation's input. Similar to this, utilizing n qubits, we could establish a combination of state as an input and processed the information in one step to solve a problem which usually requires multiple stages in a standard computer. Throughout this respect, a quantum computer has the capacity of processing n inputs after adopting their superposition state. Admittedly, before we can make benefit of this hugely useful ability of quantum computers, a big difficulty looms. We combine one superposition state, which represents four input states, with one processing step to produce the superposition of four results. As a qubit is a two-state system, the quantum mechanical superposition collapses when we measure the output qubits, causing each qubit to be viewed as either 0 or 1. As a result, given the same probability, we can only expect to get one of the four results: 00, 01, 10, or 11 (for n = 2). We can construct quantum circuits to perform specific operations on the quantum state of a system. This problem arises from the application of quantum mechanical superposition, but we can utilize the quantum theory combination property if we can create an algorithm that enhances the chances of attaining the desired result. This is how we might use quantum computers, as was stated previously, to address an issue that would otherwise need a lot of computing time as well as energy on classical computers.

INTERFERENCE:

In this subsection [21], we give a clear illustration of interference which is a fundamental concept in quantum mechanics and is crucial to how quantum algorithms work. Interference in quantum computing refers to how quantum states interact to produce either a beneficial or a detrimental interference. Unquestionably, any traditional computer can be imitated by a Turing machine, a mathematical model of a general computer. Before discussing the quantum Turing machine (QTM), we first suggest a processing tree utilizing a classical probabilistic Turing computer (PTM) [22]. Each vertex in the tree reflects the state of the machine, and each edge in the tree represents the possibility that a transition will take place (Figure 19.7).

The tree's root represents the initial state, and each level represents a calculation step. After two computing steps, we can calculate the likelihood that state 0 will change to state 1 by adding the probabilities of the two alternative routes from the root to state 1 as follows:

$$P(0 \rightarrow 1) = \left(\frac{2}{3} \times \frac{1}{3}\right) + \left(\frac{1}{3} \times \frac{1}{4}\right) = \frac{2}{9} + \frac{1}{12} = \frac{11}{36}$$

Similarly,

$$P(0 \rightarrow 0) = \left(\frac{2}{3} \times \frac{2}{3}\right) + \left(\frac{1}{3} \times \frac{3}{4}\right) = \frac{4}{9} + \frac{3}{12} = \frac{25}{36}.$$

This outcome can be interpreted in the manner that follows (Figure 19.8). The PTM will occupy state 1 with probability 11/36 in two steps, starting from state 0, and state 0 with probability 25/36.

We provide an explanation of a QTM calculation that uses the computation tree shown (Figure 19.9), much like the PTM calculation. Every edge of the tree in the PTM describes probability, whereas every edge in the QTM describes a probability amplitude. One state only occurs at the same time in the equal level of the PTM tree, whereas all states occur

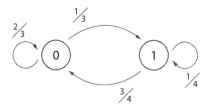

Figure 19.7 PTM's state transition diagram.

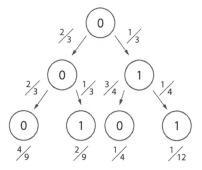

Figure 19.8 A PTM computation tree.

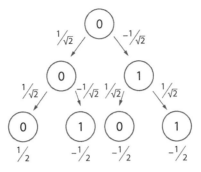

Figure 19.9 QTM begins in state 0.

concurrently in the equal level of the QTM tree. After one calculation, the probability of 0
1 from the root in this example is [14]:

$$\left(-\frac{1}{\sqrt{2}}\right)^2 = \frac{1}{2}$$

where, after one computing step, the likelihood of the root being 0 is

$$\left(-\frac{1}{\sqrt{2}}\right)^2 = \frac{1}{2}$$

Let us calculate the likelihood of a transition occurring after two steps (Figure 19.10).
The probability amplitudes of the two potential routes must first be determined:

$$\Psi\left(0 \rightarrow 0 \rightarrow 1\right), \text{ and } \Psi(0 \rightarrow 1 \rightarrow 1).$$

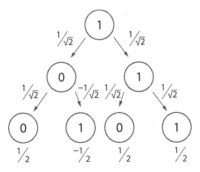

Figure 19.10 QTM begins in state 1.

$$\Psi(0 \to 0 \to 1) = \frac{1}{\sqrt{2}} \times \left(-\frac{1}{\sqrt{2}}\right) = \frac{1}{2},$$

$$\Psi(0 \to 1 \to 1) = \left(-\frac{1}{\sqrt{2}}\right) \times \left(\frac{1}{\sqrt{2}}\right) = -\frac{1}{2}$$

We add both amplitudes.

To compute the probability of transition $0 \to 0$ after two steps, we need to calculate the probability amplitude for this transition and then take the absolute value squared of that amplitude. We can use the same approach as before:

$$\Psi(0 \to 0 \text{ after two steps}) = \Psi(0 \to 1 \to 0) + \Psi(0 \to 0 \to 0) = (-1/2) + (1/2) = 0$$

The probability of transition $0 \to 0$ after two steps is then:

$$P\,(0 \to 0 \text{ after two steps}) = |\Psi(0 \to 0 \text{ after two steps})|2 = 02 = 0$$

This means that there is no probability of finding the system in state 0 after two steps, as the probability amplitude for this transition is zero. The system must instead be in state 1 after two steps with probability 1.

$$\Psi(0 \to 0 \to 0) = \frac{1}{\sqrt{2}} \times \frac{1}{\sqrt{2}} = \frac{1}{2}, \Psi(0 \to 1 \to 0) = \left(-\frac{1}{\sqrt{2}}\right) \times \left(\frac{1}{\sqrt{2}}\right) = -\frac{1}{2}$$

$$\Psi(0 \to 0 \text{ after two steps}) = \Psi(0 \to 0 \to 0) + \Psi(0 \to 1 \to 0) = \frac{1}{2} + \left(-\frac{1}{2}\right) = 0$$

$$P(0 \to 0 \text{ after two steps}) = |\Psi(0 \to 0 \text{ after two steps})|^2 = |0|^2 = 0$$

Using the computation tree shown in Figure 19.3, there are two types of density matrices that are commonly used in quantum computing [23–26]: the quantum state density matrix (QTM) and the process tensor density matrix (PTM). The QTM describes the state of a single quantum system, such as a single qubit or a collection of qubits. The QTM is calculated by taking the outer product of the state vector with its complex conjugate: $\rho = |\psi\rangle\langle\psi|$ where $|\psi\rangle$ is the state vector. The QTM is a square matrix with the same dimensions as the number of basis states in the system. The PTM describes the action of a quantum operation or gate on a quantum state. The PTM is calculated by taking the outer product of the input state with the output state after the operation or gate has been applied: $\Phi = |\psi\_out\rangle\langle\psi\_in|$ where $|\psi\_out\rangle$ and $|\psi\_in\rangle$ are the output and input state vectors, respectively. The PTM is a rectangular matrix with dimensions equal to the number of basis states in the input and output systems.

19.6 Experimental Results

➢ With the help of a computer program, the researchers were able to create a model of the human brain that could be used to study the brain's connections to its various regions.

➢ A group of scientists from the Science and Technology University of China announced in 2021 that they had demonstrated particle acceleration over a distance of 27 miles, breaking the previous record for the maximum distance.

➢ According to Monroe, qubits made of similar atomic ions are incredibly clean by nature, explains College Park Professor of Physics and Fellow of the Joint Center for Quantitative Computing and Information Science at the University of Maryland.

➢ Eventually though, errors must always be further minimized when many qubits and operations are needed, and it is easier to add additional quantum bits and encrypt data in a novel way. Error-correcting systems for atom ions are attractive in that they are highly functional and readily operated without software controls.

➢ It has never been shown before that a logical qubit is more reliable than the step that makes errors most frequently. Although the experimenters used six quantum operations that have a combined success rate of just approximately 98.9%, they were still able to initialize and measure the logical qubit with a fidelity (i.e., accuracy) rate of 99.4%. This suggests that, while the success rate of each individual operation was probably lower than 98.9%, the quantum error correcting code was able to fix the mistakes that each individual operation brought.

➢ Although it might not seem like much of a difference, it is a crucial step in the creation of quantum computers that are far larger.

➢ The logical qubit in the quantum computing experiment was supported by quantum error checking, which allowed several physical qubits to cooperate to rectify faults and increase the precision of the outcome. This is comparable to how attentive co-workers can help each other recognize and correct each other's faults, leading to a better product.

➢ The results were obtained using Monroe's ion-trap technology which, at UMD, utilizes up to 32 different charged atoms (ions) hung above electrodes on a chip and cooled with lasers. Then, using lasers, they can control each ion to function as a qubit.

➢ The numerous physical qubits that make up the logical qubit can detect and repair errors with a better success rate when they cooperate rather than when they work alone. This is a crucial step in the development of more reliable and scalable quantum computers and one of the main benefits of quantum error correction.

Rectifying Mistakes and Accepting Faults:
No matter how skilfully you construct a computer, something will ultimately go wrong according to Murphy's Law. This makes it essential to create fault-tolerant qubits that can

remedy errors. Any bit or qubit in a computer has a chance to malfunction occasionally. Most of the qubits in a practical quantum computer suggest that there are various opportunities for errors to enter the system. Unfortunately, engineers can construct a computer so that all of its parts cooperate to find issues. You can back up key data to a second hard drive or have someone else read crucial emails to ensure they are error-free before sending them. A mistake must be made by both the people and the drivers in order for it to be perpetuated. Redundancy makes the task more difficult to perform yet helps to ensure its quality. Redundancy involves duplicating or triplicating certain parts of a system in order to reduce the risk of errors or failures. The risk of an error, for instance, can be decreased from one in 100 to less than one in a thousand by transferring or storing data in three copies and relying on the majority vote. Yet quantum error correction has particular difficulties since qubits have a greater level of complexity than the normal bits and have more potential for error. A qubit cannot be simply copied or even checked at the center of a calculation. Qubits can exist in a quantum superposition of several states and can contact each other in a quantum mechanically meaningful way, which is the entire reason why they are advantageous. You need to physically measure a qubit in order to know what data it is currently holding in order to duplicate it and use various widely used technology, including high-speed modems and cell phones, to guarantee the accuracy of communications. It is true that error correction codes are frequently utilized in traditional communication systems to guard against noise and other error causes. Finally, the remark accurately draws attention to the fact that the only computing model now understood to be capable of exponentially outperforming classical computers for some tasks is that of quantum computers. This is because quantum computers are able to do some computations far more quickly than classical computers by utilizing quantum superposition and entanglement.

19.7   Conclusion

In summary, quantum computing is a new discipline that has the potential to transform computing by discovering solutions to issues that are currently beyond the capabilities of classical machines. Quantum computers use quantum bits (qubits), which can exist in numerous states concurrently, to execute computations. This enables for parallel computing and exponential speedup for several jobs. This pace is projected to increase when additional research is used in practical contexts. This formerly outlandish idea is starting to look plausible despite the fact that practical devices remain years away. Instead of building a full quantum computer right once, the current goal is to move from experiments in which we can just observe quantum events to experiments in which we can control these occurrences. Systems using quantum information have the potential to outperform any conventional computer by a wide margin. There is both a chance and a reward. The first quantum computer may be developed this year, possibly during the next 10 years, or even within a few hundred years; no one can predict when that will be the case. Yet there are a number of significant technological and philosophical issues that should be resolved first before the incredible level of computer power may have any evident economic, industrial, or scientific repercussions.

Finally, the use of quantum systems has the potential to revolutionize computation by providing solutions to some hitherto unsolvable problems. Much progress is being made even though there are currently no classical computers that can carry out operations that a computer program cannot.

References

1. Fei, S.-M., Li, M., Luo, S., Quantum information and computation. *Entropy*, 25, 463, 2023.
2. Li, W., Ma, X., Lee, Y., Zhang, Y., Gu, Y., Finding new multipartite entangled resources for measurement-based quantum computation. *Quantum Inf. Process.*, 22, 3–5, 2023.
3. Feng, Y., Miceli, R., McGuigan, M., Quantum walks, Feynman propagators and graph topology on an IBM quantum computer, *arXiv:2104.06458*, 6–10, 2021.
4. Rabinowitz, M., Is quantum mechanics incompatible with Newton's First Law. *Int. J. Theor. Phys.*, 47, 936–948, 2008.
5. Samrin, S.S., Patil, R., Itagi, S., Chetti, S., Tasneem, A., Design of logic gates using reversible gates with reduced quantum cost. *Global Transitions Proceedings*, vol. 3, 2022.
6. Aaronson, S. and Chen, L., Complexity-theoretic foundations of quantum supremacy experiments, *arXiv preprint arXiv:1612.05903*, 2016.
7. Feng, J. and Yu, K., Moore's law and price trends of digital products: The case of smartphones. *Econ. Innov. New Technol.*, 29, 1–20, 2019.
8. Xiao, L., Qiu, D., Luo, L., Mateus, P., Distributed shor's algorithm. *Quantum Inf. Comput.*, 23, 27–44, 2023.
9. Hoekenga, B., Mind over machine: What deep blue taught us about chess, artificial intelligence, and the human spirit, 31–35, 2008.
10. Yousif, M.E., Explaining the stern-gerlach experiment: Using the spinning magnetic field (SMF). *IOSR J. Appl. Phys.*, 13, 43–69, 2021.
11. Montoya, M., Making Posters for the Third World Liberation Front at UC Berkeley. *Ethnic Stud. Rev.*, 42, 162–168, 2019.
12. Li, Y. and Ren, Z., Quantum metrology with N-qubit W superposition state under local and nonlocal operation, 2, 2022.
13. Wang, M.-H., Hao, S.-H., Qin, Z.-Z., Su, X.-L., Research advances in continuous-variable quantum computation and quantum error correction. *Acta Physica Sin.*, 71, 160305, 2022.
14. Rina, and Godara, Dr., Quantum computing: Recent trend in computing. *International Journal of Creative Research Thoughts (IJCRT)*, 11, 2320–2882, 2023.
15. Raffah, B., Berrada, K., Abdel-Khalek, S., Alhadeethi, Y., Entanglement and fisher information for two superconducting qubits interacting with a deformed field. *Opt. Quantum Electron.*, 55, 3–5, 2022.
16. Häner, T., Kliuchnikov, V., Roetteler, M., Soeken, M., Vaschillo, A., QParallel: Explicit parallelism for programming quantum computers, *arXiv:2210.03680*, 4–5, 2022.
17. Wang, D.-S., Universal resources for quantum computing, *arXiv:2303.03715*, 4–6, 2023.
18. Touchette, D., Ali, H., Hilke, M., 5-qubit quantum error correction in a charge qubit quantum computer, *arXiv:1010.3242v1*, 3–5, 2010.
19. Radhika, L. and Raja, T., Shor's algorithm – How does it work on perfect squares, 2–6, 2023.
20. Vemula, D.R., Konar, D., Satheesan, S., Kalidasu, M., Cangi, A., A scalable 5, 6-qubit Grover's quantum search algorithm, *arXiv:2205.00117v1*, pg no: 6–7, 2022.
21. Gu, X., Krenn, M., Erhard, M., Zeilinger, A. Quantum experiments and graphs II: Quantum interference, computation and state generation, *arXiv:1803.10736*, 2, 2018.

22. Simonović, S., On capabilities of quantum-mechanical computer models. *Tehnika*, 77, 337–344, 2022.

23. V., S.A., Soni, G., Tyagi, A.K., A Review on recent trends in quantum computation technology, in: *Handbook of Research on Quantum Computing for Smart Environments*, A. Tyagi (Ed.), pp. 48–64, IGI Global, Hershey, Pennsylvania, 2023, https://doi.org/10.4018/978-1-6684-6697-1.ch003.

24. P., S., Soni, G., Tyagi, A.K., Kakulapati, V., J. S., S.M., Singh, R.K., Quantum computing and the qubit: The future of artificial intelligence, in: *Handbook of Research on Quantum Computing for Smart Environments*, A. Tyagi (Ed.), pp. 231–244, IGI Global, Hershey, Pennsylvania, 2023, https://doi.org/10.4018/978-1-6684-6697-1.ch013.

25. Deshmukh, A., Patil, D.S., Soni, G., Tyagi, A.K., Cyber security: New realities for industry 4.0 and society 5.0, in: *Handbook of Research on Quantum Computing for Smart Environments*, A. Tyagi (Ed.), pp. 299–325, IGI Global, Hershey, Pennsylvania, 2023, https://doi.org/10.4018/978-1-6684-6697-1.ch017.

26. Deshmukh, A., Patil, D.S., Pawar, P.D., Kumari, S., P., M., Recent trends for smart environments with AI and IoT-based technologies: A comprehensive review, in: *Handbook of Research on Quantum Computing for Smart Environments*, A. Tyagi (Ed.), pp. 435–452, IGI Global, Hershey, Pennsylvania, 2023, https://doi.org/10.4018/978-1-6684-6697-1.ch023.

20

Future Technologies for Industry 5.0 and Society 5.0

**Mani Deepak Choudhry[1]*, S. Jeevanandham[2], M. Sundarrajan[3], Akshya Jothi[4],
K. Prashanthini[5] and V. Saravanan[6]**

[1]Department of Information Technology, KGiSL Institute of Technology, Coimbatore, Tamil Nadu, India
*[2]Department of Information Technology, Sri Ramkrishna Engineering College, Coimbatore,
Tamil Nadu, India*
*[3]Department of Computer Science Engineering, SRM Institute of Science & Technology, Ramapuram,
Chennai, Tamil Nadu, India*
*[4]Department of Computing Intelligence, SRM Institute of Science & Technology, Kattankulathur,
Chennai, Tamil Nadu, India*
*[5]Department of Robotics and Automation, Sri Ramakrishna Engineering College,
Coimbatore, Tamil Nadu, India*
*[6]Department of Computer Science, College of Engineering and Technology, Dembi Dolo University,
Dembi Dolo, Oromia Region, Ethiopia*

Abstract

Industry 4.0 reshaped the production and manufacturing landscape by enhancing operational efficiency and introducing novel business models, services, and goods. With Industry 4.0, we set out to improve the manufacturing processes in two key areas: productivity and longevity. With the focus on digitizing and digitalizing systems, more progress is feasible. As technology advances, it becomes more concerned with automating and optimizing processes than improving the human condition. The augmentation of technology channels is substantially enhanced by the increasing efficiency with which cutting-edge informatics insights and linked devices may be extracted. Civilization 5.0, on the other hand, involves a human-centered organization capable of juggling social responsibilities and economic expressions through a foundational blend of cyber physical environment. Similar to the implementation of technology change throughout all areas of engineering by Industry 4.0 (I4.0), Society 5.0 (S5.0) encourages people to embrace a digital makeover of their daily lives. Indeed the movement and part of the technological initial plan and the rapid development of ICT suggesting that they are mutually supportive is the favorable interpretation of Society 5.0. This research delves into the challenges and opportunities that have arisen as a consequence of I4.0 and S5.0 and discusses how these phenomena will progress in the near and far future.

Keywords: Industry 5.0, cognition, H2M collaboration, digitized society, intelligent automation

*Corresponding author: manideepak.c@kgkite.ac.in

Amit Kumar Tyagi (ed.) *Automated Secure Computing for Next-Generation Systems*, (403–414) © 2024 Scrivener
Publishing LLC

20.1   Introduction

Beginning with the start of the Industrial Revolution, people have known that technology may be used to further progress (Industry 1.0). The use of water, steam, and fossil fuels to generate mechanical power kicked off Industrial Revolution 1.0 in the 1780s, at the end of the 18th century. In the 1870s, during the second phase of the revolution, business owners who relied on assembly lines and fast production welcomed electrical power (Industry 2.0). In the 1970s, the Industry 3.0 era, electronic and information technologies were initially used to create the concept of combining automation into industrial sectors (IT). Cognitive cyber-physical systems function as a linkage among the actual physical and virtual realms [1–5], and they are made more feasible by the usage of the Internet of Things (IoT), cloud services, and the fourth industrialization with artificial intelligence (Industry 4.0, I4.0). I4.0's focus on the technical development of manufacturing and production systems and networks has advantages, but it also has problems [6] due to the fact that it puts corporate innovation and effectiveness ahead of corporate stewardship and employee wellness. As this is the case, there is an ongoing global economic upheaval. Engineers in this phase will have the opportunity to fully use the state of the art in technology to improve the human condition and democratize production. To debunk the idea that I5.0 would not be seen as an independent industrial revolution, it must be hassled that I4.0 is still a continuing sci-tech progress and that Society 5.0 (S5.0) is still in the planning phases.

An essential component of I5.0 is the use of collaborative robotics to minimize danger. Robots like this can identify their human operators, understand their intentions, and pick up on the context of the jobs that they are doing. The goal is to have these robots aid human operators by seeing and learning how a job is done. Additionally, I5.0 seeks to maximize human potential by integrating artificial intelligence (AI) into everyday routines. In Industry 5.0, technically advanced innovations such as the IoT, robotics, AI, and AR are actions that take place for the satisfaction and pleasure of human employees [7].

Industry 5.0 recognizes that, by prioritizing worker health and adapting output to environmental constraints, industry has the potential to serve collective targets outside service and evolution, fetching a sustainable source of development. The corporate world needs a technological update, and Industry 5.0 is part of that. It will help businesses become more trustworthy systems for individuals seeking satisfying and healthy careers. It prioritizes worker wellness and uses cutting-edge technology to produce money outside service and progress while being mindful of the earth's finite resources. It gives workers a voice and helps them acquire the knowledge and abilities that they need in the workplace. It raises competitiveness and attracts the best and brightest in the business. It is now generally accepted that the goal of the movement known as "Industry 5.0" is to attract workers again to the production phase. It is driven by the consumers' need for granular personalization. Industry 5.0 goods, in this view, allow the consumers to indulge their need for self-expression at a price that they are willing to pay more for. To sum up, Industry 5.0 is a corporate philosophy with the long-term goal of fostering more resiliency, human focus, and sustainability in the marketplace. Some people think of Industry 5.0 as a whole new paradigm, while others see it as an incremental improvement upon the practices and principles established by I4.0. The "industry 5.0" technology of the next phase is designed for highly effective and intellectual devices. Figures 20.1 and 20.2 shows the development of business from I1.0 to I5.0 and S5.0, respectively. The goal of the Industry 5.0 idea is to

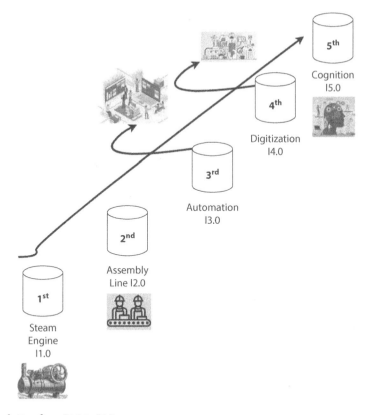

Figure 20.1 Evolution from I1.0 to I5.0.

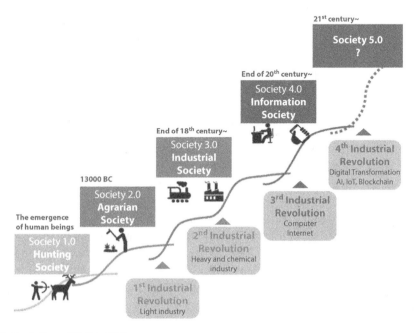

Figure 20.2 Evolution of S1.0 to S5.0.

Table 20.1 I4.0 vs I5.0.

Parameters	I4.0	I5.0
Goals	• Intelligent optimization • Intelligent work	• Societal benefits • Human-centercity • Societal guidance
General methodologies	• Real-time data control • Integrated chain	• Moral use of innovation to further humanity and desires
Humanoid dynamics	• Interaction of human-computer • People trustworthiness	• Employee management and protection
Empowering strategies and perceptions	• IoT • Cyber physical systems • Digitization • Cloud services	• Collaborative robots • Resolution sustenance schemes • Human–machine Interaction • IoT • Cloud

make businesses more sustainable, human-centered, and resistant to disruption. The aims, systemic methods, human elements, empowering expertise with ideas, and ecological concerns of I4.0 and 5.0 are compared in Table 20.1. Due to the novelty of the concept, there is no generally accepted definition of "Industry 5.0". However, it has been highlighted that the key tendencies of Industry 5.0 are the creation of a smart society and the outline of a work culture for humans as well as robots.

Contribution to the Chapter

The importance of the investigation has centered on identifying the descriptions and qualities of I5.0, which has allowed us to better comprehend the stint "Industry 5.0" from the viewpoints of many writers. The similarities and differences between Industry 5.0 and other industrial revolutions are also discussed. Applications for healthcare, supply chains, industrial production, cloud manufacturing, and others are discussed as potential outcomes of I5.0. Big data analytics, IoT, accommodating robots, Big Data Technology (BDT), and upcoming 6GN are just some of the key technologies that are covered in this research as they pertain to Industry 5.0. This dissertation also shows how hard it is to understand the conflicts that arise when people and machines work together in the same manufacturing setting.

Organization of the Chapter

The journal article definitions of Industry 5.0 are discussed in Section 20.2, along with other characteristics of I5.0 in comparison to earlier technical epochs. Section 20.3 discusses the applications as well as the empowering expertise for I5.0, such as big data, IoT, cloud computing, 6G networks, and blockchain. In the last division, we draw conclusions based on the evidence presented.

20.2   Related Work

A. Various Depictions of I5.0

- Workers who use intelligent devices and robots are referred to as "Industry 5.0". Modern tools, such as big data analytics, are used so that robots may speed up human labor [8, 9].
- The term "Industry 5.0" refers to the paradigm shift towards more human and technological cooperation in the workplace with the purpose of boosting both the methodological sophistication and the overall industrial output [10].
- Ocicka and Turek [11] claim that engineers, intellectuals, and other organizations from a wide range of sectors are pressuring Industry 5.0 to prioritize the social aspect and technology in smart factories.
- I5.0 is characterized by mortal and robotic collaboration in production [12, 13]. Human-to-human and electronic-to-electronic communication is facilitated by means of social networks.

B. Additional Features of I5.0

Machine labor is more efficient than human labor; hence, Industry 5.0 is replacing previous innovations as it advances towards perfection [14]. Several benefits of Industry 5.0 motivate business enterprises to use it despite the challenges. Proactive maintenance is essential for intelligent products, the Internet of Things, and bespoke software since it requires effective supervision and maintenance of defects in smart equipment. Using a timetable as a foundation will reduce the likelihood of machine failure [15, 16]. The I5.0 plans to make use of adapted resources to suit the demands of the modern manufacturing sector. When humans and machines work together, it may lead to more adaptable business structures. Waste elimination necessitates regulating output levels. New initiatives and long-term economic health are both products of local manufacturing [8, 17]. Thanks to modern technology, workers are once again able to return to the industrial heartland. Collaborative robots do risky and boring activities [18], while humans focus on innovation and successful commercial solutions. An actual anticipated image of the environment, temperature, resource use, and certain other characteristics is provided by intelligent, interconnected devices and specialized applications [19]. Businesses may benefit from loss prevention and enhanced production. Sustainable manufacturing requires constant iteration aimed at maximizing asset recovery, recycling, and reusing. We must lessen our impact on the planet. Sustainable manufacturers may improve customization, waste reduction, and source productivity by using state-of-the-art technology like artificial intelligence.

C. Depiction of Society 5.0

This section, which expounds on the concepts introduced in the previous section, will focus on the analysis needed to define S5.0. S5.0 was demarcated after the social upheavals shown in Figure 20.2 were compiled. Society has progressed with industrialization. Comparing the revolutionary changes in the industry with those in the society reveals striking parallels between the two (as outlined in the preceding part). Thus, Society 5.0 is a more comprehensive notion than the well-acknowledged Industry 4.0.

According to the book of Deguchi *et al.* [20], "Society 5.0" is an ultra-smart society where the actual world and the Internet are seamlessly integrated to facilitate the creation, meting out, and propagation of required details.

D. I4.0 and S.4.0: From the Conventional Environment

I3.0 was paved with the discovery of the transistor and microprocessor (1960). Such progresses allowed for the early stages of process automation and the rapid development of computer and communication technology. As a consequence, people started putting more emphasis on the creation of knowledge and the enlargement of facility diligences rather than the production of goods and money. The digital revolution, which emphasizes companies and serves as coercion, is post-industrial and has undergone a transformation since the advent of digitalization in the 1980s.

Figure 20.3 depicts the fast structural upheaval that the Fourth Industrial Revolution is creating in traditional society. A state-of-the-art AI system will evaluate and analyze massive volumes of data generated from devices and sensors dispersed across the physical environment. As a result, the research has far-reaching implications for the interaction of humans and machines in the real world. There is a growing convergence between the online and offline worlds. Thus, modern professional preparation, skill building, and cooperation should be emphasized in higher education [21]. To be clear, society is a social framework in which people gain influence and produce goods and services primarily via the acquisition, organization, and sharing of knowledge.

While it originated in Japan, the Society 5.0 framework may be implemented in any nation to promote long-term, sustainable growth. Thus, the parts of the notion associated with industrial growth must be prioritized while thinking about its adaptation. The majority of the adopters of the Industry 4.0 strategy are located in Europe, although the focus of the initiative is strictly on the industrial sector. On the contrary, societal concerns are also addressed in Society 5.0. Thus, we may use the unique constituents of the Japanese approach which are envisioned to update the non-industrial aspects of society.

Many types of industrial innovation are encouraged by the low-cost availability of large-scale data collection, transmission, storage, and analysis [22]. The data points out

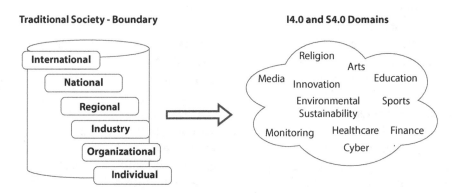

Figure 20.3 Transformation of the traditional domain to the I4.0 and S4.0 domains.

the problems and provides ideas on how to fix them. When this information is quickly disseminated across borders, it may help address management and societal problems. DX uses data-based technologies like blockchain, AI, 5G, robots, and IoT to effect societal transformation [23, 24].

S5.0 will need people with vivid imaginations and creative minds to pinpoint the wide range of societal needs and problems plaguing today and imagine workable solutions. It will also be necessary to implement publicly available data and digital-based strategies. It will be simpler to handle problems and create profit by fusing digitalization with the creative ideas of many individuals, heralding in a prosperous society. S5.0 will be an "inventive community", where digitalization works in tandem with human ingenuity and creativity to address social issues and develop fresh profit. Hence, in S5.0, individuals will utilize their ingenuity to find methods to coexist peacefully in order to keep making great strides forward.

20.3   Comparative Analysis of I4.0 to I5.0 and S4.0 to S5.0

The healthcare, industrial, textile, academic, and culinary sectors are just a few wherein Industry 5.0 is now taking shape. Most industries are adopting industry 5.0 as they make the shift to the intelligent societal plant. I5.0 is a term used to describe a business that is innovative, flexible, culturally sensitive, and efficient and that operates within its means while minimizing its negative impact on the environment. It raises many fresh questions in the areas of creativity, economics, rules, and management.

Some of the key enabling technologies (KET) that are facilitating the evolution from the current fourth industrial revolution to the fifth industrial revolution are as follows:

- Human-centered innovations that combine the best of both the digital and analog worlds.
- Products with integrated sensors and improved functionality are made possible by smart components and bio-inspired advancements.
- Whole-system modeling and simulation in real time using digital twins.
- Technologies that ensure the integrity of data at every stage of its life cycle, from collection to analysis to storage, and are capable of managing system and data interoperability in cyberspace.
- Knowledge production and the capacity to identify causal linkages in complex, dynamic systems are two examples of artificial intelligence.
- Because of its high power consumption, the KET necessitate the development of energy-saving and trustworthy autonomous technologies.

When combined with perceptual innovation and creativity, multiple facilitating technological developments can help sectors expand the supply and implement innovative products more quickly. Industry 5.0 is a state-of-the-art manufacturing model that places a premium on human–machine collaboration because of the technology that underpins it. The crucial technologies that will allow Industry 5.0 to flourish are shown in Figure 20.4.

The developments in digital technology are increasingly influenced by the society at large. The main points of S5.0 are laid forth in Table 20.2.

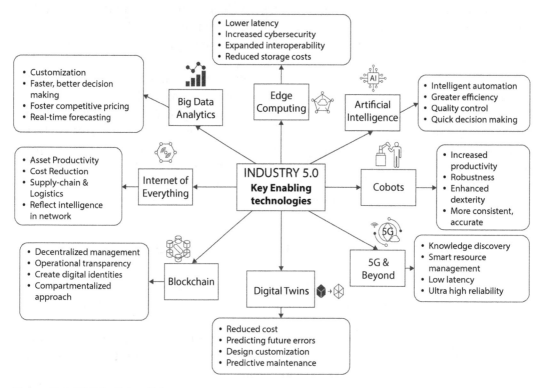

Figure 20.4 KET for I4.0 to I5.0.

Table 20.2 Focus of S5.0.

Characteristics	S4.0	S5.0
Concentration on industry	Merchandise and object categories	Values understood; problems solved
Applications	Construction, logistics, finance	Mobility, eco-friendly energy
General objective	Make the switch to a co-creation model that is more distributed and autonomous, where industry sectors create a business edifice considering customer morals and mix technology and networks from their very own competence sphere.	

Co-creation is a new kind of cooperation that goes beyond traditional commercial and corporate ties by focusing on the needs of the consumers and the solutions to problems facing the society. It relies on the introduction of novel commercial prototypes and bionetworks in which distinct businesses may generate income by combining diverse strategies to complement one another's weaknesses and maximize their own strengths. Businesses work together to create new business opportunities by using one or more of these techniques. In order to support co-creation, it is essential to set up platforms and channels for involvement from various industries to define the goals and expectations of the intended audience, to ensure multi-level communication, and to design suitable governance structures.

A. Management of the Future

- The digital and technological revolution is definitely leading the way in the wave of change that is presently sweeping over almost every facet of modern life.
- Just like every coin that has two sides, it has been shown that the exponential rise of breakthroughs has numerous positive effects on people's lives. There are also detrimental effects on the surrounding area.
- The growth and development of society are profoundly affected by the methods through which we seek to shape it.
- When societies experience such a dramatic shift into an utterly rationalized and automated sociological strategy, changes are possible at all levels of management, legislation, and tradition.
- One of the most important variables impacting the forthcoming management practice is how we manage and data dealing. This finally paved the way for the common man to recognize the many marketing categorizations and provide the groundwork for the construction of a transformation journey.
- There can be little question those standard procedures for both marketing and administration need to depart from what has worked in the past.
- The "marketing mix", "4P" for short, is one such example. Access to the product is increased with this method because a detailed description of the product is provided, including information that is often left out of advertisements.

B. Essential Competencies for Industry and Society 5.0

The improvement of machinery and manufacturing processes is only one aspect of industrialization fueled by AI. Investment in people to back up such new ventures is far more important for the long run. When it comes to getting the most out of their smart factory investments, 36% of businesses say that the lack of technical skills is the biggest roadblock. Additionally, 57% of industry executives believe that their organizations lack the AI competence necessary to implement all of the self-directed and intellectual elucidations that will replace 3D labor. The current and prospective top five essential skills are shown in Table 20.3.

Table 20.3 Skillsets required for I5.0 and S5.0.

Present skillset	Future skillset
Basics of programming	Deep knowledge on programming
Manufacturing skills	Flexibility to leverage enabling technologies
Communication skills	Cognitive skills

Table 20.4 Challenges and opportunities of I5.0 and S5.0.

Challenges	Opportunities
Population aging factor	Humanoid cyber physical system
Shortcomings in resources	Eco-intelligent manufacturing
Societal pollution	Humanoid collaboration
Complex solutions	Futuristic jobs
Constrained frameworks	Humanoid digital twin

20.4   Risks and Prospects

As mentioned in I5.0 and S5.0, one of the key objectives of the digital and green transformations is to guarantee that individuals could remain to have fulfilling, productive lifestyles. As a result, institutions like companies and colleges will play a more pivotal role in achieving this objective. Initiatives to promote industrial innovation and enhance everyone's information literacy must go hand in hand with the expansion of information technology if we are to make progress towards a genuinely individual-based way of living. In order to mend the domestic culture that defines S5.0, institutions of higher education must continue to be responsible for producing technology, but they must also be liable in promoting knowledge amid evidence handlers via a common curriculum and targeted insight and training.

In conclusion, it is important to stress that Industry 5.0 is a fundamental part of the broader Society 5.0 movement. At this point about to come, the fifth industrial revolution will speed up the process of societal progress. The ensuing Industrial Revolution (IR) will be aided by the general expansion of civilization. Table 20.4 provides a concise summary of the challenges and possibilities that have been identified among I5.0 and S5.0.

20.5   Conclusion

In this chapter, we analyzed the literature on the topic of Industry 5.0 and Society 5.0 to better understand their potential impact on the future. This review of enabling technologies advances a methodological approach in a sector which has not yet been meticulously studied by researchers while also attempting to produce a detailed study of current researches and provide an early overview of the most beneficial technology components for the transformation from I4.0 to I5.0 and S5.0. An examination of the recent empirical research and materials from public agencies working on similar measures suggests that I5.0 is more than just a passing trend and that the advent of Society 5.0 will provide brand-new possibilities for the development of an extremely smart globalized world. By analyzing the data provided, we can project how I5.0 will change the background of manufacturing in the next existences and plan for it accordingly. It is hoped that, in a later study, data crawling methods and a more in-depth analysis would shed light on what I5.0 actually is and the way the intellectual world sees it.

Acknowledgment

I thank the co-authors, Mr. S. Jeevanandham, Dr. M. Sundarrajan, Mrs. Akshya Jothi, Mrs. K. Prashanthini, and Dr. V. Sarvanan, for their valuable contribution to this chapter and helping me in bringing this chapter to be a good work.

References

1. Zengin, Y., Naktiyok, S., Kaygın, E., Kavak, O., Topçuoğlu, E., An investigation upon Industry 4.0 and Society 5.0 within the context of sustainable development goals. *Sustainability*, 13, 2682, 2021.

2. Mourtzis, D., Angelopoulos, J., Panopoulos, N., A literature review of the challenges and opportunities of the transition from Industry 4.0 to Society 5.0. *Energies*, 15, 17, 6276, 1–29, 2022.

3. Adel, A., Future of Industry 5.0 in society: Human-centric solutions, challenges and prospective research areas. *J. Cloud Comp.*, 11, 40, 2022.

4. Akundi, A., Euresti, D., Luna, S., Ankobiah, W., Lopes, A., Edinbarough, I., State of Industry 5.0—Analysis and identification of current research trends. *Appl. Syst. Innov.*, 5, 1, 27, Feb. 2022.

5. Nair, M.M., Tyagi, A.K., Sreenath, N., The future with Industry 4.0 at the core of Society 5.0: Open issues, future opportunities and challenges. *2021 International Conference on Computer Communication and Informatics (ICCCI)*, Coimbatore, India, pp. 1–7, 2021.

6. Xu, X., Lu, Y., Vogel-Heuser, B., Wang, L., Industry 4.0 and Industry 5.0—Inception, conception and perception. *J. Manuf. Syst.*, 61, 530–535, 2021.

7. Skobelev, P.O. and Borovik, S.Y., On the way from Industry 4.0 to Industry 5.0: From digital manufacturing to digital society. *Industry 4.0*, 2, 307–311, 2017.

8. Javaid, M., Haleem, A., Singh, R.P., Haq, M.I., Raina, A., Suman, R., Industry 5.0: Potential applications in COVID-19. *J. Industr. Integr. Manag.*, 5, 04, 507–530, 2020.

9. Martos, V., Ahmad, A., Cartujo, P., Ordoñez, J., Ensuring agricultural sustainability through remote sensing in the era of agriculture 5.0. *Appl. Sci.*, 11, 13, 5911, 2021.

10. Imoize, A.L., Adedeji, O., Tandiya, N., Shetty, S., 6G enabled smart infrastructure for sustainable society: Opportunities, challenges, and research roadmap. *Sensors*, 21, 5, 1709, 2021.

11. Ocicka, B. and Turek, J., Supply chain sustainability risk management in a digitally VUCA changing world, in: *The Economics of Sustainable Transformation*, pp. 167–190, Routledge, London, 2021.

12. Masood, T. and Sonntag, P., Industry 4.0: Adoption challenges and benefits for SMEs. *Comput. Ind.*, 121, 103261, 2020.

13. Carayannis, E.G., Christodoulou, K., Christodoulou, P., Chatzichristofis, S.A., Zinonos, Z., Known unknowns in an era of technological and viral disruptions-implications for theory, policy, and practice. *J. Knowl. Econ.*, 13, 587–610, 2022.

14. Adadi, A. and Berrada, M., Peeking inside the black-box: A survey on explainable artificial intelligence (xai). *IEEE Access*, 6, 52138–52160, 2018.

15. Ali, M.H., Issayev, G., Shehab, E., Sarfraz, S., A critical review of 3D printing and digital manufacturing in construction engineering. *Rapid Prototyping J.*, 28, 7, 1312–1324, 2022.

16. Sherburne, C., Textile industry 5.0? Fiber computing coming soon to a fabric near you. *AATCC Rev.*, 20, 6, 25–30, 2020.

17. Saraswa, V., Jacobberger, R.M., Arnold, M.S., Materials science challenges to graphene nanoribbon electronics. *ACS Nano*, 15, 3, 3674–3708, 2021.

18. Yu, M., Lou, S., Gonzalez-Bobes, F., Ring-closing metathesis in pharmaceutical development: Fundamentals, applications, and future directions. *Org. Process. Res. Dev.*, 22, 8, 918–946, 2018.
19. Peck, M.E. and Moore, S.K., The blossoming of the blockchain. *IEEE Spectr.*, 54, 10, 24–25, 2017.
20. Deguchi, A., Hirai, C., Matsuoka, H., Nakano, T., Oshima, K., Tai, M., Tani, S., What is society 5.0?, in: *Society 5.0: A People-Centric Super-Smart Society*, pp. 1–23, Springer, Singapore, 2020.
21. Mourtzis, D., Development of skills and competences in manufacturing towards education 4.0: A teaching factory approach, in: *Proceedings of the 3rd International Conference on the Industry 4.0 Model for Advanced Manufacturing*, Belgrade, Serbia, pp. 194–210, 5–7 June 2018.
22. Mamasioulas, A., Mourtzis, D., Chryssolouris, G., A manufacturing innovation overview: Concepts, models and metrics. *Int. J. Comput. Integr. Manuf.*, 33, 769–791, 2020.
23. Mourtzis, D., Angelopoulos, J., Panopoulos, N., Smart manufacturing and tactile internet based on 5G in industry 4.0: Challenges, applications and new trends. *Electronics*, 10, 3175, 2021.
24. Mourtzis, D., Simulation in the design and operation of manufacturing systems: State of the art and new trends. *Int. J. Prod. Res.*, 58, 1927–1949, 2020.

Futuristic Technologies for Smart Manufacturing: Research Statement and Vision for the Future

**Amit Kumar Tyagi[1]*, Anand Kumar Mishra[2], Nalla Vedavathi[3], Vijayalakshmi Kakulapati[4]
and Sajidha S. A.[3]**

*[1]School of Computer Science and Engineering, Vellore Institute of Technology,
Chennai, Tamil Nadu, India
[2]Computer Science and Engineering, NIIT University, Neemrana, Rajasthan, India
[3]Department of Fashion Technology, National Institute of Fashion Technology, New Delhi, Delhi, India
[4]Sreenidhi Institute of Science and Technology, Yamnampet, Ghatkesar, Hyderabad, Telangana, India*

Abstract

Industry 5.0 is an era of Internet of Things, artificial intelligence, and digital twin technology for smart manufacturing. The integration of futuristic technologies in smart manufacturing presents endless opportunities for manufacturers to increase efficiency, reduce costs, and improve product quality. However, to fully realize the benefits of these technologies, manufacturers must embrace automation, data, collaboration, training, and flexibility. The successful implementation of futuristic technologies in smart manufacturing requires a culture of innovation and continuous improvement as well as a willingness to take risks and try new approaches. By using data to make data-driven decisions, manufacturers can improve product quality and reduce waste, creating a positive impact on the environment. Smart manufacturing also creates new job opportunities in programming, data analysis, and robotics. Ultimately, the integration of futuristic technologies in smart manufacturing is essential for the continued growth and success of the manufacturing industry.

Keywords: Smart applications, futuristic technologies, smart applications, blockchain technology, Industry 5.0, Society 5.0

21.1 Introduction About Futuristic Technologies

Futuristic technologies refer to advanced and cutting-edge technologies that are currently in development or have the potential to be developed in the future. These technologies are often seen as transformative and can radically alter the way we live, work, and interact with each other and the world around us. Some examples of futuristic technologies include artificial intelligence (AI), quantum computing, biotechnology, nanotechnology, robotics, space exploration, renewable energy, and blockchain technology. These technologies are

---
*Corresponding author: amitkrtyagi025@gmail.com

Amit Kumar Tyagi (ed.) *Automated Secure Computing for Next-Generation Systems*, (415–442) © 2024 Scrivener Publishing LLC

expected to shape the future of various industries, from healthcare and finance to transportation and entertainment.

Futuristic technologies are often driven by the desire to solve complex problems and make our lives easier, more sustainable, and more efficient [1]. However, they also raise important ethical, social, and environmental questions that need to be addressed. As these technologies become more prevalent and integrated into our lives, it is crucial to consider their potential impact and ensure that they are developed and used responsibly. A few of these technologies are discussed in the following sections.

Internet of Things: The Internet of Things (IoT) refers to the growing network of physical devices, vehicles, buildings, and other objects that are connected to the Internet and can exchange data with each other. These devices often have sensors or actuators that allow them to gather and transmit data, receive instructions, or interact with their environment [2].

The IoT is a rapidly growing field with an enormous potential to transform various industries, from healthcare and manufacturing to transportation and agriculture. It can enable the development of smart homes, cities, and factories, improve supply chain management, and facilitate the remote monitoring and control of devices and systems. However, the IoT also raises important challenges related to privacy, security, and data management. The sheer amount of data generated by these devices requires advanced analytics and machine learning algorithms to extract meaningful insights and value [3]. Additionally, ensuring the security and privacy of IoT devices and data is crucial, as they can be vulnerable to cyberattacks and data breaches. In summary, the IoT represents a major technological shift that has the potential to revolutionize the way that we interact with the world around us. As more devices become connected and data-driven, it is important to carefully consider the ethical, social, and environmental implications of this trend and work to address the associated challenges.

Cloud/Fog/Edge/Grid Computing: Cloud, fog, edge, and grid computing are all forms of distributed computing that involve processing data and performing computations across multiple interconnected devices and systems.

- Cloud computing refers to the delivery of computing services, such as servers, storage, databases, and software, over the Internet. Cloud computing allows users to access computing resources on demand, pay only for what they use, and scale up or down as needed [4].
- Fog computing is a type of distributed computing that extends cloud computing to the edge of the network. It involves the use of intermediate devices, such as routers, gateways, and switches, to provide computing, storage, and networking services closer to the devices and sensors generating data [5].
- Edge computing is a form of distributed computing that involves processing data and performing computations at or near the edge of the network where the data is generated [6]. It enables faster response times, reduces network traffic, and improves data privacy and security.
- Grid computing is a type of distributed computing that involves the use of geographically distributed and heterogeneous resources, such as computers, storage devices, and networks, to perform large-scale computations and solve complex problems [7].

In summary, these forms of distributed computing have become increasingly important in the age of big data, IoT, and AI, as they provide scalable, cost-effective, and efficient ways of processing and analyzing large amounts of data and performing complex computations.

Parallel Computing: Parallel computing is a type of computation that involves dividing a large computational task into smaller sub-tasks that can be performed simultaneously on multiple processors or computing devices [8]. This allows for faster execution times and improved performance compared to traditional sequential computing, where tasks are performed one after the other on a single processor. Parallel computing has become increasingly important in recent years due to the increasing amount of data and the growing complexity of algorithms in fields such as scientific computing, data analytics, and artificial intelligence. Parallel computing can be implemented using a variety of architectures, including multi-core processors, graphics processing units, clusters, and distributed computing systems [9]. There are two main types of parallel computing: shared memory and distributed memory. In shared memory systems, multiple processors access a shared memory pool, while in distributed memory systems, each processor has its own private memory and communicates with other processors using message passing. Parallel computing can significantly accelerate computations and enable the development of more accurate and sophisticated models and simulations [10]. However, it also requires careful consideration of issues such as load balancing, data partitioning, and synchronization to ensure that the computations are performed efficiently and accurately. In summary, parallel computing is a critical technology for advancing scientific research, engineering, and computing in general.

Blockchain Technology: Blockchain technology is a decentralized digital ledger that records transactions in a secure and immutable manner [11]. It was invented in 2008 by an anonymous person or group of people known by the pseudonym Satoshi Nakamoto as the underlying technology for the cryptocurrency Bitcoin. A blockchain consists of a series of blocks, each containing a set of transactions, and is distributed across a network of computers, known as nodes. Each block is linked to the previous one, forming a chain of blocks, hence the name blockchain. The decentralized nature of blockchain technology means that there is no need for a central authority or intermediary to validate transactions, which reduces the risk of fraud and corruption [12]. The security of the blockchain is maintained through a consensus mechanism, which ensures that all nodes in the network agree on the state of the ledger. Apart from its application in cryptocurrencies, blockchain technology has potential uses in a wide range of industries, including finance, healthcare, logistics, and supply chain management. It can be used to create smart contracts, improve transparency, reduce costs, and increase efficiency in various processes.

Artificial Intelligence: Artificial intelligence, commonly referred to as AI, is a branch of computer science that focuses on the development of intelligent machines that can perform tasks that typically require human-like intelligence [13]. AI technology involves the creation of algorithms, programs, and computer systems that can learn from and adapt to data, make decisions, and perform tasks autonomously. AI can be classified into two main categories: narrow or weak AI and general or strong AI. Narrow or weak AI is designed to perform a specific task, such as image or speech recognition, and can only operate within its predefined parameters. General or strong AI, on the other hand, is designed to perform any intellectual task that a human can do, with the ability to learn and reason like a human. AI has numerous practical applications in various industries, including healthcare, finance, manufacturing, transportation, and more. It can be used to automate repetitive tasks, enhance decision-making processes, improve customer service, and create more personalized experiences.

Digital Twin Technology: Digital twin technology refers to a virtual representation of a physical object, process, or system. It is a software-based model that simulates the behavior and performance of the physical entity in real time. Digital twins can be used to optimize the design and operation of complex systems, such as buildings, manufacturing equipment, and infrastructure [14]. Digital twin technology uses a combination of technologies such as IoT, AI, and machine learning to create a virtual model of the physical system. The digital twin can be used to monitor and analyze the performance of the physical system, predict maintenance needs, optimize operations, and identify opportunities for improvement. The potential applications of digital twin technology are numerous, from improving the efficiency and sustainability of industrial processes to enhancing the design and construction of buildings and infrastructure. With the rapid advancement of technology, digital twin technology is expected to become increasingly common across industries, providing new opportunities for innovation and growth.

Quantum Computing: Quantum computing is a rapidly advancing field of computing that seeks to exploit the fundamental principles of quantum mechanics to perform certain types of calculations much faster than classical computers [15]. Quantum computers use qubits, or quantum bits, which are quantum systems that can exist in multiple states simultaneously, to perform calculations in parallel and quickly solve complex problems that are beyond the reach of classical computers. Unlike classical bits, which can only represent either 0 or 1, qubits can represent a superposition of both states at the same time, allowing for a much faster computation. Additionally, qubits can be entangled, which means that they are intrinsically linked and their states are correlated, even when separated by large distances. Quantum computing has the potential to revolutionize many fields, including cryptography, chemistry, materials science, and machine learning, by enabling faster and more accurate simulations and calculations [16]. However, quantum computers are still in the early stages of development, and many technical challenges remain to be addressed before they can be widely used. Despite the challenges, quantum computing is an exciting and rapidly evolving field that has the potential to transform computing as we know it, and many researchers and companies around the world are working to develop and improve quantum computers and algorithms.

In last, this chapter has been summarized in 12 (twelve) sections.

21.2   Related Work Towards Futuristic Technologies

There is a large area of research and development in the area of futuristic technologies, as companies and governments seek to push the boundaries of what is possible and drive innovation in a wide range of fields. Some of the key futuristic technologies being explored and developed include the following:

- Quantum Computing: Quantum computing is a rapidly evolving field that seeks to use the principles of quantum mechanics to perform calculations much faster than classical computers. Quantum computers have the potential to revolutionize fields such as cryptography, chemistry, and machine learning [17].
- Artificial Intelligence: AI is a broad field that includes a wide range of technologies, from machine learning and natural language processing to computer vision and robotics [18]. AI is being used in a growing number of applications, from autonomous vehicles and virtual assistants to medical diagnosis and financial analysis.
- Nanotechnology: Nanotechnology involves the manipulation of matter at the atomic and molecular scale and has the potential to transform many fields, from electronics and materials science to medicine and energy production. Nanotechnology is being used to develop new materials, sensors, and devices that are smaller, faster, and more efficient than ever before [19].
- Augmented and Virtual Reality: Augmented and virtual reality technologies are being used in a growing number of applications, from gaming and entertainment to education and training. These technologies have the potential to transform many fields, from architecture and design to healthcare and tourism [20].
- Robotics: Robotics technology is being used in a wide range of applications, from manufacturing and logistics to healthcare and exploration [21]. Advances in robotics technology are enabling the development of increasingly sophisticated and versatile robots that can perform a wide range of tasks.

Hence, the development of futuristic technologies is a rapidly evolving field, with many companies and researchers working to create new and innovative solutions to some of the world's most pressing problems. The potential applications of these technologies are vast, and their impact on society is likely to be profound.

21.3   Related Work Towards Smart Manufacturing

There is a growing body of research and development in the area of futuristic technologies for smart manufacturing, as companies and governments seek to optimize production processes and increase efficiency through the use of advanced technologies. Some of the key technologies being explored and developed for smart manufacturing include the following:

- Internet of Things: IoT technology involves connecting physical devices, such as sensors and actuators, to the Internet, allowing for real-time monitoring and control of manufacturing processes. IoT can be used to collect data on machine performance, energy consumption, and other variables and use that data to optimize production and reduce waste [22].
- Artificial Intelligence: AI can be used to analyze large amounts of data generated by manufacturing processes and provide insights into production

efficiency and quality control [23]. AI can also be used to develop predictive maintenance models, which can help to prevent equipment breakdowns and reduce downtime.

- Additive Manufacturing: Additive manufacturing, also known as 3D printing, is an innovative manufacturing technology that involves creating 3D objects by adding a material layer by layer [24]. This technology can be used to create complex parts quickly and with high precision and can also reduce waste by using only the necessary amount of material.

- Augmented Reality (AR): AR technology can be used to provide workers with real-time information and guidance during manufacturing processes, reducing errors and increasing efficiency [25]. AR can also be used for remote training and collaboration, allowing workers to connect with experts in other locations.

- Blockchain: Blockchain technology can be used to securely store and share manufacturing data, such as production records and supply chain information. This can help to improve transparency and accountability in manufacturing processes and ensure that all stakeholders have access to accurate and up-to-date information [26].

In summary, the development of futuristic technologies for smart manufacturing is a rapidly evolving field, with many companies and researchers working to create new and innovative solutions for optimizing production processes and increasing efficiency.

21.4   Literature Review Towards Futuristic Technology

Futuristic technologies refer to the emerging and rapidly evolving technologies that are expected to significantly impact society, business, and individuals in the future. These technologies are likely to revolutionize the way we live, work, and interact with one another. This literature review aims to explore some of the most promising futuristic technologies and their potential implications.

- Artificial Intelligence: Artificial intelligence has been one of the most discussed and hyped futuristic technologies in recent years. AI refers to machines and algorithms that can perform tasks that typically require human intelligence, such as recognizing speech, identifying images, making decisions, and learning from data [27]. The potential applications of AI are numerous, including healthcare, finance, education, transportation, and more. However, there are concerns about the ethical and social implications of AI, such as job displacement, bias, privacy, and safety.

- Internet of Things: The Internet of Things is another futuristic technology that is rapidly gaining popularity. IoT refers to the interconnected network of physical devices, vehicles, home appliances, and other objects that can collect and exchange data. The potential benefits of IoT include increased efficiency, improved safety, and enhanced convenience [28]. However, there are also concerns about security and privacy risks associated with IoT as well as the potential for misuse and abuse of data.

- Blockchain: Blockchain is a decentralized and secure digital ledger that allows for secure transactions without the need for a central authority. Blockchain technology has gained significant attention due to its potential applications in finance, supply chain management, healthcare, and more [29]. The potential benefits of blockchain include increased transparency, reduced costs, and enhanced security. However, there are also concerns about scalability, interoperability, and regulatory issues associated with blockchain.

- Augmented Reality and Virtual Reality (VR): Augmented reality and virtual reality are two futuristic technologies that are rapidly gaining popularity in gaming, entertainment, and education. AR refers to the overlay of digital information on the real world, while VR refers to the creation of immersive, simulated environments. The potential applications of AR and VR are numerous, including education, healthcare, training, and more [30]. However, there are concerns about the potential negative effects of the prolonged use of AR and VR on physical and mental health.

- Quantum Computing: Quantum computing is a futuristic technology that uses the principles of quantum mechanics to process information. Quantum computers are expected to be much faster and more powerful than traditional computers and could potentially revolutionize industries such as finance, cryptography, and drug discovery. However, quantum computing is still in its early stages of development, and there are significant technical and practical challenges that need to be overcome before it becomes a widely used technology [31].

Hence, futuristic technologies have the potential to significantly impact society, business, and individuals in the future. While there are many promising applications of these technologies, there are also significant concerns about the ethical, social, and technical implications. As these technologies continue to evolve and develop, it will be important to carefully consider their potential benefits and risks and to ensure that they are used in a responsible and ethical manner.

21.5 Motivation

The motivation behind writing this chapter to identify, detect, explore, etc., essential issue and challenges in the respective domain. We can explain each points here as:

- Exploring Emerging Technologies: Provides an opportunity to explore emerging technologies in the field of manufacturing, such as artificial intelligence, machine learning, and the internet of things. This can help to broaden one's understanding of the field and identify new opportunities for research and development.

- Addressing Current Challenges: Smart manufacturing can help address current challenges in the manufacturing industry, such as reducing costs, improving efficiency, and enhancing quality control. By exploring futuristic technologies, this paper can help identify potential solutions to these challenges.

- Advancing the Field: Smart manufacturing is a rapidly evolving field, and this work can contribute to its advancement by proposing new research directions, identifying key challenges and opportunities, and highlighting promising areas for collaboration.
- Building Interdisciplinary Collaborations: This paper can bring together experts from different disciplines, such as engineering, computer science, and business, to explore the potential of futuristic technologies in smart manufacturing. This can lead to new collaborations and partnerships that can advance the field.
- Informing Policy and Practice: Inform policymakers and industry practitioners about the potential of futuristic technologies in smart manufacturing and the implications of adopting these technologies. This can lead to more informed decision-making and better outcomes for the industry as a whole.

21.6   Smart Applications

Smart applications refer to software programs and systems that use artificial intelligence, machine learning, and other advanced technologies to automate tasks, personalize experiences, and enhance efficiency [32]. With the increasing prevalence of connected devices and the Internet of Things, smart applications are becoming more widespread and are expected to play a significant role in shaping the future of technology. This literature review aims to explore some of the most promising smart applications and their potential implications.

Smart Home Automation: Smart home automation refers to the use of connected devices and sensors to automate and control the various functions of a home, such as lighting, temperature, security, and entertainment. The potential benefits of smart home automation include increased comfort, energy efficiency, and convenience. However, there are also concerns about the security and privacy risks associated with these technologies, which can be included here as:

a. Personalized Health Applications: Personalized health applications refer to software programs and systems that use data analytics, machine learning, and other technologies to tailor health recommendations and interventions to an individual's unique needs and preferences. The potential benefits of personalized health applications include improved health outcomes, increased patient engagement, and reduced healthcare costs. However, there are also concerns about the accuracy, privacy, and ethical implications of these technologies [33].

b. Smart Transportation: Smart transportation refers to the use of connected devices and sensors to optimize and automate transportation systems, such as traffic management, public transit, and logistics. The potential benefits of smart transportation include increased efficiency, reduced congestion, and improved safety. However, there are also concerns about the reliability, security, and ethical implications of these technologies [34].

c. Smart Agriculture: Smart agriculture refers to the use of connected devices and sensors to optimize and automate various aspects of agriculture, such as irrigation, fertilization, and pest control [35]. The potential benefits of smart agriculture include increased productivity, reduced costs, and improved sustainability. However, there are also concerns about the potential negative environmental and social impacts of these technologies.

d. Smart Education: Smart education refers to the use of technology to enhance and personalize learning experiences, such as adaptive learning systems, virtual classrooms, and gamification. The potential benefits of smart education include increased student engagement, improved outcomes, and reduced costs [36]. However, there are also concerns about the potential negative effects of excessive screen time and the need for appropriate regulation and oversight.

e. Smart Manufacturing: Smart manufacturing refers to the use of advanced technologies such as IoT, AI, machine learning, and automation to optimize and streamline manufacturing processes. Smart manufacturing systems are designed to be more efficient, flexible, and responsive to changing market demands and are expected to play a key role in the future of manufacturing. This literature review aims to explore some of the most promising smart manufacturing technologies and their potential implications [37] as:

- Industrial Internet of Things (IIoT): The industrial Internet of Things refers to the use of connected devices, sensors, and machines to collect and exchange data in real time, allowing for more efficient and optimized manufacturing processes [38]. IIoT technologies can help manufacturers monitor and control the performance of equipment, optimize production schedules, and reduce downtime. However, there are also concerns about security risks and the need for appropriate data management and analysis.

- Artificial Intelligence and Machine Learning: Artificial intelligence and machine learning technologies can be used in smart manufacturing systems to optimize production processes, predict maintenance needs, and improve product quality [39]. AI and machine learning can also be used to analyze data collected from connected devices and sensors to identify patterns and make predictions about future trends. However, there are concerns about the need for appropriate data governance, transparency, and ethical considerations.

- Robotics and Automation: Robotics and automation technologies can be used in smart manufacturing to perform repetitive or dangerous tasks, increase productivity, and reduce costs [40]. Robotics and automation can also help manufacturers respond quickly to changing market demands and product requirements. However, there are concerns about the potential for job displacement and the need for appropriate training and education for workers.

- Additive Manufacturing: Additive manufacturing, also known as 3D printing, is a technology that allows for the production of complex and customized parts using a layer-by-layer approach. Additive manufacturing can be used to reduce waste, increase production efficiency, and reduce lead times [41]. However, there are also concerns about the need for appropriate quality control and the potential impact on traditional manufacturing supply chains.

- Digital Twin: A digital twin is a virtual replica of a physical manufacturing system that can be used to monitor and optimize performance in real time [42]. Digital twins can help manufacturers predict maintenance needs, improve product quality, and reduce downtime. However, there are concerns about the need for appropriate data management and analysis as well as the potential for security risks.

Smart manufacturing technologies are expected to play a key role in the future of manufacturing, offering significant potential benefits in terms of efficiency, productivity, and responsiveness [43]. However, there are also significant concerns about the need for appropriate data governance, security, privacy, and ethical considerations. As these technologies continue to evolve and develop, it will be important to carefully consider their potential benefits and risks and to ensure that they are used in a responsible and ethical manner.

Smart applications are becoming increasingly prevalent and are expected to play a significant role in shaping the future of technology. While there are many promising applications of these technologies, there are also significant concerns about their accuracy, security, privacy, and ethical implications [44]. As these technologies continue to evolve and develop, it will be important to carefully consider their potential benefits and risks and to ensure that they are used in a responsible and ethical manner.

21.7   Popular Issues with Futuristic Technologies for Emerging Applications

As futuristic technologies continue to evolve and gain traction in various industries, they also face several challenges that must be addressed to ensure their successful integration into emerging applications. Some of the popular issues with futuristic technologies for emerging applications are as follows:

- Security Concerns: With emerging technologies, security concerns are always a significant issue. As these technologies become more connected, they become more vulnerable to cyber attacks [45]. Companies must take measures to ensure data privacy and secure the systems from potential threats.
- Ethics: With advancements in AI and machine learning (ML), ethical considerations become crucial. It is essential to ensure that these technologies are used responsibly and not in ways that may harm society or individuals. Regulations must be put in place to govern their use [46].
- Limited Access to Infrastructure: Many emerging technologies require high-speed Internet connectivity, specialized equipment, and power supply, which may not be accessible in some areas [47]. Lack of access to the required infrastructure may limit the deployment of these technologies.
- Cost: Some futuristic technologies require significant investment, which may be a challenge for startups or small businesses. The cost of developing and implementing these technologies must be balanced with the potential benefits that they provide [48].
- Integration with Legacy Systems: In many industries, emerging technologies need to work seamlessly with existing legacy systems. Ensuring compatibility with these systems can be a significant challenge, as it may require significant modifications and upgrades to the existing systems [49].
- Adoption: Even with the potential benefits that emerging technologies offer, adoption may be slow. This may be due to a lack of awareness or understanding of these technologies or a reluctance to change established processes [50].

- Data Privacy: Emerging technologies, such as IoT devices, collect vast amounts of data. Ensuring that the data is stored, processed, and transmitted securely and with consent is crucial to protecting individual privacy [51].

In summary, addressing these issues is crucial to the successful integration of futuristic technologies into emerging applications. Companies must consider the potential challenges and develop strategies to overcome them, ensuring that they can maximize the potential benefits of these technologies while minimizing their risks.

21.7.1 Popular Issues with Futuristic Technologies for Smart Applications

There are several popular issues with futuristic technologies for smart applications that are currently being discussed and debated by researchers, policymakers, and the public. Here are some of the most significant ones:

- Privacy and Security: As smart devices and applications become more prevalent, the risk of privacy breaches and cyber attacks also increases [52]. There is a growing concern that these technologies may gather and store sensitive data about individuals, leading to potential violations of privacy. Additionally, cyber criminals could exploit these technologies to access personal data and exploit them for their own purposes.
- Ethical Concerns: There are concerns about the ethical implications of advanced technologies, such as AI and ML [53]—for example, some worry that AI algorithms could perpetuate biases, discrimination, and inequality. There are also questions about the moral responsibility of AI and autonomous systems and how they should be held accountable for their actions.
- Energy Consumption: The proliferation of smart devices and applications could lead to increased energy consumption, which could have negative consequences for the environment [54]. There are concerns about the sustainability of these technologies and how they can be made more energy-efficient.
- Health Risks: There is a growing concern about the potential health risks of exposure to electromagnetic radiation from smart devices and networks [55]. Some studies have suggested that prolonged exposure to these electromagnetic fields could increase the risk of cancer and other health problems.
- Social Impacts: The widespread use of advanced technologies could have significant social impacts—for example, there are concerns about the impact of automation on jobs and the workforce [56]. There are also questions about the impact of social media and other online platforms on mental health, social interactions, and democracy.
- Technological Dependence: As people become more reliant on smart technologies, there is a risk of technological dependence. This could lead to a loss of critical thinking skills, creativity, and problem-solving abilities as well as a loss of independence and self-reliance [57].

In summary, the development and adoption of futuristic technologies for smart applications bring with it a range of challenges and opportunities. It is essential that these issues are addressed through responsible and ethical practices to ensure that the benefits of these technologies are maximized while minimizing the potential harms.

21.7.2   Popular Issues with Futuristic Technologies for Smart Manufacturing

Smart manufacturing is the integration of advanced technologies such as artificial intelligence, machine learning, IoT, and robotics into manufacturing processes [58]. While these technologies have the potential to revolutionize manufacturing and bring significant benefits such as improved efficiency, reduced costs, and increased productivity, there are also several challenges and issues that need to be addressed. Here are some of the issues that may arise with the use of futuristic technologies for smart manufacturing:

- Security and Privacy Concerns: Smart manufacturing involves the use of vast amounts of data collected from machines, sensors, and other devices. This data can be vulnerable to cyber attacks, and there is a risk of sensitive information being compromised. Therefore, security and privacy are critical concerns that need to be addressed [59].
- Complexity: Smart manufacturing systems involve the integration of various technologies, which can make the systems complex and challenging to manage. Ensuring that all the components work together seamlessly requires significant expertise and resources [60].
- Skilled Labor Shortage: The adoption of futuristic technologies requires skilled labor, and there is a shortage of such workers in many parts of the world. This can limit the ability of companies to take full advantage of smart manufacturing [61].
- Cost: While futuristic technologies have the potential to improve efficiency and reduce costs in the long run, their implementation can be expensive [62]. The cost of upgrading existing systems and investing in new technologies can be a significant challenge for many companies.
- Ethical Concerns: Smart manufacturing can bring benefits such as improved efficiency and reduced costs, but it can also lead to job losses and increased automation [63]. Therefore, ethical considerations need to be taken into account, and strategies need to be developed to address the impact of these technologies on the workforce.
- Integration With Legacy Systems: Many manufacturing companies have legacy systems that are incompatible with the latest technologies. Integrating these systems with smart manufacturing technologies can be challenging and requires significant resources [64].

In summary, while the adoption of futuristic technologies in smart manufacturing has the potential to bring significant benefits, it also poses several challenges that need to be addressed. Companies need to be aware of these issues and develop strategies to overcome them to fully realize the potential of smart manufacturing.

21.8   Legal Issues Towards Futuristic Technologies

As futuristic technologies continue to evolve and are increasingly being integrated into various industries, they also raise several legal issues that must be addressed to ensure compliance with laws and regulations. Some of the legal issues with futuristic technologies for emerging applications are as follows:

- Intellectual Property: Futuristic technologies are often the subject of intellectual property disputes, including patents, copyrights, and trademarks. Companies must ensure that they have the necessary rights to develop and use these technologies, and they may need to defend their intellectual property rights against infringement by others [65].
- Liability: As futuristic technologies become more prevalent, the question of liability becomes more complex [66]. Who is responsible for the actions of an autonomous vehicle, for example, in the event of an accident? Companies must consider potential liability issues and take steps to mitigate them.
- Data Protection: Emerging technologies, such as AI and IoT devices, collect vast amounts of data, raising concerns about data protection and privacy [67]. Companies must ensure that they comply with data protection regulations and that they obtain the necessary consent for the collection, processing, and use of personal data.
- Cybersecurity: With emerging technologies becoming more connected, the risk of cyberattacks increases [68]. Companies must take measures to protect their systems from potential threats and ensure that they comply with cybersecurity regulations.
- Regulatory Compliance: Many futuristic technologies are subject to regulations, such as those governing healthcare, transportation, and energy. Companies must ensure that they comply with these regulations and obtain the necessary permits and approvals [69].
- Discrimination: Emerging technologies may have the potential to discriminate against certain individuals or groups, such as facial recognition technology being biased against certain skin tones [70]. Companies must ensure that their technologies do not violate anti-discrimination laws.
- International Laws: With futuristic technologies being developed and deployed globally, companies must also consider international laws and regulations. They must ensure that they comply with the relevant laws in each jurisdiction where their technologies are used [71].

Addressing these legal issues is crucial to the successful integration of futuristic technologies into emerging applications [72]. Companies must consider the potential legal implications of their technologies and develop strategies to comply with relevant laws and regulations while maximizing the benefits of these technologies.

21.9   Critical Challenges with Futuristic Technology for Emerging Applications

As technology continues to evolve and advance at a rapid pace, it brings with it a number of critical challenges that must be addressed in order to ensure that these emerging applications are developed and deployed in a safe and responsible manner. Some of the most significant challenges include:

- Ethical Concerns: One of the biggest challenges associated with futuristic technology is the ethical considerations that come with it—for example, there are concerns about the use of AI and machine learning in making decisions that could have significant impacts on people's lives, such as in hiring, medical diagnosis, and criminal justice [73]. There are also concerns about the use of advanced biotechnology, such as gene editing, and the potential for unintended consequences.
- Data Privacy and Security: With the increasing use of technology, the amount of data being collected and stored is also increasing. This data is often sensitive and personal, and there are concerns about how it is being used, who has access to it, and how it is being protected. As such, data privacy and security are major challenges that must be addressed [74].
- Regulatory and Legal Frameworks: The regulatory and legal frameworks surrounding futuristic technologies are often still in their infancy, which creates uncertainty and ambiguity around issues such as liability, intellectual property, and governance. Developing effective regulatory and legal frameworks that can keep up with the rapid pace of technological change is a significant challenge [75].
- Skills and Talent: As technology continues to evolve, there is a growing need for individuals with specialized skills and expertise to develop and deploy these emerging applications. However, there is often a shortage of skilled talent, which can limit the development and deployment of futuristic technologies [76].
- Societal Impact: Finally, there are concerns about the broader societal impact of futuristic technologies—for example, there are concerns about the potential for automation to displace human workers, the impact of social media and other forms of technology on mental health, and the potential for technology to exacerbate existing social inequalities [77].

In order to address these challenges, it is essential that stakeholders from industry, government, academia, and civil society work together to develop a comprehensive and proactive approach to the development and deployment of futuristic technologies. This should involve a range of measures, including the development of ethical frameworks, the implementation of effective data privacy and security measures, the establishment of appropriate regulatory and legal frameworks, and the investment in education and training programs to develop the skills and talent necessary to drive innovation in these areas.

21.9.1   Critical Challenges with Futuristic Technology for Smart Applications

As technology continues to advance, there are several critical challenges that need to be addressed in order to fully realize the potential of futuristic technology for smart applications. Here are some of the key challenges:

- Privacy and Security: With the proliferation of connected devices and the increasing amount of personal data being collected, privacy and security have become major concerns [78]. As smart applications become more integrated into our daily lives, it is crucial to ensure that the data being collected is secure and protected from unauthorized access.
- Interoperability: One of the biggest challenges with futuristic technology is ensuring that different devices and systems can communicate and work together seamlessly. Interoperability is crucial for smart applications to function properly and provide the desired benefits [79].
- Energy Efficiency: As smart applications become more complex and sophisticated, they require more energy to operate [80]. It is important to develop energy-efficient technologies and design smart applications that minimize energy consumption in order to reduce their environmental impact and maximize their sustainability.
- Access and Affordability: The benefits of futuristic technology for smart applications should be accessible to everyone regardless of their socioeconomic status. It is important to ensure that smart applications are affordable and accessible to all and that they are designed with a diverse range of users in mind [81].
- Ethical and Social Implications: The development and deployment of futuristic technology for smart applications also raises ethical and social concerns. It is important to consider the potential impact of these technologies on society and to develop ethical frameworks that guide their development and use [82].
- Data Bias and Fairness: As smart applications increasingly rely on artificial intelligence and machine learning algorithms to make decisions, there is a risk of bias and unfairness in the data used to train these algorithms. It is important to address these issues and ensure that smart applications are designed to be fair and unbiased [83].

Hence, addressing these critical challenges will be crucial to realizing the full potential of futuristic technology for smart applications while minimizing their negative impacts on society and the environment.

21.9.2   Challenges with Futuristic Technologies for Smart Manufacturing

Smart manufacturing is an area that is experiencing significant growth and innovation, as manufacturers seek to leverage futuristic technologies to improve productivity, quality, and efficiency. However, there are also a number of challenges associated with the adoption of these technologies in the manufacturing context. Some of the key challenges include:

- Integration and Interoperability: One of the biggest challenges associated with futuristic technologies for smart manufacturing is the need for integration and interoperability. This means that different systems and technologies need to be able to communicate and work together seamlessly in order to deliver the desired benefits [84]. However, this can be difficult to achieve, particularly when different technologies use different standards and protocols.
- Cybersecurity: As smart manufacturing systems become more connected and data-driven, there are increasing concerns about cybersecurity [85]. Manufacturing systems are vulnerable to cyber attacks, which can compromise data integrity, cause equipment damage, and even result in physical harm to workers. As such, cybersecurity is a critical challenge that must be addressed.
- Data Management and Analytics: Smart manufacturing systems generate vast amounts of data, which can be used to drive insights and improvements in performance. However, managing and analyzing this data can be a complex task, particularly when data is coming from multiple sources and in different formats [86].
- Workforce Skills and Training: Smart manufacturing systems require a highly skilled workforce capable of working with advanced technologies such as artificial intelligence, machine learning, and robotics. However, there is often a shortage of skilled workers in this area, which can limit the adoption of these technologies [87].
- Cost and Return on Investment: Finally, there is the challenge of cost and return on investment. Futuristic technologies for smart manufacturing often require significant investment in terms of both capital expenditure and ongoing operating costs. As such, it is important to carefully evaluate the potential return on investment in order to justify these investments [88].

In order to address these challenges, manufacturers need to take a holistic approach to the adoption of futuristic technologies for smart manufacturing. This means focusing on areas such as integration and interoperability, cybersecurity, data management and analytics, workforce skills and training, and cost and return on investment. It also means working closely with technology providers, industry associations, and other stakeholders to drive innovation and best practices in this area.

21.10   Research Opportunities for Futuristic Technologies Towards Emerging Applications

There are many research opportunities for futuristic technologies towards emerging applications. Here are a few examples:

- Quantum Computing: Quantum computing is a promising technology that could revolutionize computing by enabling complex calculations that are impossible with classical computers. There is a lot of research being done to develop new algorithms, hardware, and software for quantum computing, with potential applications in fields such as cryptography, optimization, and drug discovery [89].

- Nanotechnology: Nanotechnology involves the manipulation of matter on the atomic and molecular scale and has potential applications in fields such as electronics, medicine, and energy. Research in nanotechnology is focused on developing new materials, devices, and manufacturing techniques to enable these applications [90].
- Artificial Intelligence: AI involves the development of algorithms and systems that can learn from data and make intelligent decisions [91]. There is a lot of research being done in AI, including developing new algorithms for deep learning, reinforcement learning, and natural language processing as well as applications in fields such as healthcare, finance, and transportation.
- Robotics: Robotics involves the development of machines that can perform tasks autonomously or with minimal human intervention. There is a lot of research being done in robotics, including developing new hardware, software, and control systems for robots as well as applications in fields such as manufacturing, healthcare, and exploration [92].
- Biotechnology: Biotechnology involves the use of living organisms or their parts to develop new products or processes [93]. There is a lot of research being done in biotechnology, including developing new techniques for gene editing, protein engineering, and synthetic biology as well as applications in fields such as medicine, agriculture, and energy.

These are the few examples of research opportunities for futuristic technologies towards emerging applications. As technology continues to evolve, there will likely be many more opportunities to explore new frontiers and push the boundaries of what is possible.

21.10.1   Research Statements Towards Futuristic Technologies for Smart Applications

Smart applications are software programs that use advanced technologies such as artificial intelligence, machine learning, IoT, and big data analytics to improve user experiences, automate tasks, and optimize processes. There are numerous research opportunities in this field, particularly with respect to futuristic technologies that can enable even more advanced and intelligent smart applications. Here are some areas where research can be focused:

- Natural Language Processing: Research can be focused on developing natural language processing technologies that can accurately understand and respond to human language [94]. This can enable more advanced voice assistants, chatbots, and other smart applications that can understand and respond to user needs.
- Computer Vision: Computer vision technologies can be used to analyze images and videos, enabling smart applications to recognize objects, identify patterns, and even detect emotions [95]. This can enable more advanced video analysis, augmented reality, and facial recognition applications.
- Edge Computing: Edge computing can be used to process data at the edge of the network, closer to where it is generated [96]. This can help to reduce

latency and improve real-time decision-making, which is particularly important in smart applications such as autonomous vehicles, smart homes, and industrial IoT.

- Blockchain Technology: Blockchain technology can be used to create decentralized applications that are more secure, transparent, and efficient [97]. Research can be focused on developing blockchain-based smart applications that enable secure transactions, identity verification, and data sharing.

- Quantum Computing: Quantum computing can be used to solve complex optimization problems much faster than traditional computing systems [98]. This can enable more advanced machine learning algorithms, optimization algorithms, and simulations, which can be used to develop more intelligent and efficient smart applications.

- Cybersecurity: Research can be focused on developing more advanced cybersecurity technologies that can protect smart applications from cyber attacks. This can include advanced encryption technologies, intrusion detection and prevention systems, and secure communication protocols [99].

- Energy Efficiency: Research can be focused on developing smart applications that are more energy-efficient. This can include applications that use less power, such as low-power wireless communication protocols, as well as applications that can optimize energy usage based on user behavior and preferences [100].

Hence, there are numerous research opportunities for futuristic technologies in smart applications. These technologies have the potential to revolutionize the way we interact with technology, enabling more intelligent, efficient, and secure applications that improve our lives in a variety of ways.

21.10.2 Research Opportunities for Futuristic Technologies Towards Smart Manufacturing

Smart manufacturing is a growing field that involves the use of advanced technologies such as artificial intelligence, machine learning, IoT, and big data analytics to optimize manufacturing processes and improve overall efficiency [101]. There are numerous research opportunities in this field, particularly with respect to futuristic technologies that can enable even more advanced and efficient smart manufacturing systems. Here are some areas where research can be focused:

- Autonomous Systems: Research can be focused on developing autonomous systems that can manage the entire manufacturing process without any human intervention [102]. This can include robots that can assemble products, machines that can self-diagnose and repair, and systems that can optimize production schedules based on real-time data.

- Virtual and Augmented Reality: Virtual and augmented reality can be used to create simulations of manufacturing processes, allowing operators to visualize the process before it is executed [103]. This can help identify potential issues and optimize the process before it is actually implemented.

- Blockchain Technology: Blockchain technology can be used to track the entire manufacturing process, from raw materials to finished products. This can help to improve supply chain transparency, reduce counterfeiting, and enhance traceability [104].

- Quantum Computing: Quantum computing can be used to optimize manufacturing processes by solving complex optimization problems much faster than traditional computing systems [105]. This can help to reduce production time and costs and improve quality control.
- Edge Computing: Edge computing can be used to process data at the edge of the network, closer to where it is generated. This can help to reduce latency and improve real-time decision-making, which are particularly important in smart manufacturing [106].
- Additive Manufacturing: Additive manufacturing, also known as 3D printing, can be used to produce parts on demand, reducing the need for large inventories of parts [107]. Research can be focused on developing more advanced materials and processes to improve the speed and quality of 3D printing.
- Energy Efficiency: Research can be focused on developing technologies that can reduce energy consumption in manufacturing processes. This can include advanced materials that require less energy to produce as well as energy-efficient machines and processes [108].

Remember that, there are numerous research opportunities for futuristic technologies in smart manufacturing [104–120]. These technologies have the potential to revolutionize the manufacturing industry and make it more efficient, sustainable, and cost-effective.

21.11 Lesson Learned

Futuristic technologies are rapidly changing the manufacturing industry, and there are several lessons that can be learned from these innovations. Here are a few key lessons:

- Automation Is the Future: One of the biggest lessons learned from futuristic technologies in smart manufacturing is that automation is the future. With the development of robotics, machine learning, and artificial intelligence, it is now possible to automate many processes in manufacturing, from assembly lines to quality control. This can increase efficiency, reduce costs, and improve product quality.
- Data Is Critical: Another important lesson is that data is critical to smart manufacturing. With sensors, IoT devices, and other technologies, it is now possible to collect vast amounts of data about manufacturing processes, product quality, and other key metrics. By analyzing this data, manufacturers can identify areas for improvement and make data-driven decisions.
- Collaboration Is Key: Smart manufacturing requires collaboration between different departments, such as engineering, operations, and IT. This collaboration is essential for the successful implementation of futuristic technologies, as it ensures that everyone is working towards the same goals and that the technology is integrated into all aspects of the manufacturing process.

- Training Is Essential: The implementation of futuristic technologies in smart manufacturing requires new skills and knowledge. Therefore, training and education are essential to ensure that employees have the skills needed to operate and maintain these technologies. This training can include everything from basic computer skills to advanced programming and data analysis.
- Flexibility Is Critical: Finally, one of the most important lessons from futuristic technologies in smart manufacturing is that flexibility is critical. As technology continues to evolve, manufacturers must be willing to adapt and change their processes to take advantage of new innovations. This requires a culture of innovation and continuous improvement as well as the willingness to take risks and try new approaches.

Hence, the lessons learned from futuristic technologies in smart manufacturing are clear: automation, data, collaboration, training, and flexibility are all essential for success in this rapidly evolving industry. By embracing these lessons and continuing to innovate, manufacturers can stay ahead of the curve and thrive in the years to come.

21.12   Conclusion

Futuristic technologies are revolutionizing the manufacturing industry, and the opportunities for smart manufacturing are endless. By integrating automation, data, collaboration, training, and flexibility, manufacturers can take advantage of these technologies to increase efficiency, reduce costs, and improve product quality. The implementation of futuristic technologies in smart manufacturing requires a culture of innovation and continuous improvement as well as a willingness to take risks and try new approaches. It also requires collaboration between different departments, such as engineering, operations, and IT, to ensure that everyone is working towards the same goals and that the technology is integrated into all aspects of the manufacturing process. However, the benefits of smart manufacturing go beyond increased efficiency and reduced costs. By using data to make data-driven decisions, manufacturers can improve product quality and reduce waste, which can have a positive impact on the environment. Smart manufacturing also creates new job opportunities, particularly in the areas of programming, data analysis, and robotics. In conclusion, the integration of futuristic technologies in smart manufacturing is essential for the continued growth and success of the manufacturing industry. By embracing these technologies and the lessons learned from their implementation, manufacturers can stay ahead of the curve and thrive in the years to come.

References

1. Hodson, D., Time for action: Science education for an alternative future. *Int. J. Sci. Educ.*, 25, 6, 645–670, 2003.
2. Munirathinam, S., Industry 4.0: Industrial Internet of Things (IIoT), in: *Advances in Computers*, vol. 117, pp. 129–164, Elsevier, 2020. https://doi.org/10.1016/bs.adcom.2019.10.010

3. Saggi, M.K. and Sushma, J., A survey towards an integration of big data analytics to big insights for value-creation. *Inf. Process. & Manag.*, 54, 5, 758–790, 2018.

4. Bhardwaj, S., Jain, L., Jain, S., Cloud computing: A study of infrastructure as a service (IAAS). *Int. J. Eng. Inf. Technol.*, 2, 1, 60–63, 2010.

5. Hu, P., Dhelim, S., Ning, H., Qiu, T., Survey on fog computing: Architecture, key technologies, applications and open issues. *J. Network Comput. Appl.*, 98, 27–42, 2017.

6. Singh, S., Optimize cloud computations using edge computing, in: *2017 International Conference on Big Data, IoT and Data Science (BID)*, IEEE, pp. 49–53, 2017.

7. Buyya, R. and Murshed, M., Gridsim: A toolkit for the modeling and simulation of distributed resource management and scheduling for grid computing. *Concurr. Comput. Pract. Exp.*, 14, 13–15, 1175–1220, 2002.

8. Wang, W., Kosakowski, G., Kolditz, O., A parallel finite element scheme for thermo-hydro-mechanical (THM) coupled problems in porous media. *Comput. & Geosci.*, 35, 8, 1631–1641, 2009.

9. Danalis, A., Marin, G., McCurdy, C., Meredith, J.S., Roth, P.C., Spafford, K., Tipparaju, V., Vetter, J.S., The scalable heterogeneous computing (SHOC) benchmark suite, in: *Proceedings of the 3rd Workshop on General-Purpose Computation on Graphics Processing Units*, pp. 63–74, 2010.

10. Stone, J.E., Hardy, D.J., Ufimtsev, I.S., Schulten, K., GPU-accelerated molecular modeling coming of age. *J. Mol. Graph. Model.*, 29, 2, 116–125, 2010.

11. Rawat, D.B., Chaudhary, V., Doku, R., Blockchain technology: Emerging applications and use cases for secure and trustworthy smart systems. *J. Cybersecur. Priv.*, 1, 1, 4–18, 2020.

12. Peters, G.W., Panayi, E., Chapelle, A., Trends in crypto-currencies and blockchain technologies: A monetary theory and regulation perspective. *J. Financial Perspect.*, 3, 3, 2015, Available at SSRN: https://ssrn.com/abstract=3084011

13. Shukla, S.S. and Jaiswal, V., Applicability of artificial intelligence in different fields of life. *Int. J. Sci. Eng. Res.*, 1, 1, 28–35, 2013. Available at: https://www.ijser.in/archives/v1i1/MDExMzA5MTU=.pdf

14. Botín-Sanabria, D.M., Mihaita, A.-S., Peimbert-García, R.E., Ramírez-Moreno, M.A., Ramírez-Mendoza, R.A., Lozoya-Santos, J.d.J., Digital twin technology challenges and applications: A comprehensive review. *Remote Sens.*, 14, 6, 1335, 2022.

15. Outeiral, C., Strahm, M., Shi, J., Morris, G.M., Benjamin, S.C., Deane, C.M., The prospects of quantum computing in computational molecular biology. *Wiley Interdiscip. Reviews: Comput. Mol. Sci.*, 11, 1, e1481, 2021.

16. Svore, K., Geller, A., Troyer, M., Azariah, J., Granade, C., Heim, B., Kliuchnikov, V., Mykhailova, M., Paz, A., Roetteler, M., Q# enabling scalable quantum computing and development with a high-level dsl, in: *Proceedings of the Real World Domain Specific Languages Workshop*, vol. 2018, pp. 1–10, 2018.

17. Gill, S.S., Kumar, A., Singh, H., Singh, M., Kaur, K., Usman, M., Buyya, R., Quantum computing: A taxonomy, systematic review and future directions. *Softw. Pract. Exp.*, 52, 1, 66–114, 2022.

18. Wah, B.W., Huang, T.S., Joshi, A.K., Moldovan, D., Aloimonos, J., Bajcsy, R.K., Ballard, D. *et al.* Report on workshop on high performance computing and communications for grand challenge applications: Computer vision, speech and natural language processing, and artificial intelligence. *IEEE Trans. Knowl. Data Eng.*, 5, 1, 138–154, 1993.

19. Roco, M.C., Williams, R.S., Alivisatos, P. (eds.), *Nanotechnology research directions: IWGN workshop report: Vision for nanotechnology in the next decade*, Springer Science & Business Media, 2000. Available at: https://link.springer.com/book/10.1007/978-94-015-9576-6

20. Noghabaei, M., Heydarian, A., Balali, V., Han, K., Trend analysis on adoption of virtual and augmented reality in the architecture, engineering, and construction industry. *Data*, 5, 1, 26, 2020. Available at: https://doi.org/10.3390/data5010026

21. Makaya, A., Pambaguian, L., Ghidini, T., Rohr, T., Lafont, U., Meurisse, A., Towards out of earth manufacturing: Overview of the ESA materials and processes activities on manufacturing in space. *CEAS Space J.*, 15, 1, 69–75, 2023.

22. Saqlain, M., Piao, M., Shim, Y., Lee, Y.J., Framework of an IoT-based industrial data management for smart manufacturing. *J. Sensor Actuator Networks*, 8, 2, 25, 2019.

23. Tao, F., Qi, Q., Liu, A., Kusiak, A., Data-driven smart manufacturing. *J. Manuf. Syst.*, 48, 157–169, 2018.

24. Attaran, M., The rise of 3-D printing: The advantages of additive manufacturing over traditional manufacturing. *Business Horizons*, 60, 5, 677–688, 2017.

25. Rüßmann, M., Lorenz, M., Gerbert, P., Waldner, M., Justus, J., Engel, P., Harnisch, M., Industry 4.0: The future of productivity and growth in manufacturing industries. *Boston Consulting Group*, 9, 1, 54–89, 2015.

26. Javaid, M., Haleem, A., Singh, R.P., Khan, S., Suman, R., Blockchain technology applications for Industry 4.0: A literature-based review. *Blockchain: Res. Appl.*, 2, 4, 100027, 2021.

27. Drukker, L., Noble, J.A., Papageorghiou, A.T., Introduction to artificial intelligence in ultrasound imaging in obstetrics and gynecology. *Ultrasound Obstetrics & Gynecol.*, 56, 4, 498–505, 2020.

28. Borgia, E., The internet of things vision: Key features, applications and open issues. *Comput. Commun.*, 54, 1–31, 2014.

29. Saberi, S., Kouhizadeh, M., Sarkis, J., Shen, L., Blockchain technology and its relationships to sustainable supply chain management. *Int. J. Prod. Res.*, 57, 7, 2117–2135, 2019.

30. Yuen, S.C., Yaoyuneyong, G., Johnson, E., Augmented reality: An overview and five directions for AR in education. *J. Educ. Technol. Dev. Exchange (JETDE)*, 4, 1, 11, 2011.

31. Nair, M.M. and Tyagi, A.K., Chapter 11 - AI, IoT, blockchain, and cloud computing: The necessity of the future, in: *Distributed Computing to Blockchain*, Pandey, R., Goundar, S., Fatima, S. (Eds.), pp. 189–206, Academic Press, 2023. https://doi.org/10.1016/B978-0-323-96146-2.00001-2.

32. Sarker, I.H., Machine learning: Algorithms, real-world applications and research directions. *SN Comput. Sci.*, 2, 3, 160, 2021.

33. Michie, S., Yardley, L., West, R., Patrick, K., Greaves, F., Developing and evaluating digital interventions to promote behavior change in health and health care: Recommendations resulting from an international workshop. *J. Med. Internet Res.*, 19, 6, e232, 2017.

34. Iyer, L.S., AI enabled applications towards intelligent transportation. *Transp. Eng.*, 5, 100083, 2021.

35. Mohamed, E.S., Belal, A.A., Abd-Elmabod, S.K., El-Shirbeny, M.A., Gad, A., Zahran, M.B., Smart farming for improving agricultural management. *The Egyptian J. Remote Sens. Space Sci.*, 24, 3, 971–981, 2021.

36. Chauhan, J., Taneja, S., Goel, A., Enhancing MOOC with augmented reality, adaptive learning and gamification, in: *2015 IEEE 3rd International Conference on MOOCs, Innovation and Technology in Education (MITE)*, IEEE, pp. 348–353, 2015.

37. Sahoo, S. and Lo, C., Smart manufacturing powered by recent technological advancements: A review. *J. Manuf. Syst.*, 64, 236–250, 2022.

38. Shrouf, F., Ordieres, J., Miragliotta, G., Smart factories in Industry 4.0: A review of the concept and of energy management approached in production based on the internet of things paradigm, in: *2014 IEEE International Conference on Industrial Engineering and Engineering Management*, IEEE, pp. 697–701, 2014.

39. Wang, J., Ma, Y., Zhang, L., Gao, R.X., Wu, D., Deep learning for smart manufacturing: Methods and applications. *J. Manuf. Syst.*, 48, 144–156, 2018.

40. Javaid, M., Haleem, A., Singh, R.P., Suman, R., Substantial capabilities of robotics in enhancing Industry 4.0 implementation. *Cogn. Robotics*, 1, 58–75, 2021.

41. Attaran, M., The rise of 3-D printing: The advantages of additive manufacturing over traditional manufacturing. *Business Horizons*, 60, 5, 677–688, 2017.

42. Abbasi, R., Yanes, A.R., Villanuera, E.M., Ahmad, R., Real-time implementation of digital twin for robot based production line, in: *Proceedings of the Conference on Learning Factories (CLF)*, 2021.

43. Davis, J., Edgar, T., Porter, J., Bernaden, J., Sarli, M., Smart manufacturing, manufacturing intelligence and demand-dynamic performance. *Comput. & Chem. Eng.*, 47, 145–156, 2012.

44. Clements-Croome, D. and Croome, D.J. (eds.), *Intelligent Buildings: Design, Management and Operation*, Thomas Telford, ICE Publishing. Available at: ISBN: 0 7277 3266 8 2004.

45. Deshmukh, A., Patil, D. S., Soni, G., & Tyagi, A. K., Cyber security: New realities for Industry 4.0 and Society 5.0. In A. Tyagi (Ed.), *Handbook of Research on Quantum Computing for Smart Environments*. pp. 299–325, IGI Global, 2023. https://doi.org/10.4018/978-1-6684-6697-1.ch017

46. Cohen, I.G., Informed consent and medical artificial intelligence: What to tell the patient? *Geo. LJ*, 108, 1425–1469, 2020, Harvard Public Law Working Paper No. 20-03, Available at SSRN: https://ssrn.com/abstract=3529576 or http://dx.doi.org/10.2139/ssrn.3529576

47. Carlsson, B., The Digital Economy: What is new and what is not? *Struct. Change Econ. Dynamics*, 15, 3, 245–264, 2004.

48. Avram, M., Advantages and challenges of adopting cloud computing from an enterprise perspective. *Procedia Technol.*, 12, 529–534, 2014.

49. Da Xu, L., Enterprise systems: State-of-the-art and future trends. *IEEE Trans. Ind. Inf.*, 7, 4, 630–640, 2011.

50. Premkumar, G. and Roberts, M., Adoption of new information technologies in rural small businesses. *Omega*, 27, 4, 467–484, 1999.

51. Perera, C., Ranjan, R., Wang, L., Khan, S.U., Zomaya, A.Y., Big data privacy in the internet of things era. *IT Prof.*, 17, 3, 32–39, 2015.

52. Gupta, B., Agrawal, D.P., Yamaguchi, S. (eds.), *Handbook of Research on Modern Cryptographic Solutions for Computer and Cyber Security*, IGI Global, 2016.

53. Greene, D., Hoffmann, A.L., Stark, L., Better, nicer, clearer, fairer: A critical assessment of the movement for ethical artificial intelligence and machine learning, *Proceedings of the 52nd Hawaii International Conference on System Sciences*, 2019. Available at https://hdl.handle.net/10125/59651.

54. Haldar, A. and Sethi, N., Environmental effects of information and communication technology-exploring the roles of renewable energy, innovation, trade and financial development. *Renewable Sustain. Energy Rev.*, 153, 111754, 2022.

55. Jamshed, M.A., Heliot, F., Brown, T.W.C., A survey on electromagnetic risk assessment and evaluation mechanism for future wireless communication systems. *IEEE J. Electromagnetics, RF Microwaves Med. Biol.*, 4, 1, 24–36, 2019.

56. Parker, S.K. and Grote, G., Automation, algorithms, and beyond: Why work design matters more than ever in a digital world. *Appl. Psychol.*, 71, 4, 1171–1204, 2022.

57. Maley, A., Creative approaches to writing materials, in: *Developing Materials for Language Teaching*, B. Tomlinson (ed.), pp. 183–198, London: Bloomsbury Academic. Retrieved July 17, 2023, from http://dx.doi.org/10.5040/9781474211826.ch-011

58. Tran, K.P., Artificial intelligence for smart manufacturing: Methods and applications. *Sensors*, 21, 16, 5584, 2021.

59. Shah, Y. and Sengupta, S., A survey on classification of Cyber-attacks on IoT and IIoT devices, in: *2020 11th IEEE Annual Ubiquitous Computing, Electronics & Mobile Communication Conference (UEMCON)*, IEEE, pp. 0406–0413, 2020.

60. Chen, Y., Integrated and intelligent manufacturing: Perspectives and enablers. *Engineering*, 3, 5, 588–595, 2017.

61. Lee, I. and Lee, K., The Internet of Things (IoT): Applications, investments, and challenges for enterprises. *Business Horizons*, 58, 4, 431–440, 2015.

62. Hamelinck, C.N., Van Hooijdonk, G., Faaij, A.P., Ethanol from lignocellulosic biomass: Techno-economic performance in short-, middle-and long-term. *Biomass Bioenergy*, 28, 4, 384–410, 2005.

63. Fonseca, L.M., Industry 4.0 and the digital society: Concepts, dimensions and envisioned benefits, in: *Proceedings of the International Conference on Business Excellence*, vol. 12, no. 1, pp. 386–397, 2018.

64. Kusiak, A., Smart manufacturing. *Int. J. Prod. Res.*, 56, 1–2, 508–517, 2018.

65. Rapp, R.T. and Rozek, R.P., Benefits and costs of intellectual property protection in developing countries. *J. World Trade*, 24, 75, 1990.

66. Giddens, A., Risk and responsibility. *Mod. L. Rev.*, 62, 1, 1999.

67. Shah, R. and Chircu, A., IoT and AI in healthcare: A systematic literature review. *Issues Inf. Syst.*, 19, 3, 33–41, 2018. Available at: https://doi.org/10.48009/3_iis_2018_33-41.

68. Mosteanu, N.R., Artificial intelligence and cyber security–Face to face with cyber attack–A maltese case of risk management approach. *Ecoforum J.*, 9, 2020. Available at: <http://www.ecoforumjournal.ro/index.php/eco/article/view/1059>. Date accessed: 17 Jul. 2023.

69. Braithwaite, J., Enforced self-regulation: A new strategy for corporate crime control. *Michigan Law Rev.*, 80, 7, 1466–1507, 1982.

70. Leslie, D., Understanding bias in facial recognition technologies. *arXiv preprint*, 2020, arXiv:2010.07023.

71. Lee, D. and Hess, D.J., Regulations for on-road testing of connected and automated vehicles: Assessing the potential for global safety harmonization. *Transp. Res. Part A: Policy Pract.*, 136, 85–98, 2020.

72. Botta, A., De Donato, W., Persico, V., Pescapé, A., Integration of cloud computing and internet of things: A survey. *Future Generation Comput. Syst.*, 56, 684–700, 2016.

73. Wahl, B., Cossy-Gantner, A., Germann, S., Schwalbe, N.R., Artificial intelligence (AI) and global health: How can AI contribute to health in resource-poor settings? *BMJ Global Health*, 3, 4, e000798, 2018.

74. Zyskind, G. and Nathan, O., Decentralizing privacy: Using blockchain to protect personal data, in: *2015 IEEE Security and Privacy Workshops*, IEEE, pp. 180–184, 2015.

75. Scherer, M.U., Regulating artificial intelligence systems: Risks, challenges, competencies, and strategies. *Harv. JL & Tech.*, 29, 353, 2015.

76. Saxenian, A., From brain drain to brain circulation: Transnational communities and regional upgrading in India and China. *Stud. Comp. Int. Dev.*, 40, 35–61, 2005.

77. Nair, M.M. and Tyagi, A.K., Blockchain technology for next-generation society: Current trends and future opportunities for smart era, in: *Blockchain Technology for Secure Social Media Computing*, 2023.

78. Hall, F., Maglaras, L., Aivaliotis, T., Xagoraris, L., Kantzavelou, I., Smart homes: Security challenges and privacy concerns. *arXiv preprint*, 2020, arXiv:2010.15394.

79. Noura, M., Atiquzzaman, M., Gaedke, M., Interoperability in internet of things: Taxonomies and open challenges. *Mobile Networks Appl.*, 24, 796–809, 2019.

80. Palensky, P. and Dietrich, D., Demand side management: Demand response, intelligent energy systems, and smart loads. *IEEE Trans. Ind. Inf.*, 7, 3, 381–388, 2011.

81. Al Nuaimi, E., Al Neyadi, H., Mohamed, N., Al-Jaroodi, J., Applications of big data to smart cities. *J. Internet Serv. Appl.*, 6, 1, 1–15, 2015.

82. Raji, I.D., Smart, A., White, R.N., Mitchell, M., Gebru, T., Hutchinson, B., Smith-Loud, J., Theron, D., Barnes, P., Closing the AI accountability gap: Defining an end-to-end framework for internal algorithmic auditing, in: *Proceedings of the 2020 Conference on Fairness, Accountability, and Transparency*, pp. 33–44, 2020.

83. Osoba, O.A. and Welser IV, W., *An intelligence in our image: The risks of bias and errors in artificial intelligence*, Santa Monica, CA: RAND Corporation, 2017. https://www.rand.org/pubs/research_reports/RR1744.html.

84. Zeid, A., Sundaram, S., Moghaddam, M., Kamarthi, S., Marion, T., Interoperability in smart manufacturing: Research challenges. *Machines*, 7, 2, 21, 2019.

85. Tambare, P., Meshram, C., Lee, C., Ramteke, R.J., Imoize, A.L., Performance measurement system and quality management in data-driven Industry 4.0: A review. *Sensors*, 22, 1, 224, 2021.

86. Tao, F., Qi, Q., Liu, A., Kusiak, A., Data-driven smart manufacturing. *J. Manuf. Syst.*, 48, 157–169, 2018.

87. Lai, Z., Tao, W., Leu, M.C., Yin, Z., Smart augmented reality instructional system for mechanical assembly towards worker-centered intelligent manufacturing. *J. Manuf. Syst.*, 55, 69–81, 2020.

88. Quinn, J.B. and Hilmer, F.G., Strategic outsourcing. *MIT Sloan Manag. Rev.*, 35, 4, 43, 1994.

89. Al-Mohammed, H.A., Al-Ali, M.S., Alkaeed, M., Quantum computer architecture from non-conventional physical simulation up to encryption cracking, machine learning application, and more, in: *2020 16th International Computer Engineering Conference (ICENCO)*, IEEE, pp. 17–24, 2020.

90. Roco, M.C., Williams, R.S., Alivisatos, P. (eds.), *Nanotechnology Research Directions: IWGN Workshop Report: Vision for Nanotechnology in the Next Decade*, Springer Science & Business Media, 2000.

91. Jung, D., Tuan, V.T., Tran, D.Q., Park, M., Park, S., Conceptual framework of an intelligent decision support system for smart city disaster management. *Appl. Sci.*, 10, 2, 666, 2020.

92. O'Sullivan, S., Nevejans, N., Allen, C., Blyth, A., Leonard, S., Pagallo, U., Holzinger, K., Holzinger, A., Sajid, M., I, Ashrafian, H., Legal, regulatory, and ethical frameworks for development of standards in artificial intelligence (AI) and autonomous robotic surgery. *Int. J. Med. Robotics Comput. Assisted Surg.*, 15, 1, e1968, 2019.

93. Okonko, I.O., Olabode, O.P., Okeleji, O.S., The role of biotechnology in the socio-economic advancement and national development: An overview. *Afr. J. Biotechnol.*, 5, 23, 2006. Available at: https://www.ajol.info/index.php/ajb/article/view/56009

94. Hapke, H., Howard, C., Lane, H., *Natural language processing in action: Understanding, analyzing, and generating text with Python*, Simon and Schuster, 2019. Available at: https://www.simonand-schuster.com/books/Natural-Language-Processing-in-Action/Hobson-Lane/9781617294631

95. Ko, T., A survey on behavior analysis in video surveillance for homeland security applications, in: *2008 37th IEEE Applied Imagery Pattern Recognition Workshop*, IEEE, pp. 1–8, 2008.

96. Klonoff, D.C., Fog computing and edge computing architectures for processing data from diabetes devices connected to the medical internet of things. *J. Diabetes Sci. Technol.*, 11, 4, 647–652, 2017.

97. Khatoon, A., Verma, P., Southernwood, J., Massey, B., Corcoran, P., Blockchain in energy efficiency: Potential applications and benefits. *Energies*, 12, 17, 3317, 2019.

98. Ajagekar, A. and You, F., Quantum computing for energy systems optimization: Challenges and opportunities. *Energy*, 179, 76–89, 2019.

99. Chhaya, L., Sharma, P., Bhagwatikar, G., Kumar, A., Wireless sensor network based smart grid communications: Cyber attacks, intrusion detection system and topology control. *Electronics*, 6, 1, 5, 2017.

100. Berl, A., Gelenbe, E., Di Girolamo, M., Giuliani, G., De Meer, H., Dang, M.Q., Pentikousis, K., Energy-efficient cloud computing. *Comput. J.*, 53, 7, 1045–1051, 2010.

101. Li, X., Liu, H., Wang, W., Zheng, Y., Lv, H., Lv, Z., Big data analysis of the internet of things in the digital twins of smart city based on deep learning. *Future Generation Comput. Syst.*, 128, 167–177, 2022.

102. Zilberstein, S., Building strong semi-autonomous systems, in: *Proceedings of the Twenty-Ninth AAAI Conference on Artificial Intelligence (AAAI'15)*. AAAI Press, vol. 29, no. 1, 4088–4092, 2015.

103. Liu, C., Cao, S., Tse, W., Xu, X., Augmented reality-assisted intelligent window for cyber-physical machine tools. *J. Manuf. Syst.*, 44, 280–286, 2017.

104. de Boissieu, E., Kondrateva, G., Baudier, P., Ammi, C., The use of blockchain in the luxury industry: Supply chains and the traceability of goods. *J. Enterprise Inf. Manag.*, 34, 5, 1318–1338, 2021.

105. Ajagekar, A. and You, F., Quantum computing for energy systems optimization: Challenges and opportunities. *Energy*, 179, 76–89, 2019.

106. Escamilla-Ambrosio, P.J., Rodríguez-Mota, A., Aguirre-Anaya, E., Acosta-Bermejo, R., Salinas-Rosales, M., Distributing computing in the internet of things: Cloud, fog and edge computing overview, in: *Studies in Computational Intelligence, NEO 2016*. Maldonado, Y., Trujillo, L., Schütze, O., Riccardi, A., Vasile, M. (eds), vol. 731, Springer, Cham, 2018, https://doi.org/10.1007/978-3-319-64063-1_4

107. Attaran, M., The rise of 3-D printing: The advantages of additive manufacturing over traditional manufacturing. *Business Horizons*, 60, 5, 677–688, 2017.

108. Gutfleisch, O., Willard, M.A., Brück, E., Chen, C.H., Sankar, S.G., Liu, J.P., Magnetic materials and devices for the 21st century: Stronger, lighter, and more energy efficient. *Adv. Mater.*, 23, 7, 821–842, 2011.

109. Goyal, D., Goyal, R., Rekha, G., Malik, S., Tyagi, A.K., Emerging trends and challenges in data science and big data analytics. *2020 International Conference on Emerging Trends in Information Technology and Engineering (ic-ETITE)*, pp. 1–8, 2020.

110. Tyagi, A.K., Dananjayan, S., Agarwal, D., Thariq Ahmed, H.F., Blockchain—Internet of things applications: Opportunities and challenges for Industry 4.0 and Society 5.0. *Sensors*, 23, 2, 947, 2023, https://doi.org/10.3390/s23020947.

111. Tyagi, A., Kukreja, S., Nair, M.M., Tyagi, A.K., Machine learning: Past, present and future. *Neuroquantology*, 20, 8, 4333–4357, 2022.

112. Nair, M.M., Tyagi, A.K., Sreenath, N., The future with Industry 4.0 at the core of Society 5.0: Open issues, future opportunities and challenges. *2021 International Conference on Computer Communication and Informatics (ICCCI)*, pp. 1–7, 2021, doi: 10.1109/ICCCI50826.2021.9402498.

113. Tyagi, A.K., Fernandez, T.F., Mishra, S., Kumari, S., Intelligent automation systems at the core of Industry 4.0, in: *Intelligent Systems Design and Applications. ISDA 2020*, Advances in Intelligent Systems and Computing, vol. 1351, A. Abraham, V. Piuri, N. Gandhi, P. Siarry, A. Kaklauskas, A. Madureira (eds.), Springer, Cham, 2021, https://doi.org/10.1007/978-3-030-71187-0_1.

114. Goyal, D. and Tyagi, A., A look at top 35 problems in the computer science field for the next decade. 2020, 10.1201/9781003052098-40.

115. Varsha, R., Nair, S.M., Tyagi, A.K., Aswathy, S.U., RadhaKrishnan, R., The future with advanced analytics: A Sequential analysis of the disruptive technology's scope, in: *Hybrid Intelligent Systems. HIS 2020*, Advances in Intelligent Systems and Computing, vol. 1375, A. Abraham, T. Hanne, O. Castillo, N. Gandhi, T. Nogueira Rios, T.P. Hong (eds.), Springer, Cham, 2021, https://doi.org/10.1007/978-3-030-73050-5_56.

116. Pramod, A., Naicker, H.S., Tyagi, A.K., Emerging innovations in the near future using deep learning techniques, in: *Advanced Analytics and Deep Learning Models*, Wiley Scrivener, 2022, https://doi.org/10.1002/9781119792437.ch10.

117. Madhav, A.V.S. and Tyagi, A.K., The world with future technologies (Post-COVID-19): Open issues, challenges, and the road ahead, in: *Intelligent Interactive Multimedia Systems for e-Healthcare Applications*, A.K. Tyagi, A. Abraham, A. Kaklauskas (eds.), Springer, Singapore, 2022, https://doi.org/10.1007/978-981-16-6542-4_22.

118. Mishra, S. and Tyagi, A.K., The role of machine learning techniques in internet of things-based cloud applications, in: *Artificial Intelligence-Based Internet of Things Systems*, Internet of Things (Technology, Communications and Computing), S. Pal, D. De, R. Buyya (eds.), Springer, Cham, 2022, https://doi.org/10.1007/978-3-030-87059-1_4.

119. Deshmukh, A., Sreenath, N., Tyagi, A.K., Jathar, S., Internet of things based smart environment: Threat analysis, open issues, and a way forward to future. *2022 International Conference on Computer Communication and Informatics (ICCCI)*, pp. 1–6, 2022.

120. Tyagi, A.K., *Handbook of research on technical, privacy, and security challenges in a modern world*, IGI Global, 2022, https://www.igi-lobal.com/book/handbook-research-technical-privacy-security/294852.

Index